AMERICAN HOUSING

Problems and Prospects

A TWENTIETH CENTURY FUND SURVEY

The Trustees of the Fund choose the subjects for Fund surveys, underwrite their expenses, and appoint the special committees which have charge of them. The Trustees, however, assume no responsibility for the research findings or the recommendations for action.

THE HOUSING SURVEY OF THE TWENTIETH CENTURY FUND

This general survey of housing in the United States has been made under the auspices of the Housing Committee of the Twentieth Century Fund. The Committee appointed a special research staff to make an objective investigation and report on the essential facts bearing on the subject covered by this volume. These factual findings, for which the staff alone is responsible, are summarized in Chapters 1 to 11 inclusive. On the basis of these facts the Committee prepared a program for action. These recommendations, for which the Committee alone is responsible, are given in Chapter 12.

THE HOUSING COMMITTEE *

HENRY E. HOAGLAND, *Chairman*
Professor of Business Finance, Ohio State University; formerly member of the Federal Home Loan Bank Board

LILLIAN M. GILBRETH
Professor of Management, Purdue University

FRANK P. GRAHAM
President, University of North Carolina

HENRY I. HARRIMAN
Formerly President, Chamber of Commerce of the United States

ARTHUR C. HOLDEN
Architect, Holden, McLaughlin and Associates; Vice President, New York Building Congress

JOHN A. LAPP
Formerly National Referee, International Building Trades Unions

WILLIAM I. MYERS
Dean, New York State College of Agriculture, Cornell University; formerly Governor, Farm Credit Administration

COLEMAN WOODBURY
Assistant Administrator, National Housing Agency; formerly Executive Director, National Association of Housing Officials

THE HOUSING SURVEY STAFF †

MILES L. COLEAN, *Research Director*

A. B. HANDLER
J. A. VAN SWEARINGEN
CAROL W. TROSCH
LOTTIE L. WARNER
DAVID L. WICKENS

* Sir Raymond Unwin, noted authority on British housing, was a member of the Committee until his death on June 29, 1940.

† During 1940 S. B. Barber and Richard U. Ratcliff contributed to the planning and development of Survey data.

AMERICAN HOUSING

Problems and Prospects

THE FACTUAL FINDINGS

By MILES L. COLEAN

THE PROGRAM

By THE HOUSING COMMITTEE

New York

THE TWENTIETH CENTURY FUND

1944

MANUFACTURED IN THE UNITED STATES OF AMERICA
BY H. WOLFF BOOK MANUFACTURING COMPANY, INC.

FOREWORD

In March 1940 The Twentieth Century Fund began a survey of the housing situation in the United States. No authoritative over-all study of the housing problem had ever been made. The need for one was great. Furthermore, the Trustees of the Fund were convinced that revival and expansion in this field promised greater employment and general recovery than in any other, at a time when some such major stimulus was urgently called for. They hoped through this investigation to reveal the obstructions to a greater volume of building and more adequate housing and to suggest ways in which these obstacles might be removed.

Following the usual Fund practice, they appointed an eminent special committee to take general charge of the survey including persons experienced in public and private housing, with widely varying points of view: former government officials, architects, and representatives of capital and labor. Henry E. Hoagland, Professor of Business Finance at Ohio State University, formerly a Director of the Home Owners' Loan Corporation, and a former member of the Federal Home Loan Bank Board, was appointed Chairman of this Committee. Miles L. Colean, Assistant Administrator of the Federal Housing Administration, resigned from his Washington position to accept the appointment as research director. Work began in March.

By June, however, war in Europe had been recognized as a definite menace to the United States. The world situation had so drastically changed that this survey had to be modified in the light of America's vast program of national defense. It was clear that the expansion of defense industries and the resulting large-scale shifts of population would soon make adequate housing an urgent national problem.

In view of all this, the Housing Committee and the Trustees of the Fund decided to turn aside temporarily from the main survey and to prepare a brief emergency report on housing as related to national defense. The research findings showed that private industry had the capacity to provide the major part of the housing needs of the defense program as it existed at that time. Advisability of locating defense industries in the light of available housing and labor supply was stressed. Ways in which communities could make the best possible use of their existing supply of housing were listed, and there was an analysis of governmental agencies and the part they play in the total housing picture.

The survey volume was published in November 1940 under the title *Housing for Defense*. Later the Fund issued a Public Policy Bulletin, "Defense Housing in Our Town," based upon the book.

The entrance of the United States into war in 1941, with the rapid transformation of the American economy into one of relatively full-time, full-employment production that followed, has of course changed completely the setting of the housing problem. The national economy has no more need for stimulation. It is operating at peak intensity. Even the "national defense" days with which *Housing for Defense* dealt have been largely dated by the fantastic speed of developing events.

But the war will end, men and plants will be demobilized, and now is none too soon to look ahead and plan for the day—whenever it may come. When it does come, housing will present a major challenge to the nation. Housing will at once be a pressing need and a prodigious opportunity. The United States has probably never before in history been so far behind in keeping up with the demand for homes. Figures in this survey indicate a potential postwar demand for well over 1,000,000 units a year during the first decade after the war. To fill these orders will be one of the most urgent items on the nation's postwar agenda. At the same time, the wide and quick employment which such orders can create may well be a major factor in meeting the problems of demobilization.

This volume is designed to give the general reader, as well as the specialist, the background of knowledge necessary to deal with the housing question in the United States when the war is over. Chapters 1-11 give the essential facts that bear on the question. For these chapters the research staff is responsible—although the Committee passed upon the general plan of the survey and criticized the manuscript as it was being written. Anthony Netboy edited Chapters 1-11 in preparing them for publication. Chapter 12 presents a constructive program of policies to meet America's postwar housing problems. For this chapter the Committee is entirely responsible.

In presenting this volume to the public, the Fund desires to express its deep appreciation to the staff for their able handling of a difficult assignment and to Dr. Hoagland and the other members of the Housing Committee for the generous contributions they have made of their time and effort, both in furthering the research and in hammering out a useful and provocative program for action when D-Day comes.

EVANS CLARK, *Executive Director*
The Twentieth Century Fund

330 WEST 42ND STREET
NEW YORK 18, NEW YORK
DECEMBER 15, 1943

ACKNOWLEDGMENTS

THE STAFF OF THE HOUSING SURVEY wishes to acknowledge the active co-operation of a large number of individuals, government agencies and business organizations in the preparation of this report. Statistical information and published records of housebuilding experience are widely scattered among numerous government agencies and we are greatly indebted to many public officials who freely gave their aid and counsel in the task of assembling material. Much of the information was brought to light through interviews and correspondence with persons connected in one way or another with the housebuilding industry—builders, architects, labor union officials, and real-estate, financial and other businessmen. Editors, educators and research workers in this field also made generous contributions of their knowledge and experience.

The staff is especially grateful for the advice and effective criticism given by members of the Housing Committee and by Dr. J. Frederic Dewhurst, Economist of the Fund, during the period in which the work of the survey was under way. To all of these we extend our thanks and appreciation.

MILES L. COLEAN
Research Director

CONTENTS

THE FACTUAL FINDINGS

	Page
INTRODUCTION	3

Part I

The Production of Housing

CHAPTER 1. LAND FOR HOUSING	13
1. The Availability of Land	13
a. Urban Lot Vacancy	14
b. Decline of Central Cities	16
2. Barriers to the Use of Surplus Land	18
a. Effect of Location on the Availability of Land	18
b. Effects of Tax Delinquency on the Availability of Land	20
c. Legal and Financial Barriers to Utilization of Land	22
3. The Cost of Land	23
a. Prospects for Land Prices	23
b. Cost of Land in Relation to Total Property Costs	25
c. Raw Land and Improvement Costs	26
4. Trends in Land Utilization	30
a. Decline in Density and Price	30
b. Protecting Neighborhood Values	31
c. Growth of Public Control of Land Subdivision	33
d. The Movement to New Land	35
5. Summary	37
CHAPTER 2. THE HOUSE AS AN INDUSTRIAL PRODUCT	38
1. Physical Characteristics of the Dwelling	38
a. Fixed Location	38
b. Bulk	39
c. Complexity	40
d. Variety of Structural Methods	43
e. Variety of Types	44
f. Durability	45

Page

2. Some Aspects of Dwelling Costs 46
   a. Kinds of Cost 47
   b. Have Production Costs Been Reduced? 48
   c. Composition of Housing Costs 52
3. Mutability of the Dwelling 52
   a. Bulk and Form 53
   b. Materials and Structure 53
   c. Type and Arrangement 54
4. Summary 58

CHAPTER 3. THE BUSINESS OF HOUSEBUILDING 59
1. Housebuilding as an Industrial Activity 59
   a. The Processes of Housebuilding 59
   b. Housebuilding and Construction 60
   c. A Problem of Segregation 63
2. Size and Characteristics of the Housebuilding Industry 64
   a. Production in Terms of Labor and Materials 68
   b. Characteristics of Housebuilders 75
3. Seasonal Nature of Housebuilding 84
   a. Reasons for Seasonal Variation 85
   b. Smoothing the Seasonal Curve 88
4. Capacity of the Housing Industry 90
   a. Physical Capacity 90
   b. Efficiency of Operation 92
   c. Limit of Profitable Operation 93
5. Summary 93

CHAPTER 4. THE MANAGEMENT OF THE HOUSEBUILDING INDUSTRY 95
1. Initiation and General Management 95
   a. The Buyer 95
   b. The Land Developer and Subdivider 96
   c. The Architect 97
   d. The Builder 98
   e. The Subcontracting System 99
2. Management and Trade Restraints 101
   a. Purpose of Trade Restraints 101
   b. Effects of Trade Restraints and Combinations 105
3. Labor's Relations to Management 106
   a. Combating Insecurity 108
   b. Working Rules 109
   c. Effects of Labor Policy 110
4. The Role of Manufacturers and Distributors 111

	Page
a. The Rigidity of Prices	111
b. The Background of Price Rigidity	112
c. Role of the Materials Distributor	115
5. The Role of the Financier	117
a. Credit Arrangements	118
b. Dominance of Financial Institutions	119
6. The Impact of Government on Housebuilding	120
a. Government as a Stimulator	121
b. Government as Regulator	123
7. Summary	130
CHAPTER 5. INDUSTRIAL TRENDS IN HOUSEBUILDING	131
1. Simplifying and Standardizing the Product	131
a. Standardization of Parts	132
b. Standardizing the Dwelling Unit	134
2. Rationalizing the Building Process	137
a. Methods Used in Large Building Operations	138
b. Prefabricating Methods	139
3. Changes in Housebuilding Organizations	142
a. The Operative Builder	142
b. The Investor's Building Agent	144
c. The Dealer-Builder	145
d. The Factory Prefabricator	146
4. Summary	148
CHAPTER 6. PROBLEMS IN INDUSTRIAL CHANGE	149
1. The Default of Leadership	149
a. Absence of Dominant Interests	150
b. The Prefabricator's Advantage	151
2. The Skepticism of Labor	151
a. Challenge of the CIO	152
b. Change in AF of L Attitude	153
3. The Conservatism of Lenders and Buyers	154
4. Problems in Technology and Materials	155
a. New Materials	156
b. Obstacles to Technological Progress	157
5. Government and Industrial Evolution	157
a. The Problem of Land	157
b. The Problem of Building Codes	159
c. Elimination of Intra-Industry Restraints	162
d. Government Aid to Technical and Market Research	164

Page

6. Adapting Production to the Market 166
   a. Requirements of the Custom Market 167
   b. Satisfying the Urban Mass Market 168
   c. Serving the Rural Market 169
7. Summary 171

Part II

The Marketing of Housing

CHAPTER 7. THE BEHAVIOR OF THE HOUSING MARKET 175
1. Some Crucial Factors in the Housing Market 176
   a. The Variability of Demand 176
   b. The Stability of Supply 178
2. Fluctuations in the Building and Marketing of Houses 185
   a. The Pattern of Building and Real-Estate Cycles 185
   b. What Influences the Cycle 189
3. The Problem of Price Adjustment 197
   a. Slow Movement of Housing Prices 197
   b. Price Stickiness and the Violence of the Building Cycle 200
   c. Price Stickiness and Housing Surpluses 202
4. Can Market Maladjustments Be Lessened? 203
5. Summary 206

CHAPTER 8. THE MECHANICS OF THE HOUSING MARKET 207
1. Special Problems of the Housing Market 207
   a. Matching Houses to People 207
   b. Problems of Valuation and Pricing 209
   c. Problems of a Divided Market 210
2. Complexity of Housing Transactions 211
   a. Peculiarities of Real-Estate Ownership 211
   b. Title to Real Estate 212
   c. The Cost of Real-Estate Transactions 215
3. How Houses are Marketed 217
   a. The Real-Estate Broker 217
   b. Costs of Distribution 221
   c. Other Types of Distributing Organizations 221
4. Summary 224

CHAPTER 9. HOUSING INVESTMENT AND FINANCE 225
1. The Availability of Equity Funds 225

	Page
a. Funds for Use-Ownership	225
b. Investment in Rental Properties	231
c. Co-operative and Trustee Forms of Ownership	233
2. Deterrents to Equity Investment	235
a. Nonliquidity of Housing Investment	235
b. Effects of the Real-Estate Tax System	236
c. Problems of Value and Management	240
3. The Use of Long-Term Credit	242
a. The Mortgage as a Financial Instrument	242
b. The Mortgage Interest Rate	247
c. Sources of Mortgage Finance	251
4. Summary	255
CHAPTER 10. GOVERNMENT AND THE HOUSING MARKET	257
1. The Government as Salvager	258
a. State and Federal Emergency Measures	258
b. Effects of the Emergency Measures	260
2. Government and Housing Finance	262
a. The Federal Home Loan Bank Board and Affiliates	262
b. The Federal Housing Administration	265
c. Questions Raised by the Dual Financial System	269
3. Special Aid and Subsidy for Urban Housing	273
a. State Aid for Housing	273
b. Direct Federal Aid to Housing	276
c. The United States Housing Authority	277
4. Government and Farm Housing	282
a. The Farm Credit Administration	282
b. The Farm Security Administration	283
c. Urban Agencies in the Rural Field	284
5. War Housing	285
a. Operations Under the Lanham Act	285
b. The Defense Homes Corporation	286
c. Federal Housing Administration—Title VI	287
d. Co-ordination of Federal Housing Activities	288
6. Summary	289
CHAPTER 11. REMOVING THE OBSTACLES	291
1. Relations Between Production and Marketing	291
a. Unification of Production and Distribution	292
b. Problems of Used-House Distribution	292
c. Trends in the Distribution of New Houses	294

Page

2. Land Problems and Housing Distribution 296
   a. Difficulties in Obtaining Land for Low-Priced Dwellings 296
   b. Protection of Housing Values 297
   c. Reutilization of Land 298
3. Relation of Finance to the Problem of Distribution 300
   a. Encouragement of Rental-Housing Investment 300
   b. Developing New Methods of Housing Finance 302
4. Governmental Problems 304
   a. Unification of Federal Policy for Urban Housing 305
   b. Rural and Farm Housing Policy 305
   c. Simplification of State and Federal Procedures 306
5. Summary 307

THE PROGRAM

CHAPTER 12. CONCLUSIONS AND RECOMMENDATIONS OF THE HOUSING COMMITTEE 311
1. Conclusions 311
   a. The Necessity for Action 312
   b. The Backwardness of the Housebuilding Industry 314
   c. Deficiencies of the Land System 315
   d. Problems in Investment and Finance 316
   e. Halfway Measures of Government 318
   f. The Emergence of New Trends 323
2. Recommendations 325
   a. Land Utilization 326
   b. Industrial Reorganization 329
   c. Reorganization of Marketing Processes 330
   d. Investment in and Financing of Urban Housing 331
   e. Public Housing 334
   f. Special Provisions for Rural and Farm Housing 336
   g. Property Maintenance and Operation 339
   h. Timing a Program 341

APPENDIX

Appendix A

Table 1. Distribution of Population in Selected Metropolitan Districts Between Central City and Outside Central City, 1920–1940 347
Table 2. Rate of Population Change in Metropolitan Districts, Central City Compared with Outside Central City, 1920–1940 348

Page

Table 3. Valuation of Improved Land Compared with Property Valuation of New Single-Family Houses Insured by the Federal Housing Administration, 1940 349
Table 4. Cost per Front Foot of Specified Land Improvements in Selected Cities, 1941 350

Appendix B

1. Weight of Basic Materials Used in the Construction of Two Four-Room Houses 352
2. A Comparison of Two Construction Cost Indexes 352
Table 5. Weight of Basic Materials Used in the Construction of Two Four-Room Houses 353
Table 6. Basic Materials and Their Uses in the Housebuilding Industry 354
Table 7. Indexes of Construction Costs for a Frame House in St. Louis, Missouri, 1936–1941 357
Table 8. Distribution of Cost of Major Elements in the Construction of Nine Selected Houses, 1941 358

Appendix C

1. The Measurement of Residential Construction Volume 361
Table 9. Sales and Average Prices of Passenger Automobiles, Electric Washers and Household Refrigerators 362
Table 10. Number of New Residential Units Built in the Nonfarm Area Classified by Urban and Rural Nonfarm, 1900–1941 364
Table 11. Proportion of New Single-Family, Two-Family and Multifamily Units Built in Nonfarm Areas, 1920–1940 366
Table 12. Dollar Volume of Residential Construction, 1919–1940 367
2. Size of the Residential Building Industry in Terms of Gross National Product and Wages and Salaries 368
Table 13. Relative Importance of Residential Construction in the Total Economy, as Measured by Gross National Product, 1919–1935 369
Table 14. Relative Importance of Residential Construction in the Total Economy, as Measured by Wages and Salaries, 1939 371
3. Occupational Groups in Residential Construction Classified by International Unions Affiliated with the Building and Construction Trades Department of the American Federation of Labor 372
4. Wage Data for the Construction Industry 373
5. Size of Builders 377
Table 15. Distribution of Builders of Single-Family Houses and of Houses Built, by Size of Operation, in 72 Cities, 1938 380

Page

Table 16. Distribution of Builders of Multifamily Structures and of Dwelling Units Built, by Size of Operation, in 37 Cities, 1939 381
Table 17. Distribution of Single-Family Houses Built in Specified Price Classes, by Size of Operations, in 72 Cities, 1938 381
6. Number of General Building Contractors and Subcontractors 382
Table 18. Distribution of Employers and Employees in the Contract Construction Industry, by Size of Firm, Third Quarter, 1940 383
Table 19. Distribution of Work Performed by Selected Types of Contractors, by Location of Work, 1935 384
Table 20. Average Value of Building Equipment Per Employee, by Type of Contractor, 1929 385
7. Subcontracts Let on Two Major Types of Residential Building 386
8. Profits in the Construction Industry 387
Table 21. Estimated Total Construction and Net Income, Contract Construction Industry, Selected Years, 1929–1940 388
9. Seasonal Fluctuation in Construction Contracts Awarded in 37 Eastern States 388
Table 22. Building Construction Corporations Filing Income Tax Returns, 1929, 1933, and 1937 389
Table 23. Construction Industry Corporations Filing Income Tax Returns Compared with Total Manufacturing, 1938 390
Table 24. Seasonal Fluctuation in Construction Contracts Awarded in 37 Eastern States, 1929, 1932, 1940 391
Table 25. Seasonal Fluctuation in Residential Construction and Approximate Average Temperatures, by Months, in Selected Areas, 1930–1938 392

Appendix D

1. Tenure of Employment in the Construction Industry 393
2. Concentration of Ownership and the Rigidity of Prices in the Building Materials Industry 394
Table 26. Number of Workers by Trades and by Number of Weeks Worked on a United States Housing Project of 83 Units 395
Table 27. Pattern of Change in Average Realized Prices of Building Materials Compared with Other Products, 1929–1933 and 1933–1937 396
Table 28. Concentration of Production of Building Materials Compared with All Other Products, 1937 397
3. Distribution Costs of Building Materials 398
Table 29. Distribution of Manufacturers' Sales in Selected Industries, 1935 399
Table 30. Cities over 25,000 Population Having Comprehensive Zoning Ordinances, Control of Plats and Master Plans, February 1942 401

Page

Table 31. States Having Licensing Laws Applicable to Building Trades and Occupations 402

Appendix E

Table 32. Trades and Cities in Which Union Agreements Provide Separate Wage Scales for Residential Construction, June 1, 1940 405

Appendix F

Table 33. Proportion of Families in 33 Cities in Lower-, Middle-, and Upper-Income Groups, 1929 Compared with 1933 407
Table 34. Dwelling Units for Which Building Permits Were Issued in Six Selected Cities, 1870–1940 408
1. The Relation of New Building and Depreciation to the Total Supply 409
Table 35. Annual Building Rates in Nonfarm Areas, 1900–1939 410
Table 36. Effect of New Building and Depreciation on the Urban Housing Supply and Under Assumed Conditions as to the Quality and Quantity of New Houses Built, 1930–1940 412
Table 37. Indexes of Permits Issued for Residential and Nonresidential Construction, 1856–1936 414
2. Multiple Determinants of the Volume of Residential Building Activity 416
Table 38. Sales of One-Family Detached Houses in Lucas County (Toledo), Ohio, Classified by Age of House at Time of Sale, 1917–1938 417
Table 39. Annual Sales of New and Old One-Family Detached Houses in Lucas County (Toledo), Ohio, Classified by Age of House at Time of Sale, 1917–1938 418
Table 40. Annual Number of Families Added in Nonfarm Areas, 1900–1939 418
Table 41. Cost of Living Compared with Average Rents, 1914–1941 421

Appendix G

Table 42. Average Settlement Charges Compared with Property Valuation, New Single-Family Houses Insured by Federal Housing Administration, September-December, 1939 422

Appendix H

Table 43. Trend of Home Ownership in Selected Types of Cities, 1900–1940 423
Table 44. Ratio of 1940 Taxes to Average Original Loans Made by Home Owners' Loan Corporation on 400,000 Properties 423
Table 45. Relation Between Annual Income and Property Taxes for a Group of Federal Housing Administration Rental Projects, 1939–1940 424

Page

Table 46. Average Time Required to Complete Foreclosure Compared with Average Foreclosure Costs, Home Owners' Loan Corporation Experience 425
Table 47. Mortgages Outstanding on Nonfarm 1–4-Family Dwellings, Classified by Type of Lender, 1925–1940 426
Table 48. Mortgages Made on Nonfarm 1–4-Family Dwellings, Classified by Type of Lender, 1925–1940 427

Appendix I

SUMMARIES OF FINANCIAL OPERATIONS OF FEDERAL HOUSING AGENCIES, 1932–1940 428
Table 49. Financial Interest of the Federal Government in Housing to June 30, 1940 428
Table 50. Summary of Financial Operations of the Home Owners' Loan Corporation to June 30, 1940 429
Table 51. Summary of Financial Operations of The RFC Mortgage Company to June 30, 1940 431
Table 52. Summary of Financial Operations of Federal Home Loan Bank System to June 30, 1940 432
Table 53. Summary of Federal Government Investment in Federal Savings and Loan Associations to June 30, 1940 432
Table 54. Summary of Financial Operations of Federal Savings and Loan Insurance Corporation to June 30, 1940 433
Table 55. Summary of Financial Operations of Federal Housing Administration to June 30, 1940 434
Table 56. Summary of Financial Operations of Federal National Mortgage Association to June 30, 1940 436
Table 57. Summary of Financial Operations of Public Works Administration Housing Division to June 30, 1940 437
Table 58. Summary of Financial Operations of United States Housing Authority to June 30, 1940 438
Table 59. Summary of Federal Government Investment in the Farm Security Administration Housing Program to December 31, 1940 439
Table 60. Average Cost Per Dwelling Unit of United States Housing Authority-Aided Projects Compared with Public Works Administration Projects 439
Table 61. Status of the Federal War Housing Program as of December 15, 1942 440

BIBLIOGRAPHY

Page

Books and Monographs 441
Federal Government 444
Local and State Government 449
Periodicals and Year Books 450
Releases, Pamphlets, Conferences, Addresses, etc. 454

INDEX 457

LIST OF FIGURES

Figure

1. Areas of Declining Population in Cleveland, Ohio, by Decades, 1910–1940 17
2. Contrasting Costs of Land Improvements: Row Houses for Individual Ownership and for Rental 29
3. Indexes of Construction Costs for a Frame House in St. Louis, Missouri, 1936–1941 49
4. Sales and Average Prices of Passenger Automobiles, Electric Washers and Household Refrigerators 61
5. Number of New Residential Units Built in the Nonfarm Area Classified by Urban and Rural Nonfarm, 1900–1941 65
6. Proportion of New Single-Family, Two-Family and Multifamily Units Built in Nonfarm Areas, 1920–1940 66
7. Dollar Volume of Residential Construction, 1919–1940 67
8. Relative Importance of Residential Construction in the Total Economy, as Measured by Gross National Product, 1919–1935 69
9. Relative Importance of Residential Construction in the Total Economy, as Measured by Wages and Salaries, 1939 71
10. Distribution of Builders of Single-Family Houses and of Houses Built, by Size of Operation, in 72 Cities, 1938 76
11. Distribution of Single-Family Houses Built in Specified Price Classes, by Size of Operations, in 72 Cities, 1938 77
12. Distribution of Builders of Multifamily Structures and of Dwelling Units Built, by Size of Operation, in 37 Cities, 1939 78
13. Distribution of Employers and Employees in the Contract Construction Industry, by Size of Firm, Third Quarter, 1940 79
14. Distribution of Work Performed by Selected Types of Contractors, by Location of Work, 1935 81
15. Average Value of Building Equipment per Employee, by Type of Contractor, 1929 83

Page

16. Seasonal Fluctuation in Construction Contracts Awarded, 37 Eastern States, 1940 85
17. Seasonal Fluctuation in Private Residential Construction Contract Awards, 1929, 1932 and 1940 86
18. Seasonal Fluctuation in Residential Construction and Approximate Average Temperatures, by Months, in Selected Areas, 1930–1938 87
19. Seasonal Fluctuation in Construction Contracts Awarded for Single-Family and Two-Family Houses Built for Sale or for Rent, and for Owner-Occupants, 37 Eastern States, 1940 88
20. Workers Occupied at Some Time During Each of the Four Quarters of 1938, in Selected Industries 107
21. Pattern of Change in Average Realized Prices of Building Materials Compared with Other Products, 1929–1933 and 1933–1937 113
22. Proportion of Families in 33 Cities in Lower-, Middle-, and Upper-Income Groups, 1929 Compared with 1933 179
23. Dwelling Units for which Building Permits were Issued in Four Cities, 1870–1940 181
24. New Dwelling Units Added Compared with the Total Supply at the Beginning and End of Each Decade, in Nonfarm Areas, 1900–1939 182
25. Dynamics of the Urban Housing Supply, 1930–1940 184
26. Indexes of Permits Issued for Residential and Nonresidential Building Construction, 1856–1936 186
27. Sales of One-Family Detached Houses in Lucas County (Toledo), Ohio, Classified by Age of House at Time of Sale, 1917–1938 188
28. Annual Sales of New and Old One-Family Detached Houses in Lucas County (Toledo), Ohio, 1917–1938 189
29. Proportion of Sales to Number of Houses Standing in Lucas County (Toledo), Ohio, in Different Economic Periods, 1917–1938 190
30. Residential Units Built Compared with New Families and Rents in Nonfarm Areas, 1900–1940 198
31. Cost of Living Compared with Average Rents, 1914–1941 199
32. Average Settlement Charges Compared with Property Valuation for New Single-Family Houses Insured by Federal Housing Administration, September-December, 1939 216
33. Extent of Home Ownership in Nonfarm and Farm Areas, 1890–1940 228
34. Trend of Home Ownership in Selected Types of Cities, 1900–1940 229
35. Average Time Required to Complete Foreclosure Compared with Average Foreclosure Costs, Home Owners' Loan Corporation Experience 245
36. Mortgages Outstanding and Mortgages Made on Nonfarm 1–4 Family Dwellings, Classified by Type of Lender, 1925–1940 253

THE FACTUAL FINDINGS

INTRODUCTION

Adequate housing has become more difficult to provide with the increasing complexity of civilization. In primitive societies, shelter is often more easily obtained than the other two basic necessities, food and clothing. Housing standards are simple, land and materials are usually at hand and relatively little labor is required to secure acceptable accommodations.

As a rising level of culture creates new standards and as communities grow in size, the provision of shelter becomes more costly. Land acquires a scarcity value. New problems of health, safety and communication create a need for sewers, water pipes, roads, lights, and sidewalks. Structures must fulfill more functions than mere protection from the elements; they must have more parts, openings and equipment, and be stronger and more resistant to fire. Housing needs thus become more difficult to satisfy.

But this is not the whole of the housing problem. As our food and clothing requirements have expanded, human ingenuity has made them more readily available. We have witnessed astounding increases in the output of farm products and manufactured goods, and immense reductions in the effort needed to produce a given quantity of goods. In housing, however, there have been no comparable advances either in industrial capacity or productivity.

As a consequence, the average clerk or workman can afford clothes that minister alike to his comfort and self-esteem, but often a home that provides him with neither. Even the poor usually find it easier to obtain wholesome food than decent housing. Such inadequacies as exist in food and clothing are due not to failures of production, but to a system of distribution which permits restriction of output and fails to allocate goods to those who need them most. In housing, neither the production nor distribution problems have been solved.

The housing problem may thus be considered as a problem in industrial organization and efficiency, but this is not to say that all the difficulties in providing adequately for the country's shelter needs could be wholly remedied by improved industrial techniques. Pursued far enough, housing will be found to touch upon nearly every sore spot in the economic and social structure.

Delimiting the Housing Problem

The housing problem has often been confused with the problem of poverty, and the housing industry has been widely criticized for its failure to provide adequate housing for the lowest-income groups. But farmers are not blamed for malnutrition; clothing manufacturers are not accused of complicity in the wretchedness of the poor. Great as its deficiencies have been, the housing industry can hardly be held responsible for inequities in the distribution of wealth and other defects in the economy as a whole.

Housing has also been confused with the problems of slums and their removal. Housing is confused with the slum problem because slums are made up of houses, and because the deteriorated condition of slum housing, and in many ways the character of its original planning, aggravate the slum situation. Many factors, however, contribute to the existence of slums, among which are the problems of poverty and of the demoralization that comes from poverty. Almost equally pertinent are the problems arising from the structures of cities and the methods of city growth, from the techniques of land valuation, assessment and taxation, from the hopes of property owners for increases in value, and from the complicated nature of laws affecting the reassembly of scattered ownerships.

All of these things make for the creation and preservation of slums. All of them are probably more directly responsible than the dwellings of which the slums are composed. The remedy for slum conditions can never come from attempts to improve housing conditions unless the whole problem of urban organization is attacked at the same time.

Associated with slum problems are those arising from the fact that racial or religious minority groups are sometimes forced into more or less definite segregation. Where the group is small there may be little or no effective segregation, but where it becomes a sizable part of the population, social pressure, sometimes with legal sanctions, may make the segregation both real and rigid. Wherever it exists, it adds to the difficulty of those affected in finding suitable dwellings. When the groups are large and the locations available to them limited, a cruel exploitation may take place.

The problem, however, goes beyond the availability of housing. From technical and economic considerations, it is no more difficult to build houses for one group than it is for another of the same level of income. In fact, due to their frequently more modest demands, it may be easier to build for the group discriminated against than otherwise. The difficulty is one of racial and religious tolerance, of taboos, of crowd psychology or community organization, but it is a housing problem only indirectly.

There are a number of other conditions in which housing plays a part. A share of crime and delinquency has been attributed to housing conditions. Bad housing has been accused of aggravating public health problems. It is, of course, true that dwellings and, perhaps to better effect, neighborhoods can be planned so as to promote better family life and more healthful and contented living; and it is important that housing be designed with these ends in view. But the problems mentioned require more drastic treatment, just as do the problems of poverty and slums and discrimination.

All industries face limitations resulting from maladjustments in income distribution, but in many cases these limitations are not seriously aggravated by the lack of technical capacity and efficiency. In housing there is real doubt that the industry—*at this time and under traditional methods of operation*—is capable to the same extent as these other industries of providing for the general need.

The reasons for the backwardness of the housing industry have been sought in this survey—through the character of producing organizations, the complex relationships between the various groups entering into the production process, and the equally involved methods of marketing houses. Land problems in so far as they concern so immobile, or relatively immobile, a product as the house, problems of finance in their bearing both on the production and distribution of houses, and questions arising from the aggregation of laws and governmental agencies dealing with housing have all been explored, as well as the enhanced role that a rejuvenated industry might play in the national economy after war restrictions have been removed, and the means to accomplish this rejuvenation.

Postwar Housing Demands

What is the role that housebuilding may play in the postwar period? The answer, so far as it is possible to give one, must be based upon a number of assumptions. Any one of these assumptions may be challenged, not only because the data concerning our present housing stock are incomplete and in many respects inconclusive, but also because many of the factors that bear on housebuilding prospects are hidden in the future. Nevertheless, almost any approach leads to the conclusion that the role of housebuilding in the postwar years will be greater than ever played in the past.

During the postwar decade net additions to the number of families are expected to average about 420,000 a year, all in the nonfarm areas. These new families must in some way be housed. If additions to the supply are not provided they will be forced to double up with other families or live in makeshift quarters, and constitute an ineffective or unfilled demand for more housing. Another large potential demand will come from those who live in houses physically worn out or inadequately equipped.

The housing stock as a whole is in an extremely deteriorated condition. In urban areas, more than 23 per cent of all dwellings had no private bath in 1940 and over 10 per cent were in need of major repairs. In the rural communities these percentages were considerably higher, and on farms higher still. Of the houses either needing major repairs or without private bath, 6.2 million were in urban areas, constituting almost 29 per cent of the urban supply. Disregarding the lack of private baths in rural areas, 4.3 million houses, representing over 27 per cent of the rural supply, were in need of major repairs.

The following statistical picture is from the Housing Census of 1940:

	Total*	Urban	Rural Nonfarm	Rural Farm
		(In Millions)		
Total dwelling units	37.3	21.6	8.1	7.6
Needing major repairs or without private bath	18.2	6.2	5.2	6.9
No private bath	16.8	5.0	4.9	6.8
Needing major repairs	6.8	2.5	1.7	2.6
No gas or electricity	8.2	1.3	1.7	5.2
No refrigeration equipment	10.9	2.7	3.1	5.1
No central heating or stoves	4.3	1.4	.9	1.9

* Total not always exact sum of parts due to use of round figures.

These deteriorated, underequipped, out-of-date houses represent a demand for replacement and repairs that might become effective if the price structure and efficiency of the housebuilding industry were geared to the realities. The potential demand for replacement may be variously estimated. Let us suppose a replacement rate of around 400,000 nonfarm dwellings a year. At the end of a decade, (1) all the 1940 farmhouses in need of major repairs would still be in use, as well as (2) almost two thirds of all nonfarm dwellings either needing major repairs or without private bath.

Considering only population pressure, on the one hand, and existing badly deteriorated housing, on the other, 820,000 nonfarm units a year is a minimum estimate of the potential demand for new housing during the postwar decade. During the thirties, the ratio of new nonfarm dwellings to net additions in number of families was only three to five. About half the unprovided families moved into remodeled or vacant houses, but 861,000 doubled up or lived in makeshift shelters. The decade of the forties thus began with a potential backlog of demand, which through private or public effort might be brought into the market, especially in a time of relatively high prosperity.

Nonfarm vacancies in 1940 were 1.4 million units or 4.8 per cent of the total supply, chiefly in deteriorated houses or where the demand had been removed by migration. Since war conditions have almost eliminated vacancies in all but the most inactive areas, considerable new construction will be required to provide a sufficient number of vacancies to meet market requirements. Postwar readjustments will require an unusually large number to take care of internal migration.

Finally, it will be necessary to build new houses as the existing stock continues to depreciate. Therefore, in addition to the replacements necessary to catch up with past deterioration, a further replacement rate of one per cent a year of the remainder would mean 260,000 new nonfarm units annually.

No strain is required to build up an estimate of potential new housing demand amounting to 1,300,000, or even more, nonfarm units a year during the first decade after the war. There would, in addition, be a heavy demand for farm housing, repairs and alterations.

Demand in Terms of National Income

Estimates of housing volume based on the condition of the existing supply, or even on increase of population, have the dubious characteristic of ignoring the means by which demand is to be made effective. During the war, the absence of materials has prevented demand from becoming effective. The problem of materials may continue to exert an influence after the war, or the major part of the war effort, is over. But the general level and distribution of the national income and the price at which acceptable housing can be produced will be even more important.

Here we are dealing with unknowns, so that no estimate can have more than approximate validity. Nevertheless, an attempt to measure our possible ability to pay for housing will give at least some check on an estimate of the effects on housing conditions of population increase.

The end of the war is certain to see our national income at a very high level—variously estimated up to $116 billion or more. While it is unlikely—and for that matter unnecessary for a fair degree of prosperity—to maintain national income at the overstrained height of war production, it is safe to assume that a strong effort will be made both by government and private business to prevent any drastic decline. For the purpose of our estimate, let us assume a total national income of $100 billion in the immediate postwar period. This would be fairly close to the level of income in 1929, with due allowance for increases in population; and the 1929 figure was achieved, according to estimates of the Brookings Institution, with our industrial plant working only 81 per cent of capacity.

What part of this assumed income might be spent on housing? Here we have only the past to judge by—certainly not an infallible criterion, but perhaps a reasonable clue. During the past two decades the value of residential construction (comprising new dwellings of all sorts and repairs and alterations) ranged from as high as 7.2 per cent of the national income in 1925 to as low as 1.4 per cent in 1933. The average over a complete building cycle (1919-1935) was 4.5 per cent. In general, housebuilding activity has been relatively high when economic conditions were good and low when they were bad.

Thus, judged by the past, a high level of income such as may be anticipated at the war's end would permit, and in fact imply, a relatively high level of residential construction—probably at least somewhat above the cyclical average. We may, therefore, take as a possible figure 6 per cent of a national income of $100 billion or $6 billion annually for housing construction in the postwar period.

In order to get some idea of a probable division of the total between new dwellings and repairs and alterations, we must again refer to past performance. In 1925, $4,475 million was spent for 937,000 new nonfarm dwellings (about $4,800 per dwelling, excluding land) and $925 million was spent for new farmhouses, miscellaneous dwelling construction, repairs and alterations. The distribution of the total expenditure between new nonfarm and other residential construction was 83 per cent and 17 per cent respectively. To take a more recent year, in 1940, $2,276 million was spent for 600,000 new nonfarm dwellings (about $3,800 per unit, excluding land) and $628 million was spent for other residential construction and repairs, representing 78 per cent and 22 per cent respectively of a total expenditure of $2,904 million.

Looking backward, it seems evident that the 1925 unit price was much too high to permit a sustained production and that the proportion spent on repairs was much under what was needed to keep the housing stock as a whole in even fair condition. The same was true of the 1940 figures in only lesser degree. No substantial amount of replacement was taking place, and the existing supply of houses, as the Housing Census reveals, was badly deteriorated.

In view of these considerations, and, moreover, in view of recent technical progress opening the way to further cost reduction, we may take for the postwar period, a lower unit cost and a larger share of the total expenditure for repairs than has been true in the past. Suppose we assume a unit nonfarm dwelling cost of $3,400 (excluding land) and a distribution of the total estimated $6 billion expenditure at 70 per cent for new nonfarm dwellings and 30 per cent for other residential construction and repairs. On this basis we would have an annual expenditure of $4.2 billion for approximately 1,236,000 new nonfarm dwellings and $1.8 billion for farm and miscellaneous construction, repairs and alterations.

Estimates based on such tenuous premises are, of course, subject to a wide margin of error. A sharp drop in postwar income would throw them off entirely in one direction. A marked reduction in cost might upset them in the other. Changes in population growth, and the relative strength of the demand for goods other than housing may play their parts in the ultimate result. Yet the estimates are within the realm of probability and they do show that industry has a huge market to strive for—a market in excess of anything accomplished in the past.

The Turning Point in Housebuilding

This survey is published at the end of an epoch. It describes the conditions affecting the housebuilding industry as the war broke. It points out also new directions in production and finance that were revealing themselves as the decade ended. The picture is one of barriers built up from every side—from our land system, from our methods of taxation, from builder organizations, labor, real-estate operators, mortgage lenders, and even from government itself—against the maturing of housebuilding to the stature of an industry capable of producing and distributing in sufficiently large quantities and at sufficiently low costs to meet the vast housing need the country faces.

There have been many efforts made to break through these barriers. Sometimes feeble, sometimes vigorous, they have almost always been tentative or short-lived. The housing industry in 1940 remained in the grip of ancient traditions. No trends visible in that year showed sufficient strength to promise any radical break from these traditions for perhaps another decade.

The impact of war speeded up the rate of industrial change. Within two years from the war's start materials were no longer widely enough available to permit the waste and extravagance of customary building methods. The labor supply was so reduced that even with a sharp curtailment of housebuilding volume, the maintenance of archaic and restrictive handicraft methods was no longer tenable. The war thus brought about increased efficiency in the design of dwellings, in the use of materials in building dwellings, and in the building processes themselves. At the same time direct government orders permitted producers to by-pass many of the obstacles existing in the private market. Consequently, trends that were still tentative in 1940 had by the end of 1942 developed an unexpected vitality.

It was still impossible, however, to foretell whether this vitality could persist—whether it would be sufficient, against pressure of another sort, to survive a resurgence of the restriction-of-output tradition. This tradition had in the past kept housebuilding a feeble enterprise with a limited market. It might, if short-sighted policies should succeed, again lay its blight upon house production. It might force upon the country either a constantly lowered standard of housing or new and increasingly costly governmental measures to compensate for its self-imposed inefficiencies. The housing industry in the war period thus lay between two worlds. It could not be sure that it had left the old, and it was far from certain that it had gained the new.

The purpose of the survey is not only to show what the obstacles to industrial progress in housebuilding have been, but to measure the strength of the forces back of them and to face frankly the problems of their removal. In undertaking this task, the thesis is accepted that only by creating an industrial environment conducive alike to volume expansion and cost reduction can an approach to meeting the housing need be accomplished in the postwar period and can housebuilding assume its potentially great role in easing the shocks of postwar adjustment. Housebuilding must gain its new world.

PART I

THE PRODUCTION OF HOUSING

Chapter 1

LAND FOR HOUSING

THE FINISHED, usable dwelling consists of land as well as a structure. The house must have a site and environment as well as walls and roof. The character of the house is influenced by the contour, amount, and price of available land. Land is, in fact, the first thing the housebuilder needs and the first element of his costs.

Difficulties in obtaining suitable land for housing increase with the density of population. On the farm, the location of a house rarely creates a problem and the cost of land for the dwelling is usually negligible. As communities grow and houses are built closer together, environment more and more determines the character and cost of the house as well as its future value. Towns and cities not only create problems of location and surroundings but the need of providing suitable streets, sewers, water, and other improvements. In rural areas, if the drainage is good, if water can be reached at a reasonable depth, and if a road is accessible, utility problems are not likely to be important.

Urban land problems are manifold, complex, and intriguing. They affect urban families in many ways—where they live, how they live, where and how they work, and what recreational facilities they may enjoy. Urban land problems go beyond the scope of an examination of the housebuilding industry. This survey can consider only one aspect of the land situation: *Is enough land available in suitable locations and at favorable prices to make house production feasible?*

In so far as the answer is yes, housebuilding may proceed even though graver problems are untouched. In so far as the answer is no, this survey can only seek to discover the obstacles to an effective production of houses. To other inquirers must be left the study of how the urban community might be so reorganized as to remove impediments that are beyond the control of those engaged in the housebuilding industry.

1. THE AVAILABILITY OF LAND

Urban land today is not a scarce commodity. Great quantities are made available, (1) by the increased distances from the main centers of commercial and industrial activity within which land may be put to urban use, and (2) by the intensive utilization of land possible within these wide limits. With current rates of population growth, housing is not likely to be hampered for lack of land. Considering the over-all picture, the problem is no longer that of a shortage of urban land forcing values continually upward, but rather that of a surplus tending to limit the rise of values.

The change in emphasis has come about for four reasons: (1) the greater accessibility of outlying land to commercial and industrial centers, brought about by rapid transit lines, highways, busses and private motorcars; (2) the reduction in large cities of the amount of land required for a given amount of building space, made possible by the elevator; (3) speculative overdevelopment and the creation of surplus building sites in the belief that population growth would keep pace with technical possibilities; and (4) failure to overcome the economic and social barriers that prevent the proper utilization of land in the centers of cities.

As a result, there are numerous subdivided but unused sites on the outskirts of towns and cities. Vacant lots are scattered in so-called built-up sections, and idle or underimproved sites fill the depreciated areas surrounding the centers of cities—districts once marked for the expansion of commercial, industrial, or high apartment use that now seems unlikely to occur.

a. URBAN LOT VACANCY

Although nation-wide data on the number of vacant lots are lacking, information available from numerous communities indicates a general surplus of urban land.

For instance, in 1928, toward the end of the last land boom, 30 per cent of all lots in Chicago and 69 per cent in Cook County outside of Chicago were still vacant. The entire county had 335,260 vacant lots,[1] or more than all the lots subdivided in the city and county from 1914 to 1928. Chicago and its suburbs had enough lots in 1928 for an additional population of more than a million persons living in detached houses. Even in 1914 there were enough vacant lots available to have taken care of the more than 50 per cent population increase which occurred in the area between that year and 1928. Since population was almost stationary from 1930 to 1940, the rate of absorption of vacant lots during recent years was doubtless greatly decreased. All of the subdividing, therefore, around Chicago in the years 1914-1928 must, in effect, be considered superfluous. It was

1. Herbert D. Simpson and John E. Burton, *The Valuation of Vacant Land in Suburban Areas,* Studies in Public Finance, Research Monograph No. 2, Institute for Economic Research, Northwestern University, Chicago, 1931, p. 12. In 1929, 17,081 lots were added (Homer Hoyt, *One Hundred Years of Land Values in Chicago,* The University of Chicago Press, Chicago, 1933, Table LXXXIX, pp. 477-478). For some years afterward there was little subdividing.

estimated that less than one fourth of the subdivided land in Cook County that was vacant in 1928 had a prospect of utilization by 1960.[2] Yet between 1930 and 1940, 13,649 more lots were subdivided.[3]

New York City presents no brighter picture. To absorb the 61 square miles of privately owned vacant land in New York City at current rates of population increase, 41 years would be required with an over-all density of 12 families per acre; 172 years with an over-all density of 50 families per acre; while at the over-all density of 100 families per acre, common in New York City rental developments, 344 years would be required.[4] In 1934-1936 nearly one quarter of all lots in Syracuse and about one seventh in Buffalo were vacant, with Rochester and New York City between these extremes. The heaviest concentrations of lot vacancies, as might be expected, were in suburban communities. Thus, Westchester County, adjoining New York City, and Monroe County, adjoining Rochester, had about two vacant lots for each occupied lot, while the suburbs of Buffalo showed a ratio of four to one.[5]

From 1909 to 1931 the city of Grand Rapids, Michigan had a ratio of vacant lots to total lots ranging from 38.7 per cent (1922) to 45.8 (1928); in 1931 the ratio was 43.9 per cent.[6] In 1909 Grand Rapids had 21,320 vacant lots while an additional 44,124 lots were subdivided through 1931, making a total of 65,444 available for development. Actually only 25,304 lots were put into use during this period—about 4,000 more than the surplus in 1909. Therefore, practically all subdividing activity in Grand Rapids between 1909 and 1931 was superfluous.

During the second and third decades of the present century, the outskirts of Detroit were subdivided in part as far as Pontiac and Flint, twenty to fifty miles away. A sample study of the Detroit metropolitan area in 1938 revealed that four near-by townships contained 124,485 platted lots, of which only 5,412, or 4.3 per cent, were utilized. Similarly, at the end of the 1930's, the suburban areas of St. Louis had over 100,000 vacant lots out of less than 25,000 subdivided acres. For the state of New Jersey as a whole, 24 per cent of the platted area (459,153 acres) was unoccupied in 1936, and an additional 16 per cent was less than half occupied. In 1937, 21 per cent of urban Los Angeles County was in subdivided

2. Simpson and Burton, *op. cit.*, p. 25; it may be noted that even this low rate of absorption was based on an assumed population increase which did not materialize by 1940.

3. Figures supplied by Homer Hoyt, Director of Research, Chicago Plan Commission.

4. Sir Raymond Unwin, "Land Values in Relation to Planning and Housing in the United States," *The Journal of Land & Public Utility Economics,* February 1941, table and footnote, p. 5. It is probably optimistic to assume current rates of population increase. The average density of occupied residential land in New York City is about sixteen dwelling units per acre (street areas included).

5. Philip H. Cornick, *Problems Created by Premature Subdivision of Urban Lands in Selected Metropolitan Districts,* A Report to the State Planning Council of New York, Albany, February 1938.

6. E. M. Fisher and Raymond F. Smith, *Land Subdividing and the Rate of Utilization,* Michigan Business Studies, Vol. IV, No. 5, University of Michigan, Ann Arbor, 1932, Table 1, p. 471.

vacant lots, an area about two thirds as large as that utilized for residential purposes.[7]

Such instances might be multiplied indefinitely. Subdividing has generally proceeded so much faster than the absorption of land as to produce enough unused lots to take care of housing needs for many years to come. And the available land is much greater than even the surplus of subdivided acreage indicates. Earlier subdividing tended to follow rail routes, leaving wide areas in between that were often not conveniently accessible. The building of motor highways in these in-between regions has brought a tremendous additional acreage within easy reach of commercial and industrial centers.

b. DECLINE OF CENTRAL CITIES

While staggering surpluses of vacant lots were being created, chiefly beyond the rim of built-up areas, zones of declining use were appearing in the centers of cities. The centrifugal drift of urban population was first clearly indicated by the 1930 Census. Between 1920 and 1930 the increase in the central cities of "metropolitan districts" of 100,000 population and over, was 19 per cent, while in the outlying areas it was 39 per cent. Between 1930 and 1940 the corresponding rates fell to 5 and 15 per cent respectively, the suburbs on the average growing about three times as fast as the centers. Indeed, many central cities in metropolitan areas actually declined in population during the decade.[8]

Within the central cities themselves a similar outward movement exists. Figure 1 shows the widening areas of declining population in Cleveland for three decades before 1940. Cleveland illustrates the tendency of zones of declining population to form a widening band around the central commercial district. In these zones, speculation based on the expected increase of commercial, industrial, or high apartment buildings has produced the same result as in the outlying areas—

7. Sources: Detroit, Michigan: *A Study of Subdivision Development in the Detroit Metropolitan Area,* Michigan Planning Commission, Lansing, June 1939.

Flint, Michigan: Edmund N. Bacon, "A Diagnosis and Suggested Treatment of an Urban Community's Land Problems," *The Journal of Land & Public Utility Economics,* February 1940, pp. 72-80.

St. Louis, Missouri: *Regional Planning, Part II—St. Louis Region,* National Resources Committee, June 1936, p. 22.

New Jersey: *Premature Land Subdivision a Luxury,* The New Jersey State Planning Board, Trenton, 1941, Table 1, p. 21.

Los Angeles, California: *Land Use Survey, County of Los Angeles,* The Regional Planning Commission, Los Angeles, May 1938, Table VIIA. The California State Planning Board (*Tax Delinquent Land in California,* 1938, p. 55) pointed out that "Nine out of ten deeds to land forfeited to the State of California for nonpayment of taxes represent lots or *blocks* in subdivisions. In 1934 the State held deeds to 144,506 such properties, at least half of which probably are of a residential or other urban type."

8. Because of changing boundaries both of central cities and metropolitan districts, it is impossible to make precise comparisons over a period of years, but the data are sufficiently accurate to indicate the trends. See Appendix A, Tables 1 and 2, for data for twenty selected metropolitan districts having identical, or nearly identical, boundaries in the period 1920-1940.

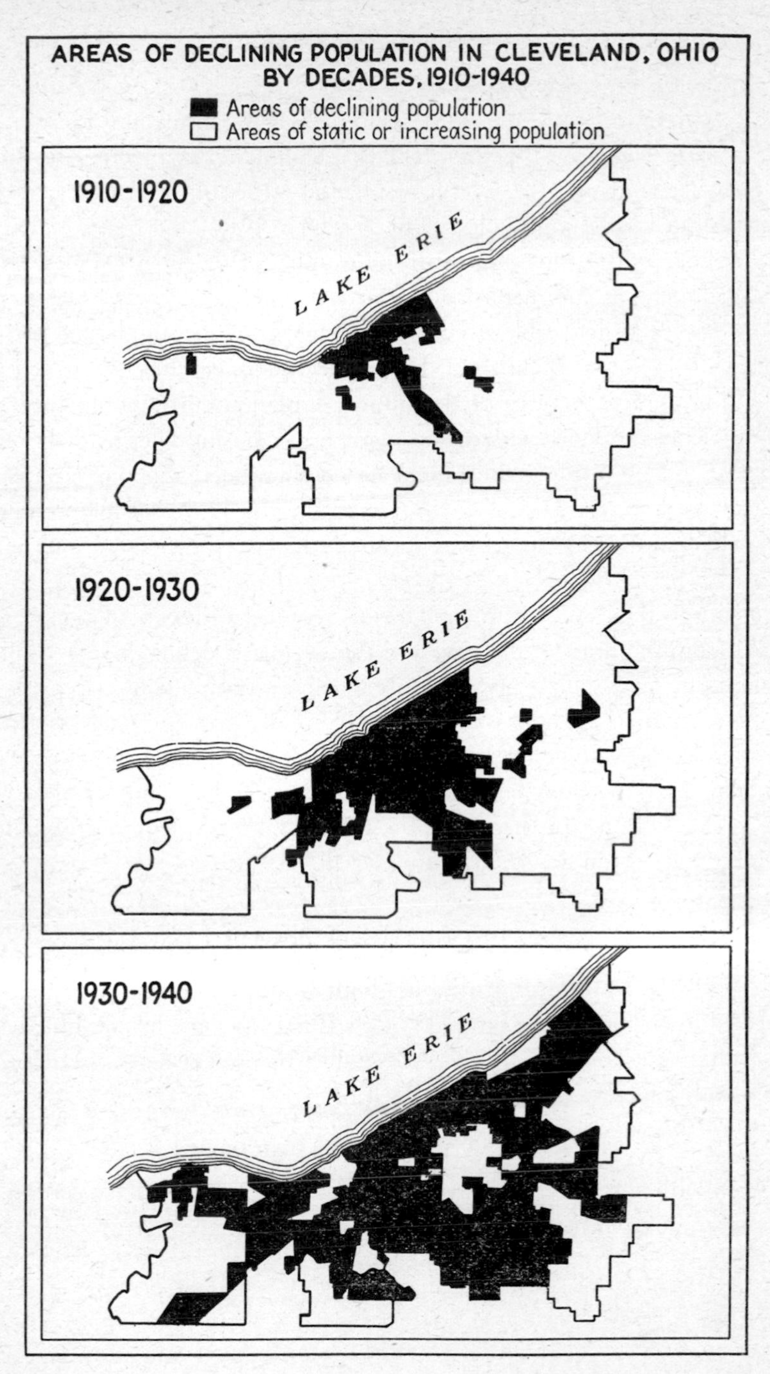

FIGURE 1. The outward movement of Cleveland's population has accelerated since 1900. This is typical of what has happened in most American cities. (*Source:* Howard Whipple Green, *Population by Census Tracts, Cleveland and Vicinity,* Cleveland Health Council, 1931; *United States Census, 1940,* Series PH–2, No. 30.)

the growth of an unwieldy land surplus. An example is the oldest part of New York City, the lower East Side of Manhattan, where population declined from 550,000 to 200,000 between 1910 and 1940. For Manhattan as a whole, the number of "old-law" tenements,[9] the typical residential structure of the area, declined from 368,000 in 1920 to slightly less than 300,000 in 1940—and probably 75,000 of these were boarded up. The decline in the number of tenements was not due to the encroachment of commercial or industrial buildings. Vacant factories and warehouses were as noticeable as empty tenements, for the number of industrial workers employed on Manhattan Island decreased by 100,000 in the same period.[10] In Chicago the area of declining population surrounding the central "loop" district has widened with each census period. Business has tended to follow population, and with the establishment of neighborhood shopping centers, the central commercial district had so contracted that by 1940 probably 15 per cent of the usable land in the "loop" was vacant or had been converted into parking lots.

In Pittsburgh the trend is similar. During recent decades population has been dispersed from the heart of the city, and the decline is definitely halted and the population rate again points upward only when we reach a zone two miles from the center.[11] Similar situations exist in such rapidly growing cities as Los Angeles, where the breakup of the commercial nucleus and the dispersion of population from the center may be seen as readily as in older, more stabilized communities like Boston. Furthermore, these trends are evident not only in the great metropolis but in the smaller city as well.[12]

2. Barriers to the Use of Surplus Land

The surplus of land for residential use both within and outside of cities might be expected to create a buyer's market. This is true to some extent, but the land already subidivided may not always be suitable for present needs, or, if suitable, adverse conditions may prevent its utilization.

a. EFFECT OF LOCATION ON THE AVAILABILITY OF LAND

To be suitable for a housing development, a location must have certain characteristics, among which the following are especially important:[13]

9. Tenements built before the Tenement House Law of 1901.

10. Data on New York based on Robert H. Armstrong and Homer Hoyt, *Decentralization in New York City,* A Preliminary Report to The Urban Land Institute, Chicago, January 1941, pp. 13, 25, 167.

11. R. D. McKenzie, *The Metropolitan Community,* McGraw-Hill, New York, 1933, pp. 175–176.

12. See Mabel L. Walker, *Urban Blight and Slums,* Harvard City Planning Studies, Vol. XII, Harvard University Press, Cambridge, 1938, Chaps. III and IV.

13. Based on "Rating of Location," *Underwriting Manual,* Federal Housing Administration, 1938, Pt. II, Sec. 9.

1. It should be in the path of urban growth for the type and class of dwelling proposed.

2. The structures already standing should be in harmony with the proposed dwellings.

3. The site should be capable of preparation without undue expense for the class of dwelling proposed. It should be free from the dangers of flood, subsidence, earthquake, or tornado, and not exposed to health hazards caused by smoke, fog, chemical fumes, stagnant ponds or marshes, poor surface drainage, or excessive heat or dampness.

4. The location should be protected from inharmonious land uses by natural barriers, zoning, protective covenants, or preferably all three.

5. It should be accessible at reasonable cost and time through customary[14] means of transportation to schools, shopping centers, religious and recreational facilities, and places of employment.

6. It should have streets and utilities suitable to the proposed development.

7. It should have some natural or created appeal as a residential neighborhood, such as attractiveness of terrain, landscaping, and layout of streets, and absence of noise, traffic hazards, billboards and other objectionable structures.

Subdividers have frequently ignored these basic criteria. Numerous areas have been platted without regard to their relation to the community or to the directions of community growth. The result is thousands of stranded lots, isolated from the community and badly equipped with urban services.

Lack of Attention to Land Planning

With some notable exceptions little attention, until recent years, was paid to the planning of subdivisions. The typical subdivision was a gridiron of streets forming blocks of about 600 by 250 feet—a pattern that was wasteful of land,[15] extravagant in street and utility installation, and destructive of natural features and of the possibility of devising pleasing housing arrangements. The gridiron pattern, moreover, does not provide for the separation of local and high-speed traffic. Because of an increasing demand for attractively planned neighborhoods free from traffic hazards, communities built on such obsolete patterns are threatened with rapid depreciation. Furthermore, the shape of the lots in the typical gridiron is often a drawback. The long, narrow lot was suitable to a period when the living part of the house preferably faced the front and when a considerable distance between the house and its outbuildings was desirable. The narrow lot does not lend itself to the compactness and privacy, both inside and outside, demanded of the modern house. Where it is impossible to increase their width, adaptation of narrow lots to new planning concepts is often difficult.

14. Customary for the intended class of inhabitants. This may vary from an almost complete reliance on private automobiles to cheap and frequent public conveyances.

15. See, for instance, Robert Whitten and Thomas Adams, *Neighborhoods of Small Houses,* Harvard City Planning Studies, Vol. III, Harvard University Press, Cambridge, 1931, and Thomas Adams, *The Design of Residential Areas,* Harvard City Planning Studies, Vol. VI, Harvard University Press, Cambridge, 1934.

The reeling light poles and vagrant fire hydrants unexpectedly encountered in abandoned fields offer bleak testimony to dormant investments in utilities. In some cases the full complement of utilities is in and paid for. But, unfortunately, the installations are often inadequate for present needs. Sometimes, though once satisfactory, they may now require repair or replacement before they can be utilized—at a cost that may be in addition to special assessments still unsatisfied. Moreover, the very existence of such utilities, even in good condition, may lessen rather than increase the value of the land because they have set an archaic street and lot pattern.

Much subdivided land is poorly protected from adverse influences. The few scattered and frequently outmoded houses found on many subdivisions may be one detriment, inadequate attention to natural boundaries another. In the older sections of cities, where the deterioration of structures creates a need for redevelopment, similar deterrents prevail and new problems are added. Existing block and lot layouts may not be suitable for desirable reconstruction, zoning may need readjustment,[16] and the large number of deteriorated and old structures, incompatible in type and appearance with possible new buildings, may offer overwhelming drawbacks. Thus bad planning and poor location prevent the utilization of a large amount of existing surplus land.

b. EFFECTS OF TAX DELINQUENCY ON THE AVAILABILITY OF LAND

Tax delinquency also tends to immobilize a considerable part of the land supply by increasing the difficulties of obtaining clear title. A Census Bureau study revealed that the average delinquency by assessed value in fifty-seven cities was highest on vacant lots (31 per cent), next highest on apartments and other multifamily structures (28 per cent), and, among residential properties, least on single-family houses (23 per cent). Delinquency by number of parcels affected 45 per cent of all vacant lots, 29 per cent of multifamily structures, and 29 per cent of single-family houses.[17]

Thus, the most prevalent cause of tax delinquency is often that which has chiefly created our surplus of urban land—excessive subdivision. Evidence for this conclusion is also found in an analysis of tax delinquency in four cities and eighteen towns of Westchester County, New York. Here, of the parcels in arrears on 1933 taxes, nearly 80 per cent were vacant lots, many of them in arrears for eight years or longer.[18] The survey notes that single-family house

16. See Chap. 4, pp. 123-125.

17. *Realty Tax Delinquency, Vol. 2, Urban Tax Delinquency,* Bureau of the Census, 1934; figures based on Table D, p. 49.

18. *Land Use and Local Finance,* prepared for the Westchester County Commission on Government by the Institute of Public Administration, New York, December 1935 (mimeographed); see Table III, p. 18a.

delinquency "would not have been sufficiently large to account for the acute crisis in local finance which existed at the end of 1933" and that "the greater part of the outstanding arrears of taxes have accumulated in all parts of the county against two types of property—vacant lands in premature subdivisions, and large multifamily and business buildings erected in premature apartment house and business zones." [19] Further evidence that speculative apartment buildings contributed greatly to delinquency is offered by a study of the second ward of Detroit, where over 75 per cent of the 1932 levy on apartment houses was delinquent on June 1, 1933, as against 35 per cent or less for other types of property.[20]

Delinquency in Slum Areas

As might be expected, slum and blighted districts frequently show high tax delinquency. In St. Louis, for example, heavy delinquency was found particularly among the vacant lots and deteriorated structures in the declining sections of the city. Delinquency in slum areas ranged from 25 to 40 per cent as against 2 to 5 per cent in newer built-up residential districts.[21] In Cincinnati, Milwaukee, Detroit, and Peoria tax delinquency and blight were closely related.[22] Cleveland's delinquent taxes in 1932 amounted to nearly a year's revenues at the 1932 rate. In one blighted area arrears were 64 per cent larger than the 1932 tax-rate income.[23] In Cambridge, Massachusetts delinquency was 43 per cent of potential income in a selected area, but only 18 per cent for the city as a whole.[24] In thirteen blighted districts in New York City the accumulated delinquency in 1938 was 16 per cent of the tax levy, or more than twice the ratio in the rest of Manhattan's residential areas.[25]

Accumulated taxes and penalties in many instances so far exceed the present or probable future value of the lots that owners abandon the land. Where market values are so low that tax sales would not cover the city's deficits, authorities are slow to take action. And even where tax liens have been foreclosed, the fre-

19. *Ibid.*, pp. 25, 35.

20. Virginia L. Eyre, *A Study of Tax Delinquency in the Second Ward of Detroit with Special Reference to Apartment House Properties,* Report No. 3, Social Science Research Council of Wayne University, Detroit, 1934.

21. *Urban Land Policy, St. Louis, Missouri,* City Planning Commission, Harland Bartholomew, Engineer, September 1936; cited in *Urban Planning and Land Policies,* Vol. II of the Supplementary Report of the Urbanism Committee of the National Resources Committee, 1939, p. 250.

22. Walker, *op. cit.*, Chap. IV.

23. *An Analysis of a Slum Area in Cleveland,* Cleveland Metropolitan Housing Authority, 1934.

24. *Cost and Income Survey of Area to the Site of Federal Housing Project,* Cambridge Planning Board (mimeographed), *circa* 1935.

25. *Ailing City Areas,* Citizens' Housing Council of New York, May 1941, Table III, p. 37.

quently doubtful legality of tax titles makes it extremely hard to dispose of the affected parcels.[26]

C. LEGAL AND FINANCIAL BARRIERS TO UTILIZATION OF LAND

Where zoning laws exist, inadequate enforcement or excessive allowance for commercial or high-density building may prevent the rational development of an area. Deficiencies in deed restrictions, where such covenants are used, may have the same effect. For instance, covenants that limit the development to costly houses may keep land idle. Rigid building codes may create economic obstacles which force builders away from otherwise desirable sites to areas beyond code jurisdiction.

Even where old subdivisions are physically satisfactory, legal restrictions may prevent the utilization of the land. It is common in many localities to find lots, scattered or in large groups, that cannot be sold because of defects in title, brought about in a number of ways. Entire subdivisions may be affected by default in an underlying mortgage. Pending proceedings or extended periods of redemption may prevent conveyance of title. If the development company has gone bankrupt and its organization is dispersed, there may be no active agent to convey title even to contract purchasers in good standing. Frequently land is tied up by defaults on land contracts or mortgages made with original buyers whose interests may never have been foreclosed, and whose present addresses are unknown. The bankruptcy of development companies and the obvious futility of holding land for price increases have often led not only to defaults in mortgage and contract obligations but to widespread tax delinquency.

Other legal deterrents to the use of land deserve mention. High taxes may discourage building on otherwise desirable sites and thus contribute to the shift of population to satellite towns or unincorporated areas, where, temporarily at least, taxes are relatively low. Land suitable for development or restoration may be kept from the market by the difficulty of reassembling individual parcels.[27] This disability affects vacant or nearly vacant subdivisions, where reassembly may be necessary in order to change the sizes of lots or reorganize street patterns to conform with good planning practices. It applies with equal force to blighted areas where rehabilitation may be accomplished only by an enterprise large enough to remodel whole neighborhoods.

These obstacles affect the availability of much surplus land. The developer of untouched land, on the other hand, escapes the costly procedure of overcoming

26. Only a few cases of vigorous municipal action in pushing tax sales can be found. In several small California cities two repossessed lots have been offered for the payment of delinquent taxes on one, provided the builder completes two new houses within six months.

27. For discussion of proposed aids to reassembly see pp. 158-159, 274-275, 298-300.

tax delinquencies, replatting subdivided lots, or reassembling land in blighted areas. So long as this is true a considerable surplus of urban land will remain.

3. THE COST OF LAND

Prices naturally influence the availability of land for housing. The drift towards the outlying sections of cities has been due to a search for land cheap enough to permit the building of apartments or single-family dwellings at attractive prices. Land costs raise two important questions. What is the current relation between the price of land and that of the completed dwelling? What is the relation between the cost of raw land and the improvements essential to an urban development?

To these questions wholly satisfactory answers cannot be given because of the lack of accurate statistical data and the difficulty of segregating the cost of raw land from that of improved land. Scattered information, however, provides some revealing clues.

a. PROSPECTS FOR LAND PRICES

The value of land is an abstruse and elusive concept. In good times the avid demands of optimistic bidders force prices beyond the real value of land as measured by the future earning power of the property. In depressions owners may sell their property at prices lower than probable earnings over a long period would justify. Moreover, there is no regular, common market place for land, where, as with many commodities, prices and trends are revealed.

Values for the more speculative types of urban land were, of course, spectacularly deflated during the depression. Apartment buildings sometimes were refinanced on a basis that would not cover the replacement cost of the structures, to say nothing of the value of the land. Vacant lots in Miami, Detroit, Denver, Chicago, and many other cities have sold for less than the cost of the streets and utilities that served them. It has been estimated that land values in Chicago declined from $5 billion in 1928 to $2 billion in 1933.[28]

Some conception of the trend of land values may be gained from revisions of tax assessments. Between 1930 and 1940 assessed values (of land and buildings) declined in Chicago by 44 per cent, in Cleveland by almost 40 per cent, and in Philadelphia, Los Angeles and Baltimore by about 30 per cent. New York showed a reduction of over 11 per cent. Declines in assessments, however, measure only part of the decline in market prices.[29]

28. Hoyt, *op. cit.*, pp. 272–273.

29. Figures supplied by Homer Hoyt. Assessment trends may not tell the whole story. As Robert H. Armstrong and Homer Hoyt say:

"The debt limit of the city of New York is 10 per cent of the assessment of its real estate. The

Deflation of land values has helped to revive building activity in some inner urban areas, as in central Manhattan, where, since 1938, there has been a notable rebirth of apartment building. But the decline of land values has usually been sufficient only to permit the construction of intensively developed high-rental structures. The limited amount of such construction that the market can support at any time is not likely to halt the long-term downward trend of urban land values. Price increases have indeed occurred in some places, but chiefly in especially desirable suburban sections. There has so far been no sign of an upward trend approaching the stratosphere prices of predepression days.[30]

There is too much land available to support a widespread speculative revival. Moreover, if the available land is to be absorbed in any reasonable period of time it must be used mainly for low-density housing developments, and if absorption is to take place on a large scale, for low-income residents. Only the very choicest land is apt to increase in value. For the owners of the rest, it is improbable, in face of carrying costs and taxation, plus the wide range of selection, that there can be much benefit in waiting; while the necessity for its ultimate use by low-income groups removes the likelihood of there being any rise in price to wait for.

Taking the supply as a whole, therefore, probably little room exists for a substantial increase in the value of improved urban land. In fact, values in the older, declining urban sections are likely to decline still further as the flight from the central areas continues.

---

outstanding debt is now within but a few million dollars of the entire debt limit and the legality of the debt is only being held up by gross over assessments. If the assessed value of New York City's real estate would be made to conform to values that exist at the present time as evidenced by income and/or sales prices, New York City would be legally bankrupt. In other words, its legal debt structure is being upheld by illegal assessments." (*Decentralization in New York City*, p. 12.)

The opposite view is expressed by William Stanley Miller, President of the New York City Tax Commission, in a letter to Mayor La Guardia (*The American City*, March 1940, pp. 35-36):

"It never was intended that the tax structure of any great city should be predicated upon the ebb and flow of a distressed real-estate market. The main requisite of any tax structure is stability, because there must necessarily be a stable revenue to be derived from real property in order to meet the bills of the municipality. . . .

"While the provision in the New York City Charter specifies value under ordinary circumstances, the difficulty in ascertaining what *ordinary circumstances* are, adds to the uncertainty of exactly what the law requires, and actual practice cannot be said to accept present market prices as the sole basis of appraisal."

30. This statement refers to land prices in relation to the whole price structure. General inflation certainly would create an upward swing in land values, along with other prices, but it is doubtful if their relationship would change greatly. In view of the present surplus land supply, general inflation might adversely affect the price of raw land. These comments, of course, do not apply to areas now experiencing a boom like Washington, D. C. Yet even there, increases have occurred in newer districts on the rim of the city. Values in the older areas have been relatively unaffected.

b. COST OF LAND IN RELATION TO TOTAL PROPERTY COSTS

Available data indicate significant changes in the relationship of the cost of land to total property costs (land, improvements, and building) over a period of years and a range of property price classifications. Thus, in the four years of increasing building activity ending with 1940 the average relationship between value of improved land and total property value for new single-family dwellings, financed with FHA-insured mortgages, dropped from over 15 per cent to less than 13 per cent. Similar ratios in 1940 varied from almost 11 per cent for properties valued between $2,000 and $4,000 to nearly 19 per cent for properties of $15,000 and over.[31]

The proportion of the total cost allocable to land (including land improvements in the completed property) declines rapidly as the total valuation declines. Thus, for new single-family properties of $15,000 or more, insured by FHA in 1940, the improved lots averaged over $3,200; for dwellings in the $6,000 to $7,000 class they averaged $834; and for small houses in the $2,000 to $4,000 class they averaged $370.[32] These lots vary in location, size, and, as we shall see later, to some extent in improvement costs. It is clear, however, that low-priced houses can be built only on low-priced lands.

The above figures reveal only the appraised value of improved land, at the time of sale with the house erected. They do not tell how much the land cost the builder, nor do they indicate the price a builder will pay for the acreage out of which he expects to obtain the ultimate appraised lot valuation. In order to cover profit, risk, taxes and loss of income during the development period, a developer or builder naturally expects to pay less than he will receive. How much less is a statistical mystery.

The question of the price that will be paid for land for apartment developments is even more obscure. Apartment builders can and will customarily pay higher prices for land than builders of houses in an equivalent rental class. In terms of land cost per dwelling unit, however, there is probably little, if any, differential between the various types of property. In 138 projects financed with FHA-insured loans land represented about 10 per cent of total valuation. The amount attributed to land, however, does not on the one hand always include improvements made within the project limits (these being included under construction estimates), nor, on the other, does it indicate the price actually paid by the developer. As with the single house, it represents the valuation of the land as part of a completed product.

Despite their limitations, the figures seem to indicate that land constitutes a

31. *Seventh Annual Report, 1940,* FHA; see also Appendix A, Table 3.
32. See Appendix A, Table 3.

declining share of total cost as emphasis in the housing industry shifts toward low-priced dwellings. (The decline shown over the past few years in the *average* value of land to total property costs is largely a result of this trend.) Looking at the situation in another way, evidence may be found of increasing pressure on land price as perhaps the most flexible element in total housing costs, i.e., the one in which a price advantage may be gained most readily.

C. RAW LAND AND IMPROVEMENT COSTS

In undertaking a new development, the builder first decides upon the price or rental range of the dwellings he proposes to construct. Then, after roughly estimating the cost of the selected structure, he tries to find land at suitable prices. Before land may be used for urban housing, it must have some degree of preparation, such as surveying, platting, clearing, grading, filling, draining, planting, installation of sewers, water lines, gas and electric lines, paved streets and walks, curbs, and community services and transportation. The builder must, therefore, know the costs of these before he can make an allocation for the land itself.

Improvement costs vary greatly. Flat land obviously requires less preparation than rough terrain. Land on which workingmen's houses are to be built involves less elaborate streets and landscaping than luxurious subdivisions. Land for relatively dense rows of houses or apartment buildings requires concrete sidewalks, wide, heavy streets, and auxiliary pavements for automobile parking, while land for detached dwellings may need only narrow, light street paving and no curbs or walks. Dense developments require fewer linear feet of utilities per dwelling unit, although their capacity will necessarily be greater than a dispersed arrangement. In general, however, no single standard of improvement specifications or costs can be established.

One characteristic of improvement costs deserves special attention. It is not possible to vary the nature and cost of improvements in relation to the buying power of the prospective occupants of the area as much as some of the other costs. For example, the size and quality of sewers or water mains depends upon the density of the population, not its income. Similarly, the material, width, and thickness of streets and the need for curbs and walks are determined primarily by the amount of traffic, not by the economic status of the prospective residents.

Improvement costs, therefore, must be considered in terms of the traffic load, number of families per acre, the character of the land layout, and disposition of the structures. Nevertheless, the buying power of the residents cannot be wholly ignored. Standards in land improvements are subject to the same general economic limitations as standards for house planning and construction. Just as building codes may make it almost impossible to construct low-cost dwellings, so regulations governing the quality of land improvements make the most needed types of housing development very hard to produce. Here, as elsewhere, the engineer's ideal has to be tempered by a recognition of what the public can pay.

Savings through Land Planning

Land planning has a direct influence on the standards of land improvements. For instance, a neighborhood may be so designed as to divert heavy traffic to a few streets, preferably at the boundaries, permitting the interior streets, limited to local traffic, to be narrower and of lighter construction. The use of minor streets and cul-de-sacs branching from main thoroughfares may not only lessen the amount of trunk sewer and water mains required, but permit most of them to be of smaller diameter. Planning may also assure more efficient utilization of land, eliminate unnecessary grading by laying out streets to conform to land contours, and provide parks where preparation costs for building purposes would be excessive. The careful designing of blocks may also eliminate unnecessary utilities and pavements.

The economies of careful planning are limited, however, by traditional methods of platting individually owned lots. So long, for instance, as individual ownership, through custom or regulation, requires that each small unit front upon a public way, builders cannot achieve the savings that might be made by using off-street groupings reached by permanent easements. Where rental housing is contemplated, off-street groupings, illustrated in Figure 2, will reduce costs. Here the absence of individual lots for each separate unit permits a single connection to the trunk sewer and a common branch line to serve a number of dwellings. The same is true of the connections for water, gas and electricity. The ability to group the dwellings in courts, obviously decreases the length of street and of service mains under that required where each unit must front the thoroughfare.

Minimum Costs of Land Improvement

The costs of streets and walks are the largest elements in the improvement bill. To these must be added the costs of sanitary sewers (and, except in areas of very low density, storm sewers) and water mains. Grading, draining, and landscaping costs, varying with the characteristics of the site, must also be added, together with the cost of engineering service. The cost of gas and electric service, while frequently calling for advance payment, is usually reimbursed as the service is put into use.

For single-family houses the minimum cost of preparing land for a 50-foot lot fronting on a 50-foot right-of-way with a 25-foot paved street would probably be not under $240.[33] The figure would be less or more depending on the improvements installed.[34] For multifamily [35] construction, the improvement cost per family unit will probably correspond rather closely to the minimum for single-house developments. Costs for multifamily housing are much more difficult to judge because of the range in density encountered, and because in most multifamily areas the land has already been to some degree improved so that improvement costs cannot be separated from the price of land. For 107 projects built on vacant land the United States Housing Authority found that improvement costs per family unit ranged from $178 to $932, with an average of $521.

Costs of Raw Land

If improvement costs on a given property are known, it is possible to estimate the approximate sum that can be paid for the land itself. There are difficulties, however, in getting accurate figures. For example, land suitable for urban purposes is rarely found in a completely raw state. It is likely to be partly improved even before the transition to urban use occurs, though perhaps by only a highway, trunk sewer, or electric power extension. As the centers of cities are approached, more improvements are found. Hence, it is rarely possible to estimate exactly just how much of quoted prices are attributable to land and how much to existing improvements.

For all new single-family properties valued between $2,000 and $4,000, financed by the FHA, the average value of lots was $370. Assuming the above minimum of $240 for improvements, the average price of raw land would be $130 a lot. With 5 houses per gross acre for this type of property (the FHA average being 3.3), the builder would be able to spend a maximum of $650 an acre for raw land for low-priced dwellings. At the rate of 3.3 lots per gross acre, his maximum allowance would be about $430 per acre. Land at either price, however, is rarely available except in outlying districts, and the increased building activity in these areas is, therefore, undoubtedly affected by the low price of land.[36]

33. This is based on $1.75 per front foot as the minimum road cost suitable for average single-house developments, $0.85 per front foot for curb and gutter, $0.95 for sanitary sewer, $0.25 for planting and seeding, and $1.00 for water. These estimates are based on averages for New York, Philadelphia, Baltimore, and Washington areas as published in *Insured Mortgage Portfolio,* FHA, Vol. 5, No. 3, First Quarter, 1941, or as provided by the Land Planning Division, FHA. See also Appendix A, Table 4, for variations in improvement costs.

34. It should be noted that the cost of installing a satisfactory septic tank and a driven well with electric pump for each lot will ordinarily equal or exceed the lot's share in community facilities. In many cases a public water supply is available, but sewage disposal must still be privately supplied.

35. This term is used throughout to denote not only apartment structures but group housing.

36. The movement to new land is discussed on pp. 35-37. The average cost of raw land for *all grades of development,* in seventy-seven New York subdivisions checked by FHA was $769 an acre, ranging from $1,300 in White Plains to $502 in Buffalo. Since all price classes are included, and costs in New York subdivisions are relatively high, the average is probably somewhat higher than for low-cost dwellings in the country as a whole.

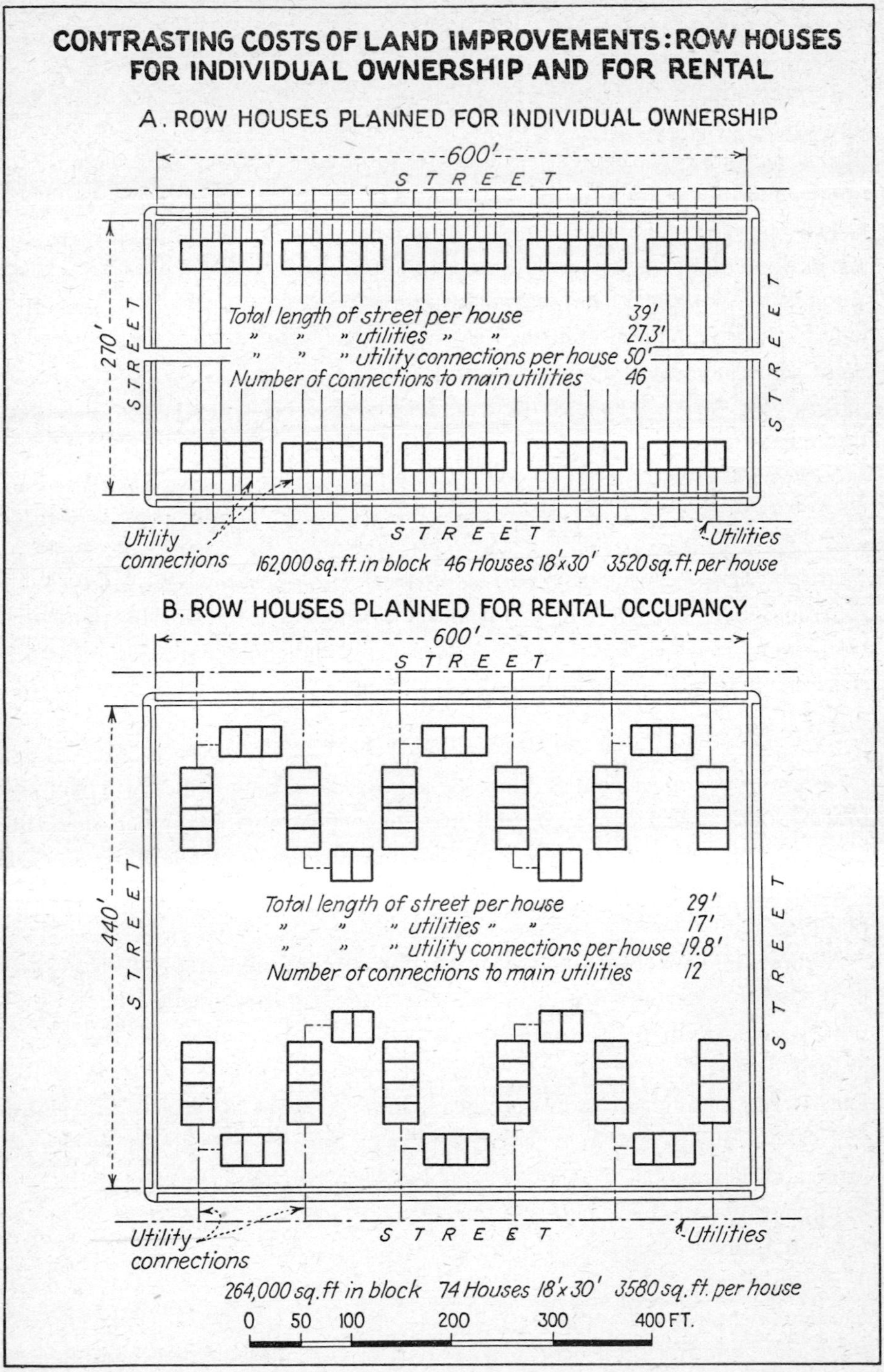

CONTRASTING COSTS OF LAND IMPROVEMENTS: ROW HOUSES FOR INDIVIDUAL OWNERSHIP AND FOR RENTAL

A. ROW HOUSES PLANNED FOR INDIVIDUAL OWNERSHIP

600'
STREET
270'
STREET
STREET
STREET

Total length of street per house 39'
" " " utilities " " 27.3'
" " " utility connections per house 50'
Number of connections to main utilities 46

Utility connections
Utilities
162,000 sq. ft. in block 46 Houses 18'x30' 3520 sq. ft. per house

B. ROW HOUSES PLANNED FOR RENTAL OCCUPANCY

600'
STREET
440'
STREET
STREET
STREET

Total length of street per house 29'
" " " utilities " " 17'
" " " utility connections per house 19.8'
Number of connections to main utilities 12

Utility connections
Utilities
264,000 sq. ft in block 74 Houses 18'x30' 3580 sq. ft. per house
0 50 100 200 300 400 FT.

FIGURE 2. Off-street groupings of row houses for rental occupancy result in considerable economies in street frontage and utility service costs. (*Source:* Staff of Twentieth Century Fund Housing Survey.)

Many things, of course, affect the price which the builder can afford to pay for land. Foremost are the allowable density and the price he can get for the finished dwelling. The building of row houses permits a developer to pay more for land than if he were constructing detached houses of an equivalent sales price. Location, while of less importance than formerly, is still a considerable influence. (FHA experience indicates that failures are greatest among remote, poorly serviced subdivisions.) Land that is easily improved will ordinarily be more valuable than rugged land necessitating costly improvements. On the other hand, attractive natural features may more than offset high cost of improvement, especially for high-priced dwellings. Nevertheless, it is clear that for most of the housing market the price at which land will move is definitely limited.

4. TRENDS IN LAND UTILIZATION

In spite of the enormous variations in local situations, there is a remarkable consistency in current trends in the development and use of urban residential land, some of which have a profound bearing on housebuilding and in turn reflect the influence of changing modes of living.

a. DECLINE IN DENSITY AND PRICE

Future urban development may be expected to follow the current trend toward lower-priced dwellings and more open planning. Light and space are no longer found exclusively in the high-priced suburb. The threat of air attacks may be counted on to intensify the trend toward decentralized, open planning.

According to the Federal Housing Administration, lots fifty feet wide, and in the South, even sixty feet wide, are becoming standard for detached houses, with an average in 1941 of only 3.5 lots per gross acre in new subdivisions approved by that agency. This contrasts sharply with former practices in the Detroit and Chicago areas, for instance, where frontages for detached dwellings were frequently as low as twenty-five feet, permitting as many as 15 lots per gross acre. Change in the width of lots has been the most common method of modifying old subdivisions.

Multifamily areas also tend to have lower population density than formerly. The garden-type apartment, often with twenty-five families or less to the acre, has figured prominently in new projects, both public and private. Even in New York City, which accounts for a major part of current apartment building, the high structure, crowded on a small plot, while not altogether a thing of the past, is being supplanted by the garden type, frequently low in height as well as in the percentage of land covered.[37]

Although trends in land values are hard to trace, there is a noticeable trend toward the use of cheaper land. FHA reports a decline of over 27 per cent between 1937 and 1940 in the average value of lots used in new single-family houses.[38] This decline is probably representative of the single-family house situation as a whole. Unfortunately similar data for land for apartment structures do not exist. But here again, the building of apartment houses in the outlying districts of cities and the increasing popularity of garden projects indicate that low-priced land is readily available, and often it is cheap enough to permit open development.

b. PROTECTING NEIGHBORHOOD VALUES

Before the 1930's the characteristic method of developing land was to sell vacant subdivided lots. The subdivider was only a retail land merchant. Sometimes he arranged for and carried out the installation of pavements and utilities, usually with the aid of municipal special assessment financing or outright gifts from the city. More often, however, the subdivider undertook nothing more than a land survey; he placed street markers to identify the future gridiron amid the stubble, and little flags to designate lot boundaries. Improvements and building were usually far from his interest. Subdividing was thus separate from building, and more often than not its methods were harmful to the development of attractive neighborhoods.

Yet there were notable exceptions. Some of the finest examples of residential land planning and co-ordination of building and subdividing date from the period 1890 to 1930, like Riverside and Lake Forest near Chicago, Roland Park in Baltimore, the Country Club district of Kansas City, Missouri, River Oaks in Houston, and the Jemison properties in Birmingham, to mention only a few outstanding examples. Such developments provided a pattern quite in contrast with that offered by the free-ride and barbecue type of subdivider. These residential parks, however, were restricted in price and clientele and did not markedly influence the general methods of subdividing and developing land.

Changes in subdividing methods have occurred because vacant lots are increasingly unmarketable to the individual buyer, and because lot selling, as such, offers less chance of high rewards than formerly, either to the subdivider or to

37. The low-density public housing projects (PWA and USHA—Local Authority) and the private projects subject to FHA financing have contributed to this trend. On the basis of about eighty USHA public housing projects, the modal project had a gross density of between 12 and 19 families per acre. The average population density for FHA rental projects was 17.8 families per acre. (FHA projects generally are not in central urban areas.)

38. See Appendix A, Table 3.

the speculative buyer. Subdividing is now, in fact, ordinarily profitable only when associated with a building operation. Today land is apt to be purchased and prepared by the operative builder, or by an independent developer who sells lots at wholesale to builders. Frequently the builders are in effect the building agents of the land developer, who may be the real director of the entire project. The closer relations of subdividing and building have helped to keep land prices adjusted to other housing costs and thus to put a damper on land speculation for its own sake. They have tended to adapt land planning to the character of the structures, rather than, as in the past, to force housing to adapt itself to a preconceived lot pattern, designed for speculation rather than utility. They have also helped to keep new subdividing down to the possibilities of utilization.

Methods of Retarding Neighborhood Depreciation

With decreased speculative profits through change to more profitable uses of the land, the developer is more likely to become interested in preserving the original residential value as long as possible—at least for the normal period of mortgage amortization. To attain this end, the low- and medium-cost projects are now often planned as carefully as the exclusive residential developments of a former era. Indeed, safeguards as a means of preserving values are applied to a wide range of neighborhoods—those with $3,000 properties as well as sumptuous houses—and to rental developments as well as to individual dwellings for sale.

Several methods are commonly used to preserve and stabilize values. The land may be laid out so as to discourage the encroachment of undesirable uses. Natural barriers, public parks or other permanent open spaces, dedicated planting strips, or main highways, may be utilized as boundaries. The streets may be designed to discourage through traffic; the development may have its own parks and, where size permits, its own shopping and community facilities, and perhaps even its own churches and schools.[39]

Physical and social homogeneity may, in part, be achieved by planning the land so as to produce a self-contained community. It may also be fostered by harmonious architectural treatment of the dwellings. Wide variations in the type and price of dwellings are avoided. But sometimes this tendency has been pushed so far that it results in either snobbish exclusiveness or the monotonous sameness of a single economic level. The latter characteristic may be found in its most exaggerated form in the mammoth public housing projects. In some cases, however, the desired end is achieved with a considerable variety in both price and type. The River Oaks development in Houston, for instance, con-

39. See Clarence Arthur Perry, *Housing for the Machine Age,* Russell Sage Foundation, New York, 1939, Chaps. III–V, for an excellent presentation of the neighborhood-unit idea and the planning methods that may be used in its achievement. See also, Adams, *op. cit.,* Chap. X.

tains houses that cost from $8,000 to over $100,000 and the Ford Foundation development at Dearborn, Michigan combines both rented and owned dwellings in one general neighborhood scheme.

Deed restrictions, or protective covenants, are often used to preserve the original features of the development. These are now frequently applied to many types of subdivisions, both high-priced and low-priced. Deed restrictions frequently regulate the minimum construction cost,[40] and sometimes provide for architectural control. They almost always establish, for the period to which the covenants apply, the residential character of the neighborhood by regulating the size of lots, use of the land, the placing of the structure, and the space between houses.[41]

Shortcomings in Subdivision Practices

Not all current subdividing follows these standards. Land-planning skill is too scarce or too little utilized and its benefits insufficiently appreciated to prevent inept and wasteful planning in which the seeds of neighborhood obsolescence are planted as the streets are laid. Moreover, much ill-advised and unneeded subdividing has undoubtedly taken place in recent years. But perhaps the darkest part of the picture is the heritage of the past.

The freezing of a considerable part of the land supply has often forced new development into places far out of touch with the built-up sections, and here isolation is likely soon to produce discontent. Although distance means less than it used to, it may still mean inconvenience and transportation costs that, partly at least, offset the original advantage of cheaper land. Even the tax problem—one of the prime incentives to the outward shift of urban population—cannot be wholly escaped. The demand for education and sanitation facilities, for traffic control and other community services, is bound ultimately to increase taxes in the new neighborhoods, while the central city, burdened with the costs of maintaining services in unremunerative districts, is certain to levy on the commuter some direct or indirect taxes—such as the New York City sales tax—to compensate for the loss of realty tax revenues. Furthermore, the immense surplus of land is a constant challenge to the security of new developments.

C. GROWTH OF PUBLIC CONTROL OF LAND SUBDIVISION

Since the community as a whole is the principal victim of excessive subdivision, it is natural for the community to attempt to protect itself against unneces-

40. Due to cost variations, this type of covenant is likely to interfere seriously with building when the market is out of line. A more satisfactory way of regulating the character of the structure is by setting a minimum square-foot area for the house.

41. For typical restrictions, see FHA Form No. 2084B, "Mortgage Insurance Requirements with Respect to Protective Covenants."

sary land speculation. Public control of subdividing in this country dates from the 1880's. The village of Oak Park, Illinois instituted a form of control as early as 1882. In 1888, the Commissioners of the District of Columbia were authorized to regulate the platting of subdivisions. At the present time, thirty-one states and the District of Columbia authorize the establishment of regulations covering subdividing practices.[42]

The usual forms of regulation provide some control over the *way in which land is subdivided,* but do not limit the *quantity to be subdivided.* From the point of view of an orderly land market and the economic burden to the community, the latter is, of course, a vital necessity. The constitutionality of regulating quantity, however, appears doubtful since subdividing land for residential purposes has not yet been regarded as a type of activity for which evidence of public necessity may properly be demanded.

Since communities thus find it difficult to limit the quantity of subdivisions, they have recently sought some indirect means of control. This has usually taken the form of requiring the subdivider to provide essential improvements or post some form of guarantee for their installation within a limited period. "The requiring of improvement construction coincident with platting," says Harold W. Lautner, "provides a moderate restraint upon such tendencies toward unwarranted land speculation. In marketing the improved, usable lot, subdivision activity tends to direct itself toward the production of lots for human habitation and building purposes in a volume more directly related to consumption needs and demand."[43]

Thus far the results of subdivision control have not been commensurate with the seriousness of the situation. Of the 215 known places where some form of improvement installation was required, 35 per cent required the installation of storm sewers and drainage, 24 per cent sanitary sewers, 22 per cent water supply, and only 4 per cent road paving.[44] Even where the municipality's jurisdiction extends sufficiently beyond corporate limits to cover most of the actual or potential adjoining land supply, the methods of control do not yet assure adequate protection against excessive subdividing.

In view of the inadequacies of local control as a means of diminishing the risks of mortgage insurance, the federal government through the Federal Housing Administration has sought to exercise some influence over the additions to the land supply. It has required the submission of subdivision layouts for all undeveloped areas where FHA financing was to be used. It has also endeavored to

42. Harold W. Lautner, *Subdivision Regulations,* Public Administration Service, Chicago, 1941, pp. 302, 317-342. See Chap. 6, pp. 157-159, for discussion of other methods of land use regulation.
43. *Ibid.,* p. 238.
44. *Ibid.,* p. 246.

limit the number of new lots to some reasonable rate of absorption, required the installation of improvements as a prerequisite to mortgage insurance, and often succeeded in improving the quality of subdivision planning. But FHA procedure exercises only remote and partial control and is not a substitute for vigorous, rational local regulation.

d. THE MOVEMENT TO NEW LAND

Although there are large quantities of vacant subdivided land in the United States, overwhelming handicaps prevent the utilization of much of it. The result is that already, after a few years of building activity, there is a considerable revival of subdividing. The FHA has reported steady increases in the proportion of loans insured in new areas. In St. Louis, Atlanta and Washington, D.C., for instance, more than 95 per cent of all insured loans during the first half of 1941 involved new areas. In Detroit and Chicago, well over half the insured loans were located in new subdivisions.[45]

It is estimated that during 1939 and 1940 the new areas approved by FHA for insured loans would have accommodated about 530,000 families in single-family houses, or almost twice the number of all new dwellings actually insured. Allowing for the fact that many houses might be built in these areas without FHA loans, there is still evidence of the accumulation of a new surplus of subdivided land. In 1939, probably half the areas examined by FHA represented the revival of subdivisions dating from the twenties or earlier. During the first six months of 1940 the percentage of revivals had dropped to just over 20 per cent.[46] FHA land planning officials estimate that the market has already absorbed the better part of the carry-over *that is readily available and suitable for use under present-day conditions.*

Such an interpretation does not deny the existence of a tremendous surplus of frozen low-grade subdivided land. New platting would be unprofitable if there were a surplus of property well-suited to market requirements, for this would tend to keep prices below the costs of new developments. But the poorly planned, legally involved, and financially distressed areas do not offer active competition to new subdivisions. Moreover, many older areas suffer from lack of promotion. A new, well-designed, well-merchandised subdivision may therefore occupy a strong competitive position compared to an area that was indifferently planned, weakly promoted, and marred by existing scattered houses of an earlier era. In any event, only a small portion of the old subdivisions is utilized as builders and developers push into new areas.

45. Source: Land Planning Division, FHA.
46. *Ibid.*

Unavailability of Centrally Located Land

Similar conditions are visible at the declining urban centers, which from many points of view may be better located for housing projects than new areas. Except for the work of public housing agencies, no effective means has yet been developed to encourage the restoration of areas containing marginal or submarginal housing.[47] In some cases lending institutions—the unwilling owners of foreclosed property—have done piecemeal rehabilitation. In others, particularly in the large eastern cities, private operators have entered the field, sometimes successfully.

Occasionally, as in several Manhattan areas, in the Georgetown section of the District of Columbia, or the Beacon Hill section of Boston, notable revivals have taken place over a period of years. Usually, however, rehabilitation has been a scattered process and has had a negligible influence on the neighborhood in general. Usually, too, rehabilitation has been undertaken only if there was a likelihood of attracting higher-income occupants. Since this prospect is exceptional, restoration activities have not offered an effective counterattack to the strong outward shift of urban populations.

Generally, neither land values nor taxes have yet declined to a point where the older central areas have attained anything like price parity, even for apartment building, with outlying locations. The outward movement of city residents, therefore, continues at an accelerating rate. The continued disability of a considerable proportion of the vacant lots in districts closer to the circumferential area has pushed housing developments even farther out.

The persistence of this trend may be counted on, as well as the tendency of developers to build houses where land is relatively cheap and ample.[48] Such land may not always be ideally located nor best suited to sound urban organization; it may also suffer from high taxes and other disabilities created by urban disintegration. To encourage the most suitable use of urban land, we must replan and reintegrate many communities, revise the tax system and abandon concepts

47. In the "Waverly district" in Baltimore, the Home Owners' Loan Corporation in co-operation with property owners, municipal authorities, and lending institutions inaugurated a plan for restoring a declining neighborhood. Although the major features of the plan have not been undertaken, a considerable amount of rehabilitation has proceeded. During the second year of the program the number of paid-in-full HOLC loans in the area nearly doubled while the ratio of HOLC borrowers in default declined by more than 50 per cent. Outstanding is the utilization of a section of vacant land for 118 dwelling units costing about $500,000. The plan is described in *Waverly—A Study in Neighborhood Conservation,* Federal Home Loan Bank Board, 1940. See also *Federal Home Loan Bank Review,* September 1941, p. 416. A similar project has been undertaken in the Woodlawn area of Chicago.

48. This outward shift does not necessarily mean extreme remoteness from populated centers. Old subdivisions have left great gaps of untouched land between suburban rail lines, which now are tapped by motor highways. Moreover, it is well to keep in mind that in a circle, the area increases with the square of the distance, so that doubling the distance from the center quadruples the possible usable area.

of land values based on untenable assumptions of population growth and density. In order, however, to maintain a sufficient volume of building activity, it is necessary to use the best available land. At the present time, this is generally found in the untainted areas at the peripheries of cities.

5. SUMMARY

This brief examination of the land situation shows the waste and disorder that traditional subdividing practices have created. The most immediate effect is the freezing of intrinsically desirable land which, if existing disabilities were removed, builders might use with advantage to themselves, their customers, and the community as a whole. This unavailable surplus is found at the edges as well as in the centers of cities. Its availability for housing must await fundamental changes in public policy toward land and urban organization. In fact, this is not a housing problem, but a major social, economic, and political problem, calling for far-reaching research and carefully considered action.

Pending such action, plenty of other land is available for housing projects. There seems little danger that either increasing shortage or increasing cost will be a drawback. Nevertheless, in numerous indirect ways the housebuilding industry will suffer handicaps as a result of the indigestible surplus of close-in land. These will be felt in various concealed costs, in hazards to property investments and in limitations on effective housing demand, caused by increasing remoteness from the centers of community activity. The public measures so far taken to cope with the problems of surplus land and deterioration of neighborhoods are inadequate. The efforts of builders to protect their developments, while often marking a great advance over former practices, can hardly overcome factors beyond their control. Until fundamental readjustments of the land problem can be made, housing problems cannot be fully solved.

Chapter 2

THE HOUSE AS AN INDUSTRIAL PRODUCT

Among the factors that influence the cost of producing an article, the nature of the product itself is most important. The house, reduced to its simplest forms, is large, ponderous, complex, and expensive. Producers must contend with numerous climatic and economic factors as well as wide variations in personal tastes. These forces have a profound bearing on the character of the housebuilding industry.

1. Physical Characteristics of the Dwelling

The house—whatever the form it takes—is the center of family life. It must provide space for cooking and eating, living and sleeping, and frequently the raising of children. It should be so arranged as to facilitate these activities, foster harmonious family life, and, so far as it can, minister to the privacy and integrity of the individual. The house should create an atmosphere of comfort and quiet, be fresh and cheerful, commodious within and have ample surrounding space, yet not be too large or complex for the scale of living of its occupants.

No other industry must translate so many ideals into material terms as housebuilding. In such terms, the house is a fixed, durable enclosure, providing protection from the elements and including the spaces and facilities necessary for carrying on family life. Even a one-room cottage or cabin is a bulky commodity with a complex function. The modern dwelling is often as intricate as the functions it serves, in its type and layout, the materials of which it is made, and the ways of assembling them.

a. fixed location

The house, unlike other consumer products, is ordinarily put together and used at the same place. Fixity of location is its primary quality.[1] The house is not only identified with a plot of ground, but, especially in the city, depends upon

1. A considerable amount of wartime housing is demountable with a high degree of salvability. The extent to which demountable houses solve some of the problems created by fixed location awaits demonstration. Obviously, demountability cannot solve all the problems arising from location, as pointed out later.

utilities, such as streets, walks, water and sewer pipes, gas mains, and electric cables as well as such community facilities as schools, stores, churches, fire and police protection, and hospitals.

This situation would not be much different if dwellings were readily demountable, or if, like trailers, they remained on wheels. No matter how short its stay in a locality, a mobile or semimobile dwelling must have a definite site, be dependent upon the services provided for that site, and subject to the limitations, charges and conditions prescribed for the use of the site. Consequently, all aspects of the urban economy associated with land—land values, taxes, changing uses—become part of the housing picture, and directly or indirectly affect dwelling costs.

Fixity of site, moreover, subjects the house to numerous local regulations covering land use, construction, character of occupancy and the like, as well as to equally numerous customs and practices that are sometimes as deep-seated as the law. A builder must know these requirements thoroughly. Often they are so complicated that only long experience provides the necessary knowledge. Consequently the nonlocal builder is placed at a disadvantage, and building organizations that might operate over a wide territory are discouraged. Except in the largest and most active areas, the creation of housebuilding companies large enough to use industrialized methods is handicapped. Fixed location has thus tended to keep the building industry a local as well as a costly business.

As we have seen in the last chapter, the house and the land must be adapted to each other. It is, of course, possible through grading, filling, terracing, or retaining to fit the land to the house; but this has fairly definite limits. More frequently, the house must be adjusted to the conditions of the site. Here, fixity of location tends to limit the possibilities of standardization, and to make each house a unique product at least to some degree, involving special and sometimes unpredictable costs.

b. BULK

Even if the house were not attached to the land it would not, because of its mass and weight, be easily moved. A four-room, one-story, basementless frame dwelling that can be built to sell (without land) for around $3,000 to $4,000 may weigh slightly over 92,000 pounds, or a little more than 12 pounds per cubic foot of enclosed volume. A three-foot wall foundation of six-inch concrete on concrete footings, accounts for about 45 per cent of the total weight. Such a house, of course, could be lightened by using isolated pier foundations. If, however, a full basement were included, about 85,000 pounds would be added to the weight. If the exterior walls were built of eight inches of brick, about 83,000 more pounds would be added, bringing the whole structure to more than 260,000 pounds, or more than 21 pounds per cubic foot of enclosed volume. Such a house is about the smallest considered practicable for commercial production during the past decade.

This minimum four-room house contains (including the chimney) over 52,000 pounds of mason materials, and almost 24,000 pounds of lumber and wood products—showing that, by weight, even a basementless frame house may still be dominantly masonry. Plaster (including gypsum lath) runs to nearly 14,000 pounds; and metal of various kinds amounts to at least 3,000 pounds, of which the plumbing system and fixtures account for more than a third. If the house has a basement and brick walls, the masonry may weigh over 225,000 pounds, while the amount of wood used will be over 18,000 pounds.[2] This small house is twenty-six times the weight of the car its occupant is apt to own.

Bulk constitutes a major problem in the housing industry. Because it must be adapted to a particular site, the mass and weight of a house have made it difficult to produce at a distance. Moreover, since in their unassembled state the materials of a house are both heavy and cumbersome, it has been customary, in order to reduce transportation costs, to ship them in as small and compact forms as possible. This, however, as we shall see later, has made the assembly of the parts at the site difficult and costly.

C. COMPLEXITY

Because of the multiplicity of its functions, fixity of location, and bulk, the traditional dwelling is exceedingly complex and varied in type and arrangement, in the number and relationship of its parts, materials of which it is composed, equipment, and methods of its construction.

Complexity of Arrangement

The interior of the house must be arranged to provide for its numerous functions. Space must be found for cooking, eating, recreation, and sleeping. Except under primitive rural conditions, sanitary facilities are necessary, sometimes on an elaborately duplicated scale. In addition to kitchen, bedrooms, bath, there may be a living room, library, nursery, game room, music room, workshop, and the like. Storage space is essential; a laundry room and garage are frequently required, and space for the heating plant, water heater, and fuel are almost universal requirements.

Not every house has all the rooms mentioned, but some, especially on farms and in small towns, may include others not listed, such as special accommodations

2. Specially prepared data, by the Technical Division, Federal Housing Administration; see also Appendix B, 1 and Table 5. The war situation has resulted in much variation in the amounts of certain materials used. The effect of this on standard practice, however, cannot yet be measured.

for preserving and storing food. In elaborate mansions space for the various functions may be so completely separated that privacy borders on loneliness. Elsewhere, cooking, eating, and recreation may sometimes go happily together; sleeping in the living room may not always be a hardship, while a single bathroom may serve several people. Unless he is building to order, the builder must know, or guess, how much and what kind of space his prospective buyers will want.

In a detached dwelling or flat the essential rooms may be on one floor or piled up over four or five stories as in costly town houses. They may be arranged in a compact cube, or in a rambling manner, with little thought of land or structural economy. Here again there is infinite choice and almost limitless possibilities of individual expression.

The housebuilding industry, for the most part, has not only accepted but encouraged and exploited individual preference in the selection and arrangement of dwelling space. Architects and contract builders thrive on the heterogeneity of housing design. The operative builder has only hesitantly departed from it, and has usually tried to disguise his standardized plans by means of personalized gadgetry. The result is to entrench the custom-built tradition in house construction, and to discourage the introduction of repetitive methods that have led to the reduction of costs in other fields.

Multiplicity of Parts

One of the large mail-order houses normally stocks about 9,700 items used in a moderately priced house. This stock excludes masonry parts, and counts as single items many articles like window sash and frames that consist of numerous subparts. If we count all the items that are ordered in one piece, but exclude separate pieces of assembled parts, as in a lock or medicine cabinet, pieces cut in two on the job, loose items like nails and screws, and plastic materials like plaster, the parts going into a detached house of average size exceed 30,000.[3] By comparison an automobile, with its 5,000 parts is a simple contraption. A military tank can be produced from 17,000 parts (exclusive of rivets).[4]

The forms and sizes of the parts of a house are extraordinarily extensive. Such standardization as has occurred in their manufacture still leaves a bewildering multiplicity of window sash, doors, plumbing fixtures and fittings, cabinets, slate, tile, lumber, hardware, and other items.[5] This multiplicity is stimulated by the desire for individual expression on the part of owners and architects and

3. "The Integrated House," *Architectural Forum,* April 1937. See also Peter A. Stone and R. Harold Denton, *Toward More Housing,* Temporary National Economic Committee, Monograph No. 8, 1940, pp. 132–133.

4. "The Integrated House," *loc. cit.;* and *The New York Sunday Times Magazine,* March 2, 1941, p. 12.

5. See Chap. 5, pp. 131-134, for a report on progress in standardization.

by the efforts of manufacturers to obtain an advantage, however temporary, for their special products.

It is impossible for the builder to estimate with complete accuracy the cost of such a diversity of items, especially where the final product is not often duplicated. Contractors are forced to safeguard themselves against inaccuracies on the one hand, and wastage of materials on the other. What this means in the final cost of the house is suggested by the wide variation among bids submitted by a number of bidders.[6] The multiplicity of housing parts also poses for the manufacturer and distributor problems of gauging demand, warehousing and handling, and maintaining stocks for replacements and repairs.

Variety of Materials

A large number of common materials enters into the parts of a house.[7] These materials represent numerous sources of raw material supply and processes of manufacture. Some materials, such as wood and stone, reach the building site after only one or a few intermediate processes. Others, like many metals and components of paint and plastics, pass through five or more stages before they can be included in the house.[8] In short, housebuilding touches practically the whole field of raw material production, while the processing of the materials used involves at least sixty-nine manufacturing industries.[9]

The builder has a considerable choice of materials in normal times. Window sash may be made of wood, steel, bronze, or aluminum; floor tile of clay products, stone, rubber, cork products, magnesium compounds, wood fiber, or other things; roofing tiles or shingles of wood, clay, stone, asbestos, cement, or bituminous compounds. Sometimes one part is compounded of many materials. Thus, the asphalt shingle is made of felt, bitumen, and stone chips; the assembled window may have a wood sash, glass panes, steel glass clips, nails and screws, putty, aluminum weather stripping, bronze hardware, iron sash weights, cotton sash cords, glue, and lead and oil paint.

Because of the diversity and complexity of parts and materials, the housebuilding industry is confronted with an intricate assembly job. The builder cannot hope to have more than a general acquaintance with the properties, uses, and

6. An unpublished study by the FHA of estimates submitted by bidders on public buildings, including public housing projects, showed that the average range between low and high bids was 30.5 per cent, and between the low bids and the averages in each case 15.3 per cent. Presumably, estimates on public works are more accurate than on average private construction, since plans and specifications are provided in great detail and wage rates are predetermined.

7. See Appendix B, Table 6.

8. Stone and Denton, *op. cit.,* Chart XX, p. 189.

9. According to the Census of Manufactures' classification which divides all manufacturing concerns into about 440 separate industries. See *Biennial Census of Manufactures, 1937,* Pt. 1, pp. V-XI.

methods of installing such an array of materials. He must rely, therefore, upon numerous separate skills and a variety of labor and subcontracting organizations.

Complexity of Equipment

The pipes, ducts, wires, heating apparatus, plumbing equipment, and facilities for the preservation and preparation of food provide the body of the structure with its nerves and entrails. More than other components, they make the average modern house a greatly different structure from that of a century ago. Moreover, they add at least a ton to the weight of the average small dwelling, and account for about one fourth of its cost.

Every house, even when new, does not contain, of course, all the equipment we have listed. In many rural areas and small towns modern equipment is only used to a limited extent. Nevertheless, standards for all classes of new housing, except in remote areas, call for at least some provision for a mechanical water supply and sanitation facilities, and usually for lighting, heating, cooking, and refrigeration. Even in the South, some mechanical heating device is commonly desired.

The introduction of mechanical equipment has greatly improved the quality of housing. It has also greatly increased housing costs. It has multiplied the tasks of fitting, adjusting and assembling at the site, thereby adding to the army of highly skilled specialists on whom the builder must rely.

d. VARIETY OF STRUCTURAL METHODS

The multitude of materials and parts that go into a house may be assembled in many ways. Brick, wood, concrete, steel, all dictate corresponding structural systems, and for every such material there is a choice of assembly methods.

Brick, for example, may be laid solid or with an internal cavity. If the first method is used, the wall may be bonded in half a dozen ways; if the second, the bricks may be set and the inner and outer surface crosstied in several ways. Brick or stone may be veneered against cinder block, hollow tile, poured concrete, or wood or steel frames. Concrete walls may be poured in place or built in blocks. In traditional construction a wood stud frame of the house may be one of three types—balloon, platform, or braced frame,[10] but each has a considerable variety of detail. Steel frames may follow wooden prototypes; in the larger, multifamily structures, skeleton steel construction may be used; and again, reinforced concrete columns and beams may be substituted for steel.

10. In the balloon frame, the wall studs run through two stories. In the other types the studs are one story in height, the main distinction being whether the second-floor studs rest directly on the plate over the first-floor studs (braced) or on a sill laid over the rough second floor. See *Recommended Minimum Requirements for Small Dwelling Construction,* National Bureau of Standards, Building and Housing Publication No. 18, 1932, pp. 53–57.

Floors, ceilings and roofs are ordinarily made of wood anchored and braced in a variety of ways; but even in small structures, steel, in pressed or expanded shapes, may replace wood. Reinforced concrete for floors and framing is a commonplace in apartment buildings and is sometimes used in single-family dwellings. Lately, walls and floors of preassembled panels, rather than continuous frames made of wood or steel, have challenged the older methods.[11]

While some building methods are rather generally accepted, others have only local popularity. Those favored in one region may actually be banned in another. Thus the balloon frame, almost universally used in the Middle West, is forbidden in parts of New Jersey for no discernible reason. Climate may justify different construction methods. In parts of California, the structure may be lighter than in colder regions, but it must have special bracing to withstand earthquakes. Florida must build walls to defy hurricanes, and in the northern states roofs must be strong enough to bear the weight of snow.

This variety of construction method fosters and is in turn fostered by local building practices. Regions and towns develop customary ways of doing things, and sometimes these practices, with little rationality, are frozen in building codes. Tradition, law, and the accustomed procedures of workmen tend to combat the introduction of new methods. And higher costs may actually result from the attempted use of systems which are intrinsically more economical but with which the builder and his workmen are unfamiliar.

e. VARIETY OF TYPES

The numerous materials, parts, equipment, and methods of house construction are, of course, not combined in a standard product. The astronomical number of possible combinations is further increased by the variety of dwelling types.

The *single-family house* is the most common type, according to census figures, representing well over half the existing dwelling units in the United States and an even greater proportion of each year's production. It assumes a great diversity of forms, as determined by style, size, number of rooms, layout, and cost. The *detached house* is by far the favorite single-family dwelling, certainly with most builders, and apparently with both the buying and renting public. Locale and climate create architectural distinctions—like the sturdy, compact New England houses, the wide verandas of the South, the bungalows of the Middle West, and the different type of bungalow of the Pacific Coast.

In order to save on land, utilities, and, under certain circumstances, on the structure itself, separate dwellings may be joined together. Thus we have the *double house* (or, more technically, the *semiattached house*), and when three or more are combined, the *row* or *attached house* (the most aristocratic of which

11. See Chap. 5, pp. 140-141.

are called *town houses*). The double house probably represents but a minor proportion of the total stock. The row house is common in the older cities of the Middle Atlantic states; elsewhere it is much less popular than the detached dwelling.

Multifamily structures range from the humble two-family house to the grandiosity of the Park Avenue apartment. Like single-family houses, apartment structures may stand alone or be joined by side walls. Often they have distinctly local features. Thus the two-, three- or four-flat buildings of Chicago differ from the three- or four-deckers of Boston, and from the small apartment houses of Washington or St. Louis.

Land crowding has perhaps been the most common characteristic of apartment buildings, East, West, or Central, particularly for the highest- and the lowest-income groups. The requirements of building and zoning codes and the ingenuity with which the building plan may be contorted to come within the letter of code provisions produce a new range of variation. Efforts to combat land crowding, first through philanthropic and publicly subsidized projects and more recently in commercial undertakings made possible by cheap land, have brought into favor the *garden apartment*. In reality this is a hybrid type, consisting of a group of flats, row houses, or both. The garden apartment usually has fifty or more units, is generous in its use of land (usually 30 per cent or less of the plot is covered), and generally is not over three stories high.

Other varieties of housing might be mentioned, such as dwellings connected with stores or workshops, but the examples cited suffice to show how versatile builders must be.

f. DURABILITY

Annual house production will average about 2.5 per cent of the total supply; the remainder consists of old houses. Many old houses, to be sure, are not very good but they endure, and make up, in one way or another, for the lag in new construction.[12] The unusual durability of houses has numerous effects on the industry that produces them.

As a result of the preponderance of old houses in the market, changes come slowly. Drastic architectural innovations meet with only gradual acceptance. We find nothing like the high rate of replacement in, for example, the women's clothing and automobile industries. Even in housing equipment—where novelty has been most frequent—innovations become established at snail's pace. A practicable water closet, for instance, was invented as early as 1778, but it did not come into wide use, except among the upper classes of the larger cities, for almost a century.

12. See Chap. 7, pp. 182-185.

In 1934, 15 per cent of urban dwellings were still without private indoor flush toilets. Electricity was introduced at a much faster rate, rising from almost zero in 1880 to 95 per cent of all urban dwellings in 1934.[13] But, even here progress has been slow compared with that of the radio or motorcar.

Changes in structural methods are phenomenally slow. The major innovations of the late nineteenth and early twentieth centuries—steel and reinforced concrete skeleton construction—appeared first in commercial buildings, where obsolescence was greater and replacement more rapid than in residential dwellings. In the residential field, steel and reinforced construction has been applied chiefly to tall apartments, the type most nearly resembling commercial structures. Yet even in New York City the majority of apartment buildings between 1920 and 1940 were built with load-bearing walls and wood floors in the traditional manner. Row and detached house construction has been almost wholly unchanged, except for a limited use of reinforced concrete and of steel shapes, usually patterned after wood members and used in the same way.

Another marked effect of the durability of buildings is in the perpetuation of the established land pattern. Buildings are rarely demolished and then usually one by one. The vacated lots often restrict new construction to the types of building designed for the original lot pattern. The persistence of old buildings, often long beyond the possibility of obtaining an economic return, helps to force new developments into fresh, outlying areas. Durability thus tends to limit the manner in which the builder may use land for new houses as well as the amount and location of available acreage.

The maintenance and alteration of the huge stock of continually deteriorating dwellings is a large and special phase of the housebuilding industry. Since the house is a complicated structure repairs are complex and difficult. Few houses are so built as to be easily repaired, and a tremendous number of their vulnerable parts are hidden and sealed. The complicated nature of the house thus makes its maintenance unnecessarily costly, forcing the industry to carry a huge supply of parts, for which there may be an infrequent and incalculable demand, and to handle small orders for a great variety of special operations.

2. Some Aspects of Dwelling Costs

No commodity required by the average consumer is so large, so complex, or lasts so long as a house. If purchased, it is the most expensive article acquired by the average family. If rented, the monthly bill is larger for those in the lower half of the income scale than any recurring expenditure except food.

13. *Urban Housing,* Works Progress Administration, 1938, pp. 30, 32.

a. KINDS OF COST

Housing costs may be viewed from three angles: (1) the construction of the house, (2) its acquisition by the user or investor, and (3) operation and maintenance of dwellings. All three are interrelated. Use of inferior materials or skimped workmanship may lower production costs but will raise maintenance costs. On the other hand, in order to assure long life and low maintenance, production costs may be too high for most prospective buyers. Again, the mortgage interest rate and terms of prepayment greatly affect the kind and quality of houses that may be produced. These, however, affect initial purchasing power rather than the cost of production. Lowering the interest rate and extending the life of the mortgage may make the house easier to acquire, but not less expensive.

Production and Operating Costs

Part of the production-cost problem is obviously one of how long the product must last and how much may be spent on it during its use period. The data on maintenance costs, however, are even more nebulous than on production costs. No recorded experience reveals what it costs to maintain houses of different qualities and types.[14] Good materials and careful workmanship, of course, simplify the problem of maintenance as well as operation. Attempts are often made to show that lower operating and maintenance costs more than offset a substantially higher original cost.[15] Such assertions may be true in specific cases and if so the additional initial cost would be repaid out of maintenance. But the components of a house are so diverse in nature and durability that a perfect balancing of the elements of costs is hardly possible. Moreover, the variety among houses is so great that averages, even if obtainable, would have little meaning.[16] The cost of maintenance and operation depends partly upon the amount of wear to which the dwelling is subjected by its occupants and the weather, and the kind of upkeep it receives. Such variables cannot be accurately measured.

If the problem is narrowed to the relative merits of certain basic structural

14. Annual maintenance expenditures on residential property have been roughly estimated as about 0.8 per cent of its value. *Construction Activity in the United States, 1915–37,* Bureau of Foreign and Domestic Commerce, pp. 20–21.

15. See "It's Not the First Cost But the Upkeep—'Bargain Homes' Are Costly to Own," *American Builder,* April 1941, p. 179; Emerson Goble, "Better Houses Can Cost Clients Less," *Architectural Record,* July 1941, p. 80.

16. Data on maintenance costs of apartment buildings are somewhat better than on single-family houses. See, for example, *A Survey of Apartment Dwelling Operating Experience in Large American Cities,* FHA, 1940. Unfortunately, even here, such a range of type and experience is revealed that average figures become almost meaningless. The United States Housing Authority and the FHA Rental Housing Division in the course of time will have excellent data on the maintenance of properties subject to their inspection. But again, this will cover special if numerous types of buildings, so that comparisons may be made only in details.

and exterior materials, the answers are still not very definite. Undoubtedly, in some areas, the added cost of brick walls as compared with wood frame and siding is more than offset by lower maintenance costs, but in many regions this is certainly not true. Stucco is a satisfactory and economic material in some parts of the United States; in others, owing to climate and the prescribed methods of application, it may be unsatisfactory and expensive. A completely fireproof one-story house would be extremely durable and require little maintenance for the basic structure. But its life might be longer than justified by changing urban requirements, while the cost of carrying the additional financial burden might well be out of proportion to the cost of a lighter structure, especially where the occupant could make some repairs with his own hands.

Durable houses can be built of various materials and the advantages of each vary with circumstances. Every case must be considered separately with regard to original and continuing costs. Cost is profoundly affected by the size and arrangement of the house, and the complexity and manner of assembly of its materials. These factors contribute to initial costs without necessarily affecting maintenance, and it is among them that the most concerted effort to lower production costs may be made.

b. HAVE PRODUCTION COSTS BEEN REDUCED?

Few valid generalizations can be made about trends in construction costs. The possibilities of using substitute materials, changes in structure, variations in type and arrangement, are so great that a so-called typical house is really typical of nothing at all. The problem is even more complicated if construction costs are studied over a period of time. In order to measure price changes it is necessary to adopt some scheme for weighting price components. In the usual index of house construction costs a typical house is assumed. The prices of the components are then weighted according to the quantities of materials and labor needed to build that house. Aside from the fictitious character of the typical house, changes in construction methods and materials over a period of years make the measurement of prices on the basis of a selected house entirely unrealistic. The effect of this, as of the numerous other variables, is illustrated in Figure 3, in which construction costs are plotted according to two different indexes.[17]

Average building permit values are frequently used to show fluctuations in costs. This practice, however, is subject to serious limitations, since average value depends as much on the *changing proportion* of high-cost and low-cost housing as on *actual fluctuation* of labor and material costs. A greater demand for smaller and simpler houses might considerably lower the average value, even with rising

17. See Appendix B, 2 and Table 7 for an analysis of construction cost indexes.

material and labor costs. This in part explains the fact that from 1936 to 1940 the average construction costs of nonfarm residential units apparently declined about 14 per cent, despite a slight rise in basic costs.[18]

Neither prices nor average permit values, then, provide a dependable measure of the trend in housing costs. About all that can be said is that home buyers, on

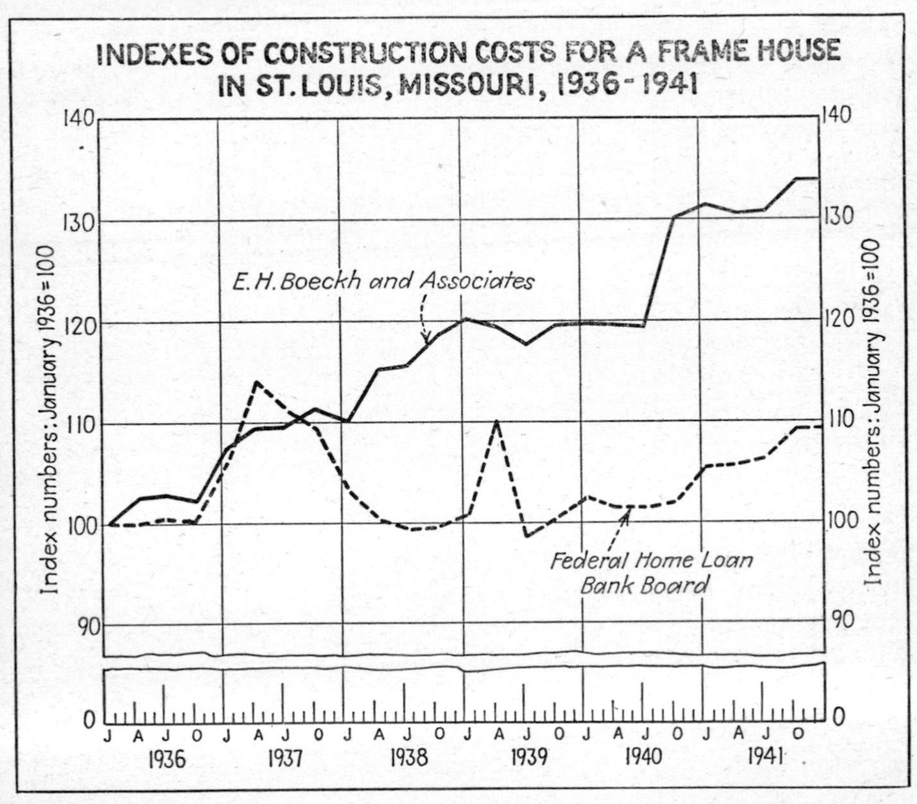

FIGURE 3. Trends in construction costs are difficult to measure owing to the variable components of a "typical" house. These two curves, which attempt to measure trends in the cost of constructing a frame house in the same city over an identical period of time, show a wide dissimilarity. (*Source:* Appendix B, 2, Table 7.)

the average, were satisfied in 1940 with a product that cost, on the average, less than that built and sold in 1936. What does this mean in terms of satisfactory housing? How was it possible to bring about the sharp reduction in average

18. Data for 1936 are derived from D. L. Wickens, *Residential Real Estate,* National Bureau of Economic Research, New York, 1941, Tables E 1 and E 2, p. 296. For comparable 1940 figures, see "New Dwelling Units in Nonfarm Areas During 1940," *Monthly Labor Review,* April 1941, Tables 1 and 7, pp. 1008, 1014. The average value of contract awards on single-family houses in 37 eastern states declined 17 per cent in this period according to the F. W. Dodge Corporation. The data include all such houses having a contract value of $4,000 or more; below that figure the coverage is incomplete.

values? Was there a marked improvement in technology? Did competition among builders result in a significant narrowing of the profit margin? Was the quality of the average house lowered?

The Ways in Which Costs Have Declined

Federal Housing Administration records supply some significant clues to these questions.[19] The average valuation of new single-family houses on which loans were accepted for insurance declined from $5,978 in 1937 to $5,199 in 1940, or about 13 per cent. Probably the most important factor in this decline was a shift of FHA financing from houses catering to the high-income classes to medium-priced dwellings. The average annual income of borrowers on new and existing single-family insured mortgages declined from $3,133 to $2,665, or about 15 per cent, between 1937 and 1940 inclusive. Even though the character of the house at a given price level remained the same, the shift to medium-priced houses would reduce the average cost. Marked changes in character, however, can be noted.

A large part of the decline in average FHA property valuation is due to cheaper land. Improved lots for new single-family houses declined on the average from $913 to $662, or 27.4 per cent, during the four-year period, a trend probably associated with the movement of city populations to outlying undeveloped areas.[20] The decreasing proportion of high-value properties has also undoubtedly resulted in a small reduction in the average size of lot, and hence in the cost of land and utilities. A third factor may be a lower quality of land improvements, particularly pavements and sewage disposal facilities.[21] Judged by these figures, the reduction in the cost of improved land accounts for more than 30 per cent of the decline in average total valuation.

The reduction of the average house from 5.5 rooms in 1937 to 5.1 rooms in 1940 may account for as much as 40 per cent of the total decline in valuation.[22] Most of the remainder of the decline is fairly easy to account for. About 39 per cent of FHA-insured structures were built with wood exteriors in 1938; by 1940 the proportion increased to 45 per cent, a shift probably accounting for 10 per cent of the reduction in average property valuation. The decrease in the proportion of

19. *Seventh Annual Report*, 1940, FHA.

20. See Appendix A, Tables 1 and 2.

21. Omission of sewer or water facilities may not represent a complete saving on public utilities, however, inasmuch as the cost of a septic tank or well, or both, must be included in the cost of the house.

22. The average valuation in 1937 of the typical 5.5-room FHA house (exclusive of $913 for land and an assumed $500 for plumbing) was $4,565. In 1940, for the typical 5.1-room FHA house (exclusive of $662 for land and the same $500 for plumbing) it was $4,037. If, therefore, in 1937 a 5.5-room house (without land or plumbing) was built for $4,565, a 5.1-room house could then have been built for $4,233, or a difference of $332, due merely to a 0.4 reduction in the number of rooms. The difference between the actual 1940 cost of $4,037 and the hypothetical 1937 cost of $4,233 is accounted for by other factors than reductions in land costs and the number of rooms.

houses with garages—from 80.5 per cent in 1937 to 75.6 per cent in 1940—may account for 10 per cent of the decline.

In this way practically all the change in valuation of the average FHA house may be explained without allowing for increased efficiency or advanced technology. The basic qualities of the traditional house are hardly touched. The shift toward less expensive materials does not mean that fewer or less complex parts and materials have been used or that assembly methods have become less intricate.[23] The evidence reveals not that production costs for an equivalent house have been reduced during the period, but simply that a smaller, more compact, and consequently less expensive house in a more outlying location has become a greater favorite in the market.

Public housing experience is somewhat similar. The over-all cost (including land) of the average family unit in public housing projects built prior to 1938 (Public Works Administration Housing Division) was $5,418. The average cost of projects finished during 1940 (United States Housing Authority) was $4,082.[24] Some of this reduction is due to the larger proportion of developments in small places, especially in the South, where land and labor costs are relatively low; some to a trend toward lower buildings and lighter construction. Since the USHA has decided that wood floors and wall framing are eligible for amortization over a sixty-year period, many developments have abandoned the fireproof ideal. Finally, some reduction has been due to elimination of basements, finished floors over concrete, plaster on concrete ceilings, or less frequently, on cinder block walls, doors on closets and kitchen shelving, and similar items.

Again, this involves no basic attack on the nature of the house. Instead, it reflects a changed attitude toward the relationships between initial and maintenance costs and toward structural systems and materials, and results in a definite simplification of standards.[25] Reduction in quality, however, should not be confused with lower basic costs. There is little conclusive evidence of cost reductions resulting

23. The extent to which FHA experience is representative cannot be determined, but it is possible tentatively to appraise the situation. In the first place, about one third of the single-family houses built in the period 1937–1940 had FHA-insured loans, and many builders qualified under FHA, even though FHA insurance was not obtained. An examination of building permits in a few selected cities indicates that where FHA has a dominating position the decline in the average number of rooms is about the same for total single-family houses as for FHA-insured construction. Even in cities where less than half the construction is FHA-insured, this situation appears to be true. More complete data from the 1940 Housing Census will shed additional light on the subject, but even on the basis of present evidence the FHA experience is significant since it covers an important part of all house production.

24. The PWA figure is for 48 projects as of June 30, 1938; the USHA figure is based on 178 projects for the calendar year 1940. For all USHA projects, numbering 338, the average over-all cost per unit was $4,305. See Chap. 10, pp. 277-282, for a description of the functions of the USHA and their transfer to the Federal Public Housing Administration in 1942.

25. This does not imply that the simplification of standards is unsound or unjustifiable.

from major changes in materials or production methods such as have permitted many industries to lower prices and yet improve quality.

C. COMPOSITION OF HOUSING COSTS

The reductions in housing costs outlined above have gone about as far as may be expected. The question remains: are the basic elements of the house hopelessly resistant to cost reductions; if not, where would an attack be most effective? To answer this question we must know the composition of housing costs.

An analysis of three traditionally built houses in three cities [26] shows that none of the cost components is dominant and that the omission of any one of them would not drastically change the picture. Any considerable cost reduction, therefore, must come from an accumulation of many relatively minor items, no one of which, taken by itself, is of outstanding importance. This is a fundamental principle. In the housing industry, every reduction consonant with sound construction, no matter how small it may be, is significant.

A few of the more sizable components deserve special attention. The basement and foundation—the bulkiest part of the dwelling—are important elements of cost, but the omission of a basement, while feasible from a structural viewpoint, usually means that space for heating equipment, laundry and storage must be provided elsewhere. An attack on costs must plainly go further than mere omission. The wall frame with its exterior finish, while important, is by no means the largest factor in construction costs. The proportionate cost of mechanical items (including stove and refrigerator), totaling over 25 per cent of the whole, has tended to rise rather than decline.

There is no simple solution to the problem of reducing costs. Each component is not only small but resistant to change, if the traditional form and composition of the house as well as methods of construction are considered immutable. In seeking reductions, there are two basic approaches: changing the nature of the house itself, including its materials, and modifying the processes of assembly.

3. MUTABILITY OF THE DWELLING

The house develops slowly, piecemeal, and erratically. Nevertheless, it does alter; and in some respects fairly radically. Certainly we have no reason to believe that the possibilities of change have been exhausted.

In examining the possibilities of evolving a more economical product we are, of course, particularly concerned with the kind of dwellings most adaptable to the lower-priced markets. There will always be a luxury trade that can, and will, pay for an indulgence in personal expression. The main task is to find some way

26. Based on data especially prepared by FHA; see Appendix B, Table 8.

of producing more houses for the lower-income groups that are now being neglected.

a. BULK AND FORM

Fixity and bulk are housing qualities that seem unchangeable. The house is likely to remain fixed to the land. This does not mean, however, that a comfortable and durable house might not be built with lighter materials which are easier to handle and transport and require fewer operations at the site. Moreover, as the war housing program has demonstrated, "demountability" (a high degree of salvability) is practicable in a small house without sacrificing basic standards. Out of this experience may come new ways of escaping some of the defects of fixed location.

It seems possible, also, to achieve greater compactness without impairing the function or utility of a house. In fact, much has already been done through more effective use of space. The modern house plan, while more complex in many mechanical respects, is usually much better arranged for living purposes than the typical plan of a generation ago. The ornamental parlor has disappeared. The dining room is often combined with the kitchen or living room. The pantry disappears as kitchens become more efficient. Halls are simplified and reduced, and storage space is more closely related to the particular use to which it will be put.

These trends are more than mere elimination. Surplus space, to be sure, is eliminated, but the really usable areas, through scientific arrangement have become more commodious. The possibilities and the need for further developments along these lines are very great.

b. MATERIALS AND STRUCTURE

Even though we reduce the bulk, simplify the arrangement, and concentrate on fewer types, the house remains an agglomeration of a vast number of parts and materials. The complexities of the house, however, often result from the grafting of innovations upon old forms. The result is an agelong accumulation of elements with a minimum of integration and simplification. Competition among manufacturers has increased the number of materials in common use, often with little regard to their suitability, or concern for building and maintenance costs. Incompatible materials are frequently combined for no better reason than the dictates of custom.

The use of wet and moisture-absorbent materials together, for instance, delays construction, increases the number of skills required, produces subsequent structural faults, and hence involves unnecessary costs both in production and maintenance. The twisting of wood, the cracking of plaster and delays in finishing caused by the need for drying plaster present familiar difficulties. Yet it is possible to reduce or eliminate wet materials in dwellings built principally of wood, to diminish drastically the use of wood in structures composed chiefly of concrete or plaster, and to precast the wet materials that must be used with materials adversely affected by moisture.

Again, the typical wood frame wall has five to seven layers—siding, paper, sheathing, studs, insulation, lath, plaster; or brick, waterproofing, furring, lath, plaster.[27] This method of construction has been developed out of successive attempts to correct faults in the underlying system. Until recently, the wall has not been approached as a thing in itself with certain definite functions to perform, such as support, exclusion of wind and rain, retention of heat, admission of light, and so forth. Investigated from this point of view, it is possible to find a much more limited combination of materials or parts to perform the necessary functions.[28] The same may be said of the customary methods of building floors and roofs. Thus, the structure of the house offers numerous opportunities for simplification of this kind. Some materials in common use may be replaced, others better combined, either by modification in manufacture or merely by changing dimensions. Research in this field is vital to progress in the housing industry.[29]

In the realm of equipment the problem is not so much that of eliminating certain items but achieving better balance and integration. A return to more primitive standards to obtain lower costs is unnecessary but the amount and type of equipment should be suitable to the character of the dwelling. As recently as 1936, manufacturers of heating equipment, for instance, could not provide a satisfactory unit for a compact, one-story, basementless house or individual apartment. Since then at least a start has been made.

Mechanization has gone far in the manufacture of housing equipment, but considerable handicraft work is still used in fitting and installing heating and plumbing systems. Here the difficulty is mainly that of adapting a manufactured article to an unpredictable variety of job conditions; but unnecessary costs also arise because the manufacturer's interest is limited to the main equipment unit instead of the whole system.

C. TYPE AND ARRANGEMENT

The possibilities of reducing and simplifying parts and materials depend to some extent on the degree to which the house itself is simplified. Actually, there is much standardization of housing types today. Many communities, as already indicated, have a characteristic form of dwelling. The units of large apartment

27. Under certain circumstances one or more of these layers may be omitted, but under the climatic conditions prevailing in most parts of the country all of them are generally considered essential to sound construction, comfort, and low operating cost.

28. See Robert L. Davison, "New Construction Methods," *Architectural Record*, October 1929.

29. See Chap. 5, pp. 139-142, for further discussion.

structures are usually repetitions of only a few arrangements. The houses in many subdivisions are repetitious to the point of monotony. The experience of the housing agencies of the federal government proves that the needs of large numbers of families may be readily accommodated by comparatively few basic arrangements.[30] Many public and private developments demonstrate that if skill and imagination are used in grouping and land planning, monotony need not accompany simplification and standardization.

If the variety of types and arrangements is reduced, it is possible greatly to increase the simplifications of parts. For example, the mechanical section of the house—bathroom, kitchen, and heater space—could be built as a unit. Shapes and sizes of materials could be more easily related to one another. The utility of a smaller number of parts could be increased.[31]

What types of dwellings are most susceptible to economical arrangement and simplification of parts? The answer is determined by many factors—the price of the land, the cost of land improvements, size of the house, selection of materials and methods of construction. Other factors include building code provisions, craft restrictions, and industrial practices. Finally, the cost of operation and maintenance in relation to original costs must be considered.

The Detached House

Until now, the detached house has been more susceptible than other kinds of dwellings to standardization of layout, parts, and off-site assembly. This type of house is usually easy to maintain—in many cases repairs may be made by the occupant—and as a rental property, it requires relatively little servicing.

The detached house usually needs a greater length of streets and utilities per unit than other types of dwellings, but the low density of single-house development allows for comparatively inexpensive improvements. The detached house also requires more land per unit than any other type, a factor that restricts the range of available locations.

The Row House[32]

The row house permits of a greater economy in the use of land than the detached dwelling, and often less material for the same size. It is also usually cheaper to heat and, having less ground and exposure, its exterior costs less to

30. See *Principles of Planning Small Houses,* Technical Bulletin No. 4, revised July 1, 1940; *Low Rental Housing for Private Investment,* 1940, FHA; *Planning the Site,* Policy and Procedure Bulletin No. 11, 1939; and *Dwelling Unit Planning,* Policy and Procedure Bulletin No. 12, 1939, USHA.

31. See "The Integrated House," *loc. cit.,* for an excellent discussion of the means of simplifying and co-ordinating the structure of the house. See also Chap. 5 for the possibilities of standardization.

32. Here, for convenience, are included all types of single-family units in combination with other similar units, irrespective of the number in the combination.

maintain. On the other hand, it usually requires more fire-resistant materials than does the detached house, a factor that may offset some of its other economies. Generally, however, the row house (in groups of three to eight) is practicable for medium- and low-income markets.

Apartment Buildings

The place of the flat or the apartment in the stock of housing is a subject of unending controversy incited by a lack of cost data. Apartments must usually be constructed with a larger proportion of heavy and fire-resistant materials than the detached or row house. They usually have certain public spaces—stairs, halls and lobbies—to be heated and cared for by the landlord. In addition, the services of the landlord for grounds maintenance, garbage collection, and minor repairs will be increased. These items tend to increase both original and maintenance costs. On the other hand, the apartment is economical in the use of land and in improvements and undoubtedly offers the most economical means of producing very small dwelling units and of accommodating families demanding considerable service.

The most economical size of apartment building depends almost entirely on the cost of maintenance and the risks of vacancy. Experience seems to indicate that the two- to four-unit, or even six-unit building is an uneconomical structure to maintain unless operated by a resident landlord who performs most of the service himself. But a continued vacancy of even one unit may mean the difference between profit and financial disaster. Apartment buildings of from six to twelve units are often even more dubious ventures since these are too large for resident landlord maintenance, without being large enough for adequate paid service, and they still carry a high vacancy risk. It is questionable whether any apartment structure or group under fifty units provides a proper balance between risk and servicing cost.

Lowering Servicing Costs

Abroad, the cost of servicing flat buildings is often reduced by using exterior rather than interior stairs, and connecting balconies instead of hallways, and by omitting central heating. Walk-up buildings both in England and on the Continent are frequently four stories or higher, and in Italy an ingenious use has been made of ramps to overcome the objection to high walk-up buildings. In the United States it is generally agreed that three stories is the maximum for walk-ups; not many tenants care for the higher levels. Balconies instead of interior stairs have not usually proven acceptable outside of California. In two-story buildings, however, the problem of maintaining interior public spaces has frequently been solved either by making the individual family unit two stories high (making it a variety of the row house) or by providing an individual stairway for each second-floor unit. These arrangements obviously reduce the costs of janitor service and light and heat of public spaces, although they may add somewhat to the cost of stairways.

In almost every section of the country some form of heating is necessary for part of the year; and, from a rental standpoint, it is generally impracticable to leave the method of heating wholly to the tenant aside from providing a flue or possibly a fireplace, as is common in even middle-class European houses.[33] The development of gas and oil-fired heating systems suitable for individual apartment units has, however, in the past few years offered an acceptable alternate to central heating. These units also eliminate the expense of building the long horizontal mains needed for central heating of a large development of low buildings.

The Question of Height

The question of height in apartment buildings is still a subject of debate. The prime excuse for high buildings has been high land costs. It may be argued, however, that because of their increased earning power, high buildings have been a principal cause of high land costs. In any case, with the wide choice of outlying acreage available it is doubtful whether land so expensive as to demand multistoried structures need now be used, except where other considerations enter the picture.

The tall building offers some economy in plumbing and heating lines. Where building codes do not greatly differentiate between high and low buildings in their specifications for wall construction, degree of fireproofing, or number of stairs, this saving may tip the balance in favor of the tall building. The latter also allows for concentration and economy in service and because of its occupant density usually involves less ground maintenance per unit.

The question of optimum height is equally debatable. If elevators as well as all the usual fire protection are necessary, the four- to six-story building probably does not achieve maximum economy. The six-story building is popular in New York City because nonfireproof floor construction is allowed up to that height. In other places the differential between the height of walk-up and elevator buildings is usually greater. The Parkchester (New York City) development of the Metropolitan Life Insurance Company varies from nine to thirteen stories, but little evidence can be found that the one height is more economical than the other. Today twelve-story apartments are being built in New York City and occasionally elsewhere, but pueblos of twenty stories or more are now rarely constructed.

33. In parts of California, and in Texas and other Gulf regions, where climatic conditions are not severe and gas is cheap, the tenant provides gas heaters.

In the absence of definitive data, judgment of the most economical height must rest upon observable trends. Today the trend appears to favor the low walk-up building; and, outside New York City, the elevator building has become a rarity. Despite the fact that the New York City Housing Authority has built elevator buildings and has advanced claims for their economy, it appears doubtful that the high structure can satisfy much of the country's housing needs, particularly in the low-cost field. Except where artificial barriers like restricted location, expensive land, or excessive code requirements exist, the walk-up type seems most economical.

The low apartment building shares with the detached and row house great possibilities of simplified and standardized arrangement. There is little choice among them on this score alone. In fact, it is possible, as several prefabricators have shown, to design units that serve equally well as detached houses, row houses, or apartments.[34]

4. SUMMARY

A house is a large and complex product and its construction is as tied to tradition as to the land on which it rests. Traditional forms require a tedious installation of numerous parts and materials at the site. The industry's cost problems are connected with the unwieldiness of the product. Yet the character of the house suggests possibilities for simplified layout, composition, and structure; less bulk and even less fixity might result in greater economy without decreasing essential comforts.

So far, the form of the house has been considered without definite relation to methods of production. The search for lower costs, therefore, leads to an examination of the building industry, an industry whose organization has been influenced by the character of the house. By taking advantage of the possible modifications of the structure, new developments may also become possible.

34. See *Preliminary Report on a Study of House Standardization*, Technical Bulletin (Form No. 2373), FHA.

Chapter 3

THE BUSINESS OF HOUSEBUILDING

Although ordinarily considered a branch of the construction industry, housebuilding differs in many ways from other construction operations. In some respects it more nearly resembles manufacturing, yet some of its characteristics and practices set it apart from manufacturing. Any judgment of the potentialities of housebuilding must consider its special characteristics.

1. Housebuilding as an Industrial Activity

In discussing housebuilding, it is necessary to deal largely with the *processes* required rather than with *producing organizations*. Centralized producing organizations, combining all or even most of the essential processes, are extremely rare in housebuilding. Ordinarily, housebuilding must be defined as a series of activities that ultimately result in the production of houses.

a. the processes of housebuilding

Housebuilding can be separated into the following activities:

1. Acquisition of land.
2. Planning the land to accommodate a housing operation.
3. Improvements of the land through installation of roads, sewers, water, gas, and electrical facilities.
4. Design of the dwellings and selection of materials and equipment, i.e., the preparation of drawings and specifications.
5. Financing the building operation (as distinct from financing the purchase of the completed product).
6. Purchase of materials and equipment.
7. Employment of labor.
8. Assembly and installation of materials and equipment to make the finished house.

Usually some of these functions are carried on separately; sometimes nearly all are. Land may be planned and subdivided without regard to building. The prospective householder or apartment owner may acquire a site independently of the builder; and even when the builder operates on his own account he often merely buys, or contracts to buy, a number of lots to be prepared by someone else. Architectural and engineering services are often supplied on a professional basis or they may be offered by the builder or the materials dealer. Again, the architect may assume the function of a general contractor; or the houseowner may make separate contracts for parts of the work.

The builder or contractor, even when nominally in charge of the work, rarely undertakes much of it with his own organization. The purchase of materials, the hiring and direction of labor and, to a great extent, the responsibility for the completed house are assumed by subcontractors. Although the supplying of materials is sometimes combined with their installation, more often suppliers stand entirely apart from the building operation. Since few builders can wholly finance their operations, capital is usually borrowed from outside sources.

Lack of Integration

The loose organization of housebuilding activities is in marked contrast to the integration of processes characteristic of many other industries. The degree of integration varies, of course, with the industry and with the firm. In its most advanced form, all operations, from design to final assembly of the product, and frequently also the distribution of the product to consumers, are subject to centralized control. Basic to centralized control is *producer initiative*—that is, the determination by the producer of both the quantity and nature of his product in *advance* of sale. This contrasts with *buyer initiative* commoner in custom industries like tailoring, shipbuilding, and, to a large extent, housebuilding where the kind and quantity of the product are largely determined by purchasers before production is begun. The greatest possibilities of expanding markets and lowering costs are present in industries where producer initiative is predominant (see Figure 4).

There is no such control of housebuilding processes as is found in industries where custom production has advanced to mass production, where handicraft methods have given way to machine methods, and where dependence on separately manufactured parts has been supplanted by the integrated manufacture of the final product. The builder generally adapts his product to, or takes the design from, his customer. He assembles what his suppliers provide, cutting and fitting materials and parts to his plan when he is able to, and adjusting his plan to them when he is not. He usually finds labor and distribution patterns firmly established and resistant to technical or industrial changes. He meets with public attitudes that tenaciously demand the maintenance of the traditional type of product.

b. HOUSEBUILDING AND CONSTRUCTION

Not only are the processes of housebuilding not integrated, but the business as a whole lacks distinct identity. Indeed, it is almost inextricably entangled with,

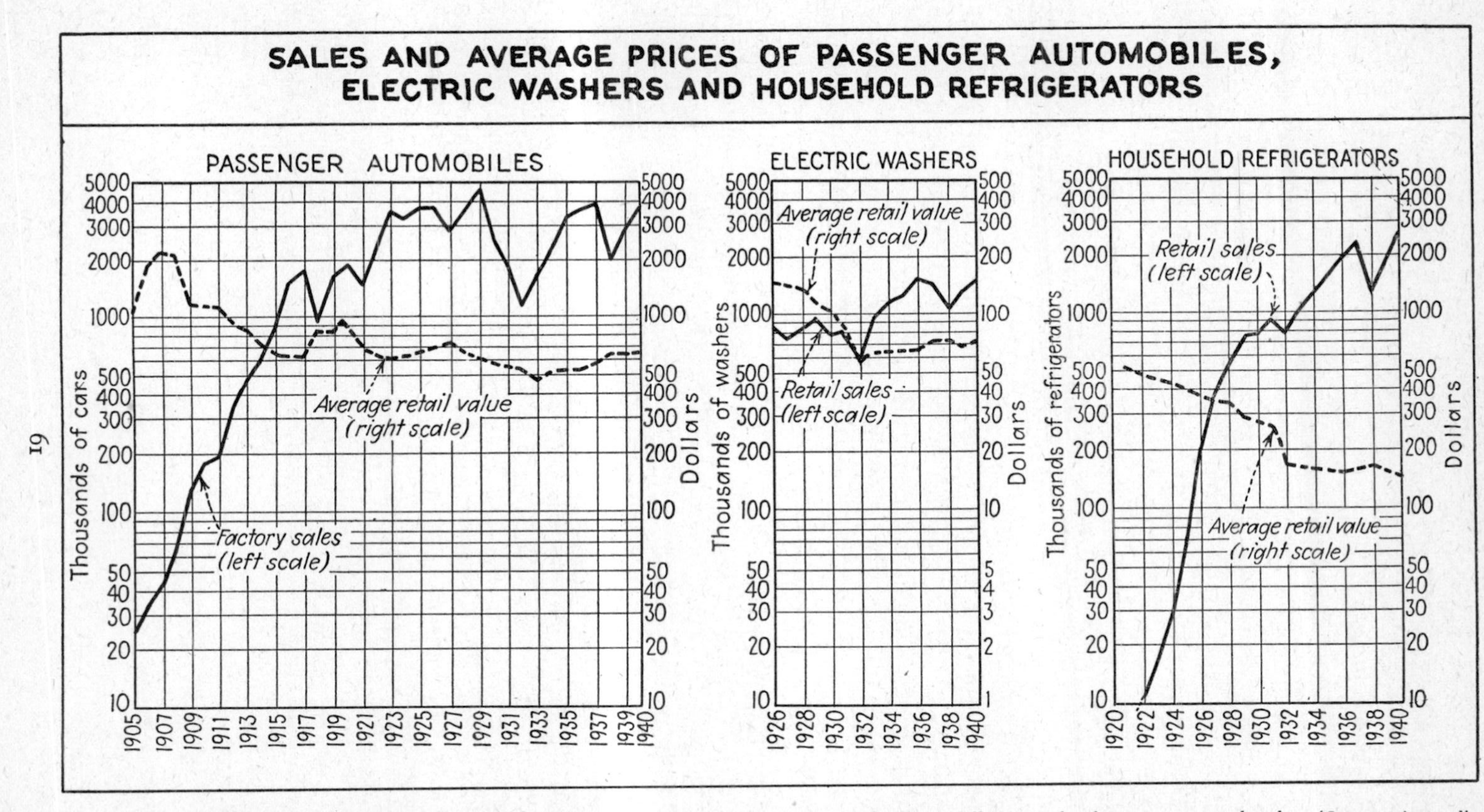

FIGURE 4. In contrast to housebuilding, industries producing passenger automobiles, electric washers and household refrigerators have been able to lower prices and substantially expand sales over recent decades. (*Source:* Appendix Table 9.)

and usually dominated by, the general construction industry—something that in itself is difficult to define clearly.

During the life of the National Recovery Administration's Construction Code, for instance, problems of definition arose at numerous points where construction shaded into manufacturing, land development, or something else.[1] Construction can be defined as the assembly at a given location, of a great variety of manufactured articles to produce any fixed structure ranging from a dam to a chicken coop, from a highway to a house, from a pipe line to the plumbing system of a cottage.

Since the products of construction can be used in only one place, construction must be planned for specific local needs, which are subject to great irregularity. A limited number of business buildings, factories, or apartments may satisfy the demand of a community for a number of years. Consequently, there is little or no uniformity in demand or rate of production. The necessity of carrying on many operations in the open—a condition imposed by fixed location—also tends to make the flow of production in the construction industry uneven.

The variety of sites and uses for buildings has multiplied the ways of erecting structures. Each site condition and each building calls for a special congregation of specialists, for each structure may have special problems in foundation, frame, use of materials, equipment, insulation, and so forth. Moreover, each may suggest its own type of assembly operation. Fifty [2] or more types of special trades and contractors may be used in a single building. These may be wholly or partly united under one general contractor, or all the work may be carried on by subcontractors working directly for the owner. No uniform pattern exists.

Except on the craft level, there is little specialization in construction work. We find carpenters, plumbers, bricklayers, and the like, but the "housewright"

1. In "The Code of Fair Competition for the Construction Industry," as approved January 31, 1934, by the President (*Construction Industry Code Manual,* Vol. 1, No. IV), The Construction League of the United States, Washington, April 1935, uses the following definition: "Section 1.—The term 'construction industry' or 'the industry' as used herein shall include the designing and the construction of (and the installing and the applying, including the assembling at the site, of manufactured parts and products incorporated in and to): (*a*) building structures, including modifications thereof and fixed construction accessory thereto, intended for use as shelter; and other (*b*) fixed structures and other fixed improvements and modifications thereof, intended for use in industry, commerce, sanitation, transportation, communication, flood control, power development, reclamation and other similar projects or services; and such related divisions or subdivisions thereof as may be defined in chapters hereof, and included hereunder with the approval of the President.

"Section 3.—The term 'member of the industry' as used herein includes any individual or form of organization or enterprise engaged in any phase, or undertaking to perform any of the functions of the industry as defined in Section 1 hereof either as an employer or on his own behalf, including also but without limitation, architects, engineers, contractors and subcontractors."

That these definitions were by no means clear is evidenced by the "explanations" that from time to time were issued in connection with them, *ibid*. See also Leverett S. Lyon and others, *The National Recovery Administration,* The Brookings Institution, Washington, 1935, pp. 150–151.

2. See Appendix C, 7.

of former days is as obsolete as the water clock. Architects, engineers, contractors, and workmen may move from dams to bridges, to skyscrapers, to apartment houses, and government and institutional buildings. The lack of specialization in the industry is evident in the Census Bureau's classification [3] of builders of (1) one- and two-family houses, (2) other residential building, (3) building other than residential, (4) heavy construction, and (5) highways. No clear distinctions are made among these groups and the allocation of contractors to one or another is determined merely by the work in which they are principally engaged.[4]

C. A PROBLEM OF SEGREGATION

Although the NRA could not find sufficient special attributes in housebuilding to warrant a distinct classification, the industry does have some characteristics that separate it from other kinds of construction. In the first place, housebuilding is concerned with a consumers' product, whereas other construction may generally be classed as capital production.[5] Its financial and merchandising problems are, therefore, different from those of other forms of construction. In the second place its products are more uniform and adaptable to repetitive operations than is generally true of construction; hence a larger proportion of housebuilding operations may be performed off the site. In all these respects, housebuilding shades from construction into manufacturing.

Despite such distinctions, it is not easy to segregate housebuilding from construction. If we attempt a classification on the basis of producers, we are confronted with the anomaly that dwellings are neither necessarily, nor commonly, constructed by a special class of producers. To be sure, operative builders, that is, builders constructing houses on their own land for future sale or rent, may form

3. See Census of Business: *Construction Industry,* 1935 and 1939.

4. In preparing a code for the construction industry the NRA had difficulty not only with a general definition but with subdivisions (Lyon and others, *op. cit.*). Divisional codes were authorized for general contractors and for the various classifications of subcontractors. The general contractors' divisional codes endeavored to distinguish between types of construction, such as building, heavy construction, and highway-construction contractors. But again no clear-cut divisions could be made. A general contractor found it necessary at times to operate under all three subdivisional codes or even some of the subcontractors' codes. So unreal was the concept of specialization that general contractors and subcontractors occasionally found themselves subject to the codes of the Distributing Division as well as of the Construction Division.

Under the NRA, housebuilding was not designated as a specialized activity, and certainly few facts could then be marshaled to support a claim for separate consideration. The National Association of Real Estate Boards stressed the preparation of land and the merchandising of completed units, arguing that these, along with dwelling construction, constituted a separate industry (Proposed Code of Fair Competition for the Land Development and Home Building Industry [revised draft, June 19, 1934] and accompanying statement submitted to NRA by the National Association of Real Estate Boards [mimeographed]). On the basis of these claims, a temporary stay of compliance with the Construction Code was granted to housebuilders, but the proposed separate code was never approved.

5. The dwelling is a commodity for direct consumer use, irrespective of its ownership, and as such may be distinguished from stores, factories, and warehouses, which are used in the production of capital, or from institutional structures designed for general public service.

such a class. But such builders, although growing in importance, do not dominate the industry. The small group of prefabricators, unknown to the NRA, has only with the impact of the war become more than a promising innovation.

Except for these groups, few specialized housing producers exist. The firm that has built the largest number of dwellings in the country entered housing as a depression stopgap. Even at the height of its operations it was not limited to housebuilding. Similarly, the builder of one of the largest private housing developments in California has constructed everything from pipe lines to public monuments. The field is open to all comers and they are a motley lot. There are men who, as a side line, construct one or two houses a year, artisans who become contractors for a time and then return to day labor, dealers in materials and land operators who enter housing as a means of sales promotion, and individuals who actually build their own homes, or who act as general contractors in constructing houses for their own use.

It is even more difficult to segregate subcontractors. Here there is specialization by trades but, with few exceptions, not by the type of finished product. A plumbing contractor goes wherever pipe is installed and a mason contractor is concerned with walls, not buildings. This kind of specialization is also true of the building artisan. A plasterer or a plumber may work on a cottage this week, and on a factory next week.

The manufacture and distribution of dwelling parts are even less specialized than housebuilding. Producers of materials and equipment do not ordinarily design their products for specific types of structure. Manufacturers of plumbing fixtures, for example, offer their wares without distinction to the hotel, office building, or apartment house. The same brick, lumber, and cement go into a workingman's cottage as into a post office or hospital.

The distributors of materials are equally catholic. The glass jobber and the plumbers' supplier cover territories, not types of buildings. In all industries manufacturing and distributing building materials there is a lack of specialization in products designed solely for houses, just as in the field of erection we find a multitude of separate crafts. Only among a small class of operators do we find any specialization on an end product—the house.

2. SIZE AND CHARACTERISTICS OF THE HOUSEBUILDING INDUSTRY

The importance of an industry can be measured in several ways: by the value of its product—or better, the "value added" by the industry's processes; by the quantity produced; by the number of workers employed; by the amount of wages paid; or by the industry's contribution to the national income.

Statistics are available, for nonfarm areas, on the number of units added by

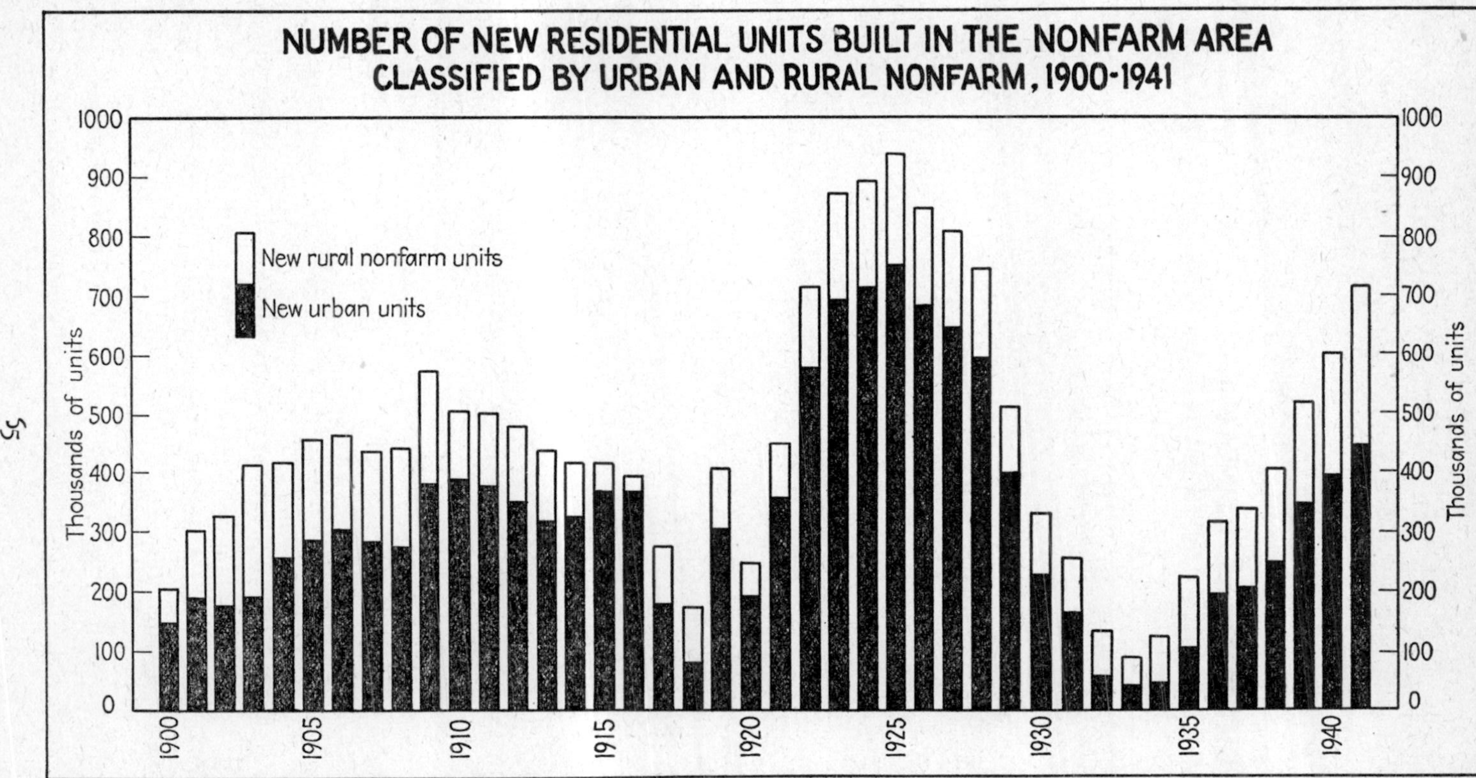

FIGURE 5. Residential construction has experienced two distinct cycles since 1900, the first reaching a high point in 1909 and the second in 1925. From the 1933 low, the volume of housebuilding again climbed steadily upward and in 1941 exceeded 700,000 units. (*Source:* Appendix C, 1, Table 10.)

new construction and by conversions (Figure 5) and on the number of new units classified by broad structural types (Figure 6). There are also data on the value of construction in the United States as a whole, classified broadly by kind of construction and by areas (Figure 7).[6]

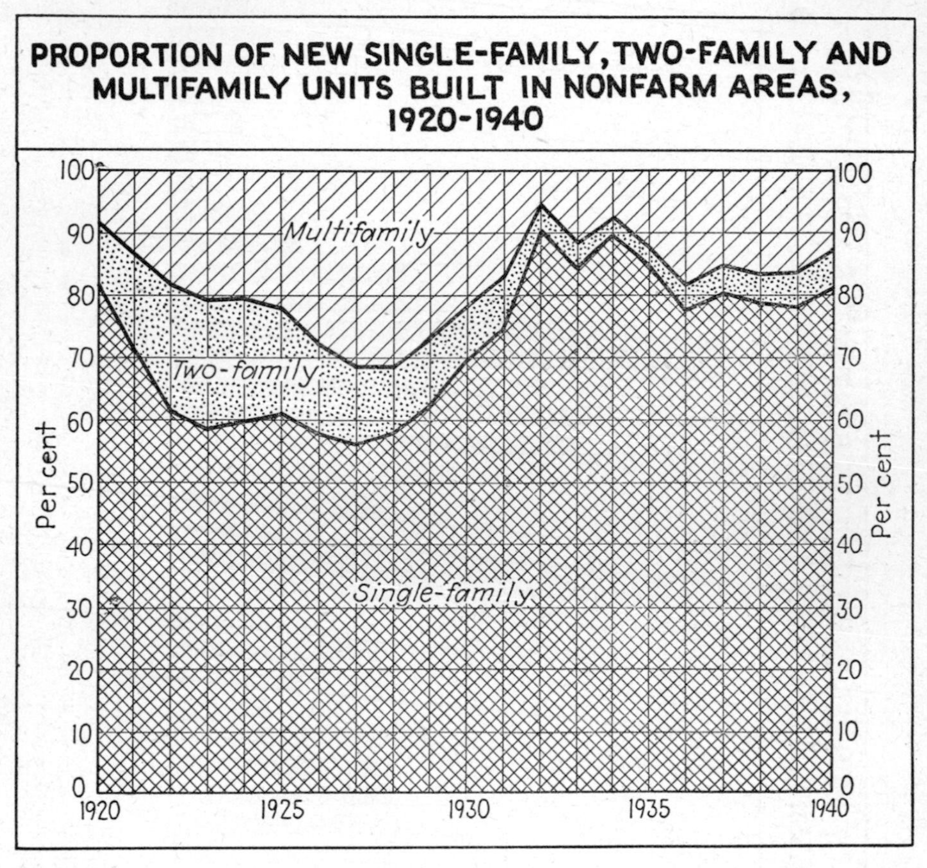

FIGURE 6. Single-family houses represented 80 to 90 per cent of total family units erected during the thirties, in contrast to the building boom of the twenties when two-family houses and apartments ran to 40 per cent of the total number of family units built. (*Source:* Appendix C, 1, Table 11.)

The Over-all Picture

The wide fluctuations in production revealed by the charts mentioned above show that the housebuilding industry is subject to sudden and violent shifts in demand.[7] Thus, the peak of production was reached in 1925 under the impulse of growing population, prosperity, optimism and speculation. The all-time low

6. Land costs are excluded from the estimates of value of farm construction. See Appendix C, 1 and Tables 10, 11 and 12.

7. See Chap. 7, pp. 185-197, 200-202, for an analysis of these fluctuations.

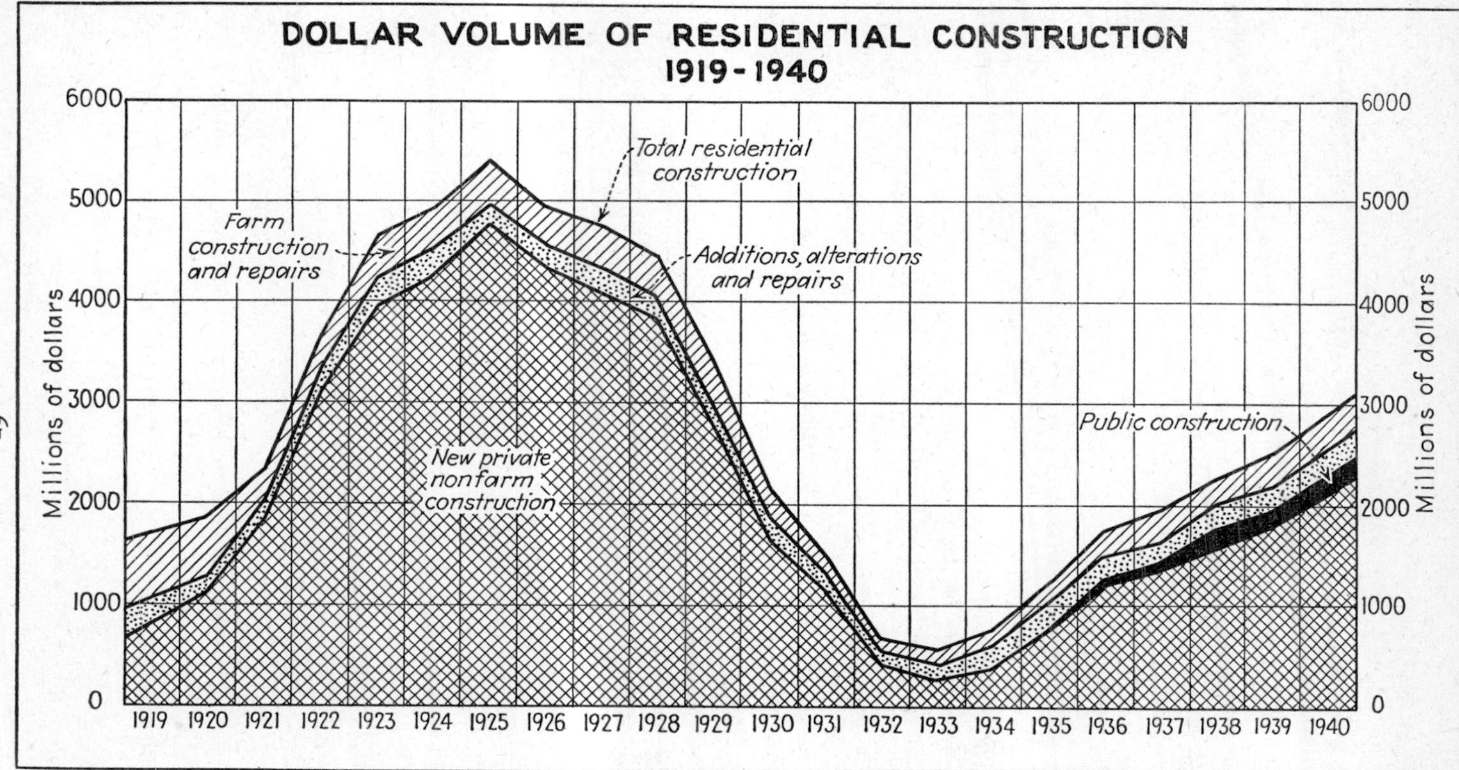

FIGURE 7. Total residential construction, including farm and nonfarm and new and converted dwellings, reached a peak of $5.4 billion in 1925 and a low of $570 million in 1933. The number of units built thereafter increased rapidly, but with the average value of homes lower than in the twenties, the dollar volume of construction had climbed no further than the $3.0 billion mark by 1940. (*Source:* Appendix C, 1, Table 12.)

was reached in the depression years. At its best housebuilding has been a $5.4 billion industry producing 937,000 nonfarm dwelling units; at its worst it shrank to less than $600 million and 93,000 units, averaging in the period 1919–1935—from the beginning of the postwar recovery to that of the postdepression recovery—around $2.9 billion and 506,000 units annually. For this period, residential construction (as shown in Figure 8) accounted on the average for 3.9 per cent of the gross national product—that is, of the total value of all goods and services produced—which averaged over $73 billion a year.

Housebuilding is thus a large and important industry, but its place in the national economy has hardly justified the claims of those who would use it as a panacea for an industrial depression, or as a dominant factor in cushioning an economic collapse. Many other industries bulk larger in the economy. For instance, in 1939 nonresidential contract construction was more than 25 per cent larger, the manufacture of metal and metal products seven times larger, and the manufacture of foodstuffs and tobacco more than twice as large.[8]

a. PRODUCTION IN TERMS OF LABOR AND MATERIALS

The figures given above cover, in addition to builders' and subcontractors' overhead and profit, money spent for materials and labor. From available data, however, it is impossible to discover the exact amounts of labor or materials going into residential building. Figures exist only for construction as a whole, and even these are inaccurate. The best opinion divides the total housing expenditure on the following basis: 35 to 40 per cent for labor used at the site, 45 to 50 per cent for materials delivered at the site, and the remainder for builders' and subcontractors' overhead and profit.

What is the Materials Bill?

With an average annual expenditure from 1919 to 1935 of $2.9 billion for housebuilding, the expenditure for materials at the site would probably not exceed $1.3 billion.[9] This sum includes not only the cost of materials and their fabrication, but handling and transporting them to the site. Since handling and transportation, plus profits, may absorb nearly half the total materials bill, the value of manufacturers' products drawn upon by housebuilding comes to about $650 million.[10]

Of the principal housing materials only a small proportion of total production

8. These comparisons are made in terms of the national income for 1939 rather than the gross national product, since the latter figures are not available on an industry basis. See Appendix C, 2 and Tables 13 and 14.

9. *Ibid.* Assuming materials to represent 46 per cent of the average value of residential construction. See Appendix C, 2.

10. See Chap. 4, pp. 115-117 and Appendix D, 3 and Table 29 for a discussion of costs of distribution.

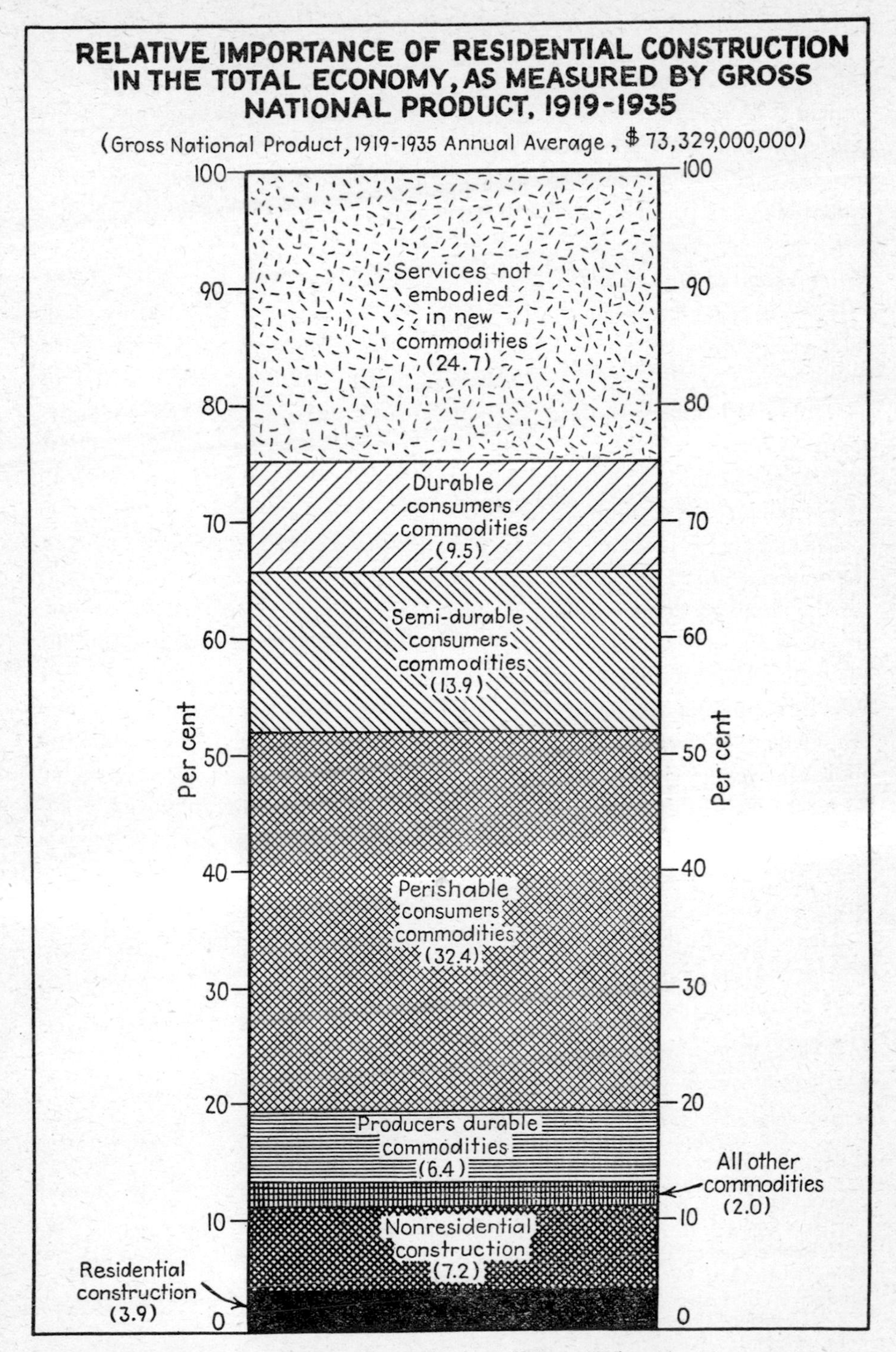

FIGURE 8. During the entire major business cycle from 1919 to 1935, residential construction averaged 3.9 per cent of the gross national product. But demand for houses fluctuated widely, with the industry's share in the total economy ranging from 6.5 per cent in 1925 to 1.2 per cent in 1933. (*Source:* Appendix C, 2, Table 13.)

is used in house construction, for example, 23 per cent of lumber, 15 per cent of cement.[11] During the period 1919–1935, materials used in residential construction represented about 2.5 per cent of the value of all finished products entering into the gross national product. In contrast, other consumers' durable goods represented about 13 per cent of all finished manufactured products.[12]

Employment in Housebuilding

If 38 per cent may be taken as a reasonable [13] estimate of labor's share of the total expenditure on housebuilding, then the average annual pay roll at the building site for 1919–1935 probably ranged from $212 million to $2 billion, averaging $1.1 billion. In the same period, the annual average of all wage payments was about $45 billion.[14] In 1939 the housebuilding pay roll was probably around $738 million or less than 2 per cent of the total national wage payment of $44 billion [15] (See Figure 9).

So enmeshed is housebuilding with all types of construction, and so poor are the data for construction as a whole, that no satisfactory figure can be given for the number of men working in the industry. Rough estimates by the Bureau of Labor Statistics on the basis of expenditures for nonfarm residential building place the 1939 monthly average at 521,000 workers.[16] In the peak months of the year this figure would undoubtedly rise by 25 to 30 per cent giving a maximum employment of perhaps 650,000. For all nonagricultural industries combined, monthly average employment in 1939 was 34,624,000, and in the peak month, 35,928,000, according to estimates by the Bureau of Labor Statistics.[17] The latter figures, however, include both full-time and part-time workers, whereas the figure for workers in residential construction is based on the estimated number required to build a certain number of houses.

There is a further difficulty in establishing a direct relationship between workers in the housebuilding industry and all employed workers, because the peak of construction in 1939 came in May, while the peak for all nonagricultural employment came in December. Nevertheless, it would seem that only 1.5 to 2 per cent of the employed nonagricultural workers were engaged in residential

11. Lumber: Frank J. Hallauer, *Lumber Requirements for Nonfarm Residential Construction,* Forest Service, Department of Agriculture, Miscellaneous Publication No. 347, 1939. Cement: Portland Cement Association.

12. Derived from Appendix C, 2 and Table 13, assuming the average value of materials used in residential construction (1919–1935) at $1.3 billion per year.

13. See Appendix C, 2.

14. Simon Kuznets, *National Income and Capital Formation, 1919–1935,* National Bureau of Economic Research, New York, 1937, Table 17, p. 58, with revisions for housebuilding wages as discussed in Appendix C, 2.

15. Appendix C, Table 14.

16. Division of Construction and Public Employment, Bureau of Labor Statistics.

17. Division of Employment Statistics, Bureau of Labor Statistics.

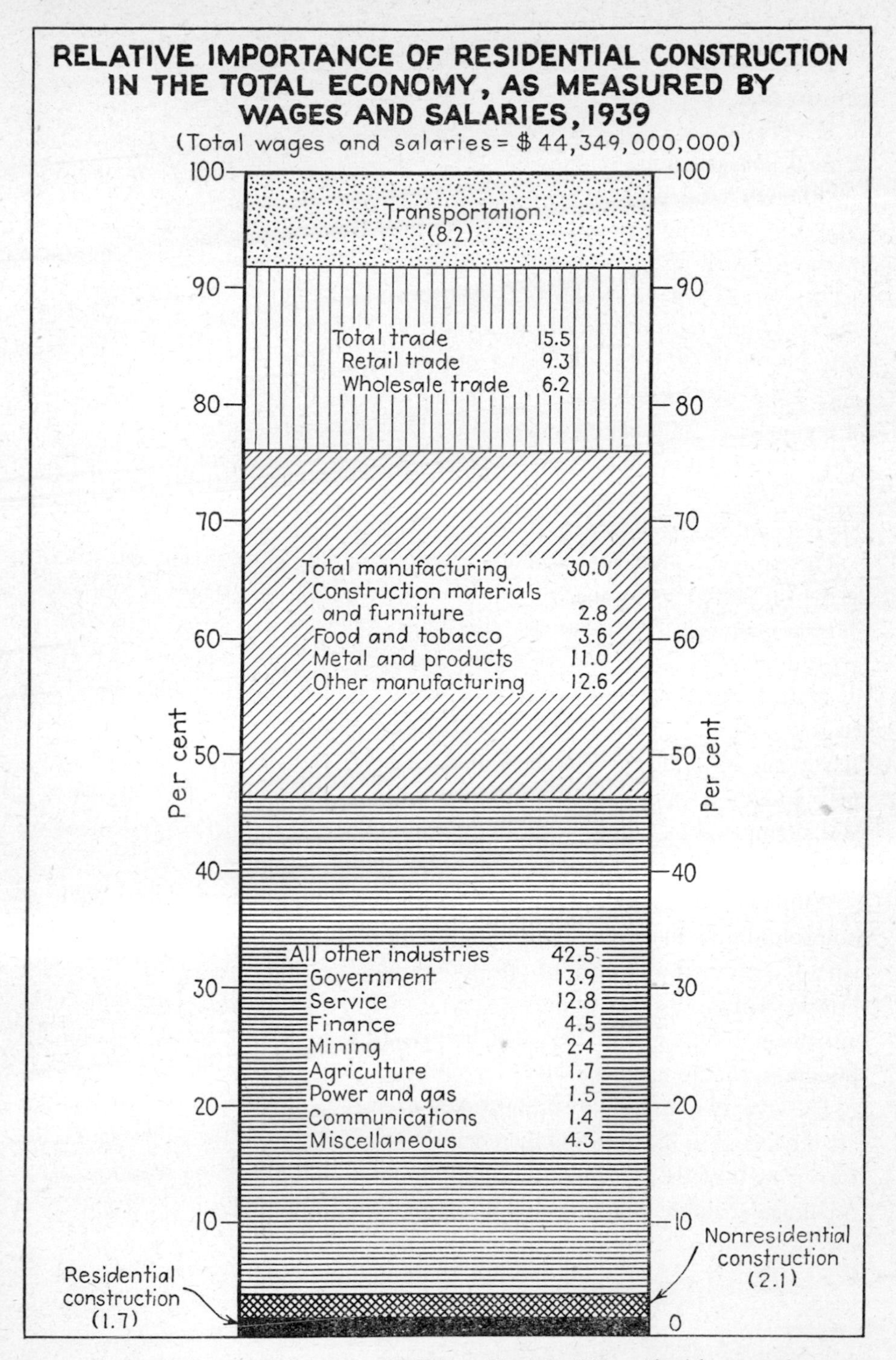

FIGURE 9. Measured in terms of wages and salaries paid out in 1939, residential construction represented 1.7 per cent of the total for all industries. Nonresidential construction accounted for an additional 2.1 per cent and the manufacture of construction materials and furniture for 2.8 per cent. (*Source:* Appendix C, 2, Table 14.)

construction. Employment in the iron and steel industry averaged about 856,000 in 1939, or 2.5 per cent, and in the automobile industry 394,000, or 1.1 per cent, of total nonagricultural employment.[18]

Although housebuilding apparently employs only a small portion of the American working force in prosperous years, the extreme cyclical fluctuations in the industry result in a disproportionate unemployment during a business depression. According to the BLS estimates mentioned earlier, the number of workers employed on nonfarm residential building totaled 842,000 in 1929, but only 184,000 in 1934. The difference of 658,000 workers is probably a minimum since some construction workers were idle even in 1929. Since there was a total of about 10,500,000 unemployed workers in 1934, according to estimates of several agencies, housebuilding accounted for at least 6.5 per cent of the total.

Housebuilding Labor

The estimated proportion of the total housebuilding costs attributable to labor at the site is high as compared with labor costs in the final stages of fabrication in most manufacturing industries. It is difficult, however, to arrive at the relative expenditures for labor at corresponding stages of fabrication in different industries. In building construction as a whole, skilled labor accounts for 71 per cent of all building labor.[19] This high figure is partly due to the practice of classifying as "skilled" all workers in designated crafts, even though their work may actually be semiskilled or even unskilled. The amount of skilled labor is also augmented by the fact that, under union restriction, operations demanding little skill are often required to be done by skilled workmen.

With due regard to such qualifications, the proportion of skilled labor in housebuilding remains high because the numerous materials and multiplicity of parts require many specialized operations. About seventy-five or eighty occupational classifications may be drawn upon during the erection of a large multistory apartment building. For detached houses, row houses, or small walk-up flat buildings, the number of crafts may range from twenty-five to forty-five.[20]

The seventy-five or eighty occupational groups used in residential construction are organized in nineteen international unions, comprising the Building Trades Department of the American Federation of Labor.[21] Although organization is presumably along craft lines there are obviously more distinguishable crafts

18. *Ibid.*

19. *A Social-Economic Grouping of Gainful Workers in the United States, 1930,* Bureau of the Census, Table 32, pp. 124–141.

20. See Appendix C, 3.

21. *Ibid.* At the present time, with the exception of the recent efforts of the Congress of Industrial Organizations to organize portions of the field (see Chap. 6), the Building Trades Department of AF of L controls all organized labor in the construction industry.

than unions. Similarity of materials handled and of tools used has been the principle of organization. The unions, for the most part, are neither strictly craft nor industrial organizations, but subindustry groups. No differentiation is ordinarily made by type of construction.

Extent of Organization

Although, according to best-informed opinion, the building trades unions control well over half the eligible workers in the construction industry, the extent of unionization varies with communities, regions, types of construction, and trades. The mechanical trades unions, for instance, frequently dominate areas and classes of work where other crafts are weakly organized. William Haber notes that:

> Union organization in the industry is not uniform throughout the country or in the several building markets. It is strongest in the larger building centers of the East, North, and Far West. Southern cities are not well organized. Unions are successfully entrenched in commercial, industrial, public, semipublic, apartment, and high-cost residential building. Small house construction in many large cities and most work in small towns and rural areas are largely nonunion; repair and maintenance work is frequently nonunion.[22]

Opinions of the extent of unionization in housebuilding vary. On the basis of questionnaires sent to contractors and labor leaders in seventy-two cities, the Bureau of Labor Statistics reported:

> In only four cities was it universally agreed that union rates prevail upon practically all residential construction. In two additional cities the contractors agreed that union conditions were nearly universal, although the union officials in these cities were not so sure. The contractors in twelve other cities and the union officials in sixteen cities estimated that union conditions prevail on over half of the smaller residence jobs. The union officials in forty-seven cities and the contractors in fifty-two cities estimated that less than half the small-dwelling work in their localities is done under union conditions. In forty-nine of these cities the contractors placed the proportion of union work at less than 25 per cent for the small-house construction, while union officials agreed that it was under 25 per cent in twenty-five cities.[23]

D. W. Tracy, Assistant Secretary of Labor, believes that union laborers working on dwellings costing $15,000 or less comprise only 10 per cent of the total employed.[24] The open shop was common among operative builders studied in connection with this survey, with unionization most frequent in the mechanical

22. See William Haber, "Building Construction," in *How Collective Bargaining Works,* The Twentieth Century Fund, New York, 1942, p. 203.

23. *Union Wages, Hours, and Working Conditions in the Building Trades,* Bulletin No. 674, Bureau of Labor Statistics, June 1, 1939, pp. 25–26.

24. *Hearings Before the TNEC,* Pt. 11, *The Construction Industry,* p. 5264.

trades. On the other hand, in private multifamily rental structures undertaken between 1935 and 1940 with the aid of Federal Housing Administration financing, over 70 per cent of the operations were conducted under dominantly union conditions.[25] Multifamily construction financed directly by United States Housing Authority and other public housing agencies has been almost entirely subject to union conditions. Since single-family rather than multifamily building dominates the industry, it must be concluded that union labor is less entrenched in the residential field than in construction as a whole, although in many localities union control is fairly complete.

Housebuilding Wages

Statistics on the wages of construction labor are difficult to obtain. The methods of reporting are less reliable than in other industries, the variations wider, and the means of concealment greater. Nevertheless, it appears reasonably clear that average hourly rates in construction are higher than in most other industries. This is due to the high proportion of skilled labor, the seasonal character of employment, and the strength of unionization in the construction industry as a whole. Even when translated into annual earnings, construction labor still fares rather well by comparison with other industries, although the difference is smaller than the high hourly rates would lead one to expect.[26]

It is, of course, the total of annual earnings that is important to labor, and here a moderate annual income—considering the large proportion of skilled labor involved—can be earned only by maintaining high hourly rates during short periods of employment. Yet it is the hourly wage, not the annual income of the workers, that fixes housing costs. Lower labor costs can be obtained only by reducing hourly wages. Under the present system of house production, however, reductions are difficult to justify and more difficult to effect.

Where the building workers are unorganized or poorly organized, wage rates for corresponding crafts may be lower for residential work than for other types of construction. Even in well-organized areas, a lower scale may be accepted by the unions for residential work.[27] While the differential between housebuilding and other construction wages varies, the general pattern among crafts usually corresponds to the union setup, and the differential diminishes with the growth of unionization. The wages of unorganized construction laborers thus tend to be influenced by the union scale in the community.

25. Division of Economics and Statistics, Federal Housing Administration. Prior to 1939 there existed no legal provision that might have favored union conditions.

26. See Appendix C, 4 for an analysis of the available data, and for a discussion of the difficulties of separating housebuilding wages from construction in general.

27. See *Hearings Before the TNEC*, testimony of D. W. Tracy, Pt. 11, pp. 5263–5266; see also Appendix E, Table 32.

b. CHARACTERISTICS OF HOUSEBUILDERS

Housebuilding is carried on through numerous organizations. Only a few account for many units annually. Most of them are financially weak as well as limited in the geographic scope of their operations.

Size of Housebuilders

The average builder of single-family dwellings in seventy-two cities examined by the Bureau of Labor Statistics for the year 1938 constructed only 3.5 houses a year. Only about one fourth of the builders, however, produced as many as the average. Quoting from the report:

> Even in the largest cities, more than half the builders took out permits to build only one house each inside the city limits. In some cases they may have built homes outside the city, or may have done other kinds of construction work. In many instances they were owner-builders, deriving their incomes from sources other than the construction industry. A large number were subcontractoı or construction craftsmen, dependent on construction activities for the bulk of their incomes, but not solely as general contractors or speculative builders.
>
> Except in cities of a half-million population or more, over one-fourth of the new 1-family houses were put up by 1-house builders, and over half the new homes were constructed by builders of fewer than 5 houses per year each. Even in the 13 biggest cities, less than half of the 1-family houses were erected by builders who constructed as many as 15 such houses in the year 1938.[28]

The small scale of housebuilding organizations is emphasized by the fact that of the twenty-eight cities in the BLS survey with a population of 100,000 or more, four did not have a builder producing ten or more houses a year, and thirteen did not have a builder who constructed twenty-five houses a year.

Number of Housebuilders

On the basis of this study, we may conclude that for the country as a whole there are 70,000 to 80,000 urban builders who construct one or more units annually.[29] Obviously only a relatively small proportion of these—probably not more than one fourth—can depend upon one-family house construction for their entire income (see Figure 10). Yet, under present circumstances, the part-time builder performs an important function in the low-priced field. In the seventy-two cities mentioned above, approximately 43 per cent of all urban one-family houses under $3,000 were constructed by one-house builders, and 67 per cent by

28. *Builders of 1-Family Houses in 72 Cities,* Serial No. R 1151, Bureau of Labor Statistics, 1940. A special investigation by the BLS indicated that the grouping of builders by production would not be materially altered if houses outside the city limits were included; see also Appendix C, 5 and Tables 15, 16 and 17.

29. See Appendix C, 6.

builders erecting not more than four houses a year. This is hardly enough to provide an adequate living. The bulk of the self-sustaining housing business is, for the most part, limited to the middle-priced field—houses that sell from $3,000 to $8,000. Above the latter amount, the one- to four-house builder again becomes dominant (see Figure 11). This suggests that the most efficient group of builders tend to operate in the middle-priced field.

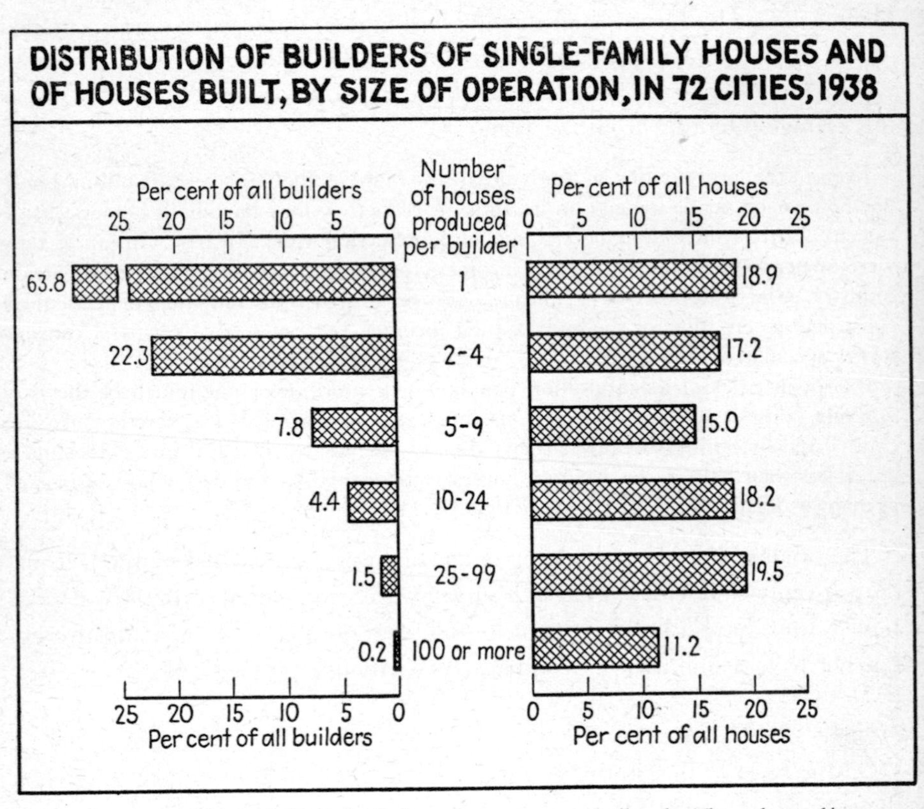

FIGURE 10. Most builders of single-family houses operate on a small scale. Thus, almost 64 per cent of the builders in 72 cities constructed only one house a year, and another 22 per cent from 2 to 4 houses. Taken together, however, these small builders—almost 90 per cent of all—produced little more than a third of all houses built in these areas. In contrast, the 2 per cent of the contractors building 25 or more houses annually accounted for over 30 per cent of all units built. (*Source:* Appendix C, 5, Table 15.)

The situation in multifamily construction,[30] while showing more units per builder, is basically the same as in the single-family house field. In the later 1930's an increasing proportion of multifamily units were produced by public housing agencies. Since these projects generally contain hundreds of units, the

30. For convenience, the term multifamily structure covers not only apartment buildings but all types of grouped dwellings not intended for separate ownership.

total production per contractor contrasts greatly with that for the single-family housebuilder.[31] Yet, the average production per builder is not spectacular. Studies of the thirty-seven largest apartment-producing cities show that the average number of family units per builder in 1939 was forty-eight, or about two buildings each.[32] Even where large projects are most characteristic, housebuilding is usually a small-scale business.

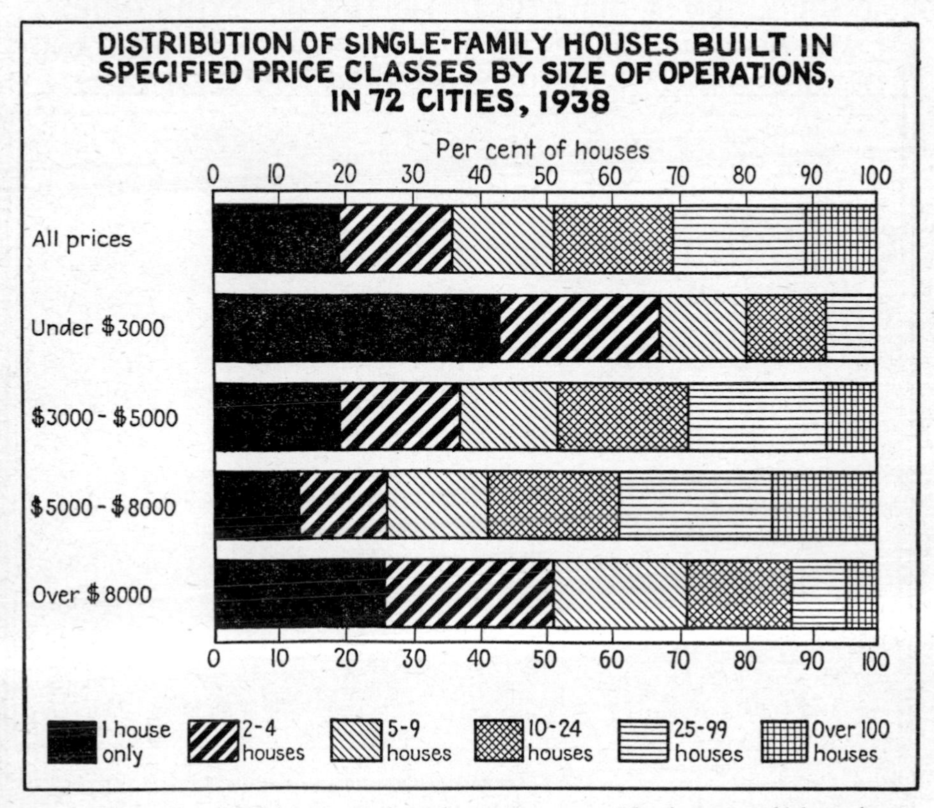

FIGURE 11. Small-scale builders apparently tend to concentrate on either low-cost or high-cost houses. Only in the middle price brackets—from $3,000 to $8,000—do builders of ten or more houses per year claim a large share of the total business. (*Source:* Appendix C, 5, Table 17.)

The scale of the typical housebuilding organization is indicated by the generally small number of employees per organization. While there are no data for housebuilding alone, the figures for the construction industry as a whole are conclusive enough. The relationships between employees and employers by size of organization for all types of construction is shown in Figure 13. Moreover, the small operator is known to be more dominant in housebuilding than in the

31. It may be noted that the builders of public housing projects are usually large general contractors who undertake other forms of construction.

32. See Figure 12.

construction industry as a whole. Except for builders of large public housing projects, some large private rental dwellings, as well as a few operative builders, not many organizations have a hundred or more employees. The majority have ten or less.

The tendency to subcontract has grown as new materials, parts and equipment

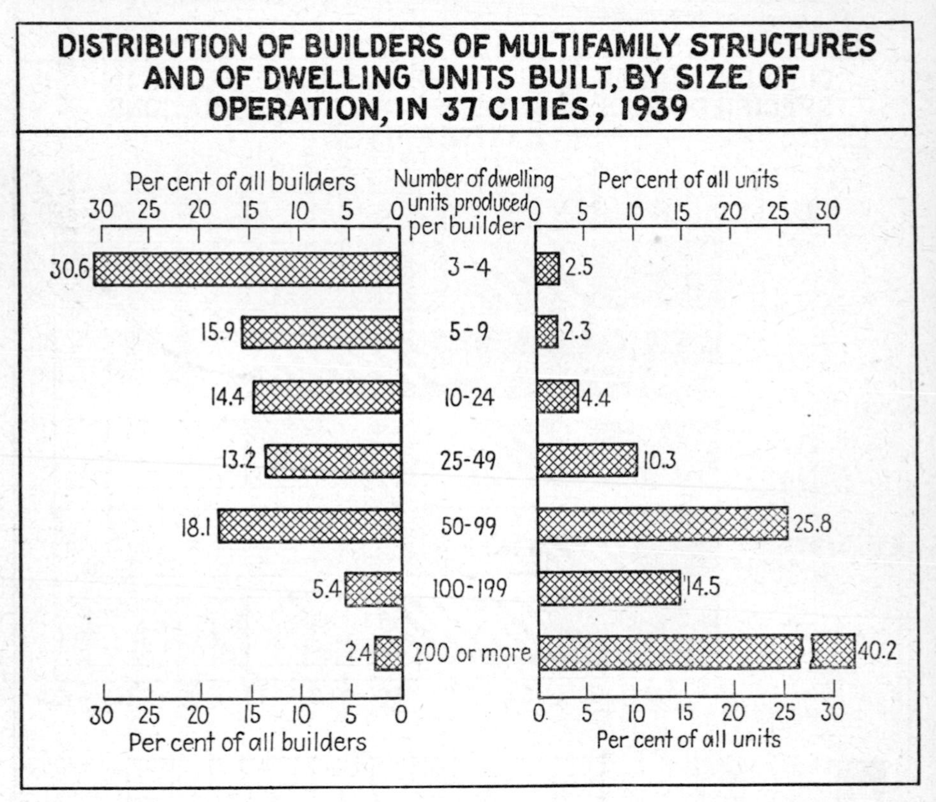

FIGURE 12. The dominance of the small operator in multifamily construction is less marked than in the case of single-family dwellings. Almost half of the contractors surveyed in representative cities built less than ten dwelling units in 1939 and together they accounted for only 5 per cent of the units built. But almost 40 per cent of the builders concentrated on 25-or-more-unit structures and together accounted for over 90 per cent of the total built. (*Source:* Appendix C, 5, Table 16.)

have come into use. The extent of subcontracting varies somewhat with the size of the community. In small towns, the builder may be a Jack-of-all-trades, depending upon subcontractors principally for mechanical work. Such builders, however, are not typical. The extent of subcontracting also varies with the size and character of the job. In a small detached house there are at least sixteen to twenty operations, and in a large apartment building well over fifty,[33] any or all of which may be subcontracted or sub-subcontracted.

33. See Appendix C, 7.

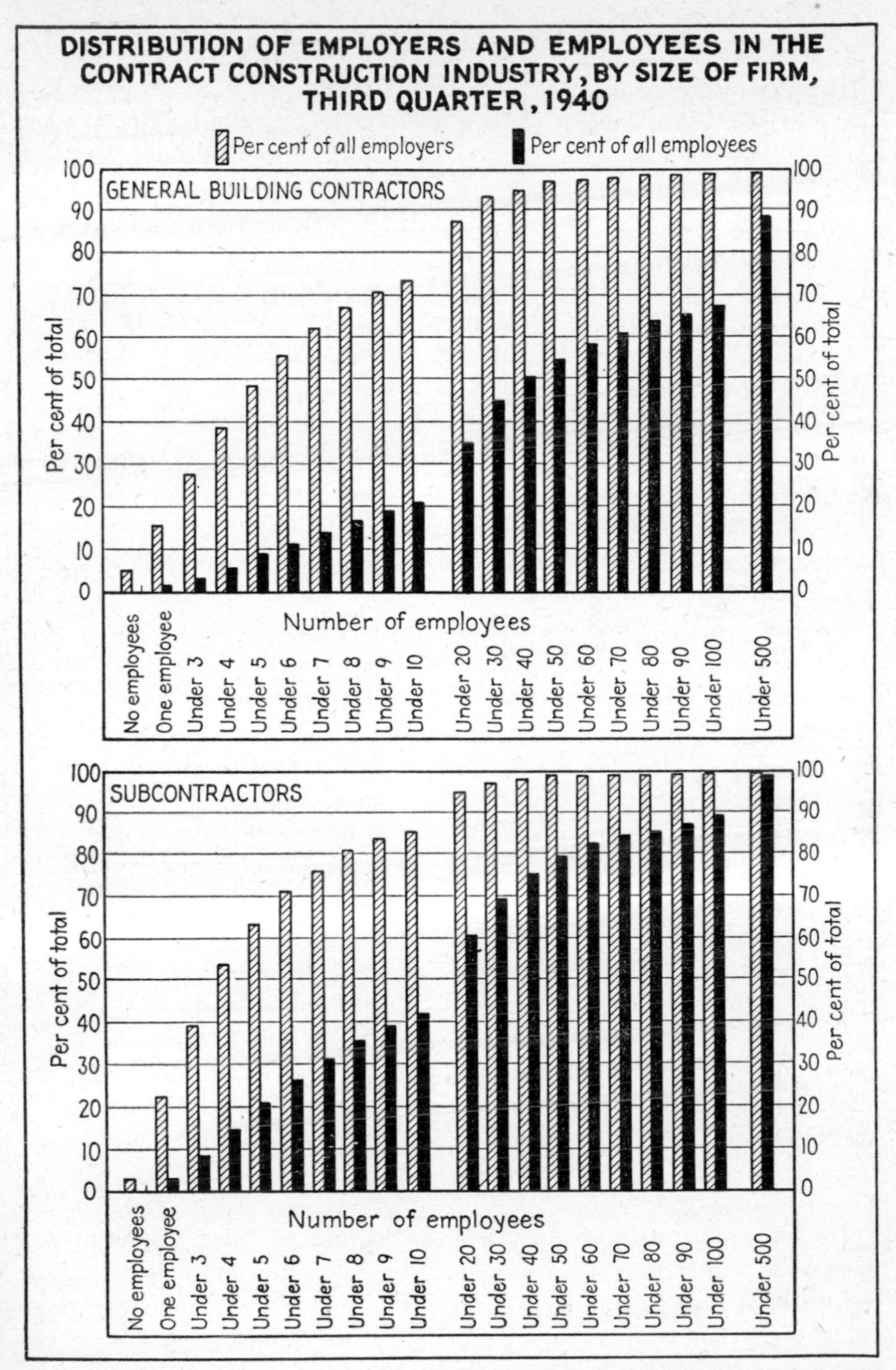

FIGURE 13. More than 70 per cent of the general building contractors employed less than ten workers each and in the aggregate they accounted for only 20 per cent of all employees in the industry in 1940. Subcontractors operated on an even smaller scale, with about 85 per cent employing less than ten workers. (*Source:* Appendix C, 6, Table 18.)

There are probably 176,000 subcontracting organizations in the whole construction field.[34] We cannot tell how many of these engage in housebuilding, or of those who do, what proportion of their work is in residential structures. Probably, however, all but a small percentage are to some degree connected with housebuilding. Subcontractors, like builders, operate on a small scale, as shown in Figure 13.

Localism of Housebuilding Operations

Housebuilding is essentially a local enterprise, as indicated by Figure 14. Although here, too, we cannot segregate the data from that for general construction, the degree of localism for housebuilders is probably somewhere between that for the entire group of building contractors and for carpenters, as shown in the chart. Thus at least 80 per cent or more of all housebuilders operate in their home city or adjoining area. Similarly, the localism of subcontractors principally engaged in house construction is probably somewhat higher than that of all subcontractors.

Localism ordinarily means a restricted market. Even in larger communities, where the prospects for continuous operations are best, builders rarely construct houses much in advance of known demand. Producer initiative, characteristic of the mass-production industries, is generally nonexistent or tentative in housebuilding. A large producer is one who completes twenty-five houses annually. At this rate, the market may be carefully explored as the work proceeds. Many substantial operators frequently begin to build only after accumulating orders from plans, model houses, or on the basis of previously completed work.

The extreme localism of the housebuilding industry confines it to small-scale operations except in the largest centers. Even here, the scale is small compared with mass-production enterprises. Hence the industry is forced into a retail relationship with suppliers. Furthermore it is subjected to many forms of local pressure that could not be applied to a more flexible industry. For this reason, housebuilders try to protect themselves by creating obstacles to the entry of outsiders in their market, and in so doing intensify the local, small-scale character of the industry.

Financial Resources

The numerous small producers, and the difficulty of differentiating housing from other construction or real-estate activity, make it extremely hard to gauge the financial basis upon which the housebuilder operates. With the average housebuilder, and even among the better organized operative builders and contractors, accounting methods are woefully inadequate.

34. See Appendix C, 6.

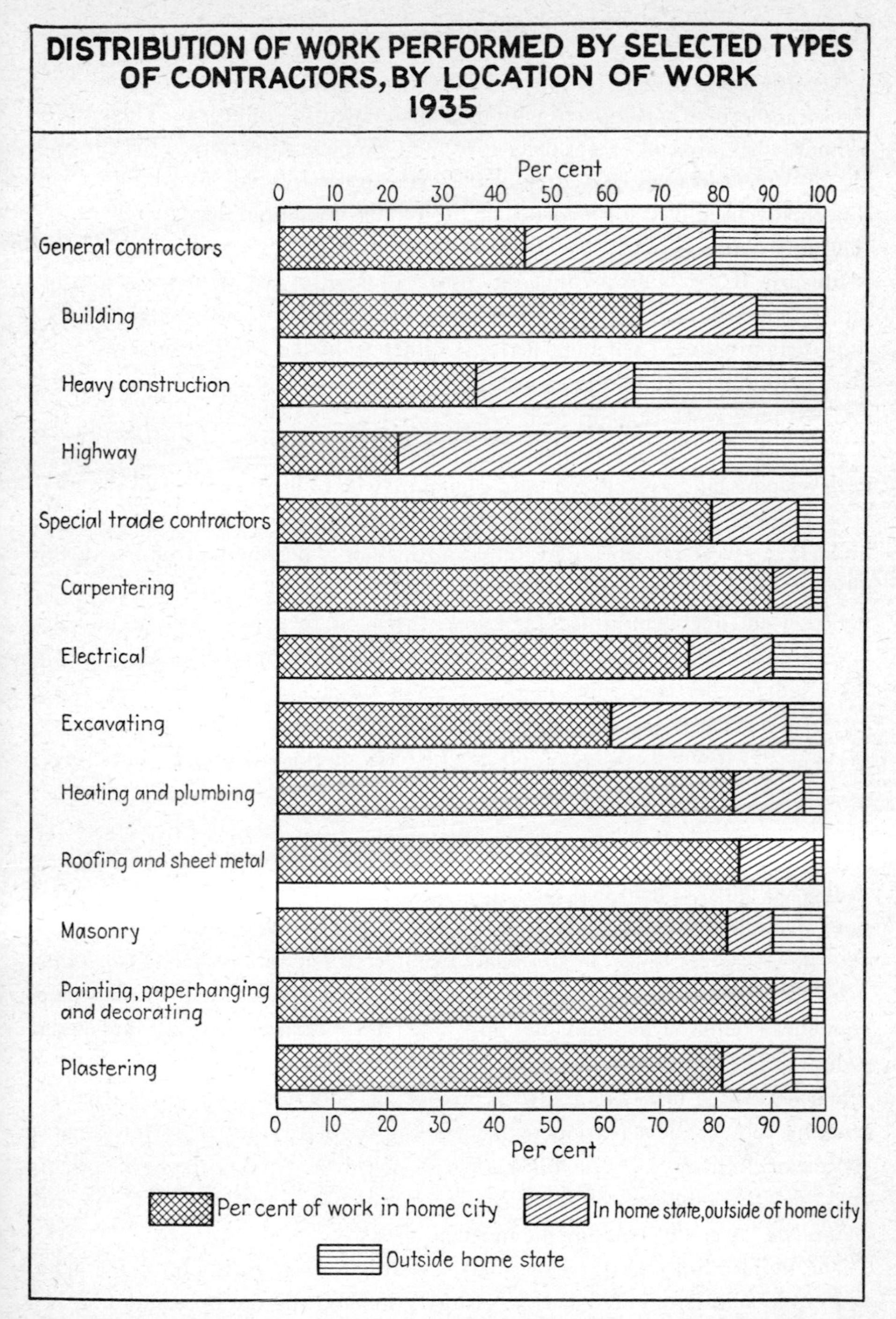

FIGURE 14. General building contractors and special trade contractors—in contrast to heavy construction and highway contractors—tend to operate largely in their home city. (*Source:* Appendix Table 19.)

Nevertheless, it is plain that the capital permanently invested in housebuilding enterprises is small as compared with most manufacturing industries. The builder ordinarily has no plant except office space and temporary quarters at the site and his investment in tools and equipment is comparatively small. Working capital is normally assembled for a particular project, as among old-time merchant adventurers, and it is returned with gains or losses when the specific undertaking is finished. If the house is built on contract for an owner or buyer, working capital of as little as 10 per cent of the total cost may suffice—just enough to carry construction between payment periods (either from the contracting agency or the mortgagee) and to take care of the "hold-back," or that part of the payment retained until work is completed.

Where the builder has a proprietary interest in the transaction and is engaged in developing land as well, working capital may be 15 or 20 per cent of the total at some time during the operation. Some of the better established operative builders have greater working capital and may only borrow half or less of the total construction cost. Indeed, some housebuilders wholly finance both the construction and merchandising operations with their own funds. Some builders also invest considerable sums in land, although a subordination of the land by the original seller is a common practice. For the majority, however, working capital is extremely limited and dependence upon borrowed funds correspondingly great. Most housing operations are financed on the proverbial "shoestring."

Financial Position of the Subcontractor

The Temporary National Economic Committee discovered that corporations in the construction field had the smallest average assets of all types of corporations, including those engaged in agriculture.[35] The average value of equipment per employee was lower for residential builders than for contractors in other fields (see Figure 15). Subcontractors carry the major investment in plant and equipment required for housebuilding, and the subsidiary organizations in the industry have relatively more capital than the so-called principals.[36]

Subcontracting firms often have to provide not only their own equipment and working capital but a portion of the working capital required by the general contractor. In many cases, of course, the reverse is true. Among the better organized operative builders, the subcontractor may depend greatly on the principal contractor for credit, equipment, and materials.

The builder can operate with small resources because little outlay for plant and equipment is required for the ordinary methods of site operation and be-

35. *Hearings Before the TNEC,* testimony of Willard L. Thorp, Pt. 1, *Economic Prologue,* p. 106.
36. *Ibid.,* Pt. 11, p. 5185.

cause it is usually possible to borrow ample funds or to use the open-book credit of the building material dealer. During 1940, for instance, operative builders in the most active areas (the eastern and far western regions generally) could borrow construction money at 4 to 6 per cent. Rarely was it necessary to pay fees or commissions. On the other hand, by combining the construction loan with the

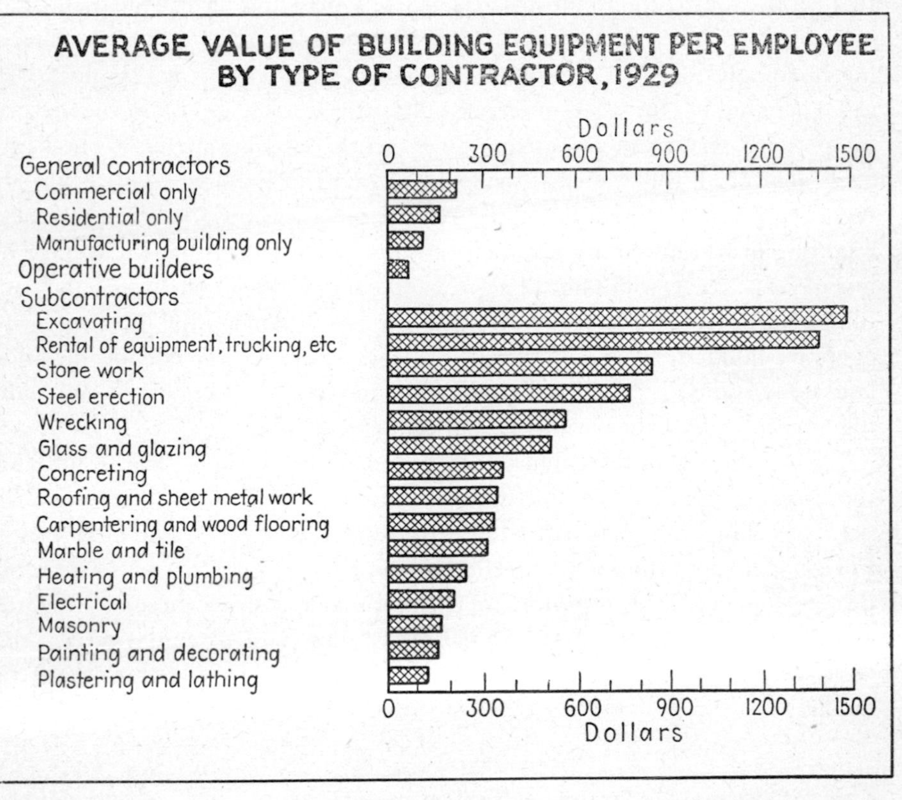

FIGURE 15. General contractors own very little equipment and the burden of maintaining a going plant rests mainly on subcontractors. Even for these, the average value of equipment per employee is lower than in other industries. Only two types of subcontractors—those engaged in excavating and in rental of equipment—own equipment whose value per employee exceeds $900. (*Source:* Appendix Table 20.)

so-called "permanent" financing, builders were able, particularly in the North Atlantic region, to lower the effective interest rate or take an additional profit by obtaining 1 to 2 per cent discounts as a premium for the business.

Failures and Profits

The small size of the average housebuilding organization and its meager operating capital result in a large number of failures. We might speak of *turnover* rather than *failure,* however, since the small amount of invested capital often makes formal bankruptcy unnecessary. The disappointed builder simply withdraws from the industry and seeks more lucrative employment.

Data on builders' profits indicate the hazards of housebuilding. Although again it is impossible to segregate housebuilding from general construction, the picture would doubtless be less favorable to the housebuilder if this were done. In 1929 the construction industry as a whole (including incorporated and nonincorporated firms constructing dams, bridges, roads, etc., as well as those erecting buildings) made a profit of 6.7 per cent of gross value; in 1933 profits fell to 1.4 per cent, but increased to 7.5 per cent in 1940. These figures include returns for personal services of proprietors of unincorporated businesses.[37] The aggregate profit of all corporations principally engaged in building construction and reporting incomes in 1929 was 2 per cent of gross receipts. Only 55 per cent of reporting firms showed a profit. In 1933 those filing returns had an average net loss of 7.5 per cent, with only 12 per cent showing a net profit. In 1937 the firms filing returns had an average profit of 0.5 per cent.[38] Among the more successful operative builders, a net of 5 per cent on gross revenue (frequently including land transactions) is considered satisfactory. In fact, for all building firms showing a profit in 1929, the net was 5.9 per cent.

The significance of these figures can be gained from comparison of profits in the construction field with those in other industries. In 1938, all construction corporations filing income tax returns showed a profit of 0.8 per cent on total receipts. For general contractors only, the figure was 1.3 per cent; for subcontractors a *loss* of 0.6 per cent was recorded. In 1938, all manufacturing industries reported an average net profit on sales of 2.6 per cent.[39] The construction industry is thus weak in resources and organization, and its low rate of profit reflects these conditions.

3. SEASONAL NATURE OF HOUSEBUILDING

In order to make the fullest use of equipment and labor and maintain a favorable bargaining position with workers and suppliers, an industry should be able to operate rather evenly throughout the year. But housebuilding is notoriously seasonal, like the construction industry as a whole. The monthly distribution of contract awards for houses, as indicated in Figure 16, varies somewhat in timing but not greatly in amplitude from that of other privately financed construction. The form and amplitude of the curve, as shown in Figure 17, do not vary much from year to year. There is a major concentration in the spring, a minor con-

37. See Appendix C, Table 21.
38. See Appendix C, Table 22.
39. See Appendix C, Table 23.

centration in the fall, a minor decline in the summer, and a major slump in midwinter.[40]

a. REASONS FOR SEASONAL VARIATION

Ordinarily three causes account for seasonal variation in industry: weather, the necessity for retooling to meet style changes, and the public's buying habits.

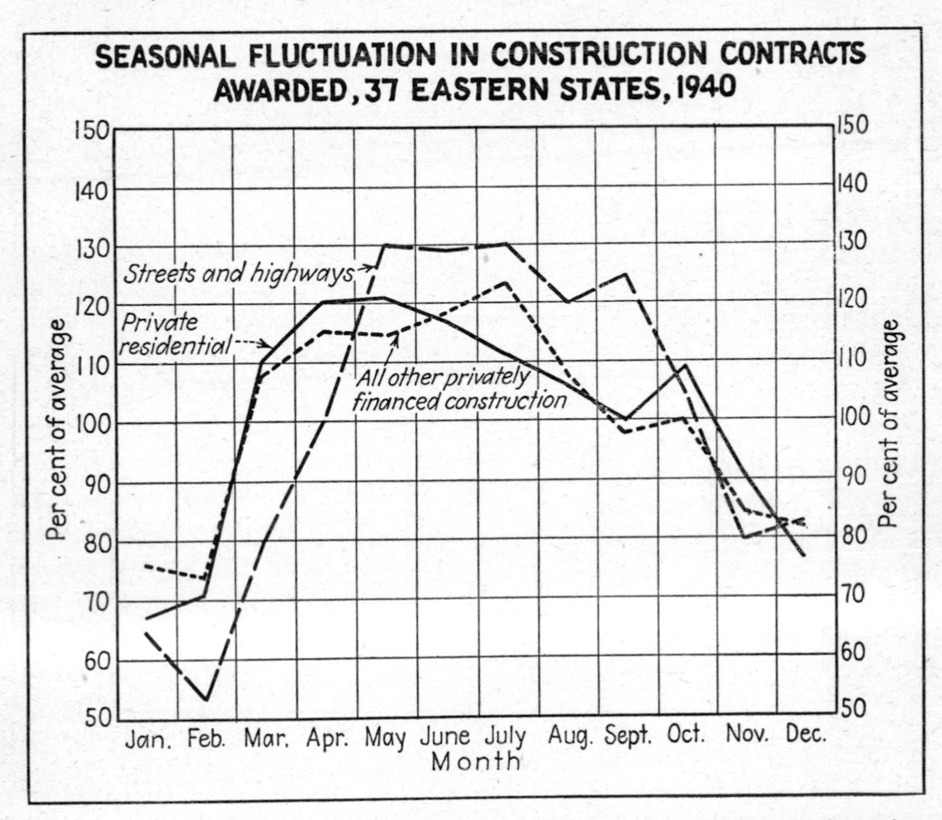

FIGURE 16. The seasonal nature of the construction industry is shown by the sharp rise from a low point in winter to a peak in spring and early summer. A minor recession in midsummer is followed by renewed activity in the fall for both privately and publicly financed construction. (*Source:* Appendix C, 9, Table 24.)

In housebuilding and construction generally, weather is the major influence not only on consumer habits but on operating conditions. The necessity for retooling and restyling obviously does not enter the picture.

How the seasonal curve for building permits varies under differing climatic conditions is shown in Figure 18. A study by the Federal Works Agency of public building projects, including a number of large public housing projects,

40. For a discussion of the data used in Figures 16, 17 and 19, see Appendix C, 9.

shows that weather was an important factor in the progress and cost of construction [41] in spite of the fact that in this class of work it would presumably be possible to use all known means of combating both cold and rain.

Since seasonal variation occurs even where winters are mild, weather alone cannot be blamed for seasonality. Custom, in its many guises, is an important factor. According to builders and brokers, the buying market is generally most

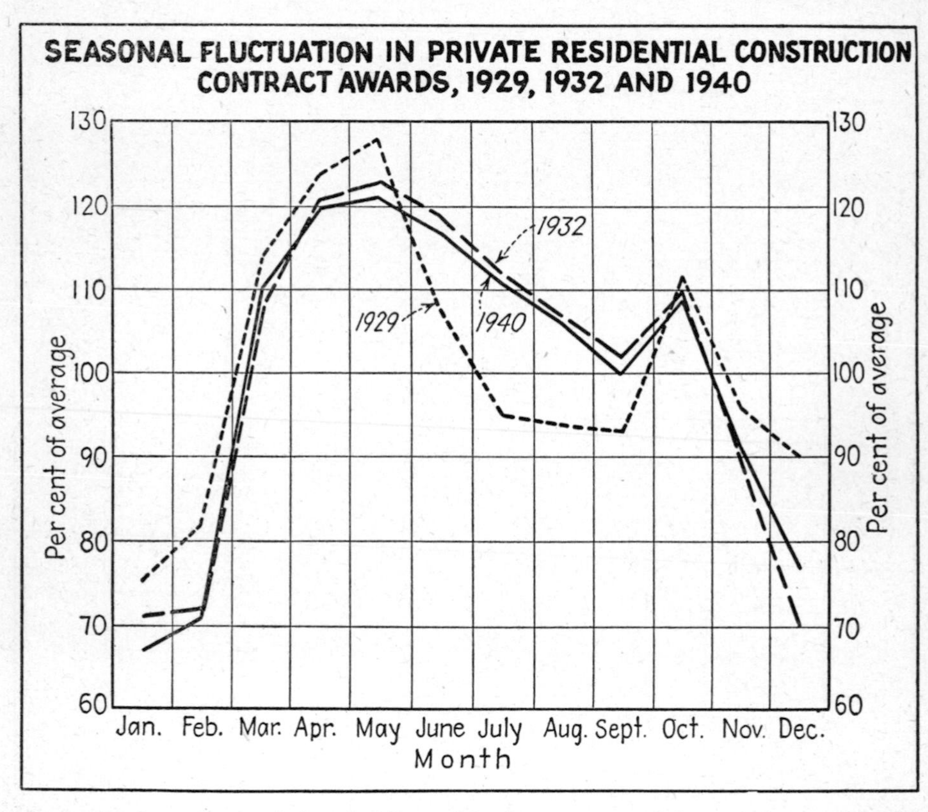

FIGURE 17. Seasonal curves in housebuilding activity do not vary much from year to year. The depression year 1932 follows substantially the same pattern as 1940, while the relatively prosperous year 1929 shows a more pronounced summer recession than the other two years. (*Source:* Appendix C, 9, Table 24.)

active in the spring, a trend that is encouraged by their advertising campaigns. Houses are generally repaired and painted in the spring, thus adding to the peak load in certain trades. Uniform leasing dates also tend to concentrate house hunting in definite seasons.

It is impossible to segregate and measure such diverse influences. Houses built

41. *Engineering Management of Project Planning and Construction.* Address before Engineers' Club of Hampton Roads, Va., September 27, 1940, by George N. Babcock, Director of Engineering Management, Federal Works Agency (mimeographed).

SEASONAL FLUCTUATION IN RESIDENTIAL CONSTRUCTION AND APPROXIMATE AVERAGE TEMPERATURES, BY MONTHS, IN SELECTED AREAS, 1930-1938

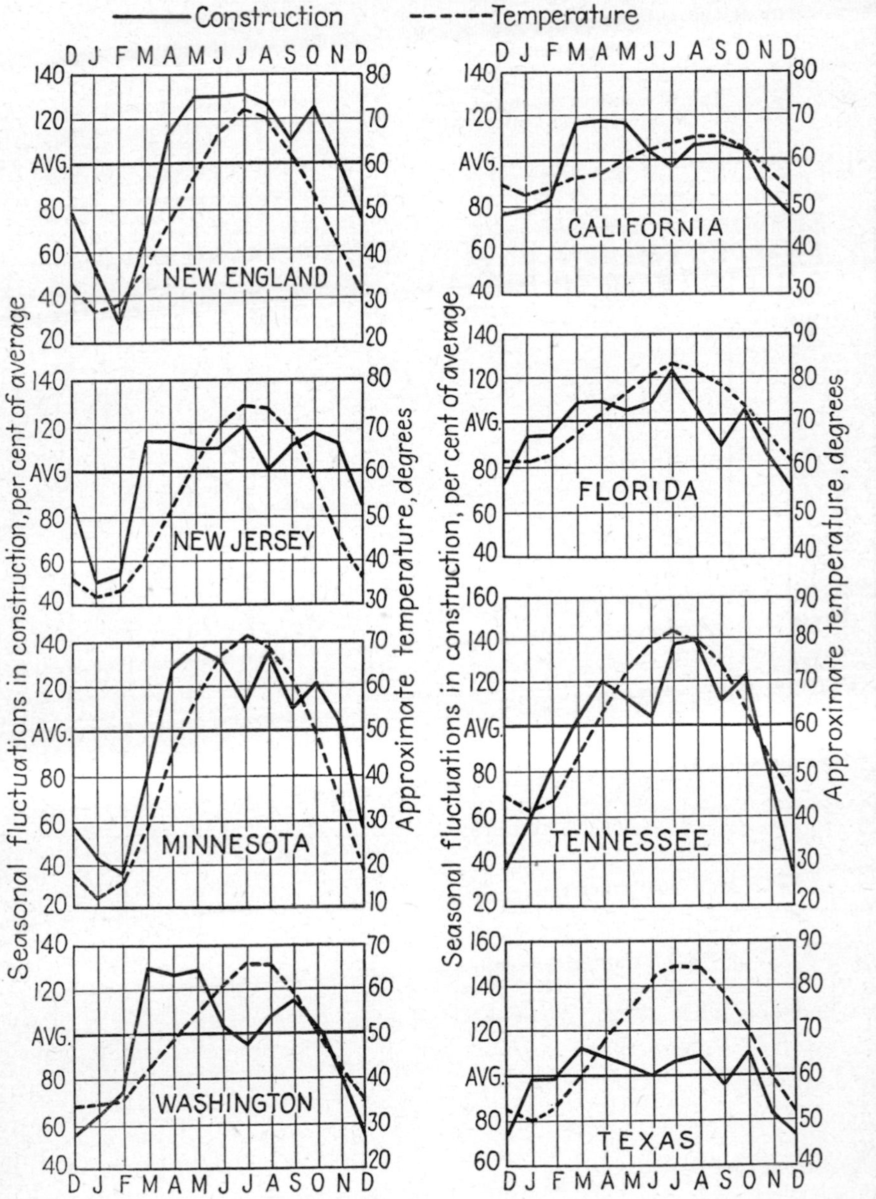

——— Construction - - - - - Temperature

FIGURE 18. Seasonal fluctuation in construction volume in different parts of the country tends to show a rough correlation with the seasonal range in average temperatures. Thus, New England and Minnesota show wider variations in construction volume than California and Florida. (*Source:* Appendix Table 25.)

on contract seem to show a slightly more marked seasonality than those produced by operative builders (Figure 19), indicating the influence of buyer initiative under the spell of spring. The secondary peak in the autumn is more noticeable in apartment than in single-family dwelling construction. This suggests a relationship between the incidence of demand and the start of construction. Since the main renting season is in the fall, the bulk of construction begins in the spring. The secondary spring rental season is reflected by a secondary autumnal initiation period.

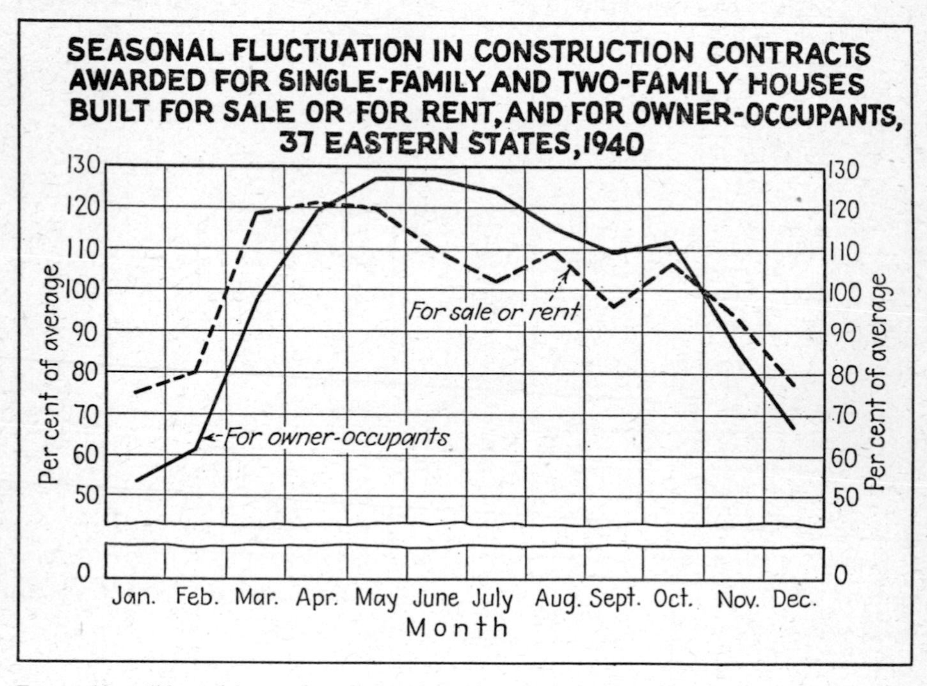

FIGURE 19. Builders of houses for sale or rent have a relatively higher rate of winter construction and operate more steadily through the year than do contract builders. (*Source:* Appendix C, 9, Table 24.)

b. SMOOTHING THE SEASONAL CURVE

The inevitability of such marked seasonal variations has been frequently challenged. It is contended, for instance, that in most parts of the country rain or cold actually make work impossible for a comparatively small number of days annually, that even for exposed work precautions may be taken to reduce this number, that labor is more efficient in cold weather, and that wages and the price of materials are apt to be lower in the off season.[42]

42. For an able presentation of these arguments, see *Seasonal Operations in the Construction Industry,* Report and Recommendations by Committee of the President's Conference on Unemployment, Washington, 1924.

Such arguments tend to ignore the circumstances under which building must be conducted. For example, although in a ten-year period only 5.3 days of 24° F. or lower temperature in one month were recorded in New York,[43] the distribution of those days was important. If they alternated with warmer days, they might cause a loss of 10 or more working days because of the difficulty of organizing operations on so erratic a schedule. Moreover, the marked variations in the number and distribution of inclement days from year to year make it difficult to plan operations for completion within a given time. In a ten-year period, days of lower than 24° F. throughout the winter averaged only 14 annually, but the range varied from 7 to 23 days. Rainfall affecting outdoor construction averaged only 13 days per year for the ten years, but the range was 7.5 to 19 days.[44]

The builder cannot afford to gamble with long-term averages. He is likely, if working on contract, to base his price on the worst probable weather condition; if he builds on his own account, he may defer construction to a period of good weather. This is particularly true of the typical small builder with little capital and without the equipment for adequately combating unfavorable weather conditions. Working on a narrow and frequently indefinite margin, the average builder cannot assume extraordinary risks.

In spite of contrary opinions, the risks of bad weather do not appear to be offset by lower labor and materials costs in the off season. Lower rates for winter work have never been granted officially by labor unions; even in unorganized areas, no evidence of such rates has been found. Cool weather probably increases the efficiency of labor, but it is doubtful whether very cold weather does, or whether greater efficiency offsets time lost because of inclement weather. There is also no evidence of special concessions in the price of building materials during the winter. Even the Work Projects Administration, which purchased in large quantities, did not obtain discounts that show any seasonal pattern.[45] Moreover, the costs of the measures needed to protect materials and workers in cold weather must not be ignored.

Persistence of Seasonal Pattern

The conditions described above will probably remain true so long as most fabricating and assembly work is done in the open. Some of the best operative builders continue to confine their work to three seasons, spring, summer, and autumn. Builders who endeavor to maintain winter operations try to arrange for inside work during bad weather. But this still results in considerable seasonal

43. *Ibid.*, p. 16.
44. *Ibid.*
45. Unpublished report by Peter A. Stone, WPA, Washington, 1938.

unemployment among workers engaged on exterior work. It is exceptional indeed for new construction to proceed at a normal rate during the winter.

Efforts to modify the seasonal pattern by staggering lease dates [46] have not been successful. Leasing habits are less easy to explain than construction practices. Beyond the influence of the school year, and the inconvenience of moving when it is very hot or very cold, there are few good reasons for the present May and October leasing arrangements. In fact, many arguments may be offered against them. Yet the attempts by real-estate organizations in the late 1920's to alter the custom were unsuccessful.

One important exception may be noted. The experience of government agencies has generally shown that the concentration of leasing dates is less marked in low-rental property than in the higher-priced accommodations. Data covering the sales of houses foreclosed by the Home Owners' Loan Corporation show no distinct seasonal pattern. While inconclusive, the data suggest that sales as well as rentals are less seasonal for low-priced than for more expensive dwellings, indicating that builders catering to the lower-income groups may count on a steadier year-round demand than exists in the market as a whole.

4. CAPACITY OF THE HOUSING INDUSTRY

Is the contribution of the industry to the general economy limited to the relationships noted earlier? Can its average production be measurably increased to meet added demand? These questions are related not only to the industry's ability to satisfy normal housing requirements, but to the possibility of using it as a major instrument in maintaining the economy in the postwar period.

a. PHYSICAL CAPACITY

In industries characterized by large capital investment and regularized methods of employing labor, the total possible output may be measured with fair accuracy. Thus, we may measure the physical capacity of the textile industry by the number of spindles in existence and the daily run per spindle; of the sheet glass or steel plate industries from the number of feet per machine per day and the total number of existing machines. In housebuilding there are no such criteria. The product is too varied to fit this type of measurement neatly and there is, besides, no way of calculating the total amount of productive equipment. The physical capacity of housebuilding depends upon the available supply of labor, materials, and managerial skill, none of which can be accurately measured.

At the peak of residential construction in 1925, the industry obviously could

46. See "The Economic Fallacy of the Peak Leasing Seasons," a circular published by the Chicago Homes Economic Council, *circa* 1928; also *National Real Estate Journal,* October 28, 1929.

produce a minimum of 900,000 nonfarm units per year. There has been no such effective demand since, and whether that capacity remains is unknown. Certainly, during the decade of 1930-1940 there was ample labor to meet all housing requirements. Complaints were heard from time to time about the shortage of apprentices, and the increasing age and lower efficiency of workers, but there is no proof that lack of labor was a major factor in hampering housebuilding operations.

The adoption of a war economy has grave implications not only for the maintenance of the housebuilding industry's capacity during the war but for its role in postwar readjustments. In an extended period of arms production the volume of housing as of all commodities not essential to war is sharply curtailed. For most industries the conversion to war materials does not greatly impair their underlying capacities. The plants and equipment remain, the labor force can be readily recruited and management is at hand. If demand exists, a return to normal manufacturing involves no serious readjustments.

Housebuilding presents a different situation, since it is not really a unified industry with a given physical plant, but a heterogeneous group of builders, subcontractors, and laborers brought together for a unique purpose. The components of the industry are easily dispersed in a period of idleness, and can be reassembled only with difficulty. Thus, workers who are not drawn into other fields lose their skill. The labor supply in the building trades is bound to deteriorate sadly as the industry endures a wartime slump. In the first World War, the building trades suffered in areas not involved in war production. According to one authority,[47] "Building labor, especially the typical home-building mechanic of the smaller cities and suburbs, has to be employed *on local building work*—if at all. It cannot readily migrate or change over to other types of defense work." The high proportions of unemployed building trade registrants with state employment offices during the expansion of war industries in 1940-1941 recalls the experience of the last war.

Building management is equally susceptible to dispersion and deterioration. Organizations disappear in slack periods and only after general recovery has proceeded for some time do capable builders again become numerous. Because houses are built by a great variety of organizations ranging from ambitious day laborers and heavy construction contractors, to adventurers from other fields, it is often forgotten that to satisfy large demands for new houses numerous experienced builders are needed. With all the stimulus that government could provide, it took nearly five years after the bottom of the depression was reached before the housebuilding industry achieved a fair degree of recovery.

47. Samuel O. Dunn, "Building Activity, Employment and Taxable Wealth," *American Builder,* July 1941, p. 35.

The war may thus seriously reduce the capacity of housebuilding especially in its traditional form. On the other hand, the war is promoting new techniques, involving a greater use of fixed plant, mechanized factory methods, and off-site fabrication of house sections. Organizations using the new methods will be ready and anxious to devote their facilities to peacetime housing. Unfortunately, their number is still small, their over-all capacity but a fraction of total requirements, and their methods of distribution not well adapted to normal marketing conditions.[48]

b. EFFICIENCY OF OPERATION

Just as there is no convenient way of measuring the physical capacity of the traditional housebuilding industry, so there is equal difficulty in measuring its efficiency. Trends in man-hour production can be found in numerous other activities.[49] In housebuilding an attempt to establish trends would be meaningless. The great variety of the product, the separation of crafts and the heterogeneity of parts and materials, prevent us from finding a basis of measurement. For instance, over a period of years, the number of bricks laid per man per day has declined. But this may not indicate a decrease in productivity, because less care and skill were required by thick masonry construction than in thin, many-windowed walls applied to a skeleton frame. Similar problems are found in nearly every craft associated with housebuilding.

In spite of the difficulties of measurement, it is clear that the usual housebuilding methods are not efficient. A study of industrial waste in 1921 revealed that the building industry was nearly twice as wasteful as other durable goods producers.[50] Among the prominent sources of waste were:

1. The seasonal pattern, which requires a labor force sufficient to meet peak conditions, thus wasting man power in the off season.
2. The predominance of site operations, resulting in idleness of workers due to weather interruptions, delays in the delivery of materials, and difficulties in scheduling sequential operations, and in waste of materials due to lack of opportunity for using odd pieces.
3. The continuance of unnecessary hand operations where mechanical means are available thereby causing more labor waste.
4. Certain craft restrictions, resulting in the use of more labor—especially skilled labor—than a particular operation may warrant.
5. Inefficient management of producing organizations.

48. See Chap. 5, pp. 131-148, for a further discussion of these problems.

49. See Spurgeon Bell, *Productivity, Wages, and National Income,* The Brookings Institution, Washington, 1940.

50. *Waste in Industry,* Committee on Elimination of Waste in Industry of the Federated American Engineering Societies, McGraw-Hill, New York, 1921, p. 9. Unfortunately, there is no later information on this important subject.

Although such wastes cannot be accurately measured, their existence proves that available resources in the housebuilding industry are not fully exploited under existing methods of production.

C. LIMIT OF PROFITABLE OPERATION

Industries find it profitable to make full use of their physical capacity only under the most extreme demands. In the sheet steel industry, for example, it is ordinarily no longer profitable to use hand-fed plants. With the pressure of war orders, however, such plants help to expand operations. Similarly, before the invention of the Bayer and Hall processes, aluminum could be profitably produced only as a semiprecious metal. With the introduction of the new methods costs were lowered and the use of aluminum expanded greatly, both for industrial and domestic articles.

Over a long period of time the housebuilding industry has been unable profitably to supply enough adequate housing. There has been no general downward trend in the actual costs of production over the past two or three decades.[51] On the contrary the introduction of more mechanical equipment, increasingly stringent building codes, and rising labor and materials costs, have made it more difficult to produce low-priced dwellings. Rising costs have not been offset by compensating technological advances. In spite of some reversal of trend in the past few years, rising costs over a long period have tended to limit new production to a small portion of the total potential demand. As a result, it has been possible to expand building activities only when the number of relatively high-income families increased, making housebuilding a prosperity phenomenon. Recent efforts to reach wider markets by building more compact houses and stripping them of nonessentials cannot fully solve the problem of attaining greatly expanded production. So far there has been no definite evidence of the industry's ability to operate profitably under conditions of lower prices and higher quality, or to maintain volume in the face of declining national income. This situation may be contrasted with the household refrigerator industry (see Figure 4) where technical improvements and parallel price reductions permitted an expansion of volume during a period of depression.

5. SUMMARY

Housebuilding is an important employer of labor, purchaser of materials and user of capital. Yet on the basis of past performance it does not occupy a large enough segment of American economy to warrant relying upon it as a decisive

51. See p. 48ff.

factor in a period of economic readjustment. The question is, can housebuilding become more influential in the general economy?

At present, builders are poorly organized, deficient in financial resources, wasteful of materials and labor, and dependent upon a number of elements beyond their direct control. Even with its retreat to cheap land, its search for cheaper materials, and smaller size of product, the housebuilding industry in 1940 and 1941 could not apparently meet a major portion of the potential demand, especially for lower-priced dwellings. With few exceptions, housebuilding has retained its primitive organization and a technology restricted to small and local operations.

Housebuilding is not in the ordinary sense a special type of business, capable of clear-cut separation from other enterprises. As carried on today, it has few specialized producers and fewer specialized suppliers and manufacturers. It is, in fact, a group of related activities to which many forms of business enterprise contribute. In the industrial sense, it is less a unity than a series of relationships, frequently diverse in interest and subject neither to strong nor continuous direction.

Under such circumstances, it is not surprising that the men and materials normally available have never been fully utilized. Even in the prosperous twenties capacity was restricted by seasonal operations. The search for the causes of the industry's backwardness must follow a devious path through production and marketing processes and conditions outside the industry proper. It may well begin with an examination of the relationships among the components of the industry.

Chapter 4

THE MANAGEMENT OF THE HOUSEBUILDING INDUSTRY

MANAGEMENT IN THE housebuilding industry is as nebulous, difficult to define, and lacking in identity as the industry itself. Just as housebuilding is an agglomeration of many activities, so many elements contribute to its management. These have separate and often conflicting interests, and they operate with uncertain responsibility and temporary and limited control over the diverse phases of the industry.

Every participant in the industry has some managerial influence, and frequently this has more than one aspect. One group, consisting of the land developers, architects, builders, and buyers, controls chiefly, though not exclusively, the initiation of work, its design and general direction. Another group, among which labor perhaps is pre-eminent, with subcontractors and builders playing somewhat lesser roles, is principally concerned with the methods of construction. Bankers and government influence the number of houses produced, their location and general characteristics. Manufacturers of materials determine the kinds, shapes and sizes of materials which builders must use, and along with their dealers, decide on the methods of distributing materials.

1. INITIATION AND GENERAL MANAGEMENT

Superficially, the first group mentioned above provides the real managers of the industry, but by and large each of them has only limited managerial power.

a. THE BUYER

Behind all the management elements stands the buyer, whether he buys a house for personal use or investment. His directional influence varies from one of considerable importance to one of insignificance. In traditional housebuilding the buyer is the primary initiating force. He acquires the land, employs an architect, selects a general contractor (by competitive bids or otherwise), inspects the work, makes changes as his fancy dictates and his pocketbook permits, and pays as the work proceeds. This is a typical pattern in the construction industry, though followed less consistently in housebuilding than in other types of construction.

This pattern applies closely in large buyer operations such as those of local authorities, the federal government, and in other large private operations such as those of the Metropolitan Life Insurance Company. In these cases, the buyer sometimes controls not only the character of the product, but the details of production.[1] Construction of high-priced dwellings and apartment structures for private investors also usually follows this pattern.

But the procedure has many variations. The owner may dispense with an architect, or he may negotiate with a materials dealer or builder for the design as well as the construction. Some owners even dispense with a builder or general contractor and deal directly with special trades contractors. Or they may go so far as to buy their own materials and do most of the work themselves, hiring laborers or special contractors only for the more intricate tasks.[2]

Frequently through clever selling, the owner is allowed to imagine that he has greater control of the operations than is true. In fact, as the operative builder and prefabricator become more prominent, control of the product and of production processes tends to pass to the producer. On the other hand, the growth of large investor-buyers, both public and private, keeps the balance weighted on the side of owner control. At present owner initiation controls perhaps a majority of the houses produced and influences the character of the rest.

b. THE LAND DEVELOPER AND SUBDIVIDER

In the traditional pattern the subdivider was not directly a part of the housebuilding industry. After he laid out the streets and prepared the lots, restricting them, perhaps, in the better class of subdivision with covenants running with the land, he sold them to speculators, builders, or prospective owners. Housebuilding then proceeded under other auspices.

The independent subdivider has left his mark in the form of a surplus of vacant lots in almost every large American city. Today the subdivider has often assumed the more dignified role of land developer—that is, he lays out and develops lots in a more or less comprehensive neighborhood plan with definite types of dwelling in mind. Homeowners who want to build on contract, or with their own labor, generally purchase their land from him. Similarly, most operative builders prefer to buy a few improved lots from an independent developer rather than assume the risk of carrying a large inventory of land.

Subdividing methods, as noted in the first chapter, have generally been much

1. In government-housing operations, this extends to the determination of wages paid and hours worked by the laborers.

2. Owner-built houses seem to be confined chiefly to small towns and rural areas. This, however, is not always true. For instance, in the environs of Peoria, Illinois, a metropolitan area of 160,000 population, several hundred small houses were constructed in this manner in 1938–1941. See Chap. 5, p. 145.

improved over the free-ride and barbecue days. Land planning is now more closely related to building and neighborhood needs, and developers and builders work more closely than formerly. The developer is less inclined to sell to speculators, and is more apt to require the buyer to construct a house after the sale is made. Yet because he is first on the scene, the developer determines the pattern and, to a great extent, the cost of the house. As long as his function is separated from that of the builder, house production cannot become a unified process. The land developer sets limits on the final product without being responsible for it.

C. THE ARCHITECT

Although the architect's influence on management may be great, he seldom has any real control over production. Yet, because of his professional status, he is never completely subordinated to management. Of the 20,869 [3] architects in the country, a large majority undoubtedly are to some extent engaged in designing dwellings, but architects probably specialize in houses even less than builders do. Moreover, as independent practitioners, their services are probably not used on more than 20 to 25 per cent of all housing units built.[4] Architects' license laws have not forced the use of their services in the residential field, because low-cost houses are usually exempt, and the preparation of plans by nonarchitects is never wholly prevented.

The architect has usually preferred to devote his attention to the more expensive dwellings. This is due no doubt to the fact that his fee, calculated as a percentage of construction costs,[5] is so small on low-priced dwellings as to make it difficult for him to operate profitably. Various schemes of modified architectural service to individual clients and builders, carrying lower unit fees, have been tried. The most notable recent one is the *Registered Home Service* sponsored by the Federal Home Loan Bank Board.[6] Like previous efforts, however, it has received

3. *Population Census:* 1940, Series P–16, No. 8: *Wage or Salary Income in 1939 by Occupation.*

4. In the opinion of Federal Housing Administration and Federal Home Loan Bank Board officials, probably not more than 5 to 10 per cent of private individual house construction is built with the help of an architect's designing and supervisory services. The percentage for private apartment buildings is somewhat higher and most public-authority projects employ independent architects for design, thus raising the total to the above figure. These estimates do not include architects in building organizations or architects in the regular employ of governmental agencies.

5. The minimum fee prescribed by the American Institute of Architects is 6 per cent "plus the architect's cost of providing competent heating, ventilating, mechanical, and electrical engineering services." Source: *Standards of Practice of the American Institute of Architects.* It is extremely doubtful that this fee is maintained on large projects. Lower fees have been approved by the AIA on public housing projects. On high-priced dwellings, however, the fee may be as high as 10 per cent, or as much more as the traffic will bear.

6. It was initiated experimentally in 1937 and became a recognized function of the board in 1939. Under this plan, a group of architects, working through a local home lending institution, agree to prepare for selection by prospective owners a limited number of designs and working drawings and specifications. The architects further agree to aid in selecting a site and contractors, and to supervise the execution of the work for a small fixed fee. Changes in the basic plans are made on the basis

only limited support from the architectural profession and thus far has had slight influence on the industry. A few architects, on their own initiative, have sometimes profitably worked in the small-house field by using standard plans, simplified specifications, and similar devices.

The Architect's Contribution

On the whole, the architect has been able to guide public taste and to influence house planning and structural trends in many ways. His influence has improved the house plan, producing better room arrangements, less waste space, and greater comfort, convenience and privacy. Architects are responsible for the wide acceptance of certain architectural styles—for instance, English Colonial in increasingly simplified versions—on the basis of which manufacturers have been enabled to introduce standardized windows, doors, moldings, mantels, and other decorative features of a quality unknown two decades ago. Credit for more radical departures from the bondage of obsolete styles must go almost entirely to pioneering architects and adventurous owners. Architects have also helped to shape planning techniques for low-cost dwellings and construction processes which permit greater standardization and prefabrication of parts.

The architect has played many other useful roles besides a strictly professional one. He has prepared house-plan books for materials dealers, thereby influencing a field of construction where good design was sadly lacking. By entering dwelling-design competitions of manufacturers and preparing material for magazines architects have enormously influenced public taste. The architect appears increasingly as associate, retainer, or employee of the operative builder, to whom his services were once almost entirely unknown. He has taken a prominent part in the government's housing programs, and he has frequently worked alone, and without remuneration, to advance building technology.

d. THE BUILDER

In a delicate balancing of forces, the builder is probably the principal single managerial factor in house production. He may be a general contractor working for an owner, with or without an architect, or an operative builder working on his own account. In the latter case he may act not only as a general contractor,

---

of the architect's cost. The lending institution protects the architect in the use of his plans. On completion, the owner is given a certificate of quality by the institution.

Up to June 1, 1941, 524 architects and other technicians had been approved for participation in the program, 1,046 house designs had been accepted for use, and 388 institutions had agreed to sponsor the proposal in connection with their lending operations. Certificates had been issued, or were in the process of issuance, to 649 homeowners who had used this service. Source: Federal Home Loan Bank Administration.

but as the owner and architect as well; sometimes he is also the land developer and the merchandiser of the completed property.

Although bearing the weight of responsibility, the builder rarely controls all housebuilding processes. He may work under the direction of the owner or his architect, or the real-estate man, or materials dealer who sponsors the enterprise. Often he shares responsibility with other contractors acting in an independent capacity for the owner. Mechanical work is thus frequently performed through direct contracts with the owner. Even when the builder is the principal, he usually does not have full charge of subsidiary processes. Land development may be carried on independently of him; his own force may do little work on the structure, which will be built for the most part by subcontractors. Only to a minor extent—in the fabrication of special milled items—will the builder have direction over the manufacturing of the parts he uses.

Within his jurisdiction, the builder or contractor is circumscribed by contractual relations with his subcontractors, and by the relations between the latter and their sub-subcontractors and laborers. In all these relations he has only restricted authority and limited responsibility.

e. THE SUBCONTRACTING SYSTEM

Production is ordinarily carried on through a series of subcontracts, whether the builder owns the house or is under contract to an owner. Evidence shows that the operative builder makes greater use of subcontracting than the general contractor.[7] The general contractor or builder rarely handles other work than carpentry and masonry with his own force. He is more likely to assume only one of these tasks, often neither.

Independence of Subcontractor

Within his own sphere the subcontractor is largely his own master. He furnishes most of the equipment to erect the building. He buys the bulk of the materials and hires and directs the greater part of the labor. The quality of the work depends upon him; the processes (except as controlled by the laborers themselves) are largely under his jurisdiction. The builder or general contractor tends to become a mere co-ordinator of production, rather than a producer in his own right.

The use of numerous subcontractors on a single job makes it difficult to arrange a sequence of work, to avoid conflicts in jurisdiction, and to prevent waste and

7. *Census of the Construction Industry,* 1930. For residential contractors accounting for $246 million worth of business in 1929, $106 million, or 43 per cent, was subcontracted (Table XIV, p. 29). For operative builders doing $131 million worth of business, $89 million, or 68 per cent, was subcontracted (Table IX, p. 23). Unfortunately later figures are not available since a similar breakdown was not included in subsequent censuses.

damage. This situation creates problems not only for the general contractor but for the subcontractor as well. The latter can only roughly forecast when his services will be needed and he may experience delays beyond his control. He not only depends upon the general contractor for the job but for the circumstances under which his work can be performed. Custom as well as variations among jobs usually prevent him from anticipating requirements by performing advance work in his shop. His dealings with suppliers and laborers are necessarily uncertain and irregular.

The relationship between the builder or general contractor and his subcontractors is temporary, shifting from job to job. The builder selects subcontractors for a particular job rather than as part of a permanent operating organization. Subcontractors are rarely certain of future work with the same contractor, while builders are seldom sure of obtaining the same group of subcontractors on successive jobs.

The bidding system is the most common way of selecting subcontractors. This impersonal method creates a temptation to put price above quality, or to lower quality to fit price. Above all, the bidding system tends to keep organizational relationships unstable. The constant shifting of elements in the housing industry militates against the efficiency that comes from familiarity and continuity of association. Since the builder's hold on the subcontractor is weak and transitory, he must bargain with, rather than control him.

Effects of the Subcontracting System

The subcontracting system in construction is unique. In other industries the subcontracted article is supplied to the manufacturer of the finished product and is installed by him. It may be accepted or rejected before it is incorporated in the final product. In housebuilding, the subcontractor actually makes the article, except, of course, for certain premanufactured equipment, as he incorporates it into the final product. As a result, co-ordination of the work of subcontractors is vastly complicated, and the rejection of a defective item or its repair may create a serious problem. For instance, if a faulty pipe joint is not replaced immediately after installation, it may mean work for the carpenter, lather, plasterer, and painter. Similar circumstances greatly add to the costs and difficulties of dwelling upkeep.

Subcontracting hampers the technical progress of the housebuilding industry. Because the general contractor is principally engaged in umpiring subcontractors, and each of the latter is interested only in one aspect of the one dwelling, integration and mechanization of production processes are thwarted at the start. As long as the materials, labor, and assembly of the parts of the structure are controlled by several independent organizations it is impossible to treat the unit as a whole. Conversely, as long as the dwelling is not treated as a whole, the subcontracting system must prevail.

2. MANAGEMENT AND TRADE RESTRAINTS

The problems of management are further aggravated by the existence of numerous self-protective combinations among the groups comprising the building industry. These combinations differ somewhat from those encountered elsewhere. In the manufacturing industries generally, combinations designed to control prices or production are, where they occur, usually initiated by the leading companies and are often nation-wide in scope. In construction, such agreements tend to correspond to the small scale and local character of the industry.

Restrictive combinations are rare among builders and general contractors,[8] but common among subcontractors, dealers, and manufacturers of materials. They are frequent between subcontractors and labor unions, dealers and subcontractors, and manufacturers and dealers. Except where national manufacturers and their distributors are involved, combinations almost invariably concern a single locality. This type of local combination is usually designed to restrict competition, to maintain prices, and exclude persons and products considered harmful or undesirable to the parties concerned.

a. PURPOSE OF TRADE RESTRAINTS

Restraints in housebuilding can be partially explained as efforts of the subsidiary groups in the industry to acquire stability and security that cannot be obtained from chronically weak and unstable management in a restricted local market. Each group strives to protect itself as best it can. But interests are diverse and alliances shift. Manufacturers of building materials strengthen themselves by mergers or mutual agreements. These, in turn, endanger the position of local distributors, who consequently combine in self-protection. Subcontractors generally cannot individually resist the price pressures of distributors of materials on the one hand and of general contractors on the other. Hence they make intratrade agreements. Finally, labor unions, faced with seasonal and sporadic employment, have often consented to act as the enforcing agents for restrictive agreements of subcontractors or suppliers in the hope of protecting their jobs and earnings.

Housebuilding suffers from arrested industrial development. It has not created a national, or even a regional market, and within its local markets there is an

8. The recent campaign of the Department of Justice against restraints in the building industry has resulted in only one indictment involving general contractors. The files of the Federal Trade Commission reveal no complaints involving general-contractor combinations. Similarly the other material studied is notable for the lack of evidence of combinations among general contractors.

intense struggle among various components of the industry—more for preservation than dominance. Fearing for its own position, each group resists innovations and prevents the domination of the industry as a whole by any one of them.

Bid Peddling and the Bid Depository

The motive for combination is clear; the forms which it may take are naturally varied. The most common perhaps is the subcontractor's *bid depository*.[9] This device is a defense against *bid peddling* by general contractors and builders. Under this practice, general contractors receiving bids from several subcontractors use low bids to bargain for still lower ones, setting one subcontractor against another in ignorance of each other's quotations. Subcontractors have no individual protection against this practice and, moreover, must constantly face bids from new entrants who will take jobs at prices allowing little or nothing for overhead and profit.

The bid depository, which is essentially a reporting system, offers subcontractors some measure of collective security. In its simplest form, duplicates of all bids in a given trade are filed with a central office. Here they are opened after the date on which bids are submitted to the contractor. Each competitor thus knows his relative position. The reporting of bids, however, does not offer assurance against bid peddling. It merely gives subcontractors knowledge helpful in improving their bargaining position and mitigating the effects of cutthroat competition. But the reporting of bids has a more important consequence. The identification of subcontractors who reduce their original bids under pressure makes it possible for other members of the depository to retaliate against them. Often the next step is for subcontractors to reach an agreement not to submit new bids unless there is a change in the specifications.

Prevention of bid peddling may lead to controlled bidding, the manipulation of estimates, the fixing of prices, and the allocation of jobs. Estimates may be sent to the depository to be used in preparing the bids that go to the awarding authority. There is evidence that this practice was, and in some instances is still employed by marble, sheet metal, electrical equipment, excavation, and painting contractors.[10]

9. During 1939–1940 suits involving bid depositories were instituted by the Department of Justice against twenty-four subcontractor and dealer-contractor groups in eight metropolitan areas.

10. Consent decrees have been entered in the following federal cases under the antitrust laws: *U.S.* v. *Sheet Metal Ass'n et al.*, Civ. 261, E.D. La., Feb. 5, 1940; *U.S.* v. *Engineering Survey & Audit Co., Inc., et al.*, Civ. 276, E.D. La., Feb. 21, 1940; *U.S.* v. *Excavators' Administrative Ass'n, Inc., et al.*, Civ. 5227, D.C., Dec. 22, 1939; *U.S.* v. *Union Painters' Administrative Ass'n, Inc., et al.*, Civ. 5225, D.C., Dec. 22, 1939.

At least some of the defendants have entered pleas of *nolle contendere*, in the following federal cases: *U.S.* v. *Associated Marble Companies, et al.*, Cr. 26796-L, N.D., Cal., indictment returned Feb. 16, 1940; *U.S.* v. *Southern California Marble Ass'n, et al.*, Cr. 14279-H, S.D. Cal., indictment returned Dec. 20, 1939.

Bid depositories can do no more than reveal the violators of agreements. Nothing short of violence can prevent a subcontractor from submitting any bid he pleases, or accepting any award offered to him. Members of a combination, however, may take steps to see that the nonconformist is unable to perform the work. If they are strong enough they can boycott the manufacturers who sell him materials.[11] Or, they may see that he is unable to get labor.

Labor's Part in Combinations

Employers' associations are thus often willing to accept union wages and rules restricting the supply and use of labor provided the union agrees not to work for nonmembers of the association. Unions are often willing to accept such an agreement.[12] This use of the power of unions creates lush opportunities for corruption. The result in any case, of course, is higher production costs. But if the combination is strong, the added cost can readily be passed on to the consumer.

Labor unions, sometimes independently or in combination with employers, seek to protect their crafts or to shift the burden of unemployment to other communities. Thus, subcontractors and labor organizations have worked together to bar "foreign" [13] fabrication of materials and equipment, or forbid the assembly of parts except on the site. A union in carrying out such a policy often secures the collaboration of unions in other crafts; at times violence has been employed to supplement other pressures.[14]

Manufacturers' Part in Local Restraints

Although the most common tie-ups are the local ones between subcontractors and labor unions, the most effective are the general trade agreements that affect

11. *U.S.* v. *Southern California Marble Ass'n, et al., op. cit.*

12. The Department of Justice has proceeded successfully against a number of combinations of subcontractors and labor unions, involving the use of such materials as tile, cut stone, electrical equipment, heating, piping, air conditioning and plumbing, plaster and laths, marble and masonry. *U.S.* v. *Pittsburgh Tile & Mantel Contractors' Ass'n,* Civ. 806, Dist. Ct., W.D. Penna., complaint filed and decree entered Feb. 29, 1940; *U.S.* v. *St. Louis Tile Contractors' Ass'n,* Civ. 521-2, Dist. Ct., E.D. Mo., complaint filed and decree entered July 1, 1940; *U.S.* v. *Chicago & Cook County Building & Construction Council,* Cr. 32069, Dist. Ct., N.D. Ill., indictment returned Feb. 1, 1940; *U.S.* v. *Harbor District Chapter National Electrical Contractors' Ass'n,* Cr. 14280-Y, Dist. Ct., S.D. Cal., indictment returned Feb. 16, 1940; *U.S.* v. *Heating, Piping & Air Conditioning Contractors' Ass'n of Southern California,* Cr. 14250-Y, Dist. Ct., S.D. Cal., indictment returned Jan. 26, 1940; *U.S.* v. *Voluntary Code of the Heating, Piping & Air Conditioning Industry for Allegheny County,* Civ. 698, Dist. Ct., W.D. Penna., complaint filed and decree entered Dec. 8, 1939; *U.S.* v. *Plumbing & Heating Industries' Administrative Ass'n,* Civ. 5226, Dist. Ct., D.C., complaint filed and decree entered Dec. 22, 1939; *U.S.* v. *Employing Plasterers' Ass'n of Allegheny County,* Civ. 840, Dist. Ct., W.D. Penna., complaint filed and decree entered March 18, 1940; *U.S.* v. *Marble Contractors' Ass'n,* Civ. 805, Dist. Ct., W.D. Penna., complaint filed and decree entered Feb. 29, 1940; *U.S.* v. *Mason Contractors' Ass'n of D.C.,* Civ. 6169, Dist. Ct., D.C., complaint filed and decree entered March 12, 1940.

13. Any locale other than that of the combination.

14. See footnote 12, *U.S.* v. *Chicago & Cook County Building & Construction Council;* see also *U.S.* v. *Glass Contractors' Ass'n,* Cr. 32233, Dist. Ct., N.D. Ill., indictment returned Nov. 10, 1940.

a whole section of the industry from manufacturer to subcontractor. For instance, the Department of Justice contends that manufacturers who provide 80 per cent of the plumbing supplies in the United States sell only to jobbers who agree to resell only to plumbing contractors, while refusing to deal directly with consumers or builders. In this combination, jobbers will buy only from manufacturers who sell exclusively to jobbers who in turn refrain from selling directly to consumers or builders. Plumbing contractors buy only through recognized jobbers and refuse to install equipment purchased through other channels and refuse even to work for general contractors who deal with unrecognized jobbers or manufacturers.[15]

There is evidence of a similar combination in the tile industry. The national subcontractors' association and the international union of tile workers together have created clearinghouses in numerous localities in the form of joint arbitration boards. In order to control tile installation, the unions submitted to the boards lists of contractor dealers with whom they had agreements. Such lists naturally excluded jobbers who made no installations and who consequently had no agreements with the union. Manufacturers then refused to sell to persons or firms not on the lists. Approved contractors boycotted those manufacturers and their distributors who did not enter the combination; and the unions refused to install the tile of boycotted manufacturers.[16] Such practices have long been fairly widespread in the construction industry.[17]

Restrictive Practices Under the NRA

Most of the combinations outlined above, which the Department of Justice now regards as violating laws against restraint of trade, were accepted under the NRA as reasonable protection in the face of the merciless competition fostered by the depression. The *Code for the Builders' Supplies Trade Industry* approved a uniform system of accounting, prohibited sales below cost and regarded deviations from published prices and terms of sale as "unfair competition." The *Code for the Retail Lumber, Lumber Products, Building Materials, and Building Spe-*

15. *U.S.* v. *The Central Supply Ass'n,* Cr. 16750, Dist. Ct., N.D. Ohio, indictment returned March 29, 1940.

16. *U.S.* v. *The Tile Contractors' Ass'n of America,* Civ. 1761, Dist. Ct., N.D. Ill., complaint filed and decree entered June 10, 1940; *U.S.* v. *Wheeling Tile Co.,* Cr. 25537, Dist. Ct., E.D. Mich., indictment returned Dec. 5, 1939; *U.S.* v. *Mosaic Tile Co.,* Cr. 32027, Dist. Ct., N.D. Ill., indictment returned Jan. 15, 1940. See also Thurman W. Arnold, *The Bottlenecks of Business,* Reynal & Hitchcock, New York, 1940, p. 258.

17. *Intermediate Report of the Joint Legislative Committee on Housing,* New York Legislative Document No. 60 (1922); *Report of the Illinois Building Investigation Commission,* 1923; see also R. E. Montgomery, *Industrial Relations in the Chicago Building Trades,* University of Chicago Press, Chicago, 1927; and Frederick L. Ryan, *Industrial Relations in the San Francisco Building Trades,* University of Oklahoma Press, Norman, 1936.

cialties Trade had similar provisions. These two codes covered all the materials distributed for building construction.

The *Code for the Construction Industry* prohibited bid peddling and required a big depository to check bids.[18] The *Painting, Paperhanging and Decorating Division* also prohibited work below cost. The *Electrical Division* gave its Code Authority power, under certain circumstances, to determine "lowest reasonable cost" below which sales were prohibited and provided for the circulation of price and discount lists. The *Roofing and Sheet Metal Division* prevented members from making fixed-fee or guaranteed-cost contracts which did not protect them against loss. The *Tile Division* forbade its members from selling tile unless they could also set it. All other divisions of the construction industry provided for bid depositories as well as for one or more of the above practices. Thus, when the industry was permitted to combat its deficiencies as revealed by the depression, it established many of the practices for which it has been condemned before and since.[19]

b. EFFECTS OF TRADE RESTRAINTS AND COMBINATIONS

The effect of the kinds of combination described is to freeze the pattern of the housebuilding industry in its local mold and to deprive it of the flexibility and growing space that an aggressively expanding industry must have. New types of producing organization, new techniques and materials, and alternative methods of distribution as a consequence find difficulty in making headway.

Manufacturers who engage in price fixing not only may keep prices high but avoid the necessity of introducing new techniques. In distribution, the effect of many combinations is to bolster the position of established groups against efforts to reroute materials around them, open up new channels of distribution, eliminate unnecessary steps, and, in short, supply materials more economically. Subcontractors have not only protected the local building industry, thus preventing the growth of organizations that could operate over wider market areas, but they have upheld the cumbersome system of distributing materials and resisted the integration of building operations. Labor unions, which developed along craft lines in conformity with historical production techniques, resist innovations in order to perpetuate their status. All in all, combinations among the various groups which comprise the building industry tend to strengthen the position of each and to thwart the progress of the industry as a whole.

Even with the inauguration of the gigantic defense construction program in

18. Some of the depositories recently prosecuted by the Department of Justice were recognized by the NRA.

19. It should be noted, however, that NRA officials soon became alarmed at many of the code provisions. As a result, when the formulas for "lowest reasonable cost" were presented to the administrator, approval was withheld.

1940, the organization of the industry made it impossible to increase efficiency and lower costs through centralized management. Attempts to eliminate subcontracting were thwarted by labor unions whose agreements for the most part were with subcontractors. Electric workers and bricklayers—among others—so strongly opposed any deviation from established practices that the attempt was soon dropped.

Combinations obviously affect prices. A restricted output tends to raise prices, or at least prevents their decline. Monopolistic agreements are aimed at those whose prices are low. Publication of identical price lists usually means an agreement not to sell below certain levels. Allotment of quotas for work may involve the fixing of prices. Bid depositories tend to raise prices. The addition of a uniform overhead to all bids prevents management from taking advantage of efficient operations while the prohibition of sales or contracts below cost, through the medium of bid depositories or dealer combinations, frequently accompanies the fixing of arbitrary costs for all parties to the agreement. Consequently, those whose actual costs are below the fixed figure cannot bid or sell as cheaply as they might. Combinations which prohibit the elimination of unnecessary middlemen also increase distribution costs.

Partly due to such practices, housebuilding is a relatively expensive undertaking. At 1940 prices it was extremely difficult, if not impossible, in most parts of the country to build a house that was within reach of a majority of the population. More economical housing depends upon the extent to which, under strong management, all costs entering into the production of a dwelling can be reduced. The restraints described have grown up as a result of weak managerial control. They are likely to persist until the industry is convinced that greater stability and steadier employment than the present combinations offer can be achieved through other forms of organization.

3. Labor's Relations to Management

In the diffuse and unco-ordinated organization of the building industry, a high degree of managerial responsibility is relegated to labor. As in any handicraft field, assembly methods are largely determined by the workmen on the job. They select and frequently own their tools and lay out their own work. New processes or equipment are often shunned because of labor customs and craft rules.

The contracting group in a typical operation acts as a business manager rather than a production manager. The product is designed by the owner or his architect, so that contractors have little control of the initial phase of production. Their part in directing production is also limited. Contractors supply workmen with materials and the heavier tools and equipment; they exercise general supervision and issue general instructions. But the detailed operations, however, are often left largely to the men themselves.

The average housebuilding operation is on such a small scale that any other arrangements would be impracticable. To keep overhead low on a small job, men, tools, and materials must be handled with a minimum of direction and

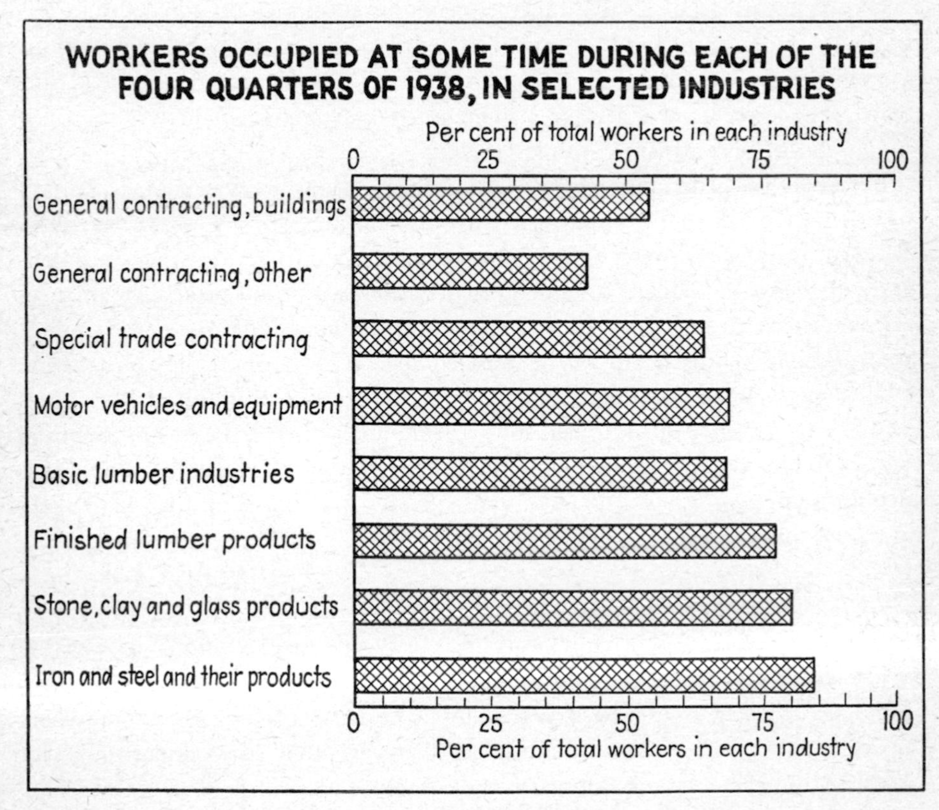

FIGURE 20. Employment in building contracting is relatively unstable; only about half of the workers in this industry worked at some time during each of the four quarters of 1938. In the manufacture of finished lumber products, stone, clay, glass and iron and steel products, on the other hand, around 80 per cent had regular employment. (*Source:* Appendix D, 1.)

this can only be done by relying upon the skill of the mechanics. In this way the craft rather than the product tends to become standardized. The industry requires numerous skills, but it has no effective means of providing continuity either in employment or in employer-employee relationships. The position of labor in the construction industry tends to be less secure than in other industries (see Figure 20),[20] a situation more common in housebuilding than in other types

20. See also Appendix D, 1, for data on labor turnover.

of construction where the opportunities for extended employment are often greater. The only exceptions are large project builders and the more important operative builders—both of whom are relatively rare and limited to a few localities.[21]

a. COMBATING INSECURITY

It is natural that labor should in these circumstances seek, by whatever means it can, to acquire some kind of security. The frequent appearance of labor unions as enforcing agents for subcontractors' restrictive agreements is evidence of this effort. The agreement is always a *quid pro quo* arrangement between a labor union and a subcontractor group.

Because of the general insecurity of the industry, labor follows a course common to other elements in the industry. It avoids housing work wherever possible. Workmen, likewise, prefer other types of construction because wages are generally higher, employment is longer, organization easier, and protective alliances are simpler to arrange and enforce. Consequently, housebuilding at the time of peak demand tends to fall to the least competent sections of the construction labor force or to be faced with an actual shortage of housebuilding labor. Thus, with the upsurgence of industrial construction in 1940, even the most substantial housebuilding organizations maintained their crews with difficulty. There was no dearth of workers for defense construction, but housebuilding in defense areas was impeded by a shortage of men.

Effectiveness of Labor Organization

Labor's usual means of combating insecurity and strengthening its position is through organization. The diffusion of managerial responsibility in the housebuilding industry might be expected to favor labor organization, but where management is so weak and unstable, there is often little opportunity for organization. The large contractor and subcontractor with considerable capital investment and comparatively permanent organization—the types most thoroughly unionized—are not often drawn into residential work except under government contract. The small builder and the small subcontractor, so common in the housing field, are almost beyond the reach of unions. As one labor leader observed, there is no way of controlling the type of builder that erects one or two houses and then disappears from the picture.[22] Large operative builders who have flourished principally in communities where labor is wholly unor-

21. Even on such projects only a small fraction of the jobs last as long as it takes to complete the project and few last as long as even half that time. For an example of employment continuity on a United States Housing Authority project see Appendix D, Table 26.

22. *Hearings Before the Temporary National Economic Committee*, testimony of D. W. Tracy, Pt. 11, *The Construction Industry*, p. 5266.

ganized or but poorly organized, are still comparatively new, and no concerted effort to unionize their organizations has yet been made.

The influence of labor organizations, however, cannot be judged wholly by the extent of unionization in the housebuilding industry. Their strength in the construction field as a whole is so great, and their control over the better artisans so extensive, that even when their direct control does not extend to housebuilding, they may nevertheless determine the general level of wages and conditions of work. This influence becomes stronger as unemployment declines and the volume of construction rises. Union practices, perhaps somewhat attenuated, thus often have the force of custom, even where the sanctions of organization are absent.

b. WORKING RULES

In order to regularize working procedures and control working conditions, unions have established rules governing the activity of their members. In the building industry union rules and regulations are a curious blend of measures to maintain the quality of the work, to protect the health and safety of the workmen, to keep wages high and to maintain the union's bargaining power. Because of management's dependence on labor for working out most operating procedures, union rules frequently become powerful instruments for advancing and consolidating the special interests of labor.

It is not always easy to distinguish the purpose of a particular rule. For example, rules specifying the distance between pull boxes on an electric line, and the number and kind of joints in a plumbing stack, may be regarded as methods of maintaining the quality of workmanship. They also, however, add to the work to be done. Similarly, rules which limit the width of a paintbrush or prohibit the use of a spray brush are excused as safeguards to the workers' health but their make-work character is patent.

Many of the rules are devised to protect jobs or increase work. Some restrict membership in the union by charging high initiation fees and requiring work permits for nonmembers (particularly from "outside" localities). Others endeavor to spread work and to overcome some of the effects of seasonal employment by prescribing limits to a "fair day's work," a standard that is hard to define in the absence of any real basis for determining efficiency. Similarly, piecework and bonuses for above average production are outlawed and even the sizes of capacity setting tools are prescribed.

Technological unemployment is combated by curbing the use of power tools and labor-saving devices, by designating the number of men who may be used on specific jobs, by requiring skilled artisans for tasks which could be performed by unskilled labor, and by ordering work at the site which might be done more cheaply in a shop. Many union regulations try to prevent the evasion of established wage rates. In this category are the rules which limit a day's output, forbid the "lumping" or subcontracting of labor, and prohibit employers or foremen from using tools or taking part in construction operations.[23]

Limitations on Management

All such regulations limit the initiative of management and its control of production. Union rules often also restrict the employer's control of his foremen and his right to "hire and fire." Materials prepared under nonunion or competing union conditions are frequently barred. The local emphasis of many of the rules increases the difficulties of the outside builder. Disputed regulations governing the jurisdiction of unions over specific types of work (satisfactory methods of settling them have not yet been found) may either limit a contractor's choice of materials or actually paralyze his operations.

Rules that arbitrarily increase the force or amount of work on a given job obviously raise costs. The same effect is achieved by regulations which prevent the utilization of cost-reducing machinery or methods, and eliminate or equalize the advantages of large-scale building organizations.

Most union restrictions can be traced either to the default of certain managerial functions by managing agencies—contractors or subcontractors—or to the insecurity that building trades workers feel. The right of labor, for instance, to insist upon safe and healthful working conditions, to protect itself against capricious and irresponsible employers and to implement wage agreements by rules which defy circumvention, are certainly essential features of collective bargaining. But when—as often happens—craft regulations hamper technical progress and freeze an industry into an archaic mold, they are injurious to the best interests of society.

C. EFFECTS OF LABOR POLICY

Since the proportion of unionization among housebuilding workers is relatively small, union rules are sometimes said to have little influence on residential construction or the cost of housing. As we have suggested, this conclusion is hardly warranted. In the first place, the public housing program and much relatively high-priced private housing is built under union conditions. Secondly, there are many areas where unionization does embrace the whole field of construction, and in many of these highly unionized areas production of low-priced dwellings has lagged, except with government subsidy. The direct effects of union policies on housebuilding are therefore undeniable.

23. See William Haber, *Industrial Relations in the Building Industry*, Harvard University Press, Cambridge, 1930, pp. 197–237; also Sumner H. Slichter, *Union Policies and Industrial Management*, The Brookings Institution, Washington, 1941.

Craft restrictions intensify the localized, technically backward, and retail character of the industry. Too often they discourage all builders except those who gamble on narrow margins, who resort to shoddy workmanship, and who can easily withdraw from the field at the threat of unionization. More substantial firms, restrained by union agreements, cannot face such competition. Although labor conditions help to divert unionized builders from the low-priced housing field, they also contribute to the average producer's reluctance to enter this huge market where the maximum economies are required.

Working rules, consequently, tend to aggravate the very conditions they are supposed to remedy. The potential demand for low-cost housing is so great that labor would probably benefit in the end by relaxing restrictions that raise the price of shelter. The development of a more advanced technology and more efficient management would undoubtedly improve the conditions of labor and strengthen the unions. To attain these goals, however, labor policies must be thoroughly understood and those forces which impede the rational and orderly development of the housebuilding industry should be eradicated.

4. THE ROLE OF MANUFACTURERS AND DISTRIBUTORS

The housebuilder assembles numerous parts and materials supplied by others. His ability to produce at a low cost depends upon his bargaining power in the materials market. Actually he faces a relatively rigid price structure against which his limited bargaining strength is of little avail.

a. THE RIGIDITY OF PRICES

It has long been contended that the price of building materials is well sustained in a depression and increases more rapidly with recovery than other commodity prices. Thus, Willard L. Thorp told the Temporary National Economic Committee that during the depression, "building material prices fell to perhaps 76, with reference to the 1929 level (taken as 100), while all commodities fell to about 62. While they came closer together again briefly in 1935 and 1937, we have a very wide spread at the present time (July 1939), when the building materials prices are perhaps 92 as against a general index of 78." [24] This statement was based on the indexes of wholesale prices compiled by the Bureau of Labor Statistics. Such indexes do not take account of factors like special price arrangements, concessions, rebates, and the like. Subsequent studies by the TNEC, however, based on the average realized prices of 407 commodities, including 70 building materials, do not greatly modify this general picture.[25]

24. *Hearings Before the TNEC,* testimony of Willard L. Thorp, Pt. 11, p. 5231.

25. Walter F. Crowder, "The Concentration of Production in Manufacturing," Pt. V, *The Structure of Industry,* TNEC Monograph No. 27, 1941, Appendix E, Table IE, pp. 562–571.

According to TNEC data, building material prices on the average declined 15.8 per cent between 1929 and 1933, while all other commodities declined 28.6 per cent. Figure 21 shows that between 1929 and 1933 a smaller proportion of building materials than of other commodities showed drastic price declines, and that between 1933 and 1937 a smaller proportion showed drastic price increases. Thus in 1933, prices of 30 per cent of all building materials, but only 12 per cent of other commodities, were 90 per cent or more of their 1929 prices. In the period 1933–1937, price increases of 35 per cent or more occurred in 16 per cent of building materials, but in 30 per cent of other commodities. The corresponding ratios for price increases of 65 per cent or more were 6 and 12 per cent, respectively.[26]

We may conclude then that the prices of building materials were well sustained from 1929 to 1937 in comparison with other commodities. Construction declined much more rapidly than most industries, recovered more slowly, and even by 1940 was lagging behind other industries. All sources tell the same story. The relatively rigid prices of building materials between 1929 and 1937 tended to retard the industry's recovery.

b. THE BACKGROUND OF PRICE RIGIDITY

Not only are there fewer materials manufacturers than builders, but large manufacturers play a much greater role in the construction industry than do large builders. Among 68 per cent of 283 important building materials, four leading manufacturers in each line account for over 50 per cent of the total output.[27] Since these figures cover national distribution, they do not reveal fully the concentration in such products as sand, gravel, brick, and planing-mill products where the market is almost entirely local. Thus, although the four leading common brick producers accounted for only 7 per cent of the total value of the product in 1937, builders in Washington, D. C., for example, had only three local brick manufacturers to choose from. In the Chicago area, four mills produce nearly 60 per cent of the window frames and doorframes used in the region, in Milwaukee 53 per cent, and in Los Angeles 52 per cent.[28]

Among housebuilding organizations, on the contrary, no such concentration exists. A year's production in the colossal Parkchester project of the Metropolitan

26. The 407 products included in the TNEC analysis adequately represent all manufactured products. Of the building materials, lumber is omitted. However, the best data available—that compiled by the National Lumber Manufacturers' Association—indicate that the average realized price for all lumber fell about 31 per cent in 1929–1933, and increased about 30 per cent in 1933–1937.

27. Crowder, *op. cit.*, Appendix Table 9D, p. 561. See Appendix D, Table 28 for a comparison of concentration of production between building materials and other products.

28. *Hearings Before the TNEC,* Pt. 11, pp. 5223–5225.

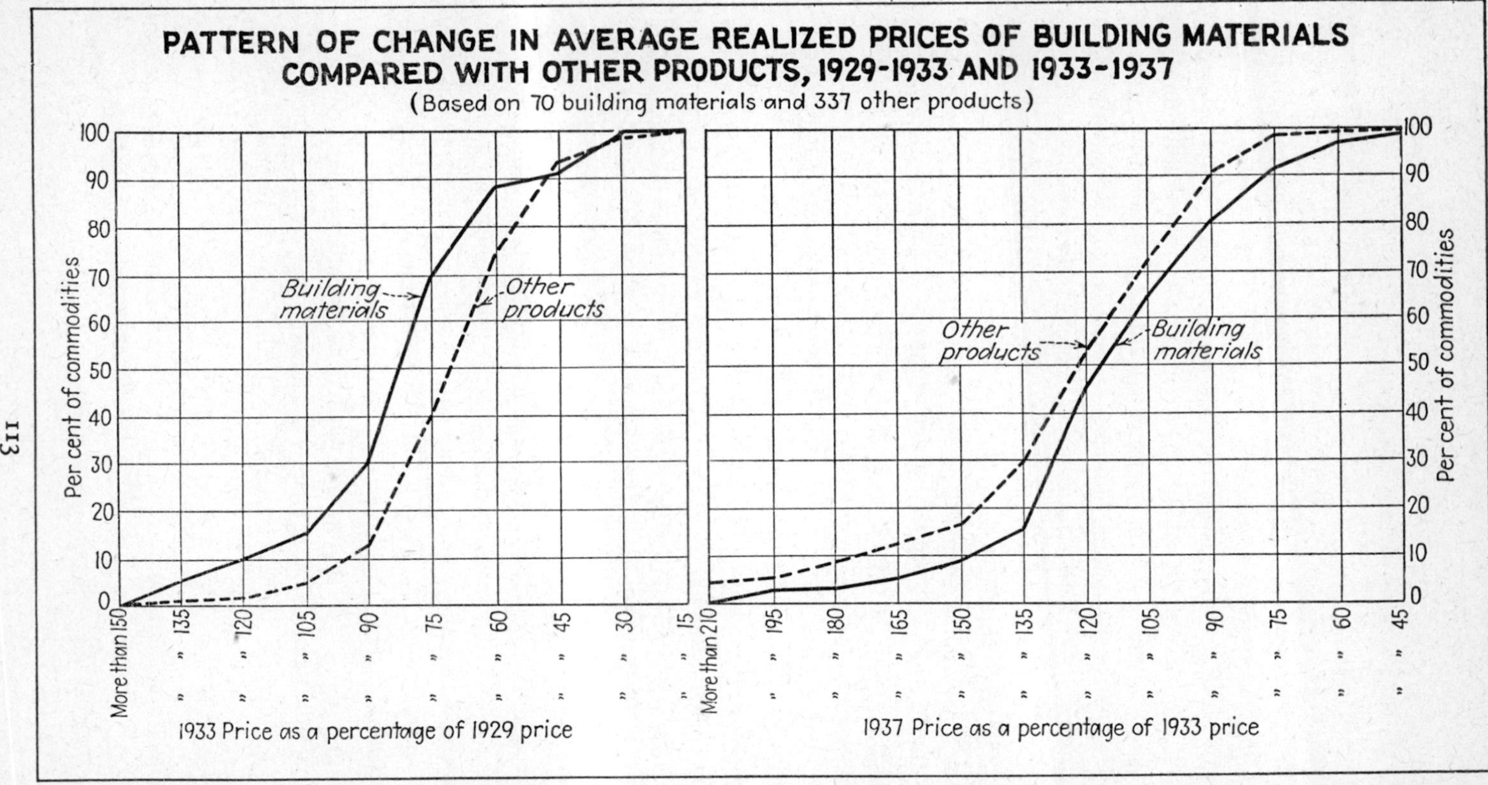

FIGURE 21. Building materials prices are more sluggish than other prices during periods of both decline and recovery. Thus by 1933, 70 per cent of all building materials—but only 40 per cent of other products—had been held to a price decline of less than a fourth from 1929 levels. On the upturn, the recovery in building materials prices was less pronounced than for other products. (*Source:* Appendix D, 2, Table 27.)

Life Insurance Company accounted for only about one per cent of the total residential units produced in the United States in 1940. On a local basis concentration is, of course, higher, yet not spectacular. Parkchester, which accounted for about 13 per cent of the new units erected in New York City during 1940, was unique. An operative builder who produced 4 per cent of the annual New York City units would be extraordinary.

Concentration of manufacturing may not always result in rigid prices.[29] But the financial strength of the manufacturer as compared with the builder unquestionably gives the former an economic advantage in negotiating prices. The limited operations of the average builder not only affect his bargaining position, but make him dependent upon the materials manufacturer for numerous services.

Services of the Manufacturer

The manufacturer must take the initiative in determining the varieties and quantities of materials and equipment that are made available for house production. He must warehouse his products until they are sold, organize an intricate network of dealers to take care of small purchases, and with them take the risks of overproduction. He must bear a considerable part of the expense of promoting housebuilding, independently or through trade associations, and undertake most of the research in new materials and techniques.

There are few builders who can assure the manufacturer a sufficiently large and steady flow of orders to warrant the production of parts adapted to special dwelling designs or to warrant any deviation from the regular distributing pattern. For example, the automobile maker orders in advance large quantities of glass in a few specified shapes. For the housebuilding trade, the glass manufacturer must make his own guess as to size, quantity, and time of demand.

Because of the services mentioned, the builder finds himself in a different distribution channel and subject to a different price structure than the manufacturer or other industrial customer. There is little doubt that the materials manufacturer charges the builder more than other types of customers. Naturally it costs him more to supply the builder than other customers. But the builder's dependence upon the manufacturer probably enables the latter to keep prices at higher levels than are justified by the service rendered. The builder can rarely find new sources of supply, as often happens in other fields. This problem is aggravated by the isolated markets in which he usually operates.

The relative durability of houses may also contribute to inflexible prices. In depression years, when incomes drop, individuals are unwilling to buy at any

29. See Appendix D, 2 for the relationship between concentration of ownership and price rigidity.

price. It is commonly believed in the trade that even large reductions in the price of materials would not bolster a demoralized market. Hence producers keep prices high. This trend is natural where parts rather than the completed product are involved. Reductions by the manufacturer of any one material cannot affect total housing costs sufficiently to stimulate the volume of building. It is natural then for each manufacturer to try to get as large a share as possible of the limited volume of business by maintaining or even increasing his prices.

The fact that most building materials are used for many purposes enhances this tendency and makes the manufacturer independent of the housebuilding trade. As previously noted,[30] housing is but a minor, and not usually the most profitable, outlet for building supplies and involves the greatest uncertainty and the most servicing. When other markets are active, housebuilding is not likely to receive any special consideration in price or otherwise.

C. ROLE OF THE MATERIALS DISTRIBUTOR

The most usual channels of distributing building materials are from manufacturer to wholesaler or jobber, to retailer, to consumer [31]as with other products for sale to diversified consumer markets in small quantities.

The principal distinction—and an important one—is that in housebuilding the retailer does not ordinarily reach the consumer directly but sells to a builder, who (through his subcontractors) assembles the materials. In most industries the assembly of the parts, corresponding to the function of the builder, is undertaken by the manufacturer, who controls the channels of retail distribution. By comparison with the more common industrial and distribution patterns, therefore, the builder is out of place in the distributing pattern. Producers in other fields do not ordinarily buy from retailers.

Variety of Distributive Relationships

The relationships between manufacturers and distributors show considerable variety. Some manufacturers maintain complete jobber and retail agency organizations, thus encompassing the whole distribution field. Others merely maintain jobbers who, in turn, sell to independent dealers who may be subsidiary to, or independent of, them. Some manufacturers retain no direct control over distribution channels, but deal with independent wholesalers who sell to independent retailers. A wide range of materials is handled by the lumber dealer—

30. See Chap. 3, pp. 64, 68-70.

31. For some types of building supplies it is difficult precisely to segregate wholesale and retail functions. See *Hearings Before the TNEC,* testimony of Willard L. Thorp, Pt. 11, p. 5190. This situation is, of course, also evident in other industries. See *Does Distribution Cost Too Much?,* The Twentieth Century Fund, New York, 1939, pp. 105–107.

or, as he is more properly called, the building materials or supplies dealer.[32] Except in large cities, he usually also sells brick and sometimes concrete materials also. The "hard materials" dealer is now found principally in the larger towns, although the development of ready-mixed concrete has prevented the absorption of the cement dealer by the general materials establishment. Hardware, paint, wallpaper, and glass are commonly sold separately, sometimes in one or more establishments. Usually the dealers mentioned above undertake no construction.[33]

Some housing materials, such as plumbing fixtures and pipe, sheet metal, interior tile, linoleum and composition tile, are installed by the dealer. This is often also true of heating equipment and wiring. For a few materials, such as steel, concrete, and brick, usually sold in large quantities for sizable structures, contractors customarily go directly to manufacturers.

Although the distribution pattern is well recognized and firmly established, and manufacturers ordinarily respect and adhere to their dealer relationships, there is constantly increasing pressure from builders to change existing procedures. Secret and varied discounts are commonly given by manufacturers to the more substantial builders; and arrangements are sometimes made between builders and manufacturers involving modified or, less often, no compensation to dealers. Occasionally a builder maintains a dealer establishment for his own use. But, even when this occurs, the form of the system is almost always observed. With the majority of builders both the form and the substance alike are maintained.

The role of the materials dealer is unique in modern industry—except where small handicraft or home production is concerned, he is a retailer who sells to a producer. He does not ordinarily sell directly to the ultimate consumer, nor is direct-to-consumer distribution possible for many of his wares. His outlets are the host of builders and subcontractors, large and small, who seek out the market and decide what and how much of his stock will be used. The dealer's position in the construction industry permits the builder to operate without inventory and frequently with little capital. This system also permits the manufacturer to produce without immediate concern with numerous erratic local markets or the hand-to-mouth builders' purchases.

The dealer also serves in other ways. As an expediter, warehouser, sorter and handler of the numerous small items which are sold in numerous small orders, he provides a service that few builders can or would choose to perform themselves. Because of his wide contacts with local conditions, the dealer can fre-

32. A comparatively small percentage of miscellaneous materials is sold to builders and consumers by department stores, 5 and 10 cent stores, and other general stores. The great mail-order houses, of course, break across the whole distributing system, reaching builder or consumer directly. Local combinations, however, frequently prevent the installation of certain materials sold in this way. For the distribution of manufacturers' sales, see Appendix D, Table 29.

33. See Chap. 5, p. 145, for a discussion of new developments.

quently judge markets better than the builders, and so help guide the production both of builders and manufacturers. The dealer promotes business by local advertising and personal contact. He often provides or arranges for the financing of building operations, and not only offers plans, but gives advice on the selection and use of materials.

The building materials distributive pattern is so intricate and variable that only a very rough indication of distribution costs is possible. According to the best available data, the manufacturer's markup over production costs is 16 per cent, the wholesaler's markup is 23 per cent (or 27 per cent of production costs), and the retailer's is 40 per cent (or 57 per cent of production costs)—making a total of 100 per cent.[34]

Dominant Position of the Dealer

In the smaller communities and rural areas the materials dealer is probably the dominant factor in the housebuilding industry. In the construction of individual houses and repair work he is indispensable. Only unusually large operations may put him in a subordinate position. Builders may grumble at his prices but nearly all of them need many or all of his services. Manufacturers, aware of the importance of their dealers, regard with skepticism or hostility any efforts to modify the distribution system.

The cost of distributing materials is generally considered high, but the dealer's markups do not apparently yield extraordinary profits. In the relatively good year, 1939, retailers of lumber and building materials averaged only 3 per cent net profit, according to a sample survey. Of the 793 concerns reporting only 32 per cent showed any profit at all.[35] The distribution system may be wasteful in the strictest economic sense, but it does perform costly and often unrewarded functions.

5. THE ROLE OF THE FINANCIER

Housebuilding in its present form, requires a comparatively large proportion of working capital in relation to the value of the unit produced. The business consists chiefly of the assembly of purchased parts over a considerable period of time before the final product is paid for. Few builders can supply all the needed working capital, and, generally speaking, the uneven rate of production and the slow turnover add to these difficulties. As a result, builders depend heavily upon credit for operating funds.

34. These figures are subject to considerable qualification. See Appendix D, 3.
35. Dun and Bradstreet, Inc., *1940 Retailers' Operating Costs Survey.*

a. CREDIT ARRANGEMENTS

In most industries the distinction between *producer credit* and *consumer* or *purchaser credit* is clear.[36] Manufacturers usually finance their production with their own capital or with short-term bank loans. The buyers of their products, if they require loans for financing the deal, borrow from the banks or finance companies. The two types of transactions are distinct. The producer's loan is not ordinarily contingent upon assurances of consumer credit, nor is consumer credit advanced in such a way as also to finance production. The institutions interested in consumer credit do not influence the product manufactured or the quantity supplied. In a few industries, manufacturers through their own control of finance companies, sometimes assure the consumer of ample sources of credit and prevent outside forces from dominating the retail market.[37]

Influence of Consumer Credit

In housebuilding, however, consumer credit in the form of mortgage financing, directly or indirectly provides the means of financing production. Since most house purchasers require high percentage loans, the consumer is dependent upon the lender for funds. As a result purveyors of consumer credit, by controlling funds for producing the house, exercise a strong influence on the character and quantity of the product.

Credit is usually made available to the builder for a specific house, group of houses, or an apartment structure, only after the project is already sold, or the lender is convinced that it can be promptly sold or rented.

Variety of Financing Procedures

There are several procedures in financing housebuilding. The prospective owner (whether of a single house or apartment building) may negotiate a loan —almost invariably secured by a mortgage on the property—the proceeds of which may be paid out as the work progresses. In some cases, particularly in the eastern market, the operative builder who erects houses in advance of sale may go on the note as owner, the mortgage later to be assigned to the purchaser.[38] This results in complete fusion of producer and consumer credit, even in the identity of the loan instrument.

Under another procedure, the owner negotiates the loan as above, but instead of obtaining payments during construction receives a commitment from the

36. See Chap. 9, pp. 225-256, for a discussion of consumer credit for housing.

37. For examples of control of consumer financing by automobile manufacturers, see *Report on Motor Vehicle Industry,* Federal Trade Commission, June 5, 1939, pp. 279-286.

38. Where the operative builder obtains the loan in his own name, the lender usually pays out only 60 to 80 per cent until the assignment takes place.

lender to pay the proceeds on completion of the property. Armed with such a commitment, the owner or builder may readily obtain an interim commercial loan to cover construction. Rental as well as owner-occupied properties are often financed in this way. In the East, the first method is probably more common among builders of single-family houses and apartments.

A builder may also obtain through a lending institution an FHA *conditional commitment* to insure a loan on completion of the structure and its sale to a satisfactory owner-borrower. Such a commitment may then be used as the basis for interim borrowing for construction purposes.

Although these devices are cumbersome, there was enough money available for mortgages in the later 1930's to carry on a sizable building program. In many cases, however, operative builders found it difficult to obtain funds for production in advance of sale. Here the materials dealer often came to the rescue, borrowing from the bank on his own credit and advancing funds as construction progressed, protected by his right of lien on the property. Sometimes subcontractors provided construction funds. Only in such arrangements do we find any real departure from the consumer-credit pattern of financing housebuilding. Yet even here the dealer's or subcontractor's security—the mechanics' lien—is similar to the mortgage in that the property itself is the ultimate security.[39]

b. DOMINANCE OF FINANCIAL INSTITUTIONS

No financial pattern especially designed to meet the producer's requirements has ever been successfully devised for the housebuilding industry. Without fixed plant and equipment, there is no security in the industrial sense, except the ability and good will of the producer. The only real security is the property constructed. Consequently, the financial institutions—the savings and loan association, the savings bank, the commercial bank, or the insurance company—assume a commanding position in housebuilding finance. The lender, usually the dominant party in the negotiations, exerts his power in several ways.

The lender may influence the volume of construction, although there is no way of telling how directly, consciously, and concertedly this is done. For example, there was a general withdrawal of credit at the end of the twenties when builders were still seeking capital. On the other hand, the expansion of mortgage credit in the middle thirties helped to increase building operations. At that time credit seems to have been available before demands for it arose. The lack of credit indexes makes it extremely difficult to compare the supply of credit with the demand for it.

39. The mechanics' lien is a striking commentary on the irresponsibility of the building industry. In the manufacture of no other product are the laborers and suppliers able to look to the purchaser to satisfy a claim. In no other case is the purchaser put in jeopardy by the producer's defaults.

Lenders have a profound influence in directing production into houses for owner occupancy or for rent, or into dwellings for families of high, or of low income. The apartment-building boom of the twenties was directly influenced by lenders, as several later investigations plainly revealed.[40] That the more recent emphasis on production for homeownership is largely a policy of lending agencies and government agencies standing behind them seems equally clear.

Lenders have been reluctant to make loans for low-priced houses. The problem of directing builders into production for the low-income groups is often a problem of persuading lending institutions—reluctant to impair the security of their existing mortgages on high-cost property—of the safety and profitability of loans on inexpensive property.

Probably in no other industry are the bankers so influential in determining the nature of the product. They influence not only matters of type and price, but such details as location, arrangement, architectural style, materials, and character of construction. Many large lending institutions maintain architectural departments or employ consultants to review plans, suggest changes, and inspect construction—practices most frequently found in the larger cities. That lenders find it necessary to exercise such wide authority over operations is evidence of the lack of managerial direction and responsibility in the housebuilding industry itself.

6. THE IMPACT OF GOVERNMENT ON HOUSEBUILDING

In housebuilding a close relationship between industry and government is not new.[41] Governmental intervention has tended both to stimulate and restrict activity. In this country, housing has been regulated at all levels of government—by local, state, and federal agencies. Yet rarely do we see any direct contact between government and a definitely recognized housebuilding industry. Government has been chiefly concerned with products, not with organizations, and

40. See the following reports of investigations of realty finance: U.S. House of Representatives—Select Committee to Investigate Real Estate Bondholders' Reorganization. Preliminary report and supplemental report (H. Rep. No. 35 Pt. I (1935) and II (1936), 74th Cong.).

Securities and Exchange Commission—Report on the study and investigation of the work, activities, personnel and functions of protective and reorganization committees. Pursuant to section 211 of the Securities Exchange Act of 1934, Pt. III, Committees for the holders of real-estate bonds, 1936.

New York State Legislature—Report of the Joint Legislative Committee to Investigate the Guaranteed Mortgage Situation, March 15, 1938, J. B. Lyon Co., Albany, 1938. Legislative Document No. 87 (1938).

41. The curious reader may go back as far as 2250 B.C. See R. F. Harper, *Code of Hammurabi*, University of Chicago Press, Chicago, 1904. For other early building regulations see F. Burton, *History of Building Codes*, Proceedings Fifteenth Annual Meeting of the Building Officials' Conference of America, 1929, p. 40.

with consumers, not with producers. It has rarely been directly interested in the effect of its acts on the industry itself.

a. GOVERNMENT AS A STIMULATOR

Except for public construction during the first World War, and for important research conducted by the Division of Building and Housing of the Department of Commerce during the twenties, the federal government's interest in housing dates from the depression. Housebuilding had never been singled out as an activity for which public stimulus was important. Housebuilders did not receive land grants, like railroad builders, nor bounties for serving pioneer areas or rehabilitating deteriorated regions. Nor were tariffs designed to benefit them.

Housebuilding as a local enterprise was of interest only to local government, which confined its interest to safety regulations, frequently at the same time conniving to make dwellings expensive. The cost of land improvements in new subdivisions was often borne by the municipality; but this bounty generally helped the speculative subdivider, rarely the builder. Departures from these policies prior to the depression came in a small number of states which enacted measures to encourage house production, usually by making it easier to buy or rent houses, rather than by making it easier or cheaper to build houses.[42]

Financial Aid to Consumers

The depression measures of the federal government followed the same approach of stimulating building indirectly by aiding the users of housing. This was done in two ways. On the one hand, the flow of mortgage credit was facilitated by the Federal Home Loan Bank System (created in 1932) and the Federal Housing Administration (established in 1934), and on the other, the government financed and sometimes contracted for the building of dwellings for low-income groups presumably beyond the reach of private enterprise.[43] The objective of the federal government was to make adequate dwellings available to more people, not by renovating the housebuilding industry, but by lowering interest rates, extending amortization periods, and providing subsidies. The only deviation from this approach was the limited use of labor furnished by the Work Projects Administration in installing streets and utilities in new areas, particularly where low-priced dwellings were to be erected. Even this was merely a government subsidy of labor costs.

The housebuilding industry, of course, has received other benefits from government. Financial practices have been regularized and a national mortgage

42. See Chap. 10, pp. 273-275, for more detailed discussion of these and later measures.
43. The federal agencies dealing with housing are discussed more fully in Chap. 10, pp. 257-290.

market, for the time being at least, has been created. Planning techniques and building standards, especially for low-cost construction, have been improved under governmental leadership. But, up to the war, the industry had not been encouraged to improve its technology or increase efficiency. The FHA, it is true, was largely responsible for the growth of operative-builder organizations and has recognized prefabrication to the extent of providing a means for examining and ruling on new methods of construction (a policy frequently nullified by field officials). The Farm Security Administration has utilized prefabricating methods in rural areas, and under the wartime housing program prefabrication has received considerable recognition. The Justice Department's intensified campaign against monopolies, inaugurated in 1938, has clearly revealed the numerous obstructions in the building industry, and has effected at least temporary modification of restrictive practices in some localities.[44]

In many ways, however, the national housing agencies have tended to preserve the archaic foundation of the industry. The dependence of production upon consumer credit has increased. The policy of facilitating buying or renting of houses through liberal financial terms and subsidies tends to discourage the industry from cleaning house, and encourages a demand for still lower interest rates and an expansion of the subsidy program as substitutes for technical progress and lower costs.

Technical and Market Research

The technical and market-research activities of the federal government have made important contributions to the housing industry. The publications of the Federal Housing Administration and the Federal Home Loan Bank Board on new building methods, house planning, standards, and neighborhood and city planning have been particularly beneficial. The National Resources Planning Board has helped to outline current and future problems.

Among the older departments technical research in housebuilding has been principally concentrated in the National Bureau of Standards (Department of Commerce), and the Forest Products Laboratory (Department of Agriculture). In the former, the now defunct Division of Building and Housing issued many pamphlets designed to improve the quality and simplify the methods of house construction, and develop model regulatory legislation. The Bureau of Standards has studied building materials and methods and tested numerous new structural

44. Prior to its new drive, the Department of Justice had instituted about one suit a year in this field. During the history of antitrust prosecutions (1890–1940) about one quarter of the 500 cases concerned some phase of the construction industry. The Federal Trade Commission has examined unfair practices in the building field and has issued a number of "cease and desist" orders. Neither agency has in the past had adequate means for effectively handling the situation.

systems.[45] The Forest Products Laboratory, concerned wholly with wood, has made a signal contribution in its development of the structural uses of plywood. The design of farm housing has received considerable attention from the Agricultural Engineering and Home Economics bureaus (Department of Agriculture).[46]

Before the depression, knowledge of the housing market (aside from a few items gathered in connection with the Census of Population) was limited to occasional local surveys and the opinions of real-estate men. In 1934 the Real Property Inventory and the Financial Survey of Urban Housing, conducted with relief funds by the Bureau of Foreign and Domestic Commerce (Department of Commerce), revealed for the first time the housing conditions of the country, and provided a basis for orienting the production of builders and materials manufacturers. This information has been vastly augmented and brought up to date (April 1940) by the 1940 Census of Housing, so that we now have a greatly improved basis for estimating housing needs and possibilities. The Bureau of Labor Statistics (Department of Labor) gathers invaluable data about current building activity. Among the administrative agencies, the FHA and the Federal Home Loan Bank Administration make available important information about the housing market.

b. GOVERNMENT AS REGULATOR

An industry which affects the safety and health of the people in so many ways as housebuilding does must expect to be regulated in the public interest. Few industries have, in fact, been regulated in so many ways, or through so many agencies, with the result that attempts to stimulate housebuilding and to improve building methods have often been nullified by the diverse regulations to which the industry is subject.

The location and type of buildings are subject to an array of state and municipal legislation—zoning laws, city-planning laws, and laws regulating the subdividing of land. These three types of legislation are fairly new in this country; the oldest—zoning (except in the limited sense of fire districts and height limitation)—only goes back to 1914.[47] This general class of legislation follows

45. The reluctance of Congress to appropriate funds for technical housing research reflects the government's indifference to the basic problems of housing. The recent work of the National Bureau of Standards would not have been possible without regular, though hopelessly inadequate, contributions from the administrative housing agencies.

46. See Bibliography for publications issued by these agencies.

47. Edward M. Bassett, *Zoning*, Russell Sage Foundation, New York, 1940. Provision for zoning in all counties or in specified counties, towns or townships is in force in twenty-one states. Enabling legislation for local planning exists in thirty-six states for all cities and for metropolitan areas, counties, groups of counties, or towns and townships in twenty-eight states. Legislation providing for the control of land subdivision has been enacted in thirty-two states. The actual number of administrative bodies set up under these enabling acts is unknown. The adoption of specific local measures

certain rather well-established forms,[48] so that there is a considerable uniformity in function and procedure.

a. *The Planning Law* provides for the development of a master plan and the preparation and enactment of an official map of the area affected by the legislation, covering such features as roads, streets, bridges, and other public improvements, parks, public buildings, and other matters relating to the structure of the city.

b. *The Zoning Law* provides for the regulation by districts (of the municipality, county, or other area) of the location, height, bulk, size of structures, percentage of lot coverage, size of yards and courts, use of structures, and sometimes the density and distribution of population.

c. *The Subdivision Regulation Law* provides for public control over the manner in which land is laid out for urban uses.

These laws and the regulations growing out of them create the physical and, to a great extent, the economic framework within which the housebuilding industry must operate. They enable the community to determine what types of housing are desirable, as well as to protect itself from undesirable developments. Their influence is, on the whole, beneficial, although they reveal several notable shortcomings.

Shortcomings in Planning Procedures

Planning and zoning regulations are not universally applied throughout a given area. At present, land outside the corporate limits of cities—the very land most sought by developers—is often beyond the jurisdiction of the regulatory bodies. This increases the difficulties of maintaining consistent and economical urban growth.

Zoning that allocates excessive areas to commercial or industrial uses (frequently as a result of the political pressure of special interests) makes unavailable for housing purposes land that might otherwise be attractive to developers. Zoning that fails to differentiate between the various kinds of residential use, either on the basis of dwelling types or population density, may increase the price of land suitable only for low-density, single-house development to a point where it becomes unavailable.

---

is less universal than the primary legislation would indicate. Even in zoning, the most widely accepted of all, several important cities have no ordinances. See Appendix D, Table 30; also *State Legislation on Planning and Zoning,* Circular No. XII, National Resources Committee, June 1, 1938; and Harold W. Lautner, *Subdivision Regulations,* Public Administration Service, Chicago, 1941.

48. See *Standard City Planning Enabling Act* (1928), *A Standard State Zoning Enabling Act* (1926), and *Preparation of Zoning Ordinances* (1931), all prepared by the former Advisory Committee on City Planning and Zoning of the Department of Commerce; also Edward M. Bassett, Frank B. Williams, Alfred Bettman, and Robert Whitten, *Model Laws for Planning Cities, Counties and States,* Harvard City Planning Studies, Vol. VII, Harvard University Press, Cambridge, 1935.

Regulations designating yard, court, and frontage requirements solely on the basis of the ordinary street and lot relationships often hamper large-scale planning that might better satisfy the objectives of the ordinance. Requirements establishing lot sizes and improvement standards that purposely, or inadvertently, thwart the building of low-priced houses may obstruct balanced community development or force the erection of such houses beyond the area of control. Master plans that rigidly delineate street lines in unoccupied areas without due regard for the economy or attractiveness of development may not only add to the cost of housing but make it difficult to organize neighborhoods properly.

All housing laws deal with some phase of planning, but their administration is commonly placed in separate and often conflicting or overlapping agencies. For the builder, the multiplication of applications he must make, the permits he must obtain, and the lapses and conflicts of administration that he encounters all add to his expenses and to the risks of doing business. Moreover, since many developers seek FHA financing, they must comply with that agency's planning and subdivision requirements. Although the FHA regulations have helped both developers and homeowners, they nevertheless add to the delays and the possibilities of jurisdictional conflicts that burden the developer.

Laws Governing Construction and Occupancy of Buildings

Legislation regulating the construction and occupancy of buildings takes the form of building codes and related ordinances, such as fire-prevention codes, electrical codes, elevator codes, tenement-house and multiple-dwelling ordinances, and housing codes. Such legislation originates in state or local jurisdictions. There are state building codes affecting housing in Indiana, Ohio and Wisconsin, but even here municipalities can establish their own more stringent regulations. County codes are uncommon. Building and related codes are almost universally municipal ordinances.[49]

It was estimated in 1938 that about 50 per cent of all places of 2,500 population or more had adopted some form of building code—meaning that over 1,800 municipal codes were then in force. In addition, about 200 localities in this population group operated under state codes or had at least established fire-limit regulations, while some towns of less than 2,500 population also had some kind of codes. Construction in practically all rural areas and about 40 per cent of urban localities in the country was not subject to codes.

Many codes omit special provisions for mechanical, sanitary and electrical work. Only about 1,300 cities had plumbing codes, while less than 800 had

49. Increased construction in unincorporated areas in connection with the war effort, however, has resulted in a movement for county building codes which has been particularly successful in Ohio.

ordinances covering electrical work. However, eighteen states had laws pertaining to one or more of the following: electrical codes and their enforcement, licensing of electricians, and control of the sale of electrical products. The condition of occupied dwellings may be regulated by building codes or may involve separate codes. Separate housing or occupancy codes exist in nine states.[50]

Some Characteristics of Building Codes

The preparation of building codes is difficult and expensive.[51] Some communities, which cannot or will not pay for the expert knowledge required to prepare their own codes, copy, in whole or in part, the codes of larger cities, sometimes with incongruous results. For reasons of economy codes are completely revised only at long intervals. It has been estimated that in 1938 over 40 per cent of existing codes were between ten and twenty years old and almost 15 per cent were over twenty years old.[52] It is obvious that this slow rate of change fails to keep up with technical advance. Moreover, because codes are chiefly concerned with heavy construction and crowded conditions, low residential buildings in open developments have not received the special attention they warrant.

The manner in which code provisions are written often proves injurious to the housing industry. Codes have, in fact, virtually become building specifications, describing in great detail the methods and materials allowable in erecting framing, installing floors, building walls, and so forth. Frequently the law does not allow building officials sufficient discretionary powers to approve new materials and methods without legislative action.[53] This increases the problems of revision. Since the specification type of code unavoidably favors conventional methods of construction, it increases the resistance to new construction processes and materials. Procedures for obtaining exceptions are not only costly and difficult but provide opportunities for political corruption. Moreover, the detailed code specifications enable special interests to conceal insidious provisions of great benefit to them.

There are many instances of what has been called "the cross-fertilization of

50. Source of data: Unpublished studies of the National Bureau of Standards; see also *Summary of Existing State Electrical Laws and Statistical Report on Municipal Electrical Ordinances,* National Electrical Manufacturers' Association, December 31, 1939.

51. See George N. Thompson, *Preparation and Revision of Building Codes,* Building Materials and Structures Report No. BMS19, National Bureau of Standards, May 1939.

52. Unpublished studies of the National Bureau of Standards.

53. The Wisconsin and Ohio state codes deal with the problem of revision through a board of building standards. In Wisconsin the board writes the code and makes changes in its provisions when it sees fit. In Ohio the board has power to suggest equivalents for materials, equipment, and processes covered in the code.

science and politics." [54] Codes may provide effective local monopolies for certain materials and manufacturers, even to the extent of specifying products by name. Manufacturers may, through building codes, exclude competitive products. Again, building interests may take advantage of the absence of recognized standards to force the installation through the codes of excessive amounts of materials. This type of provision may be due to the pressure not only of manufacturers or subcontractors but of labor unions. Labor may also secure provisions which make it difficult or impossible to introduce methods reducing the amount of labor or skill required in erection of the house or the installation of its equipment.

Variety of Code Provisions

Since the building code is a local affair, there is almost as great a variety of provisions as there are codes. Investigations of code provisions reveal a range in "live load" requirements for dwellings of from 25 to 100 pounds per square foot, minimum thicknesses of brick walls from 8 to 16 inches for the same height and load, working stresses in concrete from 500 to 1,000 pounds per square inch, and variations in pipe sizes of 150 per cent. Floor-area specifications for the same type of room vary from 60 to 120 square feet, and ceiling height from 7 to 9 feet.[55] An analysis of plumbing codes of a dozen cities selected at random shows that the community requiring the lowest amount of metal in a one-story house saves 100 pounds of cast iron, or about 30 per cent of the total required by the city with the maximum requirements. Similarly, the minimum code saves 10 pounds of metals other than cast iron out of the 50 pounds required by the maximum code.[56]

The wide range of climatic and geological conditions in the United States makes code uniformity neither possible nor desirable. The present diversity, however, is due not so much to reasonable variations as to the existence of many independent jurisdictions and the lack of recognized standards. The variety of code requirements intensifies the localism of the industry, for it places the "foreign" builder at a disadvantage—and retards the standardization of manufactured products. It forces manufacturers to keep in touch with the numerous code-

54. Introductory statements by George N. Thompson to *Restraints in Building Codes,* address by Corwin D. Edwards before the Central Housing Committee, November 28, 1940, Central Housing Discussion Papers: G: 1940 Series, Washington (mimeographed). See also report on "Building Code Revision to Lower Costs," Session of Construction Industry Conference, U. S. Chamber of Commerce, December 5, 1940 (mimeographed); particularly statements of Rudolph P. Miller and Corwin D. Edwards.

55. Data from unpublished studies by Martin Goerl of the NBS. Exceptions to the diversity of municipal codes are the national electrical safety code, the elevator safety code and the code of fire tests of building construction and materials. All have been approved by the American Standards Association and are widely accepted.

56. J. H. Ehlers, *The Conservation of Critical Materials in Construction,* Department of Commerce, December 1, 1941 (mimeographed).

making authorities in order to guard their interests, and opens a wide and well-traveled road to political corruption.

Code Administration

The administration of building codes involves equal or greater difficulties than their formulation. The standards of administration are generally low.[57] The detailed type of code results partly from the legal difficulties involved in granting discretionary power to officials and, partly from an effort to eliminate the necessity for administrative judgment. Officials are thus deprived of a desirable leeway in administering the code on the one hand, and given an opportunity to harass builders on the other. To quote Corwin D. Edwards:

> This official harassment may be of two sorts. The man may be acting *ultra vires;* he may be taking the attitude that the code is what he says it shall be. Or he may be doing exactly his duty, as prescribed by the code, against the people he does not like, because he has a code which is so complicated that any person he wants to victimize can be attacked legally and correctly.[58]

Administration difficulties arise not only from the complexity and obscurity of code provisions and the frequent incompetence or venality of enforcement officers, but from the character of the customary administrative machinery. The building regulations in a community may be covered by several ordinances, published in many documents, and administered by frequently unco-ordinated and sometimes mutually antagonistic agencies. The so-called building department of a municipality only rarely has complete jurisdiction over building activities. The health department may be responsible for compliance with plumbing and sanitary provisions, and the fire department and the bureau in charge of streets may also claim jurisdiction. In addition, builders may be forced to obtain permits or certificates of compliance from planning and zoning agencies. In extreme instances builders must secure twenty or more permits or certificates.[59]

As with land subdivision, the federal government influences building regulations through the FHA, whose *Property Standards* and *Minimum Construction Requirements* constitute a sort of supercode; compliance is incumbent on all builders who wish to qualify for FHA financing. The FHA requirements are necessary because: (1) local codes do not cover outlying areas, (2) local codes frequently pay no attention to light construction, and (3) FHA desires to im-

57. Construction Industry Conference Report, *op. cit.,* statement of Rudolph P. Miller; also Edna Trull, *The Administration of Regulatory Inspection Services in American Cities,* Municipal Administration Service, Publication No. 27, New York, *circa* 1932, p. 97.

58. Construction Industry Conference Report, *op. cit.,* Corwin D. Edwards, p. 16.

59. Rudolph P. Miller, "Economic Housing as Affected by Building Codes," mimeographed Appendix to Report of Committee on Construction, *President's Conference on Home Building and Home Ownership,* p. 9.

pose conditions that are usually beyond the authority of local codes. Local building regulations based on police power are concerned only with matters affecting safety and health. The FHA, in order to strengthen mortgage security, adds stipulations covering the physical and economic durability of structures. In spite of the additional public protection that FHA requirements afford, they add to the number of regulatory bodies and therefore to the builders' problems.

Licensing Laws

Closely related in their effects are licensing laws.[60] In some states architects, engineers, contractors and workmen in the plumbing and electrical trades and less often general contractors and builders are licensed in order to protect public health and safety by controlling the quality of work performed. Despite the beneficial aims of licensing, it creates many problems for the building industry. Thus, licensing is used to promote combinations and restraints—a situation that is facilitated by the fact that examining boards almost invariably consist of members of the group to which the particular law applies.

Licensing may thus restrict the number of contractors and artisans and place "foreign" competition at a disadvantage. For instance, in one locality the license fee for a local plumbing contractor was $1 per fixture for each installation, while for a nonresident contractor the fee was $1 for each fixture plus $25 for each dwelling unit.[61] License laws may be used, alone or in conjunction with building codes, to enforce subcontractor or labor union restrictions.[62]

Any regulation that establishes minimum standards of quality is bound to raise costs. This is unavoidable and understandable, but when regulation is irrationally or ignorantly applied, or is perverted (as in the above example) to serve special interests, the added costs cannot be justified. The extent of these illegitimate costs cannot always be measured. Requirements of excessive materials in land improvements and structures are plain enough, and the costs to

60. See Appendix D, Table 31.

61. Edwards, *Restraints in Building Codes, op. cit.*, p. 4.

62. *Ibid.*, pp. 3–4. "Thus, the code in a particular city requires that electrical work be done by licensed electricians; and electrical work is so broadly interpreted that the city holds that even the connection of a welding-machine cord to an outlet by plugging it in constitutes electrical work and must be done by a licensed electrician. The skill required for this operation is the same as that required to plug in a toaster on a breakfast table.

"Here is what actually happens. A builder who uses electric welding must employ a licensed electrician to plug the cord in. Licensed electricians in that city are unionized. Under the rules of the union plugging in a cord is not construction but maintenance. Further, union rules provide that a maintenance electrician must not do construction work and (once employed) must remain constantly on the job until its completion. Accordingly the builder must hire a full-time maintenance electrician to be idle when not plugging in the cord. The welders in that town work an eight-hour day; the electrician, who must be present continuously during the eight hours, works a six-hour day, with overtime pay thereafter. The consequence is that on one job it cost $1,000 to get that plug plugged in by a licensed electrician."

the builder of multiple permits, of duplicated administration, and of delays and harassment can also be measured in dollars and cents. But these are probably the least serious results of our regulatory methods. The effects of restricted competition, restricted labor supply, and intensified localism, of retarded building techniques and hampered industrial development, are beyond computation.

7. SUMMARY

The relationships among the housebuilding groups—including the materials manufacturer, dealer, builder, laborer and buyer are diffuse and complex. As a result, the industry lacks unity and integration, is localized in its operations and backward in its technology.

These chaotic relationships are largely due to the weakness of management, and to the absence of the managerial power necessary to weld housebuilding into a cohesive, efficient and progressive industry. Housebuilding is now directed by many unco-ordinated, uncontrolled groups—each trying to protect itself. As a result, production in the housing industry is restricted and costs are high. Reviewing the situation in 1938, *Fortune* magazine aptly noted: [63]

> . . . there is one primary necessity of a good life that $30 a week will *not* provide in most urban communities . . . and that is adequate shelter. And where it *will* provide adequate shelter it will not provide housing on a scale even approaching the standards of comfort, convenience and luxury that the $30-a-week man obtains from his other expenditures. The spending of $30 a week and less very largely supports U. S. industry, with one important exception. That exception is the disorganized and warring group of organisms known euphemistically as the building industry. In fact, the building industry by and large does not look on the mass market as a primary or even possible market for housing, and whatever technical advances it has made have been in the field of ornamentation rather than of cost reduction. Whether the fault lies with the industry itself, or with uncontrollably high basic building costs, or with government-housing policy, the fact remains that the situation is bad for the building industry, bad for society, and most immediately and painfully bad for the $30-a-week family and its less prosperous neighbors.

This indictment has been justified. Yet amid its extraordinary obstacles, the housing industry does make progress. In the past few years we have noted a ferment and experimentation. Whether this will be sufficient to create, after the war, an industry geared to the needs of American society remains to be seen. The housebuilder's major problem is to modify his product, and renovate, adapt, and augment his production to meet the potentialities of a vast unexploited market.

63. "The House Not-So-Beautiful," *Fortune,* May 1938, p. 64.

Chapter 5

INDUSTRIAL TRENDS IN HOUSEBUILDING

THE HOUSEBUILDING INDUSTRY is old but not mature. Its patterns, established before the industrial revolution, remain those of a contractor-adventurer system of enterprise. Mechanization has not gone far enough to change its ways fundamentally. More than any other industry, with the exception of agriculture, it is still in the handicraft, small-scale, local stage. Even agriculture has been more fully mechanized than housebuilding.

Nevertheless, the pressure for change has been growing steadily. In some cases it has led only to freakish or impracticable innovations. But trends of fruitful modernization are discernible. The effective developments have evolved cautiously and quietly. The new industry sensationally proclaimed by the prophets of mass-production houses in the early thirties has not appeared. The acceptance of change has come almost unknowingly, although hardly any element in the industry—design, labor, assembly, manufacturing or distribution—has been untouched by the newer trends.

Most prominent is an increasing specialization in housebuilding as a distinct form of enterprise and the growing industrialization of production methods. This has come about through standardizing and simplifying the parts of a dwelling, the mechanization of building processes, realignment of managerial relationships, and differentiation of products and processes to suit the various needs of the housing market. The trend, though uneven, has been toward industrial integration.

1. SIMPLIFYING AND STANDARDIZING THE PRODUCT

By simplifying and standardizing the parts of the house the greatest advantage can be taken of mechanization, of repetitive labor operations, and of large-scale purchasing—all of which are necessary to the maintenance of uniform quality and the reduction of unit costs. During the last few decades standardization has made notable strides. Initiated during the first World War, it was aided thereafter by the Department of Commerce and by new types of building organizations. It is receiving fresh impetus from the materials and labor shortages created by the second World War. Standardization appears at two industrial levels: the materials manufacturer and the builder.

a. STANDARDIZATION OF PARTS

Parts have been standardized primarily by the manufacturer. There has been a gradual development of the concept that a house is a unit in which the parts must fit easily rather than be shaped and assembled wastefully on the job.[1] Most manufacturers, especially of the more complicated building items, have tended to standardize their lines, although in order to obtain a competitive advantage they have often sought to make their products somewhat different from those of their rivals. The first major advance away from this latter tendency was the extension of standardization from products of individual manufacturers to groups of similar products and industries. In this, government made a notable contribution.

Following a start made by the old War Industries Board, a regular procedure for *Simplified Practice Recommendations* for groups of producers was established in the National Bureau of Standards late in 1921.[2] While this procedure is available to all industries, the manufacturers of building materials and equipment have been among the foremost users of it. Up to 1940 the NBS had made nearly forty recommendations affecting items used in house construction. Under some of the most spectacular of these, common and face brick would have been reduced from 75 sizes to 2; steel boilers, from 2,328 varieties to 38; eaves-trough and conductor pipe elbows and fittings, from 110 types to 76; metal lath, from 125 to 29; lavatory and sink traps, from 1,114 to 76; concrete building units, from 45 to 18; roofing slate, from 1,260 possible sizes to 309.[3]

1. See A. F. Bemis, *The Evolving House,* Vol. III, *Rational Design,* Technology Press, Massachusetts Institute of Technology, Cambridge, 1936; "The Integrated House," *Architectural Forum,* April 1937; and *Preliminary Report on a Study of House Standardization,* Technical Bulletin (Form No. 2373), Federal Housing Administration, for a discussion of these points of view.

2. The procedure is described as follows:

Simplified Practice is a method of eliminating avoidable waste in industry.

A Simplified Practice Recommendation may be defined as a simplified method or list of sizes, varieties, types, or grades of products which has been approved for regular stock purposes, after superfluous styles have been eliminated.

A Simplified Practice Recommendation originates with the industry. Here the term "industry" is used in its broadest sense, and may mean a manufacturer, distributor, or a consumer group. The Division of Simplified Practice of the National Bureau of Standards, United States Department of Commerce, receives a suggested recommendation from one of these groups and refers it to the others for consideration and signed acceptance, on a voluntary basis.

The procedure of the National Bureau of Standards includes promulgation, publication and revision of standards, when necessary in cooperation with a representative Standing Committee composed of manufacturers, distributors, and users of these commodities.

Quoted from: *Simplified Practice—Its Purpose and Application,* National Bureau of Standards, Washington, April 15, 1940, Letter Circular LC 590 (mimeographed).

3. NBS, September 3, 1937, Letter Circular LC 504 (mimeographed).

The program, so far as it has gone, has helped to make cost reductions possible. With less variety, manufacturers can increase their turnover and improve the efficiency and continuity of production. Dealers similarly have greater turnover and eliminate slow-moving stocks. Deliveries from their suppliers and to their customers are speeded up. With sales efforts concentrated on fewer items overhead and handling costs are diminished. How much the builder gains depends largely on the extent to which these savings are passed on to him in lower prices for materials; but at least the builder derives the advantage of better service from his suppliers and better quality in his materials. We may note that all these benefits can be accomplished without producing uniformity in the finished product.

But little more than a good start has been made. The recommendations have by no means received universal acceptance. Moreover, many items might be further simplified, and the procedure might be extended advantageously to numerous other materials. The simplification procedure itself contains an inherent weakness since it deals with materials separately. While it simplifies their production and distribution, it makes no provision for co-ordinating the shapes and sizes of different materials to avoid waste when they are fitted together in the structure. To overcome this defect, a further step in standardization is required.

Correlation of Dimensional Standards

In 1938 the American Standards Association in conjunction with the Modular Service Association,[4] the industry itself, and government agencies, launched a program to correlate *dimensional standards,* in an effort to bring order to the chaos in the relationships among materials. Its object, as stated in a *Progress Report* issued by the Executive Committee on September 3, 1940, was:

> . . . to make available the economies of standardization without standardizing the building itself. A practical flexibility of building layout is provided by an adequate variety of sizes for the structural parts or by varying the number of masonry units used. A suitable variety of sizes for items that are fitted into the structure, such as windows, doors and stairs, is also provided. Since these sizes are predetermined, they may be used as standards for the manufacture or factory assembly of building materials, or for the precutting or pre-assembling of parts before field erection. Variations in building dimensions are created by and must be correlated with the variations in available sizes of materials and structural parts.
>
> Coordination is defined as a relationship of sizes and dimensions that will permit

4. The American Standards Association is a private body, composed of representatives of industry, industrial associations and governmental agencies. Its purpose is to establish industrial and commercial standards. The Modular Service Association, successor to Bemis Industries, Inc., the holder of Bemis patents on modular design and structural methods, is devoted to the promulgation of the principles enunciated by A. F. Bemis. It co-operates with the NBS and other interested governmental agencies.

the parts that are assembled during the erection of a building to fit together without field cutting. This coordination is accomplished by applying a uniform size increment to the variations in building dimensions and sizes of parts. The proper fitting together is established by sound assembly details. The use of a single size increment permits these assembly details to apply as standards to the entire range of alternate sizes and dimensional variations that are made available.[5]

Six special committees have been set up covering: brick and tile masonry, wood doors and windows, concrete masonry, metal windows, natural stones, and structural wood. It would be hard to overestimate the benefits of such a program if carried forward to include the principal elements of the dwelling. It would be worth while if it only eliminated the cost of material wasted in site assembly and the cost of the labor wasted in wasting the material. Other benefits would involve more uniform quality of the completed work and a shorter construction period.

This is perhaps as far as simplification and standardization can go at present in the production of housing materials. Because of the smallness of housebuilding organizations and the importance of the custom-built house, the manufacturer must still aim at the market as a whole rather than at the special requirements of individual producers. But even if the simplification and co-ordination movement stops here, definite progress will have been made toward lower housing costs. In a system where manufacturers collectively standardize their products for co-ordinated use, considerable latitude is left to the builder who devotes himself to the custom trade. At the same time further standardization is not impeded by those housebuilders who choose to undertake it.

Prefabricators, operative builders, and large contractors have experimented with standardized and co-ordinated units, embodying standardized wall, floor and roof sections, roof trusses, partitions, and even plumbing stacks, to the advantage of cost and time. When this stage is reached further standardization of parts becomes more and more closely related to a standardized dwelling unit.

b. STANDARDIZING THE DWELLING UNIT

The oldest form of standardization known to housing is the repeated use of the same or similar house plans and exterior designs, as in Baltimore and Philadelphia with their row houses, Chicago and St. Louis with their small flat buildings, Detroit with its frame bungalows, and so on. This kind of standardization has been carried far enough to give the housing of a community a typical character. It has often produced notable savings. It has reduced the cost of design. It has enabled the builder to estimate his materials with greater accuracy, and often

5. See also *Progress Report,* June 1941.

to order in larger quantities. It has also increased the efficiency of labor through the familiarity with the work gained by repetitive operations.

These advantages have too generally been obscured by the ugliness of the designs and by the failure to create attractive block and neighborhood layouts. Of course, standardization of plan has not always produced ugliness. Many examples may be cited where almost complete standardization in the hands of the skillful designer has produced exceedingly fine results—Adelphi Terrace in London, the houses at Bath, England, and the houses on the north side of Washington Square in New York City, to name only a few.

While not often achieving the beauty of these examples, many recent housing developments have utilized standardized plans without either ugliness or oppressive monotony. We have had a more critical analysis of the elements and the functions of the house than was common in the old speculative builder's unimaginative repetitions. Basic in this newer development has been the simplification of the dwelling plan—especially in low-priced structures, whether detached houses or apartment units. Layout has been studied in terms of the stock sizes and shapes of materials in order to save time and waste in erection. These technical improvements have in many instances been accomplished without sacrifice of amenities in either arrangement or appearance. In fact standardization permits the quantity builder to afford higher skill in design than can possibly be paid for by the producer of the nonstandardized, low-priced unit.

Apartment Designing

The development of carefully designed and thoughtfully engineered unit plans has led to the treatment of the dwelling as a unit in the larger design of the project as a whole. This is particularly evident in current apartment designing. The units of an apartment building have always, of course, been considerably standardized, especially apartments in the same tier. Former apartment designs were often based on the mistaken notion that the key to savings in cost was in reduction of the volume or area of the structure. This theory doubtless arose from the unscientific method of estimating costs on the basis of cubic contents or floor area, which put a premium on the maximum use of space.

Now it is recognized that ease of handling materials in the erection of the structure and of establishing repetitive operations frequently more than compensates for savings in space. Under the old theory, the character of the apartment was dictated by the shape of the lot and the character of the building as a whole, considered in terms of the maximum permissible volume. Today the dwelling unit is the basic element in the plan, and the character of the total structure is derived from combinations of the selected units. The building is *made up of* units rather than *cut up into* units. All the United States Housing

Authority's planning centers around this principle, and practically all private rental developments financed through the Federal Housing Administration, as well as an increasing number of those beyond governmental influence, have adopted it. The growing popularity of garden apartments has greatly influenced this rational method of design.

Single-Family House Subdivisions

The same principle has been applied to single-family house subdivisions. The rigid gridiron with its waste of land, crowded lots, and excess pavements and utilities is being replaced by less formal, more logical, and simpler methods of laying out land. Through the use of ingenious ways of providing variation within standardization, it has been possible to avoid the monotony of the earlier examples of repetition.

Commonly a few basic plans, perhaps from two to five, are selected. This permits an initial variation in the appearance of the houses and allows for diversity in the number and size of rooms required by the potential buyers. The street façade may be further diversified by using the same plans in reverse, thus slightly changing the elevations that face the street, or by staggered setbacks or different orientation. Inside the dwelling individuality may be attained by arrangements of wall colors, furniture and draperies. Outside, different surfacing materials and modifications in the ornamental features—porches, doorways, windows, shutters, corner treatments, and color—may disguise the fundamental sameness of the house designs without destroying the technical advantages obtained from standardization. In fact, from an aesthetic point of view, a more restrained use of these rapidly multiplied possibilities frequently produces a more harmonious street picture.

It must be emphasized that an aesthetically satisfactory use of standardization is possible only if the land is skillfully planned. If the dwelling is treated as a unit in a neighborhood or block design, and the neighborhood is endowed with a distinctive character through the pattern and contour of its streets and landscaping, considerable standardization of the houses is not only tolerable but essential to the harmony of the whole.

In spite of the tendency of builders to exaggerate the variation of a basic plan, the design of exteriors has been notably simplified. This trend has not been accompanied by such radical architectural treatments as extreme modernists advocate. But the best new houses do fulfill the essential requirements of functionalism: a frank expression of plan in the exterior design, the adaptation of the form of the house to the climate, and the selection of materials primarily for their structural rather than decorative purpose. That such houses often have a traditional cast does not invalidate this statement. The most popular prototypes are those that in their time were essentially functional and that today may be used with a minimum of violence to functional principles.[6] The growth of standardization and the gradual extension of new housebuilding methods and materials may bring further stylistic simplifications. This trend, however, need not be accompanied by aesthetic sterility, but can provide the designer with an unusual opportunity to combine beauty with utility, as in the motorcar.

The trend in housebuilding is not only toward simplicity in layout and architecture, but in the structure as well. Walls have been lightened. Bulk is reduced as surplus space is eliminated and layouts become more compact. The number of materials, parts, and operations has frequently lessened, as in the elimination of plaster in favor of "dry-wall" construction utilizing wallboard or plywood.[7]

2. RATIONALIZING THE BUILDING PROCESS

As a result of the tendency to simplify and standardize modern housing, the building process is being rationalized. This is, perhaps, most evident in the increased use of mechanized methods. Mechanization, of course, is not entirely new in the construction industry. Among the makers of brick, cement, lumber, paint, and other important materials, as well as equipment, mechanization has followed the general trend in manufacturing processes.

Similarly, there has been considerable progress in the last fifty years in the use of mechanized devices on the site. Power excavating and grading machinery, now employed even on small operations, has reduced the cost of excavation and has permitted work to go on when the ground is frozen. Power hoisting equipment and the pneumatic riveter have made tall buildings possible. Concrete mixers are commonly used; mortar and plaster mixers are somewhat less familiar. The cement gun is available for stucco, and the spray brush for paint where labor unions do not prevent their use. In carpentry we find the electric skill saw, the electric drill, and the power sander in frequent use. Materials produced by mechanized processes have often reduced hand operations at the site. For instance, the development of patent plaster has simplified the mixing operation; and the increased use of prepared paints has not only lessened the painter's job but the skill required for mixing paints.

Nevertheless, hand work still characterizes housebuilding. Writing in 1930, William Haber stated, "Very few machines are used on light tasks. The work of the mason, roofer, tile setter, carpenter, plasterer and painter is commonly a

6. For instance, the overworked "Cape Cod Cottage." For a fuller treatment of this development see *Modern Design*, Technical Bulletin No. 2, FHA (revised March 1, 1941).

7. Since plaster involves four and frequently five processes (lathing, scratch coat, brown coat, finish coat, and painting or papering) while dry wall requires but two (application and painting or papering), a saving in three operations may be effected.

hand operation, even on large work, and is always performed manually on small buildings."[8] Mechanization for the most part has been superimposed upon a handicraft system. It has not fundamentally altered the system. Today, however, the system of site assembly itself is gradually being changed, and rigid craft distinctions are being broken down as men are employed in repetitive tasks and more work is done under shop conditions. Change in the building process ranges from better organization of more or less conventional methods to radical modifications of process and structural system.

a. METHODS USED IN LARGE BUILDING OPERATIONS

On large projects, whether individual houses or apartment buildings, operations are divided and specialized somewhat like the assembly-line technique in automobile production. In housebuilding, however, the workers move and the line remains stationary. One or more model units are usually erected to familiarize the workmen with their jobs. The sequence of operations is then carefully broken down into excavating, laying the foundation, constructing the first floor, the framing, sheathing, roofing, roughing-in, and so forth. Comparatively small crews specializing in one or more operations are organized, and begin to move in sequence along the "production line"; that is, from one unit to the next. The efficiency gained by repeating familiar tasks is much greater than is possible if all the houses are erected at once, in uniform stages, from foundation to roof with a large labor force for each stage.

The extent to which this method may be used varies, of course, with the project. It can be utilized best in large developments, where a year or more of continuous production is scheduled. The method must be modified for developments which are small or of short duration. Ordinarily it cannot be used on the isolated house, and only to a limited degree on the single multistory apartment building. In certain large market areas, small builders can use specialized labor crews by subcontracting to labor contractors organized for this purpose.

Considerable preparatory work may be done away from the structure, if not off the site, thus supplementing and facilitating rationalized building. Large-scale builders frequently precut all structural lumber, build stairs and door frames, mortise and fit doors, and fabricate roof framing in shops that are sometimes erected temporarily at the site, sometimes in a permanent establishment elsewhere. Precutting leads naturally to the preassembly or prefabrication of parts. As a result, there is an increasing tendency to shift operations from the site to the shop.

8. William Haber, *Industrial Relations in the Building Industry,* Harvard University Press, Cambridge, 1930, p. 34. With comparatively minor exceptions, the same statement may be made today.

b. PREFABRICATING METHODS

Although more than a decade of serious effort has gone into the development of prefabricating methods, the movement is still in its infancy. This is due to the necessity of finding suitable materials and then of fitting the materials to economical methods of processing. The early prefabricators worked principally with steel. But steel in housebuilding raises as many problems as it solves. Steel is difficult to protect, if exposed, hard to insulate, and relatively expensive. This, plus the fact that machinery for processing steel requires a large investment, has hampered its use in prefabricated houses. To be successfully used, steel requires mass production on a scale too great for any present undertakings. In commercial production, with one or two exceptions, its recent use has been confined almost entirely to framing members, and due to war shortages even this limited use was necessarily abandoned. We must not assume, however, that the possibilities of steel, and of other metals or plastics have been fully explored. Future experiment, likely to be prompted by excess capacity for producing these materials after the war, may considerably change the picture.

There have been numerous experiments with concrete, from Thomas Edison's integrally poured concrete house to the latest forms of vibrated concrete, either poured integrally (sometimes solid, sometimes with removable cores) or precast in slabs and structural shapes. Generally such methods have not been cheap enough to compete with ordinary methods of construction even when all the work is done at the site. Where transportation of precast sections is involved, the weight of concrete has been so serious an obstacle as practically to eliminate it as a material suitable for factory prefabrication.

Wood was used in "precut" or sectional houses long before the term prefabrication was first used. It was not, however, until the difficulties presented by other materials became apparent that attention was redirected to this earlier development. And then progress came usually not from the older firms but from organizations that had been experimenting with steel and synthetic materials. Usually the older firms had not simplified their product sufficiently to make mass manufacture possible or had failed to refine it sufficiently to make it suitable for other than temporary or seasonal shelter. They generally provided materials only for the shell of the house, and attempted to sell on a factory-to-customer basis, leaving the buyer to erect and procure the remaining items. Moreover, since these sectional house manufacturers used wood in traditional forms, put together with little modification of traditional methods, they offered little, if any, economy over ordinary field methods, even in the limited portion of the dwelling supplied by them.

Use of Plywood

Some recent developments still cling closely to the traditional principles of wood framing but have succeeded in reaching more extensive markets by simplifying the design, purchasing the bulk of all materials and equipment at wholesale, and distributing the "package" thus assembled through dealers or operative builders. In this type of operation, the most radical departure is usually the substitution of plywood for boards as sheathing for wall panels. The weight and bulk of sections made from traditional framing members has limited the amount of off-site fabrication that could be done economically under this method. The success of this method has been largely due to economical design and to mass purchasing.

Early in the thirties, the Forest Products Laboratory began to experiment with plywood, adapting the principle of *stressed covering* to wall and floor construction.[9] This involves the union of covering material with framework by a continuous glue bond, making a structural unit of the entire panel, in which the covering as well as the frame absorbs the stresses. The effect is that of the box girder, made possible by the rigidity obtained from the glue joint and not attainable by any other known means of joining wood members. The Laboratory's first results were announced in 1935 and with its methods panels of great strength and comparative lightness could be manufactured. The panels could be used to provide structural support, weather resistance, and inside and outside finish.[10] Here was a new structural principle, opening the way for a new industrial development. A commercially practicable method of factory prefabrication was at last available.

The problem of factory-produced parts, however, was not wholly solved. Plywood lent itself well to shop methods but could not be exposed to bad weather; it was not until synthetic resin glue (phenol-formaldehyde) was introduced that a board at all reliable for exterior use could be obtained. The resin glue, however, required both heat and pressure for setting. The process was readily adaptable to making plywood, but its use in attaching plywood to a panel frame required more costly equipment than the prefabricator could usually afford. The recent development of cold-setting resins solves this difficulty, with the result that water-resistant plywood can now be made into water-resistant panels without costly machinery.[11] When it is realized that suitable methods and materials for

9. See Geo. W. Trayer, *Forest Products Laboratory Prefabrication System, A New Departure in All-Wood Housing,* and R. F. Luxford, *Progress Report on Prefabricated House System Under Development by the Forest Products Laboratory,* Forest Products Laboratory, May 1935 and December 1937, respectively.

10. To create a more conventional appearance, siding, shingles, or masonry veneers are sometimes applied over the exterior plywood.

11. For a discussion of plywood, see "Plywood: $80 Million Industry that Wants to Revolutionize the Construction of Everything," *Fortune,* January 1940, pp. 52–55, and "Plywood," *Architectural Forum,* March 1941, pp. 197–206.

prefabrication at low cost have been at hand for hardly more than five years the progress of prefabrication must be considered rapid indeed.

Other Materials

Other materials, such as certain types of wallboard, also are adaptable to stressed-panel construction. In addition to systems in which the wall panel provides structural support, other principles have been adapted to prefabricated operations. Especially notable is a system of framed panels or horizontal construction, in which the structure itself is carried by widely spaced columns of wood or steel and the wall is enclosed by horizontal panels extending from column to column. These wall panels may be structural or nonstructural. In the former case, the panel, built of plywood, is used as a deep girder to support the floor or roof beams, with continuous window sills and heads forming the flanges and the plywood itself the web of the girder. In the case of nonstructural wall panels, floor and roof beams are carried on girders of the same material as the columns, and the spaces are filled with a material whose structural properties may be limited to self-support and stiffening of the main structure. In existing examples "cemesto-board"[12] has been used as the filler panel. This greatly simplifies the shop processes. With framed panels, the structural members require milling and sizing, while the filler panel, composed of one material, need only be cut to size.

Prefabrication has accelerated mechanization in the housebuilding industry. Power tools are used more extensively, and the spray booth, the conveyor line, and the jig table have made their appearance. The jig table is probably the most important tool recently introduced in housebuilding. It consists of a platform so calibrated and fitted as to permit exact cutting or joining of members without repeated hand measurements. It may be used in preparing lumber or steel members, in the construction of wall, floor, and roof panels, the mortising and fitting of doors, the assembly of plumbing stacks, and similar work customarily performed as separate hand operations on the structure itself. Jigs facilitate the use of power tools, greatly increase the accuracy and speed of operations, and are at the basis of the savings possible under shop conditions.

The use of jigs vastly increases the responsibility of the designer and engineer. Under a thoroughgoing handicraft system the designer may be called upon to give only a general outline of what he wants produced. The rudimentary plans

12. A material composed of one or more layers of fiber wallboard, covered on both sides with asbestos cement. This composite board provides insulation, weather resistance, inside and outside finish, and strength for its own support. The framed panel system, a development of the John B. Pierce Foundation, has notably reduced the weight of the house, the superstructure of which totals only ten and a half tons while traditional dwellings of the same size weigh about twenty-six tons. See Chap. 2, pp. 39-40.

and specifications under which a large proportion of housebuilding still is done are adequate in the hands of highly skilled workmen. Even with more comprehensive directions, the architect frequently relies on the workmen's ability to make changes and corrections as the work proceeds.

Where the jig is used, however, every detail must be completely and accurately worked out in advance. Each piece must be related to the other pieces. Nothing can be left to whim or chance. Thus, while two or three drawings and a six-sheet specification may suffice for a small one-story house constructed by ordinary methods, a hundred or more carefully engineered drawings may be required for a similar house if jigs are used in the assembly. The need for standardization and repetitive operations under such conditions is evident.

3. Changes in Housebuilding Organizations

The technical developments outlined have been used by relatively few organizations. These organizations fall into several classifications, but all show progress in integrating building processes and, with their increasing size and efficiency, in obtaining greater advantages in purchasing materials than was found with the traditional small builder tied to an unintegrated subcontracting system. It is these organizations, therefore, that have been able to take greatest advantage of the hidden flexibility of the price structure, and to add savings on materials to economies in production.

a. THE OPERATIVE BUILDER

Foremost among this group is the operative builder—representing an organization that constructs dwellings on its own land and usually according to its own designs. The operative builder, who predominantly produces houses for sale, derives from the speculative subdivider and speculative builder of the past, but he has developed characteristics far different from those of his progenitors. Besides combining the development of land with the building operation—a union formerly known principally in a few luxury subdivisions—the operative builder has helped to increase the production of medium- and low-priced dwellings. This he has effected by integrating his operations; that is, by purchasing the land, exercising usually a greater control over his subcontractors than is customary in traditional housebuilding, and by taking advantage of the buying power afforded him by the size and continuity of his production.

The growth in number and importance of operative builders was one of the features of the recovery period of the late thirties. In 1939 about 35 per cent and in 1940 over 50 per cent of Federal Housing Administration applications came from such builders.[13] Because volume and continuity are necessary to their success, however, operative builders are confined to the largest urban centers. In such areas the industrialized methods that these conditions permit enable them to produce a better house for the money than other types of producers. Their influence, however, has scarcely been felt in the smaller, nonmetropolitan centers.

The Operative Builder in the Rental Field

A special group of operative builders build and operate dwellings for rent, usually garden apartments. This, too, is an old form of activity with a new twist, characterized by a more thorough integration of construction and the management of completed projects in one organization, and greater concentration at the medium-rental level than was common among apartment promoters in the boom era. These organizations are less numerous than builders-for-sale and their total volume is smaller, but their average size and volume of production are greater. The more successful companies operate on a scale that was once almost unknown and is still rare in the housebuilding industry.[14] Some have expanded over a considerable region. One of the largest, for instance, operates projects in six states and the District of Columbia.

Again, the scale of the rental operative builder's business gives him unusual purchasing power and permits him to negotiate directly with manufacturers of materials and equipment. Frequently, the size and continuity of his operations have allowed him to develop closely integrated subcontracting organizations. This may take the form of a mutually satisfactory working association among financially independent organizations, but it often involves varying degrees of financial and administrative dependence up to the actual ownership of subcontracting units. Strong and centralized management characterizes this type of establishment. Many have made notable technical contributions. Through their influence the garden apartment, with its union of effective land planning and building design, appears to have become a favorite in private rental housing. Many rental builders have outdistanced the builders-for-sale in standardizing the preparation of materials and in handling labor.

13. This does not mean, however, that builders always proceeded without greater assurance of sales to the production of the number of committed dwellings. Commonly one (or a group of model houses) was erected, orders were then obtained from these houses, and a considerable production program was undertaken. Sometimes a percentage of construction is undertaken in advance of actual orders. But rarely is any considerable volume of work beyond the known prospects of sale kept in process. Small builders, moreover, seem more likely to gamble than large organizations. The FHA tentative commitment is important to the builder, since it provides assurance that, on finding a buyer acceptable to FHA, the purchase can be financed. It is a potent sales instrument, but it does not necessarily indicate that the builder actually proceeds much in advance of sales. The 1941 amendment to the National Housing Act (Title VI), by making 90 per cent mortgages in "defense areas" directly available to the builder (in contrast to the purchaser), has somewhat changed this picture.

14. See Appendix C, 5 and Tables 15, 16 and 17.

The rental builder often operates over a wider area than the builder-for-sale. Both groups, however, are confined to communities of sufficient size to support large enough projects to permit the economies of large-scale production and purchasing. Though the large rental builder is less dependent on a single local market than the builder-for-sale, the market he serves is chiefly a metropolitan one.

b. THE INVESTOR'S BUILDING AGENT

A unique type of producing organization has been developed by the Metropolitan Life Insurance Company and its builder. Here the builder is not, in the ordinary sense, a contractor or independent producer, but rather the technical and building agent for the investing institution. The builder also investigates market conditions, recommends projects, selects sites, and prepares the financial prospectus. He directs the preparation of plans, chooses the materials and determines building methods, operating on a cost-plus-fixed-fee basis. Since 1938 some 17,000 dwelling units [15] have been built under this arrangement.

The subcontracting system is followed in this scheme, with three salient exceptions: (1) subcontractors are not ordinarily selected by competitive bidding, but for their assumed competence; (2) they are remunerated on a fixed-fee basis; and (3) they cannot enter into sub-subcontracts, or make purchasing agreements, without the approval of the building corporation. Subcontractors thus become strictly the agents of the builder, who assumes responsibility for negotiating subcontracts on the basis of his own predetermined estimates of cost, and negotiates directly with manufacturers for the principal materials and equipment.[16] The organization and direction of the work at the site is subject to the same centralized control and supervision.

The large scale of this building company's operations gives it a tremendous buying leverage. Not only does the size of the order give the buyer an advantage, but the ability to accept delivery according to regular schedules over a considerable period (three years in Parkchester) carries enormous weight. The large quantity of materials purchased also facilitates standardization of materials to suit particular job requirements. A notable instance was the special size of brick used on the entire Parkchester project, which brought savings both in labor and mortar. Repetitive operations plus the extended tenure of employment not only increase the efficiency of labor but attract the best workmen.

15. New York City (Parkchester), San Francisco, Los Angeles, and Alexandria, Virginia. The same builder has begun an operation of the same type (1,200 units) with the Equitable Life Assurance Society in Brooklyn.

16. It may be noted that the traditional procedure is observed. After negotiations are completed by the builder, the orders are placed under the subcontractor's name in the usual manner.

C. THE DEALER-BUILDER

In the organizations so far discussed, industrialized techniques and increased buying power have been associated with a large local market. The isolated small city has been neglected. Another type of organization, representing a combination of the function of materials dealer and builder, has been able to bring some of these advantages to smaller centers, although its operations are not confined to them.

This union of dealer and builder may take place in two ways. Builders sometimes become distributors of materials by setting up separate supply houses which deal with the general trade, but are established for the primary purpose of achieving control of sources of supply and the advantages of buying in a dealer's rather than a builder's capacity.

More recently the materials dealer has become a merchant of houses rather than of materials. He finds the prospective home buyer, arranges financing, undertakes (directly or indirectly) the building operation, and supplies the materials. This kind of organization is becoming increasingly important, especially in places of 25,000 population or less. The dealer-builder not only constructs new houses but repairs and alters old structures.

From the home buyer's point of view, the dealer-builder arrangement has several advantages. He can negotiate with one firm instead of several, as under the conventional contract-building pattern. Moreover, he usually deals with a well-established firm, with greater responsibility than the typical small builder. And finally, the homeowner is apt to save money. For the small builder employed by the dealer, the arrangement may result in greater continuity of work with less financial risk or sales effort.

There are several variants in the dealer-builder's operations. He may be able to introduce advanced methods of fabricating materials, thus saving money on construction as well as materials. Lumber may be precut and frames and sash assembled; or he may do a good deal of preassembly work on structural sections or panels, or in handling the units furnished by a factory prefabricator. He may also provide precut materials or sections directly for customers building their own houses. In one notable instance, the dealer provided plans, laid out the structure, contracted for plumbing, heating, and plastering, supplied precut lumber and fitted sash and doors to the owner-builder and supervised the work. Dwellings thus erected were at the lowest prices for new houses in the community.[17]

17. It should be noted that the success of this scheme has been due largely to the availability of a large number of at least semiskilled industrial workers and to the lack of competition apparently because of tight local labor and subcontractor restraints.

d. THE FACTORY PREFABRICATOR

Prefabrication, as a method of construction, involves the performance of a considerable part of the cutting and assembly operation away from the structure, either in a central shop or one erected on the site of a specific building project. The use of prefabricating processes is not confined to specialized factory producers, but has been increasingly employed in large projects by contractors and operative builders. Indeed some large builders carry prefabrication further than do some factory prefabricators, but the factory method involves some features that can rarely be wholly duplicated in the on-site operation.

The factory prefabricator maintains a central manufacturing establishment. He purchases all or most of the materials required in a dwelling, processes and partially assembles them into units, and transports them to the building site. The proportion of materials and equipment handled and the extent of processing vary. The oldest organizations in the field confine their operations to precutting and partly preassembling lumber for floor and wall construction. They usually sell directly to the consumer, who arranges for the supplementary parts and materials and the erection of the structure.

Among the newer prefabricating organizations (as they were operating before war orders supplanted their private business), a few supplied assembled cubic sections—units comprising as much as one half the house; some provided completely finished walls, partitions, floors, and ceiling panels; some sold partially finished wall panels only, and supplied the remainder of the structure above the foundation in precut or, for such parts as roofing, in measured packages. Most of the prefabricators included the heating unit and the stack, if in metal, and all or part of the kitchen equipment (except, usually, the range and refrigerator). Some furnished plumbing fixtures, and at least one was prepared to supply a completely assembled plumbing stack where local regulations permitted its installation.

Only a few firms have attempted to carry prefabrication beyond the construction of panels. Applying the principles previously described, wall sections are usually of a standard height of eight feet and from four to twelve feet in width. Floor, ceiling, and roof panels vary in width up to eight feet with the length usually being determined by the design of the house.[18] Generally the foundation and chimney (if made of masonry) are not supplied by prefabricators. In some cases the rough lumber for the floor, ceiling and roof, and usually the plumbing and wiring, are also bought separately.

The factory prefabricator is thus not wholly a producer of houses nor simply

18. It is not possible here to mention all of the variations. See *Recent Developments in Dwelling Construction*, Technical Bulletin No. 1 (revised July 1, 1940), FHA.

a producer of materials, although he inclines more toward the latter at the present time. Prefabricators have tended to disassociate themselves from the task of preparing land and erecting the structure, leaving these functions to local dealers or agents, or to operative builders to whom they sell their manufactured parts. This division of functions results not only in divided responsibility, but in the loss through increased distribution costs of part of the savings effected by factory production methods. The prefabricating business is still too young to have solved all its problems, and the problem of a satisfactory method of distribution is one of its greatest. At the beginning of the war this problem, probably more than any other, retarded a more rapid expansion of factory operation. War orders have served to provide a temporary by-pass and at the same time to push productive capacity beyond the ability to distribute through any private channels so far devised. The new industry will thus face a critical situation when it is thrown back on its own resources at the war's end.

Size of the Prefabricating Business

There are no accurate figures as to the number of concerns or the volume of business done by prefabricators. The FHA has examined more than 500 proposed methods of construction, involving varying degrees of prefabrication, and has accepted 232 as eligible for insured mortgage financing.[19] In 1940 only a dozen firms were regularly producing and marketing prefabricated houses along the lines described above, and probably less than 10,000 prefabricated houses had been produced between 1935 and 1940.[20] Prefabrication has received great impetus from the defense housing program. In January 1942 the Federal Works Agency listed over eighty prefabricating firms with some claim to consideration. Many of these were organizations only temporarily diverted to prefabrication, but the growth of the industry during 1940 and 1941 was in any case much greater than in all its previous history. The Federal Works Agency estimates that over 14,500 units were produced by factory prefabricators between July 1, 1940 and January 1, 1942.[21]

Argument continues as to the advantages of the factory prefabricating organization. Since there is ample evidence that substantial and attractive structures can be built with the methods of prefabrication most widely in use, the argument is reduced to the question of relative costs as compared with more conventional forms of construction and building organization. Since the economies of shopwork (whether at a factory or in a field shop set up for a large project) are reasonably obvious, the question remains: is prefabrication in a central manufacturing

19. Source: Technical Division, FHA.
20. This does not include houses constructed by builders using prefabricating methods of their own.
21. Source: Defense Housing Division, Federal Works Agency.

plant with a roving erector organization, or a number of local dealer-erectors, more economical than prefabrication by a large operative builder under shop conditions?

There is more than one answer to this question. The large operative builder who constructs a hundred or more houses a year can probably take advantage of most of the important technological improvements employed by the prefabricator, and in addition save on transportation and overhead costs. On the other hand, the prefabricator, because of centralized purchasing power, can undoubtedly serve the small project or small community more economically than the local builder. One prefabricator, for example, has been able to sell houses in the $3,000-$5,000 price class in a midwestern town at prices ranging from $40 to $500 less than comparable houses built by traditional methods.[22] The character of the prefabricator's operation gives him a special buying advantage. As a manufacturer, he can deal directly with the producer of materials entirely outside the distribution system provided for the builder and can generally obtain greater discounts from the materials manufacturer. Moreover, where union wage scales are involved, the generally recognized differential for shopwork usually works in favor of the factory as against the site operation.

4. SUMMARY

Although bound by tradition, the housebuilding industry shows distinct trends toward new types of organization and new techniques of production. These trends, while tentative in many respects, point toward lower costs and wider distribution. They indicate that from a technical point of view the ancient industry of housebuilding is capable of employing mass-production techniques; they also show that the industry can create organizational forms suited to its new techniques. But so far, mass-production organizations are still relatively few although the war has given a powerful stimulus to their formation. Many problems, however, must be solved before the various elements in the industry can be thoroughly integrated and the restraining influence of the local market overcome.

22. Based on a comparison between contract selling price and FHA valuation of a 25 per cent random sample of 125 houses.

Chapter 6

PROBLEMS IN INDUSTRIAL CHANGE

IN SPITE OF the variety of new trends now discernible, most dwelling construction still follows the traditional methods described in preceding chapters. Change so far has come slowly and partially. Old impediments remain and old resistances continue. The traditional housebuilding patterns are observable in the operations of the largest producers; even the prefabricators with their group of local dealer-erectors, subcontract locally from 20 to 50 per cent of the work. Moreover, despite the changes that have occurred, the bulk of house production is still not designed for that part of the population which needs it most.

1. THE DEFAULT OF LEADERSHIP

To a much greater degree than most industries, housebuilding continues to take its traditional processes for granted. A handicraft industry does not care to give up its handmade product. There is apparently little faith in the compensatory advantages that might follow the introduction of new methods. A special report to the Temporary National Economic Committee states: [1]

> The belief that there is only a limited amount of work to be done prevails throughout the building industry. It serves both to raise money charges in the industry to uneconomic levels and to restrict productivity. Manufacturers of building materials maintain prices at sufficiently high levels to insure a profit at comparatively low rates of operation. Labor sets its rates of wages at high levels upon the assumption that there is only a certain amount of work to be done. Both labor and manufacturers are sufficiently well organized to enforce their demands. These excessive money charges, although they do not yield their recipients a necessarily large return, at least in the case of labor, add to the money cost of each house that is built, restrict demand, reduce employment, and encourage further efforts toward wage and price increases.

The supposed limitations of the housing market discourage the investment of production capital on a permanent basis. Yet only a well-capitalized industry,

1. Peter A. Stone and R. Harold Denton, *Toward More Housing,* TNEC Monograph No. 8, p. 134.

with possibilities of continuous production, can support the research and experimentation essential to developing techniques for expanding markets.

a. ABSENCE OF DOMINANT INTERESTS

An industry composed of many parts, none of which exerts a completely dominant influence, or is wholly responsible for the final article, offers a tremendous handicap to industrial co-ordination. The type of voluntary co-ordination, for instance, involved in the simplified practice procedure of the National Bureau of Standards, requires so great a balancing of diverse and unevenly matched interests that progress is disappointingly slow, or is stalled altogether. The machinery for co-ordination is cumbersome and its enforcement beset with legal hazards. Manufacturers are reluctant to alter established patterns, or to give up a real or fancied competitive advantage.

There are great difficulties in financing the research upon which co-ordination might be based since the resulting benefits are so unevenly distributed. No single manufacturer has a sufficient stake in housebuilding to warrant his undertaking the task of consolidating the industry by unifying production management; his attempt to do so might endanger too many equally vital interests. Nor is it logical that the materials manufacturer should assume the initiative. His job is the production of his specialty. That he should find it necessary to go beyond this to promote and guide the production of the article in which his product is a minor part is evidence of a default in leadership at the level of the house producer.

The beginnings of a dominant managerial force at the house-assembly level are evident in some operative builder establishments and among some factory prefabricators. But neither group has devised a universally effective formula. While the operative builder is often large enough to cut through the distributing and price systems, he cannot often guarantee to buy continuously a large enough volume of goods to influence the character of the manufacturer's product. The builders of large projects, particularly in the rental field, sometimes reach a scale of operations that justify price concessions from the manufacturers, but the continuity essential to a complete control by the builder of all parts of his product is either not present or not predictable.

All in all, the point of view of the average builder is still predominantly local, and construction is planned on a project rather than on an annual basis. The attention of the housebuilder is on the completion of the project more than it is on the future development and improvement of his product. Because of the necessity of speedily completing his current project and his uncertainty about the size, character, and timing of the next, he has little opportunity to exert steady directional pressure on the unco-ordinated elements of the industry. To achieve this, continuity of operations is essential.

b. THE PREFABRICATOR'S ADVANTAGE

In some ways, the factory prefabricator overcomes the disabilities that affect even the largest operative or project builders. He has freed himself at least from the restrictions of a local market, since the uniformity of his product permits him to shift his sales effort from one community to another, without disrupting his production. Similarly he has escaped the irregularity of project-by-project operations, since his orders are pooled in one assembly-line process. While the prefabricator has not been able to smooth out his annual production curve, he has overcome the worst effects of seasonality and reduced the delays due to weather disturbances. Thus, in three midwestern factories, visited shortly after several weeks of rain in the summer of 1941, a rush of orders was being filled without difficulty from stocks built up during the inclement period. Meanwhile, other building operations in the region had practically come to a standstill during some of the most crucial weeks of the construction season.

There appears to be a tendency today for the prefabricator to consider his job complete when he has forwarded a bill of lading. The local builder is still responsible for assembling the house, and contracting for the parts that are not factory-made, as well as for merchandising the completed dwelling. Thus his position has not been greatly changed, even if the builder is called a dealer. Leadership in integrating the industry cannot come from the factory prefabricator so long as he is content to be a sort of super materials manufacturer and ignores the crucial elements of location, land planning, and the unification of land and building design.

2. THE SKEPTICISM OF LABOR

Many labor leaders have been aware of the problems of the industry. Some effort has been made by the unions to gain more direct control over housebuilding but in general they have been skeptical of making concessions for this purpose without assurances of increased employment. From time to time unions have made concessions without any noticeable gains. Thus wage cuts and demoralization of union rules failed to halt the downward trend of construction during the depression. Like other elements in the industry, labor knows that its part in the cost picture is not enough to affect the whole in proportion to its own sacrifice. Furthermore, it has no guarantee that its concessions will be paralleled by those of other members of the industry.

Nevertheless, there has been some recognition of the fact that housebuilding justifies a lower wage scale than commercial construction. The Bureau of Labor Statistics reports that in twenty-seven cities one or more unions have established wage differentials for residential work. In this the electricians come first, with thirteen agreements, followed by the carpenters and lathers with seven each, plumbers, painters and plasterers with four each, and several other trades with single agreements.[2] In some places differentials apply only to helpers and attendants. These concessions have undoubtedly facilitated labor organization in the housebuilding field, but their effects on housing costs are difficult to measure.[3] Whatever the benefits of wage differentials, they are offset by the absence of a co-ordinated labor policy. No uniform wage policy for residential construction has ever been announced by the Building Trades Department of the American Federation of Labor. And even if one were formulated the national organization would have no means of enforcing it.

a. CHALLENGE OF THE CIO

No labor concessions made so far have recognized the right of management to eliminate or combine crafts, or to reallot operations among special trades craftsmen. Challenging the traditional organization of building trades, the Congress of Industrial Organizations announced in 1938 that it would organize workmen engaged in dwelling construction along industrial union lines.[4] Its justification was the alleged neglect of the field by the American Federation of Labor and the specialized nature of housebuilding. It appealed to housebuilders on the basis of lower wages (as compared to those generally applicable under AF of L standards), a guarantee against intercraft disputes, and the privilege of using skills interchangeably under certain circumstances. Despite this attractive bait, little progress was made by the CIO in the construction field, and subsequent progress was seriously affected by dissension within the CIO ranks. The larger operative builders to whom the program was principally directed remained aloof. Where some of their operations were organized under the AF of L, as in the mechanical and electrical trades, these builders feared that serious disruption might result from the introduction of a competing labor organization.

In October 1940 the Housing Committee of the CIO issued a statement strongly advocating the use of prefabrication in building defense housing, and has since advocated the use of industrialized methods that cut drastically across craft

2. See Appendix E, Table 32 for further details.

3. Where the workers were previously unorganized costs may have increased.

4. Work on other types of small structures, on building maintenance and on roads was included. In the schism of 1942, the construction workers generally followed the United Mine Workers in breaking away from the CIO.

lines.[5] At the same time, the CIO has had some success in organizing prefabricating plants.

b. CHANGE IN AF OF L ATTITUDE

The AF of L has opposed the intrusion of the CIO into the construction field, and AF of L workers have occasionally refused to work on jobs in connection with which CIO workers were employed. For some time AF of L leaders were hostile to prefabrication on the ground that it would bring technological unemployment, but no official policy has ever been announced. The attitude varied somewhat with the union. Electricians, who are well organized, both for shop and exterior work, appear to have been the least opposed to new construction methods. Plumbers, while generally successful in preventing the prefabrication of their own work, have not hesitated to make installations on houses in which the work of associated craftsmen was reduced or eliminated.

The pressure of war has tended to modify the early attitude. On October 31, 1941, Richard J. Gray, Acting President, Building and Construction Trades Department, AF of L, wrote to Sidney Hillman, Associate Director of OPM:

> In response to your request for information as to whether or not any American Federation of Labor unions have refused to work on prefabricated defense housing projects or on defense housing construction using prefabricated materials, I wish to advise you that in the entire record of defense housing construction there is no single instance of such refusal. This has been verified and fully confirmed by labor relations directors of all agencies of the Federal Government engaged in the construction of defense housing.
>
> In no case has there been a stoppage of work because of the use of prefabrication on a defense housing project employing our membership. Nor has prefabrication itself ever been an issue involving our unions in any labor dispute in defense housing.

AF of L workers have not only installed CIO prefabricated parts, but have been employed in prefabricating factories on shop-installed wiring and shop-fabricated plumbing. Moreover, AF of L unions have accepted prefabrication in on-site shops in large defense housing projects. Recently they have even begun to organize prefabricating plants, thus recognizing the need of modifying their rigid craft union concepts.

These new trade union trends are still the exception rather than the rule, however. In many localities, the old labor restraints remain, and there is no machinery for dealing with them except gradual education, persuasion, pressure, or special inducements. The problem of the reorientation of labor to new in-

5. See Memoranda of the Housing Committee of the CIO to the National Defense Advisory Committee, Office of Production Management, and Office of Emergency Management, October 14, 1940, January 23, 1941, and April 14, 1941, respectively (mimeographed).

dustrial procedures remains on the whole unsettled, and a high degree of statesmanship on both sides will be required to solve this complex situation.

3. The Conservatism of Lenders and Buyers

The strong influence of institutional finance is partly responsible for the laggard advancement of housebuilding techniques. In this industry the financier has a stake in the product, not in the producer. He lends on the durability and marketability of the house, and is interested in the capacity of the product to provide good security throughout the mortgage period. He is rarely concerned with the profitability of the builder's enterprise except as it may affect the outlet for more investments.

Long-Term Investment versus Innovation

The lenders have sometimes helped to maintain high standards of construction. Often they have aided operative builders to expand their organizations. Since, however, their primary interest is often in the preservation of property values, on which the safety of their investments depends, the institutional lenders sometimes oppose innovations. They are usually best satisfied when the new houses on which their mortgages are made are not much unlike older ones both in appearance and price. They certainly do not encourage style changes that hasten the obsolescence of the properties in which they already have a stake and are inclined to fear that rapid cost reductions may depreciate the value of mortgaged properties in the resale market. In the housebuilding industry this ultraconservatism constitutes a great handicap to technological progress because other sources of funds to finance innovations are not readily available.

Somewhat similar considerations influence the public, which is generally more conservative when it buys a house than when it makes other purchases. Since housebuilders have limited financial resources for experimentation, they experiment on the public. There is little doubt that the readiness of experimenters to place on the market unproven, or only partially tested products, has made buyers profoundly skeptical toward marked innovations.

For the average man, buying a house is the major financial transaction of his life. He expects to use it a long time, and hopes to be able to find a purchaser easily when he wants or has to sell. He cannot take chances. Yet, because of his usually limited experience with housing transactions, he has little to depend upon but his own preconceived notions of the kind of house that will prove satisfactory, or the experience of his friends. The buyer also relies on nationally advertised products whose merits he takes for granted. He is satisfied if the bathroom is equipped with a certain manufacturer's fixtures, the kitchen equipment is of a known make, and the pipes, windows, floors, and heater are of certain familiar types.[6]

This situation reflects the lack of integration and leadership in the industry. But the buyer has been so thoroughly indoctrinated with the idea that a house is put together like a child's blocks that he almost instinctively opposes simplification and standardization of the product as a whole. The average consumer accepts novelties, as a rule, only if they have been extensively advertised, as in bathroom, kitchen, and heating equipment. Innovations in housing design and arrangement have been introduced so far chiefly in the highest-priced dwellings where the luxury of experiment can be afforded. Novelties have appeared infrequently in lower-priced houses, and less frequently in owner-occupied dwellings than in rental properties, where the consumer is not required to take the risk of a long-time purchase.

Consequently operative builders, who have been primarily concerned with medium-priced houses for sale, have rarely tried "modern" designs. Prefabricators early learned that a combination of new methods and new architectural forms faced an apparently insurmountable sales resistance, and that radical structural changes were more acceptable when clothed in traditional coverings. This compromise has speeded the commercialization of prefabrication, but it has inhibited the advancement of its techniques. It has, for example, necessitated the use of excess material in walls and partitions in order to retain conventional thicknesses,[7] prevented the application of new structural methods, especially in roof construction, and made necessary the retention of numerous site operations, such as the application of roof shingles and wall siding, which might well be dispensed with. Because of these factors, the maximum savings that might result from a thorough use of prefabrication have not been realized.

4. PROBLEMS IN TECHNOLOGY AND MATERIALS

A steady, well-balanced technical development can hardly be expected in an industry burdened with traditions, torn with conflicting interests and lacking a dominant managerial force. Of all the elements in the industry, materials manufacturers alone are able to finance technical research on a large scale. And they are interested not in the house as a whole, but only in the parts they produce.

6. Reliance on the reputation of the part, rather than the whole product, characterized the automobile buyer before the days of industrial integration. The automobile manufacturer sold his product on the reputation of a Continental motor or Bosch magneto, etc., much as today's operative builder sells on the reputation of the manufactured elements that go into the house.

7. Only one factory producing a plywood-panel system, for instance, has persisted in using the 2½-inch wall, made possible by the stressed-covering principle discussed in Chap. 5.

Consequently research in the integration of parts has been neglected, while improvements in the parts themselves have proceeded at uneven rates.

a. NEW MATERIALS

Housing, of course, has greatly benefited from the research of manufacturers. The rapid development in a few generations of mechanical, electrical, and heating equipment needs no comment. Window glass today is far superior to that even of twenty years ago, and glass block, suitable for many utilitarian and decorative purposes, has been added to the roster of materials. Insulating materials, probably the greatest single recent contribution to dwelling comfort and economy of operation, have been developed almost entirely between the two world wars. Prior to 1914 there were only a few forms of insulation—cork, which was too expensive for ordinary use; sawdust, which has many disadvantages; and quilts of seaweed. Today insulating comes in metallic sheets, in boards of various compositions, and in "bats" or loose fill made of mineral wool and spun glass. The choice is great enough to meet any need, and prices are low enough to permit a greatly expanded use.

The development of wallboard, not only as an insulator but as a base for plaster, as a substitute for plaster, and as a substitute for sheathing and even exterior covering, has been equally rapid. Wallboards are made of wood, vegetable, and mineral fibers, of reprocessed wastepaper, of gypsum, or plywood. New uses have been found for metals—steel, bronze, and aluminum in window sash, aluminum as insulation, steel in light structural shapes. The use of copper has added to the lightness, compactness and durability of the plumbing system. The development of plastics has worked a revolution in paints and glues. Numerous new and substitute building materials are now available—asbestos cement in shingles, siding, and wainscoting; bituminous products in roof covering, floor tile, and waterproofing; and rubber, magnesium, and plastics for uses too numerous to mention. In the postwar period the competition among materials, for which excess capacity will have been created, promises to add new impetus to these developments. Steel, aluminum, magnesium, and plastics are all likely to play new roles in housebuilding.

However, these developments have thus far not been paralleled by progress in either construction techniques or design so as to permit the assembly of a well-co-ordinated house. For example, manufactured plumbing assemblies and manifolds exist, but current restrictions ordinarily prevent their commercialization.[8] Manufacturers of asbestos cement shingles make them, at extra cost, look like wood shingles because housing design lags behind advances in techniques and materials. Structural progress is sometimes hampered by lack of suitable mate-

8. The exigencies of war housing are gradually eliminating some of the old restrictions.

rials. Witness the lag in factory prefabrication before the introduction of resin-bonded plywood; and the problems of handling plywood are still not altogether solved. Further progress in such systems as the horizontal framing method of the John B. Pierce Foundation depends on co-ordinated development of suitable materials.

b. OBSTACLES TO TECHNOLOGICAL PROGRESS

The evolution of building techniques is thwarted by the loose and undirected organization of the industry. Mortgage finance must "be shown" before it supplies the lifeblood of production. Labor opposes new methods of operation and new materials that threaten its precarious earnings. Manufacturers hesitate to change distributive systems to expedite the acceptance of their most advanced products. (This has been notably true in plumbing.) And housebuilders, unable to overcome the localism of the market or escape from dependence on consumer finance, cannot guarantee, either to labor or manufacturers, sufficient production to induce them to relax their rules or restraints.

Capital for house production today is generally "in-and-out capital," advanced job by job, and looking to profits on a given project rather than on continuous production. Technical evolution, however, presents quite different capital requirements. As site operations are reduced, dependence upon the contracting and subcontracting system is lessened, the shop becomes the center of operations, and the need for larger amounts of permanently invested capital becomes apparent. Creation of a favorable investment situation is thus vital to extensive technical development. The technical gains of the war period may be lost unless well-capitalized building enterprises emerge after the war.

5. GOVERNMENT AND INDUSTRIAL EVOLUTION

The housebuilding industry, with its long history of public regulation and its vital relation to the public interest, must expect that in the future government will continue to be widely concerned with its activity. What directions this will take can hardly be foreseen, although we can note instances where modifications in existing governmental attitudes and procedures would help to promote and direct technical progress in the industry. Some of these modifications consist merely in removing obstacles created or intensified by archaic methods of public regulation; others center around the provision by government of facts and guidance which the industry cannot now provide for itself.

a. THE PROBLEM OF LAND

The primary need of the urban housebuilding industry is land cheap enough to make low-priced dwellings possible and located so as to make them marketable.

Furthermore, developments must be of sufficient size to permit good planning and adequate protection from deterioration. From this point of view, existing laws and governmental policies frequently are neither satisfactory to the industry nor compatible with the best public interest.

We have indicated in Chapter 1 how the usable supply of low-priced land has been limited by: (1) the excess zoning of commercial and apartment areas and the high assessments that follow; and (2) the absence of effective control of new subdivision. We have suggested how existing tax methods help to limit the supply of land and indicated the difficulties involved in carrying land for long-range development. Finally, we have noted how the lack of adequate means for reassembling land already broken up into small parcels prevents the rehabilitation of large urban areas that are often ideally located for new housing developments.

These situations are beyond the control of the housebuilding industry, which cannot itself plan the community or always utilize the most suitable locations. It can only follow the line of least resistance. The redirection of housing development along lines more compatible with sound city planning requires realistic zoning on the one hand and stringent regulation of the subdivision and use of new land on the other. Even this would not wholly solve the problem. Reassembling the small and scattered parcels in decadent central urban areas and abandoned subdivisions is not profitable except in rare instances where high returns from the property are possible. Here again public aid is necessary if a solution is to be quickly reached.

Conserving Existing Areas

Between the new outlying subdivisions and the declining urban center there are generally scattered vacant lots and neglected old houses. Such areas do not require rebuilding or drastic rehabilitation. They simply need new interest in their completion and maintenance. Communities could encourage owners of such dwellings to keep them in good repair and could induce vacant property holders to build. To attain these ends, however, the community must provide the environment that the large operator of a new subdivision creates for himself, such as zoning protection, perhaps partial area replanning, provision of playgrounds and parks, and rehabilitation of schools.[9] The costs of these may, in the end, be less than the costs of putting in streets, utilities, and schools in new districts, and subsidizing highways and transportation facilities for outlying areas, sometimes beyond the municipality's taxing jurisdiction.

9. As an example of this type of approach see *Waverly—A Study in Neighborhood Conservation*, Federal Home Loan Bank Board, 1940; see also Chap. 1, footnote 47, p. 36.

There are indications that the public has become increasingly aware that the economic soundness of the entire community depends upon more orderly methods of land development and redevelopment. Rezoning proceeds slowly but some progress is being made. The control of subdivisions beyond existing urban limits has been authorized in some places. The passage of laws in New York, Illinois, Michigan and Kentucky to facilitate the reassembly and rebuilding of blighted land is a step forward.[10] Municipally owned land reserves as a bulwark against unneeded expansion have even been discussed, though nowhere yet created.

Effect of Assessment and Tax Policies

Difficulties in foreclosing tax liens and giving clear title to property obtained on tax sales keep quantities of land off the market. This problem is acute in abandoned subdivisions which otherwise might often be rather easily utilized, and is even more serious in blighted areas. Aside from the scattered and relatively unimportant attempts to solve the problem mentioned in Chapter 1, no significant modifications of municipal policy have occurred.

But even in new areas, current methods of assessment and taxation add to the difficulties of the builder who seeks to develop a co-ordinated neighborhood. As soon as a plot is recorded the assessment tends to shift from a rural to an urban base, irrespective of the degree of improvement. Under such circumstances the builder is forced either to risk pushing his development faster than conservative estimates of absorption would warrant, or else restrict its size to what is likely to be immediately sold—in either event to the disadvantage of sound community planning. In the past, some of the finest housing enterprises in the country have been ruined by the cost of carrying reserve land. Yet a reserve is essential not only to an orderly, long-range neighborhood plan, but to the continuity of building operations.

b. THE PROBLEM OF BUILDING CODES

The preparation of a satisfactory building code presents a threefold problem. First, there is the difficulty of reconciling engineering and social ideals with economic realities. How "firesafe" can we afford to make our dwellings? How elaborate can we make our equipment requirements and still build low-priced houses? No matter how correct they may be technically, codes that raise costs to a point where only a few can pay for new housing defeat the objectives of proper public regulation. They simply result in the retention of quantities of substandard and old housing.

10. See Chap. 10, p. 275, for a further discussion of these laws.

The second code problem is that of wording the requirements for floors, walls, structural members, etc., so as not to exclude sound new building methods and materials. This can be solved effectively only by establishing performance requirements rather than specifications for the parts of a building—thus, not the thickness and materials of a wall, but the wind load and live load it must provide for, the duration of fire it must resist, and so on. The performance basis, with the flexible and intelligent administration and the testing facilities that it implies, obviously puts a greater burden on the code authority than does the specification basis commonly used.

The third problem consists in providing for special local circumstances without hampering the operation of industry on a wider basis. Obviously California must provide special bracing for earthquakes, Florida for hurricanes, and northern cities for heavy snow loads. Most of the justifiable local differences are limited, however, to a few important matters. Existing variations in requirements for steel and lumber stresses, for thickness of walls, and sizes and weight of pipe are not warranted by any real distinction among localities.

These problems cannot be solved in the absence of adequate facilities for research in proper construction standards and for their adoption on a reasonably uniform basis. The federal government entered this field in 1921 with the establishment of a Building Code Committee of the Department of Commerce whose work was centered in the National Bureau of Standards. The Committee initiated a program, including a series of supporting tests, which sought to develop more rational code recommendations.[11] Several preliminary reports were published, devoted especially to the construction of small houses. Economy measures curtailed this work in 1934.[12] Tests were left uncompleted; and the task of drawing up recommendations for code sections was taken up by the Building Code Correlating Committee of the American Standards Association. Under this procedure work has progressed slowly with little direct benefit to the housing industry up to the present time.

The Work of the Bureau of Standards

At the instance of the federal housing agencies, acting through the Central Housing Committee, the Bureau of Standards in 1936 renewed its testing of

11. Some work on building codes had been started earlier. The Committee was named as a result of a report by the Senate Committee on Reconstruction and Production, issued in 1921. It is interesting to note that the impetus for this work came from the problems of a postwar economy.

12. See Bibliography. When the research was abandoned the Committee was consolidating its reports in the form of a model code. It has been estimated that the Committee's recommendations were wholly or partly utilized in at least 350 municipal codes, and helped to shape the Pacific Coast Building Officials' Model Code and the Model Code of the Board of Fire Underwriters (see Chap. 4, pp. 125, 127). Source: National Bureau of Standards.

building materials and methods. Code problems again were taken up, and as a result a new plumbing manual was issued in November 1940.[13] Among other things the manual recommended diminution of pipe sizes and simplification of roughing-in design, resulting in an appreciable reduction in plumbing installation costs.[14] This manual with some modification provided the basis for the *Emergency Plumbing Standards for Defense Housing* issued by the Division of Defense Housing Coordination, which became mandatory for all public projects and for private builders seeking priority ratings.

Aside from the use of wartime powers, no regular means for the adoption of the Bureau of Standards' recommendations and co-ordination of building codes have been devised. Several efforts, however, have been made by other agencies. One of the most successful was the Pacific Coast Building Officials' Conference, organized in 1922. The Conference has helped communities to adapt its model code to local needs. In June 1941, the Conference Code was being used with modifications in 291 cities in twenty-nine states. About one hundred cities have adopted the code prepared by the New England Building Officials' Conference.

There are good reasons for increased federal activity in this field. The central position of the federal government makes it an ideal clearinghouse for the best current thought and practice. The government's laboratories and planning bodies provide ideal facilities for making tests and developing standards. The prestige of the federal government should be helpful in gaining acceptance of the research findings. Adoption of more uniform building requirements might be further aided by the government's ability to dispense or withhold benefits, after the practice of the Public Roads Administration, or through the use of such agencies as the Commission on Interstate Cooperation of the Council of State Governments.[15]

13. *Plumbing Manual,* Building Materials and Structures Report BMS66, National Bureau of Standards, 1940, Report of Subcommittee on Plumbing, Central Housing Committee on Research, Design and Construction.

14. See "Plumbing Progress," *Architectural Forum,* February 1941, p. 4, where it is estimated that the savings would average around $125 in a one-bathroom house. It must be recognized that savings are exceedingly difficult to estimate. The National Bureau of Standards would not hazard a guess, and warns also that not all building-code revision can be expected to reduce costs, the reverse in many cases being unavoidable. The Federal Housing Administration has estimated that the code would save about 8 to 10 per cent of the weight of critical materials in the plumbing installation.

15. For the methods used by the Commissions, see *The Book of the States,* 1939–40, Vol. III, The Council of State Governments, Chicago.

The defense housing co-ordinator endeavored to secure the adoption of wartime code modifications by states and localities, using the co-operation and assistance of the American Municipal Association, National Institute of Municipal Law Officers, International City Managers' Association, American Public Works Association, American Society of Planning Officials, National Association of Housing Officials, and United States Conference of Mayors. Supplementing voluntary co-operation, priorities for housing in defense areas were subsequently issued only on a basis that made compliance with the wartime code mandatory if materials were to be available.

C. ELIMINATION OF INTRA-INDUSTRY RESTRAINTS

In the task of recreating the housebuilding industry, government has another important responsibility—that of aiding in the removal of the trade restraints and combinations among subcontractors, labor unions, dealers, and manufacturers. The antimonopoly drive initiated by the Department of Justice in 1938, revealed serious shortcomings in the existing laws, while the extreme localism of the industry puts many cases beyond the reach of the federal government. Indeed, a local government's approval of building code provisions designed to maintain local monopolies constitutes a conflict with federal policy directed at the removal of such restraints.

Perhaps the most serious difficulties, however, have arisen in the cases involving labor. The Department of Justice has attempted to formulate a new public policy on union activity, summarized in the following statement to the Temporary National Economic Committee:[16]

> The United States has decided that it wants high wages, short hours, and good working conditions, and that it can obtain these results by encouraging collective bargaining and arming those who represent labor in the bargain with the right to use strikes and boycotts. It has not decided that it wants price fixing, the driving out of independent enterprise, the stoppage of improvement in technology, the private imposition of work relief programs upon business enterprise, or the conversion of unions into dictator-ridden bodies closed to the great mass of workers who are not yet members. Self-restraint by labor groups is not enough to prevent such developments. The problem of public policy is to maintain the legal immunities of the collective bargaining process without granting organized labor the privilege of collective action for the undesired ends. Labor's freedom to use coercive devices, if unchecked, is a freedom to serve any purpose whatsoever. For the most part, the ends of monopoly and unreasonable restraint of trade to which these devices may be made to contribute are contrary to no laws but the anti-trust laws. The alternatives are to apply these laws to labor whenever labor acts outside its legitimate sphere or else to devise new legislation affording the public an equivalent safeguard.

To this the American Federation of Labor replied that the alleged restraints in the building trades were merely legitimate means of protecting not only the wage scale but the very livelihood of the workers.[17]

These are the problems of industrial evaluation. "They are not," as Brandeis said in the *Duplex* dissent, "for judges to determine and certainly not for prosecutors to decide." They are properly the subject for negotiation and collective bargaining where both sides have the opportunity to present the facts and work out policies to mitigate

16. *Hearings Before the TNEC,* Supplemental Data Submitted by Corwin D. Edwards to the TNEC, Pt. 31–A, p. 18194.

17. *Ibid.,* pp. 18175–18178, 18186 *et seq.,* for a detailed account of the restraints charged and a detailed reply.

whatever harm may exist in industrial change. . . . We can ask with Henry Epstein, Solicitor General of New York: "Is it the purpose of the law or the courts to determine from what method best results will accrue to society? Is this not the very field of economic combat into which with the absence of violence, deceit or misrepresentation, the courts should not tread without legislative or constitutional mandate?" And again: "Is this within the omniscience of an administrative official? Will prosecutor now supplant the courts and become a new legislative authority? Having had judicial legislation, are we now to have administrative legislation?" . . . Labor's struggle to supply greater spread of employment, the struggle which, in the classic dictum of the New York Court of Appeals, barring "violence, deceit or misrepresentation," the courts must leave to the field of economic conflict, has now been outlawed. . . . Labor clearly recognizes that the antitrust laws are directly aimed at conspiracies to raise or fix prices, and that individuals found to be so conspiring are guilty of violating these laws. It is a wholly different matter, however, to charge that *labor unions acting as unions in the pursuit of their basic purpose of collective bargaining for mutual aid and protection* are engaged in such conspiracies. . . . "The antitrust laws should not be used as an instrument to police strikes or adjudicate labor controversies." [18]

The Supreme Court of the United States has refused to uphold the views of the Department of Justice on union activity. In the words of Mr. Justice Frankfurter: [19]

So long as a union acts in its self-interest and does not combine with non-labor groups, the licit and the illicit . . . are not to be distinguished by any judgment regarding the wisdom or unwisdom, the rightness or wrongness, the selfishness or unselfishness of the end of which the particular union activities are the means.

This would seem to grant a labor union immunity from the antitrust laws where it can clearly show that it is acting on its own behalf and in its own interest. If this is true it appears that if a new public policy with respect to labor is to be established, it will have to be through some other medium than the antitrust laws.

The problem of intra-industry restraints is not easily solved. Some restraints are beyond the reach of legal attack by the federal government under existing statutes. Others must be attacked at so many points and so continuously as to make it extremely difficult, if not impossible, to enforce a national policy. Independent state action has been desultory. After each attack by the courts the practices reappear in a pattern that has varied little in half a century.

The situation gives rise to two serious questions: Can these restraints be successfully removed while the industry remains in its present form? If not, can the industry be so modified as to make their ultimate removal possible? The future development of housebuilding depends upon the answers to these questions.

18. *Ibid.*, pp. 18182–18183.
19. *William L. Hutcheson, et al.*, 312 U.S. 219.

d. GOVERNMENT AID TO TECHNICAL AND MARKET RESEARCH

An outstanding weakness of the housebuilding industry is its inability to advance its techniques concurrently on many fronts. Materials manufacturers have spent large sums in developing their own products; as a result, there is a steady increase in the variety as well as constant improvement in the quality of building materials. The components of the industry, however, are too diffuse and too limited in their interests to undertake jointly the kind of industrial research the situation requires, nor can private-research organizations be expected to solve the problem, even though many of them such as Purdue University, the Bemis Foundation and the John B. Pierce Foundation, are making important contributions.

In certain industries vital to the public welfare which have been unable to carry on essential research the federal government has stepped into the breach. The most outstanding example is agriculture. During 1938 and 1939 the Department of Agriculture received more than $20 million for research activities. In commercial aviation, too, the government has assumed responsibility for a huge program of research, supplementing that of airplane manufacturers. Federal expenditures for new laboratory facilities in aeronautics in 1939 and 1940 amounted to $18.4 million. By contrast the total amount allocated by the federal government to technical housing research during the six-year period, 1935-1940, was only $852,000.

Even this small research program has suggested the important results that might follow from greater attention to the industry's needs.[20] The major example of technical housing research initiated by the government—the development of the stressed-covering principle by the Forest Products Laboratory—has become a mainspring of progress in prefabrication. The work of the National Bureau of Standards in simplifying materials standards has been the principal force for industrial co-ordination. The Bureau's tests of new structural methods have been not only the chief means by which prefabricators could learn the real properties of their systems of construction, but a way of obtaining public confidence in them.

Until the industry is able to support a program of continuous research, such as characterizes the automobile industry, for example, government might carry a large part of the burden.[21] The interest of the federal government in housing is obvious, not only from the point of view of the general welfare, but as a large-scale buyer of dwellings.

20. See Chap. 4, pp. 122-123.

21. For further discussion of government-sponsored research, see Stone and Denton, *op. cit.*, pp. 141–148.

Supplementing Technical With Market Information

Without thorough market information it is impossible to adapt production techniques to demand. Yet such knowledge is woefully lacking in the housebuilding industry. In 1935, the Division of Economics and Statistics of the Federal Housing Administration listed a series of data on real-estate and housing activity.[22] The subjects covered were: rents, occupancy and vacancy, building operating expenses, real-estate values, real-estate transfers, subdividing activity, new construction, construction costs, mortgages, foreclosures, real-estate taxes and delinquencies, population data (growth, shifts, marriages, etc.). The report acknowledged that on none of these was satisfactory information available. Seven years later, in spite of the expansion of the research facilities of the housing agencies and the broadening interest of the Bureau of Labor Statistics, the same conclusion was inescapable. The war has strikingly revealed the importance of data. The difficulties of determining the amount, type, and location of war housing and the problems of rent and price control have all been greatly complicated by the absence of accurate indexes of the condition and needs of the housing market.

Not only is there inadequate basic quantitative data, but the industry has very little information about the way people live at different economic and social levels—the number of rooms they want; how they use their rooms; the size of rooms; the amount and kind of storage space, basements, garages, dining room and laundry space required. These and other questions have a direct bearing on housing design, and on the extent to which standardization may be carried or production projected in advance of sale.

The lack of market information is a serious impediment to the development of large-scale production. It accounts, in part, for the caution with which even the most experienced builders proceed and for their reluctance to change models that have been found to be acceptable. It forces unsuitable housing upon many people and accounts in large measure for the maladjustment of the housing supply to family needs. Until adequate data are compiled our conceptions of housing standards must continue to be based on opinions rather than supportable facts.

In many industries large and well-organized establishments spend huge sums in studying consumer preferences.[23] Housebuilding organizations do not have much money for consumer research, yet without such knowledge they cannot judge their markets in advance, either quantitatively or qualitatively. Even the largest operative builders, except in a few unusually active areas, cautiously edge their way into the market and begin construction only after they have a number

22. *Report of the Committee on Current Real Estate Data,* Division of Economics and Statistics, FHA, May 25, 1935 (mimeographed).

23. General Motors before the war spent around $300,000 a year on consumer research alone. *Fortune,* March 1939, p. 138.

of orders on hand. In short, building in advance of sale and for unknown buyers is still not characteristic of the bulk of the housebuilding industry.

In rental housing, where the prospective occupant is necessarily unknown before production starts, caution toward the market also prevails. The boldness of rental enterprise characteristic of the unfounded market assumptions of the late twenties has not reappeared. And it may well be that inadequate market data, under which that boom proceeded, accounts in part for its subsequent collapse and contributes to present caution. Moreover, the size of the average rental project during the thirties has been generally small so that the speculative element is kept at a minimum.[24]

6. ADAPTING PRODUCTION TO THE MARKET

Producers, no matter how efficient, must always keep a weather eye on the market—or, in other words, on the prospect of disposing profitably of their products. Because of inadequate consumer data building techniques have been developed and house production has been carried on with insufficient attention to the peculiarities of the market.

Housing offers not one but several fairly distinct markets. The farm market cannot be satisfied in the same way as the metropolitan market; the luxury buyer is distinct from the mass market; and there is a demand for alterations and repairs separate from the demand for new construction.

The opportunities offered by any of these markets, of course, vary greatly over periods of time. The decade of the thirties was, on the whole, not a period in which any spectacular expansion of housebuilding was possible. The luxury market, particularly in the rental field, was burdened by surpluses carried over from the previous boom era. Low incomes and savings and archaic and costly building techniques kept the great bulk of city dwellers out of the market for new houses. It was only toward the end of the decade that agricultural recovery and the extension of electrical facilities in rural areas began to make it possible to develop the latent demand for farmhouse improvement.

The opportunities of the postwar period may be much better. The stoppage of construction during the war in the face of increased incomes and savings should add greatly to the backlog of demand. At the same time, technological advances and the development of new materials arising from the war should put the industry in a better position to supply postwar demands, particularly in small towns, on farms and among low-income urban families.

24. The production of small rental projects has predominated over large orders even where FHA financing was used (*Seventh Annual Report*, 1940, FHA, p. 88).

a. REQUIREMENTS OF THE CUSTOM MARKET

The acceleration of the development of mechanized methods during the war, and the probability of still further departures from traditional techniques in large-scale housing enterprise does not mean that the days of the custom builder are over. Made-to-order work will always be required to a great extent by the higher-income groups. With the release of war restrictions, the pent-up demands of these groups are likely to be the first and one of the most important stimuli to postwar building. Moreover, no transition in production methods can be so rapid or extensive that traditional methods can immediately be displaced for more modern types of construction.

Even where traditional building patterns prevail, some advantage may be taken of the new technical and organizational trends. Co-ordinated sizes and dimensions in materials could be used without hampering individualistic expression. Standardized parts can be used with widely varied arrangements and appearance. Even such large standardized units as the four-foot wall section can be used in a great variety of special designs.[25] Nor must we assume that the custom market is inevitably tied up with the traditional housebuilding organizations. The success of operative builders and even prefabricators in the custom field indicates that special market demands are not incompatible with industrial modifications.

Repair and Alteration Work

In the postwar period, repair and alteration work should be an important source of business for the custom builder—with 29 per cent of urban houses alone either in need of major repairs or lacking private baths and 6 per cent still without gas or electricity. Deferred maintenance and increased income should greatly stimulate demand at the close of the war.

Though ordinarily carried on by establishments primarily engaged in new construction, repair and alteration work is often unprofitable except in exceedingly slack times, or in cases of major alterations. For the individual house or apartment owner, the ordinary methods of repairs and alterations are equally unsatisfactory. Except for multifamily structures which can afford to keep their own maintenance crews, a repair or minor alteration usually requires special trade contractors, and this frequently means a delay because the contractor often tries to fit the work into idle time.

25. The sales folder of one prefabricator shows nine basic plans, any one of which might have eight variations. Another does not even issue any general sales brochures, on the theory that it is providing materials and a system of construction rather than houses. Other prefabricators make similar claims.

There is need for specialized service organizations, equipped to investigate the maintenance demands of dwellings and handle repair, maintenance, or alteration jobs promptly. Such organizations might also provide regular inspection and service. The magnitude of this work is often obscured by the small dollar volume of the separate items. Efficiently organized and administered, the specialized maintenance establishment should be able to operate profitably in almost any medium-sized or large community.

b. SATISFYING THE URBAN MASS MARKET

Important as the made-to-order market for both new construction and alterations is likely to be, the great possibilities of industrial expansion are in those areas where full advantage can be taken of standardized mass production. No matter what the distribution of incomes may be in the postwar period, the so-called mass market will come from the lower three quarters of the nonfarm population. The more equable distribution of income that may well prevail at the end of the war will somewhat increase the rent-paying capacity of the lower three quarters; but these families (plus the increase since 1940) will provide the largest potential market for new houses. This mass market varies in nature according to the size and character of the community.

The greatest progress in industrial organization and price reduction has been made in the concentrated metropolitan market. Here the operative builder has flourished. He could systematize operations, introduce efficient processes, extend standardization, use shop or field prefabrication, and combine the functions of land development and frequently subcontracting and materials supply with that of house erection.

Up to the present time, no other method of wholly private operation has gone further toward satisfying the mass demand for housing, particularly for individual ownership.[26] But the operative builder is best suited to the large community. He requires large tracts of land, capable of fairly rapid development. He must have considerable prospective demand and continuity of operations. In the smaller communities or with a slackening of demand, the effectiveness of operative builder organizations diminishes.

The Scattered Mass Market

Only the smaller part of the mass market, however, permits such concentrated operations. Almost 60 per cent of the nonfarm families live in communities of 25,000 population or less, and these places, unless they are part of a metropolitan area, can hardly offer much opportunity for large-scale site operations. More-

26. Included, of course, is the factory prefabricator with operative builder outlets. See Chap. 5, pp. 146-148.

over, in even the largest cities the demand for houses on scattered vacant lots—most of them in low-priced areas—cannot be met practicably by operative builder methods. This demand has fallen to a large group of part-time builders who erect only a few houses annually and who are often guilty of bad design and shoddy construction.

The factory prefabricator offers a potentially effective means of satisfying this demand. He may easily cover a market area with a radius of 300 to 500 miles, including many small communities, none of which could support a large operative builder. The prefabricator enjoys all of the advantages of standardization and quantity buying of the more progressive operative builders. Various means can be developed for erecting prefabricated houses—the traveling erection crew, the local dealer or agent, or subsidiary erection organizations.

The Rental Market

In 1940 over 56 per cent of all occupied dwellings were rented, a proportion that had increased from around 52 per cent in 1930. In cities the shift was from 56 per cent in 1930 to over 62 per cent rented in 1940. Yet, during the decade, comparatively little effort was made to provide new accommodations for this increasing market. In the unsettled period following the war's end, the rental demand will probably continue to be strong and should offer excellent opportunities to producers.

The rental market readily accepts standardization, and, except in the relatively few cities where high buildings are needed, the technical problems presented by rental housing do not differ greatly from those of houses for sale. In fact, as previously pointed out,[27] rental housing, because of savings possible in land planning, may be produced more economically than houses for individual ownership.

The type of builder-manager organization associated with Federal Housing Administration rental financing seems well adapted, from a production standpoint, to serve large portions of the rental market. The special problems here do not involve production so much as finance and investment—problems that will be discussed in Part II of this survey.

C. SERVING THE RURAL MARKET

Producing houses for farms and small isolated communities presents special problems.[28] The special skills required to build good houses under traditional methods are rarely found in rural areas. Nor is the purchasing power necessary

27. See Chap. 1, p. 27.
28. The finance and distribution of dwellings for the rural market will be discussed in Pt. II.

to pay for such elaborately assembled structures readily available. The newer methods of production have neglected the rural field. The operative builder obviously cannot function here. The prefabricator's product is still too expensive and its assembly methods still too complicated for sale and erection in widely dispersed locations.

The primary requirement in producing for the rural market is a drastic reduction in cash outlay of the purchaser. This may sometimes be accomplished by using the labor of the purchaser or of groups of buyers, and the materials available in the locality, preferably on the property. This method, widely used for rural housing in the past, is less suitable today because local materials are less readily available and the average farmer is less skillful in construction.

The methods developed by the Farm Security Administration in its rural housing program suggest an approach to the problem.[29] Portable sawmills, set up temporarily in a convenient central location, combined with simple forms of panel jigs, have been used to precut and preassemble wall, floor, and roof sections. These, carried to the site, were erected with a minimum of labor. The labor of the occupants was used for all but supervision and the most skilled of the operations. Costs, including allowances for labor, have been as low as $400 a room for houses with bathrooms, and $250 a room for houses without bathrooms.

The difficulty in expanding such methods is the absence of a central organizing, directing, and purchasing agency that might perform the functions of the FSA. The extension of governmental activity in this field might help, though private enterprise need not be kept out of this market. A low-priced and simple system of prefabricated panel construction, including essential plumbing, could be devised which would permit the use of farm labor for site erection with a minimum of supervision.

While the number of new farmhouses needed has been estimated at well over a million,[30] probably the most important feature of the rural market is the potential demand for repair and modernization. In 1940, over 90 per cent of 7.6 million farm dwellings were either in need of major repair or had no private bath, and nearly 70 per cent lacked gas or electricity. The trend toward larger farms has produced a surplus of farm dwellings in many areas. Where this has occurred, there is a need not so much for new dwellings, as for the renovation of the best existing structures. The spread of rural electrification has made possible the introduction of modern lighting, water supply and sanitary facilities and other improvements which formerly were found only on the most opulent farms.

29. *Small Houses,* Farm Security Administration, 1939.

30. U.S. Department of Agriculture, Interbureau Coordinating Committee on Post-Defense Programs, "The Need for Rural Housing" (mimeographed), October 20, 1941, p. 12.

The increased farm income resulting from the war should create a demand for considerable repair work even where sizable new construction is not called for.

7. SUMMARY

In spite of many forward-looking trends, the housebuilding industry is still held back by numerous deficiencies in organization and techniques. The leadership necessary to create a well-integrated industry has not yet emerged. Technical progress is held back by land problems and by the conservative attitudes of labor, financiers and the public. Public regulation often continues to enshrine traditional practices to the detriment of more advanced building methods; and trade restraints, beyond effective legal control, still flourish.

The war has broken down much of the resistance to change, temporarily, at least. Carried into the postwar period, these gains, together with pressure to use excess manufacturing capacity, should result in substantial expansion of housebuilding. And the demand for housing in the postwar years promises to be so large and varied that all types of producers will be needed.

The housing question cannot, however, be solved merely by a better organization of production. Serious financing and distribution problems must also be solved if the industry is to attain its full development. Our survey must proceed, therefore, to the marketing of houses.

PART II

THE MARKETING OF HOUSING

Chapter 7

THE BEHAVIOR OF THE HOUSING MARKET

THE FUNCTION OF THE housing market as with other markets is to establish the price at which buyers and sellers can be brought together. It exists to balance supply with the effective demand at any given price level. While in many industries price controls market activity and a lowering of price stimulates demand, in housing, price changes do not always have this effect.

Housing has not one but several markets, as determined by type of house, tenure and location. Moreover, houses are not uniform products but as diverse as a local, handicraft production system can make them. Price changes in a local market may have no general influence, since the product cannot be used elsewhere. Again, reductions in the price of upper-class houses—if production is largely limited to them, as it frequently is—may have only minor repercussions on the general price structure of housing and little or no influence in increasing effective demand and production.

In housing, as in other durable goods, the concept of price is complex. Since most houses are bought on credit, the terms at which money can be borrowed are an important aspect of the price. The amounts of the down payment and of the monthly payments for interest and amortization are likely to be even more important to the house buyer than the total price.

Since a very large proportion of houses are rented rather than bought, price to the majority of families means rent rather than purchase price. Even home buyers usually consider monthly principal and interest payments, taxes and maintenance costs as a rental equivalent; and the amount of home buying will tend to be governed by the relation between rents and the rental equivalent under a time purchase plan. Since investors in rental property also depend on mortgage credit, the terms at which loans are available play as important a role in the rental as in the home-purchase price.

The complex price situation and other peculiarities of the housing market—such as the ability of consumers to postpone purchases and the inability of producers to gauge future demand—make adjustments of supply to demand slow and difficult and result in violent fluctuations in building activity. Every part of the industry is affected by these movements. Investors and lenders are subjected to unanticipated losses, and are always uncertain about the value of their investments. Consumers are uncertain about the extent to which their needs can be met. Producers cannot plan effectively for advance production, and, in fact, may be forced rapidly to liquidate not only their products but their very organizations.

1. SOME CRUCIAL FACTORS IN THE HOUSING MARKET

Purchasers of shelter are either owner-occupants or renters. Physically the house presents the same appearance to both, but it has a different economic impact on them. To the ordinary buyer a house represents a large commitment. It involves a down payment which may equal all his savings. It means borrowing up to twice and perhaps three or more times his annual income. It usually requires that he obligate himself to make fixed monthly payments until the debt is paid, which may take as much as twenty-five years. The renter, on the other hand, commits himself only for the duration of his lease. He pays for shelter out of current income, neither borrowing nor utilizing his savings. The buyer puts his savings into his house and may obtain a measure of security in his declining years. The renter can relinquish his present quarters if his income declines or he can move to another locality if opportunity beckons, without risking his savings.

Because of the large commitment involved, the buyer considers the possibility of resale. He tries to protect his savings should he be forced to sell his house, whether it be because of loss of income, the necessity of moving to another locality or any other reason. A successful buying transaction, therefore, requires expert knowledge about the local housing market. The renter is faced with no such problem. If he does not like the house in which he is living, he can in a short time simply move out without loss to himself.

Fortunately for the buyer, the purchase of a house is almost always deferable. He can usually continue living in the house he occupies or rent another one. He can still choose between buying and renting. Whether he postpones his purchase depends largely on his expectation of his future prospects. He thinks twice before embarking on such a large commitment and frequently refrains from buying until he has assurance of income stability.

a. THE VARIABILITY OF DEMAND

Since the need for some kind of shelter is always present, the demand for housing in its broadest terms, as for other basic necessities, remains fairly constant—but with a difference. Changes in price and purchasing power lead to changes in doubling up and vacancies, thereby affecting the number of houses used and their quality. The standard of housing that families will accept is remarkably flexible. When housing prices rise, or depression forces incomes down, people cling to their housing standards as long as possible, then double up with other families, or accept fewer rooms and conveniences and even dilapidated structures. On the other hand, when the price of housing declines or incomes improve and the more favorable price-income ratio is expected to continue, families seek better and more commodious dwellings and absorb vacancies.

Demand at Different Price Levels

The demand for low-priced shelter is more affected by price changes than is the demand for high-priced shelter. So long as incomes remain fairly constant, considerable changes in the price of housing may occur before the upper-income demand is seriously affected. The relative sum available for housing among families with incomes of $10,000 or more is usually much greater than among families with $1,500 or less. Moreover, the income distribution is such that in the lower-income groups there are more families at the margin ready to enter or leave the market when prices change.

Among lower-income groups the maximum amount available for shelter is relatively fixed. Low-income demand is consequently more sensitive to small price changes, and the market readily expands or contracts with fairly small reductions or increases in price. This situation is aggravated by the low quality of housing generally available for this group and the relatively large number of families affected.

Demand in Depression and Prosperity

During a depression drastic changes occur in the demand for housing. Many families dispossessed through foreclosure seek rental quarters. Others, once in the $5,000 and over income group, forced to move into cheaper quarters, prefer to rent because they do not want to buy a house below their accustomed standard. The depletion of savings reduces the number of families who can make the requisite down payment on the purchase of a house. The market for owner-occupied houses may become demoralized. Prices may decline and no buyers appear. Surpluses may remain for a considerable time, almost irrespective of price. At the same time the demand for rental housing increases, particularly for the lower-priced units where the greatest increase in doubling up occurs. In short, the depression market is primarily a rental market.

The demand for houses for sale responds to price changes in quite a different manner in prosperity than in depression. In prosperous times ownership increases. Larger incomes and accumulated savings induce some renters to buy homes. An increasingly large number of marginal buyers also enter the market as prices, credit terms or other recurring costs become favorable. On the other hand, the demand for rental housing may decline, although it tends to hold up better through all phases of the business cycle than the demand for houses for sale.

At the turning points of the cycle, demand acts somewhat differently than in its prosperity and depression stages. In general, families hesitate for a while to make prospective changes in their existing housing conditions at the turning points. After the downward phase of the cycle is well under way, however, declines in family income may force quick changes to inferior housing. During the upward phase, increased incomes, coupled with infectious optimism and social pressures, are ready inducements to better and more expensive housing; but at the same time, lack of savings postpones purchases and it takes time for confidence to be restored. At the downturn, expectations of future income begin to become shaky, buyers become wary of mortgage commitments, and a wait-and-see attitude prevails.

Another important aspect of demand is its varying stability at different income levels. Despite the changing patterns of family income in prosperity and depression, there is at all times a range of income within which the number of families is relatively stable. In thirty-three cities studied, this range (as shown in Figure 22) was between $950 and $1,950. During the depression the number of families with incomes above $1,950 declined sharply, while those below $950 increased. As prosperity returned, the high-income group increased, the lowest-income group declined and the group between remained stable.

This middle group is, of course, not always composed of the same families, but recruits from below in good times and from above in a depression. Thus a tabulation of Financial Survey data for six large cities shows that of 28,000 families with incomes of $1,000-$2,000 in 1929 less than 12,000, or about 44 per cent, remained in that group in 1933.[1] The loss, however, was made up by families brought down from former incomes of more than $2,000.

Obviously the steadiest demand for housing will be found in the group having the most constant number of families. But the great shift of individual families within this group indicates that, on the whole, its demand for rental housing is apt to be better sustained than for homes for sale.

b. THE STABILITY OF SUPPLY

Only a portion of the houses standing appear on the market in any one year. Figure 29 shows that in one city annual sales between 1917 and 1938 average 9 per cent of the existing stock, with a range from 4 to 16 per cent (data for other cities and for rental transactions are not available). Under certain circumstances,

1. The six cities were selected from thirty-three for which data are available. None showed much deviation from the average.

any house may appear for sale or rent. The whole existing stock of houses plus newly constructed ones constitute the potential market supply.

Fixed Location of the Supply

The housing market is *not* like the grain market, for example, which operates through central exchanges on an international scale. Nor is it like the market for standardized consumers' goods, the producers of which can seek outlets in

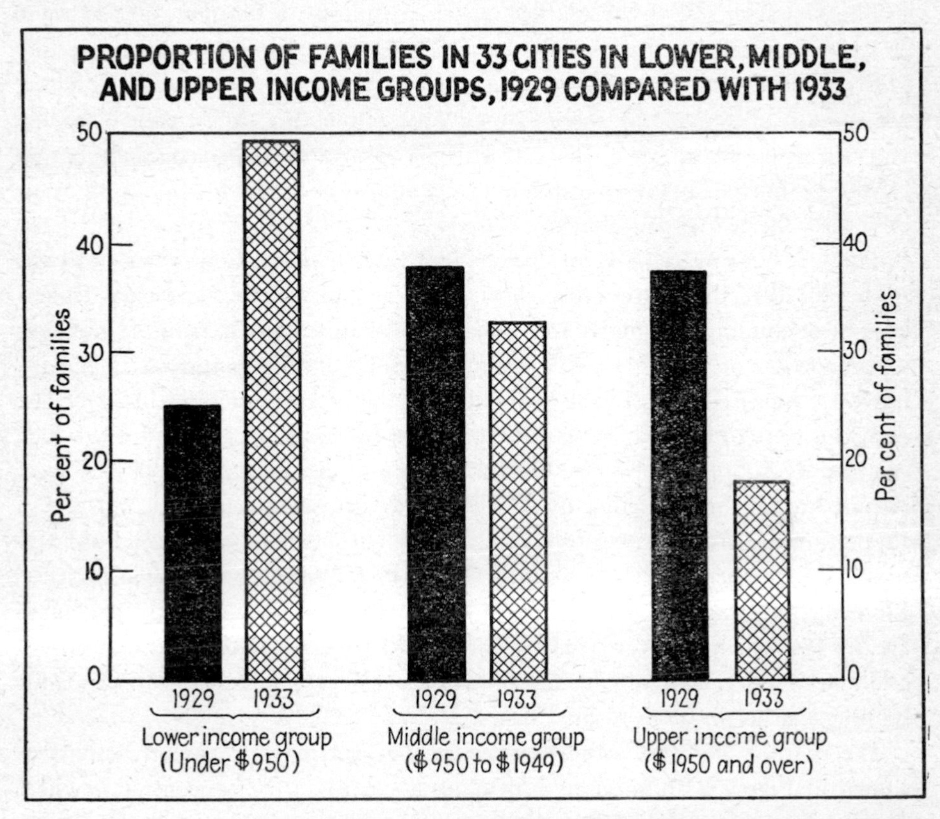

FIGURE 22. In good times and bad the number of families in the middle income group is relatively stable, although the composition varies with changes in family income. (*Source:* Appendix Table 33.)

numerous communities, concentrating their distribution in one place or another to meet demand. The housing market is rarely regional, and often not even city-wide. Dwellings must be accessible to their occupants' place of employment, and the boundaries of the market area are largely determined by traveling time between home and work. This is particularly true of the market for low-priced dwellings, in which cheap and quick public transportation, and proximity to schools, shopping centers and municipal services are major factors.

Although the improved transportation of the last two decades has widened market areas, their essentially local nature has not been modified. There is often considerable overlapping between markets—one merging into another with no clear demarcation between them. A new highway or bus line, the extension of a suburban railway, may enlarge the market area but at best the prospective buyer must confine himself to a restricted locality and the seller must have a house located there.

This characteristic of the market creates a rigidity in the flow of goods (in this case, houses plus their lots) such as is found in no other industry dealing with a consumer product. It retards the adjustments of supply to demand that are more readily made in goods having greater mobility. It increases the difficulty in disposing of surpluses and in overcoming shortages. Because houses cannot be moved, many may remain vacant in one locality while a shortage exists elsewhere.

The war housing crisis is an exaggerated case in point. It was not until the middle of 1942 that commodity shortages began to develop, and then largely because of absolute shortage of materials rather than from defects in the methods of production or distribution. The shortage of housing in industrial centers, however, appeared almost at the very start of the defense program in 1940. The demands were often far beyond the capacity of the local housing industry which customarily supplied the area. Outside building and financial resources were required to fill the gap. Since many investors and lenders were reluctant to risk supporting the erection of future indisposable surpluses, governmental aid was required to finance outright or assume the risk involved in building war housing. However, while a few communities had large shortages, others (usually in areas from which the war workers had come) had plenty of vacant dwellings and idle capacity. The same conditions, in lesser degree, are characteristic of the housing market in more normal times.

The marked geographical variation in the rate of construction activity is shown in Figure 23. Housebuilding naturally tends to be concentrated where there is a potential demand and favorable building and financial conditions. Thus, in the last decade, large operative builders have generally been prominent in populous centers. Prefabricators did their best business (prior to the war) where they encountered little resistance to new building techniques. Generally builders and lenders preferred metropolitan areas and neglected the small isolated communities. During the upward movement of the late thirties, production was consistently high in the Southwest and far West, with a lower and more uneven rate through most of the Great Lakes region, where business recovery was sluggish.

The unevenness of production results in considerable geographical variation

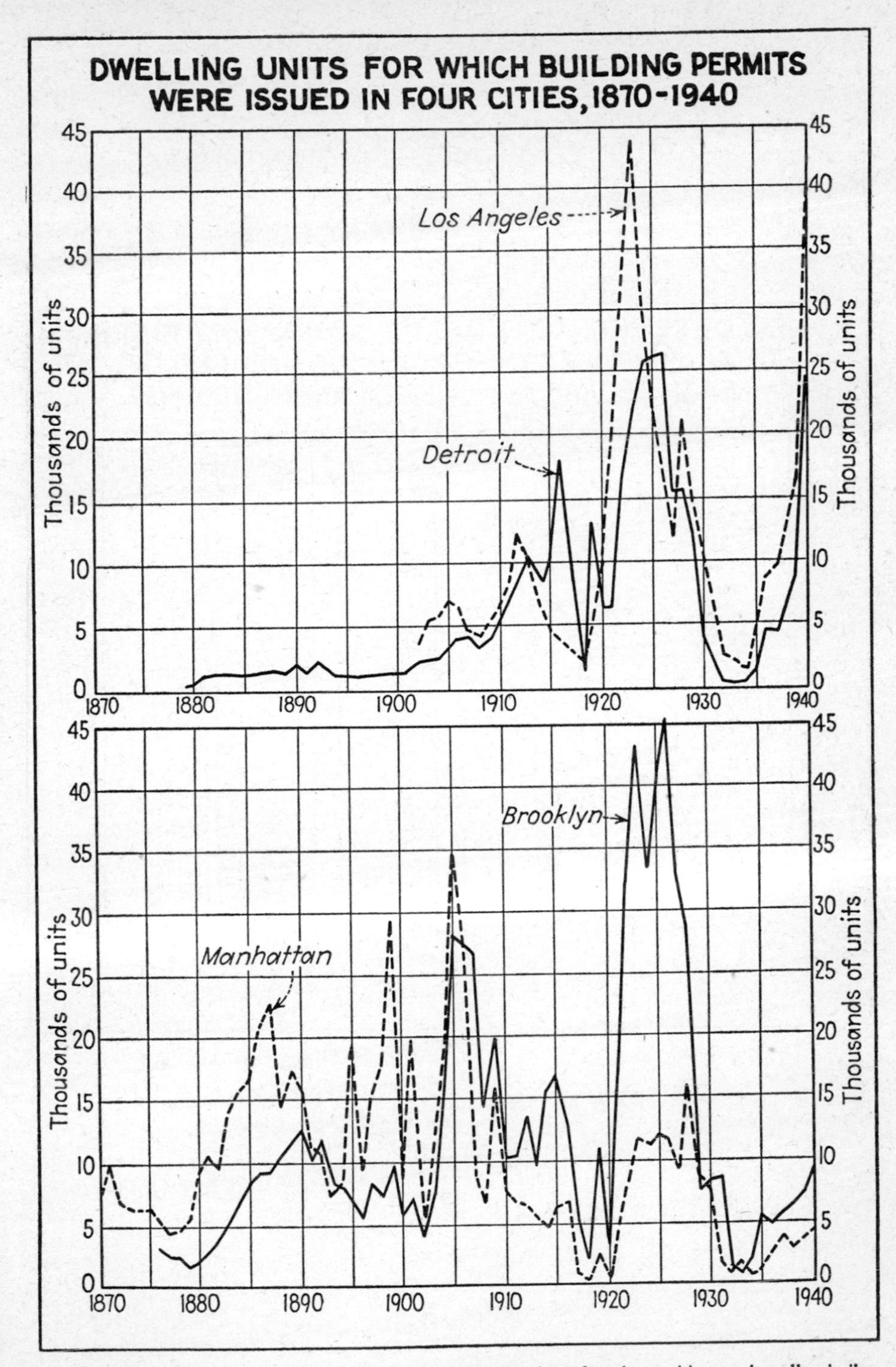

FIGURE 23. Cyclical movements in residential building in these four large cities are broadly similar, although some rather marked differences appear. During the twenties, for example, the peak in Los Angeles came three years before the peak in Detroit and Brooklyn, and five years before the high point in Manhattan. (*Source:* Appendix Table 34.)

in the condition of the housing supply. Where few houses are built, the rate at which houses are demolished or fall into disuse is retarded by the absence of new buildings. Therefore the average quality of the existing supply of houses declines. On farms and in isolated small towns the replacement rate is usually extremely low. Where there is much building activity obsolescence and turnover are likely to be more rapid. Since builders usually shift the center of their opera-

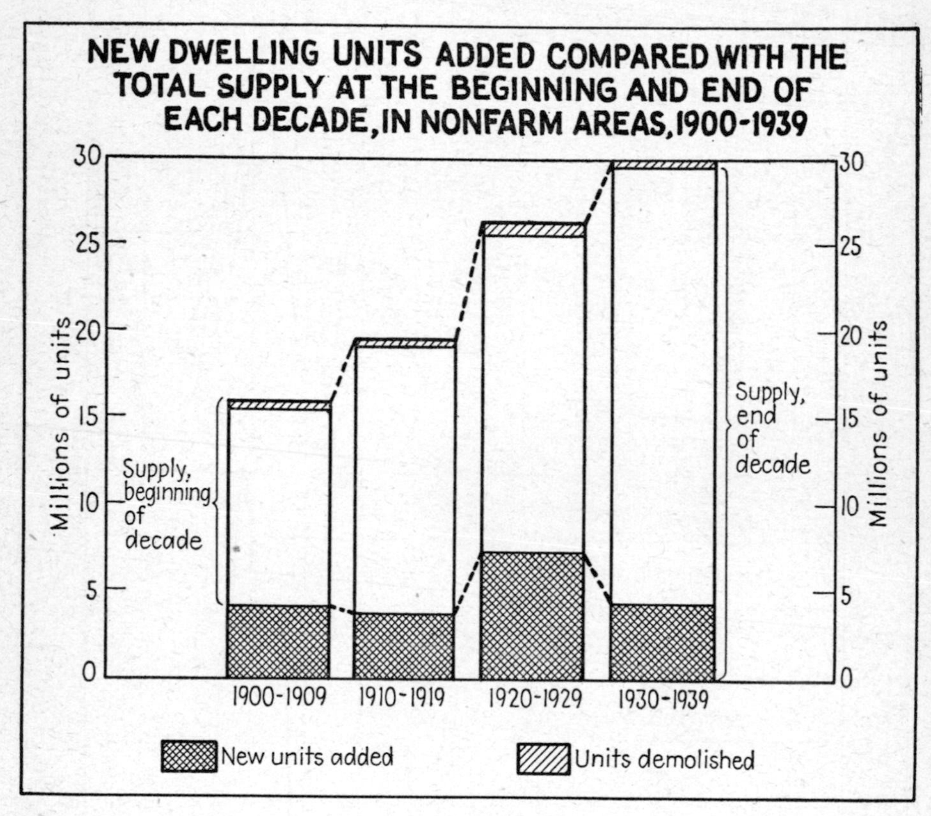

FIGURE 24. The total supply of housing increases fairly slowly, with considerable variation from one decade to another. The annual additions of new units to houses standing at the beginning of each decade averaged 2.6 per cent over the period but the percentages varied from as high as 3.7 per cent in the twenties to 1.4 per cent in the thirties. (*Source:* Appendix F, 1, Table 35.)

tions gradually, if at all, to meet changes in demand, and since the supply itself cannot be shifted from place to place, local maladjustments are hard to remedy when they occur.

Slow Change in Quantity of Supply

The great mass of the housing supply consists of used houses. As Figure 24 shows, the average ratio between the annual production of nonfarm dwellings and total supply was 2.3 per cent from 1900 to 1940, ranging from 1.3 to 3.2 per cent. It takes a long period of sustained demand to add significantly to the total stock. Annual new construction, even if doubled and trebled, as it has been since the depression, adds only a relatively small number of dwellings to the supply. With a curtailment in demand, reductions in the supply are even slower in taking place. Thus, in the period 1930-1939, demolitions have been estimated at only 400,000 units, or 40,000 annually—less than 0.2 per cent[2] of the 1930 stock.

New construction constitutes not only a small portion of all houses, but a smaller percentage of the low-priced than the high-priced supply. As shown in Section A of Figure 25, urban houses added by new construction and conversion in the decade of the thirties constituted the following proportions of the 1940 housing stock: 47.5 per cent of the over $50 rent ($5,000 value) class, 8.5 per cent of the $30-$50 ($3,000-$5,000) class, and 3.2 per cent of the under $30 ($3,000) classes. The annual building (including conversion) rates are accordingly 4.8, 0.9 and 0.3 per cent, respectively. Thus, in the last decade the lower the price range the smaller was the proportion of new and converted houses to total supply. Though the data are not available for distributing the dwellings built during the twenties according to price classes, a comparison of their average value with the average for those built during the thirties indicates an even greater concentration of new house production in the upper-price brackets.

To satisfy the demand for low-priced houses, higher-priced dwellings had to be filtered down, converted or made to serve more families. As shown in Figure 25, Section A, the whole of the 1940 supply of upper-priced houses could be replaced by new and converted ones in twenty-one years, even at the low rate of building activity which prevailed in the thirties. In each of the two intermediate price classes, well over 80 per cent of the 1940 supply consisted of houses which had depreciated into that price class during the last decade, while only about 10 per cent were there prior to 1930. In the lowest price class, however, only 41 per cent of the supply consisted of recently depreciated dwellings and almost half of the supply were houses already in that price class by 1930.[3] Here even the recent replenishment of the supply was from houses already pretty well worn out. There was little replenishment with adequate houses, but a settling and retention in the low-priced brackets of the worst of the supply. This meant only one thing—a deterioration in the quality of low-priced dwellings.

2. "Housing and the Increase in Population," *Monthly Labor Review,* April 1942, pp. 869–880; see also Appendix F, Table 35.

3. These large movements from one price class to a lower should not all be interpreted as filtering down. For a large part, they are indications of a general lowering of the price level during the decade of the thirties. For a discussion of Sections B and C of Figure 25, see pp. 204-205.

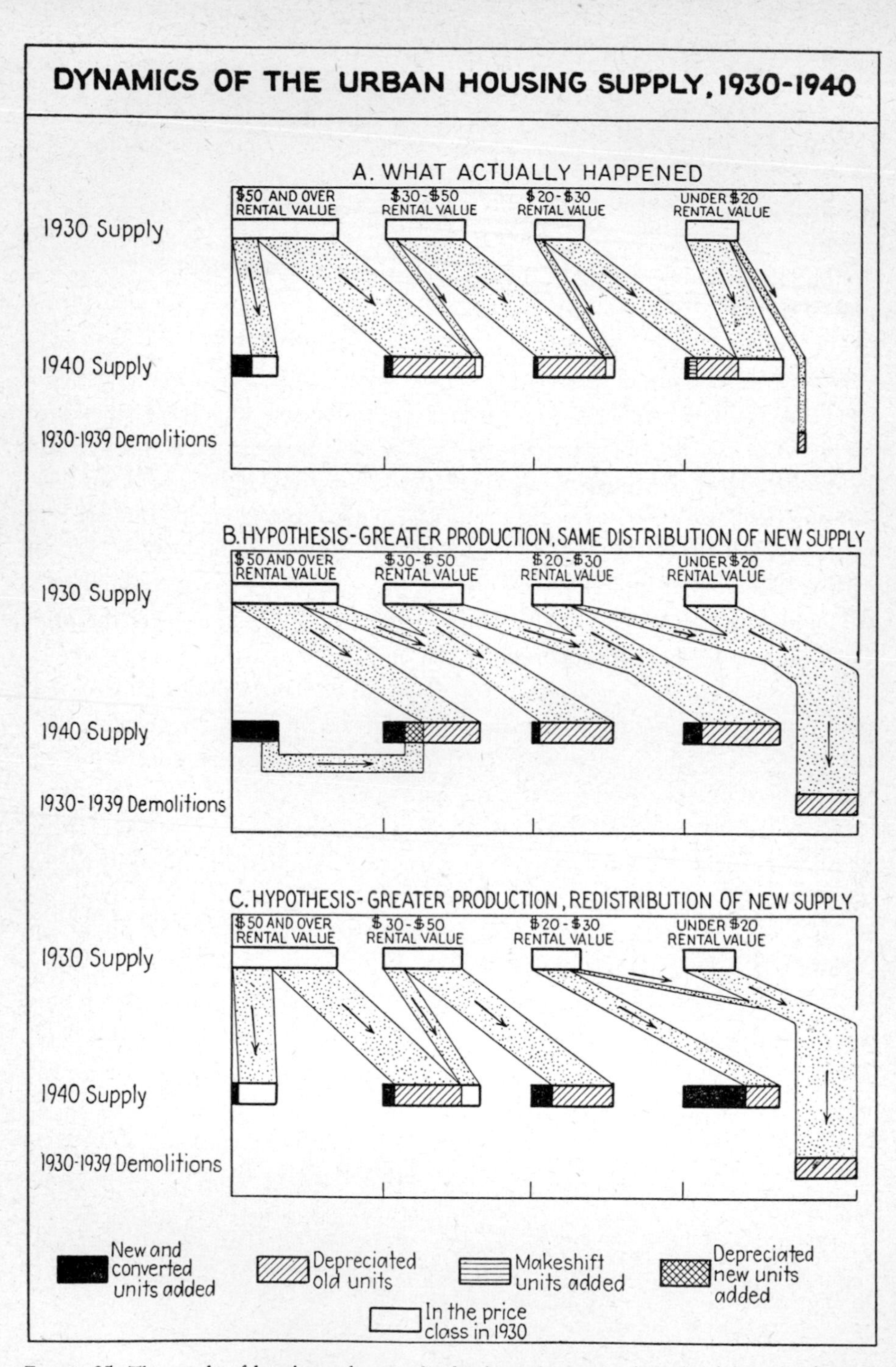

FIGURE 25. The supply of housing at lower value levels consists preponderantly of depreciated structures "filtered down" from higher levels. Increased production during the decade would have greatly speeded up demolitions but, unless the production had been concentrated on low-priced houses, the rate of depreciation would have been very high. (*Source:* Appendix F, 1, Table 36.)

The Filtering Down Fallacy

Moreover, many of these depreciated houses are not particularly well suited to the low-income groups. They may have too many or too few rooms; the rooms may be too large and inconveniently arranged to suit simpler modes of living; or they may require too much maintenance and service. In the filtering down process, therefore, a large number of houses are bound to lose their utility. Conversion of large single-family dwellings into units for more than one family usually leaves much to be desired. The resulting accommodations may be poorly arranged, badly lighted, and frequently have unsatisfactory sanitary, heating and cooking facilities. Under existing circumstances, however, such conversion is necessary.

There are relatively so few families with high incomes that filtering down begins from too small a supply. Even though high-priced houses depreciate rapidly, their number is not large enough to improve the condition of low-priced houses, unless supplemented by an adequate building program.[4] While filtering down is an important means of satisfying housing demand, we do not now have an article that filters well or in sufficient quantity.

2. FLUCTUATIONS IN THE BUILDING AND MARKETING OF HOUSES

Considerable responsibility for the inadequacies of low-priced dwellings is due to the periodic declines in the building and marketing of houses. When demand falls off, when vacancies become numerous and foreclosures increase, building activity all but ceases. Replacements, filtering down and demolitions are retarded. At the same time the amount spent on repairs declines. Thus the quality of the supply deteriorates at the same time that overcrowding increases.

a. THE PATTERN OF BUILDING AND REAL-ESTATE CYCLES

The housing industry is characterized by wide and violent fluctuations in building and marketing. With some important differences, the housebuilding cycle roughly parallels the general construction cycle. Since the Civil War, as shown in Figure 26, the low points in housebuilding came approximately in 1864, 1880, 1900, 1918 and 1933, the high points in 1871, 1889, 1915-1916 and 1925.

Nonresidential building is also subject to wide cyclical movements (see Figure 26), but these are not quite as violent as in residential construction. In the residential field, the variations are greater for multifamily than for detached dwellings. A variety of short-time movements, superimposed upon the main swings,

4. Even the very large number of expensive houses standing in 1930 and the drastic decline in values during the last decade proved insufficient.

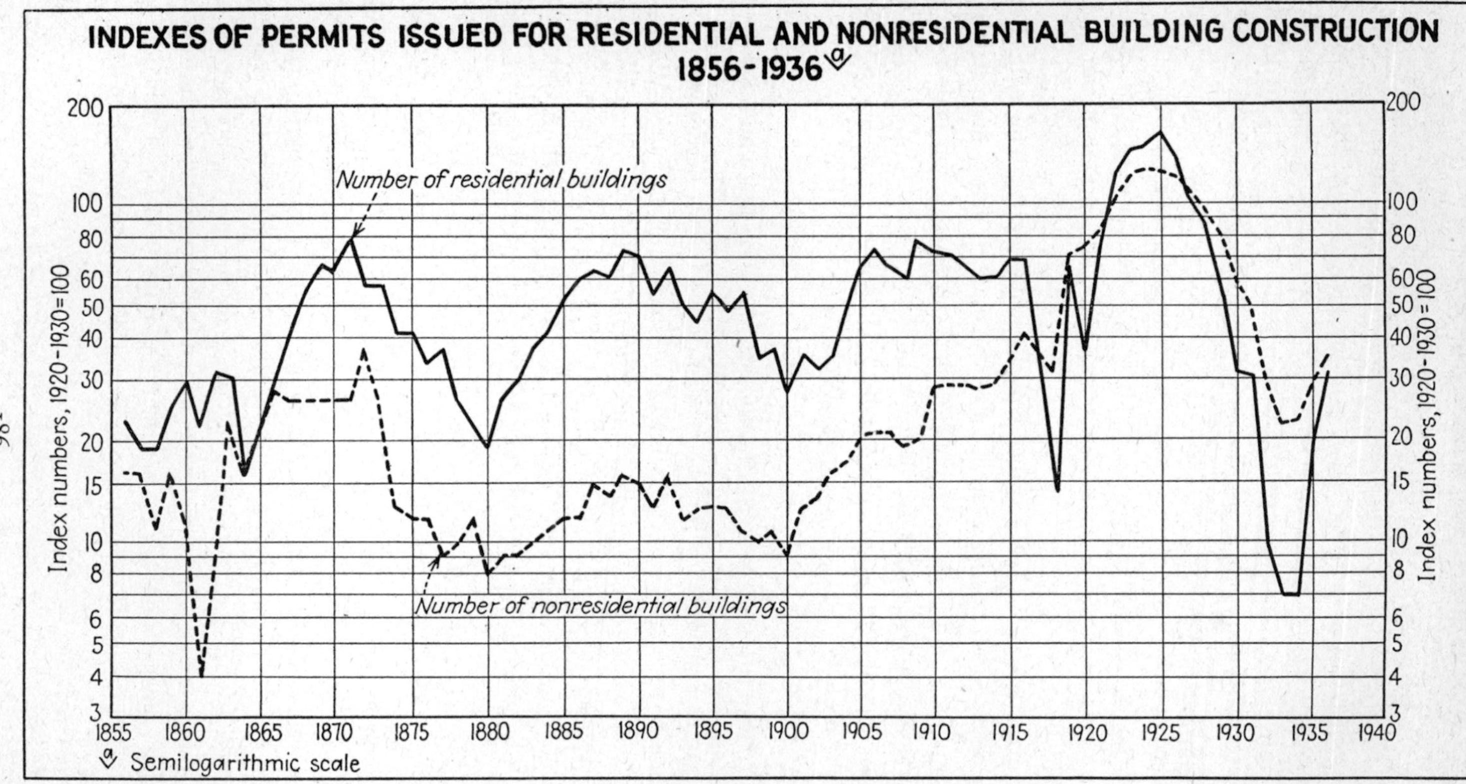

FIGURE 26. The housebuilding industry is subject to marked cyclical swings, with the variations in the last 25 years appearing more pronounced than in earlier periods. Nonresidential building cycles are somewhat less marked. (*Source:* Appendix Table 37.)

appear for the most part to be random. These are more pronounced in nonresidential than in residential construction.

The cyclical fluctuations seem greater in residential building than in most other industries.[5] The small amount of available evidence suggests that the residential real-estate cycle is as violent as the residential construction cycle. Available data for the most part provide only indirect measures of the residential real-estate cycle.[6] One of the few exceptions is a series depicting the annual volume of single-family house sales in Lucas County (Toledo), Ohio, for the period 1917-1938.[7] Although these data do not include transactions in the rental market, in multifamily dwellings and in land, they provide good evidence of the relative importance of new and old houses in the residential real-estate market.

Figure 27 shows that new dwellings, even in boom times, never accounted for much more than 30 per cent of the annual transactions in one-family houses in Lucas County; for the entire period 1917-1938, they accounted for only 20 per cent. The year-to-year trends of new and old house transfers are similar only in a general sense, as Figure 28 indicates. During 1919-1921, few houses were constructed, mainly because of the great rise in building material and labor costs during and shortly after the war. Transfers of used houses, on the other hand, increased sharply during this period, reflecting existing shortages. Apparently buyers found old houses much more attractively priced than new houses.

The year 1921 brought a sharp slump in old house transfers, while sales of new houses continued at about the same pace as in 1919-1920. After the 1921 depression, sales of both new and old houses increased, but the maximum annual volume for the former was not reached until several years after the peak in the

5. In his study of ninety-nine industries, A. F. Burns found that only a few industries experienced wider fluctuations than building. Variations in building permits for all types of construction combined were at least twice as wide as those of seventy other industries and at least three times as wide as those of forty industries. Among these were beet sugar, sulphur, cement and locomotives. See A. F. Burns, *Production Trends in the United States Since 1870,* National Bureau of Economic Research, 1934, pp. 230–233.

6. Some studies use deeds recorded, residential and nonresidential combined; others measure land subdividing or such other indirect evidences of residential real-estate activity as residential foreclosures and vacancies. See, for example: Roy Wenzlick, "Problem of Analyzing Local Real Estate Cycles," *Journal of the American Statistical Association,* March 1933 Supplement, pp. 201–206; Lewis A. Maverick, "Cycles in Real Estate Activity," *The Journal of Land & Public Utility Economics,* May 1932, pp. 191–199 and February 1933, pp. 52–56; E. M. Fisher, "Real Estate Subdividing Activity and Population Growth in Nine Urban Areas," *Michigan Business Studies,* Vol. I, No. 9; Homer Hoyt, *One Hundred Years of Land Values in Chicago,* The University of Chicago Press, Chicago, 1933; "Home Financing in Relation to Business Fluctuations," *Federal Home Loan Bank Review,* IV, 7, April 1938, pp. 245–247; James S. Taylor, "City Growth and Real Estate Cycles," *Insured Mortgage Portfolio,* II, 1, July 1937, pp. 10–24; Helen C. Monchow, *Seventy Years of Real Estate Subdividing in the Region of Chicago,* Northwestern University, Chicago and Evanston, 1939.

7. William M. Hoad, "Real Estate Prices: A Study of Residential Real Estate Transfers in Lucas County, Ohio." (Unpublished doctoral dissertation, University of Michigan, 1942.)

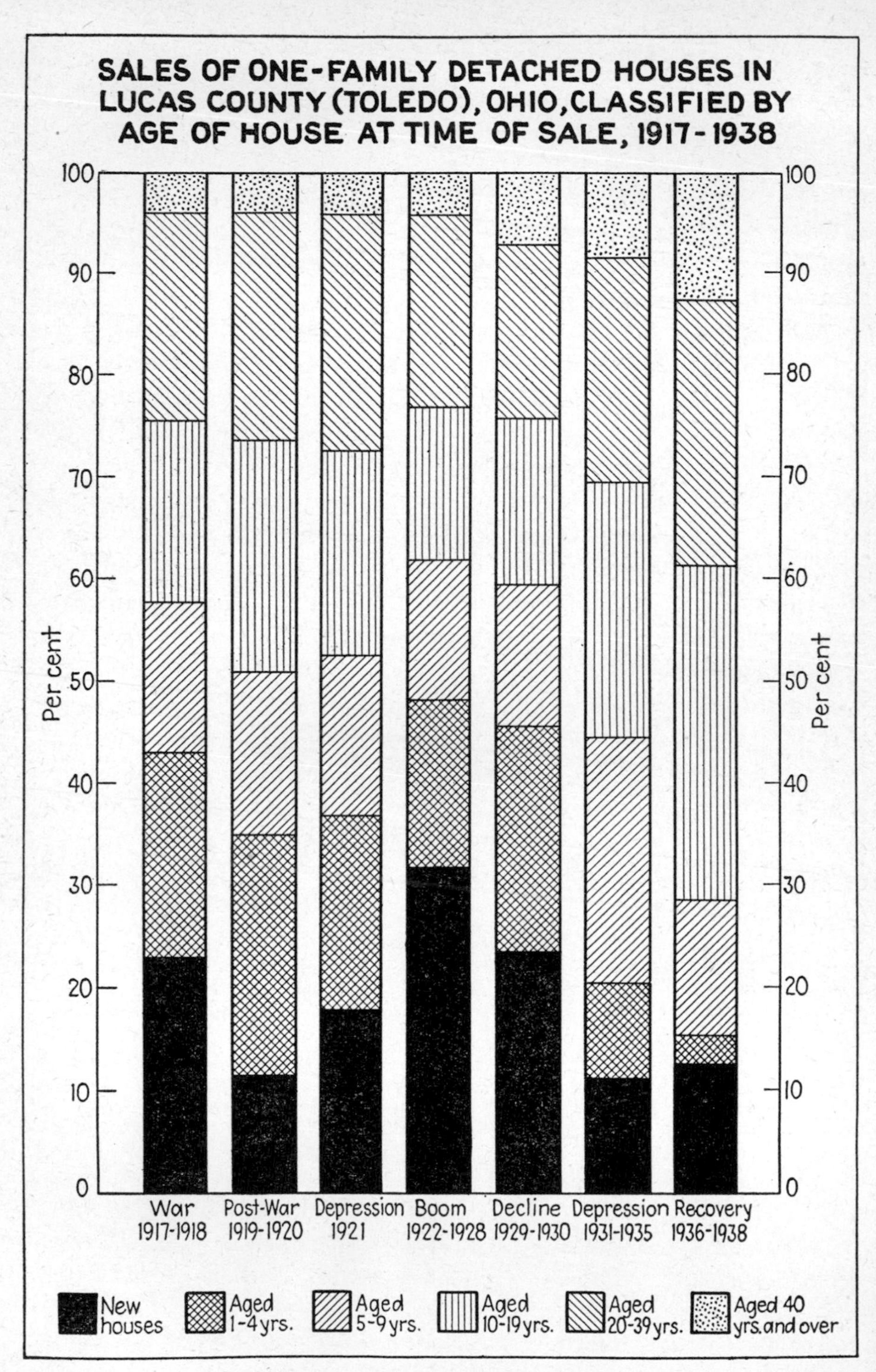

FIGURE 27. New houses accounted for only 20 per cent of all market transactions in Toledo over the period 1917 to 1938. Houses over 10 years old constituted a substantial part of total transactions, particularly in recent years and immediately after World War I. (*Source:* Appendix Table 38.)

latter. After 1933, sales of new houses were low for several years until the large supply of old houses available at relatively low prices had been absorbed.

b. WHAT INFLUENCES THE CYCLE

The causes of the periodic fluctuations in housebuilding are hard to isolate. The industry itself is complex and unorganized. Influences have varied in the

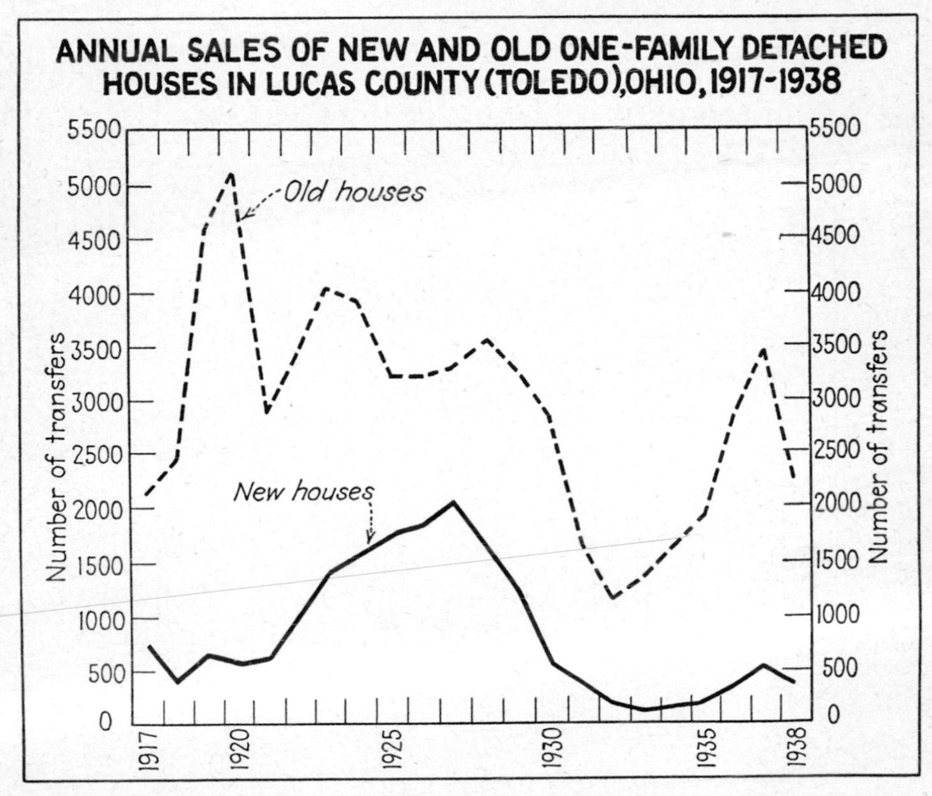

FIGURE 28. On the average 3½ times as many old houses as new houses were sold during the period shown on the chart but the ratio varied widely at different times. Sales of new houses gained rapidly during the building boom of the twenties and the ratio of old to new houses fell to 2 to 1. In the recovery period of the thirties, on the other hand, new building remained at a low level while sales of old houses went sharply ahead. (*Source:* Appendix Table 39.)

combinations in which they appeared from one cycle to another; and new ones, such as the government recovery programs of the thirties, have from time to time been introduced. Probably never before the early thirties had such a concentration of adverse factors been brought to bear upon housebuilding and real-estate activity. Likewise, probably never before the late thirties had such a concentration of government stimuli been brought to bear upon the housing market. It is consequently extremely difficult to isolate the effects of individual influences or to interpret any correspondence between fluctuations in the housing market and other economic phenomena.

Costs and Prices

It is frequently claimed, for example, that the volume of building varies inversely with costs, and that high prices are responsible for a downturn in the

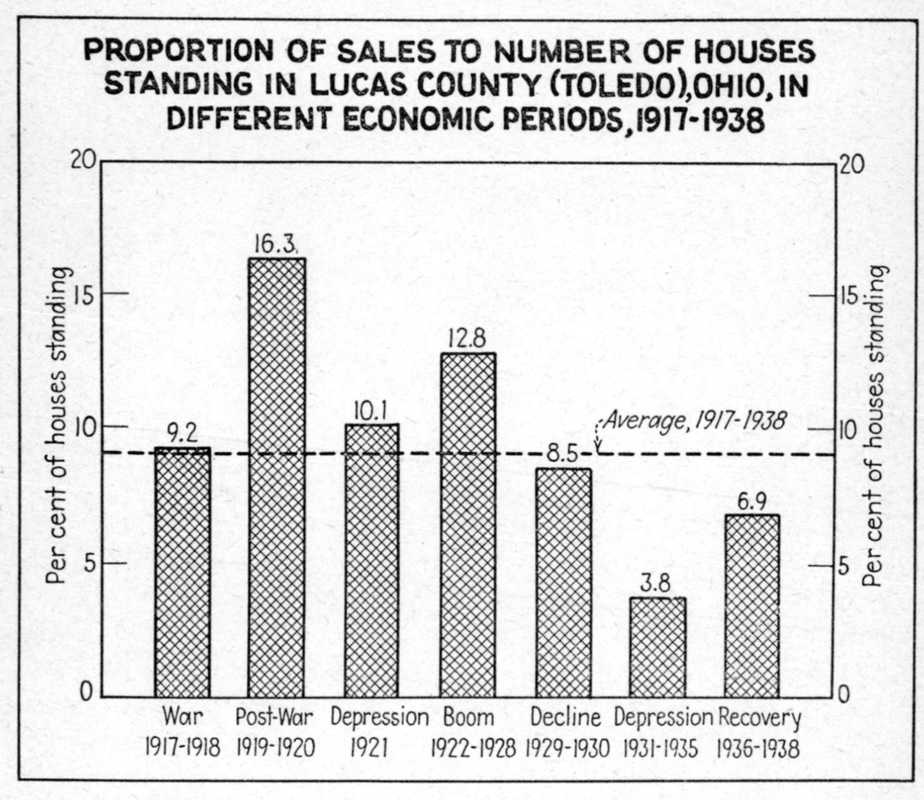

FIGURE 29. The proportion of the total stock of houses sold annually shows wide variations at different periods. At one extreme, the depression of the thirties witnessed average annual sales of 3.8 per cent of the supply—or a turnover of once in 26 years. This contrasted with an average annual turnover rate for the entire period of once in 11 years and with a high point of once in 6 years following World War I. (*Source:* William Hoad, *Real Estate Prices,* unpublished doctoral dissertation, University of Michigan, 1942.)

volume of housebuilding. The situation in the last half of 1937 and early part of 1938 has been cited in support of this contention. To be sure, building costs rose sharply in the winter of 1936-1937, and building subsequently recorded a marked recession. But practically every other form of business also dropped off. Factory production suffered one of the sharpest contractions on record. There are good indications that the rise in building costs played, if anything, a minor part in a building recession, which was only part of a general downturn that included most elements in the economy.

Indeed, W. H. Newman found that "during the major movements of building, both up and down, costs typically followed an independent course, showing but a slight tendency to move with, rather than against the direction in building activity." He concludes, "This does not mean that, other things remaining the same, costs will not affect building volume. It does show, however, that other factors in the situation were far more important than the level of building costs—so much so that the expected connection between costs and building was often reversed." [8]

The mortgage interest rate (being a critical element in price) is regarded by some authorities as determining the direction in which building activity moves. Interest rates on mortgages, however, have changed very slowly. In one hundred years, Homer Hoyt found only eleven significant changes in interest rates on new loans secured by Chicago business property.[9] This rigidity, according to certain authorities, indicates that mortgage interest rates have had little effect on building cycles.[10]

The constancy of a factor in the economic equation does not, however, necessarily mean that it had no influence. The interest rate (as an important element in the cost of purchase and the level of rent) must at least have an influence similar to other costs. The slow changes in costs, particularly interest rates, probably helped to determine the long-time volume of construction even though they had no demonstrable effect on the turning points of the cycle.

Some indication of the influence of mortgage rates may be found in the recovery from the last depression, although the changes did not come soon enough to show any relationship to the actual turning point. Thus the 5 per cent rate of the Home Owners' Loan Corporation, instituted in 1933, represented a marked decrease from current mortgage rates, but it was applicable only to relatively few existing houses. It affected new construction only to the extent to which it helped to reorganize the distressed sector of the market and thereby

8. William H. Newman, "The Building Industry and Business Cycles," *Journal of Business*, University of Chicago, July 1935, pp. 20, 24.

9. Hoyt, *op. cit.*, p. 347.

10. ". . . We must come to the conclusion that under the most extreme circumstances interest can only exercise a minor role in the inducement to invest in residential building. [This] must be even more true of the less durable nonresidential building, except notably for public building and building in certain protected industries," Clarence D. Long, Jr., *Building Cycles and the Theory of Investment*, Princeton University Press, Princeton, 1940, p. 29; "The interest rate . . . showed very little influence [on the volume of residential building]," J. B. D. Derksen, "Long Cycles in Residential Building," *Econometria*, University of Chicago, Vol. 8, p. 106; Wolfgang F. Stolper in his "British Monetary Policy and the Housing Boom," *Quarterly Journal of Economics*, Vol. LVI, No. 1, Pt. II, November 1941, effectively disproves the widely held view that the British housing boom of the thirties was caused by a reduction in the mortgage rate.

stimulated new building. In 1935 building-and-loan interest rates still averaged over 6 per cent. The Federal Housing Administration rate became a factor in the beginning of 1935, but it stood at slightly over 6 per cent. Important reductions did not come until 1937 and 1938, after housebuilding had begun to increase. The upturn in the cycle was due to other causes than the mortgage rate, but rate reductions undoubtedly contributed to the strength of the upward movement.

Similar considerations apply to the other elements that enter into the price of shelter, such as down payments, amortization periods, repair and maintenance costs. Principal and interest payment provisions remain unchanged over long periods of time; while the cost of upkeep follows the same rigid course as building prices.[11] While they probably cannot be held responsible for the fluctuations in housebuilding, these price factors have unquestionably exerted an influence on the violence of these fluctuations.

Population Changes

In spite of the possibilities of doubling up, there is obviously a close relationship between the number of families and changes in the total available housing space. It is therefore reasonable to expect that changes in the number of families have affected the volume of residential building.

The Chawner data on family formation provide an adequate basis for such an analysis, when used in conjunction with the data on new units built.[12] For the short period for which data are available, the increase in the number of families began to occur before the upturn in new building, as shown in Figure 30. There was a tendency for the peaks in family growth to be reached before the residential building peaks and for the decline in family formation to set in first.[13] Despite the fairly close relationship between building and changes in the number of families, the suggestion of causation cannot be carried too far. Aside from the fact that other influences are constantly at work, the increase in the number of families may be merely an expression of more fundamental factors. For instance, the formation of new families is influenced by the general income level and to

11. See pp. 111-112.

12. Lowell J. Chawner, "The Residential Building Process," *Housing—The Continuing Problem*, National Resources Planning Board, December 1940. See also Appendix C, Table 10. The only important limitation of these figures is that they do not reflect the need for new housing occasioned by the migration of population, which, as the war experience has shown, may be an overwhelming factor in stimulating demand.

13. Newman's comparison, *op. cit.*, which is somewhat less refined but covers a longer period, yields the same general results. The curves for population (rather than number of families) and building both show three major cycles; the turning points of the former anticipate those of the latter quite consistently, and the amplitudes of the cycles are similar.

a very considerable extent changes in the number of families may be merely symptomatic of income changes.

Multiplicity of Factors Affecting the Cycle

The foregoing examples show the difficulty of attempting to find causal relationships between the housebuilding cycle and any single factor, whether rents, vacancies, taxes, the cost of living, or what not. It is a combination of many forces operating with varying strengths at different times that causes the cyclical fluctuations in building. Thus, if all other influences remained unchanged an increase in building costs might lead to a downturn in building activity. But a change in other factors might offset the increased building costs sufficiently to prevent a downturn from occurring. The swings from depression to recovery and from prosperity to decline depend not on any single factor but on many interrelated elements.

Attempts have been made to express mathematically (through the technique of multiple correlation) the interrelationships between such basic factors as rents, vacancies, interest rates, taxes, family formation, incomes, cost of living.[14] However, this method of analysis, while helpful in suggesting general conclusions, has obvious weaknesses.

In the first place, any multiple correlation represents only the mathematically calculated effects of factors selected on the basis of observed correspondences to movements in housebuilding. For instance, trends in the increase in families have been observed to bear a certain relationship to residential building. However, other series of data entirely unrelated to the number of families or family incomes would, if they moved in a similar way, yield the same results in the correlation analysis. The correlation technique itself cannot distinguish between family income and so unrelated a series as the price of radishes if they both happen to have corresponding trends from month to month or from year to year.

Not only are the possible factors numerous and the underlying influence of some of them of a doubtful character, but the data concerning the various possible influencing factors are rarely exact. The critical factors have combined in different ways at different periods; new ones have appeared and old ones disappeared from time to time, and what combinations may appear in the future no formula can forecast. The housing market does not operate according to immutable laws capable of statement with mathematical precision, but amid constantly changing circumstances.[15]

14. Chawner, *op. cit.*, pp. 97-116; J. Tinbergen, *Statistical Testing of Business-Cycle Theories*, Vol. I, League of Nations, Geneva, 1939; and Charles Frederick Roos, *Dynamic Economics*, Monographs of the Cowles Commission for Research in Economics, No. 1, Bloomington, Indiana, 1934, pp. 69-110. See Appendix F, 2 for discussions of several of these analyses.

15. See Appendix F, 2 for a further discussion of this topic.

Despite these reservations, the multiple correlation studies reveal the wide range of influences that impinge on the housing market, including such external ones as trends in income, family formation, and general economic conditions as well as internal ones like construction costs and rents.

Of all the factors considered, family income seems to be the most important. Its influence, however, is largely indirect. For example, it has already been suggested that family formation is considerably influenced by the level of income.[16] The situation is somewhat the same with regard to rents. Rents apparently play an important part in determining the number of dwelling units built, but the level of rents is determined chiefly by the ratio of families to available dwelling units. This does not vitiate our conclusion that no single factor determines the volume of building. Rather, it merely suggests that of all influences, income seems to be most important.[17]

Housebuilding and the Business Cycle

No pronounced similarity can be discerned between housebuilding activity and the movements of general business. The former is much more erratic than the latter and its swings much wider. There is, however, some indication that the business depressions were preceded by declines in building, but that business picked up before building.

It is difficult to portray this sequence graphically because of the great difference in the length of the cycles shown by the two curves, the variations in amplitudes, the maze of random movements, and the different techniques used in compiling the data. The available evidence, however, indicates that since the 1870's building, after a depression, usually did not start an important upward movement until general business had begun to recover.[18] General business and building turned upward together in 1933, but the recovery of the latter was very slight. A decline in general business was usually preceded by a diminution, or leveling off, of housebuilding. The major exception to this also reflected the war situation; residential building began to decline in 1916 and reached a comparatively low level in 1918 because of the war and government limitations on building. General business, on the other hand, increased rapidly during this period under

16. For a more detailed discussion of this, see Appendix F, 2.

17. "Income is the determining factor in the demand for housing. It fluctuates with the business cycle. . . . Rentals and vacancies, purchases and refinancing, are elements caught in the resulting vortex." Quoted in *Federal Home Loan Bank Review,* IV, 7, April 1938, p. 245, from John H. Cover's survey of the Seventh Federal Home Loan Bank District.

18. The only exception occurred in the period immediately following the first World War. This does not necessarily mean that *all* business recoveries were followed by upturns in building, since building may have already been at a relatively high level, as in the 1880's.

the stimulus of war buying. It should also be noted that in two instances (1881 and 1920), building continued to rise after business had begun to decline.[19]

In explaining the relationship between building and business cycles, it is useful to explore the connection between the demand for housing, family incomes and general business conditions. As we have seen, vacancies and doubling up increase during depression, and decrease in periods of prosperity. In so far as business conditions are reflected in family incomes and the latter is reflected in the demand for housing, to that extent does the demand for housing depend upon general business conditions. The effect of changes in business conditions on the demand for housing may be offset by contrary influences. For instance, unsatisfied demand for housing, such as occurred after the first, and will probably occur after the second World War, may continue even if a decline in general business activity should occur. Again, the demand for housing may continue to rise while general business declines, if the recession is not too long or severe or is limited to a part of the economy. Such situations, however, cannot continue for long, since any prolonged decline in business is bound sooner or later to curtail incomes, postpone purchases and retard the formation of new families, and consequently reduce the demand for housing.

Why Business Picks up before Housing

It is not difficult to explain the improvement of general business before housebuilding. At the bottom of a depression the housebuilding industry becomes completely disorganized. Because producing units are small and capital investments negligible, entrepreneurs tend to disappear and building workers to seek work in other fields. In addition, vacancies are high and there is a large supply of foreclosed houses. In a sense the housebuilding industry has to be created anew after a prolonged depression. The initial stimulus to recovery must, therefore,

19. Most authorities recognize this pattern, at least in part. Thus, Long states that "Building tends to precede general business on major downturns," *op. cit.*, p. 155; and that "Except after great wars building has been slower to recover from great depressions than has business activity in general . . ." *Ibid.*, p. 156. J. B. Hubbard states that "Building movements have corresponded with similar changes in general business conditions, [and] have preceded corresponding general business conditions . . ." "An Analysis of Building Statistics for the United States," *Review of Economic Statistics*, Vol. VI, Harvard University, Cambridge, 1924, p. 32. J. M. Clark believes that "(1) Industrial building shows the most regular timing and is most nearly synchronous with the general business cycle; it tends to lead on the upturn but not on the downturn; (2) Commercial construction shows less conformity with the building cycles, but does show a lead on the upturn; (3) Residential building shows a clear tendency to lead the business cycle," *Strategic Factors in Business Cycles*, National Bureau of Economic Research, New York, 1934, pp. 27–29. On the other hand, J. R. Riggleman has observed that while a change in general business is quite often preceded by a corresponding minor movement in building, sometimes a business change precedes a building change and vice versa, "Business Cycles in the United States, 1875–1932," *Journal of the American Statistical Association*, June 1933, p. 174, *et seq.* Also, Newman says, ". . . we are impressed . . . with the absence of major fluctuations [in business] comparable to the major cycles in building . . . it is the minor fluctuations which correspond in nature and time limit to business cycles," "The Building Industry and Business Cycles," *op. cit.*, p. 13.

be given by industries that are still relatively intact. Moreover, before substantial housebuilding begins, vacancies must be absorbed and the real-estate market revived somewhat—a situation which cannot occur before general business begins to improve. Because housing demand is usually postponable and because large capital outlays are involved, other necessities are likely to be acquired first by consumers. This is particularly true of houses built for sale. Buyers must have sufficient savings and reasonable expectation of future income. As a result housebuilding tends to lag behind general business recovery.

A possible explanation for the tendency of housebuilding activity to fall off in advance of general business is the drastic effect which small changes in the total demand for housing have on the demand for newly produced houses. This may be illustrated by a hypothetical example: Let us assume that a given community has 1,000 occupied houses and no vacant dwellings, and a normal replacement demand of 2 per cent representing new houses built to replace an equivalent number demolished each year. If the number of families in the community requiring housing accommodations neither increases nor decreases, and the replacement demand remains steady year after year, twenty new dwellings will be required each year. If, however, in one year thirty new families move into the community, the total demand for dwellings would increase from 1,000 to 1,030, or by 3 per cent; but the demand for new dwellings would increase from twenty to fifty. Thus an increase of only 3 per cent in the total demand for dwellings would result in an increase of 150 per cent in the demand for new dwellings to be supplied by the construction industry of the community.

The demand for *new housing* cannot be maintained at the new rate, however, unless the *total demand* for housing *continues to increase*. Thus, if there were no additional new families demanding housing accommodations in the community in the following year, the total demand for dwellings to be supplied by the construction industry would fall to the replacement rate of twenty—causing a decline of 60 per cent in the demand for new dwellings. Even if the total demand continues to increase, but at a lower rate, the demand for new housing will decline from the level of the preceding year. For example, if twenty additional families move into the community, instead of thirty, the demand for new houses would decline from fifty to forty.

From this it can be seen how a small change in the over-all demand for housing is greatly magnified in the demand for new dwellings. In a period of general activity when the total demand for housing accommodations has been increasing, a mere slackening in the rate of increase will cause a falling off in the demand for new structures. This characteristic of the demand for housing (which is described in technical economic language as the "acceleration principle," applying to all durable goods) may help to explain the fact that the housebuilding industry may suffer from a shrinking market for its products, even at a time when total demand for housing accommodations continues to increase, though at a declining rate.

A change in the *demand* for new housing, however, will not necessarily be reflected immediately in the *building* of new houses. If all houses were built to order, the housebuilding industry would react at once to demand. Since they are not, the builder who erects houses in advance of sale must gauge demand. It is difficult for him immediately to recognize changes in demand and adjust his production accordingly; his expectations may turn out to be wrong. Consequently, even if demand falls off, housebuilding may continue to increase—but not for long. In the past, residential building has generally begun to drop before a decline took place in the over-all demand for housing or in general business.

The prior change of direction by housebuilding on the downturn is merely an indication that small changes in general business conditions profoundly affect housebuilding. Of course, a decline in housebuilding will be felt by general business—one reacts upon the other. The first impetus, however, appears to come from general business. Provided that builders are aware of what is happening a slowing up in the rate of business improvement is sufficient to cause a decline in housebuilding.

3. THE PROBLEM OF PRICE ADJUSTMENT

The price of housing must, of course, be considered in relation to other forces already described: the violence and length of the business cycle, the durability and immobility of the house, and the general inflexibility of the supply coupled with the deferability and variability of demand. But taking all things into account, the pricing pattern seems to be mainly responsible for most of the maladjustments in the housing market, just as the cost pattern lies at the root of the problems of the housebuilding industry.

a. SLOW MOVEMENT OF HOUSING PRICES

There has been much less fluctuation in housing prices than in the volume of building (Figure 30) and somewhat less than in the prices of consumer goods taken as a whole. This was due to a number of reasons. The relative stability of construction costs, examined earlier,[20] affected the prices of new houses. Important also has been the prevalence of credit in the housing market. Until the past decade interest rates and other mortgage terms were comparatively static over long periods of time. Moreover, the long life of mortgages and their inflexible provisions have created a rigidity in the monthly amount paid for shelter by

20. See pp. 111-112.

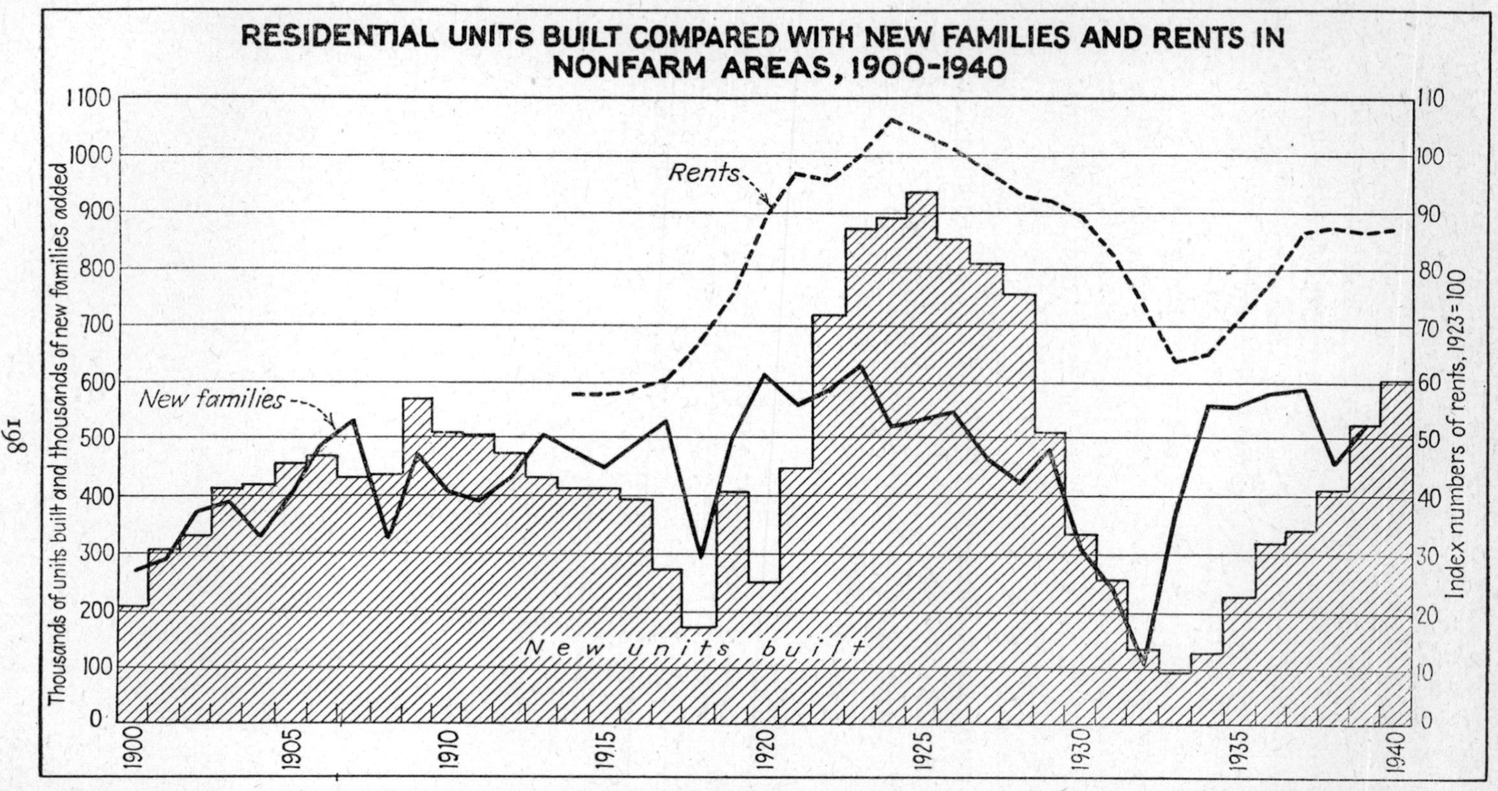

FIGURE 30. Formation of new families and changes in rentals are only two of the many factors affecting housebuilding. Although not showing a consistent relationship for the entire period, building volume tends to lag after changes in the number of new families and to move in accordance with changes in rent levels. (*Source:* "New Units Built," Appendix Table 10; "New Families," Appendix Table 40; "Rents," Appendix Table 41.)

homeowners and have had a steadying effect on housing prices in general. The influence of credit has also been evident in the policies of financial institutions, particularly when they have held large numbers of foreclosed houses. The tendency has been to set prices for such dwellings on the basis of outstanding indebtedness rather than market conditions.[21] Rents have been more responsive than sales prices to changing market conditions, but they too are fixed for definite periods by leases.

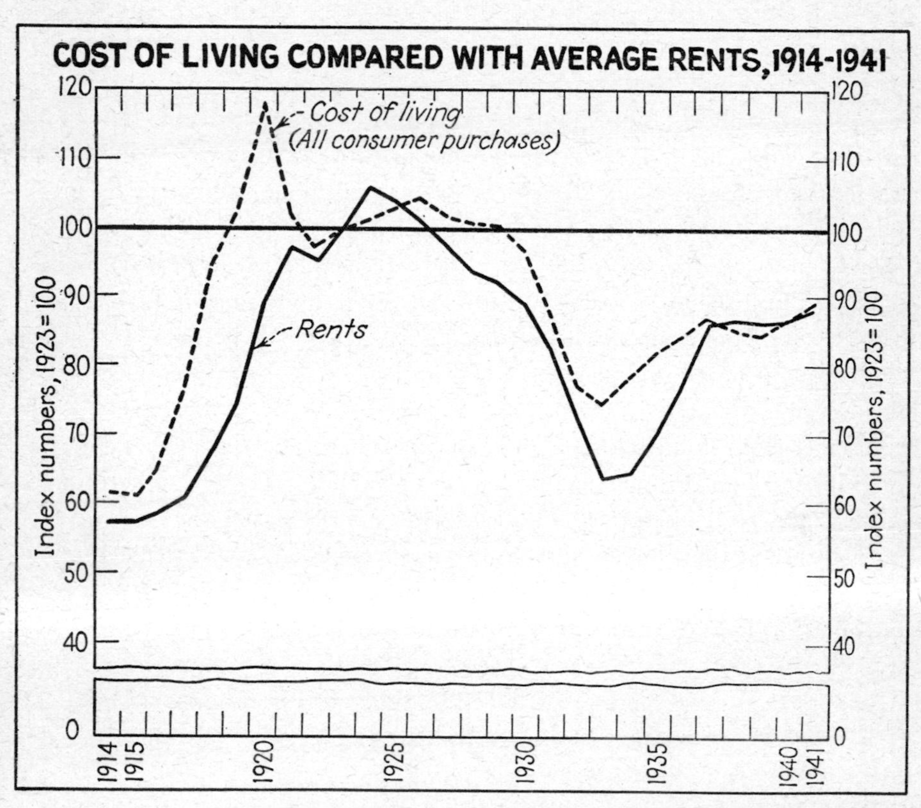

FIGURE 31. During the period 1915–1920, the cost of shelter lagged behind the general cost of living. But after 1923 rents fell faster and further and subsequently climbed more sharply than other consumer prices. (*Source:* Appendix Table 41.)

At the top and bottom of the building cycle, prices have been slow to change direction, but once started they have moved with considerable rapidity, though, in relation to other prices, for comparatively short distances. Part of the explanation for the slow movement at the turning point lies in the fact that the housing

21. With the increasing use of the amortized mortgage, this practice may become a less important factor in price rigidity, since mortgage lenders can, without loss, reduce prices by the amount of principal returned.

supply has not been able to respond readily to changes in demand. Under prevailing building and marketing conditions, there is a considerable time lag between the emergence of demand and its fulfillment, as well as between decline in demand and diminution of supply. This has led to price stickiness in the following manner:

In the early stages of recovery, the large number of vacancies have prevented prices from rising in response to increased demand until the oversupply was absorbed. During the remainder of the recovery stage supply has tended to lag behind demand. It has taken four to six months to erect a dwelling. Before construction has begun, land was bought, title searched, plans drawn up, and contracts signed—all time-consuming processes. Moreover, where the building industry, local and small in scale, has been confronted by a large increase in demand for shelter, its facilities have been so taxed as to postpone fulfillment for a considerable time. The tendency for building to lag behind demand has frequently resulted in a continued shortage. This shortage has tended to persist despite a downturn in demand, as long as the demand (even though moving downward) exceeded the supply. Prices have consequently tended to be firm, and at the turning point of the cycle remained high so long as demand continued greater than supply.

Another factor contributing to price stickiness has been the lack of satisfactory market data. Builders, who to a large extent operate for a spring market, might, for instance, have interpreted an actual decline in demand as a mere seasonal phenomenon. If their financial position was strong enough, they tended to hold their unsold houses at the same price until the next season. Even if they could not afford to hold their houses, the result was about the same, since the decline in the price of such houses, when taken over by financial institutions, was limited by the amount of the mortgage. Builders and financial institutions have realized only belatedly that demand had actually declined and that they had to accept lower prices.

What happens is that demand shifts to lower price levels and from owner-occupied to rental housing. Because prices have not been lowered to keep pace with the changing demand, people either move into inferior dwellings or double up, or both—thereby creating many vacancies chiefly at the top and bottom of the price range.

b. PRICE STICKINESS AND THE VIOLENCE OF THE BUILDING CYCLE

The violence of the building cycle ultimately depends upon the fluctuations in family income, which in turn bears a close relationship to general business conditions. There are, however, contributing forces within the housing market, among which the stickiness of housing prices is of prime importance. The influence on price of the unresponsiveness of supply to demand has just been discussed. The relationship, however, is not entirely one-sided. Sticky prices have also contributed to the maladjustments between supply and demand. Indeed, each reacts upon the other, at the same time exerting a profound influence on the violence of the building cycle.

In the early stages of business recovery, the oversupply of dwellings has kept prices from rising in response to increased demand. This in turn has retarded building activity, until a closer relation between supply and demand has led to an upward movement of prices. With continuation of the upturn, the other factors making for a lag of building activity behind demand have tended to come into operation. Housing shortages appeared and persisted; prices remained favorable to builders; and building increased rapidly in an effort to supply unfilled demand. When demand finally declined, the unresponsiveness of supply led once more to an oversupply. Then the stickiness of prices aggravated the oversupply and caused a drastic drop in building.

Other internal factors have played roles of varying importance. Unlike those industries where the bulk of the supply is newly produced, small changes in the total demand for housing will, as we have seen, have a drastic effect on the demand for new housing.

The violence of the building cycle has been further affected by the immobility of the housing supply and the inability to shift surpluses to places where shortages existed.

The violence of the cycle has also been intensified by the fact that when prices have declined, the housebuilding industry has preferred to restrict output rather than lower prices or produce a cheaper line of houses. On the upturn, producers have waited for what they considered a favorable price position before recommencing operations. Because of the little capital required by builders and the small risk they have usually assumed, speculative overbuilding has tended to be common, once activity was under way.

Easy credit terms have also stimulated the volume of building and, as optimism grew, have resulted in what amounts to gambling on future income. Hence, when a reaction sets in, the housing market has tended to become panicky and demoralized. Not only does building fall off, but defaults on existing contracts aggravate the situation and impede the task of reorganizing and restoring the market.

The importance of the sales market has also added to the violence of the building cycle. During depressions, when the demand for houses for sale practically disappeared, rental dwellings in the lower and middle price brackets have come into greater demand. If the industry had been producing a larger proportion of rental houses, it would have had a better opportunity for sustained activity.

C. PRICE STICKINESS AND HOUSING SURPLUSES

Housing surpluses have been intimately connected with the characteristic movement of housing prices. The rapid rise of prices during prosperity has helped to create a surplus which was then translated by sticky prices at the downturn into a high vacancy rate during a depression. This lack of responsiveness at the turning point has led to the early appearance of vacancies, while the failure of prices to fall far enough, even at the depth of the downswing, has led to a high vacancy rate until prosperity began to return. In other consumers' goods industries surpluses have tended to disappear more quickly through drastic price reductions.

Of course, this is not the whole explanation for the long-continued existence of housing surpluses. Food, for instance, has been taken off the market by destruction and by government storage, but an adequate house demolition program has not yet been developed. The inability to shift the housing surpluses from one locality to another, along with the unsuitability of the more expensive homes for low-income families, has also increased the difficulty of clearing the market.

The method of handling surpluses has aggravated the situation. Housebuilders have rapidly transferred new dwellings to consumers or financiers. Except when builders have had large financial resources, few new houses have remained with them. Because it is usually the house, not the builder, that is financed, the house—not the builder—has gone into default. The house has gone to the lender, and the builder has been able to escape further responsibility.[22]

In other industries surpluses must be carried and disposed of by manufacturers and distributors. In housebuilding they come into the hands of investors and financiers. Thus the supply, at the very time it requires expert management, is likely to be in the control of groups not equipped to distribute it.

Although these other factors have been important in the creation and continuance of housing surpluses, the influence of prices can hardly be exaggerated. Surpluses have been for the most part artificially induced by high prices. Abso-

22. This, of course, depends upon the builder having a properly designed corporate organization. There are several ways of doing this, but a typical example will serve for illustration. The builder incorporates his various projects (subdivision developments or apartment buildings) separately from his construction organization. The assets and liabilities of each project are segregated, and those of the building corporation kept free from all. The failure of one enterprise, therefore, cannot affect the others or the builder as such. If a specific operation fails, the surplus dwellings are soon transferred to the mortgagee and become his concern rather than the builder's. The dealer, or broker, as distinct from the builder, is even less likely to have a financial stake that will force him to carry the risk or burden of houses which cannot be sold or rented.

lute surpluses have occurred in a given market area only under special circumstances, such as rapid decrease in population.

In times of prosperity the industry continually built new housing for the upper-income groups, often in excessive quantity. During depressions a further surplus was created in this class by the vacating of high-priced dwellings as families were forced to seek cheaper accommodations. At the other end of the income scale, there was greater overcrowding and doubling up accompanied by increased vacancies because of the failure of values and rents to decline sufficiently to meet the curtailment of income. In prosperous times, as incomes increased, undoubling occurred, vacancies were reduced and a housing shortage tended to appear. In the higher-priced markets the shortage was apt to last only until construction got under way. On the lower level, high prices hindered the building of sufficient dwellings to eliminate the shortage.[23]

4. CAN MARKET MALADJUSTMENTS BE LESSENED?

Cycles in housebuilding, as in other industries, are a feature of our general economy. The phenomenon is too widespread to permit us to assume that changes in any single industry or its market mechanisms could bring striking modifications in the timing and occurrence of cyclical swings.

On the other hand the different degrees of violence that distinguish the movements of one industry from another may be caused by peculiar internal maladjustments. These, if corrected, might at least ease the effects of cyclical changes on the industry in question, and aid somewhat in the general leveling of business cycles.

The peculiar maladjustments of the housing market are manifested in the violence of the cyclical movements. Problems of pricing and of production in relation to price are at the root of these maladjustments. The tendency has been to produce more houses than were required for sale to the upper-income market. The demand for such houses is unresponsive to price changes, while the houses themselves are not generally adaptable to lower-income occupants. The shifts in the emphasis of production to meet changes in demand have not taken place. If the housing industry is to move toward more sustained activity it must produce a greater proportion of low-priced and rental housing.

Patterns of Production and Distribution

The effect on the housing supply of changes in the production pattern is illustrated by Figure 25. Section A shows what actually happened to the urban hous-

23. For the incidence of vacancies and doubling up by price classes in prosperity and depression see Appendix F, Table 41.

ing supply in the decade of the thirties in terms of rental value or price. Sections B and C show what would have happened if the production of new houses had (1) increased or (2) increased and been differently distributed among the value groups, while the number and price distribution of houses existing at the beginning and the end of the decade remained the same. As has already been indicated,[24] the residential construction pattern of the thirties failed to keep low-income families supplied with adequate housing.

Section B of Figure 25 shows what would have happened if the number of new urban houses built had been 5,613,000 (a number no larger than was built during the decade of the twenties) instead of 1,735,000, while the price distribution remained unchanged. Under this assumption, the whole of the 1940 supply of higher-priced houses would have been less than ten years old; and over 10 per cent of the new houses built in that price class during the thirties would have depreciated to a lower price group by 1940. In each of the remaining price classes, the total 1940 stock would have been composed solely of a small amount of dwellings built, plus a large number added through depreciation since 1930. The whole 1930 stock of lowest-price houses as well as a substantial number in the next price class would have been demolished. Such a production pattern and high rate of depreciation would be so financially damaging to investors in housing and mortgage lenders as to completely disrupt the real-estate market.

Section C shows what would have happened with both an increase in residential building activity to 5,613,000 units and a price distribution which placed the bulk of new construction in the lower price classes and the smallest amount in the highest price class. Compared with what actually happened, there would then have been an increase in the rate at which all but the highest-priced houses were replaced by new ones. The rate of depreciation would have been slowed up in the two upper price brackets and accelerated in the two lower ones. Placing the bulk of construction in the lower price classes would have meant that as a house deteriorated and became progressively worse in quality, the less time it would have stayed in any one price class and the faster it would have moved toward demolition. Instead of depreciation slowing up with age as is now the case, it would have increased. The houses at the bottom of the price scale would have been rapidly replenished through new construction and filtering down and the bad ones rapidly eliminated through demolition. Though the worst of the supply would have found its way into the lowest price group, it would not have been long retained there. Without disrupting the market through an excessive rate of depreciation of high-priced houses, there would have been a great improvement in the quality of low-priced dwellings.

24. See above, pp. 183-185.

The production pattern envisaged in Section C of the chart would not lead directly to a high rate of depreciation in high-priced houses. Low- and high-priced houses do not compete directly with each other; they are two different products. Because good low-priced houses are available does not necessarily mean that high-income families would demand them, for they would not suit the scale of living to which such families are accustomed. At most, some of the new techniques utilized on low-priced might be applied to high-priced housing. If this occurred, it would lead, as it has in the automobile industry, to price reductions all along the line, so that everybody would be spending a smaller proportion of income on shelter. But, generally speaking, a greater concentration of production on low-priced dwellings should improve rather than hurt the investment quality of existing housing for the higher-income groups.

In recent years housebuilders, partly because of more favorable credit terms to buyers, and partly because of changes in design, have begun to tap the low-priced market. Up to now, as the demand for high-priced houses became saturated, builders have attempted to speed the obsolescence and thus the turnover of existing houses by the introduction in the new houses of superficial novelties. When such expedients failed, rather than build for lower-income groups, they have shut down or gone out of business—steps easy to take because of the small capital investment in their enterprises. In spite of some progress recently toward a wider view of the market, this traditional attitude persists, as may be seen from the storm of protest raised in 1941 by limiting priorities, under the defense program, to houses under $6,000.

Balancing Ownership and Rental

Increased construction of cheaper houses would help greatly to adjust supply to demand. However, although it would result in a more adequate supply of housing, it would not by itself diminish the violence of the building cycle. If houses continue to be produced chiefly for sale to owner-occupants, demand would still fall off sharply with any general curtailment of business. Production would better be able to keep up, however, in the face of a business decline or pick up rapidly after a depression only if the industry were geared to the production of a considerably larger proportion of rental housing.

Construction of houses principally for sale results in a diminution of production during periods of economic decline commensurate with the severity of the depression. Home buying for any income group is a prosperity phenomenon. Moreover, people cannot buy houses until prosperity has existed long enough to permit an accumulation of savings. The effect of this lag on the violence of the building cycle has been noted. By lowering the down payment on houses during the past decade this lag has been somewhat shortened. But the extension of the mortgage period and the inflexible mortgage terms are apt to aggravate distress in a subsequent depression. So long as the housebuilding industry is directed mainly to homeowners rather than renters, it cannot be expected to adjust itself to the preponderately rental demand that exists during a depression.

5. SUMMARY

Previous chapters have shown that the development of a well-organized and integrated industry is essential to provide a greater number of low-priced houses. This chapter indicates that from the point of view of the market the production of more low-priced dwellings would be highly desirable. If, in addition, proportionately more rental houses were built, and a better geographical distribution could be devised, we would go far toward eliminating the maladjustments in the housing market.

Why are these possibilities unrealized? It is easy to blame the shortcomings of the housing industry upon the stupidity, shortsightedness, or venality of the persons who comprise it. But our examination of the processes of production has revealed formidable obstacles to the reorganization of the production process. The distribution system is similarly hamstrung.

It is easy also to say that better adjustment of supply to demand could be effected only if more production were undertaken by public agencies. But until other avenues are explored this proposal simply dodges the issue. We cannot overlook the vital part that government can play in stimulating the market and in building adequate low-income housing that can be provided in no other way. However, even the efforts that government may make in these directions are rendered more difficult by the obstacles that hamper the production of houses and the operation of the housing market.

Every phase of the housing industry is beset with obstacles. Those affecting production, serious as they are, arise in large part from lack of faith in the profitability of expanding construction for a lower-priced market. The obstacles found in the market, therefore, stand as perhaps the greatest deterrent to a more adequate supply of dwellings. These will be examined in the following chapters.

Chapter 8

THE MECHANICS OF THE HOUSING MARKET

THE HOUSING MARKET always works against the frictions of complex and often hazardous procedures, which tend to keep production within higher price ranges, where the margin to cover special risks and costs is sufficiently large. The development of simpler and more efficient methods of distributing houses is impeded by the costly and immobile nature of the house and the intricacies of law and custom surrounding transactions in real property.

1. SPECIAL PROBLEMS OF THE HOUSING MARKET

The fixed, durable, and costly nature of the house makes it difficult to acquire in a legal sense—much more difficult than goods that can be examined and compared in a central market place, that are rapidly consumed (and hence regularly traded in), and that can be paid for immediately or in a comparatively short time. Lacking these characteristics, the housing market has had to face special problems of its own.

a. MATCHING HOUSES TO PEOPLE

Houses have to be found for millions of families differing widely in size, composition, income, and preference. The differences among families are not only wide but inconstant, so that what may be salable today may become a drug on the market tomorrow. Families grow and shrink in size, changing their housing needs with the passage of time. Over long periods, changes occur in important group characteristics, such as the increase in the proportion of small families, profoundly affecting the ease with which the existing housing supply can be distributed.

Families often change locality, sometimes one by one, in quest of better income or living conditions, or in mass movements like the gold rush, the exodus from the dust bowl, or the defense migrations. These sweeping changes create indisposable surpluses of houses in some places, and shortages in others. Family incomes change, and consequently result in an improvement or lowering of housing standards. During the last depression, a large part of the population became unemployed or reduced to a low level of income, thus complicating the problem of fitting the supply of dwellings to changing demand. Family tastes change. Individuals seek to enhance their prestige by moving into more elaborate quarters. Houses that seem out of style in one generation may become popular in the next—and vice versa.

Shifting Demand and Slowly Changing Supply

The vagaries of housing demand are no greater than is the demand for other goods. But with housing, changing demands must be accommodated by a relatively fixed supply. Only the relatively few houses erected each year can be closely related to current needs. For the rest, consumers must choose from the mass of old houses, which constitute around 97 per cent of the total.

Used houses on the average account roughly for three quarters of annual sales.[1] In the rental market old houses are even more predominant. Probably half of all rented dwellings in the United States are used, single-family houses.[2] The remainder of the rental supply, consisting of a few new single-family dwellings, and most of the flats and apartments, rapidly falls into the secondhand class because of the high turnover of tenants. Only a very few new houses are rented upon completion. Thus, the major part of housing distribution is concerned with secondhand and partially out-of-date products.

Handling a Scattered Supply

The market supply of houses is fixed in widely scattered locations, and for the most part is in the hands of a widely diversified ownership. Only with new buildings in new developments is there a concentration either in location or ownership of the houses for sale that produces anything like a central market place. For rental dwellings it is only in large new apartments that distributing effort can be concentrated. The only other situation providing centralization of the ownership of dwellings offered in the market is after a wave of foreclosures when large mortgage lending institutions may have large numbers of houses for sale or rent. But a geographical concentration of supply, after the first sales or rentals take place, is rarely restored.

Once the initial selling or renting program is over, the units become part of

1. In Lucas County (Toledo), Ohio, used houses accounted for 80 per cent of sales from 1917–1938. See Chap. 7, pp. 187-190. See also Appendix F, Table 39.

2. According to unpublished data compiled in connection with the 1934 Federal Real Property Inventory in sixty-four metropolitan districts, 42 per cent of all rental units (assuming all vacant units to have been available for rental) were single-family houses. Practically all of these can be considered old houses, since few new single-family dwellings are built to be rented. Data for the sixty-four cities are not representative of small communities, where the proportion of single-family units in the rental market is undoubtedly higher than in the cities. The assumption that half of all tenant-occupied units were single-family houses therefore appears reasonable (Real Property Inventory records in Federal Housing Administration files).

the great mass of houses among which transactions are diffused both in time and location. Selling and renting, consequently, are costly and time-consuming. Purchasers must tediously go from one house to another and back again to make comparisons. House hunting, once undertaken, may become something of a career unless pressure is urgent. Its cost in lost time and lost motion to both buyer and seller is rarely considered in true relationship to the final price.

b. PROBLEMS OF VALUATION AND PRICING

The absence of a market place, the private and secret nature of transactions, the want of comprehensive market data, all combine to deprive the housing market of the benefits of a visible price structure. Both buyers and sellers, in varying degree, operate in the dark. The pricing situation is complicated by the variety of houses offered for sale or rental, and by the peculiarities of location which put each house in a class by itself.

The ultimate uniqueness of every house makes it impossible to establish uniform sales units or standards of value. No regular basis for valuing the heterogeneous mass of houses is possible. In spite of some advances in the technique of appraisal, buying and selling houses remains pretty much on a horse trading basis. As a result prolonged negotiations are frequently necessary to arrive at the terms of sale or rental.

Inexperience of Buyers and Sellers

Price setting is made more difficult by the inexperience of the average buyer and seller. Most of the transactions are in old houses. The seller is usually unfamiliar with the market. His only gauge is often the amount he originally paid for the dwelling. The buyer is apt to be even less experienced, for house buying is an infrequently repeated process. Buyers and sellers have little way of obtaining a comprehensive view of the market. Each approaches the transaction in ignorance and suspicion, and the services of a third (and more expert) party—the broker—are usually necessary.

But the broker's expertness does not relieve the market of all its hazards. In few other types of transactions is the principle of *caveat emptor* so thoroughly applicable. The purchaser at best can obtain only a limited guarantee even in buying a new house from a builder; in purchasing an old house, he does not get even this protection. He cannot easily judge the quality of the product or discover all the possible defects in construction or operation. The inspection of an expert may not be wholly revealing. Yet the sale is usually made without recourse, and since the producer has long since vanished from the picture, his guarantees, if they ever existed, will have run out. The broker, so long as he does not knowingly misrepresent the facts, cannot be held responsible.

Similar conditions arise in renting a dwelling. Buyers and sellers, landlords and tenants thus move in an atmosphere of distrust, which is apt to produce resistance on the one side and high pressure on the other.

C. PROBLEMS OF A DIVIDED MARKET

The high price of houses, the nomadic habits of the population, and other considerations, make it impossible for large numbers of families to own their homes. The Housing Census of 1940 shows that about 41 per cent of non-farm dwellings were owner-occupied and 59 per cent were rented. Even in more prosperous times, the ratio did not reach 50-50. A major part of the housing supply must therefore be maintained on a rental basis.

A relatively small proportion of the rental market is supplied by apartment buildings. Few single-family houses are built expressly for rental occupancy. Hence a large number of rented units are dwellings that have been vacated by their owners. These are usually the oldest part of the housing stock and are not as well maintained as owner-occupied dwellings. They generally have begun to decline in value before coming into the rental classification.[3] The transition from a neighborhood of owner-occupied to predominantly rented houses invariably depreciates the individual properties. If more families can be crowded into the area through conversion to, or replacement by, apartments, values of course may be maintained for a while. But these opportunities are less frequent now than during the peak of urbanization. Rental dwellings are not only apt to be step-children; they are often problem children.

The neglect of the rental market is at least partly due to the present organization of the market as a whole.[4] Except for relatively few dwellings—mostly in the apartment class—neither the investment in, nor management of rental property is professionalized. Rental houses are largely owned by people who have been unable to sell them or who look forward to reoccupying them. In many instances such dwellings are managed by real-estate men who regard their rental business as a side issue.

Selling a piece of property may be a tedious process, but once the deal is closed and the commission collected, the agent's responsibility is ended. He may even derive, with comparatively little effort, some income from the property through insurance renewals and mortgage servicing. Rental transactions, although less intricate legally, involve on the whole greater overhead, skill, and expense. Except for large apartment buildings, the task of finding a tenant and making a lease is often as arduous as that involved in selling a house, while the remunera-

3. Data from the Real Property Inventories reveal clearly that in any age group the proportion of deteriorated dwellings is greater among rented than owner-occupied dwellings.

4. For effects of investment and credit policies on the market see Chap. 9, pp. 225-256.

tion even over the term of a long lease is usually less. Moreover, throughout the term of the lease, the operator must not only collect rents but handle tenant's complaints and the endless problems of maintenance in which the owner's interest is likely to grow progressively less. As a result of these conditions, the average agent generally prefers sales to rental business.

2. Complexity of Housing Transactions

The housing market is not only difficult to serve, but every step is surrounded by elaborate legal ceremonials. Fixed as they are to the land, dwellings must be bought, sold, leased, and financed as real estate. Consequently housing transactions are more hedged about with legal prescriptions and more subject to contingent liabilities and responsibilities than those in other kinds of goods. Houses cannot be bought as easily and held as securely as automobiles, cattle, or other kinds of property.

a. PECULIARITIES OF REAL-ESTATE OWNERSHIP

Ownership of real estate is never absolute, but consists merely of rights to the use, enjoyment, and disposal of property. These rights are precisely defined by law, and their possession must be evidenced by legal documents. The peculiarity of real-estate ownership derives from the fact that one piece of land can be identified from another only by a description of its boundaries, usually only platted lines. Such descriptions may err and descriptions made at different times may not precisely correspond. The chance of doubts as to the validity of ownership may thus exist from the record of the first transaction. Ownership is also subject to the prior rights of the state and of other persons, which may restrict the freedom of using the property, or even make it impossible to maintain possession.

The rights of the state are usually readily ascertainable. They are expressed in building codes, zoning and planning laws, subdivision and health regulations limiting the use of property in the public interest. The purchase of property without full knowledge of these limitations, or their change after the property is acquired, may seriously affect the investment. Moreover the state may at any time acquire the property for some public purpose, with compensation, to be sure, but not necessarily with the consent of the owner. Limitations to the ownership and use of other goods are usually simple and unimportant to their enjoyment, while such goods cannot be commandeered by the state except under direst emergencies. With real property the reserved rights of the state are always present.

In addition to public rights there are numerous private rights in land. A wife has rights in her husband's real property, and sometimes the converse is true. Mortgagees acquire interests. Unpaid laborers, subcontractors, or materials men may have a lien right even though the owner may not have caused the default on which the lien is based. There may be easements granting limited use of the property to others, or restrictive covenants forbidding the owner to do certain things. In order to become aware of all these possible infringements on ownership, the buyer (or lessor under a long-term lease) must be acquainted with all the past transactions affecting the parcel. Since public records are often incomplete and usually difficult to trace, ignorance of some unsettled claim may result in subsequent loss of the property. No other form of property carries such risks.

Transactions are often impeded by the seller's or lessor's inability to carry out the proposed deal. The property may be tied up in estates or life interests, dower rights may not be released, and similar disabilities may exist in addition to possible unsettled claims. Sometimes a serious disability is discovered only after considerable negotiation has occurred.

The difficulties and uncertainties in the disposition and ownership of real property are largely traceable to a legal system inherited from a precommercial society. The law of real property matured in a feudal environment, where land was closely held and where the whole social structure depended upon its continuing to be closely held. Changes in ownership were few, and the complex procedure helped to restrict transactions. The fluidity of modern commercial and industrial society has failed to change the legal concepts involved in the ownership of land. Indeed the dispersion of ownership and the frequency of turnover under changed conditions have added to the complexity of the records and the difficulty of assuring valid claims to ownership. The legal system, like the construction system, has stubbornly maintained many vestiges of medievalism.

b. TITLE TO REAL ESTATE

Evidence of ownership is known as *title,* and consists of legal instruments, public records, or facts that can be proved. Ordinarily, the instruments or records are the final basis of judgment, unless they are controverted by other facts.

Yet the records are so complex that their examination is a laborious and expert task. An *abstract of title* is made by searching the deed books, mortgage books, plat books, and miscellaneous records for the whole history of transfers, encumbrances, liens, judgments, covenants, subdivisions, and devises in the hope of finding a complete chain of ownership without gaps or disputed claims. The procedure is obviously time-consuming and there is always a risk of missing some important item. Every time the land is sold, mortgaged, or subdivided, the process must be repeated. The building up of *title plants* by abstracters and lawyers, consisting of copies of previous abstracts, may save some labor in succeeding cases, but the creation and maintenance of these plants is difficult and costly and the cost must be paid by the buyers.

Public records may be incomplete as well as complex. Important records may be lost. Lapses may occur owing to the failure to record or indicate clearly the disposition of all interest in past transactions. Frequently facts affecting the validity of title are not only absent from the records but cannot be discovered by reasonable search outside the records.

The title abstract merely states the facts as they can be found. It gives no assurance of the validity of title. Judgment of the facts covered by the abstract requires thorough knowledge of the law of real property. Consequently, after the abstract has been brought down to date, it is essential to obtain a lawyer's *opinion of title* pointing out any defects in the record and certifying to its clearness otherwise. If defects are discovered, they may be removed through a suit to clear title. But just as the abstracter is responsible only for exercising reasonable care, skill, and diligence in preparing the abstract, so the attorney is liable only for failure to use reasonable care and diligence in examining it. The buyer may still be subject to loss due to unrevealed defects in his title.[5]

As a consequence, title insurance companies have been established to protect owners and mortgagees against hidden risks accompanying the purchase of real estate. The title insurance company often prepares and examines the abstract. It then issues a *title insurance policy* to the purchaser or mortgagee, under which it contracts to indemnify him for losses resulting from defects in the title other than those specifically excepted in the policy. Since known defects are excepted, unless they are removed by legal action, the risk that might arise from them remains. Title insurance thus usually does not insure against any ascertainable risk. Without a high premium for special protection the insurance is limited to such adverse claims as the title examination may have failed to disclose.

Title Registration

These methods of transferring ownership of land, inherited from an age when buying and selling property was rare, are poorly suited to contemporary needs. Real-estate transactions would be greatly simplified, and serious deterrents to investment removed, if transfers could be based on simple forms of title registration providing conclusive proof of ownership, as in the purchase of automobiles.

Simplified methods of title registration are widely used in central Europe, Australia, New Zealand, Canada, in parts of England and Ireland, and many other parts of the British Empire. They are permissive in this country in seventeen

5. He may get some protection by requiring the seller to give a full warranty deed—provided the seller is willing and is able to make good his guarantee.

states and Hawaii. Generally known as the Torrens System, title registration provides that, once officially registered, the property cannot be taken from an owner because of a title defect, but any person deprived of a valid interest because of the registration may be reimbursed out of a public fund created under the statute. In this country title registration has faced powerful opposition from those benefiting from the existing chaotic conditions. Nowhere has registration been made compulsory, and where it has been enacted permissively the arrangements for obtaining initial registration have been made so tedious and costly that acceptance has been discouraged.

Acquisition and Transfer of Title

Closely connected with the obsolete methods of proving clear title to real property are the cumbersome procedures for transferring or conveyancing title. Two separate steps are required, an agreement to transfer and the actual transfer, when one could serve the purpose just as well if the securing of evidence of title were not such a lengthy business. First a binding and enforceable purchase and sale contract is drawn up and signed. Then, when all is ready for the actual transfer it is superseded by a deed. There are several kinds of deeds, depending upon the degree to which the seller protects the buyer from possible claims against the property—a contingency that may always arise where title registration is not used.

The validity of a deed depends upon the strict observance of such legal requirements as the following. It must be in writing; no verbal deed or agreement is valid. The parties must be competent to execute the deed and their identity must be stated in the document. Their marital status must be indicated. If more persons than one are grantees, the conditions under which they take title (whether as joint tenants, tenants in common, etc.) must be stated. While a consideration is not essential to the validity of a deed, the acknowledgment of one is desirable. The deed must clearly indicate the grantor's intention to pass title, include a full and correct description of the conveyed property, and be signed and usually sealed by the grantor, witnessed or attested, and acknowledged before a notary or other qualified official. Finally, the deed must be delivered by the grantor and accepted by the grantee.

Despite this ceremonial, ownership is often only a legal fiction. The buyer may have given a mortgage representing as much as 80 per cent or more of the property's value, so that economically his interest is relatively small. Although the so-called owner's rights are qualified by the rights of the mortgagee, the qualifications still leave the mortgagee in a secondary position. In order to enforce rights against a defaulting owner, the mortgagee must go through the long and costly procedure of foreclosure.[6]

6. See Chap. 9, pp. 244, 245.

To give the seller a simpler means of repossession in case of default than is possible under the mortgage laws, property has often been sold on the basis of a *land contract* or *contract for deed.* These may provide that title passes only upon payment of the entire purchase price or a specified amount plus a mortgage for the remainder. Efforts to escape the complications of the mortgagor-mortgagee relationship, however, have not been very successful. The courts are inclined to recognize that the buyer under a land contract has an equitable right in the property and to require that regular foreclosure proceedings follow any default.

Leases

The lease of property is somewhat less formal than the transfer of title. But even the common year-to-year lease usually covers two pages, and leases become more complicated and the consequences of misunderstanding more serious as the term is lengthened.

All leases represent the temporary transfer to the lessee of certain rights to the property, other rights being retained by the owner or landlord. The lease recites the rights and obligations of both parties. Since it is usually prepared by, or on behalf of the landlord, he obtains most of the advantages in the transaction. Leases contain two kinds of clauses: those relating to the laws of the state regarding lessor-lessee rights and relationships and those intended to get around some specific court decision or to avoid the effects of the statute by agreement to the contrary. The tenant rarely knows into which class a particular clause falls and in fact he is rarely able to understand the legalistic language of the lease. He may therefore be easily duped by an unscrupulous landlord.

Most leases for residential property are of short duration, the one-year lease being typical. Long-term leases are rare, except those involving *ground rents,* which are for the most part limited to a few cities in the Middle Atlantic region. In Baltimore, for example, the long-term ground lease, under which the purchaser takes title to the house only, is a common form of tenure for residential property. The lease usually runs for ninety-nine years and carries an option to acquire title to the land after five years. Particular care must be taken to determine the ability of the grantor of a long-term lease to give title, since a defect in the title might cause the loss to the lessee not only of the land but of the dwelling.

C. THE COST OF REAL-ESTATE TRANSACTIONS

Aside from the cost of the house and of any commission paid to a broker, the transaction itself involves special costs. The buyer in a sense must pay for the privilege of buying. Anything comparable to this situation is rarely found in the transfer of other goods. And it is rare also that these special charges, or *closing costs,* as they are frequently called, are included in the quoted purchase price.

The usual charges include some or all of the following items: mortgagee's appraisal fee (and perhaps also an FHA appraisal fee), cost of title search or abstracting, title insurance, survey charges, attorney's charges, recording and filing

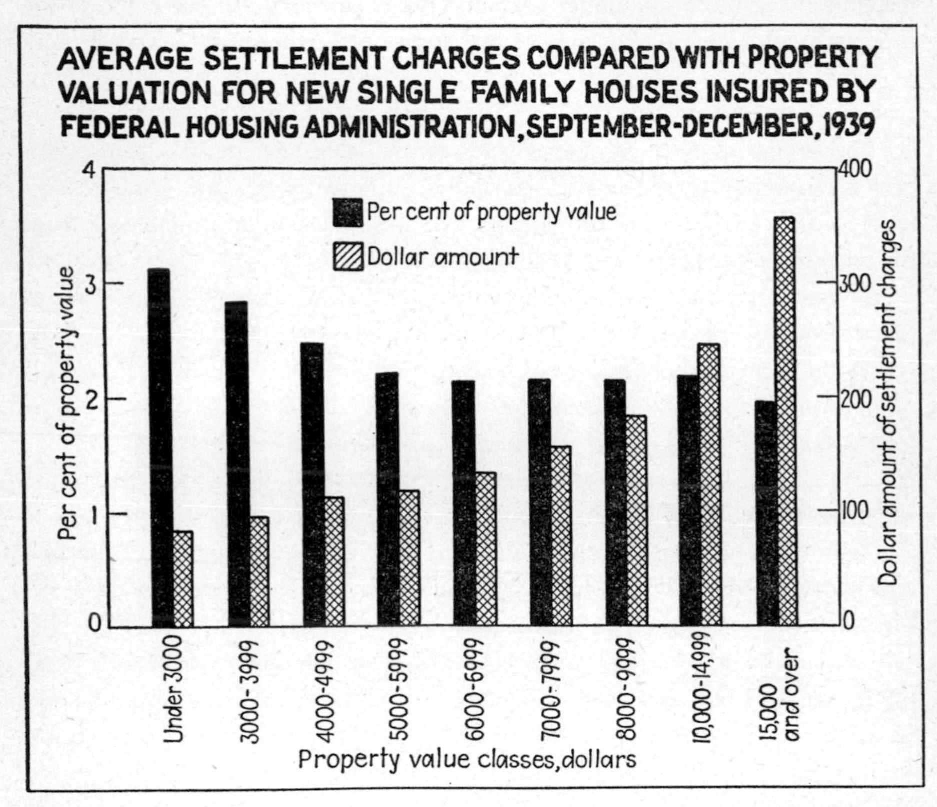

FIGURE 32. Settlement charges, or closing costs, bear most heavily on purchasers of low-cost houses. These charges represent about 3 per cent of the dollar value of houses costing up to $4,000, about 2.5 per cent for the next price class, and around 2 per cent for price classes over $5,000. (*Source:* Appendix Table 42.)

fees, revenue stamps, initial service charge, credit report, closing fees, notary fees, and possibly certain other fees besides. If a mortgage is involved, few of these fees can be escaped. Figure 32 shows the relation of these costs to the value of the property, according to FHA experience. Since many of the fees and charges are absolute, rather than based on a percentage of the house price, they bear most heavily on the low-priced house where they may amount to as much as half the minimum down payment.

In addition, the buyer at closing, if a mortgage is given, may be required to make advance payments for real-estate taxes, special assessments, hazard insurance, and perhaps FHA mortgage insurance. The highly advertised small down payment is thus only a part of the initial outlay.

In large transactions, such as the purchase of an apartment building or of land for a large development, the legal technicalities may be more complex and the charges correspondingly higher. There may be protracted negotiations with public officials and lenders in regard to zoning, planning, and financing. These necessitate options for the period of negotiation and the time it takes to make preliminary drawings. Heavy costs may be involved, with the risk of loss if all the loose ends cannot be satisfactorily tied together and the deal falls through.

This situation may bring waste and industrial inefficiency. Because of the risks of negotiation, preliminary planning is often on a sketchy scale. Then, because of time lost in negotiation and the necessity of completing the plans in a specified period (as for recording a subdivision) final plans are often drafted without adequate study.

3. HOW HOUSES ARE MARKETED

The diverse and scattered supply of houses, the complexity of transfer procedures, and the inexperience of buyers and sellers, creates a need for a special distribution system to help the prospective purchaser or renter in the difficult task of finding a house. The distribution system must provide the market judgment needed to arrive at going prices, guide the parties through involved negotiations, and arrange for financing the transaction. For rental property provision must also be made for collection of rents and handling of maintenance.

a. THE REAL-ESTATE BROKER

The adjustment of housing demand to supply is to a great extent accomplished through the system of real-estate brokerage. The broker's function makes up for the absence of a central market place by bringing buyers and sellers together. Though usually paid by the seller, the broker's service is used by both buyer and seller. His service consists on the one hand in judging the market, that is, considering the value of the property in relation to supply and demand. On the other, he analyzes the buyer's needs and the extent to which they can be satisfied within the limitations of the market. It is his task then to bring about a meeting of minds and, through his knowledge of the mechanics of the market, to avoid the pitfalls that might prevent a consummation of the deal. As the market is now constituted, the broker is often an essential part of the distribution mechanism.

Licensing of Brokers

The importance of the broker's function and his public responsibility has been recognized by the thirty-two states that, up to 1940, had enacted laws for licensing real-estate brokers. Pressure for this has come from the real-estate people themselves, and the legislation has to a great extent followed the model act, the so-called MacChesney Act, sponsored by the National Association of Real Estate Boards. The small capital needed for establishing a real-estate office, the public's ignorance of the complexities of the real-estate market and the gullibility of buyers bent on profiting from real-estate speculation have created vast opportunities for fraudulent real-estate transactions.[7] Hence, the need for licensing.

The purpose of licensing legislation is to regulate the participants in the real-estate business, including brokers, property managers, subdividers, mortgage brokers, as well as the salesmen who represent any of these. The laws exempt certain types of transactions, and usually owners at least are excepted if they deal in their own property.

Administration of Licensing Laws

Licensing legislation provides for the establishment of state commissions, consisting usually of brokers, to receive and pass on applications for licenses and otherwise to administer the provisions of the statute. The commission is empowered not only to require letters vouching for the suitability of the applicant, but to hold public hearings on his qualifications. In some states oral or written examinations are also required. The commission may usually revoke licenses for misrepresentation, double-dealing, fraud and similar unbecoming conduct, including an individual's use of the term "Realtor" without being a member of the National Association of Real Estate Boards.[8] The commission's findings may be appealed to the courts which may also impose penalties, other than revocation, on violators of the licensing laws.

Any licensing scheme based, like that of real-estate brokers, on so many fine shadings of practice, can never be completely effective. Furthermore, a licensing system administered by members of the trade can be improperly used to protect existing enterprises from new competition. Nevertheless, real-estate licensing has improved the ethics of the business and reduced the number of fraudulent transactions.[9]

7. For examples see Robert W. Semenow, *Survey of Real Estate Brokers' License Laws,* National Association of Real Estate Boards, Chicago, 1936.

8. The detailed offenses for which licenses may be revoked are given in the MacChesney Act (1927 edition).

9. See E. M. Fisher, *Advanced Principles of Real Estate Practice,* Macmillan, New York, 1930, pp. 349–351.

Number and Size of Brokerage Enterprises

The 1940 Census lists over 467,000 persons as engaged one way or another in real estate activity.[10]

A special report of 1935 which listed only 47,689 full- and part-time employees [11] provides the only general source of information about the size and character of real-estate firms. It reveals a business with striking parallels to the housebuilding industry. The typical real-estate firm is small, renders highly personalized service, but does not specialize in any particular type of property, and often carries on other activities.

The 47,689 workers embraced in the 1935 report were employed by 36,137 firms —an average of 1.32 workers per organization. The number of firms has, of course, multiplied since 1935, but there is no reason to believe that the average number of employees per firm has greatly increased. Active proprietors accounted for approximately 40 per cent of the total personnel of real-estate and brokerage offices. Many proprietors reported that they had no paid employees, and others only one.

Large organizations were concentrated in large cities, where property turnover is more rapid. Offices located in cities of over 500,000 population, represented only 21.6 per cent of all establishments, but accounted for 40.5 per cent of the income and nearly 36 per cent of total employment. Even in these cities, the ratio of employees to proprietors was only about two to one. The large firm employing more than a dozen persons is exceptional. The small broker, like the small builder, is typical even of the metropolitan center.

Of all establishments reporting, over 49 per cent were located in six states: California, New York, New Jersey, Pennsylvania, Illinois, and Ohio. These accounted for 54 per cent of total income and 53 per cent of employment. Like housebuilders, real-estate brokers seem to thrive most in densely populated areas, especially in metropolitan centers.

10. Sixteenth Census of the United States: 1940 Population, Series P–14, No. 6.

11. Census of Business: 1935, *Real Estate Agencies,* Table 1, p. 1. The total of 47,689 includes some insurance workers. The inclusion of such workers results from the fact that the Census of Business is conducted on an establishment basis wherein the employees of a particular establishment are all counted regardless of their activity. The conduct of the Census on an establishment basis also resulted in the omission of an unknown number of brokers and agents who did not have a regularly established place of business which could be identified as such, or were employed by firms not engaged primarily in real estate and brokerage or in real estate and insurance. This accounts for a considerable part of the undercounting as is indicated when comparison is made with the Census of Occupations. The latter report was a part of the 1930 Population Census in which *all* workers were covered. Another factor of considerable importance in explaining the difference in the two totals is the varying dates of the two studies. By 1935, many of those reported as real-estate agents in 1930 were no longer so engaged.

Specialization and Sources of Income

Real-estate brokers do not generally handle a special type of property.[12] Because of the predominance of residential properties in the urban housing market, however, the majority of brokers probably engage, in part at least, in housing transactions and receive a substantial part of their income from them. It is also safe to assume that the smaller firms are chiefly devoted to the residential business. The brokerage business often has allied with it several other forms of activity which are extremely useful in making a living in an uncertain and competitive business. Many firms sell fire and casualty insurance and manage rental property. Some engage in property appraisals, land development or housebuilding. Others buy and sell on their own account, act as loan agents for life insurance companies, or conduct a mortgage business.

Nevertheless, according to the census figures, commissions from real-estate sales, even in the poor business year of 1935, constituted the largest single source of income, 42 per cent, for brokerage establishments and insurance and real-estate offices.[13] Although this figure was slightly topped by the combined income from straight rental commissions and rental commissions taken under management contracts, this situation undoubtedly reflects the relatively small volume of sales during the depression. It is almost certain that figures for the decade 1930-1940 would show a higher income from sales, a substantial increase in income from mortgage placement (which was of little importance in 1935), and a corresponding reduction in the proportion of income from rentals and management.

Cost and Compensation of the Broker's Service

The broker is usually paid a fee based on a percentage of the sales price or rental involved. Fees vary, but local real-estate boards usually establish certain minimum commissions. Five per cent on a sale, and for a rental half the first month's rent plus 5 per cent of the gross rental thereafter are common.

Such commissions apparently do not yield spectacular incomes. The average gross income of establishments dealing exclusively in real estate was $3,971 in 1935; and the average gross income attributable to real estate of firms engaged both in the real-estate and insurance business was $2,781. The average income of employees in both types of offices was under $1,250.

12. As an exception, it may be noted that brokerage in farm and industrial properties is more or less specialized, and is recognized as such by the National Association of Real Estate Boards. There is also a tendency to specialization according to other types of property and transaction in the larger cities.

13. That is, 42 per cent of income from real-estate activities only. Total income does not include insurance commissions received by insurance and real-estate offices. Census of Business: 1935, *Real Estate Agencies,* Table 3, p. 22.

b. COSTS OF DISTRIBUTION

If we assume that the broker's commission represents distribution costs, housing makes a good showing as compared with many highly organized industries. If the closing charges are also counted among distribution costs, the total may run to 10 per cent of the price of the house. Comparisons of distribution costs of different industries are difficult to make, but local handicraft industries generally have lower distribution costs than highly centralized and mechanized industries producing standardized products. But this is not the whole story.

A relatively low distributing cost is not a criterion of an efficient and economical industrial operation. Compared with the present distributing costs of shoe manufacturers, those of the handicraft cobbler who sold from his workbench were negligible. His total cost for producing and selling a pair of shoes, however, was much higher. The reduction in shoe prices was made possible not only by centralized and mechanized production but by a more elaborate system of distribution. Centralization of manufacture involved additional transportation, warehousing, advertising, and selling costs, but the net result was lower prices to the consumer.

In housing, the distribution system is still in the "cobbler stage," except that it is necessary to employ intermediaries to bring buyer and seller together. Visible distribution costs in housing are only a part of total distribution costs. For instance, the cost of carrying inventory, which is concealed in the builder's price, is properly attributable to distribution. Advertising is another element of distribution cost that does not appear in the broker's operating expenses, since it is usually paid for by the owner.

C. OTHER TYPES OF DISTRIBUTING ORGANIZATIONS

Although the brokerage system is dominant, it does not have exclusive control of housing distribution. A considerable number of transactions take place directly between seller and buyer. Auctioning, once a common method of selling lots, is occasionally used with houses, but usually only under distress conditions. The special groups discussed below also have varying importance in the market.

Real-Estate Operators

Distinct from the real-estate broker who negotiates deals for others is the real-estate operator who engages in the purchase and sale of property for profit or income. He handles his own deals or uses brokers. His profit may be derived from the difference between the purchase and selling prices, or it may come from rentals on his investments, or from both. Traditionally, the real-estate operator[14]

14. Not to be confused with the operative builder or the land developer who actually prepares land for use.

is a speculator in land. In flush times, as during the Florida boom of the twenties, he may deal in options to purchase rather than in land which he actually owns. With declining prospects of speculative profits in land this type of activity has tended to disappear. Nevertheless, where sudden increases in population occur he quickly returns, with a resulting artificial stimulus to land values that may create difficulties for sound development.[15]

In some large cities the real-estate operator has dealt in apartment buildings, occasionally building up sizable investments. The tendency in this type of activity, however, has been to pick up bargains wherever they exist rather than to assemble related groups of properties. Thus many of the advantages of large-scale management have been lost and little progress, through this means, has been made toward the comprehensive neighborhood rehabilitation that might be possible through concentrated ownership.

Where ground rents are common, the operator may remain in the picture as the holder of leased fees and may deal in such properties even after their improvement. In Baltimore, for instance, there is fairly active trading in ground rents. There appears, however, to have been little tendency for operators to deal in individual houses on a large scale, or to build up sizable holdings for rental purposes.[16]

Operative Builders' Sales and Management Organizations

During the last decade, some of the large operative builders have set up their own sales organizations, with salesmen paid on a salary basis or receiving a fixed fee—usually around one per cent of the sales price, in contrast with the broker's traditional 5 per cent.[17]

For new dwellings produced in sizable groups, this method of distribution has proven practicable and economical. The large operative builder is in a very real sense a merchant. He owns his houses and sets his prices. Because the houses are concentrated in location and can be readily inspected by prospective purchasers, his selling expenses are not predicated on extended search and protracted negotiation. But selling can be integrated with production in this way only in large-scale operations carried over a considerable period. Such operations are most common in large cities, and perhaps more in medium-priced than other types of houses. The consequent savings are often considerable and help the producer to reach a wider market.

The operative builder's organization is, of course, designed to sell new houses.

15. Thus largely because of land speculators, the average prices around Washington, D. C. rose from 100 to 200 per cent and more. Similar conditions prevailed in other defense areas.

16. See also Chap. 11, p. 294.

17. In arriving at the operative builder's total distribution costs, the cost of carrying inventory, advertising, and other miscellaneous expenses should be added to the salesman's commission.

It deals with old dwellings usually only in the case of trade-ins or defaulted purchases. The amount of used-house business done by operative builders during the past few years appears to be small and, with trade-ins particularly, the builder often prefers to call in brokers rather than to use his own specialized organization.

The last decade has produced a number of organizations that build properties for their own investment and management. These properties have in the main been on a relatively large scale, usually of the garden apartment type. The union of management and building functions has undoubtedly helped to keep building costs down and associate property management more closely with the design and construction of houses. Though affecting only a small part of the total supply, these operations point the way to a new pattern of distribution in which the producer, by leasing his product, maintains control of it. Similar operations are found in such widely different types of industrial organizations as the Pullman Company, International Business Machines Corporation, and United Shoe Machinery Corporation which also lease rather than sell their products. The growth of this kind of operation in housebuilding has been retarded by the unfavorable investment situation, which will be discussed in the next chapter.

Dealers in Prefabricated Houses

Although up to the war an insignificant factor in the market as a whole, the prefabricated house dealer deserves attention as a new and unique type of organization. As pointed out in Chapter 5,[18] the dealer is also a part-builder. He usually finds the purchaser for his house, places an order with the factory, pays for the parts on delivery, contracts for, or undertakes on his own account, the assembly of the house (including parts not furnished by the factory), and conveys the finished job to the buyer. His income is derived from a markup over the factory price of the prefabricated parts and from a contractor's profit on the rest. All in all this may total 10 or 12 per cent of the selling price of the dwelling.

Essentially this kind of dealer is a small-scale builder. He may receive technical guidance, both in selling and construction, from the factory organization, but ordinarily he receives no financial support from it. In fact, the prefabricating factory's terms may be more rigid than those exacted by the suppliers of miscellaneous materials.

There are, of course, still other variants of the dealer pattern. The factory prefabricator may distribute through regular operative builders, thus combining mass manufacture with large-scale erection and distribution. Or the prefabricator may develop his own organization for site assembly. This method has been used in connection with government contracts, and might be adapted to private opera-

18. See Chap. 5, p. 145.

tion involving large rental properties. The materials dealer[19] often becomes a dealer in houses, sometimes distributing for a factory prefabricator, sometimes fabricating on his own account or employing local builders.

4. SUMMARY

The new departures in housing distribution suggest that even within the tradition-bound limits of housebuilding, there are opportunities for organizational ingenuity similar to those that have been seized upon in other fields of American industry.

Nevertheless, development has been slow and piecemeal. The lingering dominance of handicraft methods in production results in the continued prevalence of a small-scale and costly system of distribution. This situation, combined with the intricate and disorganized nature of the market (especially as complicated by its large proportion of old houses) is reflected in the mechanisms commonly used in carrying on the marketing process. The entanglement of the dwelling in the real-estate complex, making the transfer a matter of involved and intricate legal observances, adds other inhibitions to the spread of simpler and more efficient methods.

Although the mechanism is the creature of the market, it in turn exerts an influence upon the market. It reacts upon the character and extent of housing production. It adds to the frictions of the market, which in turn create serious questions of public policy. It affects the attitude of purchasers toward housing investment and the form and character of investment. In searching for possible resolutions of these difficulties, all of these factors must ultimately be considered together.

19. See Chap. 5, p. 145.

Chapter 9

HOUSING INVESTMENT AND FINANCE

AMONG THE critical factors in the marketing of houses are: (1) the character of the product, (2) its price, and (3) the terms of purchase. With housing, the last has special importance because its price is generally high and its use extends over a long period. Inducements to make long-term investments and the availability of long-term credit consequently govern housing distribution.

There are two classes of house buyers: those who intend to occupy the dwellings they purchase, and those who plan to rent to others. The prospective buyer-occupant is influenced by comparison with the rent he would otherwise have to pay and with possible alternative uses for his savings; but he is swayed also by other than financial considerations: the prestige of ownership and the qualities of environment, amenity, and newness that are difficult to find in rented houses. The buyer-occupant may, therefore, remain in the market despite situations unfavorable to investment as such and is apt to be influenced more by the terms on which he can finance his purchase than by the total price.

The rental-buyer, on the other hand, is generally disinterested in sentimental values but is guided almost wholly by the comparative returns from housing and other possible investments. The risks and rewards of investment are paramount to him, and conditions that unfavorably affect an investment will deter him to a greater extent than they will the home buyer. When inducements to investment are lacking, therefore, the result is likely to be an unbalanced emphasis on building houses for owner-occupancy as against dwellings for rent.

1. THE AVAILABILITY OF EQUITY FUNDS

A striking phenomenon of the thirties was a general lack of equity, or venture money, seeking investment. This was particularly true of housing.

a. FUNDS FOR USE-OWNERSHIP

The outstanding evidence of the timidity of investors is the small proportion of rental housing built during the decade. The increase of housebuilding during the later 1930's was stimulated principally by the demand for owner-occupied dwellings. Yet even in this class of housing the initial investment was usually small.

The small down payment now common seems to climax a long-term trend. Sample studies in fifty-two cities indicate that of one-family houses held by their original owners in 1934, those purchased in the nineties involved an average equity of 78 per cent of the dwelling's value, compared with 47 per cent for those bought during 1930-1934.[1] While indicative of a trend, these averages undoubtedly understate the amounts generally borrowed in the periods referred to. By 1934, buyers with the most substantial investments would have been most able to weather the depression, while many small equity purchasers, particularly those who in large numbers had been forced to use second and third mortgage financing, had already been foreclosed. Were it possible to show accurately the increase in the use of second and third mortgages (a characteristic of boom finance during the twenties) the indicated decline in initial equities would be much greater.

The increasing use of secondary loans was not the only evidence that the statutory limitations on the percentage of a first mortgage loan to value—if rigidly adhered to—did not provide enough credit to permit the market to function on a considerable scale. Pressure to expand sales along with decreasing equities also led to fictitiously high appraisals. Recognizing this, postdepression measures tended to relieve this pressure by increasing the percentage of the first mortgage loan.

Thus, refinancing by the Home Owners' Loan Corporation was on the basis of a maximum 80 per cent loan ratio, with second mortgages eliminated. Then, facing the fact that high ratios were needed not only to rehabilitate distressed loans under HOLC but to revive the housing market as a whole, the maximum ratio for federal savings and loan associations was set at 75 per cent. Shortly after, the 80 per cent loan became a feature of residential mortgage lending through the insured mortgage system of Federal Housing Administration. Subsequent amendments to FHA legislation permitted 90 and even 95 per cent loans for certain classes of property. Finally, FHA was authorized to insure loans on low-priced developments in defense areas against which the purchaser of a new house might make little or no down payment.[2]

Increasing Importance of Borrowing

The recent downward trend of equity investment may actually have been somewhat less sharp than the figures indicate. Improvements in appraisal methods probably tend to give a more accurate picture of the value of a house than in the

1. D. L. Wickens, *Residential Real Estate,* National Bureau of Economic Research, New York, 1941, Table D 10, pp. 216–217.

2. See Chap. 10, pp. 287-288.

past. If the same standards were, therefore, applied to predepression lending, we might discover higher loan ratios than the figures show. However, the small down payment is accepted as normal today.

An obvious reason for the high-ratio loan is that houses are expensive in relation to the buyer's annual income, representing sometimes much more than he can save out of several years' earnings. Without heavy borrowing most families could never purchase homes. Since the depression served to deplete savings, the importance of borrowing was undoubtedly increased during the recovery period. Moreover, the success of low down-payment installment selling for other industries influenced the housing market. Demands for a higher standard of housing than would be possible with the same equity on a lower percentage loan may also have influenced the trend. And finally, easy terms have in themselves tended to increase the incentive of homeowners to borrow rather than increase their equity.

Limitations of the Home-Buying Market

The decline in equity ratios was accompanied by an increase in the owner-occupancy of nonfarm housing during the first third of the century. Between 1900 and 1930 (see Figure 33) the percentage of owner-occupied dwellings rose from 36.5 to 45.9 per cent.[3] This figure declined during the depression, reaching a low point around 40 per cent in 1934, and, in spite of some recovery in the later thirties, the ownership ratio in 1940 was only 41.1 per cent of all nonfarm houses.[4]

During the period 1900-1940, the ownership ratios (as shown in Figure 34) were much higher in small towns than in large cities. It is in many of the larger and the older of the larger cities, however, that the increase in the ownership ratio has been most marked. The recent homeownership drive had the most marked results in the metropolitan centers. The decline in the ratio of owner-occupied to rental housing was apparently a depression phenomenon, and governmental policy on the whole has, since 1933, sought to promote homeownership. On the other hand, there has been vehement controversy about the desirability of encouraging ownership under present conditions of mobile population and uncertain income.

3. Fifteenth Census of the United States: 1930 *Population,* Vol. VI, *Families.* "Tenure unknown" has been proportionately distributed. During the same period farm ownership declined from 63.9 per cent to 52.5 per cent.

4. In an attempt to measure changes in tenure during the last decade, 1934 preliminary Census of Housing data for sixty-one cities in which Real Property Inventories were taken were compared with census data for the same cities in 1930 and 1940. The ownership percentages were as follows: 1930, 41.4 per cent; 1934, 36.9 per cent; and 1940, 38.7 per cent. Census figures are 1930, 45.9 per cent; 1940, 41.1 per cent. The sixty-one cities thus understate the proportion of homeownership, but less in 1940 than in 1930. If we assume (lacking any indication to the contrary) that the bias in the sixty-one cities decreased at a constant rate from 1930 to 1940, the understatement in 1934 was about 8.2 per cent. Applying this to the 1934 figure, we get an ownership ratio of 40.2 per cent.

The advocates of homeownership emphasize its long-run economy over renting, and its importance as a means of saving and as a force for social stabilization. An equally articulate group, however, argues that the long-run costs for the small homeowner are greater than those of the renter, and that the risks of losing his equity are inordinately high in a world of fluctuating employment. This group

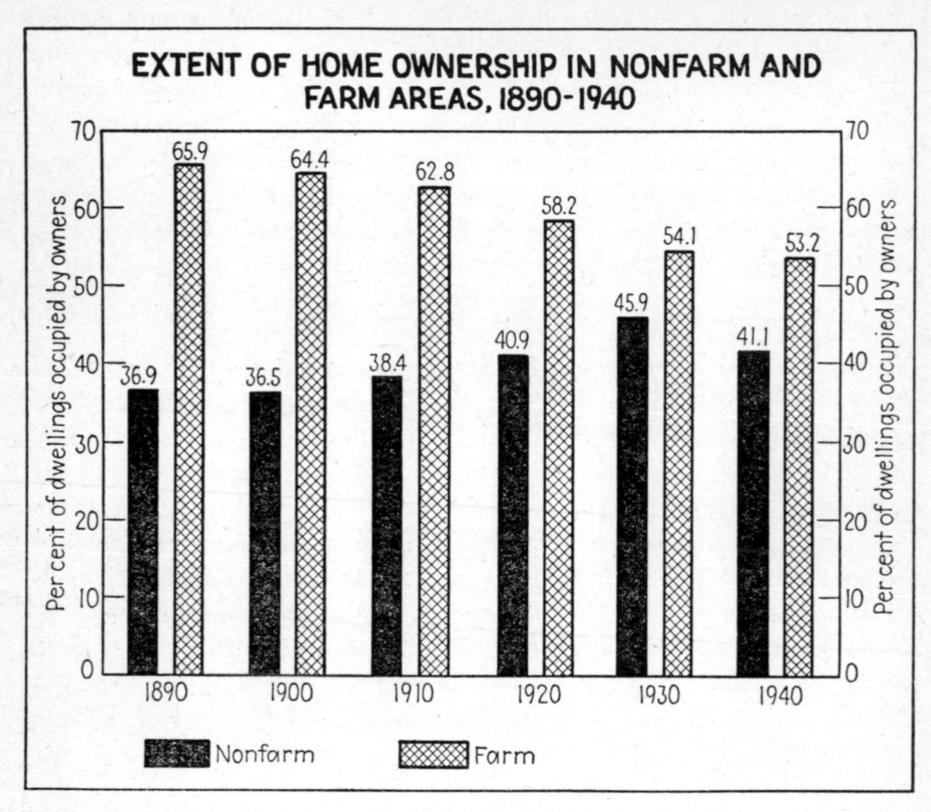

FIGURE 33. Homeownership in farm areas has declined steadily since 1890 while an upward trend has occurred in the case of nonfarm families. The depression brought a reaction from the 1930 peak of about 46 per cent homeownership for nonfarm areas, with the low point in 1934 and some recovery occurring since that year. (*Source:* Census of Population.)

insists that homeownership among the lower-income classes has already been carried too far.

To Buy or Rent?

Neither side can present thoroughly convincing arguments. A perfectly valid comparison could be made only by considering all the expenses of maintaining two identical properties, one rented and one owner-occupied, over the same period of time. No such data exist. Obviously comparisons showing the advantage

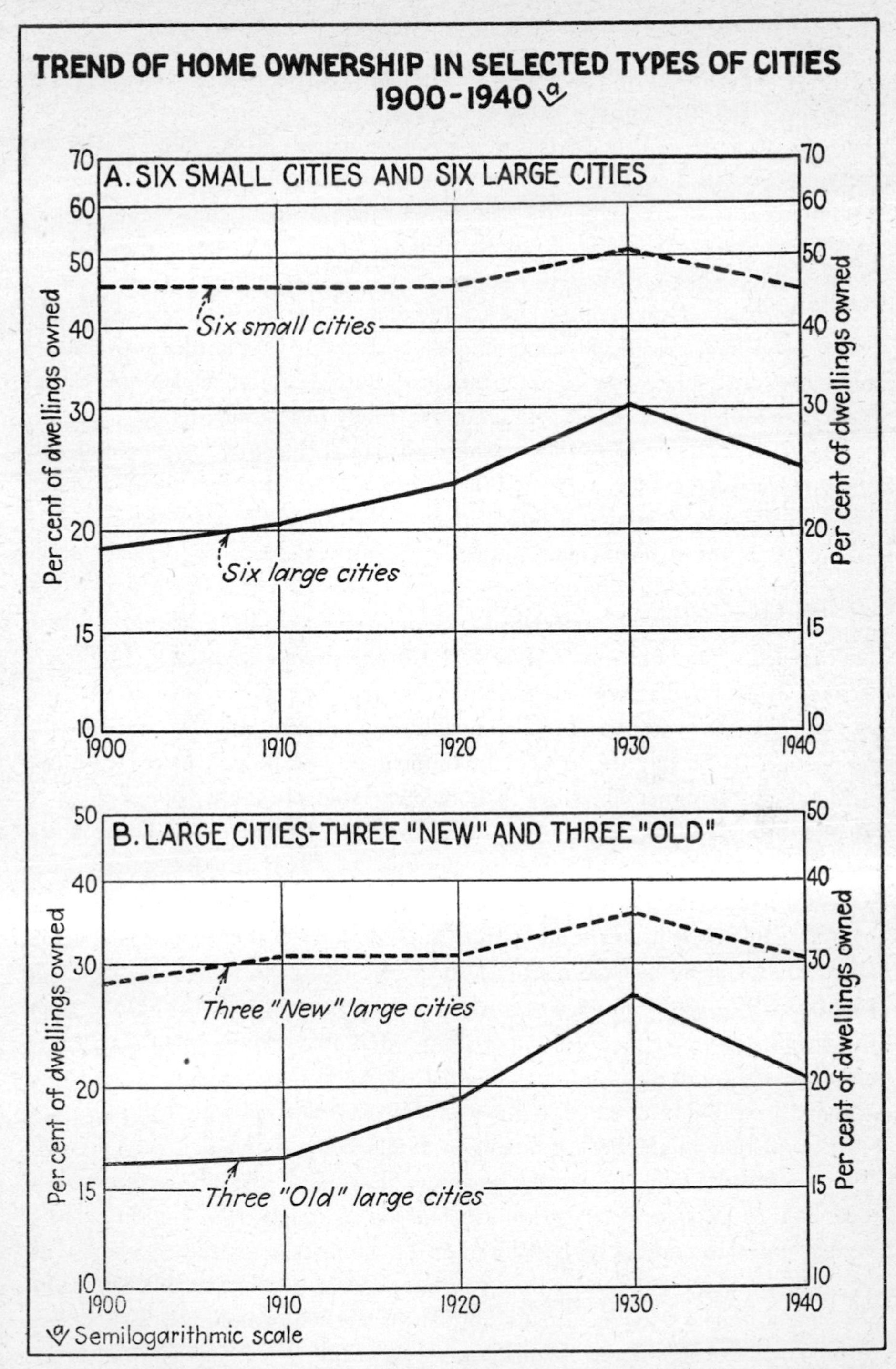

FIGURE 34. Although the proportion of homes owned by occupants has averaged much higher in the small cities than in the large ones, the trend toward homeownership has been more rapid in the larger centers. The proportion of homes owned has been less, but the rise in ownership more rapid, in the three "old" cities—New York, Philadelphia and Boston—than in the "new" cities of Chicago, Detroit and Los Angeles. (*Source:* Appendix Table 43.)

of ownership but leaving out unavoidable maintenance and replacement costs have little validity. On the other hand, there are unique expenses in rental housing, such as frequent advertising, leasing costs and losses from vacancy and defaulted rentals that are not incurred in the case of the owned house. Similarly, maintenance costs are higher for the rented house than for the owner-occupied dwelling because of the more frequent turnover of rented houses and the greater wear and tear they are likely to receive.

On the basis of two houses costing the same, and receiving the same care, with the general price level remaining static during the amortization period, a favorable case can be made for home purchase. But the argument cannot rest here. Price levels are unpredictable and are never steady over a long term.

The relative advantages of ownership and rental, therefore, vary greatly with the time the calculation is made and the period over which the estimate is carried. An individual who bought a house in 1928 was almost sure to lose money if forced to sell in the thirties, and, in the depths of the depression, probably would have found his carrying charges burdensome in comparison with current rentals. By contrast, a person who purchased a home in the early 1900's would probably have reaped a handsome profit if he sold it in the twenties. Anyone who bought a house in 1935 had a good chance of beating rental prices for at least a decade. His principal risk was that of not being able to sell or rent quickly for an amount based on a reasonably depreciated investment in case he was forced to move.

Moral and sentimental values in homeownership no doubt have a deep influence throughout the social and political structure. The desire for homeownership is widely diffused. Though thin equities and fixed payments may prove hazardous, it is argued that the risks on the whole are compensated by the broader gains both from the individual and community point of view. On the other hand, during a wave of foreclosures the intangible values of ownership may be small consolation for a serious financial loss; and, even in normal times, the inability to move freely as opportunity offers may detract from the lure of homeownership. In the last analysis no flat generalization can be made as to the advantages or disadvantages of homeownership as compared with renting.

The question might be less vexing if families could choose freely between ownership and rental. Generally speaking, the rental market is restricted to older houses or apartment buildings. The average apartment building has a limited appeal to families with children or the family desiring some contact with the ground. The older houses may be outmoded or poorly located. These disadvantages undoubtedly lead many families to buy who would continue to rent if the rental market offered them the same choice of new houses and attractive neighborhoods.

b. INVESTMENT IN RENTAL PROPERTIES

Rental construction did not show as great a postdepression recovery as houses for sale. Since few single-family urban houses are built for rental purposes, a fair clue to rental production is the number of new dwelling units in multiunit structures (three or more families).[5] During the period 1920-1929, dwellings of this type made up around 24 per cent of all family units built in nonfarm areas, reaching a peak of 32 per cent in 1927 and 1928. During the following decade this ratio dropped to 16 per cent. In 1940 it was 13 per cent.[6] These figures do not include a large number of two-family houses. If we assume conservatively that half of all such units are built for tenants, the above percentages rise to 32 per cent for 1920-1929 (with a peak of 38 per cent in 1927), and 19 per cent in 1930-1939. The 1940 figure would be 16 per cent. The figures for the twenties represent privately financed construction entirely. Those for the thirties include increasing amounts of publicly owned houses, amounting in 1940 to 30 per cent of all new rental structures having three or more units.

During the thirties about 510,000 rental dwellings (mostly two-family and multifamily buildings) were built out of a total production of 2,734,000. In addition, about 725,000 units provided in converted structures,[7] and probably 2.5 million used single-family houses were transferred from owner-occupancy to a rental status, indicating a preponderant dependence on old houses to supply the increasing rental market. By contrast the new units built for tenants in the twenties were apparently sufficient to accommodate increased demands, so that it was not necessary to draw to anywhere near the same extent on old houses.[8]

Most of the new rental construction, especially in the thirties, was apparently confined to a few large cities. Thus according to the Bureau of Labor Statistics Building Permit Survey, New York, Washington, Philadelphia, Chicago and Los Angeles accounted in 1939 for 60 per cent of private rental construction, and

5. The number of owner-occupied units in small flat buildings probably balances the number of single-family units built for rent.

6. See Appendix C, Table 11.

7. Single-family dwellings and structures of other types altered so as to obtain additional family units.

8. About 3,984,000 tenant-occupied nonfarm units were added from 1930 to 1939, according to census data, as follows: (a) 510,000 new units were built (all structures of three or more units, plus half the units in two-family structures). It is assumed that only a small number of single-family rental units were built, and that the omission of these is offset by the inclusion of a few owner-occupied units in the 510,000 apartment buildings (see Appendix C, Table 11). (b) About 250,000 vacant units were rented, or half the decline in vacant units reported by the Bureau of Labor Statistics. (c) About 725,000, according to the BLS, were added by conversion. This indicates a total of 1,485,000 units made available for the 3,984,000 new tenant families. The difference, 2,499,000 units, was evidently supplied by the transfer of formerly owner-occupied houses to a rental basis.

In the decade 1920–1929 relatively few owner-occupied units were transferred to a rental basis, since the new units built for rental (2,217,000) were enough to accommodate the 2,163,000 tenant families added in the ten-year period.

nearly half of total rental construction, including public dwellings. This geographic concentration of new dwellings for rent suggests a starvation of the rental market and a decline in the incentives to hold or invest in rental property.

Absence of Incentive to Rental-Housing Investment

Certainly during the thirties private rental housing did not receive as much stimulus as homeownership. Except for the brief mortgage bond hysteria of the late twenties, rental housing has never been able to obtain credit as easily as has ownership. The federal government's efforts to make credit available for residential property have been aimed almost wholly at homeownership, and in some places may even have created a situation unfavorable to the building of rental properties. The efforts of a few states, especially New York, to encourage investment in limited dividend rental property have been only slightly effective. State authorization of insurance companies to invest in rental housing has so far been used by only three institutions.[9]

The relative success of a few private companies devoted to the ownership and operation of rental properties, such as the City and Suburban Homes Corporation of New York City, the Washington Sanitary Housing Company and the Washington Sanitary Improvement Company of Washington, D. C., and the Cincinnati Model Homes Corporation has not resulted in establishing this activity on any wide basis. The success of such investors in rental housing as the late Julius Rosenwald in Chicago and the Buhl Foundation in Pittsburgh has not encouraged others. In short, only a few large investors have turned to the rental field, and most of the cases mentioned above antedate the depression of the early thirties.

Formerly a fruitful source of funds for rental housing was provided by the small investor who made a substantial down payment on a small flat building, perhaps occupying one of the units himself, and managing the rest. In Chicago, for instance, a large amount of rental property has been owned in this way. In New York City speculative apartment builders traditionally built up a rent-roll, then sold their properties to investors. The depletion of savings during the depression, and the declining popularity of the small apartment structure with the decentralization of cities and the competition of more popular types of structures, seem to have seriously diminished these investment sources.

Problems of Landlordism

The rental market thus stands in an uncertain position. As compared with the past the new supply is deficient. With the increasing mobility of the population

9. See Chap. 10 for further discussion of federal and state influence on rental-housing investment.

there is continued need for a large amount of housing on some other tenure basis than ownership. However, rental on a month-by-month or year-by-year basis does not always offer a satisfactory alternative to ownership. Such tenure, under ordinary circumstances, breeds little or no sense of responsibility in the tenant for the occupied property and tends to hasten its depreciation. Tenants also have little interest ordinarily in maintaining neighborhood or community values.

Landlordism thus raises its own problems no less than homeownership. In weak hands, it results in poor management, neglect of the property, and dissatisfied tenants. Large operating companies or financial institutions can assure efficient management and good maintenance, but they only serve a small part of the rental market. Moreover, large-scale landlordism may magnify the problems of tenant relations and remove the tenant even further from a direct interest in, and sense of responsibility for, his dwelling and community. There is danger that governmental landlordism may become paternalistic and create new political problems. Such problems call for a critical study of the questions of tenure and of relationships between the householder and the landlord or financing agency with which he must deal.

C. CO-OPERATIVE AND TRUSTEE FORMS OF OWNERSHIP

Even during the boom period of apartment construction in the late twenties, dissatisfaction with landlordism led to the rapid, if temporary, development of co-operative ownership. With this form of ownership, the interests of the equity investor and the user were combined, as in owner-occupied houses, with the profits of operation presumably going to the occupants.

In the usual co-operative, a corporation held the equity in the property, the stock being distributed according to the appraised rental value of the apartments. The tenant-owners received long-term "proprietory" leases, the rental covering debt service, taxes and operating costs. All the apartments might be occupied by tenant-owners, or some might be rented to non-members of the co-operative, thus supposedly adding to the profits of the stockholders. The latter elected the directors of the corporation who selected a management organization or managed the property themselves.

Co-operative apartments became popular, principally in the higher rental brackets during the period of rising rents in the middle twenties. The number of units built under co-operative ownership is not known, but the promotion, selling, and management of such structures was sufficiently widespread to warrant establishing a Co-operative Division in the National Association of Real Estate Boards.[10]

10. The division was formed in 1924 and was discontinued in 1930. At its peak it had ninety-five members from eleven cities.

Pros and Cons of Co-operative Ownership

Theoretically the co-operative idea had considerable merit. The tenant-owners supposedly stood to save by the absence of speculative profits ordinarily going to outsiders. Normal returns on equity investment would accrue to the tenant-owners. Maintenance costs should be lower than in rental buildings because the occupants could be expected to do some of the work and take a greater interest in the property. Ownership in the form of stock was presumably more liquid and more easily transferable than ownership in fee.

Actually, however, unforeseen difficulties frequently appeared. The directors of co-operatives often failed to provide competent management or eliminate disagreements or factionalism among the owners. Few co-operatives had a substantial equity investment, and in many instances the speculative gains of the promoters consumed the entire amount of the supposed equities. Probably no form of real estate was so exploited by unscrupulous promoters. As a result values were inflated to untenable levels and the resultant thin equities left no margin when rentals declined.

Failures were consequently widespread, and it was often said that the owner came out best who defaulted first. Tenants who tried to save their interests had to carry their share of the defaulted leases on apartments that could neither be resold nor relet at prices equal to the charges allocated to them. During the depression numerous failures occurred and the co-operative plan fell into discredit. Some conservatively financed, nonpromotional structures, however, survived the depression despite hard sledding; perhaps the most noted are the co-operatives sponsored by the Amalgamated Clothing Workers in New York City. Efforts during the later 1930's to revive co-operative housing, inspired by the success of the idea in Sweden and other countries, have not been fruitful.

Co-operation Under Trustee Ownership

A variant of the co-operative pattern which came into some prominence in the middle twenties involved trustee ownership instead of corporation ownership —the so-called Massachusetts Trust.[11] Under this plan the tenant-owners received trustee certificates as evidence of their interest in the property. Direction was placed in the hands of a self-perpetuating group of trustees, selected from the beneficiaries. Sometimes a corporate trustee with veto power was also included, particularly where mortgage financing was involved. This form of operation was apparently more successful in maintaining competent management and avoiding tenant disagreements than the typical co-operative. Although less widely used than the corporate form, the trustee plan appears to have been relatively success-

11. See Nathan William MacChesney, *Principles of Real Estate Law,* Macmillan, New York, 1927, Chap. 8, for description of the trust form.

ful on the whole. Nevertheless, little use has been made of it in the postdepression period.

Problems of organization and finance have been the strongest deterrents to co-operative housing in recent years. Where the group must be assembled before the prospect is initiated, the problems of organization and direction, of deciding on architectural and engineering aspects of the project, and of raising equity funds have in many cases proven insurmountable. Where the scheme depends upon professional promotion, the bad record of the past has generally prevented the raising of initial equity funds or getting a mortgage.

The success of co-operative housing in Sweden, by contrast, seems to lie in (1) public familiarity with co-operative methods both in production and distribution of commodities, and (2) the existence of a central producer co-operative in the housebuilding field which can assume responsibility for the planning, construction, and initial financing of the project. Neither of these important factors is found in the United States.

2. Deterrents to Equity Investment

The decline of equity investment in new residential property raises serious questions about the future course of the housing market, and the devices that may be necessary for its stimulation and operation. In part, of course, the decline is attributable to external forces although special conditions surrounding the production and marketing of houses have been sufficiently adverse to limit equity investment in housing even under more favorable general conditions. In fact, housing might not have fared as well as it did during the thirties if the general investment market had been more attractive.

Several real drawbacks to housing investment are evident—relative nonliquidity, as compared with many other types of investments, the special forms of taxation that affect real estate more directly than other types of investment, special problems of maintenance and operation, and the unique factors affecting future values.

a. nonliquidity of housing investment

The increasing demand for liquid investments has placed housing at a considerable disadvantage. The local nature of the market and the absence of a market place in the usual sense creates special difficulties in finding buyers. Complex legal procedures in conveying and protecting title impede transactions and produce contingent risks for the buyer. Selling opportunities arise sporadically and often do not coincide with a homeowner's desire to sell. Since housing is fixed in location and can usually be managed at a distance only with difficulty, inability to sell quickly is especially burdensome to the owner who has to move away. These considerations may account partly for the home purchaser's reluctance to pay down any more than necessary, so as to minimize his risk. In the rental field the result is to restrict investment to those who do not regard nonliquidity as a serious drawback. Such investors are apparently few in number.

Except for some ill-fated efforts in the late twenties to create stock ownership of housing (through co-operatives or publicly offered stock issues) no attack has been made on the problem of liquidity. Investors who require liquidity or are unwilling, or unequipped, to assume managerial responsibility are thus generally excluded from the housing field. At the same time investors for whom liquidity is not essential, such as insurance companies and other fiduciaries, not subject to incalculable demand payments, are still largely deterred by law and by their own caution from acquiring equities in housing.

b. EFFECTS OF THE REAL-ESTATE TAX SYSTEM

The property tax, which bears rather lightly or not at all on most forms of investment, falls with full force upon real estate. That the property tax has in effect become almost wholly a real property tax causes many investors to look upon it as discriminatory, placing real estate at a special disadvantage in comparison with other forms of property. This attitude is accentuated by the fact that the property tax forms the principal source of income for local government, the benefits of which go not only to real estate but to all the activities of the community.

A recent study made by the Home Owners' Loan Corporation revealed that the average annual taxes of HOLC borrowers amount to about 2.7 per cent of the original loans. In twenty states the ratio is above 3 per cent and in eight of these it is 4 per cent or more.[12] Relating the tax load to other fixed charges, the Home Owners' Loan Corporation found:[13]

> For the United States as a whole, the average monthly tax installment represents about 33 per cent of the average monthly loan payment. However, in four states real estate taxes are equivalent to 50 per cent or more, and in an additional twelve states they constitute between two fifths and one half of the loan payment. If the tax bill is related to interest alone, the average tax is equal to about 80 per cent of the interest portion of the regular loan payment, and there are ten states where it actually exceeds the total interest charges to the borrower.

12. *Federal Home Loan Bank Review*, July 1941, p. 336. The *Review* states:

In an evaluation of the results of this comparison it will be well to keep in mind that HOLC loans were made in the emergency period from 1933 to 1936 and were permitted to be equal to 80 per cent of liberal appraisals. They were intended to be generous and may have frequently approached or sometimes exceeded market values at that time. Meanwhile market prices for old properties generally have been on the decline. The figures presented [see Appendix H, Table 44], therefore, *under*state rather than overstate the annual tax in relation to present property values.

13. *Ibid.*, p. 335.

The determination of an economically sound ratio of tax to value or of tax to other charges cannot be undertaken here. The HOLC data, however, clearly indicate that the tax load may have an important bearing on the homeowner's ability to maintain his obligation. Generally, a larger percentage of HOLC loans had to be foreclosed in high-tax states than in low-tax states. Moreover, sales of foreclosed properties were proportionately greater in the latter states.[14]

The real-estate tax bears more heavily on housing investment than on investments in most other forms of enterprise because the earnings and value of a housing property depend upon a specific location. A manufacturing enterprise, suffering from heavy property taxes relative to earnings, may often move to another location, because its earnings rarely depend on operating at one specific site. Moreover, the value of a factory's site is not directly affected by the income from its operation. Even commercial enterprises, whose profitability may be more closely associated with their location, have often been able to move to lower-tax areas without suffering loss of earnings.

A housing enterprise once established cannot move. Not only are its earnings dependent upon location, but as the earnings increase, the value of the site, and therefore the tax assessment, also tends to increase. Housing consequently cannot escape from burdensome taxes by changing location or increasing earnings. With many forms of enterprise location is an incident to the business. In housing it is an essential feature of the business.

Inequality of Property Taxation

Since property values cannot be determined with mathematical exactness, assessments are bound to show considerable variation even among similar types of property. Thus, in addition to unavoidable inequalities, the way is left open for political and personal favoritism in assessment policy. In some communities large property owners, through political pressure or greater knowledge of the realty market, can sometimes obtain better ratings than small homeowners. In other communities, the small homeowner may be favored and rental and income-producing property generally placed at a disadvantage. New dwellings sometimes receive lower assessments, particularly in relation to earning power, than older houses located in supposedly higher land-value areas. Within a given community, therefore, taxes may show great inconsistency,[15] and the investor can never be sure of the basis upon which his tax is to be levied.

Variations in property taxes from one community to another are even more striking. For instance, for Federal Housing Administration insured rental projects in twenty-nine cities taxes varied in relation to gross potential annual

14. *Ibid.*, p. 337.
15. See *Facing the Tax Problem*, The Twentieth Century Fund, New York, 1937, Chap. 20.

earnings from 5 to 22 per cent.[16] Studies by the Home Owners' Loan Corporation of properties foreclosed by the Corporation also show considerable differences. In a representative number of New Jersey properties, taxes on single-family houses equaled nearly 32 per cent of gross rental, and on apartments 30 per cent. In New York State the ratios were 33 and 23.5 per cent respectively; in Chicago the average taxes for both types of property were 21 per cent and in Kansas City, Missouri, 26 per cent.[17] Tax inequalities between localities sometimes result from special legislative provisions. Thus, some states provide tax exemptions on homesteads, and others limit the tax rate on all property.

The lack of uniformity in tax policy tends to place certain communities or even neighborhoods in a more unfavorable investment position than others.[18] The effect of tax variations on the decentralization of cities has been noted in Chapter 1.

The Method of Real-Estate Taxation

The property tax is levied on an ad valorem basis. The basic disadvantage of the ad valorem levy is that it may not be related directly to the ability to pay as evidenced by the earnings of the property.

Assessments are customarily based on the supposed sales value of the property, land and buildings being appraised separately. The system is theoretically kept both current and equitable through periodic reassessments,[19] equalization boards, and boards of appeal. The determination of sales value, however, is difficult because of the absence of any regular real-estate market, where comparative values might be established, the private nature of real-estate transactions, and the frequent absence of any active buying and selling. Ultimately assessments must rest on the assessor's judgment.

Sales prices, even when known, may be a poor basis of valuation. In an active market prices may rise beyond what is justified by the property's long-term earning power, while in a dull market prices may drop temporarily far below real value. Assessments on either basis would be unfair—in the one case possibly creating a burden greater than the property could carry, and in the other permitting a levy less than realities warrant. Conscientious assessors are thus forced to take the property's long-term earning power into account. But this, too, is largely theoretical and injustice in any given year or series of years may result.

16. See Appendix H, Table 45. While these figures illustrate differences in taxing policy, they do not fairly represent the relative proportion of taxes to income as paid by apartment property. The FHA projects are for the most part in low-tax areas—frequently suburban communities. In large cities, taxes on multifamily structures may run as high as 25 to 30 per cent of gross rental.

17. *Federal Home Loan Bank Review, op. cit.*, p. 334.

18. William H. Husband, member of the Federal Home Loan Bank Board, in an address before the National Conference of Real Estate Taxpayers (Washington, April 26, 1941), noted that in Chicago taxes ranged from 16 per cent of rentals in the west zone to 25.5 per cent in the north zone.

19. Periods may run from one to four years. Not all states have definite reassessment periods.

The periodic reassessment offers little assurance that the levy will correspond to market conditions. Values are likely to fluctuate more than assessments. For obvious reasons assessments tend to lag both on the upswing and downswing; in fact they are apt to decline more slowly and to a lesser degree than property values.

Difficulties of Tax Adjustment

Municipalities are reluctant to take account of changes in market conditions that will reduce income when it is badly needed—especially when tax delinquencies make it imperative to squeeze the most from every taxpayer. The practice of relating municipal bonding power to the assessed value of real estate is another obstacle to the readjustment of taxes. In bad times falling revenues and problems of relief force municipalities to expand their debt. Yet the power to borrow, commonly limited by a fixed relationship to assessed values, would often be seriously curtailed if assessments were lowered to conform to actual market conditions.

The tax system is thus fairly inflexible, while property income is subject to extreme fluctuations. As a result, taxes often have kept properties in the red and even exceeded gross income, while assessed values have exceeded sales prices.[20] The failure of taxes to decline with value or income creates a real hazard to investors. Consequently, housing tends to be less attractive than investments which are taxed more in accordance with ability to pay.

The British System

It is often said that the British system of property assessment and taxation is more equitable than ours. During recent decades the tendency in Great Britain to supplement local taxation by grants-in-aid from the central government has, to a much greater extent than in this country, diminished the proportion of local government costs carried by the property tax. Nevertheless, the British system has some similarities to ours. The method of levy, however, is markedly different from those customarily used in this country since taxes are usually assessed against the occupant of the dwelling instead of the owner, and are presumably based upon the net rental of the property.

20. The Home Owners' Loan Corporation reports that during the first half of 1940 it sold one hundred properties in Boston at an average of 73.5 per cent and eighty in New York at an average of 79 per cent of assessed value. Data collected by the local real-estate boards in those two cities show an even lower ratio of sales price to assessed value. There is evidence that in Manhattan between 1937 and 1940 the difference between sales prices and assessed values grew steadily larger. On the basis of over 2,000 sales, assessed value increased from 20.7 per cent above market value in 1937 to 37.3 per cent in 1940. (Robert H. Armstrong and Homer Hoyt, *Decentralization in New York City,* A Preliminary Report to The Urban Land Institute, Chicago, January 1941; see chart "Market Value and Assessed Valuations of Manhattan Real Estate as Shown by Open-Market Sales," p. 182.)

Assessments are made every five years, with interim assessments for new properties. Residential property is commonly rated by the so-called *comparative method*. Forms are filled out by the taxpayer, giving the actual rent paid, or, in case of an owner-occupied dwelling, the rent probably obtainable. The official rates are then determined by comparing the returns on similar properties and by further research. Hence the assessment represents not so much actual rent but rent which the property might reasonably bring.

Since the net rather than the gross rental is taxable, an adjustment of rates to take account of operating costs is necessary. This adjustment, however, is calculated on the basis of arbitrary statutory amounts, supposedly representing average expenses. Deductions vary from about 20 per cent of gross revenue for higher-rental properties to 40 per cent for lower-rental houses. The assessed or *ratable* value is thus the rent that the assessor finds the property should yield minus an amount fixed by law to represent expenses.

Responsibility for collecting the tax is often assumed by the landlord. This is usually compulsory for apartment buildings and for low-rental properties where rent is paid oftener than quarterly. Where this responsibility is assumed, the landlord must also pay the tax on vacant quarters, and in return he is allowed a rebate up to 15 per cent of the taxes levied on the property. Where the responsibility for taxes is not assumed by the landlord, vacant dwellings are not taxed. Unused land is not taxed.

Under the British system tax rates probably correspond more closely to income than under our system. At least, wide discrepancies between the levy and ability to pay are likely to occur much less frequently. On the other hand, the five-year assessment period, if applied under fluctuating market conditions, such as are common in this country, would still tend to result in inequalities. The absence of levies on vacant land helps builders who carry large land inventories for long-time developments.

C. PROBLEMS OF VALUE AND MANAGEMENT

Almost none of the circumstances affecting the long-term value of housing property are accurately calculable. The reproduction cost—one of the common criteria of value—varies with changes in the costs of labor and materials. The rate of depreciation, as used in the valuation process, is purely theoretical.

No exact forecast of actual depreciation can be made. Some parts of a house wear out sooner than others, and the over-all deterioration depends upon how well these are maintained and replaced. Depreciation depends also upon the quality of the original parts and on the way in which materials of different quality are combined. Thus, a slate roof if used with an inferior grade of nail or flashing may be more costly to maintain than a shingle roof. Moreover, maintenance costs, irrespective of changes in income or value, recur as persistently as taxes. Over a long period they remain fairly constant and tend to absorb an increasing proportion of the dwelling's income.[21]

Importance of Property Management

Value is affected not only by the wisdom with which the dwelling is originally built but by the skill with which it is taken care of. This has special meaning for rental housing. Constant attention must not only be given to the condition of the structure but to the state of the housing market and relations with tenants. Housing management requires special knowledge and ability. If the investor does not have such ability, or for other reasons cannot manage the property himself, he must depend on agents or employees. If wholly unacquainted with management problems, he is at the mercy of his agents or employees. There are many forms of investment that carry less responsibility and permit easier liquidation.

Even less calculable than physical deterioration is obsolescence. A structure may remain physically sound and yet lose value through changes in demand which affect size, arrangement, style, or equipment, or simply because its location has lost appeal. Movements of population, entirely beyond the owner's control, may sap the earning power of the property. These factors, however, are less important in the case of low-rental property.

Effects of External Conditions

Shortage or surplus of housing, the rise and fall of income, the level of taxes, the availability of investment funds and interest rates, the buying power of the dollar, all affect the value of housing property. Other investments may be similarly influenced by economic conditions, but their greater liquidity makes adjustment easier.

The prospective investor who is well enough informed to view the situation realistically must face a housing transaction with many reservations. To begin with, the very transaction is comparatively difficult and expensive. The property is subject to special taxation without assurance of relief if its earning power declines. In order to safeguard his investment the investor must provide competent and vigilant management. Notwithstanding his caution, the income from his investment is subject to many changes which he cannot control or even forecast accurately.

All these deterrents have undoubtedly helped to retard investment in housing

21. See *A Survey of Apartment Dwelling Operating Experience in Large American Cities,* Federal Housing Administration, 1940, pp. 59, 61.

property. An increase in such investment must await removal of artificial barriers to the flow of funds and the development of means for making housing a more attractive source of income.

3. THE USE OF LONG-TERM CREDIT

Because of the decline of equity investment in relation to the dwelling's cost, the housing market has become heavily dependent on borrowed money. The credit system, in fact, has exerted a profound influence on the amount and kind of houses traded in and upon the public's attitude toward equity investment.

Fortunately for the industry, loans on mortgage security have been available in the period of the thirties, which was characterized by a lack of equity funds. Housing credit, however, has not been uniformly available either among communities or types of dwelling. Metropolitan areas have undoubtedly fared best, while small towns and rural nonfarm areas outside of metropolitan areas have been relatively neglected. No strictly home-finance system has been devised for farm dwellings. Finally, credit has been more readily available for owner-occupied than for rented houses, for one-family houses than for apartments, and for medium- and high-cost than for cheaper dwellings.

One reason for the relative ease of obtaining credit is that the lender is able to escape some of the risks of equity investment. This advantage has been increased by new safeguards given to mortgage lenders by the federal government. Another reason for the diversion of lender funds to mortgages has been the relative paucity of new security issues and the smaller demand for commercial loans, both of which were formerly principal outlets for many lending institutions. If there had been greater choice among loan outlets during the thirties, and if the government had not provided special safeguards, the mortgage would probably not have become so popular for institutional investment, since it is a cumbersome, relatively nonliquid and hazardous security.

a. THE MORTGAGE AS A FINANCIAL INSTRUMENT

The mortgage goes back to a time when land was the principal form of collateral for loans. The mortgage on real property has been used for a variety of personal, commercial, and industrial loans, and in the past has been used for short-term and intermediate credit purposes probably more than for long-term real-estate investment. Until recent decades, the mortgage loan was usually of short duration, three to five years being common, with the entire amount becoming due in one lump payment.

The special significance of the mortgage in the field of housing results from its present widespread use in financing the purchase of the property. When used for a long-term purchase, repayment of the mortgage must usually depend directly or indirectly on the property's earning power. Debt service is met either from rental revenue, as in apartment buildings, or from the purchaser's "rent equivalent" in an owner-occupied house. Consequently the loan must extend over a longer period than for the traditional, strictly collateral mortgage loan. Thus, a mechanism originally designed mainly for medium-term credit needs is used for long-term purchase contracts. Many problems in housing finance arise from the fact that the mortgage is not completely adapted to its new role, for some of its historical characteristics remain and create special risks and costs both for borrower and lender.

Some Legal Aspects of the Mortgage

Legal concepts change slowly and those affecting the mortgage are no exception. The mortgage pledges the property as security for a loan. It ostensibly transfers to the creditor title to the property with the provision that the transfer becomes void if the debt is paid in accordance with the agreement.[22] Originally the transfer of title was absolute and gave the creditor the right to full ownership and possession on default by the borrower. The debtor's rights ceased if he failed to pay promptly, and, in fact, even when the debt was satisfied, it was necessary for him to prove payment before he could regain title.

Over the course of centuries the penalty incurred by the defaulting borrower has been modified. There has been a steady trend toward greater protection for the borrower, which has received fresh impetus with every period of economic stringency up to and including that of the thirties. Today, the creditor must return title immediately on full payment of the debt. Many states, in fact, permit the mortgagor to retain title during the interim rather than pass it on to the lender, in direct contrast to the original practice. The lender's interest is limited to the amount of indebtedness, including interest. To recover his money in case of default he must go through the legal process of *foreclosure*. General recognition is also given to the debtor's right to redeem his property (known as the *equity of redemption*) even after foreclosure, provided he can satisfy the obligation plus all accrued charges within a statutory period.

Complexity and Variety of Mortgage Procedures

The use of real estate as collateral for debt involves more extensive legal procedures than are usual in other forms of lending or time-payment contracts.

22. A modification of the ordinary mortgage form, known as a *trust deed in the nature of a mortgage,* conveys title to a third party to be held in trust as security for the debt. For all purposes it is the same as a mortgage and is so interpreted by the courts.

Mortgage procedures are cumbersome and costly to the lender. And, in contrast to negotiable instruments procedures, they are not uniform among the states. State laws vary in definitions of the rights of the parties in a mortgage transaction and in the form of the instrument.

Perhaps the most important variations are in foreclosure practices—the nature of the foreclosure process, the length of the redemption period, and the rights of the defaulted borrower. Thus, the time required for clearing and conveying title under foreclosure varies from a few days in Virginia, Texas and Georgia to eighteen months in Illinois and over two years in Alabama. In most cases, the debtor is entitled to possession of the property during the period of redemption, and in Kansas, he is not even obligated to pay rent.[23] The costs of foreclosure also vary, Texas providing an inexpensive and rapid procedure, while in New York and Illinois foreclosure is exceedingly costly. The Home Owners' Loan Corporation's experience, as shown in Figure 35, illustrates the delay and cost of foreclosure proceedings. Since, however, the HOLC could make favorable arrangements because of the volume of its cases, its experience greatly understates the situation faced by the average lender, both as to time and expense.

Existing mortgage procedures in many ways hamper the development of a sound and economical system of housing finance. The extreme variations among state laws not only create barriers to a national system of housing finance, but in areas where procedures are costly and time-consuming, they raise interest rates or restrict the availability of investment funds. Expensive foreclosure also discourages lending on low-priced houses since the costs may equal or exceed the actual equity. The efforts of state governments to protect defaulted debtors have thus reached a point where they create hardships for a large class of borrowers.[24]

Trends in Mortgage Practice

In spite of the variety of state laws, the practices of lending institutions during the past decade have tended to become standardized. Mortgage interest rates at the end of the thirties were generally lower and more uniform throughout the country than at any previous time. Ratios of loan to valuation were higher, with a consequent decline in the use of second and third mortgages. The payment period

23. See J. Douglass Poteat, "State Legislative Relief for the Mortgage Debtor During the Depression," and David A. Bridewell, "The Effects of Defective Mortgage Laws on Home Financing," *Law and Contemporary Problems,* Vol. V, No. 4, Duke University, Durham, 1938.

It is interesting to note that the states with long redemption periods are those which at the time of establishing these restraints were dominated by small farmers. The relationship between the period of redemption and the time needed to get in one or two additional crops is striking.

24. See Horace Russell, *Legal Problems in the Housing Field,* Housing Monograph Series No. 1, National Resources Planning Board.

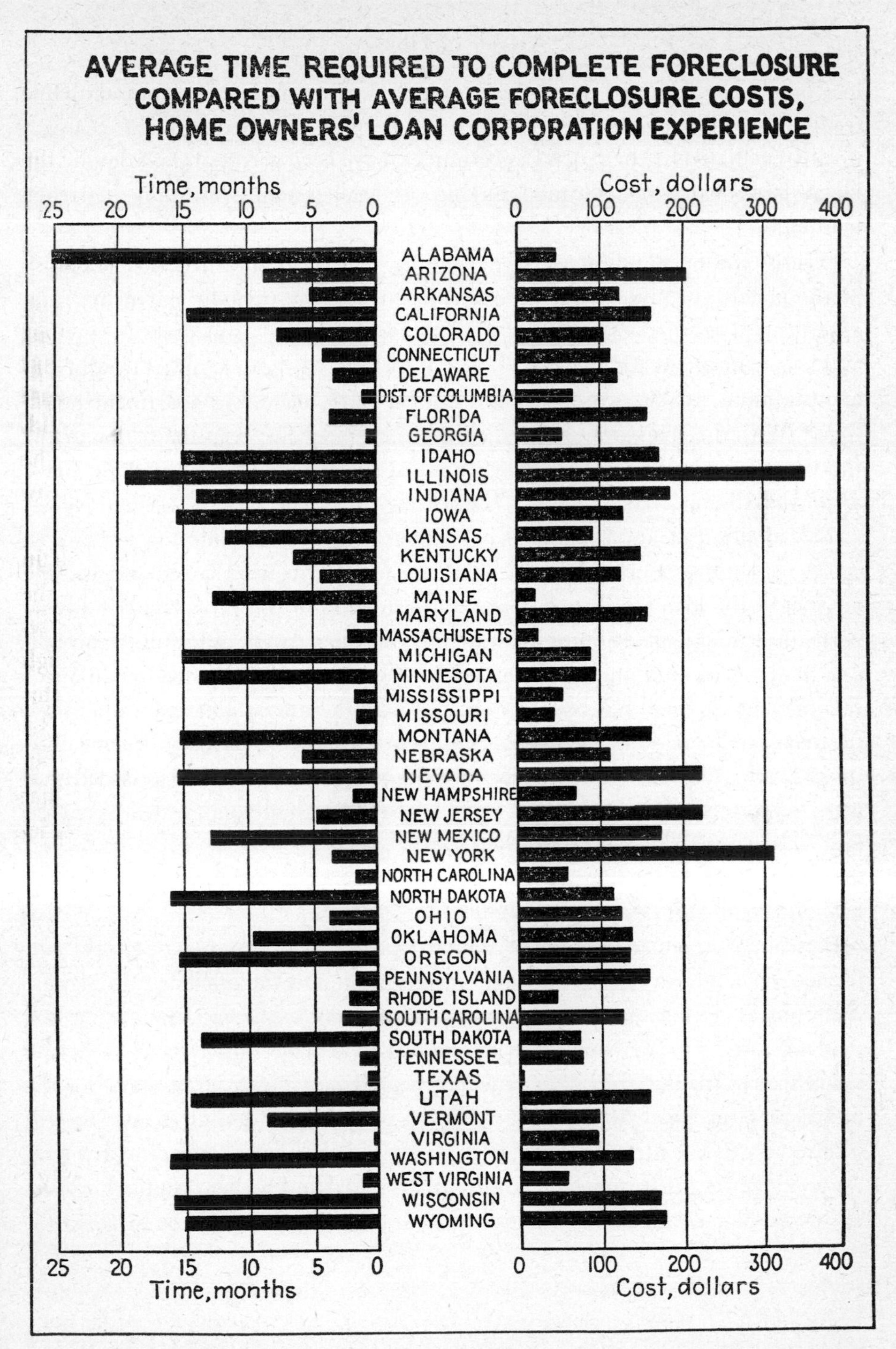

FIGURE 35. Foreclosure procedures are often time-consuming and costly and vary widely from state to state. In Alabama and Illinois, for instance, the average time required to complete foreclosure is about two years compared with less than a month in Georgia, Texas and Virginia. Average costs vary from \$5 to \$350. (*Source:* Appendix Table 46.)

has been extended and long-term original loans are more common, while trading in mortgages in the secondary market has increased.[25] These changes, greatly facilitated by the federal government, have been accomplished despite the laggardness of the states in modernizing the legal system controlling mortgage lending.[26]

Perhaps the outstanding trend in lending policies is the increased adoption of the practice of amortizing the principal in regular periodic payments. The amortization method of payment used in former years, principally by savings and loan institutions for owner-occupied properties, has been adopted by all types of institutions for loans on every kind of property, including apartment buildings.[27] With the abandonment of the lump-sum payment, even the fiction of the mortgage as a short-term loan, when used in connection with a purchase transaction, has disappeared.

The adoption of amortization has resulted in a new attitude toward risk in mortgage lending. Formerly the lender's principal safeguard lay in keeping the amount of the loan low in relation to the valuation of the property. For his security the lender looked almost solely to the probable recovery of his funds through sale in case of default and foreclosure. The depression proved, however, that this safeguard alone could not be relied on, and with the subsequent extension of the term and the increase in the mortgage-to-loan ratio, its inadequacy became even more visible. Experience with consumer time-payment credit had revealed that it is safer to rely on the borrower's ability to pay his installments and so avoid default than on the value of repossessed goods.

The Rigidity of the Mortgage Pattern

Present-day requirements are recognized in the high loan-to-value ratio and the lengthened term of payment and amortization. On the other hand, the payment plan is not flexible enough to permit adjustment to the variations in income that are sure to occur over a long period. The scheme of payment is rigidly established at the outset as if current income and rental were to be static for the duration of the loan. Actually the payment period, extended as it now is, will probably cover an entire cycle of the market and perhaps more, thus involving all the contingencies that implies. Loans on both rental and owner-occupied properties would be safer for lender and borrower, if the payments could be increased in

25. By secondary market is meant the selling of mortgages to, and the buying by, institutions not engaged in the primary writing thereof.

26. See Chap. 10, p. 258.

27. In the past some insurance-company loans on income-producing property were set up on an amortized basis. It was not often, however, that amortization was complete or the term of the payment was directly adjusted to the assumed economic life of the property or its earning power.

good times and lowered in bad.[28] The amortization plan, moreover, does not increase the likelihood of leniency to the borrower. Each monthly accumulation of defaulted payments increases the lender's chances of loss. The costs of foreclosure have not diminished, and the risk of loss from "milking [29] the property" during the redemption period has not been lessened. Where a Federal Housing Administration mortgage is involved, losses due to deferment of foreclosure are not covered by the mortgage insurance. This may tend to make the lender institute proceedings immediately on default rather than to temporize with the borrower.

The inflexibility which is the major defect of the mortgage as a financial instrument thus remains. Indeed, the old lump-payment mortgage—as long as the possibility of renewal existed—could be adjusted to new conditions faced by the borrower at its expiration. Thus, in spite of its many advantages, the substitution of periodic partial payments for a lump sum has tended to increase the rigidity of the payment pattern and to increase steadily the borrower's risk as the loan is paid off.

b. THE MORTGAGE INTEREST RATE

Since houses are usually purchased through long-term credit, the rate of interest is an important element in the total cost. Changes in interest rates, or the cost of money, thus affect the market like changes in production or distribution costs.[30]

During the past decade, the interest rate is the one element of cost that has been substantially reduced. It is estimated that in 1931 the effective rate of savings and loan association loans ranged from 6.2 per cent in Connecticut to 15.3 per cent in Tennessee. Five years later the range had been narrowed to from 5 per cent in New Hampshire to 7.3 per cent in Oklahoma.[31]

28. See D. L. Wickens, "Adjusting the Mortgagors' Obligation to Economic Cycles," *Law and Contemporary Problems,* Vol. V, No. 4, Autumn 1938, pp. 617–624.

29. The willful neglect, waste, or spoliation of the property by its owner or occupant.

30. The effect on the monthly charges of a given percentage reduction in the interest rate as compared to a similar percentage reduction in building costs has frequently been exaggerated. Clarence D. Long, Jr. (*Building Cycles and the Theory of Investment,* Princeton University Press, Princeton, 1940, pp. 26–27), states: ". . . without any allowance for maintenance or replacements, without any consideration of the costs of heating and lighting, a fall in the mortgage rate of interest from 5 per cent to 0 [assuming 20 years' amortization] would reduce the annual carrying charges of a $6,000 home by only 36 per cent. A drop of interest of 20 per cent from 5 per cent to 4 per cent would cause a fall in carrying charges of only 7 per cent; whereas a fall in building cost of 20 per cent would reduce carrying charges by nearly 15 per cent. . . . A reduction of the rate of interest from 4 per cent to 2 per cent is a reduction of 50 per cent and would reduce carrying charges less than 14 per cent; whereas a reduction of 50 per cent in the original cost would, even assuming no reduction in taxes or insurance, reduce carrying charges 35 per cent. Even zero interest would not in itself make building profitable if expected rent fell more than 30 per cent from equilibrium."

31. *Federal Home Loan Bank Review,* December 1937, p. 80. The effective rate covers all costs to the borrower, including initial fees or discounts averaged over the period of the loan. At the earlier date these initial charges made a sizable addition to the nominal rate.

These figures, however, greatly underestimate the actual changes, since they apply to first-mortgage rates only. In 1931 a second and perhaps even a third mortgage, at much higher interest rates, would have been required to reach the loan-to-value ratio possible today under a first mortgage. Consequently, where total borrowing of 70 to 80 per cent of value included secondary mortgages of 20 to 30 per cent, the actual interest rate might be double or treble the effective rate for first mortgages.

Supporting this assumption, a survey by the National Association of Real Estate Boards showed that in 1924 interest rates on second mortgages ranged from 8 to 15 per cent or more, with the country as a whole averaging over 10 per cent. A sample study by the Institute for Research in Land and Public Utility Economics indicated that in Chicago second-mortgage rates in 1925 ranged from 12.9 to 18.1 per cent. A legislative committee reported in 1925 that in New York City a 10 per cent rate was conservative and 15 per cent above average. In 1927, 10 per cent discount was often charged for a loan of one year, 15 per cent for two years and 20 per cent for three years. By 1929, 40 per cent discounts were commonly demanded and even then the supply of funds was limited. The President's Conference on Home Building and Home Ownership (December 1931) found that total initial charges for obtaining a one- to three-year loan ranged from 15 to 25 per cent. Both first and second mortgages had to be renewed frequently so that some or all of the initial costs recurred.[32]

The first breach in the mortgage rate structure was made in 1933 when the Home Owners' Loan Corporation began to refinance mortgages at 5 per cent. In 1934 the Federal Housing Administration established a nominal rate of 5 per cent for insured mortgages, plus annual payments of 0.5 per cent of the total loan for insurance and 0.5 per cent as a lender's service charge. In 1938 the service charge was eliminated and the insurance was calculated on declining balances. In 1939 the interest rate was reduced to 4.5 per cent, plus 0.5 per cent for mortgage insurance.

Except for remote communities, poorly serviced by financial agencies, second mortgages and mortgage renewals are less common than formerly; in some areas they have disappeared as more funds for housing have become available. These trends constitute a virtual revolution in the financing of housing.[33]

32. Summarized by A. F. Bemis, *The Economics of Shelter,* Vol. II, *The Evolving House,* Technology Press, Massachusetts Institute of Technology, Cambridge, 1934, pp. 367-376 *passim.*

33. From the borrower's point of view, the extension of the term of an amortized mortgage, by reducing the amount of principal payment each month and thus the total monthly payment, may have much the same effect as a lowering of the interest rate. Since the two have gone together in recent developments, it is impossible to weigh the definite influence of each. It must be borne in mind, however, that amortization is not a cost. It is a method of distributing the payment of a cost. The reduction of the amortization payment merely extends the period over which a definite amount must be paid. Since interest must be paid during the whole life of the mortgage, an increase in the

Composition of Interest Rates

In spite of this 30 to 50 per cent reduction on high-ratio loans, the mortgage interest rate has continued to be subject to attack. This is due in part to the greater ease with which the interest rate can be singled out to suit political expediency than can the more complex questions of production and marketing. Those engaged in the latter activities are likely also to find it easier to urge lower interest rates than to undertake the Herculean house-cleaning job confronting them if construction costs are to be substantially reduced. Moreover, support for demands for lower rates can easily be obtained from the extensive class of debtors—especially amid general uncertainty as to what establishes the interest rate or what, under ideal conditions, that level might be.

Traditionally, the interest rate depends on three components: the cost of money to the lender, the expense of making loans, and reserve for the risks of the business.

The average dividend rate paid by federal savings and loan associations was 3.69 per cent in 1935 and 3.39 per cent in 1939. The Home Loan Bank Board has recently advocated a mortgage rate of 3 per cent, and in New York the prevailing savings and loan association dividend rate in 1940 was 2.5 per cent. In December 1940, the average dividend (or interest) rate paid by mutual savings banks was 1.97 per cent, with many New York banks paying only 1.5 per cent.[34] A maximum of 2.5 per cent is permitted on savings and time deposits of six months or more in Federal Reserve member banks, but the actual rate paid on all time deposits averages only 1.1 per cent. In 1939 several life insurance companies reduced the guaranteed dividends on policies from 3 to 2.5 per cent.

Authorities differ as to what the minimum payment for money can be.[35] In part the rate depends upon the public's attitude toward the risk involved and the liquidity of the investment. The commercial bank rate reflects the recognized safety of deposits and their liquidity, while the higher rates of savings and loan and insurance company dividends indicate a premium paid for relative illiquidity.

---

amortization period actually increases the total amount of interest paid in the long run. Thus, the total amount of interest at 5 per cent on a $1,000 mortgage on a twenty-five-year basis is $331.20 more than that paid on a fifteen-year basis, although the monthly payment in the first case is only $5.85 as against $7.91 in the second.

34. *Eighth Annual Report, 1939–1940,* Federal Home Loan Board, pp. 46–49.

35. See *Hearings Before the TNEC,* Pt. 11, *The Construction Industry,* testimony of R. R. Rogers, Vice President of the Prudential Insurance Company, p. 5064; Morton Bodfish, Executive Vice President, U.S. Building and Loan League, p. 5098; Henry Bruère, President, Bowery Savings Bank of New York City, p. 5125; John H. Fahey, Chairman, Federal Home Loan Bank Board, p. 5390. Mr. Fahey expressed the opinion that "there is a serious question that the rate of return to savers can go any lower than 3 to 3.5 per cent without discouraging thrift." Mr. Bruère testified that his bank was offered more deposits than it would take at zero interest for the first three months and 2 per cent thereafter. Mr. Bodfish was "convinced we could not buy money cheaper than 3 per cent." Mr. Rogers declined to venture an opinion.

The quantity of savings as well as the competition offered by alternative sources of investment are a primary influence on the interest rate. The generally lower rates on securities today, in contrast to a decade ago, have, by reducing the competition for funds, permitted institutions to obtain money on more favorable terms than formerly.

Dividends to depositors or shareholders do not represent the total amount paid by the institution in assembling funds. There are advertising, clerical, and general overhead costs, varying considerably with the size and type of institution. Although general data are not available for the relation of such expenses to the total interest rate, it is obvious that the lender must take them into consideration.

Expense of Making Loans

The making of amortized mortgages is a relatively expensive type of business. The average loan is small, and the work of collecting and accounting for the small amounts collected each month involves considerable work. The Federal Housing Administration type of mortgage, for example, requires the keeping of five accounts: interest, amortization, taxes, fire insurance, and mortgage insurance. Authorities disagree on the cost of doing business.[36]

Since the Federal National Mortgage Association has found it necessary to pay 0.75 per cent per annum of the outstanding principal for servicing a mortgage, this may be regarded as a satisfactory rate for handling the details of the mortgage business after the transaction has been made. Yet this figure still leaves some overhead costs unaccounted for (for instance, those of the purchasing institution) and, of course, it does not cover the special commissions and costs of initiating the business (formerly passed on to the consumer but now generally carried by the institution) nor the expenses of foreclosure (which, even with Federal Housing Administration mortgages, must be borne largely by the lender). Part of the difference between the interest paid on savings and that charged for loans is also due to the proportion of cash reserves required of the different classes of institution to meet depositor demands. This partly accounts for the greater spread in commercial bank rates, for instance, than in savings and loan association rates.

Charges for Risk

The element of risk is one of the imponderables. The amortized mortgage has to some extent reduced the lender's risk, but the high-ratio loans partly counteract this advantage. The liquidity of insured mortgages and the borrowing powers

36. *Ibid.*, Mr. Rogers (p. 5068) accepts 0.5 per cent as sufficient, Mr. Fahey (p. 5398) considers 0.5 per cent too low, Mr. Bodfish (p. 5098) finds the cost of doing business to be 2 per cent, and Mr. Bruère (p. 5124) infers it to be in the neighborhood of 0.75 per cent.

of member institutions of the Home Loan Bank System, in so far as these features cover the mortgage structure of the country, provide new cushions against the shock of another depression. Because the principal is paid off in regular payments, the risk of loss from resale of foreclosed properties is lessened. On Federal Housing Administration insured mortgages, almost all of this risk is assumed by the government upon the payment of the 0.5 per cent premium charge.[37] Only experience can tell whether the FHA insurance rate would provide a sufficient reserve for a private institution. Nevertheless, FHA insurance is available to institutions that care to substitute it for their own allowance for this item.

Prospects of Changing the Mortgage Interest Rate

From the foregoing estimates, a probable minimum mortgage rate may be estimated. If 2.75 to 3 per cent is taken as the payment for savings and allowances for the lending institution's reserves under 1940 conditions, 0.75 per cent for handling loan collections, and 0.5 per cent for the risk, the minimum mortgage interest rate under 1940 conditions was 4 to 4.25 per cent, without any allowance for the several less easily calculated direct and overhead costs mentioned.

Although some money has been available for so-called "prime" loans at these rates, the best generally obtainable in 1940 for selected risks was probably 4.5 per cent with the average around 5 per cent.[38] The difference between the average rate and the estimated minimum is due: (1) to varying estimates by institutions of the components of the interest rate, (2) to the competition between mortgages and other investments for available funds, and (3) to circumstances surrounding individual transactions.

Unless there is a drastic change in the methods of capital finance, lower mortgage rates can result only from: (1) changes in the basic money rate due to general financial and economic conditions, (2) the growth of more efficient lending institutions, (3) lessening the risk in mortgage investment, and (4) the assumption by mortgage loans of a more favorable position in the capital market. In spite of the demands for capital created by the war, the mortgage rate shows no indication of change.

C. SOURCES OF MORTGAGE FINANCE

We do not have a group of institutions in this country principally concerned with long-term mortgage lending. Savings and loan institutions are the only type that deal principally in housing mortgages, but they do not dominate the mortgage market. As a group, commercial and savings banks, insurance com-

37. See Chap. 10 for a discussion of FHA insurance.

38. The maximum permissible FHA rate at present is 5 per cent, including 0.5 per cent mortgage insurance premium.

panies and noninstitutional lenders are today a large factor in real-estate finance.

As shown in Figure 36, "individuals and others" [39] hold a larger dollar volume of mortgages on one- to four-family houses than any single institutional lender. For the sixteen-year period 1925-1940, the average annual amount of mortgages outstanding was $18.2 billion, with the average for individuals and others being $6.4 billion, for savings and loan associations $4.6 billion, mutual savings banks $2.9 billion, commercial banks $1.7 billion and insurance companies $1.4 billion. The end of the thirties saw each of these groups holding much the same proportion of the total dollar volume of mortgages outstanding as at the end of the twenties, with the exception of savings and loan associations. These latter, which had held an average of 31 per cent in the four-year period 1926-1929, averaged only 21 per cent during 1937-1940. In 1933 the Home Owners' Loan Corporation began its operations, reaching its peak in 1935 when it had $2.9 billion worth of mortgages; in the period 1937-1940 it held an average of 12 per cent of total mortgages outstanding.

Figure 36 also shows the amount of mortgages made annually on one- to four-family homes. For the sixteen-year period 1925-1940, the average annual amount of mortgages made was $3.3 billion, with savings and loan associations making an average of $1.1 billion, individuals and others $0.7 billion, commercial banks $0.6 billion, mutual savings banks $0.4 billion and insurance companies $0.3 billion. The only significant shift in the proportionate amount of mortgage business between the late twenties and late thirties was a decline by the mutual savings banks from 14 per cent in 1926-1929 to 4 per cent of the total in 1937-1940.

Fusion of Short- and Long-Term Credit Operations

The increase in the length of the mortgage repayment period has widened the divergence between the theory and practice of mortgage lending and the traditional concepts of commercial banking. In spite of this, there has been a tendency to combine long-term mortgage credit and short-term financing in commercial banks.

This trend goes back to the beginning of the century, when state banks were already engaged in real-estate lending. To meet competition, successive changes in the federal banking laws after 1913 permitted national banks to increase their real-estate loans. Under the McFadden Act of 1927, national banks could invest

39. "Others" include fiduciaries, trust departments of commercial banks, real-estate companies, bond companies, title and mortgage companies, philanthropic and educational institutions, fraternal organizations, construction companies, The RFC Mortgage Company, etc. Although important shifts have taken place between the volume of mortgage debt held by individuals and the various components of the miscellaneous group, no specific data are available that show what these shifts were. The proportion of the total debt held by individuals has probably declined and that of the institutional group risen.

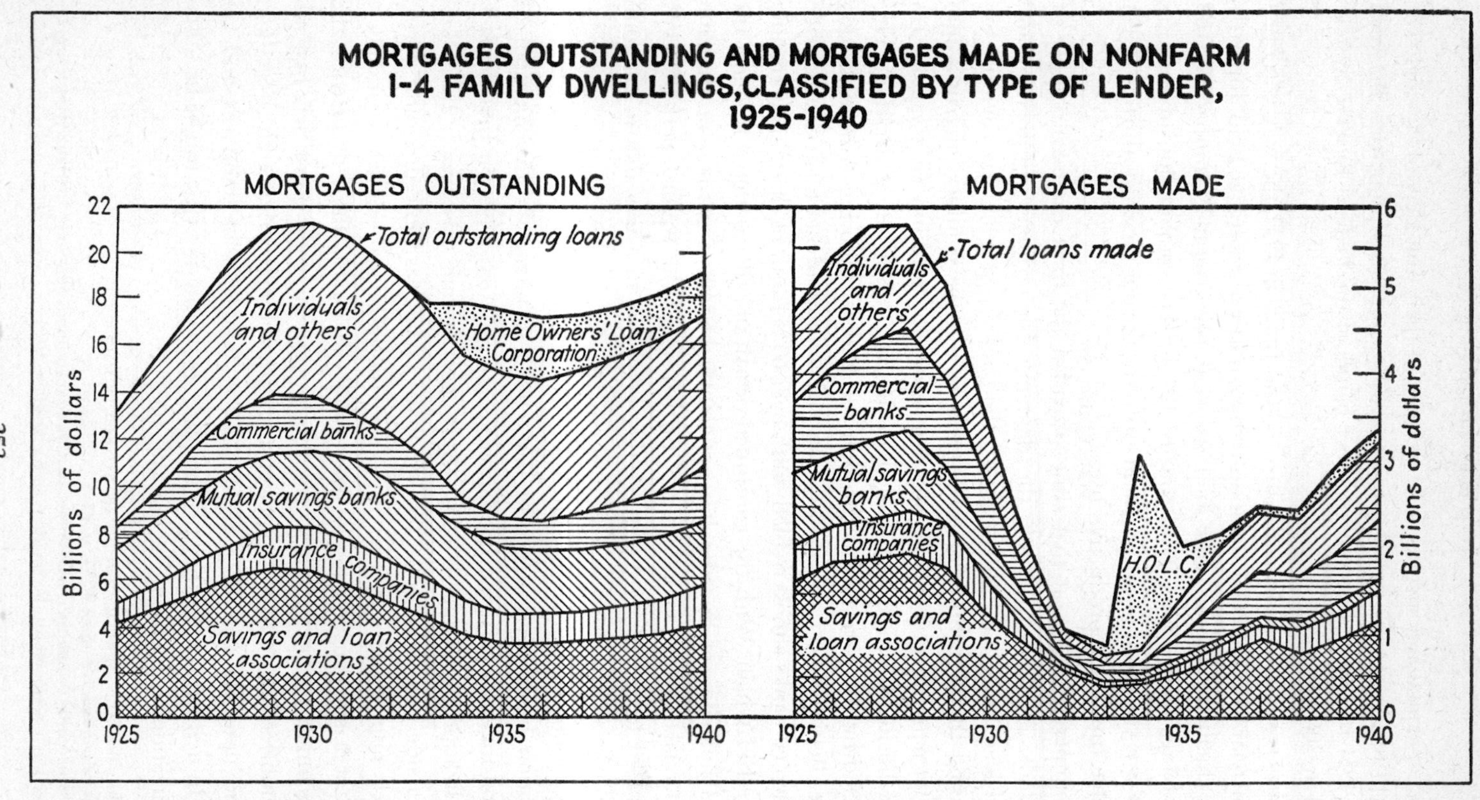

FIGURE 36. The proportion of mortgages made each year to the total volume outstanding has changed radically from the late twenties—with a ratio of 1 to 4—to the middle and late thirties. At the bottom of the depression, the ratio had fallen to 1 to 20, from which it recovered to 1 to 6. Except for a decline in mortgages made by mutual savings banks, the distribution of new mortgage business has changed only slightly. (*Source:* Appendix Tables 47 and 48.)

25 per cent of capital and surplus or 50 per cent of their time deposits (whichever was larger) in five-year 50 per cent mortgages on improved properties. Between 1920 and 1931 real-estate loans by member banks of the Federal Reserve System increased by 300 per cent.[40]

With the creation of the federally insured mortgage in 1934, the way was open for commercial banks to enter the long-term, amortized mortgage field, formerly confined chiefly to savings and loan associations, insurance companies, and mutual savings banks. This trend toward the further combination of banking functions was the result of government pressure during the early thirties to get all available funds into productive use.

The commercial banks at that time provided the most extensive supply of liquid funds. At the same time, the demands for ordinary commercial and industrial loans were too light to absorb the banks' resources. An obvious way of increasing the availability of credit, was to put the commercial banks into the long-term mortgage business, supplementing the medium (five-year) term mortgage business, which had tended to dry up during the depression. This was effected by the government through the Federal Housing Administration insurance. Between 1935 and 1940 the annual volume of mortgage loans made by commercial banks almost trebled, with over 60 per cent of these loans coming under the FHA plan. With the continued dearth of other outlets for loans, the improved financing of housing has apparently become a permanent function of commercial banks. The result is a furthering of the fusion—perhaps even confusion—of long- and short-term credit operations, in a way that is not common in European banking systems.

The situation is like that in the construction industry itself, where lack of specialization by types of structure has tended to retard the development of production methods particularly adapted to the different types. In finance, lack of specialization has similar effects.[41] Mortgage lending may simply be looked upon as a side line, to be given less emphasis as soon as more profitable forms of business appear. Institutions with which the mortgage business is merely a side line or a stopgap will rarely desire and can rarely afford to provide the special technical facilities essential to sound mortgage lending practice. Instead, in their indifference or lack of experience they may neglect thorough procedure, or depend upon the federal government for judgments of standards and appraisals. In neither case do they fill the place in the market that might be taken by organizations specializing in housing finance.

40. Morton Bodfish, "Mortgage Credits in Relation to Banking Policy," *The Journal of Land & Public Utility Economics,* August 1935, p. 219.

41. The situation is complicated by the fact that those institutions that have specialized in mortgage lending have often been among the smallest and least efficient.

British Mortgage Lending Methods

In contrast with our system, the long-term and short-term credit facilities are fairly well separated in Great Britain. There the building societies (which correspond, though on a larger scale, to our savings and loan associations) have developed along with the growing demands for housing funds. The necessity for tapping other sources of credit consequently has not existed.

The British mortgage institution has undoubted advantages because of its size and its specialization in a single field. It can acquire an expertness unknown to the small institution, or the institution that regards mortgage lending as merely a side line. It has effected reductions in overhead and servicing costs, and so has been able to operate on a very narrow spread between rate of interest charged and rate of dividend paid. Another contributing factor to the narrow spread is the practice of using a flexible interest rate, permitting the institution to increase its charges from time to time in proportion to the extent to which the Bank of England rate may have been increased. The lending institution is thus able to protect itself against increases in the cost of money to it. Thus, while the British building society interest rate has been lower than ours, the rate of payment to shareholders has been generally higher.[42]

The British system, however, may have doubtful applicability to American conditions. The fusion of lending functions is an intrinsic part of our banking structure and the reversal of so strong a trend would be difficult without drastic changes in our whole concept of long-term housing finance.

4. SUMMARY

Housing is an essential class of property and an important field of investment in which few people apparently are able or willing to put much of their own

42. *English Building Society Dividend and Mortgage Rates,* 1929–1937

Year	Average Interest Rate Paid on Shares (*Per Cent*)	Interest Rate Charged to Borrowers (*Per Cent*)
1929	4.54	6.00
1930	4.65	6.00
1931	4.62	6.00
1932	4.52	5.50–6.00
1933	3.95	5.00–5.50
1934	3.80	4.50–5.00
1935	3.64	4.50
1936	3.45	4.50
1937	3.38	4.25–4.50

Source: Wolfgang F. Stolper, "British Monetary Policy and the Housing Boom," *Quarterly Journal of Economics,* Vol. LVI, No. 1, Pt. II, November 1941, Tables XXI and XLV.

money. The shortage of equity funds is due to small savings and low income in relation to the costs of buying a house and to the unusual responsibilities and limitations that surround the ownership of real property. The cumbersome, expensive, and hazardous machinery of transfer, the nonliquidity of the investment, the heavy taxation, and the uncertainties of value over a long period of amortization—all contribute to the reluctance of investors to risk their money.

No basic solution of the problem has been undertaken. On the contrary, the only means developed for meeting the situation has been to facilitate heavier borrowing in relation to the equity investment. At the same time, the customary methods of finance have not been sufficiently modernized to meet the special needs of long-term loans dependent for payment upon fluctuating income. Instead, the trend among lending institutions has been away from specialization in housing finance and toward an increasing dependence upon government for specialized services, while government itself has, as the next chapter will show, so far failed to develop a financial program that is either consistent or comprehensive. As a result, the housing market is often handicapped at one of its most vital points.

Chapter 10

GOVERNMENT AND THE HOUSING MARKET

GOVERNMENT HAS PLAYED a much more extensive role in the marketing than in the production of houses. In production, as Part I of this survey has shown, government's function has been chiefly regulatory. Except for the occasional provision of architectural and supervisory services and research in construction, government has generally left housebuilding to private establishments.

The major impact of government upon the housing industry has been at the marketing level. Government (chiefly state government) has throughout our history established the legal procedures under which the selling, buying, and renting of real property take place. The inadequate financial system and the growing discrepancies between income and housing costs, however, induced the federal government—and to a limited extent the state and municipal governments—to offer more direct aid to the consumer.

Government has rescued homeowners who were faced with the loss of their properties. It has stimulated new building, new buying, and new lending by providing safeguards to lenders in exchange for favorable terms to borrowers. It has offered other inducements to investment in certain classes of housing property. And finally, to aid in providing shelter for families unable, under existing conditions, to obtain safe and sanitary shelter within their small incomes, government has become a financier, owner and operator of housing property.

The economic and social dislocations of the war program have increased the federal government's participation in the housing market.[1] Through direct loan or investment, contingent liabilities, and outright grant or expenditure, the varied stake of the federal government had by July 1940 reached the total of $7 billion in urban housing alone.[2]

These activities have attained an important place in public finance. Taken together, they appear to constitute a consistent and comprehensive program supplementary to private enterprise. In practice, however, this apparent consist-

1. Its supervision of design and construction, its specification requirements, and sometimes even its dictation of production methods (especially under the defense program), have influenced the technological aspects of the industry (see Chap. 5, pp. 131-132, 135-136, 147).

2. See Appendix I, Table 49, for the components of this sum. The expansion of Federal Housing Administration operations and the war housing program since July 1940 has resulted in more than a 40 per cent increase in the above total.

ency is weakened by contradictions and conflicts among agencies, and by a lack of co-ordination between state and federal activities. The benefits of government aid have therefore been lessened, and a complicated marketing system has often become more confused. The impending economic problems of the postwar period make this situation especially critical.

1. The Government as Salvager

The real-estate and financial collapse of 1929-1933 precipitated the greatest wave of urban home foreclosures in our history. In December 1931 President Hoover called the Conference on Home Building and Home Ownership.[3] Out of this came a recommendation for a home-mortgage reserve banking system, a proposal that had been under discussion since the first World War. In July 1932 Congress created a Federal Home Loan Bank System, under the supervision of a Federal Home Loan Bank Board. But the housing situation at the time called for more drastic treatment. Measures that might have helped to forestall a collapse, if enacted a decade before, were powerless to stem the mounting tide of urban foreclosures.

An even more acute situation prevailed in farm mortgage finance. Recognizing the shortage of farm mortgage credit, the federal government as early as 1917 had established a system of federal Land Banks to provide to farmers long-term mortgages at low interest rates. But again, the spread of distress in rural areas required greater aid than the Land Banks were able to provide under existing powers, and emergency action followed.

a. State and Federal Emergency Measures

Between 1931 and 1933, thirty-three states passed special laws for the relief of delinquent mortgagors. Some of these acts extended redemption periods or limited foreclosure by power of sale. Others limited or attempted to limit deficiency judgments and set minimum amounts at which properties might be disposed of under forced sale. The most important and widespread of these special measures were mortgage moratorium laws, which prevented for an extended period the ordinary functioning of foreclosure procedures. In all, twenty-eight states created mortgage moratoria, and by extensions of the original acts a number of these are still on the statute books.[4]

These temporary relief measures did little to solve the basic problems and indeed postponed the day of reckoning. New sources of credit were needed and this only the federal government was prepared to provide.

3. The reports of the conference were published in eleven volumes. See Bibliography.
4. J. Douglass Poteat, *op. cit.*, Appendix, pp. 539–544.

Federal Aid to Farm Finance

In 1933, $200 million was made available for federal Land Bank Commissioner loans to meet the urgent need for additional and more liberal farm mortgage credit. These loans could be made on either first- or second-mortgage security to an amount (including prior encumbrances) not exceeding 75 per cent of the appraised normal value of the farm property. Commissioner loans could be made for forty years, but were limited to $5,000. Since the $200 million fund soon became inadequate, the Federal Farm Mortgage Corporation was created in 1934 to assure sufficient funds for both Land Bank and Land Bank Commissioner loans. The Corporation obtained its funds through the sale of Federal Farm Mortgage Corporation bonds, guaranteed by the United States Treasury as to principal and interest. When the Federal Farm Mortgage Corporation was formed, the maximum Land Bank Commissioner loan was increased from $5,000 to $7,500; by an act of May 1935, the Land Bank Commissioner was authorized to grant loans on a "prudent investment" basis. Between May 1933 and the end of 1941, 578,544 Commissioner loans were made, totaling about $1,066 million.

Even more important than the Land Bank Commissioner's loans in refinancing farm mortgage debt were the provisions that made possible an expansion of the volume of federal Land Bank loans in order to meet the emergency. The Federal Farm Mortgage Corporation was authorized to purchase Land Bank bonds and to resell them at an opportune time in the open market at reasonable rates. Between May 1933 and the end of 1940, the Federal Land Banks granted loans totaling $1,438 million on farm mortgages. This sum plus the Land Bank Commissioner loans made a total of more than $2.5 billion of farm mortgage refinancing accomplished through these means. By 1936 the Land Banks were able to return to the open money market, thus ending the necessity for direct government purchase of farm mortgages.

The Home Owners' Loan Corporation

The best known and most spectacular of all federal mortgage relief measures was the establishment of the Home Owners' Loan Corporation by Congress in June 1933. The Corporation was placed under the direction of the directors of the Federal Home Loan Bank Board and was authorized to make direct loans to nonfarm homeowners threatened with the loss of their properties through foreclosure.[5] Summarizing the activities of the Corporation before the Temporary National Economic Committee, the Chairman of the Board stated:

5. A few loans on farm dwellings were made in the early days of the Home Owners' Loan Corporation.

Loans could be made under the law for a 15-year period at a flat 5 percent rate, amortized on a monthly basis, and on the basis of a liberal appraisal. As soon as the offices of the Corporation were opened, they were flooded with applications. A total of 1,886,491 applications were received, amounting to $6,173,355,652. When it suspended lending on June 12, 1936, the Corporation had made 1,017,948 loans in the amount of $3,093,450,641. Advances for reconditioning and taxes made subsequent to the closing of the original loans have brought the total advances made by the Corporation through May 31, 1939, to $3,167,764,388. The average loan closed amounted to $3,039. By the early part of 1935 the acquisition of mortgages by the Corporation and its disbursements of funds had so relieved the mortgage market and stabilized real estate values that the applications thereafter declined by the Corporation were invariably refinanced by the lenders without objection from any part of the country.

As of May 31, 1939, there were 862,902 accounts on the books of the Home Owners' Loan Corporation and being billed. As of that date these loans totaled $2,091,324,356. As of the same date foreclosures resulting in the acquisition of properties totaled 138,640; 50,665 of these properties have been sold and 88,801 are on hand. The total capitalized value of the properties the Corporation now holds is $506,248,027. This capitalized value represents unpaid principal, all unpaid advances including taxes, insurance, and repairs made by the Corporation for the borrower's account, foreclosure costs, accrued and unpaid interest as of the date of foreclosure judgment, charges to the property during the foreclosure period, all initial reconditioning regardless of when made and capital improvements or betterments after acquisition.[6]

The RFC Mortgage Company

To take care of urban income-producing property, which could not secure assistance from the Home Owners' Loan Corporation, the Reconstruction Finance Corporation created in 1935 a wholly owned subsidiary, The RFC Mortgage Company. This agency made some direct loans for the refinancing of mortgages on apartment buildings, hotels, and business properties and to a lesser extent for the construction of multifamily structures, where pressing need could be demonstrated and other sources of mortgage funds were not available. By June 30, 1940, The RFC Mortgage Company had loaned about $68 million.[7]

b. EFFECTS OF THE EMERGENCY MEASURES

The measures instituted by the states to meet the depression had mixed effects. They provided temporary relief to mortgage debtors but increased the difficulties of creditors, and they created a new hazard to lending. The fear of continued or repeated moratoria, especially after the emergency laws had been extended, no doubt added to the reluctance of institutions to re-enter the mortgage field, and hence contributed to the need for further federal measures which would create

6. *Hearings Before the TNEC,* Pt. 11, *The Construction Industry,* testimony of John H. Fahey, p. 5386. See Appendix I, Table 50, for summary of HOLC operations to June 30, 1940.

7. See Appendix I, Table 51. Since 1937, the activities of the company have been principally confined to the purchase of Federal Housing Administration insured mortgages from original lenders.

new confidence and new inducements. Nowhere was the opportunity taken to simplify the complicated mortgage system; indeed, if anything, the new laws made it more complex.

Federal action had generally beneficial results. It not only helped to stop foreclosures but also promoted recovery. The termination of forced liquidation saved lending institutions and property owners and halted the decline of property values. By rewriting mortgages on a long-term amortized basis, frequently with reduced principal and lower interest rates, a huge volume of defaulted loans were put on a paying basis. Evidence was given of the advantages of regular principal payments over the lump payment, with its risk of catching the borrower unprepared and unable to pay, and other features of value in a more fundamental approach to the problems of home finance were suggested.

To quote the Chairman of the Home Loan Bank Board:

> In my opinion, the most significant lesson which Home Owners' Loan Corporation teaches is that powerful financial reserve institutions are essential to the maintenance of anything like economic stability. When difficulties begin to develop, if such reserve institutions are wisely administered, they can prevent the development of panic losses. When troubles begin, if honest debtors are not pressed for immediate payment but are given a reasonable time to meet their obligations, they will invariably do so if the debt is at all within their capacity to pay.
>
> The average loan taken over by the Home Owners' Loan Corporation was more than 2 years in default on principal and interest and 3 years on taxes. Consequently these loans were hopeless when the Corporation assumed them. As a result of making over these mortgages on a 15-year basis and at a 5-percent rate, amortized monthly and without charges or commissions, hundreds of thousands of the Corporation's borrowers were able almost immediately to begin meeting their monthly payments.[8]

From Emergency Measures to a Permanent Policy

The emergency measures made the national government a vital factor in the farm and urban mortgage field. With the way paved for recovery, the government's next step was to assume responsibility for speeding up recovery and seeking the means to prevent, or at least ameliorate, future depressions. Private mortgage finance had already been reduced to about 60 per cent of the total mortgages in farming areas, and in towns and cities it was too badly shaken to resume operations without assistance. The states seemed unlikely to do much. The federal government found it advisable, therefore, to assume additional credit functions and to establish a number of new agencies or modify those already existing.

The new measures had far-reaching implications and were for the most part intended to be of indefinite duration, but they were enacted when emergency

8. *Hearings Before the TNEC*, Pt. 11, *op. cit.*, pp. 5389-5390.

conditions prevailed and had an emergency point of view. Each new housing bill was advocated as a means of stimulating the durable goods industries or putting men to work. Housing thus was looked upon as a remedy for general economic ills rather than a problem in itself. This confusion of objectives has hindered the co-ordinated development of federal housing policy.

2. GOVERNMENT AND HOUSING FINANCE

Having entered the housing stage from the financial wing, the federal government has played its part chiefly from a financial point of view. Having assumed the role of helping the consumer, the federal government began to expand its operations in this direction. Its legislative traditions and constitutional powers made a financial approach logical, while its aim to speed recovery seemed to be best advanced by increasing the public's ability to acquire or rent new dwellings.

a. THE FEDERAL HOME LOAN BANK BOARD AND AFFILIATES

The Federal Home Loan Bank System [9] established in 1932, is the oldest of the existing housing agencies. While the activities of the Bank System were overshadowed during the worst of the depression by its more spectacular affiliate, the Home Owners' Loan Corporation, it began by 1934 to take its place as part of the permanent financial organization, with its position strengthened by additional legislation and the formation of related agencies. The members of the Federal Home Loan Bank Board direct or supervise the following: the Federal Home Loan Bank System, the Home Owners' Loan Corporation, the Federal Savings and Loan Associations, and the Federal Savings and Loan Insurance Corporation.[10]

The Federal Home Loan Bank System

The Federal Home Loan Bank System was intended to provide a credit reserve banking system for urban residential mortgage institutions. The System comprises twelve regional banks and their member institutions. Originally it was planned that the stock should be held by member institutions. In order, however, to speed its establishment, the government was empowered to take up the unsubscribed balance of authorized stock. As of June 30, 1941, the Treasury still held about 73 per cent of the stock. But the number of member institutions had grown from 101 to 3,839 since January 1933.

9. Now organized in the National Housing Agency as the Federal Home Loan Bank Administration. See p. 289.

10. These agencies, under the new plan, are all directed by the Federal Home Loan Bank Commissioner.

Although membership is open to all types of institutions engaged in long-term mortgage lending, the System consists chiefly of savings and loan associations. Other types of institutions on June 30, 1941 comprised only one per cent of the membership and 12 per cent of total assets.[11] The System is thus dominated by the building and loan associations, and modifications in its structure since 1933 have been of benefit principally to them.

The Federal Home Loan Bank System, through the provision of credit, increases the capacity of its members to make home mortgage loans. Member institutions may borrow from the Home Loan banks on the security of eligible home mortgages, or of obligations issued or guaranteed by the government. The banks in turn obtain their funds through the public sale of debentures. Under existing authorizations, the banks may issue consolidated debentures not exceeding their total outstanding advances to member institutions provided the total is not greater than five times the paid-in capital of all the Home Loan banks.

The Federal Home Loan Bank System, however, has much more limited power than the Federal Reserve System. The Reserve banks not only have the lending power, but may also discount certain classes of paper without recourse (in effect, purchase them outright). In order to make such purchases, the Reserve banks also have the power to issue currency backed by their collateral. The Home Loan banks can neither discount nor issue currency, but are restricted to lending operations.[12]

Federal Savings and Loan Associations

The slow growth of the Federal Home Loan Bank System—probably due chiefly to the frozen assets of its prospective members and their inability to discount them—led to the creation of a new group of institutions able to start with free capital. These were the Federal Savings and Loan Associations chartered by the national government. In the bill establishing the Home Owners' Loan Corporation, the Treasury was authorized to subscribe $100 million for the shares of such associations, provided that not more than $100,000, or 50 per cent of total capitalization, went to any one institution. State-chartered associations were allowed to become Federal Savings and Loan Associations and receive Treasury stock subscriptions. A total of $50 million was appropriated by Congress for this purpose and subscribed by the Treasury.

Supplied with fresh capital, the federal associations became active in home

11. *Ninth Annual Report, 1940–1941,* Federal Home Loan Bank Board, p. 83. On June 30, 1941 the System consisted of: 3,798 savings and loan associations, twelve mutual savings banks, and twenty-nine life insurance companies. The savings and loan associations represent about 50 per cent of all such associations in the country, with 75 per cent of all savings and loan association assets.

12. See Appendix I, Table 52, for summary of the operations of the Federal Home Loan Bank System up to June 30, 1940.

mortgage lending, and their importance has increased from year to year. On June 30, 1941, there were 1,455 associations, of which 639 were new and 816 converted from state institutions. Their assets represented 38 per cent of total Home Loan Bank System members' assets on that date, and they did 15 per cent of all home mortgage lending during the year ending June 30, 1941. All federal associations must belong to the Federal Home Loan Bank System and are supervised by the Home Loan Bank Administration. Their shares are insured by the Federal Savings and Loan Insurance Corporation.

In 1935, Congress authorized the Home Owners' Loan Corporation (rather than the Treasury) to make additional subscriptions to shares in savings and loan associations. State as well as federal associations became eligible if they were members of the Federal Home Loan Bank System or had their shares insured. Up to June 30, 1941, the HOLC had invested almost $225 million in savings and loan shares. Including sums advanced through the HOLC, the federal government provided almost $275 million to rehabilitate or form these mortgage lending institutions. All share investments are reported to be paying dividends, and repayment of the investment itself has begun.[13]

Federal Savings and Loan Insurance Corporation

In order to maintain the competitive position of savings and loan associations as against commercial and savings banks, whose deposits were insurable by the Federal Deposit Insurance Corporation, Congress in 1934 authorized the establishment of the Federal Savings and Loan Insurance Corporation, with a capital of $100 million provided by the HOLC. Any association approved by the Insurance Corporation may, by setting up special reserves against loss and by paying a premium of ⅛ of one per cent of all share accounts, receive insurance protecting the investment of any one shareholder up to $5,000. If the insured institution fails, the shareholder may receive either a new insured account in a solvent institution, or 10 per cent in cash and the balance in negotiable non-interest-bearing debentures of the Corporation, one half payable one year, and the rest three years from the date of default.

As of June 30, 1941, the accounts of all Federal Savings and Loan Associations and 860 state institutions were insured with the Corporation. Its losses until then amounted to around $1,460,000 out of insured accounts of $2,460,000,000—somewhat under one per cent. Its accumulated surplus and reserves totaled over $29 million, and its operating expenses were paid from interest on its reserve fund. No interest, however, had been paid on the original HOLC investment.[14]

13. See Appendix I, Tables 49 and 53, for a summary of these operations up to June 30, 1940.
14. See Appendix I, Table 54, for a summary of the operations of the Federal Savings and Loan Insurance Corporation up to June 30, 1940.

b. THE FEDERAL HOUSING ADMINISTRATION

Probably no law passed during the depression so mingled emergency and long-range objectives as the National Housing Act of 1934, which created the Federal Housing Administration. Departing from the usual formulas of loans, credit control, or grants, this Act provided not for any direct use of federal funds for credit purposes but, instead, for the insurance of loans made by private institutions. The stated purpose of the Act was "to encourage improvement in housing standards and conditions," and "to provide a system of mutual mortgage insurance." But the arguments placed before Congress stressed more immediate objectives, such as the revival of construction and the reduction of unemployment. Primarily a financial measure, the National Housing Act was supported principally by manufacturing, building, and real-estate interests to whom the short-range objectives were paramount.

Insurance of Loans for Repairs and Alterations

The Act exhibited this dual point of view. Thus, *Title I—Housing Renovation and Modernization* was designed to stimulate the production and installation of building materials and equipment. Under this Title, an approved lending institution was insured against loss up to 20 per cent of the total of so-called modernization loans. Experience with installment credit indicated that this was in effect complete coverage. In 1936, coverage was reduced to 10 per cent—still ample for any reasonably conservative operation. No premium was charged for the insurance until July 1939, when a charge of ¾ of one per cent per annum of the net proceeds of the loan was provided. Outstanding Federal Housing Administration liability under this Title was originally limited to $200 million, later limited to $165 million, plus net insurance premiums collected. The outstanding amount of loans insurable thereunder is thus limited to approximately $1,650 million, so as to maintain the 10 per cent insurance coverage.

Title I of the Act now authorizes the insurance of the following: (1) for three years up to $2,500 for "the alteration, repair, or improvement of existing structures";[15] (2) for five years up to $5,000 for the alteration, repair, or improvement of multifamily structures, or conversion of single to multifamily units; (3) for fifteen years up to $3,000 for new buildings;[16] (4) for seven years up to $5,000 for repairing or remodeling existing structures to provide additional accommodations for war workers.

15. Readily detachable equipment is excluded. See *Property Improvement Loans Under Title I of the National Housing Act, Regulations,* FHA, July 1, 1941 (mimeographed).

16. This type of loan must not be confused with the first-mortgage loans insurable under Title II, as described below. It was instituted to provide for seasonal and other properties not eligible, because of location, for Title II mortgages.

No provision was made in the Act for down payments or security, but these matters were covered by FHA regulations and since 1941 by the Federal Reserve Board's rules for installment credit.[17] Except for 5 per cent equity and the taking of first mortgages on loans for new structures, neither down payment nor security has been required by the FHA on Title I loans.

Following the installment credit pattern, Title I loans have usually been made on a discount rather than an interest basis. Under current regulations, modernization and conversion loans under $2,500 may carry a discount rate equal to $5 per $100 on a one-year note, equivalent to 9.58 per cent conventional annual interest on a one-year and 9.30 per cent on a three-year loan. One-year conversion loans exceeding $2,500 are limited to a discount rate equal to $4 per $100 on a one-year note, which is equivalent to 7.61 per cent conventional annual interest on a one-year loan and 7.26 per cent on a five-year loan. Loans for new houses (under Title I) may be made at a discount rate equal to $3.50 per $100 on a one-year note, which is equivalent to 5.86 per cent conventional annual interest on a fifteen-year loan. All these rates include the insurance premium.

On January 1, 1941 loans insured under Title I amounted to $1.24 billion. The losses assumed by the government were $19.7 million, or 1.59 per cent of the total.[18] Defaults were most frequent on loans for freestanding or easily detachable equipment, permitted between May 1935 and April 1936. Up to 1938, the defaults on equipment loans amounted to 3.8 per cent of the insured total, and 2.1 per cent on loans for repairs and alterations.[19]

Mutual Mortgage Insurance

Title II of the National Housing Act provides for the insurance of mortgages (1) on one- to four-family structures, and (2) for more-than-four-family buildings designed primarily for rental purposes. Most FHA lending has involved the first.

As the law stands, mortgages on one- to four-family houses, if made by approved institutions, are insurable provided they do not exceed $16,000 or 80 per cent of the property value. There are two important exceptions: (1) Loans up to $5,400 may run to 90 per cent of the property value, and (2) loans between $5,400 and $8,600 may cover 90 per cent of value up to $6,000, and 80 per cent of the additional value up to $10,000. All loans are limited to twenty years' maturity except the $5,400, 90 per cent class, which may run to twenty-five years. Interest rates for all classes of loans, in all areas, are limited by legislation to 5 per cent

17. See *Consumer Credit, Regulation W,* as adopted on August 21, 1941, by the Board of Governors of the Federal Reserve System. This regulation limits the maturity of any note under $1,000 to eighteen months in nondefense areas.

18. *Seventh Annual Report, 1940,* FHA.

19. See *Fifth Annual Report, 1938,* FHA.

and by regulation to 4.5 per cent. No service charge by the lender in addition to the interest rate is permitted.

The insurance premium is set at ½ of one per cent per annum in advance on outstanding balances. The aggregate amount of insurable mortgages is set by law at $4 billion, although the President at his discretion can increase this to $5 billion. Not more than 35 per cent of the insurance written after June 3, 1939 may cover mortgages on existing dwellings; after 1944 all operations are to be limited to new construction.

To cover losses, the government created an initial fund of $10 million. This fund had increased by June 30, 1941 to almost $35 million through income from interest on the fund, and income from fees, and insurance premiums. Since July 1, 1939 all administrative expenses have been borne by premiums and other income of the fund. On July 1, 1941, $3.11 billion, representing over 725,000 mortgages, had been insured; about 2,900 properties had been foreclosed by mortgagees and turned over to the administrator with a net loss on those sold of $1,292,000, or less than .05 per cent of the total amount of mortgages insured.

As contrasted with Title I loans, under which claims are payable upon presentation of evidence of default and transfer of the note to the administrator, claims against the Mutual Mortgage Insurance Fund can be made only after the mortgage has been foreclosed and the property is tendered to the administrator. Again differing from Title I claims, which are paid in cash, claims against the Mutual Mortgage Insurance Fund are payable in interest-bearing debentures, secured by the Fund and the guarantee of the Treasury, maturing three years after the original maturity date of the mortgage.

Interest on the debentures is set at the current long-term government rate. The debentures are exempt from all but federal taxes, surtaxes, estate, inheritance, and gift taxes. Debentures cover the unpaid principal of the mortgage at the time of instituting foreclosure proceedings plus the net expenses of the mortgagee for taxes, special assessments and insurance. For mortgages in the 90 per cent class, $75 may also be allowed toward foreclosure costs. Otherwise, such costs are covered only by a certificate of claim, payable by the administrator out of the net proceeds, if any, from the sale of the property.

The insurance fund is mutual. Mortgages are grouped according to "sound actuarial practice and risk characteristics," and premiums are segregated for each group account. Ten per cent of the premiums are paid into a general reinsurance account. Claims are chargeable first against the group account and then against the reinsurance account. Net balances in a group account at its termination [20] are payable to the mortgagors.

20. Accounts may be terminated when the balance is sufficient to pay off the unpaid principal of the mortgages in the account, or when all the mortgages have actually been paid off.

Rental Housing Insurance

One of the compromises in the National Housing Act as originally passed was the section (207) in the Act providing for the insurance of mortgages on rental property "for persons of low income," owned either by public instrumentalities, or private limited-dividend corporations. The exceedingly broad language of the original act raised sufficient doubt about the constitutionality of this section (on the question of delegation of power) to reinforce the reluctance of lenders to enter into the type of operation it provided for.

After subsequent amendments, this part of the National Housing Act now permits the insurance of mortgages on publicly or privately owned housing for rent or sale provided the amount of the mortgage: (1) does not exceed $5 million,[21] (2) does not exceed 80 per cent of the property value or the estimated costs of the physical improvements, whichever is lower, and (3) does not exceed $1,350 per room. The owning corporation or instrumentality is subject to regulation of "rents, charges, capital structure, rate of return, and methods of operation" by the administrator or other public agency.

As evolved in practice, the limitation on rents was exercised mainly as a restraint on the proclivity of landlords to seek higher rents than the market could bear. The limitation on dividends was simply a restriction against milking the property until the indebtedness was paid. In other words, the project was permitted to earn what the market would reasonably bear, but any excess of earnings beyond the established dividend rate was required to be used for additional amortization of the mortgage. Such a scheme, along with the close inspection of plans and construction by the administrator, was foreign to speculative apartment-building practice. With the speculative element reduced, the impediments to true equity investment were clearly revealed.

The complex and costly procedure necessary under the law proved onerous, especially for small rental properties. To provide a simpler means for insuring rental mortgages up to $200,000, a new section (210) was added to the Act in 1938. Under this provision, the elaborate limited-dividend procedure was dropped, but a year later, this section of the act was repealed because of fear of abuses resulting from decreased administrative control over the operator.

Relatively little construction has been done under Sections 207 and 210. On July 1, 1941, mortgages totaling $135 million had been insured, covering 35,000 dwelling units in 335 projects. Eight properties have been foreclosed and turned over to the administrator. Of these, one has been sold and the remainder are being operated by the administration. These are all meeting operating expenses and paying interest on debentures, and in some cases payments on principal are

21. Provision was made for releasing parts of the blanket mortgage to permit ultimate individual ownership of separate units, if the project was designed to make this possible.

also being made. Up to July 1941, $303,000 arrears in operating expense and debt service had been incurred by the administration during the rehabilitating period following foreclosure of projects.

The insurance provided for these operations is not of a mutual character. Otherwise the procedure for making claims and the manner of payment are the same as for the mutual fund with the exception that in lieu of foreclosing the property himself, the mortgagee may turn over the defaulted mortgage to the administrator and receive debentures for 98 per cent of the outstanding amount, plus certain items for taxes and insurance.[22]

C. QUESTIONS RAISED BY THE DUAL FINANCIAL SYSTEM

These activities of the federal government have not only made the long-term, amortized mortgage the accepted type of instrument, but have lowered interest rates, improved methods of appraisal, advanced marketing knowledge and given aid to technical research. The federal housing agencies have also made important contributions to the study of city planning and rehabilitation, and improved standards of construction and land subdividing.[23] As a result, it is undoubtedly true that during the later thirties better houses were being built and sounder mortgages written than were characteristic of the previous decades.

Nevertheless, in the Federal Home Loan Bank System and the Federal Housing Administration the government has created two systems of mortgage finance that have many points of conflict, contradiction, and duplication. This dualism detracts from the effectiveness of the reforms and prevents the development of unified and systematic financial procedures.

The Reorganization Act of 1939[24] brought the two agencies (along with all Reconstruction Finance Corporation activities) together in the new Federal Loan Agency. This move, however, did not result in a basic reorganization. Even duplicate administrative functions were not eliminated. Research divisions and technical operations were still separate and administrative conflicts, created partly by agency rivalry and partly by fundamental differences in philosophy, remained. The creation of the National Housing Agency in 1942 has not yet resolved these conflicts.

Points of Divergence

In theory, the Home Loan Bank System is a partnership between government and the member institutions. With the final liquidation of the federal government's investment, the Home Loan banks will be owned by the members. Regular

22. For a financial summary of all FHA operations up to June 30, 1940, see Appendix I, Table 55.
23. See Chap. 4, pp. 122-123, 125.
24. Not to be confused with the final reorganization of housing agencies in 1942. See pp. 288-289.

procedures exist for consultation between the banks and the central administration on matters of policy, but the directive authority of the administration over the banks or member institutions is decidedly limited. Thus interest rates on mortgages are beyond the direct control of the administration. The methods of appraisal or the standard of housing accepted as security cannot be dictated by the administration except through the banks' supervision. The System derives its character from the numerous local institutions of which it is made up, and in turn provides a means for co-ordinating the policies and expanding the credit facilities of local institutions.

The Federal Housing Administration, by contrast, is centralized and independent of local relationships. The FHA insures only such loans as are made on the basis of its appraisals and are backed by security conforming to its standards and subject to its inspection. Its policies are internally determined and no regularized means exist whereby the locality or its institutions can influence the adaptation of national policy to local needs. The success of the system thus depends upon the administrative wisdom of FHA. It asks only that the institution with which it deals be "responsible and able to service the mortgage properly"—a purely routine task. There is, consequently, a tendency for lending institutions to offer little more than this and to become dependent upon the judgment of the FHA.

A divergence in basic policy is thus present. The Federal Home Loan Bank Administration is concerned with strengthening the lending institutions and increasing their participation and responsibility. The FHA is less concerned with the technical than with the mortgage-getting capacity of an institution, relying on its own processes to see that proper security is given. With the Home Loan Bank Administration, the institutions are the system. With FHA, they are merely the sales and service agents of a system.

Another difference between the Home Loan Bank Administration and FHA is in their attitude toward the segregation of banking functions. The former is attempting to create a specialized, long-term mortgage banking system. FHA accepts and promotes the fusion of long- and short-term lending functions in the same institution. With it the characteristics of the mortgage rather than the nature of the lending institution are the primary consideration. These differences are displayed in the insurance plans of the two agencies. Under the Federal Home Loan Bank Administration, the Savings and Loan Insurance Corporation insures the assets of an institution collectively. FHA insures each mortgage separately. Here again the Home Loan Bank Administration stresses the solvency of the lending institution, while the FHA is concerned with the soundness of the mortgage itself.

Conflict and Competition

Thus, these two governmental agencies are in some respects vying for supremacy in the same field. The lack of uniform policies on appraisals and standards has often tended to undermine the effectiveness of one agency or the other as an instrumentality for improving housing conditions and lending practices. The FHA's disinterest in specialized lending institutions has increased the Home Loan Banks' difficulties in creating a cohesive and comprehensive mortgage banking system. The FHA has often felt its efforts to maintain standards were compromised by the less directly controlled Home Loan Bank member institutions which operated outside of FHA supervision.

In addition to the separate methods of insurance, the two agencies have also established a dual system of providing reserve funds for lending institutions. The Home Loan Banks can make advances to member institutions. Corresponding facilities were sought for FHA through the authorization of national mortgage associations.[25] Such an association must have a capitalization of not less than $2 million and be formed with the approval of the administrator on a finding that the "establishment of such association is desirable to provide a market for mortgages insured under Title II." A mortgage association may lend funds on the security of FHA rental housing mortgages (Section 207) and may "purchase, service, or sell" other types of FHA mortgages. Funds for carrying on these activities may be raised through the public sale of debentures, the total outstanding amount of which may not exceed twice the amount of its paid-up capital and surplus, and in no event exceed the unpaid principal of its mortgage investments or its holdings in cash or government bonds.

The provision for establishing national mortgage associations was bitterly opposed by the savings and loan group prominent in the Home Loan Bank System. With the failure of private capital promptly to form such associations, efforts were made to use the Home Loan Bank System for a similar purpose. The Home Loan Bank Act was amended to permit loans to nonmember institutions on the security of insured mortgages, but this power was little used. The RFC Mortgage Company then agreed to purchase FHA mortgages; and finally in 1938, the Federal National Mortgage Association was formed entirely with RFC funds.[26] At the same time, insurance companies and the larger banks became heavy buyers of FHA mortgages. Original lenders thus found an ample

25. See Title III of the National Housing Act, as amended.

26. The formation of the Federal National Mortgage Association with RFC funds was due to the continued reluctance of private investors to meet the requirements of the law and the qualifications of the Federal Housing Administration. After the Federal National Mortgage Association proved successful, several offers to purchase it were made, but were turned down by FHA, which has not considered that the amount of mortgages on the market warrants the formation of additional associations.

and eager market for their paper, and, from the FHA angle, the problem was solved.[27]

Thus in the Federal Home Loan Banks we have a system for the *lending* of funds to certain types of institutions, while the Federal Housing Administration and Federal National Mortgage Associations constitute a system *buying* from any type of institution a certain type of collateral. In neither case do we have a complete mortgage banking system.

Effects of the Dual System

Out of this dualism, and the competition that has come from it, the public probably has at least temporarily obtained easier borrowing terms and more ample sources of credit for housing than if only one such agency had existed. But these benefits may not endure. For instance, if the traditional outlets for bank and insurance company funds are restored, the main support of FHA might diminish. To attempt to maintain itself under a less favorable competitive situation, FHA standards might therefore suffer. Moreover, the liquidity provided by the Federal National Mortgage Association and other mortgage buyers is illusory. There is nothing in the Mortgage Association that gives any promise of help in time of emergency. The Association in its discretion might refuse to make further purchases of mortgages. Moreover, if the financial situation were such that the Mortgage Association could only sell its debentures at a high rate of interest, if at all, it would not be able to meet institutional demands for liquid funds. Its resemblance to a discount bank might thus disappear.

On the other hand, it is doubtful whether the Home Loan Bank System can fill the gap in the demand for mortgage money should FHA activities seriously diminish. The System is neither cohesive nor comprehensive. Except for the Federal Savings and Loan Associations, member institutions are not required to insure their accounts. State associations may insure their accounts without belonging to the System. Members may also insure their mortgages with FHA. The Federal Home Loan Banks' lack of authority to purchase mortgages prevents them from providing a national mortgage market like that created by the Federal National Mortgage Association.[28] At the same time, since the banks are limited in making loans to members, and are not sure of a market for their own debentures, they are in no better position to meet emergency demands than the Mortgage Association.

Thus the federal government by 1942 had not solved the problem of providing and controlling credit for private housing operations. The FHA and HLBA did

27. For a financial summary of FNMA operations up to June 30, 1940, see Appendix I, Table 56.

28. It is sometimes argued that the creation of strong local mortgage institutions would eliminate the need of a national market.

not dominate the mortgage market sufficiently to be able to slow down a boom or prevent a depression. Moreover, there was no assurance that the two agencies could work together on essential policies.

3. SPECIAL AID AND SUBSIDY FOR URBAN HOUSING

The federal government and most states have realized that such instrumentalities as we have so far examined would not assure the production of houses to accommodate large numbers of low-income families. Consequently, a variety of legislation, both state and federal, has been passed to attain this end.

a. STATE AID FOR HOUSING

The first efforts at special aid were prompted by the acute housing shortages and high rents during and after the first World War. Most of the states did not attempt to provide housing but contented themselves with temporary limitation of rents.[29]

Massachusetts went farther in 1917 by authorizing The Massachusetts Homestead Commission to spend $50,000 in building suburban houses and selling them at cost on long amortization to workers living in congested quarters. Only twelve houses were erected and sold. In 1921 Wisconsin legislation permitted the city and county of Milwaukee to subscribe to the shares of co-operative housing companies. One company was formed to build 105 houses.

In 1921 California created a state-operated system of twenty-year mortgage financing for veterans desirous of owning their own homes. Funds were obtained through the issuance of serial bonds, and about 14,000 loans were made.[30] New York State at the same time began its long history of special aids for the encouragement of dwelling construction.

The New York Laws

The first New York law (1920) permitted cities to grant tax exemption on dwelling structures, if completed after April 1920 or (as the act was amended) begun before April 1925. Tax exemption for ten years was granted on new dwellings for sale or rent. In 1922 insurance companies were empowered to purchase land and erect dwellings in New York City for sale or rent until (as amended) 1926. Rentals were limited to $9 a room. A revival of the law in 1938

29. The following states adopted such legislation: Connecticut, New Jersey, District of Columbia, Wisconsin, New York, Illinois, Delaware and Maine (see Edith Berger Drellich and Andrée Emery, *Rent Control in War and Peace*, National Municipal League, New York, 1939, pp. 12–41, *passim*).

30. Edith Elmer Wood, "A Century of the Housing Problem," *Law and Contemporary Problems*, Vol. I, No. 2, March 1934, p. 140. Report of the California Veterans Welfare Board, 1936.

permitted the insurance companies to erect and own dwellings in cities over 300,000 population; [31] omitted the rental limitation and the provision for tax exemption. The tax exemption law resulted in a moderate expansion of house-building. The insurance company law of 1922 resulted in only one project, erected by the Metropolitan Life Insurance Company. The 1938 law has so far been utilized only by the Metropolitan and the Equitable Life Assurance Society.

In 1926 New York passed the first limited-dividend housing law. This offered exemption from all state taxes and fees and from local taxation of buildings and improvements in return for a limitation on rents ($12.50 per room in Manhattan, $11 elsewhere) and a restriction of dividends to 6 per cent. If the corporation declared that it existed to serve a public purpose and restricted its power of disposal, it might also obtain the aid of eminent domain in assembling land.[32] No companies were organized under the latter provisions and only eleven corporations, providing 6,925 dwelling units, were established under the limited-dividend housing law.

The District of Columbia Alley Dwelling Act

With the deepening of the depression in the early thirties state efforts to promote housing temporarily ceased. State or local laws were for the most part enacted only to facilitate the operation of the various federal housing measures.[33] The only important exception was the Alley Dwelling Act of the District of Columbia passed by Congress in 1934. This law established the Alley Dwelling Authority (later renamed the National Capital Housing Authority), for the purpose of clearing the inhabited alleys of Washington.

Although the Act was primarily a slum clearance rather than a housing measure, the Authority is required to see that housing is available for families displaced, and is authorized to buy and repair old houses or build new ones. The Authority may acquire slum property, clear sites, and dispose of or improve the cleared sites in any manner compatible with the logical development of the city. A revolving fund of $500,000 was provided. The Act was amended in 1938 to permit the Authority to erect dwellings on other than slum sites, borrow money from the Treasury, and receive loans and grants from the United States Housing Authority.

31. Amended in 1941 to cities over 100,000 population or within a radius of fifteen miles of any such city.

32. The original draft of the limited-dividend housing law provided for a state mortgage bank to lend money at low interest rates to limited-dividend corporations. This part was omitted owing to strong opposition from private lending institutions.

33. Federal Housing Administration enabling legislation and acts to establish local housing authorities eligible for grants and loans from the Public Works Administration and, later, the United States Housing Authority.

Apart from operations financed by the USHA, the Alley Dwelling Authority up to January 1, 1942 acquired fourteen slum sites. On five it built or rehabilitated 112 dwelling units at a total cost of $555,000. On five additional sites it built garages, parking lots and so forth. Two sites were sold for specific uses and two were retained for future development.

Recent State Legislation

The State of New York in recent years has taken important steps to promote public housing projects. Amendments to the constitution, passed in 1938 and implemented by legislation in 1939, empowered the state to make fifty-year loans up to 100 per cent of the development cost of a project at an interest rate equal to the state's cost in borrowing money. The state may also grant annual subsidies not to exceed one per cent more than the going state interest rate of the cost of each project. Each subsidy must be matched by an equal amount from the municipality. Municipalities are also empowered to build housing projects or provide loans and subsidies to housing authorities. Only New York City has so far taken advantage of this power, and its authority has borrowed directly for projects covered by city subsidy contracts. New York City subsidies are raised from an occupancy tax on other real estate. By November 1942, one development containing 240 dwelling units had been financed in this way and the city had contracted to build another with 617 units after the war. Three developments, containing 3,850 apartments, had been started under state provision, while contracts had been signed to build eleven more, containing 9,860 units, most of them after the war.

New York State has also authorized financial institutions to invest in the stock of state-supervised limited-dividend corporations. In 1941 state legislation authorized the establishment of Urban Redevelopment Corporations, the purpose of which is, through combination of property owners, to rehabilitate blighted areas by repairing and altering existing structures or building new housing or other suitable structures. Dividends are limited and corporate operations are subject to state regulation. In return, the power of eminent domain is made available and tax assessments must not exceed the current level for a period of ten years. In 1942 a second law was passed enabling redevelopment companies (when and if formed) to operate under less stringent supervision than under the 1941 law and also empowering insurance companies to make equity investments in redevelopment projects. Illinois and Michigan in 1941 and Kentucky in 1942 passed redevelopment laws having similar objectives. In 1942 and 1943 New York State passed additional legislation (called the Redevelopment Companies Act) to facilitate insurance company investment in rehabilitation projects.

b. DIRECT FEDERAL AID TO HOUSING

Except for the building of houses for war workers in 1918, the first federal measure involving direct aid for housing was in the Emergency Relief and Construction Act of 1932 which empowered the Reconstruction Finance Corporation to make loans to state-regulated limited-dividend corporations. At that time only New York had passed suitable legislation, but other states hastily followed suit.[34] But within a year only one project, Knickerbocker Village in lower Manhattan, was actually authorized. With the passage of the National Industrial Recovery Act of 1933, which, as part of a great recovery program, provided for the "construction, reconstruction, alteration or repair under public regulation or control of low-rent housing and slum clearance projects," the housing powers of the RFC were transferred to the new Public Works Administration.

The Public Works Administration Housing Division

A Housing Division was set up in the Public Works Administration to carry out this part of the Act. Here, as with the Federal Housing Administration, there was a combination of objectives, in which the improvement of housing was secondary to the use of housebuilding as a cure for the depression. The Housing Division was plagued throughout its brief career by this split purpose. The evolution of techniques for a new form of public enterprise required time. The exigencies of the depression demanded action. Between these two demands there was no satisfactory compromise.

In the beginning, the Division attempted to operate through loans to limited-dividend corporations at 85 per cent of value, 4 per cent interest, for twenty-five to thirty-five years. But the limited-dividend idea was still new to investors, and even 15 per cent equities were hard to find, especially with the limitations on income and capital gain that the regulations imposed. After a year, during which hundreds of proposals were examined, seven projects got under way.

Because of the difficulties in obtaining substantial sponsorship and the fact that rentals attained were generally far from the reach of the low-income groups, the Division abandoned this scheme of operation. Instead it embarked upon a plan of direct financing of government-owned housing. Under this new arrangement, the Public Works Administration Housing Division itself actually acquired land and retained title. Of the funds advanced for the project, 45 per cent was considered an outright grant and 55 per cent a loan to be repaid over sixty years at 3 per cent interest from the earnings of the property. Adverse decisions

34. Arkansas, Delaware, Florida, Illinois, Kansas, Maryland, Massachusetts, New Jersey, North Carolina, Ohio, Pennsylvania, South Carolina and Virginia.

in the lower courts on the federal power to condemn land for housing purposes [35] caused the PWA to encourage the formation of local housing authorities so that, through them, the problem of land acquisition might be surmounted.

From February 1934, when the limited-dividend policy was abandoned, to November 1937, when the Housing Division was succeeded by the United States Housing Authority, forty-nine developments, comprising 21,441 dwelling units, and costing $129.5 million, were completed or placed under contract by the PWA.[36] Title to these projects was retained by the federal government.

The career of the PWA Housing Division was stormy. Disappointment at the rate of its progress resulted in frequent shiftings of its funds to other emergency purposes. This permitted the Division to plan ahead only for short periods of time—yet long-term planning was the essence of its program. Local apathy (New York City was a notable exception) forced the PWA to undertake costly missionary work and also deprived it of extensive local support. Insufficient technical experience with mass housing developments forced the PWA to proceed by trial and error. Its first buildings, as is now generally recognized, were more elaborate and expensive than was necessary to serve the purpose for which they were designed and much more so than could be acceptable for a continuing nationwide program of this sort.

The average cost of the dwellings erected by the PWA was $5,927 per dwelling unit and almost $1,700 a room. Excluding the cost of demolished slum buildings, it was $5,418 per dwelling and $1,548 per room. Omitting, in addition, the cost of land, the figures were $4,975 and $1,421, respectively.[37] By comparison the costs of twelve limited-dividend projects erected in New York City between 1928 and 1935 averaged $4,933 per dwelling unit and about $1,450 a room; with land excluded, the average cost was $3,917 and $1,150, respectively.[38] Except for the use of expensive land, resulting from concentration in slum areas, the high costs of PWA houses were due chiefly to what may be called a mania for durability.

C. THE UNITED STATES HOUSING AUTHORITY

The PWA Housing Division accomplished important pioneering tasks. It dramatized the need for providing shelter for lower-income urban families who generally were crowded into the poorest of the supply. It succeeded in persuading

35. *U.S.* v. *Certain Lands in City of Louisville,* 78 F. (2d) 684, 1935; *U.S.* v. *Certain Lands in City of Detroit,* 12 Fed. Supp. 345, 1935; *In the Matter of the Acquisition of All Privately Owned Land, Etc.,* 63 Wash. Law Rep. 822, 1935.

36. In addition two PWA projects were begun and turned over to the Puerto Rico Reconstruction Administration for completion. See Appendix I, Table 57, for financial operations of PWA Housing Division up to June 30, 1940.

37. See Appendix I, Table 60.

38. *Report of the State Superintendent of Housing to the Governor and Legislature of the State of New York,* Legislative Document (1940) No. 70, Table 2.

twenty-nine states to pass enabling legislation, which resulted in the establishment of forty-six housing authorities. It advanced the science of unit design and mass planning and developed sufficient support for the principle of public housing to result in the creation in 1937 of a permanent agency, the United States Housing Authority, to finance and subsidize houses for low-income urban families.

The United States Housing Authority was established as a corporate body in the Department of the Interior, and in 1939 it was transferred on a similar status to the Federal Works Agency. In 1942 its functions were transferred to the Federal Public Housing Authority in the National Housing Agency created under the President's wartime emergency powers.

Methods of Finance and Subsidy

The public housing program is based on the assumed obligation of government to make it possible for large groups of low-income families to obtain reasonably good housing. The framers of the USHA legislation were impressed with the inadequacy of the supply needed to accomplish this purpose. However, except for admonitions that construction and operation should be economical, nothing in the legislation either recognized the shortcomings in production and marketing methods or granted any powers for correcting them. No other means of providing low-rental dwellings was considered except governmental ownership and operation. While not required to do so by law, the USHA up to 1942 had confined its activities to new structures and had made no use of existing or altered structures.

The sponsors of USHA legislation furthermore assumed that the states and cities could not solve their housing problems with their own resources. They therefore devised a system of special finance and subsidy which placed the principal financial burden upon the federal government, but envisaged local governments as permanent owners and operators of a large quantity of urban housing. Financial aid could take two forms: (1) federal loans to make up deficiencies in municipal borrowing power, and (2) grants or subsidies to make up deficiencies in family income. The grants might be: (1) a capital grant, or outright gift, of all or part of the project cost or (2) an annual grant, or gift, of part of the rental. Occupancy of the buildings was usually restricted to families with incomes not exceeding five times the established rental.

Loans and Subsidies

In the development of the USHA legislation there was little controversy on the question of loans. The USHA was authorized to make 90 per cent loans for sixty years at an interest rate ½ of one per cent higher than the going long-term government rate. Localities were required to raise at least 10 per cent of the total cost of the project from nonfederal sources. The question of subsidy was more controversial, owing to the opinion that PWA's capital grants had been partly responsible for the high costs of its housing enterprises. The Act provided outright grants not exceeding 25 per cent of the project's cost.[39] But the Act also provided annual grants, which could not exceed a percentage of total cost equal to one per cent more than the going long-term government interest rate. Localities were required to make annual contributions equal to 20 per cent of the federal subsidy. Subsidy contracts could run up to sixty years, with the right of review by USHA at the end of ten years and every five years thereafter, so that payments would not exceed a minimum necessary to maintain the low-rent character of the property. The authority has confined its operations to loans and annual grants.[40] Funds for loans to local authorities are obtained from borrowings by USHA. The present authorization permits USHA to have outstanding obligations not in excess of $800 million.

In practice the local contributions have approached 15 per cent rather than the required 10 per cent. Municipalities have obtained their funds chiefly through the sale of local authority bonds backed by rental revenues and contracts with USHA for annual subsidies. The annual USHA subsidy payment has averaged about 15 per cent less than the maximum. Local contributions have been made chiefly in the form of tax exemption or reduction.[41]

Partnership of Federal and Local Governments

Under the original law, the USHA, unlike the PWA Housing Division, cannot buy land, contract for construction, or own and manage property.[42] Except for special wartime powers it must deal entirely through local authorities. Ostensibly it is only an instrument for providing financial assistance to local housing authorities in carrying out their housing programs. At present thirty-eight states [43] have enabling legislation and, in all, over 600 local housing authorities have been established.

39. It was required that where a capital grant was made the grant plus the loan should not exceed 90 per cent of the entire cost.

40. A typical USHA-Local Authority agreement might run as follows: Assuming a proposed project to cost $1 million, financing could be through a 90 per cent loan from USHA and 10 per cent through the sale of local housing authority bonds or other means. A maximum subsidy from USHA per year on such a project (assuming a going long-term federal bond rate of 2.5 per cent) would be 3.5 per cent from USHA, or $35,000. The local contribution of $7,000 (i.e., 20 per cent of the USHA subsidy) would usually be in the form of an exemption of taxation on the structures.

41. For a summary of USHA financial operations to June 30, 1940, see Appendix I, Table 58.

42. In case of default, of course, the USHA can take over and operate the project. Amendments to the USHA legislation in 1940 gave USHA power to build, own and operate housing for defense purposes.

43. All except Iowa, Kansas, Maine, Minnesota, Nevada, New Hampshire, Oklahoma, South Dakota, Utah and Wyoming.

The USHA plan is thus one of local-federal partnership, but, because of the overwhelming dependence upon federal aid, the USHA has a dominant position. The USHA formulates standards and requires that projects built with its funds adhere to them at every stage of development—site selection, planning, contracts, construction, and management. It supervises the spending of the local authority, and has the determining voice in setting rents. It must require the removal of an amount of substandard housing equivalent to the number of new dwellings built, and it sets the period within which such removal is to be accomplished.

The very nature of the local-federal relationship implies a certain dominance by the federal agency. The financial dependence of local authorities (except possibly in New York State) upon the federal authority is virtually complete. Moreover, the weakness and inexperience of many local authorities made federal dominance, at least at the start, doubly necessary. As a result the local authority has been frequently looked upon simply as an agent of the USHA. In some places authorities seem willing to remain just that. Elsewhere, however, as the local body gains in experience and local support, a more independent attitude has been shown, with increasing chafing at what is felt to be federal dictation and paternalism. Actually this trend reflects a greater desire on the part of the locality to face its own problems and to participate in their solution.

Little if any local action has been taken, however, to strengthen the local authorities. New York State, as we have noted, has set up its own alternative public housing plan, but has specifically legislated against the mingling of state and federal funds on the same project. Many authorities are still dependent upon USHA even for operating expenses, and thus can survive only as long as the USHA maintains operations in their locality. Until the local authority is generally better recognized as an integral part of the municipal establishment with its own appropriations for operation and definite means of making its own contributions, it is hardly likely that federal domination of the program will substantially decrease.

Costs, Rents, and Subsidies

By March 1942, the USHA had advanced or contracted for $770 million of housing, against the $800 million authorized. These advances covered 747 projects, comprising about 185,000 dwelling units in 548 cities or other political subdivisions. The average development cost was $4,604 per dwelling unit. Excluding the cost of the slum buildings demolished and other costs charged to slum clearance, it was $4,234;[44] and excluding, in addition, the cost of land, it was $3,924. USHA houses have thus been built at considerably lower costs than PWA houses;

44. See Appendix I, Table 60.

furthermore, as USHA operations expanded, the unit costs have decreased.[45] The change is partly due to the use of cheaper land, not only because the United States Housing Authority has not insisted on slum locations but also because it has extended its operations to small communities where land costs are comparatively lower. The average cost of land per dwelling unit in USHA projects up to February 28, 1942 was $987 compared to $1,448 for PWA housing.[46] The total cost reduction is also due to changes in standards permitting simpler accommodations and more economical materials and construction. The PWA showed a partiality for walk-up apartments; the USHA has built mainly grouped houses, which are cheaper to construct and maintain.

Annual USHA subsidies will come to a maximum of $28 million, or over $12 a month per family. If the local contribution is added, the total maximum subsidy rises to perhaps $15 a month per family or over $175 a year. Average rentals for USHA dwellings, as of February 28, 1942, were $12.61 per month, for so-called "shelter rent" which omits charges, amounting to an additional $5.08 per month, for water, heating, cooking fuel, light, and refrigeration. By contrast, the average monthly rental of PWA housing (prior to the establishment of USHA) was $19.47 per dwelling per month with services an additional $5.51. The average annual income of USHA tenants (before income requirements in certain localities were changed by the war) was $823. Slightly more than half the tenants had incomes below this amount, 25 per cent earned $800 to $1,000 and about 25 per cent $1,000 and more.

Competition with Private Enterprise

The emergence of government agencies as large owners of huge units operated at a loss raised strong opposition, especially among real-estate owners and brokers who during the depression were having difficulty in avoiding losses on their own property. The elaborate nature of the first PWA dwellings, and their relatively high rents added fuel to the opposition. Finally, the fear of widespread tax exemption with a corresponding shifting of taxes to the remaining privately owned real estate gave public housing opponents another strong weapon.

Much of this opposition has proven groundless, however, as the USHA program has proceeded. In places USHA projects have, to be sure, competed with poor housing let at similar rents; and generally USHA rents have been low

45. The average over-all cost of new dwellings (total development less costs charged to slum clearance) to June 30, 1939 was $4,730, and to June 30, 1940, $4,414. Net construction costs (cost of the structure, including plumbing, heating and electricity but excluding movable equipment such as ranges, refrigerators, screens, etc.) averaged $2,946 to June 30, 1939 and only $2,720 to June 30, 1941. (Data supplied by Division of Research and Statistics, United States Housing Authority.)

46. These figures are the sum of the following costs: land and land acquisition, slum buildings and their demolition, site improvements. Net construction costs average $3,740 for PWA and only $2,711 for USHA projects. See Appendix I, Table 60.

enough to attract tenants who could not otherwise afford new or even habitable old housing. USHA developments have apparently prompted considerable renovation of contiguous areas, and examples can be found, as in Washington, D. C., of successful public and private developments existing side by side. The worst fears of the opponents of public housing have certainly not been realized.

The problem of tax exemption might become serious if, in the course of time, the proportion of tax-free public housing became large enough to cause a noticeable decrease in the area against which the municipal levy could be assessed. So far, the removal of public properties from the tax rolls has not been sufficient to affect the rates on the remainder. Moreover, the total tax exemption by no means represents an equivalent loss of revenue. The exemption is based on the taxes that the fully developed property might be expected to yield, and is thus income that has never been fully realized in fact. Often the area taken by the government has either had a very low tax yield or has actually been delinquent. Then, too, public housing projects by correcting unsafe and unsanitary conditions may result in actual savings to the municipal budget.

4. Government and Farm Housing

The financial problems of farm housing differ from those of urban dwellings. The typical farmhouse is part of the farm plant. Usually, farmhouse financing cannot be separated from farm financing since the ability to pay off money borrowed for a house depends on the income from the farm. As a result, no special system of farm housing finance, as separate from farm finance, has been devised. Most lenders, including the Farm Credit Administration, are reluctant to advance credit for nonproductive purposes. Several efforts have been made to remedy this situation but no satisfactory solution has been found.

a. THE FARM CREDIT ADMINISTRATION

The most important federal farm credit agency is the Farm Credit Administration—now a unit of the Department of Agriculture—which was formed in 1933 to co-ordinate and supervise several existing governmental agencies. At the present time the Farm Credit Administration supervises the Federal Land Banks and the National Farm Loan Associations through which Federal Land Bank loans are generally made; the Joint Stock Land Banks, which are in process of liquidation; the Federal Farm Mortgage Corporation; the Federal Intermediate Credit Banks; the Production Credit Corporations and the Production Credit Associations; the Banks for Cooperatives; the Emergency Crop and Feed Loan Offices; and federally chartered Credit Unions.

Of these agencies, the Federal Land Banks and the Federal Farm Mortgage

Corporation are the most closely related to farm housing. Federal Land Bank and Land Bank Commissioner loans may be made for buildings that improve farm property. Consideration can be given to farm home values where Commissioner loans are made on a "prudent investment" basis. Such loans are made when "the person occupying the property is not entirely dependent upon farm income for his livelihood but receives a part of his income from other dependable sources." Production credit association loans often include funds for minor repairs or alterations to farm homes and other buildings, or for the purchase of household or farm equipment. Production credit loans are limited to what can be repaid in a year or two through sales of crops, livestock, or livestock products.

b. THE FARM SECURITY ADMINISTRATION

The Farm Security Administration (also of the Department of Agriculture) through its concern with the resettlement of families from submarginal land and its rehabilitation of farm tenant families, has been more directly interested in rural housing than has the Farm Credit Administration. The Farm Security Administration is the successor of earlier emergency organizations such as the Resettlement Administration and the Division of Subsistence Homesteads of the Department of the Interior. The Subsistence Homesteads Division endeavored on the one hand to provide a means for industrial workers to hedge against unemployment and to supplement their wages through part-time farming and, on the other, to promote a semi-industrial mode of life for excess farm population. Created under the National Recovery Act, it acquired land, built houses, and supervised the homestead enterprises. The homesteaders acquired their property on long-term amortized loans, without down payment.

Similar attempts to solve the problems of stranded industrial populations were undertaken by federal and a few state relief agencies, but the housing problem here was part of a larger social and economic problem, which could not be solved by the subsistence homestead idea alone.

The Division's projects, personnel, and problems were transferred to the Resettlement Administration in May 1935. The Resettlement Administration was authorized to move rural families from submarginal to better land, and to finance, through long-term loans, not only farm homes and other needed buildings, but the farm enterprise as well. Aid was given to families individually and to rural communities as a whole, some of which were conducted on a co-operative basis.

The Administration also undertook the development of garden-city communities for urban workers, three of which, near Washington, D. C., Cincinnati, and Milwaukee, were carried to substantial completion. The so-called "greenbelt" towns represented a contrasting approach to the housing problem to that taken by the other public housing agencies. Instead of clearing slums and rebuilding existing communities, the Resettlement Administration built complete new suburban towns where, to quote R. G. Tugwell, its first administrator, "the old wasteful practices never have a chance to get started." The towns were laid out along advanced city-planning principles, and included not only well-designed houses but appropriate service and recreational facilities. Costs were high, partly because of the required use of relief labor, and the program fell victim to the political difficulties in which the Resettlement Administration became involved. The towns remain, however, as models in many ways for future community planning.[47]

Late in 1936, the Resettlement Administration became the Farm Security Administration in the Department of Agriculture. No more of the ambitious suburban schemes were undertaken and subsequent activity was largely confined to a continuation of the rural aspects of the program, plus the new functions of aiding the acquisition of farms by tenant farmers, under the Farm Tenant Purchase Act of 1937, and providing living facilities for migrant farm laborers. Again housing was incidental to the larger program of agricultural rehabilitation.[48]

C. URBAN AGENCIES IN THE RURAL FIELD

The Federal Housing Administration and United States Housing Authority were created to help urban homeowners and low-income urban tenants. The obvious need for better housing on farms and other rural places, together with the lack of adequate means for meeting these needs, resulted in attempts to utilize these agencies to serve broader fields than those for which they were primarily designed.

In 1938, the Federal Housing Administration was empowered to insure mortgage loans on farm properties on a similar basis to urban properties, provided that not less than 15 per cent of the proceeds were spent for construction and repair of dwellings.[49] The FHA made a costly effort to make this provision effective, but the results were negligible. The mortgage as an instrument for extended payment for housing apparently did not fit rural needs as well as it did the urban housing market.

Similarly, the United States Housing Authority late in 1938 embarked on a rural housing program, which it was able to do without special legislative enactment. It fostered the creation of county housing authorities and later some regional

47. See R. G. Tugwell, "Housing Activities of the Resettlement Act," *Housing Yearbook*, 1936; W. W. Alexander, "Housing Activities of the Resettlement Act," *Housing Yearbook*, 1937; Tracy B. Augur and Walter H. Blucher, "The Significance of the Greenbelt Towns," *Housing Yearbook*, 1938, National Association of Housing Officials, Chicago.

48. Report of the Administration of the Farm Security Administration, 1940. See also Appendix I, Table 59.

49. Section 203, National Housing Act, as amended.

authorities, and by March 1942 had made commitments amounting to $14.7 million for the rehousing of 7,717 small farm owners, tenant farmers, share croppers and rural wage earners. In this activity the USHA has co-operated with the Farm Security Administration, which determines the desirability of the project from an agricultural point of view. Land is acquired by the USHA usually through donation of the landowners; the houses are erected by contractors bidding in the usual manner; and tenants are responsible for the maintenance of the property, receiving in return a rebate on their rent. Actual cash rental payments for dwelling units average $6.21 a month. The program has proceeded slowly, and only five projects are under way. The houses are often built to form small communities. By March 1942, 1,150 dwelling units had been completed and 584 were under construction. The average cost of the units so far completed is $2,253, and the average annual rental is about $85 (less $10.50 tenant maintenance allowance), which covers little if any more than the maintenance of the property, without any allowance for the repayment of capital costs.

5. War Housing

At one time or the other, a considerable number of other governmental agencies have financed or built houses. The Army and Navy build houses on contract for their posts and stations. The Reclamation Service and Tennessee Valley Authority build towns for their workers. Special facilities (under the Reconstruction Finance Corporation) have been available for the repair or replacement of dwellings after floods or other disasters. The Rural Electrification Administration loans money for the modernization of farm buildings. Most of these operations are so specialized in character, however, as to be apart from any general pattern of house distribution and finance.

The necessity for providing dwellings for workers in war industries which became evident with the beginning of the defense program in 1940, has resulted not only in a large addition to the housing supply but in the development of procedures that may greatly influence housing after the war. By December 15, 1942, approximately $2 billion of federal funds was made available for the housing of war workers and in addition the Federal Housing Administration was permitted to insure $800 million in mortgages on war housing.

a. operations under the lanham act

Much of the war construction was needed in areas where local housing authorities did not exist, and where, consequently, houses could not be built through the federal government's existing financial and subsidy formulas. In general, defense and war housing has been provided by direct appropriations through contracts let by federal agencies. In some cases local authorities have been used as the contracting and operating agents.

The first step in the program was taken in June 1940 when the United States Housing Authority was authorized to contract directly for housing in connection with defense industries or Army and Navy establishments.[50] Some 13,232 dwellings were provided for under this provision. In September 1940, an Army-Navy appropriation act provided these departments with $100 million for building dwellings for the families of noncommissioned officers, civilian workers on military or naval establishments, and workers in vital war industries. The Navy used the portion of the funds allocated to it. The Army utilized the services of the Public Buildings Administration, turning its money over to it. No subsequent departmental appropriations were made.[51]

Direct federal operations were greatly amplified by the Lanham Act, passed in the fall of 1940, which provided $150 million ($1.3 billion by July 1943) for building dwellings for the families of noncommissioned officers,[52] and civilian workers on naval and military reservations, or in plants manufacturing articles of defense. The fund was allocated to the administrator of the Federal Works Agency who was empowered to use instrumentalities subsidiary to or outside the FWA to design and construct the dwellings. Average construction costs were limited to $3,000 per dwelling unit,[53] but questions of rental, subsidy, or final disposition of the dwellings were left open except that sale to a public authority could be made only with the consent of Congress. A special fund of $320 million was granted by Congress to the President early in 1942 for building temporary or demountable houses for war workers.

The light construction, simple materials, and reduced standards used on dwellings built under these appropriations have resulted in lower average costs than those previously obtained by public housing agencies. This has set a precedent from which it will be hard to retreat. The use of parts prefabricated in factories and on the site has given a powerful impetus to the infant prefabricating industry.[54]

b. THE DEFENSE HOMES CORPORATION

Among the first of the special means for stimulating housebuilding in defense areas, the Defense Homes Corporation offered promise of a unique means of

50. See *Housing for Defense,* The Twentieth Century Fund, New York, 1940, p. 112. Since October 1941, in USHA projects receiving priority assistance, defense and war workers regardless of income must be given first chance to occupy the dwelling units. As of December 15, 1942, 53,000 such units were programmed.

51. *Ibid.,* Chap. 6.

52. This provision was broadened to include families of commissioned officers below the rank of captain in the Army and Marine Corps and of lieutenant, senior grade, in the Navy and Coast Guard.

53. Raised to $3,750 on January 21, 1942.

54. See Appendix I, Table 61 for summary of operations under the special war housing appropriations.

combining public and private effort. In August 1940, $10 million was made available to the Reconstruction Finance Corporation from the President's special defense fund [55] for the purpose of subscribing to equities in new rental properties in defense communities where a prospect of continuing need for the housing was present. This fund might be supplemented with private subscriptions, and could be used in connection with mortgage financing. It was hoped that this device could be put into operation before the slower moving all-government programs were organized. Together with insured mortgage financing, about $100 million [56] of housing was possible under this plan if the RFC subscribed to all the equity stock.

The Defense Homes Corporation was organized to handle these operations in October 1940, and let its first contract in December 1940. By September 1942, it had entered into contracts for 9,000 family units and accommodations for 3,200 single persons in twenty-eight projects costing $57.2 million. All the equity in these projects was provided by the Corporation, for after some weeks of negotiation it had decided to retain complete control in its own hands. Mortgage funds were obtained from The RFC Mortgage Company.

Instead of providing a means for supplementing private capital, as seems to have been intended, the Corporation finally adopted an exceedingly complicated plan for producing dwellings wholly owned and operated by the government. Whether the original plan of shared private and public investment in housing corporations was practicable can hardly be judged from this experience.

C. FEDERAL HOUSING ADMINISTRATION—TITLE VI

The increase of workers earning good wages in defense areas stimulated the demand for houses for sale, but not many prospective buyers could make down payments of 10 per cent, as required by the Federal Housing Administration. At the same time, the risk on high percentage loans was apparently increased by the possibility in some places of sharp declines both in earnings and population when the emergency had passed.

Congress undertook to solve these problems by adding Title VI to FHA legislation which provided a nonmutual insurance fund of $10 million (to be augmented by the usual premiums) covering special operations in defense areas as designated by the President. Against this fund, the FHA was empowered to insure twenty-year (later amended to twenty-five year) institutional loans made to builders, on a 90 per cent loan-to-value ratio, provided the mortgages did not exceed amounts ranging from $4,000 on a single-family house to $10,500 on a four-family dwelling (subsequently increased to $5,400 and $12,000, respectively).

55. Which was reimbursed from Lanham Act funds.
56. Assuming 10 per cent equity under FHA Title VI mortgages. See below.

Previous 90 per cent financing had been available only to the owner-occupant of a single-family house. In this way builders could obtain full mortgage financing without advance sales, sell on a contract for deed with little or no down payment, or hold dwellings for rental. The FHA was authorized to insure $100 million worth of mortgages under this title in March 1941, $200 million more in September 1941 and $500 million more in May 1942. By December 1, 1942, mortgages had been accepted for insurance for about 185,000 one- to four-family dwelling units.

In May 1942 an additional section was added to Title VI to facilitate new rental housing projects. The FHA was empowered to insure mortgages on large-scale rental projects for war workers. The principal amount of any individual mortgage is limited to $5 million and may represent up to 90 per cent of value. By regulation, maximum interest chargeable was fixed at 4 per cent and maximum amortization periods twenty-seven years and seven months. By December 1, 1942, nineteen rental projects containing 2,770 units valued at $11 million were insured. The downward trend in the equity required of the purchaser or developer now reached its lowest level. In some ways the situation paralleled that in Britain during the vast housebuilding program of the early thirties. There 5 per cent down payments, or even less, were common, if the builder "stayed on the note" until the buyer accumulated normal equity or contributed to a guarantee fund established by the lender. In Britain, however, the government was not involved in the transaction.

d. CO-ORDINATION OF FEDERAL HOUSING ACTIVITIES

War housing activities have influenced not only the market but the government's administrative policy. The need of using every possible sort of aid in one combined effort accentuated the weaknesses, lack of co-ordination, and personal jealousies arising from the existence of several independent or quasi-independent federal agencies. An effort to overcome these shortcomings resulted in the establishment, first under the Advisory Commission on National Defense and then as part of the Executive Office of a Division of Defense Housing Co-ordination. However, since the power to determine and execute policy remained, under existing laws, in the agencies themselves, the co-ordinator's effectiveness was extremely limited. Conflicts of policy and personality continued.

As a consequence, the President under the wartime powers of the Overman Act, issued an order in February 1942 consolidating all housing agencies under a new National Housing Agency. This included:

1. The Federal Housing Administration and the Federal Home Loan Bank Board and its subsidiary organizations, and the Defense Homes Corporation—all transferred from the Federal Loan Agency (abolished by this order and remaining functions transferred to the Department of Commerce).

2. The United States Housing Authority, the housing activities of the Public Buildings Administration, the Division of Defense Housing, the Mutual Ownership Defense Housing Division, and the first World War U. S. Housing Corporation (still in process of liquidation)—all transferred from the Federal Works Agency.
3. The nonfarm and war housing activities of the Farm Security Administration—transferred from the Department of Agriculture.
4. All off-post housing—transferred from the War and Navy Departments.
5. The activities of the Division of Defense Housing Coordination.

In the new organization three constituent units were established:

1. The Federal Housing Administration, under a Federal Housing Commissioner, including all former FHA functions.
2. The Federal Home Loan Bank Administration under a Commissioner (superseding the former Board and Chairman), including the Federal Home Loan Bank Board agencies and the United States Housing Corporation.
3. The Federal Public Housing Authority, also under a Commissioner, comprising the functions of the United States Housing Authority, the Defense Homes Corporation, the nonfarm and war housing of the Farm Security Administration, miscellaneous war housing activities of the Federal Works Agency, and the off-reservation housing of the War and Navy Departments.[57]

6. SUMMARY

Government has become increasingly influential in the housing market. Through its powers to regulate and arbitrate financial transactions it can facilitate or impede the operation of the market. Through its ability to affect the supply of credit, it can exercise a profound influence on the volume and character of housing and through its subsidies it has set up alongside the existing system of private marketing and ownership a system of public ownership and distribution. Governmental activity in the aggregate is bound to have important effects not only on the character of housing but also on the nature of private operations. It is no longer possible for government to withdraw completely from the housing industry. On the contrary, the war has shown that with every new emergency governmental housing activities are apt to expand.

Yet in its efforts to stimulate the housing market the federal government has often taken incomplete measures, or its benefits have been nullified by the competition or contradictions among agencies. State governments, moreover, have not modified their laws to meet the special needs of long-term housing purchase, nor their taxing methods to remove some of the disadvantages of housing investment.

57. Executive Order consolidating the Housing Agencies and function of the government into the National Housing Agency, February 24, 1942.

The housing measures of the federal government have been strongly colored by an emergency point of view. The problem of housing has been approached as a means of solving some broader economic or social problem, rather than on its own merits. Measures that could not serve an immediate end have received scant attention. No serious attempt has been made to solve the basic problems of the industry. Instead steps have been taken, first in one direction and then in another, to ameliorate some surface manifestation. In doing so the underlying trouble is often not only ignored but actually intensified. Instead of removing obstacles, government aid in the past has often permitted them to go unchallenged.

The wartime program has at least faced the problem of house production as a problem in itself. Despite its emergency nature, the program has generally aimed at the production of dwellings by the most economical and expeditious methods available. Furthermore, the need for a comprehensive and single-minded approach has brought about the long-needed consolidation of federal agencies concerned with housing.

The war has thus forged new tools, both in industry and government, which should be helpful after the war in solving the problems of the housing industry. The federal government must still clarify its long-range objectives of meeting the housing need through a great expansion of housing construction, investment, and conservation, and marshall all its powers to serve those ends.

Chapter 11

REMOVING THE OBSTACLES

As THE FIRST part of this survey has shown, the production of new dwellings at costs low enough to satisfy the country's mounting housing needs has been hindered by the small scale and disorganization of the industry, by artificial restraints, and by unsatisfactory methods of distribution and finance. As our knowledge of housing needs and of the nature of deficiencies in the supply has increased, efforts to break through traditional restraints have become more frequent. Both government and industry have shared in these efforts.

We have seen the beginning of a shift toward large-scale production, centralized managerial control, simplification and standardization of the parts of the dwelling, and increasing prefabrication of parts either at the site or in a factory. These industrial trends have been aided by the increased availability of long-term, low-rate mortgage money. On the whole, however, developments in methods of distribution and finance have not kept pace with those of production. Consequently, until the war a sizable demonstration of the possibilities of mass-production techniques had not been possible.

The distribution system continues to be subject to the following drawbacks: (1) the desire to sustain the values of used houses has discouraged the construction of low-priced dwellings; (2) the complex legal machinery involved in the sale and transfer of houses throws a particular burden on low-priced dwellings; (3) the brokerage system as now organized is not well suited to marketing a low-priced product; (4) the risks of investment caused by heavy taxation on real estate and the uncertainties of the real-estate market bear heavily on the low-income home buyer as well as the investor in low-rental property.

1. Relations Between Production and Marketing

As industries develop, their production and marketing processes become more closely related. Usually industries that have moved farthest toward unified control of production and marketing are most successful in catering to the mass market. Unification may be attained under different auspices. Sometimes large retailers control the production of the articles they sell. Frequently wholesalers become the integrating element. In the automobile and many other industries, the manufacturers exercise complete control of distribution as well as of production.

a. UNIFICATION OF PRODUCTION AND DISTRIBUTION

All these trends may be found in the housing industry as it breaks away from traditional practices. Wherever large producing units have appeared, they tend to gain control of the distribution system. Large operative builders set up exclusive sales organizations, often shutting out independent brokers. Producers of rental properties often established their own operating and managing organizations, again excluding the independent broker or property manager. Factory prefabricators may distribute through operative builders (who in turn handle their own sales) or through dealer outlets, somewhat like the distributing pattern of the automobile industry.

As in other industries, unification may come through domination of some other element in the industry. For instance, the land developer who sells lots at wholesale to operative builders often retains the right to determine what kind of houses should be built. He may also undertake to sell the completed structures. In this case the producer is largely under the control of the distributor. If the materials supplier undertakes the development of a project, and directs and finances construction, the builder (or producer) may be reduced virtually to the status of an employee. In housing built by public authorities or in the housing operations of insurance companies, the buyer controls both production and distribution.

All these trends are in the direction of centralized control of production and marketing and elimination of independent agents.

b. PROBLEMS OF USED-HOUSE DISTRIBUTION

With used houses constituting the bulk of the transactions in the housing market it is clear that any system of housing distribution must be prepared to handle this part of the supply. But the satisfactory expansion of new production is bound to be retarded by a distributing system so largely dominated, as now, by the requirements of the used-house market. The latter is, therefore, a critical factor in the housing problem.

Maintenance and Elimination of Used Houses

Theoretically, the cycle of production and use of durable goods calls for (1) efficient and adequate manufacture of new products, (2) provision for maximum effective use of the product, and (3) a means for removing the outworn supply from the market. In housing this implies not only improved production methods, but more efficient management of the supply of old houses and a more rational approach to the problems of depreciation, debt extinction and replacement of supply.

By and large, the used house is an uncertain quantity. Except where properties fall into his hands through foreclosure, the mortgagee cannot properly repair and maintain used houses. Independent brokers and managers can provide only such maintenance as owners authorize. Moreover, excluding some large operators of rental properties, ownership of used dwellings is dispersed. Owners of rental properties are often more interested in getting the highest possible immediate return than in maintaining the property so as to preserve long-term investment. Dwellings occupied by owners are frequently neglected because maintenance costs prove to be more than the owners can pay. As these houses pass into rental tenure, they tend to become even more neglected.

Consequently it is impossible to measure fully the utility of the existing supply of dwellings, or to learn how much might be rehabilitated. The builders of new houses thus cannot be sure of the competition offered by the existing supply. In addition, the housing market suffers from the effects of dwellings that have deteriorated beyond the possibility of repair, that depress rents, that involve costs for police, health, and fire-protection services far beyond what they yield in taxes, and occupy land that might be better utilized. There is no means for systematically removing these outworn structures. Chance, whether in the form of condemnation or physical collapse, determines their end.

Operation of the Used-House Market

Even in so disorganized a field as the used-house market strong management is possible. The Leigh organization in London, for instance, has done a substantial business in buying, refurbishing, and leasing old dwellings at $12 to $18 a month rentals. In 1938 this company had over 12,000 tenants. Similar operations have been conducted in the United States, though on a smaller scale and usually at higher rentals.

Large organizations, specializing in the buying, renovating, and rental or sale of old properties—contrasted with the multitude of negligent, indifferent, or incompetent owners who now are the principal factors in the used-house market—might help to attain a more efficient utilization of our housing supply. The condition of used houses could then be more readily appraised, and the demand for new and old dwellings more easily determined. Such organizations, moreover, would not be likely to keep on the market dwellings that had deteriorated beyond economic maintenance. In Part I of the survey, we pointed out the need for special repair and alteration organizations. These might work with or become part of the large-scale operating company.

Difficulty of Encouraging Investment in Old Houses

The failure of such organizations to become common in American cities is due simply to the fact that the same factors that discourage housing investment generally act with added force here. The problems of shifting neighborhoods and the influence of high assessments, of fictitious land values, or unrealistic zoning, all combine to prevent the investment in and operation of used houses from being an attractive form of enterprise. So long as these drawbacks remain, some special form of inducement is required to counteract them.

The difficulty of obtaining new investment has led to proposals for improving the position of present owners of old properties, particularly in blighted areas. Under these proposals, the present ownerships in a block area or larger neighborhood unit would be pooled, the owners receiving shares of stock in a new owning corporation proportionate to the appraised value of their former properties. The corporation would then proceed progressively to restore the character of its holdings. The best structures would be rehabilitated, those beyond economic operation removed, and new structures added from time to time to replace those torn down. This process of renewal could proceed indefinitely, preventing a future relapse into blight.[1] Many difficulties have prevented a trial of this plan—complex financial relations between owners and mortgagees, failure to realize the interdependence of property values, unreal notions of the value of property, difficulties in tax adjustment, and so on.

The New York urban redevelopment law described in Chapter 10[2] is designed to overcome some of these difficulties by permitting developers to invoke the power of eminent domain in assembling land. It provides for the approval of the scheme as a whole by the planning authorities, thus assuring zoning adaptable to the new development. It also limits taxes for a fixed period. The problem of fictitious land valuations is met by permitting pooling of ownership interests based on proportionate rather than absolute values. The return of peace may offer better opportunities for testing the effectiveness of this and similar laws.

C. TRENDS IN THE DISTRIBUTION OF NEW HOUSES

Although used-house distribution has been neglected, the industry has made noteworthy progress in unifying the distribution and production of new houses. This trend parallels the efforts of producers to modify their production methods to fit special market needs.

Up to the present time, the large operative building and sales organization has developed the most economical methods of selling houses. Similarly the

1. For further details see "Group Action for Property Control, IV-V," *Land Usage, Housing and City Planning,* 1936, Land Utilization Committee of the New York Building Congress.

2. See p. 275.

large rental-housing developer appears to offer the greatest values to the tenant. The large land developer, with a consistent building program, can offer many of the economies of continuous, large-scale enterprise to those buyers who demand more individualized design than the operative builder usually provides.

All these cases point toward the growth of larger enterprises and the integration of land preparation, sales, and property management. But this is possible only in large urban markets. Except for the factory prefabricator with his dealer organization, and what we have called the dealer-builder,[3] the smaller market areas have gained little from recent developments. Furthermore, neither of the new methods mentioned appears yet to offer a wholly adequate solution to the problem of providing an adequate supply of new dwellings in these areas.

The dealer-builder usually offers no essential variation from the handicraft custom-contracting system of building houses. However, because he combines functions ordinarily separated, that is, supplies materials, builds and sells houses, the dealer-builder may reduce the cost of housing. He also offers the purchaser a relatively substantial and responsible organization to deal with, especially in small towns. But these advantages have not been sufficient to result in a marked expansion of housebuilding.

Combined with owner-labor for the assembly of the bulk of the structure, the materials supplier also offers another method of broadening the housing market, at least in localities where mechanical skills are prevalent among prospective home buyers. But unless the structure is greatly simplified, and in addition largely preassembled, there is little prospect of developing owner-built methods even in farm areas. Moreover facilities for mass purchasing and manufacturing are required which the average supplier of materials does not possess.

Prefabricators' Distributing Methods

The factory prefabricator offers a practicable method for building houses for the scattered market for medium- and low-priced dwellings where a minimum of individual design variation is acceptable. Methods of distributing prefabricated houses, however, are still in a tentative stage. The separation of producer and dealer common in the late thirties may prove advantageous neither to the producer nor consumer, since one third to one half the structure and equipment must be installed under ordinary subcontracting methods. As a result, the savings in prefabrication are frequently dissipated in the traditional assembly of unprefabricated parts. Furthermore, the prefabricator's market, being thus limited to areas where most of the traditional skills are available, does not include farms and small towns. The dealer in prefabricated parts must be a contractor as well

3. See Chap. 5, p. 145.

as a salesman, a combination that usually requires a large organization and high overhead. Finally, the acquisition and preparation of land is usually left to the home buyer.

Thus, while prefabrication represents a real advance in productive efficiency, it leaves unsolved many problems of distribution. The prefabricator often regards his task as finished at his loading platform, a situation that threatened for a time to discredit prefabrication when the government, under the war program, called upon producers to build completed houses.[4]

Prefabrication can be adapted to a dealer system if more operations are concentrated in the factory and field-assembly methods are further simplified. This is especially needed in small-town and rural markets where there are apt to be few skilled building mechanics. The prefabricator must also give greater attention to the selection and preparation of land. Indifference to location has caused as much difficulty in obtaining mortgage money for prefabricated houses as has the novelty of the structural method itself.

The housing industry is groping for solutions to its many problems. Only partial answers so far have been found. Thus the operative builder, for the most part, continues to be bound to a local market. The factory prefabricator still has difficulty in perfecting his distribution pattern. Housebuilding enterprise remains too small in scale and too discontinuous to take full advantage even of such technical advance as it has made.

In many industries the large size of the individual companies has resulted in trade restraints. In housebuilding small size has brought the same results. The development of large producing and distributing organizations seems to be the next stage in the housing industry. This development is as necessary for the scattered as for the concentrated portions of the market.

2. LAND PROBLEMS AND HOUSING DISTRIBUTION

Land problems intrude at every stage of house production and distribution. They face the owner or operative builder before construction can begin, affect the value of the dwelling at every period of its life and make it difficult to remove deteriorated structures and reassemble parcels of land for the rehabilitation of a neighborhood.

a. DIFFICULTIES IN OBTAINING LAND FOR LOW-PRICED DWELLINGS

The ability to produce and market cheap houses depends upon low-priced land. As the first part of this survey has shown,[5] so great a surplus of land is available

4. See "Building for Defense . . . Prefabricators Put on a Show," *Architectural Forum*, September 1941, pp. 188–189.
5. See Chap. 1.

for housing that a serious rise in land prices is not generally anticipated. Yet the cheapest land is usually found in outlying areas, while low-income families need cheap public transportation and access to shopping centers and places of employment. They depend upon public schools and other public services found in built-up communities. Consequently, the outlying urban areas are not always most suitable for low-priced developments. Moreover, independent suburban communities and some central cities tend to increase the cost of land by elaborate specifications for streets, lot width, and other zoning and planning provisions. As a result, low-priced developments are often excluded. Sometimes this situation arises from the zeal for durability on the part of those who prepare the requirements for public improvements, but often it is part of an avowed policy to keep out undesirable developments. Excessively stringent building codes may have the same effect.

Under present conditions, many obstacles stand in the way of balanced community development and the provision of low-cost shelter for the urban population. These obstacles will remain so long as metropolitan areas consist of numerous independently administered communities. Indeed, such problems cannot be solved by builders, even large ones, but only through public consciousness of the importance of community planning. Such planning must take into account all the groups living in the community and should lead to public policies that will help the housebuilding industry to meet all housing needs.

b. PROTECTION OF HOUSING VALUES

As a dwelling grows older its marketability depends more and more on its location. Recently much progress has been made by communities, developers, and builders in protecting locations against rapid deterioration. Improved methods of subdivision, widely used during the recent period of building expansion, promise to help sustain housing values in low-priced as well as higher-priced areas. But a good land plan can preserve the value of a house over a long period only if the community itself is well planned and administered.

Rarely can the municipal services needed by a residential neighborhood, particularly if inhabited by medium- or low-income groups, be provided solely by taxes directly attributable to that area. In a balanced community taxes on commercial and industrial real estate make up the deficits. Where low-priced properties are concentrated in communities without a normal proportion of industrial, commercial and high-priced residential property the lack of a broad tax base is almost certain to result in their neglect. The best planned developments will deteriorate if schools prove inadequate and street maintenance, garbage and trash collection, and similar services are apathetically performed.

C. REUTILIZATION OF LAND

The possibilities of making private enterprise effective in eliminating deteriorated and outmoded dwellings and redeveloping their locations largely depend upon (1) improved mechanisms for reassembling land and (2) land prices low enough to make redevelopment feasible.

Use of the power of condemnation has been recognized as a means of clearing up blighted and slum areas.[6] The urban rehabilitation acts seek to extend the power of condemnation to private corporations engaged in redevelopment work under state regulation. The power of condemnation helps to clear up titles held by minors or unknown claimants, and to force minority interests to sell, but it provides no assurance that land can be purchased at a reasonable price for the proposed development. The price is determined at the very end of the condemnation process. A private corporation, following the proposed procedures, might find—after large expenditure in surveys, land planning, architectural and legal services, and negotiations with property owners and governmental bodies—that the awarded price was too high to make the development economically sound. For this reason, private corporations are likely to be reluctant to utilize these powers.

Such difficulties may be avoided for the most part by the pooling of property interests. But pooling may not always be a practicable method of assembling land. As an alternative, the task of condemnation, reassembly and clearance might be left to municipal bodies. The corporation would then deal with one owner, the municipality, with whom it could negotiate on the basis of how much of the cleared area it wishes to use and the price to be paid. It would have the certainty that a transaction could be accomplished on an agreed basis, and would be able to tell, without excessive preliminary expenditures, whether or not a specific proposal would result in a satisfactory investment. If the municipality were able to lease instead of sell the cleared land to private corporations, the problem of financing a project as well as future public control of the area might also be simplified.

Fictitious Land Prices

Except where landowners are able to agree on a pooling of their properties, each taking a proportionate interest in a new enterprise, the fixing of land prices for a rehabilitation project is always likely to be a perplexing problem. Con-

6. *Minnie Keyes* v. *U.S.*, 119 Fed. 2d. 444. On October 13, 1941, the Supreme Court of the United States, by denying the defendant's application for a writ of *certiorari*, affirmed the decision of the Court of Appeals. This decision covering the condemnation of land for slum clearance must be distinguished from those in cases establishing the right of local government to condemn land for public housing.

demnation alone cannot provide a solution as it is based on traditional concepts of value, which assume a constant increase in land prices. Even the disaster of the late twenties and the growing realization that former expectations can never be attained, have so far failed to shake the old beliefs. Until recently many owners and mortgagees neglected to allow for depreciation on buildings on the theory that it would be compensated by land value increases.

There are no immediate prospects of drastically modifying the values which owners or the general public set upon blighted areas. The interests of numerous small owners and investors are involved in such areas either directly, or indirectly through banks and insurance companies. The problem not only of speeding redevelopment but of handling the loss facing these vested interests, which in part at least may be an innocent one, has raised a new question of public policy. As a consequence, proposals have been made that the federal government aid municipalities in purchasing blighted land and absorb a share of the difference between the current and true values as determined by prospective earnings.

Land Policy of the National Capital Housing Authority

The National Capital Housing Authority has devised a plan for writing off the fictitious element in the price of land. If the price the Authority has been required to pay in condemnation exceeds what the rental income of the new development may bring, the true value (as represented by capitalization of prospective income from a suitable redevelopment) rather than the actual purchase price, is used in the financial setup of the project. Rentals are set to allow for normal taxes, although legally the Authority's properties are tax-exempt. Instead of paying taxes, however, the Authority sets funds aside until a sufficient sum has been accumulated to pay off the excess land price. Thereafter, it is contemplated that the project will pay taxes regularly. Thus the community as a whole, through loss of taxes, gradually writes off the excess value of the land.

Need for greater public control of the use of land is evident, not only to remedy existing problems but to prevent their aggravation in the future. Several possibilities have been suggested. First, state laws might require proof of public necessity for additional housing before more urban land is subdivided.[7] Secondly, after a reasonable period for amortizing the investment has elapsed and at stated intervals thereafter owners might be required to show why an existing structure should not be demolished and the municipality should be granted power to enforce demolition if evidence to the contrary is lacking. Third, planning and zoning principles might be modified so as to prevent congestion of population,

7. Provision for proof of such necessity exists in Washington State law but has not been put into effect. The surest method of such control, of course, would be through the building up of municipally owned land reserves as is done in many places in Europe.

unnecessarily expensive public improvements, and the resulting excessive land prices. Finally, unified political administration of the urbanized area would be necessary to make the enforcement of such measures effective.

3. RELATION OF FINANCE TO THE PROBLEM OF DISTRIBUTION

Increasing recognition of the weakness of the mortgage, as an instrument for long-term purchase, has inspired proposals for the modification of financing methods. There are two approaches: (1) to make more funds available for equity investment in rental property; (2) to devise a contract payment plan for buying a home that would involve a simpler procedure and more equitable distribution of the risk than is true of current methods. These proposals would radically alter or eliminate the mortgage as it is known today.

a. ENCOURAGEMENT OF RENTAL-HOUSING INVESTMENT

Mortgage lending institutions, particularly insurance companies, have been regarded as promising sources of rental housing equities. It is contended that mortgage lending with its high loan-to-value ratio involves an outlay of funds closely comparable to what is required for outright ownership. Despite this, the legal control over the investment is largely left to equity holders with their relatively small financial interest.

Lending institutions, it is claimed, would therefore benefit by assuming at the outset full control of the property in which they invest their funds. The risks of mortgage financing would thus be removed, since the return on the property could be adjusted to varying economic conditions. The cost of writing the mortgage and of foreclosure (if that should occur) would be eliminated and the tendency to overappraise the value of the property would be discouraged. Furthermore, the need for high profits to protect a thin equity would be avoided and better management and maintenance assured. Thus the institution as well as the tenant would profit.

Institutional Investments

Lending institutions on the whole have shown, however, little enthusiasm for equity investment. Only two companies have taken advantage of the New York law making housing equity investments eligible to insurance companies. Only California and Virginia have followed New York's example.[8] Another New

8. In thirty-seven states, nonresident companies with the approval of the insurance commissioner (or similar official) can make any type of loan permitted under their home state laws, thus permitting a considerable range for equity investment for companies of the three states mentioned. All but these three states would require special legislation to make such investment legal for resident companies. In 1943 Massachusetts was added to the states definitely permitting housing investment by insurance companies.

York law permitting savings banks under certain conditions to invest in housing equities has so far evoked no action on the part of the banks.

This does not necessarily indicate the unsoundness of equity investment by financial institutions. Such institutions naturally move cautiously into a new investment field, especially one that requires specialized knowledge and constant attention. Few institutions are equipped to handle such investments or can afford the overhead involved in the supervision of construction and management of housing projects. If more large, responsible housebuilding organizations were available to construct projects and perhaps even manage them for the lending institutions, the latter might be more easily induced to invest in housing property.

State authorization for institutions to engage in equity finance does not eliminate all the disabilities of real-estate investments, such as the real-estate tax, and the possibility of rapid depreciation which can be only partly controlled by good planning and management. The nonliquidity of real-estate investment may be aggravated in the case of large projects. All these factors not only inspire caution in investors but tend to limit housing operations to the largest institutions which need only a minimum amount of liquid funds. Moreover, according to present indications, such institutions favor large rental projects in relatively large cities. Important as an expanded rental production is to the larger centers, this type of operation is not likely to be of benefit to smaller communities.

"Yield Insurance"

Various proposals have been made for inducing equity investment in rental property.[9] Most of them provide for 100 per cent equity, eliminate mortgage financing, and involve some form of insurance against loss to be provided by the federal government somewhat along the lines of FHA mortgage insurance. Some of the plans call for a guaranteed minimum income (at about the long-term government bond rate) for a number of years. On his part, the investor must accept a limited maximum annual return, excess earnings to be used to amortize the investment or build up reserves against future losses. Other proposals go so far as to protect the principal as well as the yield of the investment.

Judging from FHA experience, many institutions would invest in rental property if the insurance coverage were sufficiently attractive. The insurance plan, however, would require close supervision by the government of construction and managerial costs and methods. The result would not likely be a simple or inexpensive form of operation. Hence only an institution engaged on a scale large enough to warrant the expense of dealing with a governmental agency

9. See, for instance, *Hearings Before the TNEC,* Pt. 11, *The Construction Industry,* testimony of Henry J. Eckstein, pp. 5281–5303.

could afford to enter the rental housing field. Yet large institutions are the ones most likely to invest in housing without the benefit of insurance. The introduction of insurance of the yield as well as the principal probably would make equity investment more acceptable to institutions, but would probably not spread its use beyond a limited group of banks or insurance companies.

b. DEVELOPING NEW METHODS OF HOUSING FINANCE

In no phase of housing have more proposals been offered and experiments tried than in home finance. Many schemes suggest not only radical changes in the financial transaction but also in the tenure under which housing property is held. It is possible only to outline here a few of the suggested modifications of the mortgage system.

The traditional mortgage contract is equitable to both parties, at least in theory. The borrower can never be forced to pay more than the debt he incurred. If he defaults and the property is sold under foreclosure proceedings, he receives any excess over the unpaid amount of the defaulted loan. The lender is protected not only by the security of the mortgaged property but he can enter a deficiency judgment against the borrower if the value of the property is less than the loan.

As long as foreclosures result from occasional individual misfortunes or miscalculations, and while prices generally are trending upward, the mortgage system can hardly be called unfair and certainly does not disrupt the housing market or the economy as a whole. Most foreclosures occur, however, during a depression. Hence they may bring inordinately low prices and the defaulting borrower must take a loss out of all proportion to the long-term value of his property.

Protection of the Borrower

We have seen how mortgage law and practice have tried to give the mortgagee greater protection,[10] chiefly by increasing the cost and difficulty of foreclosure. But it is now clear that such measures not only fail in their purpose but tend to make mortgage money more difficult to obtain, particularly by low-income borrowers.

The use of regular amortization payments represents another effort to safeguard both the borrower and lender. Amortization by small monthly payments eliminates large lump-sum payments and, by providing for a regular return of capital, saves the lender from getting into a position where his assets are frozen through the inability to collect large due payments. But the monthly payment plan does not eliminate the possibility of foreclosure or the risk of capital loss.

All amortization payments, of course, do not represent the borrower's investment. A portion covers depreciation, which should be written off regularly

10. See Chap. 9.

whether the property is mortgaged or owned outright. Misunderstandings about the true "equity" represented by the amortization payments have resulted in exaggerated estimates of loss from foreclosure. But the payment above actual depreciation provides protection to the lender against unforeseen loss in case of foreclosure. To the borrower it represents investment or forced savings and means that he is paying for the house at a faster rate than he is using it up. The amount of forced savings is especially high in relatively short amortization terms.

Having paid in more than the monetary equivalent (on a long-term value basis) of the house's utility to him, the borrower may lose whatever equity is represented by the amortization payments if foreclosure occurs during a serious dip in the market. Since the borrower's equity increases the longer the mortgage has run, amortization may increase the borrower's risk. The FHA has removed the lender's risk almost entirely but it has not made the borrower's position comparably secure.

Proposed New Types of Sales Contracts

To increase the borrower's protection, proposals are offered for: (1) segregating part or all the equity from the depreciation in the amortization payment and (2) providing for the return of the equity to the borrower in cash, in case of forced or voluntary withdrawal from the contract, or (3) permitting the borrower to use his accumulated equity credit to meet regular payments during a temporary stringency. Thus the traditional relationship of borrower and lender would become that of seller and buyer on long-term contract, the latter being in possession of the property though not the actual owner. The purchaser would then in effect pay rent to the seller on the basis of estimated physical depreciation of the property, and make an additional payment which would permit the transfer of title before the end of the depreciation period. At the same time the seller would allow the buyer to use the accumulated additional payments to meet deficiencies, or take them in cash in case of withdrawal from the contract. Obviously, to protect the seller against declines in value, some penalty would be necessary in the use of the purchase or equity reserve, so that the amount returnable would not equal that paid in. Such an arrangement (with its penalties) might be similar to the terms of withdrawal from a contract for the installment purchase of an annuity or paid-up insurance.

The lack of actuarial data either on house depreciation or purchase defaults makes it difficult to determine what the payments ought to be to cover the seller's risks without overcharging the buyer. To offer greater inducements for entering this type of transaction, therefore, its sponsors usually propose government insurance of the contract. This insurance would not only guarantee the seller against losses caused by undue depreciation, but would assure the buyer that his equity would be preserved.

This scheme thus contemplates the virtual abandonment of the mortgage as a financing instrument and tends to break down the distinction between ownership and rental. The down payment, if any, would become incidental. Title, if transferred at all, would be passed only when the buyer had fulfilled his contract obligations. The seller would have control over the property's management and maintenance. At the same time, the intangible values of homeownership would be preserved and the occupant's interest in the property and the community presumably would be greater than under straight rental tenure.[11]

4. GOVERNMENTAL PROBLEMS

There is every indication that government's concern with housing problems will increase rather than diminish. We may expect more extensive controls of land use and building construction and occupancy. Problems of restraints and rackets are likely to lead to new means of policing the industry itself as well as its products. Government's interest in technical and market research may well be broadened, and it is highly improbable that it will withdraw from the responsibilities it has assumed in the fields of finance and subsidy.

The first part of the survey showed that the relationships between government and housebuilding have not always contributed to a desirable expansion of production. Thus attacks on trade barriers and restraints have for the most part been ineffective or short-lived; building codes and other ordinances of control have often thwarted technical progress; and information on housing needs has been inadequate. The examination of marketing processes reveals other places where a modification of governmental policies and procedures might benefit the housing industry. Methods of taxation, mortgage finance and transfer all need re-examination in the light of what they might contribute to the rejuvenation of housebuilding.

But even beyond these questions, the expansion of the housing activities of the federal government has created new problems of co-ordinating policy and

11. A plan involving principles along these lines was advocated by Colonel Laurence Westbrook before the Temporary National Economic Committee (see TNEC Hearings, Part 11, pp. 5340–5357). Later some of Colonel Westbrook's ideas were embodied in a number of projects initiated as part of the war housing program of the Federal Works Agency. (See "Suggested Principles Governing Execution and Operation of Mutual Home Ownership Projects," Federal Works Agency Form 7530, revised October 17, 1941.) A more elaborate plan involving a nation-wide set-up of trustee organizations, transfer of equities between dwellings in different locations, government insurance both of the equity payments and the lender's investment has been advocated by Ivan de Tarnovsky under the name of "The Equity Plan." See also "The Finite Plan" as presented by Bernard Smith, *Harper's*, July 1943.

administration and of clarifying objectives. These problems also must be solved if the industry is to go forward.

a. UNIFICATION OF FEDERAL POLICY FOR URBAN HOUSING

The housing program of the federal government has resulted in a hodgepodge of agencies sometimes contradictory in theory and often conflicting in administration. It has been a program without a policy. The National Housing Agency established under the President's war powers provides an essential mechanism for effecting the administrative co-ordination of the individual agencies. We may assume that this emergency arrangement will become permanent through future legislation, and that the present structure will form the basis of all postwar federal housing developments in urban areas.

The larger task of co-ordinating policy remains. The conflicts, for instance, between the Home Loan Bank Administration and the Federal Housing Administration remain to be resolved. The relation of public and private enterprise needs to be more clearly established. Governmental policy seems settled on the necessity for providing assistance to families whose incomes do not permit them to obtain decent shelter. It is unlikely that any combination of increased income or decreased housing costs in the near future will entirely remove that necessity. The form that public assistance may take, particularly as to the amount of new construction and as to the level of housing standards, is, however, open to question. The extent to which such assistance is to be granted is similarly an unsettled point. These questions bear directly on the problem of "competition" between public housing activity and private enterprise. The unification of interests in one governmental agency, together with the experience of the past eight years, should make this problem easier to resolve.

b. RURAL AND FARM HOUSING POLICY

The establishment of a unified housing agency reveals the absence of effective means for dealing with the housing requirements of rural areas. A comprehensive rural housing program not only involves techniques differing from urban housing but also requires procedures varied to suit the different groups of the rural population. Thus we have farm owners, tenants operating entire farms, tenants working parts of commercialized farming establishments or plantations, farm laborers with a relatively fixed abode, and migratory farm workers. Each group requires a different approach. Existing credit facilities may be ample to provide a good standard of housing for owner-operators and the more substantial tenants. But under existing economic conditions, supplemental financial aid is necessary to improve the housing of large numbers of rural families, especially in the tenant and laborer classes. Education in the desirability of better housing, as well as in simple housebuilding skills, is needed for all groups so that the family itself can do as much as possible of the building or repairing of its home.

At present the federal government aids to rural housing are scattered in many agencies. Two of the urban agencies have special provisions for rural housing. The FHA insures loans for repairs and new construction, and the USHA (now FPHA) subsidizes rural projects. The Farm Credit Administration and the Farm Security Administration touch the housing problem from different angles.[12] The Rural Electrification Administration has provided funds for the modernization of farmhouses. And the Department of Agriculture's Bureaus of Home Economics and Agricultural Engineering, and Extension Service undertake housing research and education.

Since the majority of these agencies are under the jurisdiction of the Department of Agriculture, the basis for a more closely knit organization and a greater co-ordination of policy is present. The parent agency also offers a means for providing a better relationship between housing and other aspects of the agricultural economy than has so far been achieved. Until now, the problems of farm housing have been slighted by the government in its greater concern with the urgency for increasing farm income. The improvement in rural economic conditions due to the war may permit a shift of interest to the neglected question of housing.

Although farm housing cannot be considered apart from the productivity of the land, it may still be possible better to distinguish the methods of financing farm housing from the making of loans for productive purposes. This might be accomplished through a greater use of personal credit to build or repair farmhouses, perhaps supplemented by loan insurance similar to that of the modernization credit plan of FHA. Co-operative credit unions might be developed to extend such credit.

C. SIMPLIFICATION OF STATE AND FEDERAL PROCEDURES

The increased role which government will probably play in future housing programs emphasizes the need of re-examining its relationship to private housing interests. It is, of course, difficult for government to follow as simple procedures as some critics would like. Government agencies must observe special considerations and limitations not present in private activity, and the very size of their operations necessarily results in a certain inflexibility of process. The various jurisdictional levels at which government must be dealt with, in respect to the same undertaking, add to the problem.

One difficulty is plainly the nonuniformity of state land and finance legislation. Although the states should not be deprived of their right to meet local

12. See Chap. 10, pp. 282-283.

problems or experiment with new measures, there is little reason for the divergent mortgage foreclosure laws, for instance, or for varying engineering requirements in building codes. Greater uniformity would stimulate the production of housing and development of operating enterprises, and facilitate the flow of capital on a nation-wide basis. Simplification of legal and administrative processes in buying and producing houses would benefit the industry in general. Little progress, however, has been made in these directions, either in federal or state laws.

Another problem arises from the expansion of federal-local relationships. Wherever it deals with the purchase of land, ownership and management of housing projects, supervision of mortgage institutions, insurance of savings and loan shares, mortgage insurance, appraisals, land planning and housing standards, the federal government to some extent has entered a field formerly reserved to the states. As a consequence, overlapping of jurisdiction and conflicts have frequently occurred and builders or developers have had to act as mediators between warring governmental agencies. Industry finds it difficult to operate effectively under such conditions. It is important that the jurisdiction of governmental housing agencies be defined, that contradictory policies be eliminated, and administrative procedure be simplified. This would promise greater progress toward better housing.

5. SUMMARY

Our survey of the conditions affecting the production and marketing of houses is concluded. A vast public need is being served—inadequately to be sure—by heterogeneous agencies, private and public, whose main common characteristics are their lack of comprehensiveness and capacity for mutual obstruction. In the housing field government, as well as private business, has tended to seek for compensations or partial remedies, to avoid basic solutions, to create conflicts, obstacles and costs.

The problems we have examined cannot be easily solved. No halfhearted attack can clear away the traditional obstacles in the housing industry. If housebuilding is to make a major contribution to the restoration of peacetime conditions, and serve the population more adequately, a comprehensive, many-fronted drive on these obstacles must be made. Industrial organization, and the modifications of financial and governmental policy, cannot solve all the problems of housing. External forces still produce dislocations in demand. But in so far as the internal situation can be improved, the violence of the effects of these dislocations may be lessened. A vigorous industry and an efficiently organized market are vital to the bridging of the gap between supply and need.

THE PROGRAM

Chapter 12

CONCLUSIONS AND RECOMMENDATIONS OF THE HOUSING COMMITTEE

1. Conclusions

THE MASS HOUSING MARKET has been served less effectively than the mass markets for many other goods. New house production has been generally aimed at a limited upper-priced demand. The remainder—and by far the major part of the market—has been supplied chiefly through old structures discarded by the income group for which they were built.

Sometimes these old structures provide commodious homes for the lower-income families at lower prices than for comparable accommodations in new dwellings. Sometimes, converted old houses or apartments can accommodate a larger number of families just as comfortably and more economically than can new buildings. But, by and large, the number of new dwellings fed in at the top to the upper-income third is too small and too little adaptable to make possible a reasonable standard of housing for the population as a whole. In comparison with our accomplishments in other fields, too large a proportion of the population must put up with deteriorated, inconvenient and often hazardous dwellings.

In this survey the Committee is not primarily concerned with the housing of the people who are now relatively well taken care of, or with the methods used to produce the highly individualized, custom-tailored article called for by a well-to-do demand. This part of the market is not likely to suffer often or long from an acute shortage of dwellings.

The Committee, however, is deeply concerned with the dangers to the economic system and the social structure that come from depending so largely for our housing supply upon the variable and often eccentric demands of the top third of the population and upon an industry designed to accommodate them. This traditional policy has been accompanied by: (a) an exaggerated violence in the housebuilding curve with serious repercussions throughout the business world; (b) a rapid obsolescence of dwellings at the top of the scale and an undesirable maintenance of values in the worst of the supply at the bottom; (c) unnecessarily high costs in the production, distribution and financing of dwellings; and (d) unnecessary expense, inconvenience, and even suffering for a large part of the population.

Not only would the bulk of the public benefit from an ampler production of houses for the middle- and lower-income groups, but an industry devoted to such production could hope for a more sustained activity than housebuilding has enjoyed and could play a more substantial and more dependable part in the economy as a whole. The Committee has, therefore, directed its attention mainly to the difficulties that, up to the present time, have kept housebuilding in its restricted traditional mold.

A clear understanding, not only of the production but also of the marketing factors involved, will be needed to deal with our housing problems after the war. This is the responsibility of all the groups concerned with housing:

1. The producers of houses who create shelter and keep it in repair, including labor and those who supply building materials.
2. Occupants and users of houses, both those who rent and those who buy.
3. Owners and managers who invest in houses and service them for their occupants.
4. The lenders on long-term credit who arrange for the advance payment of the cost of creating shelter and for the repayment of these advances.
5. Government (federal, state and local) which regulates housebuilding, furnishes public services to houses and often provides financial and other aid to housing.

a. THE NECESSITY FOR ACTION

The aggravated shortages of housing created by war conditions and the overwhelming need for utilizing to the fullest every industrial resource when the war is over make the housing question more than ever an urgent one.

We entered the war with a huge backlog of unfulfilled need, with which the revived building activity of the late thirties had only begun to cope. During the decade as a whole the number of new urban dwellings built was only three fifths of the net number of families added. At the time of the Housing Census, in April 1940, probably three million urban families were doubled up; about 9 per cent of all occupied urban dwellings were overcrowded and almost one fifth of them were in need of major repairs. Conditions in farm and rural nonfarm areas generally were worse than in the towns and cities.

The war period will inevitably see a further deterioration in the housing supply. New construction has been drastically curtailed. Even necessary repairs have not been made because of shortages of labor and materials. Population shifts and demobilization will create added demands.

The survey has estimated that to catch up with any substantial part of the backlog during the first postwar decade and at the same time to keep pace with family increase on the one hand and the continued depreciation of the housing stock on the other, well over a million new dwellings of good quality a year could be used. The majority of these needed dwellings should be medium- and low-priced—varying from $2,000, or even less, in some regions, to $4,000 in others, at present price levels—and a very large part of them in both rural and urban areas will be needed for rent rather than for sale.

The woeful inadequacy of the tools that we have for the task constitutes a serious indictment of the housebuilding industry. The estimated number of houses needed annually is much greater than has ever been built in the past. Houses in the price range where the need will be greatest have, for the most part, been furnished in the past through haphazard and socially costly "filtering down" rather than by new construction. The class of rental tenure where need will be heaviest has also been mostly served by "filtering down" and by the poorest of the available supply at that.

It is hard to see how the housebuilding industry in its traditional form, even with government aid, can effectively cope with such an assignment. But, to add to the difficulty, the drastic curtailment of housebuilding during the war will, if long continued, result in the disappearance of building organizations, the dispersion of building labor, and the deterioration of skills. The effect of the war on the housebuilding business will be much like the effect of a major depression. With all the stimulus that government provided to recovery from the last depression, it was nearly five years before strong building organizations were an important factor in production. We cannot afford to wait so long again.

The problem will be one not only of obtaining a larger volume of production than ever before but of creating an industrial organization geared to such production. The problem has many aspects. The housebuilding industry is itself technically backward. It must deal with a system of land subdivision, transfer, and ownership that is even more bound in costly and restrictive traditions than construction itself. It must rely upon methods of finance and distribution that are only poorly suited to mass requirements. If it is to fill the need, it must overcome these obstacles and produce adequate houses more cheaply than ever before. And even then, there will be a residue of families able to afford only substandard housing. Their need cannot be solved solely through an industrial approach but must receive special consideration.

The task before the housing industry is indeed difficult. The dead hand of the industry's past must be prevented from indefinitely thwarting its future. If the Committee's interpretation of the facts is correct, housing is on the verge of a new era. How long the transition will take depends upon the resolution and enterprise with which the industry and government are prepared to act.

b. THE BACKWARDNESS OF THE HOUSEBUILDING INDUSTRY

Housebuilding has, for the most part, been content to accept a limited market and to remain in a handicraft, merchant-contractor stage of industrial development. It has hardly qualified as a separate industry because it has continued to be a composite of loosely interrelated activities, rather than an integrated and special form of enterprise. Workmen and contractors move freely from housebuilding to other types of construction. Housebuilding operations are usually small in scale, local in character, and ordinarily require little capital investment. Such operations are perhaps well suited to the service of a limited and highly personalized demand, but they are quite incapable of meeting mass needs.

In justice to housebuilders it must be said that their product is not readily adapted to the processes of mass production. The house is a heavy and bulky article, arranged to serve many functions. It is composed of a multiplicity of parts, makes use of an extraordinary number of materials, and contains a wide range of equipment. It must be provided in a variety of types and sizes to meet family requirements. The problems of transporting and handling heavy materials and of assembling a complex and diverse product are unquestionably serious.

But such difficulties are not insurmountable, as the first utilization of mass production methods has shown. That they have not been surmounted is to a great degree due to the absence of a competent and responsible managerial force within the housebuilding industry. Although great advances have been made in engineering skill and in the production of mechanical equipment, the control of production processes remains dispersed among seven, often discordant, functional divisions:

1. *The builder or general contractor* is ostensibly the central figure in production, responsible for organizing the process of housebuilding. Yet he has not yet been able effectively to co-ordinate the subordinate elements in the production process.

2. *The special trade contractors* are responsible for organizing the installation of plumbing, heating, electrical equipment, painting, and many other specialties. The builder must rely for the bulk of the operation upon these subcontractors, whose organizations are usually independent of him, and whose labor and methods are beyond his control.

3. *Labor,* with its numerous separate trades, retains a more direct control over the manner in which work is done than in most of the more highly developed industries. As in other technically backward industries, custom and prescription help determine the ways in which work is done, resulting in a further dissipation of control over the production process.

4. *The architect and engineer* are responsible for design. Through their selection of methods and materials, they are able to influence production and assume varying degrees of managerial control.

5. *The land subdivider* exercises a profound influence on the environment of the house and establishes limitations within which producers must work.

6. *Materials producers and distributors* are able to influence construction processes in so far as they determine the types, sizes, qualities and availability of materials.

7. *Government and underwriters* influence production to the extent to which they enforce compliance with standards of construction established either by law through building codes, zoning ordinances and the like, or through underwriters' requirements for insurance against fire, mortgage loss or other risk.

Each of the first six functional groups (and sometimes the seventh as well) naturally tries to obtain the greatest possible remuneration for its services. Each tends, especially in the larger cities, to establish rules and enter into price fixing and other combinations in restraint of trade for the protection of its economic interests. In the absence of dependable and responsible management, the use of such tactics has enabled each group to perpetuate its established, quasi-independent position in the industry. As a result, a strong management is prevented, technical advancement is hindered, and the industry is frozen in its traditional mold.

The industry is thus left committed to unnecessarily costly methods of producing an unnecessarily costly product. Weak over-all management results in industrial restraints and, in turn, the restraints, particularly among subcontractors and labor, keep management weak. The industry has been so far unable to break these bonds and to develop new methods.

C. DEFICIENCIES OF THE LAND SYSTEM

It would be a mistake, however, to blame the shortcomings in production solely on the failure of house producers to set their own internal affairs in order. Our traditional system of land utilization and methods of home financing have been ill-suited to a mass market. Outmoded methods for handling real property have not only contributed to the difficulties of producers but have, in addition, had a direct influence on the ability of consumers to acquire more adequate housing.

Since the house is fixed to the land, it must share in every situation affecting land. If land costs are high, the difficulties of producing houses at low cost are increased. If land suitably located for low-priced houses is scarce, the supply of such houses will be restricted. If land is wastefully or unintelligently laid out, the problems of producing economical dwelling groups of lasting value are aggravated. It is a truism that low-priced houses cannot be provided unless properly located low-priced land is available. Yet even with the excessive subdivision of the past, that kind of land is often lacking.

Our traditional methods of uncontrolled and wastefully planned use of land resulted in subdivision activity separate and distinct from building activity.

There was no attempt to integrate site and structure, and houses were built in locations that often became entirely unsuitable for dwellings because of lack of proper land-use regulation. The centers of most of our large cities have thus become undesirable dwelling places. Slums and blighted areas have constantly spread as population moved to the outskirts. Subdivision in outlying areas has been so prolific that large quantities of land have remained vacant beyond the probability of absorption within a reasonable time. Much of it is unsuitable for use because of poor layout, faulty titles, and tax delinquency.

Land speculation and liens attached to the land have held prices up with the result that today low-priced housing can usually be built only well away from the center of cities. Speculation has produced scattered ownerships, and made land assembly difficult for planned developments. The failure of builders and land developers in the past to integrate their activities has helped to keep the building industry small in scale and consequently has retarded the emergence of the dominant managerial force with strength to open the path to innovation. Yet the small-scale operations of the industry have hampered the assembly of land for planned housing projects which would help to lower land-development costs and provide better located housing.

d. PROBLEMS IN INVESTMENT AND FINANCE

The union of the house with the land has still another aspect. The pattern of housing finance has been typically a pattern for the merchandising of real estate rather than for investment in housing. The financing of real estate has retained all the hoary legalisms characteristic of medieval land transactions. This circumstance has its bearings on the financial problem both of producers and of investors in completed properties.

The traditional mortgage as the characteristic form of security for both construction and purchase loans resulted in a fusion of producer and consumer credit not common in other forms of enterprise. In the usual construction loan it is the product rather than the producer that is financed, and the lender looks to the house rather than to the enterprise for his security. Since the lender, in his capacity of maker of the purchase loan, is often looking to preservation of values in existing houses (on which the majority of his loans are placed), credit is seldom available for any great number of houses in advance of sale. The accumulation of capital by housebuilders has been slow, and most of what has been accumulated has not remained in the industry because existing production methods have not required plowing back. Consequently housebuilders have not been able to acquire the financial independence requisite to a more complete control of production processes.

In the case of buyers of completed houses, the traditional land transaction pattern results in many drawbacks to a smoothly operating market. Scattered small ownerships, high appraisals, title insurance costs and the pricing problems arising from a lack of standardization in the product make transfers costly and time-consuming. Real-estate buyers encounter legal procedures which, having been developed in a precommercial society when transactions were few and far between, hinder rather than facilitate sales. The uncertainties in clearing title alone make the act of acquisition risky. These drawbacks affect both owner-occupiers and investor-owners.

The latter are, in addition, faced with further difficulties. Investment in housing is not easily marketable and consequently stands at a disadvantage compared with many other forms of investment. The investor in real property is faced with a special form of taxation, the real-property tax. Assessment practices often are unpredictable; and the tax itself bears no necessary relation to the earning power of the property. The investor is also faced with a management problem which requires special knowledge and ability. It is more troublesome to own real property and sell shelter than to sell the products of most other forms of investment.

So long as the prospect of rising property values could be maintained, these disabilities did not appreciably retard market operations. But the explosion of the myth of inevitable appreciation in value led to a general withholding of substantial equity investment, especially in rental properties. At the same time, widespread failure of apartment-house ventures financed during the twenties made mortgage credit for rental properties difficult to obtain except where accompanied by substantial equities. As a result, during the thirties relatively little rental housing was constructed. If this trend is maintained, there will be a continuous deterioration in the quality of rental units, with the low-income population (most of whom are renters) being affected most.

The desire for homeownership has always constituted a powerful inducement to house buying. But because of the large capital expenditure involved, such investment has been dependent upon the amount and terms of available mortgage credit. In the course of time the original harshness of mortgage law toward the borrower has been greatly modified. The lender's interest has been limited to the amount of the indebtedness; the legal process of foreclosure was introduced; and the debtor was given the right to redeem his property within a statutory period after foreclosure. This effort to protect the borrower by increasing the risk of the lender has, however, acted to restrict the availability of funds and keep interest rates high. Only the intervention of government to assume part of this risk has prevented this situation from becoming an increasing drawback to market activity.

Mortgages do not easily weather adverse contingencies. The mortgage is a rigid contractual agreement, and as such is not well suited to the increasing economic insecurity of the population and to its high mobility. It fails to protect such savings as the homeowner has accumulated in his equity. Nor does it make for the liquidity in their housing investment which families require when they move from one place to another. The fulfillment of the desire for homeownership is often incompatible with instability of employment and mobility of population. We have not yet developed a financing system adapted to the lives of modern users of housing.

e. HALFWAY MEASURES OF GOVERNMENT

Until recent years government has contributed to the housing problem largely by its inaction; and, when it has acted, its efforts have been halting and frequently inept. Government has not succeeded in maintaining the competitive conditions in the industry which would lead to lower production costs and free the way for the development and utilization of technical innovations. State antitrust laws, where they exist, have not been very effectively administered, and only recently has the federal government taken concerted action against restraints in the building industry. There is still no evidence that an adequate policing job is possible through the medium of the present antitrust laws alone.

Building Codes

Although local government long ago began to regulate the construction, location, and occupancy of urban houses in the interest of public health and safety, still about 40 per cent of the communities of the country do not have building codes, while housing codes are rare. Where building codes do exist, they frequently add to housing costs more than necessary to protect the essential public interest. Many codes are obsolete and contribute to high costs in their lack of adaptability to changing techniques. Codes often require unnecessary material and labor, sometimes at the instigation of special labor and material interests. Unnecessary local variations in code provisions hinder standardization of products and hamper the geographical extension of producers' activities. The quality of code administration tends to be low. Efforts to overcome this by making codes incomprehensible compendia of detailed specifications eliminate desirable flexibility and at the same time open the way to corruption.

Land Use

Laws regulating the utilization of land are, on the whole, inadequate to assure the availability of suitable sites for low-priced dwellings. Zoning regulations usually apply only to areas within city limits; and even where present they tend toward excessive allowance for commercial or high-density use, thereby increasing land costs for housing. In the large number of places where there are no zoning regulations, there is no barrier to undesirable intermingling of housing, factory or other uses. Public control of land subdivision, even where present, seldom goes far enough. The common form of regulation is concerned with the way land is subdivided; there is seldom any regulation of the amount that can be subdivided and only a limited control over land improvements. Seldom is there a master plan for a whole locality or area, of which housing development forms an integral part.

Promoting Greater Efficiency

Government has provided few inducements to builders to reduce costs and become more efficient in their operations. Only to a very limited extent has it engaged in technical research designed to improve quality and simplify construction methods. With few exceptions, the policy of government has been to accept the housebuilding industry in its traditional formlessness and wastefulness and to compensate for high costs by various forms of financial relief. This, for instance, was the point of view taken by the State of New York after the first World War in offering tax exemptions as a means for encouraging construction. It was the point of view taken by the federal government in the series of measures enacted following the depression of the thirties.

Federal Intervention

The federal government entered the housing field as an emergency measure during the first World War, and its subsequent activities have been the offspring of later emergencies. Direct government construction in World War I stopped abruptly with the peace. The next housing crisis came as a result of the great wave of foreclosures between 1931 and 1933. State moratorium laws provided temporary relief to debtors but offered no solution to the collapsed mortgage market. The Home Owners' Loan Corporation was created by Congress to take over distressed mortgages on nonfarm houses. Not only did it place former mortgage holders in a more liquid position and help revive the mortgage market; but, by sometimes writing off part of the debt and extending liberal credit terms to borrowers, it refinanced more than a million mortgages and helped homeowners to retain their homes. In addition, it confirmed the advantage of the amortized mortgage.

The Federal Housing Administration

Adopting the device of federal insurance of private credit, the FHA was established primarily to encourage, as a recovery measure, the revival of residential repair and construction. Under its auspices a large volume of loans has been made for the repair and modernization of existing structures. Even more important has been its influence in making institutional funds (of which the commercial banks provided a specially significant amount) available for house financing on a long-term, amortized basis, with smaller equity payments and at lower interest rates than had formerly been attained.

Through these means the FHA reduced home-financing costs. But, in addition to making home purchase attainable by a lower-income group than before, it resulted indirectly in encouraging technical and industrial advancement through the development of strong operative-builder organizations in many places. At the same time it set up a mortgage system supplementary to and, in practice, often competitive with the previously established Federal Home Loan Bank System.

The Home Loan Bank System

The Federal Home Loan Bank System (now under the direction of the Federal Home Loan Bank Administration) had been established in 1932 on principles that had been under discussion since the first World War. The System was intended to provide reserve credit facilities for all types of long-term home lending institutions. In practice, however, membership in the System has been largely confined to savings and loan associations, a number of which, under provisions of the Home Owners' Loan Act were federally chartered and, to considerable extent, federally financed. Further measures were taken to strengthen the savings and loan group (both state and federal) by federal share investment and by federal insurance of associated shares. But even these measures did not provide the stimulus to bring into the System sufficient resources to meet the home financing needs of the country.

At the present time we have, therefore, two systems of home mortgage finance, each approaching the problem from a different point of view. The Federal Housing Administration method, based on the security of the individual mortgage, irrespective of the type of institution making the loan, can exercise considerable influence on credit terms and housing standards. The Home Loan Bank method, based on the development of responsible local institutions specializing in mortgage lending, must leave a large part of the task of influencing housing costs and quality to private enterprise. The FHA plan includes no assured means for maintaining the liquidity of insured mortgages under adverse economic conditions, while the means available to the Bank System are of a limited character. Neither agency, consequently, can promise the cushion that might be needed to soften a depression or to provide funds for new lending when conditions are most critical. At the same time, the rivalry of the two for business might readily aid in carrying a boom to excess. And, even with this possibility aside, it is unlikely that existing controls could effectively restrain a boom market.

The effect of the activities of the two agencies has been to make homeownership easier and cheaper. Mortgage lending practices have undoubtedly been improved, and much of the risk has been taken out of mortgage lending and of investment in mortgage lending institutions. But aside from the conflicts and shortcomings of the dual system, there are other weaknesses. The risk of homeownership has not been greatly, if at all, reduced, for nothing has been done to safeguard the housing equities of an economically insecure and mobile population. Both approaches, in short, have been attempts to fit new patterns into an old and unreceptive fabric.

Neither agency, moreover, has provided any effective means for encouraging the production of dwellings for rent. In the rental field the efforts of the federal government have been almost wholly limited to the financing of dwellings for low-income families for whom some form of subsidy was necessary to fill out the rent required to carry the investment. Here again the emergency aspect was present. The program, as inaugurated in 1933 under the Public Works Administration, was at least as much for the purpose of increasing construction as of meeting the needs of low-income families. In 1938, the public housing function was established on a permanent basis in the United States Housing Authority (now a component of the Federal Public Housing Authority of the National Housing Agency).

Public Housing

The question of the scope and character of the aid necessary to be given to families unable under existing circumstances to obtain adequate housing is at best not a simple one, and it has been complicated by conflicts in policy and by experimental gropings. Costs and standards, particularly in the first years under the Public Works Administration, were needlessly high. Problems of the place of public housing in the housing picture as a whole and its relation to community planning have led to controversy. Yet by 1940, over 10 per cent of the total new dwelling units was produced under public auspices, and under war conditions public housing has become an increasingly important factor in the housing picture.

The public housing program has been looked upon chiefly as a matter of direct aid to the badly housed. Its broad economic significance in the pattern of an over-all housing program has received but scant attention, largely no doubt because of its administrative separation from other housing agencies. The use of public housing as an instrument for moderating the violence of the housebuilding cycle and for supplementing the controls and stimuli possible through purely financial measures has hardly been explored.

Rural Housing, Farm and Nonfarm

Compared with its housing activities in cities, government has contributed relatively little to housing improvement in small towns and on farms. The nonfarm home financing measures have been successful chiefly in metropolitan districts. The liberal facilities created by the government for farm-mortgage credit have provided only incidental aid for farm housing. Direct governmental aid for farm housing, given as part of rural resettlement and rehabilitation programs, has provided only a few houses. An effort to apply United States Housing Authority methods to the farm situation has been no more successful numerically. The problem of means for improving farm housing conditions seemed no nearer solution at the end of the decade than at its beginning.

Effects of World War II

The current war brought another housing crisis and a new series of measures. A special-risk insurance fund was given to the Federal Housing Administration, with especially liberal terms for use in war production areas. After restrictively regulating the new program for over a year, it finally became the principal means through which private housing operations were carried on under war conditions. Aside from this use of FHA, and the diversion, under special enactment, of USHA funds to war housing purposes, the war measures resulted in the assignment of the bulk of the war housing program either to agencies new in the housing field or to agencies especially created for the emergency. Finally, in the midst of an ever mounting confusion, a long-awaited amalgamation [1] of all housing instrumentalities in one National Housing Agency took place.

In spite of the possibilities for policy co-ordination inherent in the reorganization, pressure for action threatens to prevent a rapid development of consistent long-range programs. The same pressure, combined with increasing shortages of men and materials, is likely to result in an enforced indifference to costs, standards, and the future disposition of the housing itself. We consequently face the

1. Congress has taken successive steps in housing legislation, each as a result of a specific emergency presented at a particular time. Even the recent movement to "amalgamate" divergent agencies has been made without presentation to Congress of an understanding picture of the relationships and functions of long-term finance, real estate, the building industry, material supply, code restrictions, and other factors. Although there is still insufficient popular understanding of this complex problem, the attempt should be made to explain to Congress that to maintain the supply of housing at levels to satisfy demand, there is not so much need for more restriction and regulation of housing as for more adaptability and simplification in the complex industrial mechanism which produces and maintains shelter.—ARTHUR C. HOLDEN

danger that the postwar period will find us unprepared for the new housing crisis that it certainly will bring.

f. THE EMERGENCE OF NEW TRENDS

Although the impediments to industrial progress in housebuilding are manifold and deep-seated, they constitute a challenge that both industry and government have begun to meet. Industry is showing signs of emerging from its archaic mold. Government at the same time has shown greater recognition of the production problem as it is related to the whole housing picture.

Since the last war, chiefly under the auspices of the National Bureau of Standards and private technical societies, manufacturers of building materials have made progress in reducing the variety of similar products and in establishing standards of performance for materials in use. A program for correlating the dimensions of the various materials often used in combination has been started. Research in building codes, long under way in a halting manner, has received strong impetus from war contingencies. The need for conserving materials has revealed many possible economies in the use of materials and has brought into strong focus the notorious wastes enshrined in most local regulations. Model code provisions have been offered by the federal government, which has utilized the priorities system to bring pressure for the enactment of more rational regulation.

These moves to simplify, standardize, and co-ordinate the elements of the house, and to implement the findings of research in rational code requirements pave the way for the application of scientific methods to the house-production process. Much yet remains to be done, and it is encouraging to note that the executive order creating the National Housing Agency opens the way for a co-ordinated research program.

Independent research by materials manufacturers, builders, and architects has added to the range and utility of materials available for dwellings and has demonstrated the practicability of new techniques in planning and construction. For those who can pay the price, today's house is more comfortable and convenient, better equipped, and probably on the whole, more sturdily built than dwellings of the past; and the first steps have been taken to bring these qualities into lower and lower priced structures.

During the past decades a considerable amount of mechanization has taken place in the building industry, but until recently the use of new tools has been fitted into the typically handicraft system by which the industry has been carried on, sometimes resulting in the creation of additional crafts. More recent developments, however, have tended to make radical changes in the system itself. The concept of the housebuilding process as one carried on at the site has been giving way to one in which more and more of the separate assembly operations are transferred to a shop or factory, often not even in the same community in which the house is located. Since factory methods are conducive to increased standardization and simplification of both parts and processes, they are tending to reduce the variety of skill required and to increase the efficiency of labor through more highly productive, cost-reducing industrial techniques.

The same trend toward integrated assembly-line processes has been evident in large operative builder and contract builder projects—and though the factory may more or less crudely be established at the site of the development, its presence is none the less significant. As production processes become more integrated and management control more centralized, the builder's control over subcontractors and materials dealers increases and he finds new avenues for savings through direct purchases from materials manufacturers. Industrial integration has also increased in another direction to take in control of the sales or rental of completed dwellings, frequently in areas where strong operative builder organizations have grown up.

While the most spectacular evidence of these trends has been noticeable in large housing developments in metropolitan communities or war industry centers, the possibility of the use of the new methods in small towns and even on isolated farmsteads has been demonstrated. The factory fabricators found their first and—until war orders superseded normal activity—their most active markets in small towns not associated with metropolitan centers. And in the small towns also local materials dealers increasingly instituted a type of integration on their own part, taking over the building and selling as well as the supply function, sometimes using the product of a factory fabricator.

These trends indicate a ferment at work within the housebuilding industry. With the focus, as it is, on the low-priced house and with the stimulus to technical innovation brought about by the war, the prospects for developing the means for producing an increased volume of low-priced dwellings are certainly greater than they have ever been in the past.

In the public housing field an important development of local housing authorities has taken place. Many of these have achieved a competence that during the war emergency has permitted their use on a broader scope than contemplated under the original USHA program. As their projects have matured, they have evolved new practices and new standards of housing management which have opened the way to lower operating expense and an increased sense of the tenant's responsibility to the property.

There are, to be sure, serious lags. The new methods are still crude by comparison with those in more highly industrialized fields, and the houses produced by them often leave much to be desired in quality and price. No effort has been yet made to simplify the mortgage transaction. The hazardous land transfer system remains unchanged. No effective steps have been taken to encourage production for rent rather than for sale. The land problem has not been lessened in seriousness, and aside from yet unproven measures taken in a few states to facilitate the rehabilitation of blighted urban areas, no significant effort to ameliorate it has recently been made.

The demands upon housebuilding in the postwar era will be both heavy and urgent. Our progress in forging the tools necessary to meet such demands has been unbalanced and incomplete. If we are to be able to do more than risk the effects of a wastefully conducted boom, further steps must be taken in the creation of producing and marketing mechanisms, and of land- and community-planning techniques that will make possible a sustained production of low-priced houses. The Committee's proposals are offered with this end in view.

2. RECOMMENDATIONS

Though a solution to the housing problem cannot be presented in any simple formula, the basic questions that appear again and again through the survey are those of cost and price: production, financing and operating costs, land prices and market values. No matter how much our shortage of adequate housing can be laid to a maldistribution of income in the social structure as a whole, the effect of wastes, inefficiencies, and traditionalisms upon the price of housing must still be considered to be at the heart of the housing problem. Even though, as appears likely, we shall enter the postwar period with a level of national income and of average individual incomes higher than has been the case during the last decade, the existing cost of new housing will still be too great to permit a continued large volume of production.

The Committee therefore believes that the most important line of attack is on housing prices, and its recommendations for the most part are centered on the means by which unnecessary production costs may be eliminated and the various other elements entering into price reduced. But the problems of price reduction go beyond the mere statement of means. They involve also questions of incentive. People must be induced to utilize the means offered to them. They must find it desirable to create efficient production organizations, to lend on and buy or invest in dwellings, and to care for the property they hold or occupy.

The Committee recognizes that under existing circumstances there are serious obstacles to the creation of a more efficient housebuilding industry and a more orderly and comprehensive housing market. Techniques are still backward. The facts of the market are difficult to determine. The corporate tax system may not be conducive to the expansion of production capital. The property tax creates hazards both to investment and financing. Public attitudes often result in unnecessary wastes alike in production, marketing, and maintenance. Governmental policy is not always either clear or consistent in its objectives and its methods of administration. These obstacles must be overcome as part of a general endeavor to expand the volume of house construction.

Reduction of costs and the energizing of activity would serve two purposes. First, the way would be cleared for a greater production of low-priced houses of good quality where they are needed and of the type required to meet the great potential demands that lie back of the restricted market of the past decades. Second, the means would be provided for the industry to play a larger and more sustained part in the general economy than housebuilding has done in the past—an industry geared to assume an important share of the burden of postwar readjustment.

In the light of these considerations, the Committee presents a program of action summarized in the sections that follow.

a. LAND UTILIZATION

The hope of speculative gains from land transactions provides no essential stimulus to housebuilding enterprise. On the contrary, the excesses of land speculation in the past and the continued hope for speculative price increments are largely responsible for the difficulties encountered in obtaining sites suitable for low-cost dwellings. Instead of hampering legitimate activity, a more extensive public control of land utilization should serve to promote better planning and planning techniques, to stimulate enterprise, and to direct it to the areas of greatest need. The Committee, therefore, recommends:

Control of the price of land for housing through an extension of the public regulation of land use, the stringent regulation of speculative subdividing, the rationalization of zoning, the development of assessment policies based on the realities of the future uses of inlying areas, and the improvement of facilities for reassembling small ownerships in blighted areas.

The Committee urges specifically:

1. That, where advisable in the light of the prospects of city growth, zoning ordinances be revised and enforced to eliminate excess provision for commercial, industrial and multistory dwelling uses.
2. That population density be directly limited under the zoning power.
3. That a method of time zoning be studied and developed so that buildings which do not conform may be amortized after reasonable periods and demolished.
4. That zoning and planning regulations make due provision for large group

housing developments to which the customary yard and frontage requirements, suitable for individual buildings, cannot be economically applied.

5. That the control of subdividing covers the submission and approval of the street plan and the installation of land improvements by the developers, and also that the necessity for the proposed type of development be satisfactorily demonstrated before subdividing may take place. The harm done to our communities by excess subdivision has been so great that the necessity for its control [2] in the public interest makes imperative the treatment of land as a public utility.

6. That zoning for housing and the regulation of subdivision be extended by county or state enactment beyond the corporate limits of cities to areas likely to be affected by urban growth. That, if this fails, state-organized administrative bodies be created to acquire and hold reserve lands outside corporate city limits.

7. That appropriate administrative bodies be set up to prepare and, from time to time, revise comprehensive master plans for urban and regional areas, such plans to deal with highways, other transportation facilities and terminals, major recreational areas, the broad allocation of land use, etc.

8. That partial property tax limitation and the right (under public regulation) to use the power of eminent domain be granted to encourage owners of property in blighted areas to pool their interests, and private or semipublic corporations to make investments for the purposes of property maintenance or rehabilitation, provided that such redevelopment conform to a master plan. That, in addition, municipalities be empowered and (if necessary) aided, through state and federal grants, to reassemble lands in blighted areas by negotiation or eminent domain, that land so acquired be developed by the municipality or leased to private redevelopment companies.[3]

2. I believe that there should be recognition of the principle that an individual parcel of property ought not to be considered as an absolutely independent unit. Neighboring properties have an interest in the character and maintenance of the individual parcels within the neighborhood. The doctrine of "ancient lights," which has a long legal history, is based upon the principle that abutting owners possess the right to the enjoyment of certain community amenities. In planning for the control of modern communities, we should look back again and revive certain half-discarded principles, which were once used to protect community amenities.—ARTHUR C. HOLDEN

3. I am unable to agree with this recommendation in so far as it proposes to grant the right of eminent domain to private and semipublic corporations. The right of eminent domain is an attribute of sovereignty; it must be jealously guarded. To permit its exercise for the purpose of reconstructing blighted areas, by any but public bodies, violates fundamental principles.

I condemn the proposal specifically on four grounds. First, it is clearly unconstitutional to grant the power of eminent domain to private corporations for the purpose indicated. It would be a taking of property without due process of law. Second, it is immoral to take private property for other private uses, and particularly for the same uses. Third, it is impracticable and would result in non-action, thus holding back the only remedy for blighted areas, namely, comprehensive public action through the state, county, city, or other municipality. Lastly, it would be unwise because it would result in private corporations skimming off the cream and leaving the most needed rehabilitation untouched.

The only remedy for blighted areas is complete area treatment through a master plan designed to develop the whole to its best purposes in parks and parkways, streets and boulevards, dwellings, and

9. That eminent domain procedure be modified so as to improve and expedite land assembly techniques and permit the acquisition of sufficient area to provide adequate protection to the proposed re-use.

---

business and industrial establishments. To that end, municipalities should have the power of condemnation and of excess condemnation to develop and protect the whole area. Municipalities should be permitted to build any of the necessary projects or to lease land for the purpose of building to semipublic or limited-dividend corporations.

It is no answer to say that two or three states have already enacted laws granting the right of eminent domain to private corporations to develop blighted areas. These laws are merely on the books; nothing has been attempted under them, and they have not gotten into courts where their obvious unconstitutionality would be declared. But they have blocked public action and in Illinois, at least, that was the purpose of the promoters of the legislation.

It is no answer, either, to say that private corporations are to exercise the right under public supervision. This does not change the fundamental fact that it is a private corporation that takes one man's property for the private use of another and for the same purposes. Public supervision can be only superficial and the whole would open the way for an orgy of corruption.

Private corporations may be encouraged to reconstruct blighted areas by giving limited incentives but not by giving to them one of the most fundamental attributes of sovereignty.—JOHN A. LAPP

[Inasmuch as Mr. Arthur C. Holden served on the original committee, in New York, which drafted the Urban Redevelopment legislation, he has requested that the following statement over his signature be included in the report of The Twentieth Century Fund Housing Committee, opposite the dissent expressed by Mr. John A. Lapp. Mr. Holden believes that the grant of eminent domain to local incorporated neighborhoods is in accord with the best principles of public policy.]

To understand the reason for the grant of eminent domain to corporations representing properties in a neighborhood, it is necessary to study the principle upon which the New York Urban Redevelopment Law was based. The law was designed to restore local initiative to the small community. This is accomplished by permitting the incorporation of local neighborhoods within the corporate limits of our overgrown municipalities, and granting to these local redevelopment corporations, on a limited scale, powers for lack of which local neighborhoods have been unable to act for themselves.

It is important to recognize that under the American system the states are the origin of governmental authority. On the one hand, the states have delegated their nationality and the powers required to maintain nationality to the federal government; on the other hand, the states have *incorporated* local municipalities and have endowed them with the powers needed for performance of services necessary to the life and well-being of the local community.

The Corporation of the City of New York operates under a charter granted by the legislature. Before the great growth of the city, reasonable contacts were possible between its corporate members. The administrative organization of the city was small and intimate enough so that the acts of the corporation were responsive to the needs of the citizens. Originally, it must be remembered, only qualified property owners were given the vote. As the city grew and population increased, the property qualification for voting was abolished.

The Urban Redevelopment Act of New York aims to create new corporate entities which represent not whole cities but incorporated local neighborhoods where homogeneity of interest exists but has lacked means of expression. We have talked much about the restoration of neighborhood values but the urban redevelopment legislation is the first attempt on the part of the state to delegate to localities the needed powers for the control and replanning of depreciated local neighborhoods (revision of New York State Constitution of 1939, Article XVIII, makes replanning of blighted areas a public purpose).

The grant of the power of eminent domain under the Urban Redevelopment Corporations Act of 1941, is extended solely for the purpose of control. Under eminent domain, the corporation may take property outright or it may condemn merely certain interests in the property.

The legislation provides that the right of eminent domain may not be exercised by the local corporation except after full approval has been given to the local plan by the City Planning Commission, and after assent of 51 per cent of the properties.

This is the essence of the whole legislation. It stimulates local initiative. It gives the right to the

10. That land be reassessed in accordance with the proposed revisions in the zoning ordinances, but that such tax reassessment be actually made only as properties are redeveloped to comply with the new zoning provisions.

b. INDUSTRIAL REORGANIZATION

The development of industrial processes in housebuilding has lagged far behind that of other industries serving mass needs. Housebuilding remains backward in its localism, its unit-by-unit method of erection, its emphasis on hand operations. While it is true that in other fields bigness may have in cases exceeded the limits of social benefit, in housebuilding littleness is equally a social menace. The next step is one toward enlarged producing units and greater mechanization of processes. National policy should encourage the formation and development of larger-scale housebuilding enterprises and the removal of existing obstacles to such development. The Committee, therefore, recommends:

A reduction of production costs through the encouragement of larger producing organizations, through greater use of machinery and factory-produced parts, more highly productive industrial techniques, and the establishment, for the bulk of house production, of more direct and economical methods of materials distribution.

The Committee specifically urges:

1. That the federal antitrust laws and antiracketeering laws designed to remove restraints be strengthened; and that vigorous campaigns be carried forward by

---

majority in a neighborhood to guide the development of the neighborhood according to a plan agreed upon by the majority. If minority interests refuse to conform, eminent domain may be invoked to deprive owners of such rights as are antagonistic to the approved plan.

At the time the legislation was drafted, some critics advocated admitting nonproperty holders to a vote in the affairs of the local redevelopment corporation. Principal focus was placed by the drafting committee upon removing the existing legal and physical obstacles in the way of the assembly of property. Until experiment could show how effective an instrument the Urban Redevelopment legislation might prove in simplifying processes of property assembly and property control, the majority thought it inexpedient to complicate these difficult matters by giving a vote in the local corporate neighborhood to nonproperty-holding members.

It is my personal belief, however, that after reasonable experiment a way will be found to admit tenant members of the local community into a share in the control of the incorporated local district, just as nonproperty-holding citizens were in due course admitted to vote in municipal elections. Before any changes are attempted, it should be made clear that the Urban Redevelopment Corporation is not a private corporation in the old sense, but rather a co-operative type of incorporated neighborhood serving an important public interest, and helping to redivide our overgrown cities, for purposes of initiative, into smaller more workable units.

There is need for re-education as to the different types of rights involved. There are certain types of rights which unquestionably involve the tenants—others which unquestionably concern the property holders. There are, in addition, certain undistributed rights which, though a part of property rights, cannot be maintained merely through the assertion of the independent rights of each individual property holder. To prevent neighborhood decay, these undistributed rights must be given more specific recognition and improved methods of control.—ARTHUR C. HOLDEN

both federal and state government to rid the housing industry of price-fixing agreements and restraints set up to protect existing contractor, dealer, and labor groups from the necessity of adjustment to advancing techniques in production and distribution that may threaten their present interests.

2. That building codes be revised so as to eliminate the wasteful use of materials and labor and to permit the adoption of new structural methods, new materials, and new uses of materials that meet reasonable performance requirements; and that the jurisdiction of code authorities be extended similarly as recommended for zoning and subdivision control.

3. That, under the National Housing Agency, the federal government amplify its facilities for technical research (a) by providing, through experiment and test, the data essential to sound building code revision, (b) by undertaking independent investigation in the development of new materials, equipment, structural systems, industrial methods, and the co-ordination of materials in use, and (c) that the National Housing Administrator be permitted to allocate funds for these purposes to other governmental agencies, universities, and private research institutions, and that the results of all tests and investigations be made available to the public.

4. That, under the National Housing Agency, the federal government regularly assemble and publish, as a guide to housing producers, data on family income, volume of housebuilding, rents, sales, vacancies, foreclosures, and other similar critical information concerning the housing market.

5. That methods of corporate and income taxation be re-examined in relation to the provisions on undistributed surplus, capital investment, and reserves for corporations and individuals engaged in producing and maintaining housing in order to see whether they can be revised to encourage the investment and expansion of capital in new producing enterprises.

C. REORGANIZATION OF MARKETING PROCESSES

Large producing organizations can succeed only if their development is paralleled with that of more efficient methods of distributing the finished product. Obviously volume producers cannot operate on a unit-by-unit contract basis, nor can production wait upon an assemblage of individual orders. Furthermore, producers of housing cannot rely upon, nor bear the costs of, distribution by numerous independent brokers. Efficient marketing as well as efficient production of shelter requires greater concentration than is now common.

No single pattern of marketing, however, will meet the varied needs of the market. Methods that are suitable for houses for sale will differ from those adaptable to houses for rent. Methods that work well in large metropolitan centers may have little or no applicability to the small town or the open country.

Yet in every type of market a greater integration among the production, distribution, and maintenance functions can and should be developed. Producers of houses for sale, whether they operate through their own sales organizations or through dealers, should develop means for handling trade-ins and for servicing dwellings sold. Producers of rental property may, following existing successful examples, maintain their own operating organizations or work in collaboration with investor-operators or with housing authorities. In large centers at least, the used house, whether for sale or rent, should be more highly organized and combined with repair and maintenance services.

The Committee feels that the prospect for such developments is closely related to changes that may be needed in the investment and finance picture. The methods of housing distribution are so dependent upon the availability of funds for equity investment, and of loans to supplement and facilitate such investment, that recommendations in the one field can only be made after consideration of the other.

d. INVESTMENT IN AND FINANCING OF URBAN HOUSING

The increasing search for safety and liquidity in investment is an outstanding feature of current finance. Funds for venture enterprises have been relatively unavailable and equity investment generally has not proven attractive. Instead, savings have tended to flow into the hands of banks and fiduciaries, which in turn are usually prevented by law from making equity investments. Housing, which suffers, as the survey shows, from investment disadvantages peculiar to itself, has been especially lacking in appeal to equity investors. The housebuilding revival of the middle and late thirties was made possible by debt rather than equity financing.

The Committee is strongly of the opinion that the lack of substantial equity investment has been one of the important causes of housing market weakness. It tends to create an element of instability in homeownership and at the same time results in too great concentration on production for ownership rather than for rental. The Committee recognizes the necessity for and the wisdom of long-term credit as an aid to home purchase, but it feels also that, in the private market, credit has been used too exclusively for promoting the production of houses for sale rather than for rent. The result has been a lack of choice of desirable rental quarters and a tendency to force families into the ownership market in cases where inadequate savings, low income, impermanent employment, or instability of location, have added to the hazard of a long-term debt contract.

The Committee feels that sound homeownership would be served by a greater production of attractive, moderately priced dwellings for rent, and that a modification of the present emphasis on sales would reduce the violence of the production and market cycle. The Committee believes, however, that private rental dwellings at sufficiently low prices to permit any considerable expansion of volume can be provided only through substantial equity investment. It therefore urges that, as a matter of state and federal policy, steps be taken to encourage equity investment in rental-housing enterprises.

The piling up of funds in financial institutions, and the increasing difficulties of finding suitable investment outlets both suggest that these vast resources be tapped to meet the needs for equity finance. The Committee believes that, within limitations, insurance companies and other institutions predominantly concerned with long-term investment should be permitted to make equity investments in housing for rental or long-term purchase by their occupants. It has doubts, however, that such institutions are likely, without substantial guarantees, to move rapidly or extensively into this field. In case existing institutions fail to make such investment, the Committee believes that a special type of institution, designed for the purpose, should be devised.

The problems of the ownership market are not wholly solved by providing more rental housing. The desire for homeownership is strong. The achievement of that desire should, within reasonable limits, be encouraged and the means for it provided. The Committee does not believe that existing conflicts in federal policy respecting home finance, nor the existing intermingling of function in our financial system, make for a sound system of home finance. It favors a reconsideration of the place and purpose of existing instrumentalities and welcomes the formation of the National Housing Agency as a suitable medium through which more unified policies may be developed.

While the Committee considers that the wide acceptance of the amortized mortgage is one of the most important advances in home finance during the past decade, it believes that decreasing the monthly payment by extending amortization over long periods does not result in a sound basis for expanding the housing market. Shorter amortization periods on dwellings of lower initial cost would not only decrease the total amount of interest paid on the purchase contract but would somewhat reduce the risk attending rigid loan contracts over periods which are now often as long as twenty-five years. The Committee, moreover, is not satisfied that existing methods of mortgage finance, with their involved procedures, their high attendant costs (aside from the interest rate), their inflexible contracts, and their risks of inordinate loss, provide the best instruments for long-term purchase credit. At the same time, it is unwilling to endorse any of the specific proposals for drastic modifications in the credit pattern that have so far been put forward. It urges, however, that further study be given to this subject.

The Committee recommends:

A reduction of marketing costs through the greater integration of the production and marketing function, the simplification of transfer procedure, the encouragement of larger-scale owning and operating organizations in the rental field; and

A reduction of financing costs through the simplification of mortgage procedures or the creation of other less cumbersome methods of long-term finance; the development of a more unified and efficient house-financing system.

As first steps toward a more efficient marketing of houses and lower risk and cost in housing finance, the Committee specifically urges:

1. That each state take steps to eliminate the uncertainties, costs and delays in obtaining title to real property by establishing and making compulsory the Torrens System of land-title registration.

2. That methods of real-property taxation be modified so as to bring the tax into closer and more sensitive relationship to the actual or (in the case of owner-occupied houses) the estimated earning power of the property; and that, in addition, the whole basis of local revenue be reviewed with the object of lessening the dependence of local government upon the tax on real property.

3. That, following the pattern of the New York law, insurance companies be authorized by the various states to invest up to 10 per cent of their assets in the debt-free ownership of housing property; that, under a system of federal insurance, guaranteeing an average net return over a ten-year period of an amount not to exceed the current long-term government bond rate as applied to the total investment, the permissive investment be increased to 15 per cent; that similar insurance be made available to federally chartered and regulated trustee institutions organized for investment in housing property.

4. That, under the National Housing Agency, the facilities of the Home Loan Bank Administration be so modified as to secure a more inclusive membership among institutions financing long-term housing purchase and investment; that the Administration encourage the further consolidation of small lending institutions; that the federal National Mortgage Association be transferred from the Department of Commerce to the National Housing Agency under the direct jurisdiction of the Home Loan Bank Administration and that its facilities be made supplementary to those of the Bank System.

5. That, under general policies established by the National Housing Agency, the Federal Housing Administration be used not to maintain a mortgage-lending system distinct from the Home Loan Bank System but to provide additional incentives to lending institutions to extend credits to or make investment in the

type of housing considered by the National Housing Agency necessary to augment the housing supply at any given time.

e. PUBLIC HOUSING

Since a comprehensive housing program must assume the combined use of public and private resources, the Committee considers that the division of the total effort between public or private activity is one to be determined not on doctrinaire grounds, but on the basis of the most practicable means of doing a particular job.[4]

Public activity in housing (apart from regulation) has several aspects: (1) the performance, for all groups of householders, of functions that they cannot so efficiently or economically perform for themselves individually (such as the laying and maintenance of streets, sewers, etc.), (2) the provision of such public housing as may be needed to fill the gap caused by the inability of private enterprise to provide adequate housing for the lowest-income groups of the population, (3) the gathering of basic data and research in all aspects of housing, and (4) the education of the people to desire and appreciate adequate standards of housing.

The Committee believes that these forms of public activity are desirable and necessary to assure orderly community development, to provide a means for lowering housing costs, and to make up deficiencies in the general economy and in the housebuilding industry itself. The Committee, however, considers it reasonable to assume that with the advancement of the housing industry and of the development of new means for public-private co-operation the necessity for special aids and subsidies will and should be diminished.

For these reasons the Committee believes it important that (1) measures for direct aid to housing should be closely co-ordinated with, and as far as possible, act as a stimulant to, the efforts of private enterprise; and (2) as a means of keeping both the costs and subsidy picture clear and of encouraging cost reductions, the subsidies given should be in the form of a proportion of the economic rent of the housing produced. (Activities under this policy, however, would be in addition to such governmental land operations as suggested under Section I and such net expenditures by government as may be incurred in the operation of mortgage and equity insurance, secondary credit facilities, and other governmental housing activities that have been recommended.)

The present formula for annual subsidies as set forth in the United States Housing Act does not accomplish these purposes. Being limited to a percentage of the capital cost of a project, the subsidies tend to put a premium on high construction costs, amortized over long periods of time, if such costs produce or

4. See The Twentieth Century Fund, *Housing for Defense,* New York, 1940, Chap. 7, pp. 125–126.

promise lower expenses of maintenance and operation. Consequently, the present formula increases the difficulties of utilizing rehabilitated and other shorter-lived properties where costs might, however, be actually less than in the type of public housing now generally provided. The result is either to discourage the use of any but the most permanent kinds of building or to stretch dangerously the amortization period on lighter forms of construction.

The Committee is concerned about another aspect of current practice in public housing—namely, the relatively rigid relationship that has been maintained between income and rental. Under some circumstances this may tend to destroy incentive to income betterment through the fear of tenant families that they might lose a superior standard of housing if their incomes rise materially. Graded rent plans, which have been adopted by many local authorities, measurably reduce this danger. The danger will also grow less as private enterprise, and possibly unsubsidized public housing, combine to raise housing standards in the no man's land that now stretches between the poorest families receiving good housing of modern types of private enterprise and the highest-income families now served by public housing agencies. The Committee feels that public housing policy should not discourage economic improvement among its tenants and that present and future practice should be carefully studied for signs of this defect so that it may be minimized or entirely eliminated.

The Committee recommends:

That the necessity of utilizing various forms of public activity and public aid in a comprehensive attack on the housing problem be fully recognized and necessary provision for such utilization be made; but that public activity be designed so far as possible to the end of reduced costs and more efficient forms of industrial operation.

The Committee urges specifically:

1. That for application at the end of the war, carefully studied methods be established for assuring minimum standards of safety, health, and decency in housing for families unable to afford the rent necessary to obtain such quarters through the operations of private enterprise; that these methods include the construction, rehabilitation and operation of low-rent housing; that responsibility for action be placed in cities and nonfarm rural areas on local housing authorities collaborating with the National Housing Agency, and in farm areas on an appropriate agency in the Department of Agriculture.

2. That the administrators of the respective agencies carefully and clearly define the physical and economic conditions under which such aid may be given and that such conditions be regularly reviewed in the light of industrial progress and the general economic situation.

3. That the use of simple structures and of rehabilitated structures be encouraged, and that local authorities be permitted to acquire housing provided under the wartime housing program.

4. That subsidies be set as a proportion of the economic rent of a housing development; that the subsidy for any given dwelling unit within a project be graded according to the paying capacity of the family occupying that unit, provided that the sum of all subsidies does not exceed the allowed maximum for the project as a whole; that the scale of subsidies be regularly reviewed and modified as may be necessary to keep it in relationship with general economic conditions.

5. That the present requirements of the United States Housing Act for the elimination of one substandard unit for each one built with federal aid be modified to grant the federal administrator the right to make the elimination requirement for a locality depend upon its housing needs and population trends; that this administrative discretion should be exercised within limits to be established in the statute; and that the present provision for postponing elimination under conditions in which it would amount to unnecessary hardship should be kept.

6. That certain technical amendments to the United States Housing Act should be adopted to encourage the direct investment of private funds in the security of local housing authorities financed in part by the federal government; that statutes governing the investment of public insurance reserves should be amended to authorize trustees and other responsible officials to invest part of these funds in the bonds of local housing authorities on which a high degree of security is provided by annual contributions contracts with the Federal Public Housing Authority.

f. SPECIAL PROVISIONS FOR RURAL AND FARM HOUSING

The intimate relationship between the farmhouse and the farm economy places the housing that is dependent upon agricultural income in a different category from urban housing. The home financing and production facilities that are suitable for urban conditions are rarely adaptable to the rural situation.

The rural housing problem is not only distinct in many ways from the urban housing problem but it is in itself a congeries of quite separate problems, differentiated according to the way in which the householder derives his income. Thus we have: (1) individual farm owners and operators; (2) tenants or laborers attached to farms; (3) migratory farm laborers; (4) part-time farmers, whose principal income may be derived from other forms of activity; and (5) the non-farm rural resident, who derives his whole income in the city. Each of these groups requires special financial facilities and to some extent different types of houses.

Yet the quality of housing available to any of them, with the exception of those not relying on farm income, depends on the productivity of the land, the form of tenure under which the land is held, and the conditions affecting the prices of farm products. Where the land is definitely of a submarginal character, as in the exhausted and eroded sections of the South and the cutover regions of the North, there can be no satisfactory solution but a removal of the population to more productive areas. At the same time, land supporting several important crops—for instance, the large-scale vegetable and deciduous fruit areas of the Pacific Coast and the wheat ranches of the semiarid West—apparently does not yield sufficiently to provide adequate housing for the large amount of seasonal labor required. The cotton plantations, too, in large part support only the most meager shelter for their workers, though here the tenure system and the inexperience of the tenants are probably as much responsible for the deplorable housing conditions as the nature of the crop.

It is plainly unsound to encourage or to assist the building of houses on unproductive land and thus retard its proper transfer to forestry, grazing, or other extensive use. Nevertheless the problems of providing ample credit for housing on self-sustaining farms, of removing rural slums, and of giving decent shelter to rural families needed by, yet not adequately supported by, the farm economy deserve equal attention with corresponding problems in cities.

Although the Committee is of the opinion that greater recognition might be given to the better farmhouse, as a stimulus to the morale and productivity of the farm workers, it realizes that, where credit is to be relied upon, debt beyond the reasonably anticipated earning power of the land is unwise. The standard of the farmhouse must necessarily bear a relationship to the productivity of the land and the credit terms extended must take into consideration the debt situation of the borrower and fluctuations in farm prices and farm incomes. In cases where subsidies are extended, assurance should be sought that the families provided for are essential to the rural economy, that the subsidization does not constitute a premium on wasteful farm management or inordinate profits on the part of landed proprietors, and that it does not delay or prevent the transfer of definitely submarginal land to a more extensive use to which it is adapted.

In many sections of the country, the increase in the size of the farm and the decline in the number of farm families should make possible a great improvement in farm housing through repair and modernization rather than through new construction. At the same time the extension of rural electrification makes possible on a wide scale a type of modernization not before available to any but a small number of farm properties. Every effort should be made to utilize the existing stock of farm housing through repair where it is feasible to do so.

Aside from housing that is directly dependent upon farm income, the Committee does not believe that the financing of village and rural nonfarm housing has been given sufficient consideration. In the years to come this type of housing, located in a rural environment, yet depending only partly if at all upon the produce of the soil, is likely to take an increasingly important place in the total housing picture. At the present time, this housing at the rural-urban fringe constitutes a sort of twilight zone between the operations of the farm credit agencies and the agencies and institutions financing urban dwellings. The larger number of rural nonfarm dwellings are merely city homes in the country with cheaper living costs. The Farm Credit Administration finances them only when they produce and sell some agricultural products. The urban credit agencies finance them only when they meet requirements designed for city dwellings. Effort should be made to deal with this zone.

In rural housing, as in urban, the greatest hope for improvement lies in the development of a more efficient housebuilding industry which will give consumers better houses at lower cost. Since rural regions are at a disadvantage in hiring skilled workers, the opportunities for the wide use of prefabricated construction may be even greater in rural than in urban areas. Another factor favorable to the increased use of prefabrication is the absence of restrictive building codes and of tight regulation by labor unions which in large cities frequently have obstructed the use of prefabricated houses.

The Committee makes the following recommendations for the improvement of rural housing conditions:

That the farm housing problem be considered in relation to the farm income problem as a whole, and that, in the determination of farm land policies, greater recognition should be given to the farmhouse as a factor in the productivity of the farm and the morale of farm families; that the shortcomings of the rural economy should not be made an excuse for the continuance of slums in the country; that the farm population be educated in the desirability of improved housing conditions and be instructed how best to obtain good housing; and that better credit facilities be made available for rural nonfarm housing.

The Committee urges specifically:

1. That the existing means for aiding farm housing through the Farm Credit Administration, the Farm Security Administration, and Rural Electrification Administration be continued; that, for the purposes of co-ordinating and developing rural housing policy, there be established in the Department of Agriculture an Intradepartmental Housing Committee; and that the strictly farm housing functions now residing in the National Housing Agency be transferred to appropriate agencies in the Department of Agriculture. Since its loan funds and expenses are provided by the government, the Farm Security Administration could continue to

finance disadvantaged farmers who cannot get credit from business credit agencies. The FSA is also the logical agency to assist or administer programs involving federal subsidies such as those of local or regional farm housing authorities. The Farm Credit Administration is a business-credit agency, partly owned by farmers, borrowing funds from investors and operating on a self-supporting business basis without Congressional appropriation. However, it should assist in educational programs to improve housing conditions among its borrowers. It should also give sympathetic consideration to loans for financing new houses or improvements that are appropriate to the borrower's financial condition and within his reasonable capacity to repay. Production credit associations and banks should be urged to make intermediate term loans for financing farm housing improvements that are justified by sound credit policies and the borrower's capacity to repay.

2. That the proposed Committee co-ordinate all housing research functions now being carried on in the several bureaus of the Department of Agriculture and promote decentralized housing research through the State Agricultural and Mechanical Colleges.

3. That the new agency, through the state extension services and the county and home extension agents, enlarge and strengthen education programs among farm families, emphasizing adequate but economically sound housing standards and assisting farm families in obtaining suitable housing at the lowest possible cost.

4. That, as an experiment, provision be made for sale to farmers on a conditional sale basis of surplus demountable houses acquired under the wartime housing program.

5. That an extensive rural house repair and modernization program be instituted, utilizing methods based on the experience of Rural Electrification Administration and the Electric Home and Farm Authority.

6. That the Federal Home Loan Bank Board, Federal Housing Administration and the farm housing agencies co-operate to reduce and eliminate the gap in credit facilities between farm and urban housing.

g. PROPERTY MAINTENANCE AND OPERATION

The Committee recognizes the importance of maintenance and operating costs in the over-all housing picture and of the necessity of striking a proper balance between these costs and initial construction costs. It regrets that the absence of trustworthy and comparable data has prevented a more definitive treatment of this subject. As a matter of general policy, the Committee does not advocate attempts to achieve a maximum of physical durability. It considers that the prospect both of changes in the urban structure and in the character of dwellings is so great that construction designed for indefinitely long duration is as likely to result in future capital loss as it is to effect savings in maintenance.

The Committee is, therefore, less concerned with a long period of utility than it is with a nice balance of the relative durability of the parts of a house during whatever estimated physical life it may have and with provisions for the full writing off of the investment within that period. It believes that such a policy will be most conducive to minimizing repair costs during the useful life of the structure and to its removal when that period is over.

The most serious current maintenance problems arise from the following causes: (1) the shortage in the supply of low-priced dwellings, necessitating the continuance in the market of numerous structures beyond the limit of economic repair; (2) the instability of neighborhoods, caused by the constant pressure from the unsatisfied lower-priced market, the flight of higher-income families to outlying areas and the scattering of ownership with the constant losing fight of the individual against neighborhood deterioration; (3) the unknown character of maintenance costs, with the frequent inability of small owners (both of owner-occupied and rental properties) to meet unforeseen contingencies—a situation aggravated by the generally bad balance in the durability of house parts; (4) indifference to the maintenance of or willful misuse of dwellings, particularly by tenants; (5) the absence of sufficient attention to maintenance problems in the initial planning of the structure—a situation in which there has been some improvement during the past decade.

So far as the maintenance problem is aggravated by a shortage of new dwellings, the solution lies in the stimulation of the housebuilding industry and the directing of it into the areas of the market where need is sharpest. So far as bad maintenance results from small, scattered, and weak ownership, the answer can come only through the provision of such means as previously recommended for pooling ownership interests and for opening the way for stronger investment ownership. The Committee, therefore, recommends:

A reduction of the proper costs of operating dwellings through the simplification of structures and the improvement of their quality, the better balance of the durability of the parts of the structure, the acceptance of regularized policies of debt and investment amortization, the encouragement of better methods of and organizations for property maintenance, and the establishment of means for eliminating outworn and outmoded buildings.

Beyond this, the Committee urges specifically:

1. That the National Housing Agency undertake studies (a) of property operation, maintenance, and repair costs both of rental and owner-occupied dwellings;

(b) of the causes of property depreciation both as to value and physical condition and the rates of depreciation of the components of the dwelling; and (c) of means, through more scientific planning, of simplifying maintenance and operation problems; and (d) that the results of such studies be made available for the education and guidance of the producers, operators, and occupants of dwellings.

2. That local laws for the maintenance of minimum housing standards, and for the closing and demolition of substandard dwellings be strengthened and enforced.

3. That experiments in tenant maintenance be studied and encouraged.

4. That housing management's place in the housing process be more clearly recognized and that training for it be furthered by the National Housing Agency, educational institutions and housing organizations.

h. TIMING A PROGRAM

In outlining its recommendations, the Committee has developed its program in relation to over-all needs for industrial, market, legal, and administrative adjustments, without regard to the time sequence in which such adjustments might practicably be made. The program is thus a combination of short-term and long-range proposals.

At the termination of the war, in order to maintain a high level of national income, it will be necessary to take measures to accomplish as rapidly as possible a reconversion of industry to peacetime production. Inevitably housebuilding will be looked upon as an important instrument in making this shift, and every possible effort will be made to accomplish a rapid revival of house construction, reduced to depression levels by wartime restrictions.

The choice will be either to follow the pattern of the past and institute measures designed principally for emergency ends, or to adopt the parts of a comprehensive program that may serve the double purpose of providing immediate stimulation and of contributing at the same time to meeting housing needs over a long future period. The Committee strongly urges that the pressure of an emergency should not be allowed to result in purely short-time measures, but that, with the importance of immediate action fully recognized, each step taken, in so far as is possible, be a co-ordinate part of an over-all plan.

From this point of view, the recommendations may be considered in the light of what may be accomplished with the least delay. For instance:

1. There need be no delay in taking measures to assure freer competition within the housebuilding industry and to break down the policies and agreements that hold back technical advancement and maintain high cost levels.

2. Building code reform, already stimulated by war necessities, can be immediately carried forward in a joint federal-local program.

3. Rezoning need not be delayed.

4. Changes that may be necessary in corporate tax laws to encourage needed investment in producing organizations and in housing properties can be considered at once.

The aids to housing finance already in existence stand ready for immediate use and should be continued until better methods can be devised:

1. The encouragement of institutional investment in housing equities, although an ambitious undertaking, could undoubtedly be accomplished in no longer a period than the twelve months that were necessary to pass the National Housing Act and its implementing legislation.

2. Changes necessary to improve the formula for public subsidies could be quickly made.

3. With the completion of the Housing Census, the basic data for creating a market information service will be at hand.

If such a group of measures is ready when the postwar period is upon us, housebuilding might rapidly be brought to a high plateau. Many serious obstacles to a continued production and an effective distribution of houses, however, will still remain and will require attention if the results of the immediate stimulation are to be sustained.

The problems of real-property assessments and taxation will require solution. Basic land problems will remain, with the need for developing satisfactory methods of land-use control, and eliminating slum and blighted areas. A unified system of housing finance, adapted to present-day long-term credit needs, must eventually be worked out. Paralleling this are the questions of modernizing state mortgage laws and the methods of land transfer. Some time also must be required before the research and educational programs recommended can be expected to yield their most useful results, so that these, too, must be considered principally as parts of a long-range program to be continued over a period of years.

The short- and long-term parts of the program must be developed as a whole. Second steps need not be deferred for the first, for long-range objectives not only take more time to achieve but the measures implementing them also take longer to devise and institute. Both groups of measures should, so far as they can, be developed together so that those of long range will be available to provide more sustained benefits as the stimulus of the short-range measures reaches its peak. In no other way can the needs of an emergency be turned to permanent advantage or the creation of new problems out of each partial solution be prevented. With such an approach we may look forward to a rapid revival of housebuilding following the war and to the ultimate maturing of a well-functioning housebuilding industry geared to the housing needs of the country.

Henry E. Hoagland, *Chairman*
Lillian M. Gilbreth
Frank P. Graham
Henry I. Harriman
Arthur C. Holden
John A. Lapp
William I. Myers
Coleman Woodbury

APPENDIX

APPENDIX A

TABLE 1

DISTRIBUTION OF POPULATION IN SELECTED METROPOLITAN DISTRICTS BETWEEN CENTRAL CITY AND OUTSIDE CENTRAL CITY, 1920–1940

Metropolitan District	1940 Population of Metropolitan District	Central City as Per Cent of Metropolitan District		
		1940	1930	1920
East	*(In Thousands)*			
New York City—Northeastern New Jersey	11,691	72.2	72.8	77.1
Philadelphia, Pa.	2,899	66.6	68.3	74.1
Boston, Mass.	2,351	32.8	33.8	37.2
Baltimore, Md.	1,047	82.1	84.6	89.5
New Haven, Conn.	308	52.1	55.4	62.8
Wilmington, Del.	189	59.5	63.9	71.3
Portland, Me.	107	69.1	70.9	76.1
Manchester, N. H.	82	94.8	95.2	97.0
South				
Louisville, Ky.	434	73.5	76.1	71.2
Augusta, Ga.	88	75.1	77.9	79.5
Central				
St. Louis, Mo.	1,368	59.6	63.3	71.8
Des Moines, Ia.	184	86.9	88.6	90.2
South Bend, Ind.	147	68.9	71.1	77.0
Wichita, Kan.	127	90.3	93.2	95.0
North				
Detroit, Mich.	2,296	70.7	74.1	79.1
Flint, Mich.	189	80.4	87.0	89.0
Duluth, Minn.—Superior, Wis.	157	86.7	88.5	90.5
West				
Seattle, Wash.	453	81.4	86.9	90.0
Sacramento, Cal.	159	66.6	73.8	77.8
Spokane, Wash.	141	86.3	89.7	91.7

Source: See Table 2.
Note: See Table 2.

TABLE 2

Rate of Population Change in Metropolitan Districts Central City Compared with Outside Central City, 1920–1940

(*Per Cent Increase or Decrease* [—])

Metropolitan District	1930–1940 Total District	Outside	Central City	1920–1930 Total District	Outside	Central City
East						
New York City— Northeastern New Jersey	7.2	9.8	6.2	28.2	52.4	21.0
Philadelphia, Pa.	1.5	6.7	—1.0	16.1	42.2	7.0
Boston, Mass.	1.6	3.1	—1.3	15.0	21.2	4.4
Baltimore, Md.	10.0	27.9	6.7	16.1	70.5	9.7
New Haven, Conn.	4.9	12.6	—1.3	13.4	36.0	0.1
Wilmington, Del.	13.3	27.1	5.5	7.9	35.5	—3.2
Portland, Me.	6.7	13.3	4.0	9.7	33.4	2.2
Manchester, N. H.	1.6	10.6	1.1	—0.1	60.6	—2.0
South						
Louisville, Ky.	7.4	19.3	3.7	22.5	1.6	31.0
Augusta, Ga.	13.4	28.1	9.2	17.1	26.1	14.8
Central						
St. Louis, Mo.	5.3	15.7	—0.7	20.6	57.0	6.3
Des Moines, Ia.	14.3	31.2	12.1	14.8	33.6	12.7
South Bend, Ind.	0.3	8.0	—2.8	59.1	100.2	46.8
Wichita, Kan.	6.8	53.1	3.5	56.9	114.4	53.9
North						
Detroit, Mich.	8.4	22.5	3.5	68.1	108.4	57.4
Flint, Mich.	4.8	57.8	—3.2	74.8	106.4	70.8
Duluth, Minn.— Superior, Wis.	1.1	17.3	—1.0	1.4	21.8	—0.7
West						
Seattle, Wash.	7.6	53.1	0.7	20.0	57.4	15.8
Sacramento, Cal.	25.2	59.5	13.0	49.9	76.8	42.2
Spokane, Wash.	9.8	45.8	5.6	9.0	35.6	6.6

Source: Sixteenth Census of the United States, 1940, Series PH 1; Fifteenth Census of the United States, 1930, *Population and Area, Metropolitan Districts.*

Note: These districts have been selected from a total of 140 available from the 1940 Census. They include only districts for which the outside boundaries and the boundaries of the central cities have remained unchanged over the period 1920–1940, except in a few cases where such boundary changes resulted in the annexation of entire minor civil divisions. In cases where annexations involved entire minor civil divisions, it was possible to adjust the published figures so that identical areas were covered by the statistics for each of the three census periods. Because of such adjustments, the data shown here in several instances do not agree with published census reports.

TABLE 3

Valuation of Improved Land Compared with Property Valuation of New Single-Family Houses Insured by the Federal Housing Administration, 1940

Property Valuation Classes[a]	U. S. Total		Inside Metropolitan Districts[b]		Outside Metropolitan Districts[b]	
	Average Land Valuation	Land as a Per Cent of Property	Average Land Valuation	Land as a Per Cent of Property	Average Land Valuation	Land as a Per Cent of Property
Less than $2,000	c	c	c	c	$199	11.0
$2,000—$2,999	$282	10.5	$303	11.1	263	10.0
$3,000—$3,999	383	11.0	402	11.4	343	9.9
$4,000—$4,999	529	12.0	553	12.5	451	10.3
$5,000—$5,999	642	11.9	654	12.1	577	10.8
$6,000—$6,999	834	13.3	848	13.5	740	11.8
$7,000—$7,999	1,056	14.4	1,078	14.7	906	12.4
$8,000—$9,999	1,307	15.2	1,325	15.4	1,199	13.9
$10,000—$11,999	1,708	16.2	1,739	16.4	1,532	14.6
$12,000—$14,999	2,302	17.8	2,326	18.0	2,172	16.9
$15,000 and over	3,264	18.7	3,264	18.7	3,268	18.6
All classes: 1940	662	12.7	698	13.1	508	11.0
1939	724	13.5	770	13.9	534	11.4
1938	785	14.2	848	14.7	568	11.9
1937	913	15.3	1,011	15.9	691	13.5

Source: Federal Housing Administration, *Seventh Annual Report, 1940,* Table 40, p. 76.

a. Includes FHA valuation of house, other physical improvements and land.

b. Data based upon metropolitan districts established in the 1940 Census.

c. Computations excluded because of small number of cases involved.

Note: It is probable that the actual proportion of total cost attributable to improved land is higher than shown in this table. The cost of both septic tanks and wells is included as part of the construction cost when public sewer and water supply are not available rather than as part of land improvement costs. According to a special study made by FHA, the percentage of insured properties not served by a public sanitary sewer system ranges from 28 (Albany, N.Y.) to 100 (Suffolk County, N.Y.) in the northeastern area alone. The percentages are, with a few exceptions, somewhat lower in most other parts of the country. These figures cover all FHA operations through July 1, 1941. In the opinion of FHA officials, the proportion of FHA insured properties served by septic tanks and by individual water systems, or both, has increased considerably in the last few years.

TABLE 4

Cost per Front Foot of Specified Land Improvements in Selected Cities, 1941

Locale	Total Cost	Grading	Paving	Curb	Side-walks	Sanitary Sewer	Planting and Seeding	Water	Allocation for Cross Streets[a]	Engineering[b]
New York										
Elmira and Binghamton	$5.02	$.50	$1.30	$.90	$.80	$.50	$.25	$—	$.51	$.26
Nassau County	6.30	.35	1.92	.45	.80	1.60[c]	.22	—	.64	.32
Queens County	6.88	.39	2.17	.45	1.00	1.60[c]	.22	—	.70	.35
Westchester County and adjoining areas	7.28	1.00	2.45	.80	.72	.95[d]	.25	—	.74	.37
New Jersey										
Camden	7.44	.30	2.19	.60	.80	1.25	.25	.88	.75	.42
Camden County outside Camden city	6.20	.30	1.62	1.00	.80	1.25	.25	—	.63	.35
Pennsylvania										
Philadelphia, suburban areas[e]	6.25	.75	2.20	.80	.80	.65	.25	—	.55	.25
Philadelphia, outside metropolitan area	7.25	.95	2.60	1.00	.80	.75	.25	—	.65	.25
Pittsburgh, metropolitan area	8.38	1.20	1.73	1.10	.88	1.67[f]	.30	—	1.03	.47
Allegheny County, outside Pittsburgh										
Low cost development	6.85	1.20	1.73	.20	.52	1.67[f]	.30	—	.84	.39
Medium cost development	9.17	1.20	1.52	1.95	.88	1.67[f]	.30	—	1.13	.52
Delaware										
Seaford	3.66	.35	.60	.50	.70	.50	.25	—	.58	.18
Wilmington, metropolitan area	6.80	.50	2.00	.90	.80	1.00	.25	—	1.10	.25
Maryland										
Baltimore	7.10	.25	1.68	.75[g]	1.00	1.55	.25	.75	.62	.25
Baltimore County	4.98	.25	1.47	.80[g]	1.00	.60[h]	.25	—	.44	.17
Virginia										
Norfolk, Portsmouth and Newport News	4.71	.30	1.35	1.00[g]	.70	.63	.15	—	.41	.17
Richmond and vicinity	5.85	.40	1.33	1.10[g]	.80	.75	.25	.50	.51	.21
Suburban and rural counties	5.80	.40	1.37	1.10[g]	.72	.75	.25	.50	.51	.20
North Carolina										
Asheville and Charlotte	5.30	.75	1.65	.80	.60	.60	.25	—	.47	.18
Six other cities[i]	4.80	.40	1.65	.70	.60	.60	.25	—	.42	.18
Georgia										
Atlanta, metropolitan area	6.75	.75	2.20	.90	1.00	.75	.25	—	.60	.30
Atlanta, metropolitan area outside city limits	5.35	.25	1.70	.90[g]	.80	.75	.25	—	.47	.23
Louisiana										
New Orleans	4.65	.25	.96	.78[g]	.60	1.00[h]	.25	—	.58	.23

Ohio										
Cleveland and Cuyahoga County	9.10	.65	1.68	1.10[g]	.80	2.00[j]	.25	1.50	.64	.48
Indiana										
Indianapolis, metropolitan area	7.14	.90	1.75	.75	1.00	1.25	.25	—	.89	.35
Lake LaPorte and St. Joseph Counties	6.05	.50	1.75	.70	.80	1.25	—	—	.75	.30

Source: Federal Housing Administration, Land Planning Division.
a. Represents allocation of cost of cross streets to lot frontage, calculated on basis of 10-20 per cent of total for lot improvements.
b. Calculated on basis of 4-6 per cent of total for lot improvements.
c. Includes $.85 for cost of storm sewer.
d. Includes $.25 for cost of storm sewer.
e. Suburban areas of Delaware and Montgomery Counties, Philadelphia, Pa.
f. Includes $.42 for cost of storm sewer.
g. Includes cost of gutter.
h. Cost of storm sewer only.
i. Durham, Greensboro, High Point, Raleigh, Winston-Salem and Tarboro.
j. Includes $1.00 for cost of storm sewer.

Note: Data are based on FHA surveys made to determine minimum costs to the developers for the specified improvements. In some cases, part of the real cost has been absorbed by the city government; only the amounts charged to the developer are here given. The cost of water mains, for example, is frequently assumed in total by the city government; in the table, this was true for all but five of the twenty-five selected localities. Such absorption of costs is usually calculated as a percentage of the contract price for making the improvement, and is, of course, reflected in higher property taxes.

The figures are not to be taken as "typical," even for the specified cities. They are used by FHA appraisers as a guide; for a particular situation, actual conditions are likely to show a considerable variation from the figures given. Variations in terrain, for example, will affect grading costs, even within a given city.

APPENDIX B

1. Weight of Basic Materials Used in the Construction of Two Four-Room Houses

Data shown in Table 5 were supplied by the Technical Division of the Federal Housing Administration. Each house has two bedrooms, living room, kitchen and bathroom. Floor plans are identical for the two houses, except that the brick house has a basement stairway, and its outside dimensions are increased 8 inches each way by the substitution of brick for frame construction. The floor area of each house is 616 square feet. Figures in the table are based on the estimated amount of materials that would be required to build these particular houses in accordance with FHA standards.

The houses are not intended to be typical of current building. They have been selected entirely for the purpose of showing what happens in particular cases. Variations in the amounts of materials used in different houses are great. For example, the amount of metal used to produce 1,000 "average" FHA insured dwelling units has been estimated by that agency at 5,916 pounds per unit, as compared with 2,974 pounds for the four-room frame house, and 3,561 pounds for the four-room brick house, as detailed here. These wide differences are readily accounted for by variations in the size of the structure and in the weight of such items as the heating unit, plumbing equipment, and structural bracing.

A third figure on metals required for house construction is that prepared by Raymond V. Parons, Consulting Engineer, of New York City. According to his estimate, 4,945 pounds of metal would be required in the production of a four-room defense house of the type designed by the Public Buildings Administration. The house is 24 x 28 feet, one-story, gable roof, conventional wood frame construction.

All estimates are based on average prewar conditions. As a result of war shortages the amounts both of metal and lumber permitted in houses built during the war period have been much reduced. It should not be assumed, however, that the wartime standard will be applicable to houses of the future.

2. A Comparison of Two Construction Cost Indexes

The lack of certainty as to the actual trends of construction costs is well illustrated by Figure 3, p. 49, and the data shown below in Table 7. The causes for such divergence are common to all index numbers, and some understanding of these causes is essential to the interpretation of the data. Generally, two indexes supposedly representing the same phenomena, such as construction costs, will show divergent trends because of (a) differences in the method of compilation, and (b) differences in the

TABLE 5

Weight of Basic Materials Used in the Construction of Two Four-Room Houses

(In Pounds)

Elements	One-Story Frame Construction Without Basement					One-Story Brick Construction With Basement				
	Total	Masonry [a]	Wood	Metal	Other	Total	Masonry [a]	Wood	Metal	Other
Total	92,422	52,127	23,597	2,974	13,724	262,934	226,909	18,727	3,561	13,737
Per cent of total	100.0	56.4	25.5	3.2	14.9	100.0	86.3	7.1	1.4	5.2
Basement and foundation	41,712	41,688	—	24	—	126,864	126,864	—	—	—
Chimney	10,439	10,439	—	—	—	12,325	12,325	—	—	—
Outside platform framing	186	—	186	—	—	186	—	186	—	—
First floor framing	4,854	—	4,854	—	—	4,501	—	4,501	—	—
Exterior walls	5,488	—	5,488	—	—	88,669	87,720	522	427	—
Ceiling framing	1,333	—	1,333	—	—	1,333	—	1,333	—	—
Roof framing and covering	5,739	—	5,739	—	—	5,856	—	5,856	—	—
Partition framing	1,488	—	1,488	—	—	1,488	—	1,488	—	—
Basement stairs	—	—	—	—	—	349	—	349	—	—
Doors and windows [b]	2,121	—	2,121	—	—	2,161	—	2,161	—	—
Exterior trim	301	—	301	—	—	244	—	244	—	—
Interior finish, walls, ceiling, floors, trim, closets	15,658	—	2,032	—	13,626 [c]	15,658	—	2,032	—	13,626 [c]
Fixtures, cabinets, range, refrigerator	730	—	55	675	—	730	—	55	675	—
Builder's hardware	285	—	—	285	—	285	—	—	285	—
Plumbing, pipe and fixtures	1,345	—	—	1,345	—	1,415	—	—	1,415	—
Heating, warm air system	645	—	—	645	—	759	—	—	759	—
Electrical wiring and fixtures	98	—	—	—	98	111	—	—	—	111

Source: Federal Housing Administration, Technical Division.
a. Includes concrete, brick and terra cotta.
b. Includes weight of sash, frame, trim and hardware.
c. Gypsum board and plaster.

TABLE 6

Basic Materials and Their Uses in the Housebuilding Industry

- Chemicals
  - Formaldehyde
    - Preservatives
  - Linseed oil
    - Linoleum
    - Paint
    - Putty
  - Pigments
    - Flooring material
    - Glazes
    - Paints
    - Plastics
  - Resin and gum
    - Enamel
    - Shellac
    - Varnish
    - Wax
  - Tung oil
    - Paint
    - Varnish
  - Turpentine
    - Paint
    - Varnish
- Cotton
    - Canvas decking
    - Linoleum
    - Muslin wall covering
    - Rubber tile
    - Sash cord
    - Wire covering
- Forest products
  - Cork
    - Insulation
    - Linoleum
  - Paper
    - Building paper
    - Wallboard
    - Wallpaper
  - Wood
    - Cabinets
    - Door and window frames
    - Doors
    - Floors
    - Forms
    - Joists
    - Lath
    - Paneling
    - Plywood
    - Rafters
    - Sheathing
    - Shingles
    - Siding
    - Studs
    - Subfloors
    - Trim
    - Wallboard
    - Window sash
- Hair and wool
    - Felt
    - Plaster
- Metals
  - Aluminum
    - Alloys
    - Fittings
    - Hardware
    - Insulation
    - Paint
    - Roofing
    - Sheet metal
    - Weather strips
  - Chromium
    - Fittings
    - Hardware
  - Copper
    - Downspouts
    - Fittings
    - Flashing
    - Gutters
    - Lighting fixtures (in bronze)
    - Pipe
    - Roofing
    - Water heaters
    - Weather strips
    - Wire
  - Iron and steel
    - Boilers
    - Cable
    - Columns
    - Conduit

TABLE 6 (*continued*)

- Dampers
- Doors
- Downspouts
- Expanded shapes
- Finish hardware
- Flushing
- Furnaces
- Grilles
- Gutters
- Heaters
- Lath
- Lintels
- Pan forms
- Pipe
- Plumbing fixtures
- Pressed shapes
- Railings
- Reinforcing rods
- Rolled shapes
- Roofing
- Rough hardware
- Sash weights
- Ventilating ducts
- Window sash

Lead
- Caulking
- Paint
- Pipe
- Solder
- Tinning

Magnesium
- Composition flooring
- Mastic

Molybdenum
- Alloy in sheet steel

Nickel
- Alloys
- Fittings
- Hardware
- Pipe

Slag
- Concrete
- Mineral wool

Tin
- Alloy in bronze and brass
- Flux
- Solder
- Tinning

Zinc
- Alloys
- Downspouts
- Flushing
- Galvanizing
- Gutters
- Paint
- Roofing

Petroleum and coal
- Coal tar
  - Roofing
  - Waterproofing
- Petroleum
  - Asphalt products in roofing and waterproofing

Plastics
- Counter tops
- Electrical fittings
- Hardware
- Lacquers and finishes
- Lighting fixtures
- Paints
- Tile
- Wallboard
- Wire covering

Rubber
- Tile
- Wire covering

Silk
- Wire covering

Stone, clay and glass
- Asbestos
  - Insulation
  - Shingles
  - Siding
  - Wallboard
- Cement
  - Concrete
  - Mortar
  - Stucco
  - Terrazzo
- Cinders
  - Block
  - Concrete
  - Fill

TABLE 6 (*continued*)

Clay	Limestone
Adobe	Ashlar
Brick	Sills
Ceramic tile	Steps
Encaustic tile	Trim
Roofing tile	Marble
Structural tile	Fireplace facing
Tamped earth	Hearths
Terra cotta	Terrazzo
Crushed stone	Wainscot
Artificial stone	Porcelain
Concrete	Plumbing fixtures
Glass	Sand
Enamel	Concrete
Glass block	Mortar
Hardware	Plaster
Insulation	Stucco
Lighting fixtures	Terrazzo
Mirrors	Sandstone
Structural glass	Ashlar
Window glass	Sills
Granite	Steps
Ashlar	Trim
Sills	Slate
Steps	Laundry trays
Trim	Paving
Gravel	Roofing
Concrete	Shims
Roofing	Stair treads
Gypsum	Soapstone
Floor plank	Hearths and facings
Partition tile	Laundry trays
Plaster	Steps
Wallboard	Vegetable fiber
Lime	Hemp
Mortar	Linoleum
Plaster	Okum
Putty	Wallboard
Whitewash	

Note: This list of basic materials has been compiled by the staff of the Housing Survey to give a general picture of the variety of materials and their uses, and to indicate the comprehensiveness of building requirements. It is not all-inclusive either as to the number of materials or their uses.

basic data.[1] Implicit in the former is a careful definition of the *intent* of a particular index number. Thus, an index of construction costs may be intended to represent the trend over a period of time in the cost of producing a certain house according to careful specifications, or it may be intended merely to reflect the broad trends of a few of the major material and labor components entering into a certain general type of house. It may be intended to represent average conditions over the country, or to refer to a single locality. The cost of the material and labor components may be weighted and averaged several different ways, the best methods again depending upon the intent of the index and also upon the character of the data.

TABLE 7

INDEXES OF CONSTRUCTION COSTS FOR A FRAME HOUSE IN ST. LOUIS, MISSOURI, 1936–1941
(*January 1936 = 100*)

Year and Month	E. H. Boeckh and Associates	Federal Home Loan Bank Board	Year and Month	E. H. Boeckh and Associates	Federal Home Loan Bank Board
1936			1939		
January	100.0	100.0	January	120.0	100.7
April	102.7	99.7	April	119.5	110.0
July	102.9	100.3	July	117.5	98.6
October	102.1	100.1	October	119.5	100.3
1937			1940		
January	107.2	106.0	January	119.7	102.2
April	109.3	114.0	April	119.5	101.5
July	109.6	111.3	July	119.2	101.2
October	111.1	109.4	October	130.0	101.8
1938			1941		
January	110.0	103.5	January	131.2	105.3
April	115.0	100.5	April	130.5	105.4
July	115.3	99.3	July	130.8	106.1
October	118.8	99.4	October	133.7	109.2

Source: E. H. Boeckh and Associates, Inc., Cincinnati, Ohio and Federal Home Loan Bank Board (see also accompanying appendix text).

Applying these criteria, it may be stated that while the two indexes in Figure 3 attempt to measure conditions in the same locality, they differ considerably in other respects. The Federal Home Loan Bank Board index is based upon that agency's conception of the type of six-room frame house that was most *typical* over the country as a whole in 1936.[2] Indexes for a number of cities in addition to St. Louis are based

1. For a technical treatment of the subject, see Wesley C. Mitchell, *The Making and Using of Index Numbers,* U. S. Bureau of Labor Statistics, Bulletin No. 656, 1938, and Wilford I. King, *Index Numbers Elucidated,* Longmans' Economic Series, Longmans, Green, New York, 1930.

2. For a detailed description of this house, see the *Federal Home Loan Bank Review,* January and February, 1936.

on this house. The Boeckh index, on the other hand, is based upon an actual survey of an unspecified number of houses in 1928. The result was a "composite" house which is probably no more "typical" of building in St. Louis than in other cities.

The intent in both indexes is to measure the trends in the cost of producing a particular house. However, they are clearly not the same house. Moreover, the components in the FHLBB house are priced in much greater detail than are those in the Boeckh house. While it may be true that the price trends of the major components are sufficiently representative of the trend in over-all construction cost, it is likely that more detailed information would give better results.

The differences in the two houses and the varying amount of detail in pricing

TABLE 8

DISTRIBUTION OF COST OF MAJOR ELEMENTS IN THE CONSTRUCTION OF NINE SELECTED HOUSES, 1941

(In Per Cent of Total Cost)

	Atlanta, Georgia			Cleveland, Ohio			Seattle, Washington		
	Wood Frame		Brick	Wood Frame		Brick	Wood Frame		Brick
Cost Elements	1-Story 1150 sq. ft.	2-Story 2350 sq. ft.	2-Story 2350 sq. ft.	1-Story 1050 sq. ft.	2-Story 1550 sq. ft.	2-Story 1550 sq. ft.	1-Story 950 sq. ft.	2-Story 2250 sq. ft.	2-Story 2250 sq. ft.
Total	100.00	100.00	100.00	100.00	100.00	100.00	100.00	100.00	100.00
Foundations a	10.97	6.56	6.62	16.97	12.04	10.60	17.54	13.11	12.26
Chimney and fireplace	4.19	2.87	2.57	5.19	5.13	4.51	5.26	3.74	3.14
Floor construction b	10.00	12.70	11.40	8.19	9.75	8.56	9.77	13.86	11.64
Walls and partitions c	14.19	16.80	24.63	14.96	17.44	27.46	13.05	14.24	26.43
Lath, plaster and decorating	12.58	15.98	14.34	10.17	12.31	10.80	10.78	14.99	12.89
Roof and ceiling construction d	10.00	7.38	6.62	9.19	6.15	5.41	5.25	4.11	3.45
Millwork e	17.75	22.13	19.84	15.77	17.44	15.32	17.29	19.47	16.35
Special floors and wainscot	.65	.41	.37	1.80	1.80	1.59	.75	.75	.62
Plumbing	11.29	7.79	6.99	10.37	9.23	8.10	10.78	6.75	5.67
Heating f	5.48	4.10	3.68	4.19	5.64	4.95	6.02	4.49	3.78
Electric work g	2.90	3.28	2.94	3.20	3.07	2.70	3.51	4.49	3.77

Source: Special compilation for The Twentieth Century Fund made by the Technical Division of Federal Housing Administration. An effort was made to select houses that were the most typical in each area.

a. Excavation, footings, walls, basement floor and basement essentials. In Atlanta, only a partial basement is included.

b. Floor framing, subfloor and finished floor.

c. Exterior wall framing, sheathing, siding, gutters and downspouts and interior partition framing.

d. Roof framing, sheathing, roofing and ceiling framing.

e. Interior doors, trim, windows, exterior doors and detail, cabinets and interior detail and stairs. The "millwork" item includes window screens in the Atlanta houses, a mailbox and clothes chute in the Cleveland houses, and window shades in the Seattle houses.

f. Does not include range.

g. Does not include refrigerator.

result, of course, in the derivation of two entirely different sets of weights to be applied to the price series. In addition, the application of the weights to the individual price series differs markedly. In the FHLBB index the weights are applied automatically simply by obtaining at regular intervals the total cost of specified quantities of the materials needed to reproduce the selected house. In the Boeckh index the weights are on a value basis, as of 1928. That is, the relative importance of the several components in the index is measured in terms of their specific values in 1928. Thus lumber is given a weight of 36, since in 1928 lumber accounted for 36 per cent of the total construction cost of the composite house. Relative importance on a value basis, therefore, is a function of price—in this case 1928 price. Had prices in any other year been taken instead, the apparent relative importance of the components might have been different.

Thus the divergent movements between the two indexes may be partially explained by the differences in the intent of the indexes and in the method of weighting employed. A third possible factor in the divergence may involve the basic price data and the methods used in their collection. In the Boeckh index quotations are obtained from (a) subscribers to the Boeckh service, who may be presumed to be influenced by self-interest in accurate reporting, and (b) the dealers of two large producers of building materials. Special indexes are compiled for these manufacturers by the Boeckh organization, and again the element of self-interest operates to insure accurate reporting.

The FHLBB index is compiled from data collected by its field representatives. The prices are used by the Board to approximate in advance the cost of repairing and remodeling properties without awaiting the return of formal bids. The close correspondence between the prices so obtained and prices indicated by bids when received is believed by the Board to offer sufficient evidence of the accuracy of its reporting system. Both systems seem satisfactory and it is difficult to choose between them. It may be that they both obtain about the same quotations, but this cannot be verified.

Perhaps enough has been said here to make clear some of the reasons why the two indexes cannot be expected to show similar movements. There are several other factors, such as the inclusion in the Boeckh index of a correction for labor efficiency, and the inclusion in the Board's index of a one-car garage. These, however, are minor differences and need not be dealt with in detail.

There are several other indexes of construction costs available, but none of them specifically refers to residential construction. In addition, all of them have the same limitations mentioned in connection with the FHLBB and Boeckh indexes, in greater or lesser degree. They include the indexes compiled by the American Appraisal Company, the Associated General Contractors of America, the *Engineering News-Record,* the Aberthaw Company, the New York Federal Reserve Bank, the Turner Construction Company, and the Bureau of Foreign and Domestic Commerce.

In conclusion, it may be worth while to call attention to one of the fundamental difficulties in the compilation of construction cost indexes. Perhaps the greatest problem is that of selecting a "typical house" to form the basis for an index. It has been pointed out frequently in this study that houses vary infinitely as to type, size, arrangement, facilities, etc. By definition the index may be narrowed to measure construction cost trends for a particular type and size of house, such as a six-room frame structure, but variations in detail among houses of this general description are so great that a truly representative house is not to be found. This is further complicated by a weighting procedure that requires the use of constants. Thus in the FHLBB index, the various prices are weighted by the quantities of the different materials used in the construction of a specified house. This was a 1936 house. With the passage of years it will become constantly less representative. The compiler is confronted with this dilemma: shall his index represent the current cost of reproducing yesterday's house, or should it represent yesterday's cost of producing today's house? Both are artificial and the degree of artificiality increases as the period of years covered by the index increases.

Theoretically, a way out is provided by Fisher's "ideal" formula,[3] which averages geometrically formulas erring in opposite directions.[4] That is, by averaging, the errors offset each other. This is only theoretically possible, however, since in practice it would require selecting, at stated intervals, a new typical house. Only in the broadest sense would it be possible to do this.

3. Irving Fisher, *Making Index Numbers; A Study of the Varieties, Tests, and Reliability,* Publication No. 1 of the Pollack Foundation, Houghton Mifflin, New York, 1927 (3d edition, revised).

4. In the example given, an index based on yesterday's house and an index based on today's house would require different formulas. Those would yield results which would be biased in opposite directions.

APPENDIX C

1. The Measurement of Residential Construction Volume

An attempt is here made to present an over-all picture of the trend and volume of residential construction over a period of years. This has been accomplished by combining and adjusting to a comparable basis several separate series compiled by the Bureau of Labor Statistics and the National Bureau of Economic Research, and several additional series compiled by the staff of the Housing Survey.

Data shown in Figure 5, p. 65, and in Table 10 below represent the estimated number of new units added annually in nonfarm areas for the period 1900-1941. Data for 1930-1939 were compiled by the BLS. Unlike most current estimates of building volume, neither building permits nor contract awards were used, except incidentally. The basic method involved estimating a decade total, taking into consideration the increase in the number of occupied dwelling units since 1930 as shown by the 1940 Housing Census, the change in vacancies, and the estimated number of demolitions and of conversions. The resulting decade total for new units was then distributed annually, using sample data from the 1940 Housing Census showing dwelling units classified by year built. The latter data were subject to some error due to mistakes in reporting, but these have been eliminated so far as possible by a smoothing process. A detailed explanation of the methods used in making the 1930-1939 estimates appeared in the *Monthly Labor Review,* March 1942.

Estimates for 1940-1941 were made by the BLS on the basis of a large sample of cities currently reporting building-permit data.

For the period 1920-1929, basic data used are those compiled by David L. Wickens and Ray R. Foster, for the National Bureau of Economic Research and published in *Non-Farm Residential Construction, 1920-1936,* Bulletin No. 65, New York, September 15, 1937.[1]

Some error in trend results from the direct combination of these two sets of data. Thus the 1930 BLS figure for urban units is about 6.5 per cent larger than the National Bureau of Economic Research total for the same year, and for rural nonfarm units the difference is 52 per cent. Only part of this is accounted for by the redefining of urban and rural nonfarm areas in accordance with the 1940 Census. The remainder reflects undercounting of construction in the rural nonfarm areas. In the decade of the thirties the rate of growth in the rural nonfarm population was even more rapid than it was thought to be, and all existing estimates are considerably out of line. The National Bureau of Economic Research figures for the twenties art probably more accurate than those for the thirties since the bases for estimation, in the form of the Censuses of 1920 and 1930, were more adequate. It is on this as-

1. See also David L. Wickens, *Residential Real Estate,* National Bureau of Economic Research, New York, 1941, Chap. 5. Sizable revisions have been made since publication.

TABLE 9

SALES AND AVERAGE PRICES OF PASSENGER AUTOMOBILES, ELECTRIC WASHERS AND HOUSEHOLD REFRIGERATORS

Year	Factory Sales — Passenger Automobiles		Retail Sales — Electric Washers		Retail Sales — Household Refrigerators	
	Number	Average Price	Number	Average Price	Number	Average Price
	(*In Thousands*)		(*In Thousands*)		(*In Thousands*)	
1905	24	$1,062	—	—	—	—
1906	33	1,863	—	—	—	—
1907	43	2,130	—	—	—	—
1908	64	2,112	—	—	—	—
1909	124	1,288	—	—	—	—
1910	181	1,191	—	—	—	—
1911	199	1,130	—	—	—	—
1912	356	941	—	—	—	—
1913	462	865	—	—	—	—
1914	548	769	—	—	—	—
1915	896	642	—	—	—	—
1916	1,526	604	—	—	—	—
1917	1,746	603	—	—	—	—
1918	943	851	—	—	—	—
1919	1,652	826	—	—	—	—
1920	1,906	950	—	—	—	—
1921	1,468	707	—	—	5	$524
1922	2,274	657	—	—	11	498
1923	3,625	605	—	—	17	453
1924	3,185	619	—	—	29	428
1925	3,735	658	—	—	71	405
1926	3,784	697	843	$147	200	373
1927	2,937	737	776	143	375	350
1928	3,815	675	810	135	535	334
1929	4,588	620	956	113	778	292
1930	2,785	590	802	105	791	276
1931	1,973	563	812	85	906	258
1932	1,135	544	570	59	798	189
1933	1,573	470	967	62	1,016	172
1934	2,178	516	1,121	65	1,284	172
1935	3,252	526	1,229	65	1,568	162
1936	3,670	522	1,529	66	1,996	163
1937	3,916	588	1,465	72	2,310	171
1938	2,001	635	1,031	72	1,240	171
1939	2,867	634	1,320	68	1,840	168
1940	3,692	653	1,457	71	2,600	152

Source: For passenger-car sales, *Automobile Facts and Figures,* 1941, Automobile Manufacturers' Association, Detroit; for electric washers and household refrigerators, *Electrical Merchandising,* McGraw-Hill, New York, except household refrigerators prior to 1927, which are data from the *Consumer Census* of R. L. Polk & Co., adjusted to the level of "Electrical Merchandising" data.

sumption that the National Bureau of Economic Research figures for 1920-1929 have here been accepted without alteration.

The record for total nonfarm building in the period 1900-1919 is subject to a rather wide margin of error as regards the year-by-year distribution. The decade totals, i.e., 1900-1909 and 1910-1919, however, are probably fairly reliable. In any event, the data at least provide an interesting background for the more adequate figures for later years. The decade totals are by Wickens [2] and are based on the estimated increases during the two decades, in the number of occupied units, the number of vacant units and the number of demolitions and conversions in nonfarm areas. The estimated total for the ten-year period 1910-1919, 3,993,000 units, has been distributed on the basis of the year-to-year trend of an index compiled by Lowell J. Chawner.[3] Considerable adjustment was necessary to bring the trend into line with the National Bureau of Economic Research figures beginning 1920, i.e., when the decade total was distributed year by year, the 1920 figure for total nonfarm units was somewhat too high. Data beginning 1920 and extending back to 1917 were therefore progressively lowered. Figures for the early part of the decade were correspondingly raised. The basis for the latter operation may be justified by the fact that the Chawner index in the first half of the decade was based entirely on urban building. For the decade as a whole, there was apparently not much building in rural nonfarm areas, but that which did take place may have been concentrated in the first several years, which represented the concluding phase of a considerable outward movement of population from city centers during the 1900-1909 period.

For the period 1900-1909, a somewhat similar operation was performed. The decade total of 4,033,000 units, as reported by the National Bureau of Economic Research was first distributed according to the Chawner index. A rough adjustment was then made to correct the annual totals for undercounting in rural nonfarm areas, in which the population growth was quite rapid.

The breakdown between urban and rural nonfarm building in the years prior to 1920 is particularly subject to error. Here, the problem of inadequate basic data is complicated by the fact that the "urban area" and the rural "nonfarm area" have changed radically over the years through incorporation. The method of separation used here involves the backward projection of the urban series according to an index number of units built in 21-29 cities,[4] and the subtraction year by year of the resulting "urban" series from total nonfarm, to get "rural nonfarm." Fairly large arbitrary adjustments were made in a few of the years in both the urban and rural nonfarm totals.

For public construction, the data shown for the period 1935-1941 are compiled by the BLS from the records of all of the federal housing agencies. Also included are units built by the New York City Housing Authority. Activities of the United States Housing Corporation during the years 1918-1919 have not been included in Table 10 below. It is estimated, however, that in those two years the Corporation

2. *Ibid.*, Table EM5, p. 54.

3. "The Residential Building Process," *Housing—The Continuing Problem*, National Resources Planning Board, December 1940, Table IV, p. 33.

4. Clarence D. Long, Jr., *Building Cycles and the Theory of Investment*, Princeton University Press, Princeton, 1940, Appendix B, Section 3.

TABLE 10

NUMBER OF NEW RESIDENTIAL UNITS BUILT IN THE NONFARM AREA CLASSIFIED BY URBAN AND RURAL NONFARM, 1900–1941

(In Thousands)

Year	Total Nonfarm	Urban Total	Urban Private	Urban Public	Rural Nonfarm Total	Rural Nonfarm Private	Rural Nonfarm Public
1900	204	149	149	—	55	55	—
1901	303	191	191	—	112	112	—
1902	327	176	176	—	151	151	—
1903	411	191	191	—	220	220	—
1904	416	256	256	—	160	160	—
1905	459	288	288	—	171	171	—
1906	464	302	302	—	162	162	—
1907	433	284	284	—	149	149	—
1908	438	277	277	—	161	161	—
1909	573	380	380	—	193	193	—
1910	505	382	382	—	123	123	—
1911	501	376	376	—	125	125	—
1912	476	350	350	—	126	126	—
1913	435	318	318	—	117	117	—
1914	414	323	323	—	91	91	—
1915	414	364	364	—	50	50	—
1916	394	364	364	—	30	30	—
1917	277	180	180	a	97	97	a
1918	174	79	79	a	95	95	a
1919	405	303	303	—	102	102	—
1920	247	196	196	—	51	51	—
1921	449	359	359	—	90	90	—
1922	716	574	574	—	142	142	—
1923	871	698	698	—	173	173	—
1924	893	716	716	—	177	177	—
1925	937	752	752	—	185	185	—
1926	849	681	681	—	168	168	—
1927	810	643	643	—	167	167	—
1928	753	594	594	—	159	159	—
1929	509	400	400	—	109	109	—
1930	330	224	224	—	106	106	—
1931	254	164	164	—	90	90	—
1932	134	56	56	—	78	78	—
1933	93	40	40	—	53	53	—
1934	126	41	41	—	85	85	—
1935	221	106	102	4	115	114	1
1936	319	199	186	13	120	118	2
1937	336	205	201	4	131	131	—
1938	406	246	239	7	160	160	—
1939	515	342	287	55	173	172	1
1940	603	397	334	63	206	196	10
1941	715	440	370	70	275	249	26

Source: See text of Appendix C, 1.

a. During 1918-1919 the United States Housing Corporation completed work on 5,998 dwelling units and provided quarters for 7,181 single men. See *Housing for Defense,* The Twentieth Century Fund, New York, 1940, Appendix VI, pp. 156-157.

completed work on 5,998 dwelling units and provided quarters for 7,181 single men.[5]

From the standpoint of units built, a complete picture for nonfarm residential construction requires an estimate of the number of units provided by conversions. According to the BLS, total conversions for the period 1930-1939 numbered 725,000 units, of which 650,000 were in urban areas and 75,000 in rural nonfarm areas. Directly comparable figures are not available for earlier years. According to an estimate made by Wickens, totals for earlier decades were: 1920-1929, 125,000 units; 1910-1919, 103,000 units; and 1900-1909, 81,000 units.[6] There are no satisfactory means of distributing these totals annually.

Figure 6, p. 66 and Table 11 below present an approximate breakdown by major types of structure for the period 1920-1940. For the period 1920-1929 the Wickens-Foster figures are used.[7] For later years it was assumed that the undercounting in the Wickens-Foster figures, as discussed above, was with reference to single-family houses, i.e., the undercounting was for the most part in the rural nonfarm area where construction is almost entirely limited to single-family houses.

As a final measure of building volume, Figure 7, p. 67 and Table 12 below present data on the dollar volume of residential construction for the United States as a whole, 1919-1940. Estimates include value of new construction (but they do not include the value of the land), conversions, and repairs in both nonfarm and farm areas. For nonfarm areas, the basic figures are those compiled by Wickens and Foster. As already noted, these estimates of new construction were somewhat low in the decade of the thirties. They have been adjusted by the BLS by applying the average unit values of housekeeping units, as originally reported, to the revised estimates of number of units built. For rural nonfarm areas, the average unit values are slightly lower than those used by Wickens and Foster, the assumption being made that rural nonfarm units not included in the original estimates had a lower average value. For the period 1920-1929, the Wickens-Foster figures for housekeeping units have been used without alteration.

As in Table 10, the figures for public construction, 1935-1940, are compiled by the BLS from the records of the federal housing agencies and the New York City Housing Authority. Valuations are at contract prices, and the value of land, and in so far as possible the value of site improvements, are excluded. The U. S. Housing Corporation projects during the years 1918-1919 have been estimated at $52,373,000.[8] Only a few projects, however, were actually completed. The figure ($14 million) given in Table 12 for the single year 1919 is probably reasonable for work brought to completion.

The value of additions, alterations and repairs, which is here presumed to include conversions, is based on a special BLS study in representative cities to determine the relationship between such work and new construction. Over the 22-year period additions, alterations, and repairs varied from 5.5 per cent of new construction in the relatively good year 1925 to as high as 63 per cent in the depression year 1934. In Table 12 below, this series of percentages has been applied to total value of non-

5. *Housing for Defense,* The Twentieth Century Fund, New York, 1940, Appendix VI, pp. 156-157.
6. Wickens, *op. cit.*
7. David L. Wickens and Ray R. Foster, *Non-Farm Residential Construction, 1920–1936,* National Bureau of Economic Research, Bulletin 65, New York, 1937, Table 3, p. 4.
8. *Housing for Defense, loc. cit.*

farm housekeeping units constructed to obtain the figures given for the value of additions, alterations and repairs.

For the value of nonhousekeeping units a similar BLS study is available for the 1930-1939 period, and the ratios thereby obtained were applied to the value of housekeeping units to obtain annual figures for the value of nonhousekeeping construction. For earlier years, the figures shown are those of Wickens and Foster.

The value of construction work on farmhouses in Table 12 is intended only to provide some indication of magnitude. It is not to be interpreted as an accurate measure of the value of farmhouse construction. The data are derived from a recent

TABLE 11

PROPORTION OF NEW SINGLE-FAMILY, TWO-FAMILY AND MULTIFAMILY UNITS BUILT IN NONFARM AREAS, 1920–1940

	Number of Nonfarm Units				Per Cent of Total		
Year	Total	Single-Family	Two-Family	Multi-family	Single-Family	Two-Family	Multi-family
		(In Thousands)					
1920	247	202	24	21	81.8	9.7	8.5
1921	449	316	70	63	70.4	15.6	14.0
1922	716	437	146	133	61.0	20.4	18.6
1923	871	513	175	183	58.9	20.1	21.0
1924	893	534	173	186	59.8	19.4	20.8
1925	937	572	157	208	61.0	16.8	22.2
1926	849	491	117	241	57.8	13.8	28.4
1927	810	454	99	257	56.1	12.2	31.7
1928	753	436	78	239	57.9	10.4	31.7
1929	506	314	51	141	62.0	10.1	27.9
1930	330	229	28	73	69.4	8.5	22.1
1931	254	189	21	44	74.4	8.3	17.3
1932	134	121	6	7	90.3	4.5	5.2
1933	93	78	4	11	83.9	4.3	11.8
1934	126	113	3	10	89.7	2.4	7.9
1935	221	187	6	28	84.6	2.7	12.7
1936	319	246	13	60	77.1	4.1	18.8
1937	336	269	15	52	80.1	4.5	15.4
1938	406	320	17	69	78.8	4.2	17.0
1939	515	401	28	86	77.9	5.4	16.7
1940	600	485	37	78	80.8	6.2	13.0

Source: See text of Appendix C, 1.

study of the Department of Agriculture which yielded an annual series of cash expenditures on farm operators' dwellings.[9] In addition to operators' dwellings the 1935 Census reported other dwellings on farms to an extent that the total averaged 1.21 houses per farm. These extra houses are mostly those of other tenants or laborers, but many of them are the residences of nonoperator owners or the homes of retired families. Assuming that three fourths of them have the value of tenant dwellings

9. C. M. Purves and C. A. Gibbons, "Expenditures for and Depreciation of Permanent Improvements on Farms, 1910-40," *Income Parity for Agriculture*, Pt. II, *Expenses of Agricultural Production*, U. S. Department of Agriculture, March 1941 (Preliminary), Sec. 5.

TABLE 12

DOLLAR VOLUME OF RESIDENTIAL CONSTRUCTION, 1919–1940

(In Millions)

			Nonfarm Construction									
				New Housekeeping Construction								
					Urban			Rural Nonfarm				
Year	U.S. Total Residential Construction	Farm Construction Including Repairs[a]	Total Nonfarm Construction	Total New Housekeeping Construction	Total Urban	Private	Public	Total Rural Nonfarm	Private	Public	Non-housekeeping construction	Additions, Alterations and Repairs
1919	$1,701	$606	$1,095	$ 795[b]	c	c	$ 14[d]	c	c	—	$ 54[e]	$246[f]
1920	1,838	556	1,282	1,068	$ 902	$ 902	—	$166	$166	—	54	160[f]
1921	2,315	260	2,055	1,771	1,539	1,539	—	232	232	—	70	214
1922	3,643	310	3,333	2,957	2,547	2,547	—	410	410	—	157	219
1923	4,648	416	4,232	3,775	3,258	3,258	—	517	517	—	206	251
1924	4,904	397	4,507	4,065	3,526	3,526	—	539	539	—	179	263
1925	5,400	402	4,998	4,475	3,869	3,869	—	606	606	—	279	244
1926	4,954	390	4,564	4,112	3,531	3,531	—	581	581	—	202	250
1927	4,757	440	4,317	3,910	3,321	3,321	—	589	589	—	154	253
1928	4,464	426	4,038	3,613	3,042	3,042	—	571	571	—	200	225
1929	3,406	434	2,972	2,453	2,074	2,074	—	379	379	—	300	219
1930	2,158	305	1,853	1,494	1,148	1,148	—	346	346	—	139	220
1931	1,497	196	1,301	1,105	819	819	—	286	286	—	31	165
1932	687	106	581	407	231	231	—	176	176	—	7	167
1933	570	146	424	285	166	166	—	119	119	—	3	136
1934	771	161	610	368	172	172	—	196	196	—	9	233
1935	1,255	245	1,010	754	490	473	17	264	260	$ 4	10	246
1936	1,754	255	1,499	1,267	964	898	66	303	296	7	17	215
1937	1,959	293	1,666	1,382	953	937	16	429	429	—	22	262
1938	2,107	256	1,851	1,584	1,078	1,056	22	506	506	—	16	251
1939	2,520	299	2,221	1,948	1,562	1,381	181	386	383	3	26	247
1940	2,904	324	2,580	2,276	1,787	1,589	198	489	460	29	33	271

Source: See text of Appendix C, 1.

a. Excluding land costs.

b. Estimated on basis of 1919-1920 trend for 135 identical cities, as reported by the Bureau of Labor Statistics, adjusted to include U.S. Housing Corporation expenditures of $14,000,000, as reported in Lowell J. Chawner, *Construction Activity in the United States, 1915-37,* U.S. Department of Commerce, Table 50, p. 87. Total expenditures of the U.S. Housing Corporation during 1918-1919 have been estimated at $52,373,000 (see *Housing for Defense,* The Twentieth Century Fund, New York, 1940, Appendix VI, pp. 156-157). This includes the cost of many projects which were never completed, so that the figure of $14,000,000 for the single year 1919 is probably reasonable for work actually completed.

c. Data not available.

d. See note b above.

e. Assumed to be the same in 1919 as in 1920.

f. Lacking data, it is assumed that the ratio of additions, alterations and repairs to total new housekeeping construction in 1919 was the same as in 1935, and in 1920 the same as in 1931.

and one fourth that of owners and managers,[10] they would, according to 1930 data, average 80 per cent of the value of average farmhouses. The total of these would thus add 16.8 per cent to the value of operators' dwellings, and construction and repair in this group would add a similar proportion to the cash expenditures for all farm housing.

During the 22-year period cash outlays for both new construction and repairs on farm operators' dwellings ranged from a high of $461 million in 1919 to a low of $81 million in 1932, exceeding $200 million in both the beginning and closing years of the period.

Supplementing cash outlay for dwellings, substantial contributions of materials and labor were made from the farm. These amounted to about one third on repairs of farm dwellings and one sixth on new farm dwellings.[11] Other studies indicate that in a typical year about 47 per cent of expenditures are for new structures and additions and 53 per cent for repairs.[12]

Application of these percentages would indicate that cash expenditures and value contributed from the farm held the proportion of 76 per cent and 24 per cent, respectively. This relationship has been applied to the reported figures for cash expenditure on operators' dwellings after the latter were raised by 16.8 per cent to allow for construction work on houses of tenant and nonoperator owners. The results appear in Table 12. The major weakness of the series is the assumption, perforce, that a constant relationship exists between new construction and repairs. Since this is not actually the case, and since the contribution from the farm for repair work is about twice that for new work, a considerable distortion results in certain years. Then, too, the estimate of the farm contribution is on exceedingly tenuous grounds.

2. Size of the Residential Building Industry in Terms of Gross National Product and Wages and Salaries

The relative importance of residential building in terms of the gross national product is shown in Figure 8, p. 69, and in Table 13 below. In terms of wages and salaries a similar comparison is given in Figure 9, p. 71 and in Table 14 below.

The concept of gross national product, as set forth by Simon Kuznets, can best be understood by first analyzing briefly net national product, or national income, and then examining the additional elements which go to make up gross national product.

Net national product or national income may be defined as the net value of commodities and services produced by the nation's economic system. It is "net" in that the value of output of all commodities and services is reduced by the value of commodities (fuel, raw materials and capital equipment) consumed in the process of production.[13] Several concepts of gross national product are obtained by including various amounts of duplication with the net figure, i.e., the duplication that results from the inclusion of the finished products of one industry as the "raw material"

10. Wickens, *op. cit.*, pp. 84–85.

11. *An Economic Study of Farm Buildings in New York*, Bulletin 478, Cornell Agricultural Experiment Station, Ithaca, May 1920.

12. Purves and Gibbons, *op. cit.*, p. 12.

13. Simon Kuznets, *National Income and Capital Formation, 1919-1935*, National Bureau of Economic Research, New York, 1937, p. 3.

of another industry. The magnitude of the gross totals would thus vary with the amount of duplication desired.

Of these several possible concepts of gross national product one appears of greater importance than the others, that in which the value of commodities and services produced is not adjusted for the value of durable capital goods consumed in the process of production, but is adjusted for raw materials, partly fabricated products and fuel consumed.[14] It is this concept that is referred to in Figure 8, p. 69 and in Table 13.

Data for the residential construction industry as presented in Appendix C, 1, Table 12, have been substituted for those given in the Kuznets volume. As indicated in Appendix C, 1, and Tables 10, 11, and 12, they are somewhat more comprehensive, an important difference being the inclusion of an estimate for construction and repairs of farm dwellings.

TABLE 13

Relative Importance of Residential Construction in the Total Economy, as Measured by Gross National Product, 1919–1935

Class of Product	Value	
	(In Billions)	*(Per Cent of Total)*
Annual average value of gross national product	$73.3	100.0
Residential construction [a]	2.9	3.9
Nonresidential construction [b]	5.3	7.2
Services not embodied in new commodities	18.1	24.7
Durable consumer commodities	7.0	9.5
Semidurable consumer commodities	10.2	13.9
Perishable consumer commodities	23.8	32.4
Durable producer commodities	4.6	6.4
Other [c]	1.4	2.0

Source: Simon Kuznets, *National Income and Capital Formation, 1919–1935,* National Bureau of Economic Research, New York, 1937, Table 17, p. 59, except as noted in the discussion. Combinations of certain items are indicated in the footnotes below.

a. From Appendix C, 1, Table 12.

b. Business construction plus public construction (except public residential).

c. Net change in business inventories, plus change in stocks of silver and gold, plus unallocable—net change in claims against foreign countries.

In the total picture, the contribution of the residential construction industry is measured in terms of the work it performs and the *materials it uses*. In strict definition, the contribution of the industry per se should be conceived of in terms of the value added to these materials in the building process, i.e., the work performed in converting the materials to finished houses. Here, however, the comparison is on the basis of the value of final products. As has been stated, duplications have been eliminated, so that building materials once counted in the residential construction total do not again enter into the gross national product. This is also clear from the breakdown of gross national product as shown in Table 13.

14. *Ibid.* The reasons given for making no adjustments for the value of capital goods consumed are that any estimate must at best be very rough and that this replacement rate is largely at the discretion of the individual enterprise.

Estimates of income in the construction industry as a whole suffer somewhat because of a lack of satisfactory data relating to salaries, wages, interest, dividends, and other items entering into the composition of national income. Because of this, the Bureau of Foreign and Domestic Commerce uses its own data on the value of construction and attempts (as shown in Table 14) to segregate from this the items of national income.[15] In 1939, the total volume of all construction (exclusive of that on farms) was estimated at $6,286 million, of which $2,533 million represented force account work, which is covered in the income data for other industries.

The remainder, $4,753 million, represents "contract construction." Wages and salaries accounted for 35.5 per cent of this, according to a small sample comprising a variety of construction projects compiled by the Bureau of Labor Statistics. The difference between this amount, $1,689 million (column 2 of Table 14) and national income of $2,134 million (column 1) comprises interest, dividends, entrepreneurial withdrawals, and business savings (or losses) estimated from data for incorporated businesses filing income tax returns and from financial statements of corporations as given in *Moody's Manual of Investments, Industrial Securities.*

The calculation of salaries and wages for residential construction alone follows the same procedure. The total volume of nonfarm residential construction, including public residential, was estimated at $1,941 million in 1939.[16] No attempt was made to adjust the data for the small amount of force account construction. Thirty-eight per cent, or $738 million, was assumed to represent labor cost at the site of construction. Very little information is available on relative labor and material costs in the construction industry, except for certain types of construction financed by the federal government. On this work, labor and material costs and their proportionate relationships are apt to be unique rather than typical. Wage payments on a particular job are by law based on the "prevailing wage" in the area, and in practice, this wage is usually closer to the union scale rate than to the average wage actually paid in the area. Because of this, the percentages given above for labor costs are probably high.

Evidence of this may be seen in the following comparisons: The figure given for residential construction (38 per cent) is based on federal work upon which the total of *all* construction cost, including profit and overhead, was about $100 million. The principal study on this subject for private residential construction was made by the Bureau of Labor Statistics in 1931-1932 ("Relative Cost of Material and Labor in Building Construction, 1931-32," *Monthly Labor Review,* October 1932, pp. 763-772). Covering labor and material costs *only,* the study included data for six "ordinary dwelling houses" and two apartment houses in each of fifteen cities. Labor costs were found to be 37 per cent of total labor and material costs. Overhead and profit, however, were not taken into consideration. The inclusion of these items would lower considerably the percentage attributable to labor. On the public construction projects, labor was *46 per cent* of combined labor and material costs; this was lowered to 38 per cent by the inclusion of profit and overhead. Within the limita-

15. Milton Gilbert and Dwight B. Yntema, "National Income Exceeds 76 Billion Dollars in 1940," *Survey of Current Business,* June 1941, Tables 7 and 9, p. 17.

16. Does not include the revisions to residential construction occasioned by adjustment to the 1940 Housing Census, as discussed in Appendix C, 1. Neither does it include the estimated value of farm residential construction and repairs mentioned in Appendix C, 1.

tions of the small sample for private construction, it can therefore be assumed that 38 per cent is the maximum that should be assigned to residential construction as a whole, and that in all likelihood the actual percentage is lower. On the same basis, it is also roughly estimated that material used accounted for 46 per cent of total construction costs.

TABLE 14

RELATIVE IMPORTANCE OF RESIDENTIAL CONSTRUCTION IN THE TOTAL ECONOMY, AS MEASURED BY WAGES AND SALARIES, 1939

Industry	Contribution to the National Income	Total Wages and Salaries	
	(In Millions)		*(Per cent)*
Total	$70,674	$44,349	100.0
Contract construction, total	2,134[a]	1,689[a]	3.8
Residential construction	932[b]	738[a]	1.7
Nonresidential construction	1,202[b]	951	2.1
Other industries			
Transportation	4,960	3,659	8.2
Trade, total	9,585	6,887	15.5
Retail trade	6,102	4,148	9.3
Wholesale trade	3,483	2,739	6.2
Manufacturing	16,384	13,260	30.0
Construction materials and furniture	1,443	1,226	2.8
Food and tobacco	2,176	1,595	3.6
Metal and metal products	6,101	4,901	11.0
Other manufacturing	6,664	5,538	12.6
All other industries	37,611	18,854	42.5
Government, including work relief	9,934	6,197	13.9
Service industries	8,839	5,660	12.8
Finance	6,051	1,994	4.5
Mining	1,299	1,081	2.4
Agriculture	5,750	738	1.7
Power and gas	1,418	671	1.5
Communications	917	622	1.4
Miscellaneous	3,403	1,891	4.3

Source: Milton Gilbert and Dwight B. Yntema, "National Income Exceeds 76 Billion Dollars in 1940," *Survey of Current Business,* June 1941, Tables 7 and 9, p. 17, except as noted in the discussion regarding this table.

a. Does not include the revisions in residential construction occasioned by adjustment to the 1940 Housing Census, as discussed in Appendix C, 1.

b. On the tenuous nature of this breakdown of total contract construction, see the text of Appendix C, 1.

Table 14 above includes an estimate of national income derived from residential construction alone, although data on interest, dividends, entrepreneurial withdrawals and business savings are lacking. On the assumption that the relationship between (a) wages and salaries and (b) national income for the contract construction industry as a whole is also typical for residential construction, national income derived from the latter in 1939 would be $932 million, and for nonresidential construction, $1,202 million.[17] Many questions, however, can be raised as to the validity of this procedure.

In comparing Tables 13 and 14 it will be noted that estimated wages and salaries in residential construction represent only 1.7 per cent of the total of all wages and salaries, whereas in gross national product, residential construction represents about 3.9 per cent of the total. There are several factors accounting for this. Of greatest importance is the fact that the data in Table 13 are in terms of final products and represent the total values of the several classifications of products. In Table 14, on the other hand, the residential construction industry is represented only to the extent of wage payments for *site labor* (column 2); wages paid in the production of the materials entering into residential construction are in other classifications such as construction materials and furniture and metal and metal products. As a secondary factor, it will be observed that the periods covered by the two sets of data differ. In the period 1919-1935, site labor for housing represented 2.1 per cent of total salaries and wages, or 0.4 per cent higher than in 1939.

3. Occupational Groups in Residential Construction Classified by International Unions Affiliated with the Building and Construction Trades Department of the American Federation of Labor[a]

(1) International Association of Heat and Frost Insulators, and Asbestos Workers
Asbestos workers.

(2) International Brotherhood of Boiler Makers, Iron Ship Builders and Helpers
Boilermakers, welders.

(3) Bricklayers, Masons and Plasterers' International Union
Bricklayers, cement finishers,[b] marble setters, plasterers,[b] stone masons, stone setters, tile layers.

(4) International Association of Bridge, Structural and Ornamental Iron Workers
Ornamental ironworkers, reinforced steelworkers (rodmen), riggers, structural ironworkers, welders.

(5) United Brotherhood of Carpenters and Joiners
Cabinetworkers, carpenters, floor layers and dressers, form builders, saw filers, weather strippers, linoleum layers, millwrights, pile-driver leadsmen, shinglers (wood and asbestos).

Source: Classifications are based on opinions of persons familiar with residential construction. Lists of trades maintained by the Bureau of Labor Statistics, the American Federation of Labor, and others were consulted. The table includes the maximum number of occupational groups that are likely to be engaged in the construction of a large multistory apartment building. Of the 79 classifications listed, as many as 45 may be engaged in the construction of smaller structures such as detached houses, row houses, and walk-up apartments. The number of groups actually employed on a particular job will vary greatly, with one of the major determining factors the extent of unionization in a particular place.

a. Only journeymen included. The inclusion of apprentices and helpers would practically double the number of occupational groups.

b. Workers in this occupational group belong to different unions in different localities.

17. In comparing these two figures for residential and nonresidential construction, it should be recalled that the total dollar volume of *all* construction has been reduced 40 per cent by the exclusion of force account work, which is reflected in the income produced by other industries. Nearly all of this was nonresidential construction.

(6) International Brotherhood of Electrical Workers
Cable splicers, electricians (inside), linemen, welders.

(7) International Union of Elevator Constructors
Elevator constructors, welders.

(8) International Union of Operating Engineers
Air-compressor engineers, crane and derrick engineers, dragline engineers, hoisting engineers, mixer engineers, pile-driver engineers, pump engineers, roller engineers, shovel engineers, siphon engineers, trench machine engineers, firemen (portable and hoisting engine), oilers (power machinery), tractor operators.

(9) Granite Cutters' International Association
Granite cutters.

(10) International Hod Carriers, Building and Common Laborers' Union
Blasters, concrete workers, concrete puddlers, derrick men (hand), hod carriers (masons' tenders), jackhammer men (drillers), building laborers, common laborers, mortar mixers (hand), tenders, window cleaners, wreckers.

(11) International Union of Wood, Wire and Metal Lathers
Lathers (metal), lathers (wood).

(12) International Association of Marble, Stone and Slate Polishers, Rubbers and Sawyers, etc.
Mosaic and terrazzo workers.

(13) Sheet Metal Workers' International Association
Sheet metal workers, welders.

(14) Brotherhood of Painters, Decorators and Paper Hangers
Glaziers, painters, painters (sign), paper hangers.

(15) Operative Plasterers' and Cement Finishers' International Association
Cement finishers,[b] plasterers.[b]

(16) United Association of Journeymen Plumbers and Steam Fitters
Plumbers, steam fitters, sprinkler fitters, welders.

(17) United Slate, Tile and Composition Roofers, Damp and Waterproof Workers' Association
Roofers (composition), roofers (slate and tile), waterproofers.

(18) Journeymen Stonecutters' Association
Stonecutters.

(19) International Brotherhood of Teamsters, Chauffeurs, Warehousemen and Helpers
Teamsters, truck drivers.

4. WAGE DATA FOR THE CONSTRUCTION INDUSTRY

The major problems that have confronted all agencies in the collection of wage statistics for the construction industry trace back to the characteristics of the industry. Contractors are large in number but small so far as size of operations is concerned. It has proved impossible to secure even an accurate count of their number, much less obtain accurate information as to their operations. Except as regards the census, reporting to the various collecting agencies has been voluntary, and contractors are frequently reluctant to report anything of confidential or assumed confidential nature.

This was amply demonstrated in connection with efforts made to secure data on "prevailing wages" under the Davis-Bacon Act. Also, reporting is made difficult by the lack of contractors' records.

It has been impossible so far to obtain what might be considered a reasonably satisfactory sample. The Bureau of Labor Statistics in its monthly report on average weekly wages has made the only real effort in this direction, and even here the effort is limited to securing some sort of balance between different trades. No consideration is or can be given to representativeness from the standpoint of size of builder, type of construction or the proportions of organized and unorganized labor.

For residential construction alone the only data are those shown by the BLS survey of 105 cities, described below. At best, such data could cover only hourly wages, as in the case of this survey, or weekly wages. There can be no such concept as an average annual wage for residential construction workers since they work in their respective trades without regard to the type of construction.

Any conclusions regarding hourly, weekly and annual earnings of construction workers are thus subject to many qualifications. This becomes particularly evident with reference to attempted comparisons with other industries. Such comparisons are futile, not only because of inaccuracies in the data but because of wide variations in the proportion of skilled workers, in the stage of fabrication, and in the amount of full and partial unemployment, the latter reflecting different labor needs in the several industries and the lack of incidence in cyclical movements.

Hourly Wages

For hourly wages in construction, the only general reports are *Union Wages, Hours, and Working Conditions in the Building Trades, June 1, 1939,*[18] and *Local Wage Rates for Selected Occupations in Public and Private Construction, 1936.*[19]

The first of these reports represents an annual compilation as of June 1, for 72 selected cities. Annual indexes for 1907-1940 of hourly wage rates and weekly hours worked in all building trades, for journeymen, and for helpers and laborers are available. Similar data for specific building trades are also available. The major criticism that may be directed at these data is that they are union rates only. Much construction work, particularly housebuilding, is done with nonunion labor for which the scale of wages may be considerably lower than that provided for in union agreements. Even union scale rates are subject to considerable bias; in times of business adversity union workers may accept jobs below the scale, while in prosperous times some workers will be employed at rates above the scale. As a further limitation, the indexes in the tables are weighted by cities and by trades according to the number of union workers. These numbers may or may not be in accordance with actual employment of all construction workers by trades, and it can be reasonably assumed that they are not in accordance with the distribution of workers by trades in the housebuilding industry.

The Works Progress Administration study referred to above presents hourly wage rates for twenty-five occupations in over 1,000 localities, as of 1936. Basic data were obtained from the American Federation of Labor, the Builders' Association of Chicago,

18. Bulletin No. 674, Bureau of Labor Statistics. See also "Union Wages and Hours in the Building Trades, June 1, 1940," *Monthly Labor Review,* November 1940, and mimeographed statement No. 10071, BLS, giving union scales of wages and hours by trades in selected cities as of June 1, 1940.

19. Works Progress Administration.

the Solicitor's Office of the Department of Labor, the Bureau of Labor Statistics, and the Public Works Administration. The AF of L figures are union rates, and those for the Builders' Association of Chicago are from an annual survey of building construction wage rates in 125 cities, purportedly covering both union and nonunion wages actually paid. The figures secured from the Solicitor's Office of the Department of Labor were collected under the Davis-Bacon Act, which requires the payment of "prevailing wages" on federal buildings or other federal works and on Public Works Administration federal projects. One set of the BLS data represents entrance rates for common labor, obtained from employers by means of a mail questionnaire. A second set of BLS statistics included in the WPA study represents a special survey made in 105 cities in the fall of 1936. A separation was made between union and nonunion, residential and nonresidential, and public and private sponsorship. It was estimated that about 30 per cent of the construction workers were covered in this latter survey. The PWA rates were taken from the pay rolls of PWA contractors and cover the workers employed on all types of PWA projects. Also included are PWA records of local union contracts and the record of prevailing wages as determined by the PWA Housing Division.

Within themselves, however, limitations of the data render them of little value for residential construction wage rates, even in the specific localities listed. Thus, the AF of L rates are union only. The Builders' Association of Chicago apparently made no attempt to weight the union and nonunion rates for the different cities. The public hearings, which were the basis for determining the "prevailing wage" on federal construction, were not always conducive to frankness on the part of contractors. The BLS data for entrance rates for common labor have no reference to skilled workers, aside from other limitations; and the WPA special survey of 105 cities made no attempt properly to weight union and nonunion rates, with the result that in some cities rates on residential work are shown to be higher than on nonresidential construction, a most unlikely situation. Also, slightly over two thirds of the 186,000 workers covered were union members. This is considerably above the probable proportion of union workers on residential construction. Rates paid on PWA projects are obviously too limited in scope to be of much use.

Weekly Earnings

For average weekly earnings, the major source of information is the Bureau of Labor Statistics. For private construction the Bureau currently receives reports from more than 15,000 general contractors and subcontractors, who report data on man-hours worked, number of workers, and total pay roll for the pay period ending nearest the fifteenth of each month. Average weekly earnings are derived by dividing aggregate pay roll by the number of workers. The current reports cover about 30 per cent of all workers in the private construction industry, according to employment estimates made by the BLS. In early years the coverage was somewhat less. Also, the sample is overweighted with large contractors, and no effort has been made to obtain a proper distribution of residential and nonresidential work, union and nonunion workers, and skilled and unskilled workers. It should be noted that the averages are influenced by the relative degree of activity in the construction industry and by the number of wage earners working part time or overtime. Finally, some of the variation in average earnings may be attributed to changes in the size and composition of the monthly reporting sample.

It is not possible to evaluate these data with any degree of accuracy, but it can be assumed that they are higher than actual average weekly earnings on residential construction. This is both because of the underweighting of small contractors and because of the inclusion of nonresidential work on which wage rates are generally higher.

The BLS also reports data each month for average earnings on federal public construction projects. As published each month in *Employment and Pay Rolls,*[20] the data are on a monthly basis. However, it would be possible to convert these to a weekly basis. This publication also contains monthly data for state and locally financed road building which may be converted to a weekly basis. Data for other types of public work have not been brought together. Data for average weekly wages on private force account work are entirely lacking.

For average weekly earnings then, the data are limited to a sample of private construction, and a partial coverage of public construction. It is not possible to segregate from the data figures on residential earnings.

Annual Earnings

For annual average earnings the Bureau of Foreign and Domestic Commerce reports data for a considerable number of industries as a by-product of the studies of national income conducted by that Bureau.[21] The census of the construction industry for 1929 and 1935 provides the basis for these data. For the years 1930-1933, interpolated values are derived from an index of average weekly earnings in five midwestern states, as reported by the labor departments of those states; data for 1934 and subsequent to 1935 are extended by means of the Bureau of Labor Statistics data on average weekly earnings in private construction already discussed.

Limitations to these figures are inherent in the basic data rather than in the methods used in the compilation of this particular series. In the first place, the census figures include only the annual average earnings of employees of those firms whose volume totaled more than $25,000 per year. Smaller firms, being more predominantly nonunion, probably paid a smaller average wage. Second, the indexes used for interpolation, while they are the best available, leave much to be desired. The five-state index may or may not be representative of the country as a whole and the BLS sample, while large, is deficient in numerous respects as already discussed. Also, the latter is for private construction only, whereas the census figures, and possibly the five-state index, include public construction. This is particularly important in 1940 since the large volume of public defense construction was carried on at "prevailing wages," which are somewhat higher than average wages on private work.

In addition, serious question may be raised as to the validity of using average weekly earnings to interpolate average annual earnings, since the latter will be affected by changes in the average number of weeks worked per year, whereas the former will not. As a last item, "average" annual income states in effect what the average annual income would have been if the number of workers had remained at a constant level and if they had all worked the same number of hours. Actually, of course, there is a

20. Prepared by the Division of Employment Statistics and the Division of Construction and Public Employment, Bureau of Labor Statistics.

21. Gilbert and Yntema, *op. cit.*

marked seasonal movement in the number of workers engaged, and the amount of part-time work is considerable. For trade union members alone, the proportion of part-time work in building construction is considerably higher than in most other industries.[22]

Several writers have attempted to adjust annual wage estimates for at least some of these factors, usually for the purpose of making comparisons with other industries. For example, the average wage for 1935 was given as $1,149. However, if total pay roll for the year is divided by the *maximum* employment instead of the average, this figure is reduced to $940.[23] This, in effect, spreads the total pay roll among all construction workers who were assumed to be available for work during the year. It includes all workers, regardless of whether they were engaged one month or twelve months. Because the distribution of workers over the year is uneven, the average given may be somewhat in error.

Using 1929 data, Mercer Evans corrects the census figures for unemployment, according to estimates made by Paul H. Douglas. According to the census, average annual wage payments in the construction industry were $1,770 [24] in 1929. In manufacturing industries they were $1,315. Correcting for unemployment of 22 per cent in the former and 7 per cent in the latter, Evans obtains an annual average wage of $1,381 for construction and $1,223 for manufacturing industries.[25] Considering the relatively high proportion of skilled workers in the construction industry, Evans concludes that the average wage figure is not out of line.

The figures are subject to some question. Weaknesses of the census data for the construction industry have already been pointed out, and the Douglas estimates of unemployment, like all unemployment statistics, are crude. Also, they cover experience in the first quarter of the century, which does not necessarily apply to 1929, the year used in the comparison. In that year construction was well past its cyclical peak and unemployment was growing rapidly.

The first and only reasonably satisfactory figure for annual average earnings will come from the 1940 Census of Population, which, for the first time, includes data on incomes of all individuals. While subject to numerous limitations these data will give fairly reliable information by occupational classifications.

5. Size of Builders

Data relating to the size of builders of residential structures are from information collected in a special Bureau of Labor Statistics building permit survey. For builders of single-family houses (Table 15 below) data were obtained from building permits

22. According to AF of L data, 29 per cent of building trades workers were employed on a part-time basis in 1937 as compared with 20 per cent for all trades combined. Forty-six per cent of all building trades workers were employed full time, compared with 68 per cent for all trades combined. Compiled from Mercer G. Evans, "Labor and the Cost of Housing," *Housing—The Continuing Problem,* National Resources Planning Board, December 1940, Table VIII, p. 199.

23. Peter A. Stone and R. Harold Denton, *Toward More Housing,* Temporary National Economic Committee Monograph No. 8, pp. 52-53; see also Gilbert and Yntema, *op. cit.*

24. The Bureau of Foreign and Domestic Commerce figure of $1,904 includes salaried workers. Gilbert and Yntema, *op. cit.*

25. Evans, *op. cit.,* p. 198.

issued in 1938 to 13,934 builders for the erection of 47,156 houses in 72 cities.[26] For multifamily structures (Table 16 below) the data pertain to the 1939 operations of 958 builders who obtained permits for 1,827 structures in 37 cities.[27] New York City is shown separately in these tables because it varies considerably from the general pattern and because the bulk of multifamily building was concentrated there.

The data for single-family housebuilders cover about 15 per cent of all such structures built in nonfarm areas in 1938, but the sample is only fairly representative since the coverage of small places is inadequate. Because of the concentration of multifamily structures the data for such buildings are somewhat more representative. For structures containing a minimum of three units, the sample represents about 73 per cent of private multifamily construction in 1939. Excluding New York City, the coverage is about 66 per cent complete. If public construction is included, the sample, including New York City, is reduced to about 55 per cent. As in the case of single-family housebuilders, building in small places may be underrepresented. Since most, though not all, of such building is in the smaller size structures built in small numbers, it is likely that their inclusion would further emphasize the predominantly small size of apartment housebuilders. The 37 cities included in the sample are as follows:

New England
- Bridgeport, Conn.
- Stamford, Conn.
- Boston, Mass.
- Quincy, Mass.

Middle Atlantic
- Atlantic City, N. J.
- Albany, N. Y.
- New York City
- White Plains, N. Y.
- Yonkers, N. Y.
- Lower Merion Twp., Pa.
- Philadelphia, Pa.

North Central
- Chicago, Ill.
- Indianapolis, Ind.
- Dearborn, Mich.
- Minneapolis, Minn.
- St. Paul, Minn.
- St. Louis, Mo.
- Cincinnati, Ohio
- Cleveland, Ohio
- Columbus, Ohio

South Atlantic
- Washington, D. C.
- Jacksonville, Fla.
- Miami, Fla.
- Baltimore, Md.
- Raleigh, N. C.
- Winston-Salem, N. C.
- Norfolk, Va.
- Charleston, W. Va.

South Central
- Mobile, Ala.
- Shreveport, La.
- Knoxville, Tenn.
- Dallas, Tex.
- Houston, Tex.

Mountain and Pacific
- Long Beach, Calif.
- Los Angeles, Calif.
- Santa Monica, Calif.
- Denver, Colo.

The data are subject to several limitations other than the size of the sample. In the first place, only permits issued in the central cities are included. As a result, the opera-

26. For further details, and a list of the 72 cities, see *Builders of 1-Family Houses in 72 Cities*, Serial No. R1151, Bureau of Labor Statistics, 1940.

27. The analysis of builders of multifamily structures is based on tabulations made by the Housing Survey from unpublished data supplied by the Bureau of Labor Statistics.

tions of a particular builder in the suburbs are ignored and his total volume of building is understated. In a test conducted for Cleveland in 1938, it was found that when operations in the suburbs were included the number of builders who built only one single-family house decreased from 65 per cent to 57 per cent of all builders. To complete the picture, the compilers included in a third calculation builders operating only in the suburbs of Cleveland. On this basis, 60 per cent of all single-family housebuilders in the entire Cleveland area built only one house each in 1938. The error is thus of some magnitude, but it detracts little from the general picture.

A further limitation is that some builders are known to obtain permits under more than one name. Among builders of multifamily structures in New York City it was noted in many cases that the address of the builder, or the building corporation, was identical with the site of operations. Where this reflects the creation of separate corporations for each project, it is probably a method of limiting financial responsibility. This is especially desirable for the speculative builder who depends upon the sale of the completed project for the protection of his investment in the building operation. To the extent that this practice prevails, the number of builders is overstated and the number of units built per builder is understated. For builders of multifamily structures, this practice is more prevalent in New York City than in other parts of the country. In many cities, single-family housebuilders follow the same procedure, but the reasons for it are less clear than in the case of multifamily housebuilders. Also, it is not believed that the resulting distortion of size of builders is as great in the former as in the latter.

The study of single-family housebuilders was independent of the analysis of builders of multifamily structures. In each case, the objective was to determine the size of operations of builders of the specified type of structures, and no consideration was given to the other operations of the builders. Thus, while it has been shown that 64 per cent of the single-family housebuilders built only one house each in 1938, some, or perhaps many, of them carried on construction work of an entirely different type. The data, therefore, are not a measure of average *total operations,* but rather of operations in a particular type of building.

For builders of both one- and two-family structures the F. W. Dodge Corporation has made a special analysis of its record of 1938 contract awards in 37 eastern states. A summary of the findings appears below:

Houses Per Builder	Builders		Houses	
	(Number)	*(Per Cent)*	*(Number)*	*(Per Cent)*
Total	33,554	100.0	110,800	100.0
1	17,351	51.8	17,351	15.7
2–10	14,498	43.2	52,889	47.7
11–30	1,426	4.2	22,982	20.6
31 and over	279	0.8	17,578	16.0

The sample is more than twice as large as that of the Bureau of Labor Statistics for one-family structures, but it is less representative in the low-price brackets. This is because the Dodge Corporation does not collect data on awards below a minimum of $2,000. Also, the one-house builder group is understated by reason of the fact that many of such houses are built without awarding a general contract. Despite these rather important differences, together with a small variation occasioned by the inclusion of two-family structures, the general picture is the same as that shown by the BLS data.[28]

The data shown in Tables 15 and 16 below provide sufficient evidence of the small-scale character of the building industry, but an additional measure is needed of the price ranges in which builders of different sizes operate. Such data are provided in Table 17 of this appendix, in which operations of single-family housebuilders in the 72 cities mentioned earlier have been classified by permit value, and then converted to a selling price basis. The conversion was determined from special studies in each of the cities as to the relation between permit values and selling prices (including land)

TABLE 15

DISTRIBUTION OF BUILDERS OF SINGLE-FAMILY HOUSES AND OF HOUSES BUILT, BY SIZE OF OPERATION, IN 72 CITIES, 1938

Number of Houses Produced in 1938	Total for 72 Cities: Builders		Total for 72 Cities: Houses		New York City: Builders		New York City: Houses	
	(Number)	*(Per Cent)*	*(Number)*	*(Per Cent)*	*(Number)*	*(Per Cent)*	*(Number)*	*(Per Cent)*
Total	13,934	100.0	47,156	100.0	990	100.0	9,598	100.0
1	8,890	63.8	8,890	18.9	448	45.5	448	4.7
2–4	3,105	22.3	8,111	17.2	202	20.2	554	5.8
5–9	1,095	7.8	7,069	15.0	119	12.0	788	8.2
10–24	602	4.4	8,606	18.2	138	13.9	2,000	20.8
25–99	209	1.5	9,194	19.5	69	7.0	3,324	34.6
100 or more	33	0.2	5,286	11.2	14	1.4	2,484	25.9

Source: "Builders of 1-Family Houses in 72 Cities," Serial No. R1151, Bureau of Labor Statistics, 1940.

for individual properties. The relationships found were then applied to the distribution of size of builder by permit value class, in each of three regions (North, South, and West) and cities in two size groups (over 100,000 population and under 100,000 population). Table 17 presents a consolidation of these data. For the 72 cities as a whole, building permits were thereby inflated by 45 per cent, on the average. This, however, was not uniform as between permit value classes. Actually a fairly consistent inverse relationship is shown. Thus, for permits under $1,000, it was found that the average selling price was more than twice that amount. At the other end of the scale, the spread was reduced to 22 per cent for houses having a permit value of from $5,500 to $6,000.

28. The Dodge data were presented by Thomas S. Holden, President, F. W. Dodge Corporation, in a paper entitled "Integration of the Housing Function," read before the annual meeting of the American Statistical Association in Philadelphia, December 28, 1939.

TABLE 16

Distribution of Builders of Multifamily Structures and of Dwelling Units Built, by Size of Operation, in 37 Cities, 1939

Number of Units Produced in 1939	Total for 37 Cities: Builders (Number)	Builders (Per Cent)	Units (Number)	Units (Per Cent)	New York City: Builders (Number)	Builders (Per Cent)	Units (Number)	Units (Per Cent)
Total	958	100.0	46,129	100.0	295	100.0	31,329	100.0
3–4	293	30.6	1,142	2.5	10	3.4	38	0.1
5–9	152	15.9	1,065	2.3	10	3.4	65	0.2
10–24	138	14.4	2,036	4.4	20	6.8	271	0.9
25–49	126	13.2	4,764	10.3	69	23.5	2,818	9.0
50–99	174	18.1	11,911	25.8	139	47.2	9,474	30.2
100–199	52	5.4	6,678	14.5	37	12.6	4,719	15.1
200–499	17	1.8	4,438	9.6	7	2.1	2,009	6.4
500–999	3	0.3	1,603	3.5	1	0.3	545	1.7
1,000 and over	3	0.3	12,492	27.1	2	0.7	11,390	36.4

Source: Special tabulation made by the Housing Survey from unpublished data for 37 cities as supplied by the Bureau of Labor Statistics.

TABLE 17

Distribution of Single-Family Houses Built in Specified Price Classes, by Size of Operations, in 72 Cities, 1938

Price Class	Total	Builders of: 1 House	2–4 Houses	5–9 Houses	10–24 Houses	25–99 Houses	100 Houses and Over
(Number of Houses Built)							
Total	47,156	8,890	8,111	7,068	8,597	9,204	5,286
Under $3,000	5,091	2,173	1,238	655	611	414	—
$3,000–$5,000	11,094	2,122	2,022	1,605	2,078	2,363	904
$5,000–$8,000	25,575	3,201	3,474	3,726	5,062	5,987	4,125
Over $8,000	5,396	1,394	1,377	1,082	846	440	257
(Percentage Distribution by Size of Operations)							
Total	100.0	18.9	17.2	15.0	18.2	19.5	11.2
Under $3,000	100.0	42.7	24.3	12.9	12.0	8.1	—
$3,000–$5,000	100.0	19.2	18.2	14.5	18.7	21.3	8.1
$5,000–$8,000	100.0	12.5	13.6	14.6	19.8	23.4	16.1
Over $8,000	100.0	25.7	25.5	20.1	15.7	8.2	4.8
(Percentage Distribution by Price Class)							
Total	100.0	100.0	100.0	100.0	100.0	100.0	100.0
Under $3,000	10.8	24.4	15.3	9.3	7.1	4.5	—
$3,000–$5,000	23.5	23.9	24.9	22.7	24.2	25.7	17.1
$5,000–$8,000	54.3	36.0	42.8	52.7	58.9	65.0	78.0
Over $8,000	11.4	15.7	17.0	15.3	9.8	4.8	4.9

Source: Bureau of Labor Statistics, Division of Construction and Public Employment.

6. NUMBER OF GENERAL BUILDING CONTRACTORS AND SUBCONTRACTORS

On the basis of the Bureau of Labor Statistics data, given in Appendix C, 5 and Tables 15, 16 and 17, that bureau has estimated that in 1938 there were about 75,000 builders of urban *one-family* houses.[29] This figure differs considerably from data available from other sources, and it is here intended to compare the several estimates.

In making the above estimate, the BLS tabulated the names of builders in 72 cities as they appeared on building permits issued. The data given in Appendix C, 5 and Tables 15, 16 and 17 were thereby obtained. These were raised to national totals, giving all possible consideration to departures from the typical which might be expected in small places. Unlike other published figures, the BLS figure gives representation to small builders, particularly owner-builders acting as their own contractors.

This figure, however, is subject to the errors inherent in all building permit data. Also, there was evidence that some contractors, because of real or imagined advantages, obtain building permits under more than one firm name, so that in the tabulations a builder of four houses might appear as four individual builders of one house each. To the extent that this is true, the BLS figure exaggerates the actual number. On the other hand, the figure includes no estimate for rural nonfarm areas, as it is specifically for urban construction by urban builders. It should be remembered that the BLS figure is not restricted to general contractors in the usual sense of the word. The original tabulations were based on a count of names designated as builders on building permits. Many of these were of owner-builders, i.e., owners who acted as their own general contractors in the construction of houses they intended to live in. They are thus "one-time builders," rather than contractors.

For the year 1935, the Census reported only 8,337 general building contractors, including operative builders.[30] These included general contractors engaged in nonresidential as well as residential construction. However, the census figure is specifically for contractors regularly in business during the year who had established places of business. The existence of a "regularly established place of business" could be recognized as such by the enumerators only when a street sign was displayed. A supplementary mail canvass brought many concealed businesses to light, but the coverage was still incomplete and is so noted by the census. In 1940 the census coverage was clearly much better, and the supplementary lists were more complete. According to these data, there were 29,640[31] general building contractors on April 1, 1940.

The last figure to be considered is that reported by the Social Security Board. From reports of employers under the Old-Age and Survivors' Insurance provisions of the Social Security Act, the Board tabulated a total of 33,721 general building contractors in the third quarter of 1940.[32] The SSB figure includes contractors engaged primarily in the various types of building construction, alteration, and repair, including nonresidential as well as residential. However, it covers only contractors who had one or more *employees* in the third quarter of 1940.

Data on the number of subcontractors are limited to those reported by the SSB,

29. "Operations of Urban Home Builders," *Monthly Labor Review*, May 1941, pp. 1283-1285.
30. Census of Business: 1935, *Construction Industry*, Vol. I, p. XXIV.
31. Census of Business: 1939, *Construction*.
32. Social Security Board, Division of Old-Age and Survivors' Insurance (unpublished data).

TABLE 18

Distribution of Employers and Employees in the Contract Construction Industry, by Size of Firm, Third Quarter, 1940

(In Percentages)

Size of Firm By Number of Employees	General Building Contractors [a]		Subcontractors [b]	
	Employers	Employees on Last Pay Roll of Quarter	Employers	Employees on Last Pay Roll of Quarter
Total	100.0	100.0	100.0	100.0
None	4.9	—	3.1	—
1	11.0	.9	19.2	2.9
2	12.1	1.9	17.3	5.3
3	11.2	2.6	14.0	6.4
4	9.2	2.9	9.7	5.9
5	7.6	2.9	7.3	5.6
6	6.1	2.8	5.4	5.0
7	5.1	2.7	4.4	4.6
8	3.5	2.2	2.9	3.5
9	2.9	2.0	2.2	2.9
10 to 19	14.0	14.6	9.1	18.3
20 to 29	5.0	9.1	2.5	9.0
30 to 39	2.3	5.9	1.1	5.8
40 to 49	1.3	4.3	.6	4.1
50 to 59	.8	3.4	.3	2.8
60 to 69	.6	3.0	.2	2.1
70 to 79	.4	2.5	.1	1.6
80 to 89	.3	2.1	.1	1.5
90 to 99	.2	1.7	.1	1.2
100 to 199	1.0	10.6	.3	5.8
200 to 299	.3	5.0	.1	2.0
300 to 399	.1	3.6	c	1.4
400 to 499	.1	2.0	c	.7
500 to 599	c	1.7	c	.4
600 to 699	c	1.7	—	—
700 to 799	c	1.0	c	.1
800 to 899	c	.4	c	.4
900 to 999	c	.2	c	.3
1,000 to 1,999	c	2.3	c	.4
2,000 to 2,999	c	2.6	—	—
3,000 to 3,999	c	1.4	—	—

Source: Special tabulation made for The Twentieth Century Fund by the Bureau of Old-Age and Survivors' Insurance, Social Security Board.

a. Percentages are based on 33,721 employers and 435,304 employees on last pay roll of quarter.

b. Percentages are based on 92,981 employers and 611,460 employees on last pay roll of quarter.

c. Less than one tenth of one per cent.

Note: General building contractors include those engaged primarily in the construction, alteration and repair of buildings, both residential and nonresidential. Excluded are those whose primary operations are on highways, streets, bridges, terminals, harbors, and other heavy projects. Subcontractors include those engaged in all subcontracting, without regard to the type of construction.

Figures for employers cover all contractors who engaged workers at *any time* in the third quarter of 1940; data for employees refer only to the number at work during the last pay period in the third quarter of 1940. Data used in Figure 13 were derived from this table by a process of accumulation. The chart does not include data for establishments employing 500 or more workers; these statistics, however, are given in the above table.

which totaled 92,981 [33] in the third quarter of 1940, and those of the Bureau of the Census which counted 63,556 in 1935 and 176,187 in 1939.[34]

For purposes of this study, the BLS figure for housebuilders is accepted. However, since it refers only to builders of single-family houses in urban areas, it is clear that the total number of builders of residential structures is somewhat larger. For subcontrac-

TABLE 19

DISTRIBUTION OF WORK PERFORMED BY SELECTED TYPES OF CONTRACTORS, BY LOCATION OF WORK, 1935 [a]

(*In Per Cent of Total Business*)

Kind of Business	Total	In Home City	In Home State Outside Home City	Outside Home State
General contractors	100.0	44.7	34.3	21.0
Building[b]	100.0	66.1	21.4	12.5
Heavy construction	100.0	36.1	28.5	35.4
Highway	100.0	21.9	58.8	19.3
Special trade contractors	100.0	78.5	16.1	5.4
Carpentering	100.0	90.2	8.3	1.5
Concreting	100.0	79.1	15.6	5.3
Electrical	100.0	75.0	15.1	9.9
Excavating and/or foundation	100.0	60.6	32.8	6.6
Heating and plumbing group	100.0	83.1	13.1	3.8
Heating and piping	100.0	67.8	25.3	6.9
Heating and piping with sheet metal	100.0	84.7	12.9	2.4
Heating, piping, plumbing	100.0	87.5	9.6	2.9
Heating, piping, plumbing with sheet metal	100.0	79.1	14.0	6.9
Plumbing	100.0	93.5	5.5	1.0
Plumbing with sheet metal	100.0	92.8	4.5	2.7
Roofing and sheet metal group	100.0	84.0	13.8	2.2
Roofing	100.0	84.6	13.4	2.0
Sheet metal	100.0	91.1	7.8	1.1
Roofing and sheet metal	100.0	80.5	16.6	2.9
Masonry	100.0	81.5	8.3	10.2
Painting, paper hanging, and decorating	100.0	90.0	6.5	3.5
Plastering	100.0	81.2	12.9	5.9
Tile and mantel	100.0	74.2	18.6	7.2

Source: Census of Business: 1935, *Construction Industry,* Vol. III, Table 10, p. 106.

a. Based on the reports of 46,429 contracting establishments that performed work amounting to $1,330,835,000. This was about 82 per cent of the value of all work reported in the Census.

b. Includes operative builders.

tors, the census figure appears more reasonable. As a basis for this, the SSB data (Table 18) indicate that 19.2 per cent of subcontractors reporting to that agency employed only one worker. It probably follows that a considerable number employed no workers at all. As stated earlier, such employers are not included in the total of

33. *Ibid.*

34. Census of Business: 1935, *Construction Industry,* and 1939, *Construction.*

92,981 subcontractors reported by the SSB,[35] but they are included in the census figure. It is true, of course, that some of these small subcontractors may actually be tradesmen who choose to identify themselves as subcontractors. This is largely a matter of definition; in small places a tradesman working by the job rather than by the hour, as they frequently do, may logically be classified as a subcontractor, as he is in the census tabulation.

TABLE 20

AVERAGE VALUE OF BUILDING EQUIPMENT PER EMPLOYEE, BY TYPE OF CONTRACTOR, 1929

Type of Contractor	Average Value
General contractors	
Commercial only	$211
Residential building only	175
Manufacturing (industrial) building only	115
Operative builders (principally residential)	68
Subcontractors	
Excavating	1,491
Rental of equipment, trucking, etc.	1,400
Stonework	861
Steel erection	788
Wrecking	579
Glass and glazing	509
Concreting	358
Roofing and sheet metal work	347
Carpentering and wood flooring	341
Marble and tile	315
Heating and plumbing	254
Electrical	209
Masonry	169
Painting and decorating	161
Plastering and lathing	126

Source: Fifteenth Census of the United States, 1930, *Construction Industry*, pp. 96-101.

Note: Figures in the table represent average inventory value of equipment as reported by construction establishments doing more than $25,000 worth of business in 1929, divided by the average number of employees. Firms reporting "equipment" and "employees" are not identical, but since both items are on a "per firm" basis, it is not believed that the distortion is great. The distinction between types of general contractors is not clear-cut, since many contractors engaged in more than one of the several types of work specified. For census purposes, the reports are classified according to the major type of work done. It should also be noted that the averages are probably high because of the exclusion of contractors whose 1929 business was valued at less than $25,000.

It seems clear that in the 1939 census of the construction industry the Census Bureau went to unusual lengths to obtain complete coverage. For example, all contractors reporting to the SSB in 1938 were covered, and a complete list of builders obtaining building permits in cities reporting to the Bureau of Labor Statistics was obtained.

35. Table 18 includes a small number of employers who had no employees in the last pay period of the third quarter of 1940. At some other time during that quarter there were employees. The exclusion referred to relates to those builders who had no employees at any time during the quarter.

In addition, some 1,400 Chambers of Commerce were queried for mailing lists. It remains true, however, that it was impossible to identify many small operators. The extent of the undercounting cannot be determined. It is probably not of the magnitude indicated by the difference between the BLS figure and the census figure for general contractors, since the former, as explained, specifically includes an unknown number of owner-builders excluded by definition from the census figure.

7. Subcontracts Let on Two Major Types of Residential Building

a. PROBABLE NUMBER OF SUBCONTRACTS ON A MULTISTORY APARTMENT BUILDING

(1) Excavating and rough grading (including rock excavating, shoring, sheet piling)
(2) Finished grading and landscaping
(3) Special foundations—caissons, pile driving
(4) Concrete work (including reinforcing and ready-mixed concrete)
(5) Concrete-form work
(6) Fireproofing
(7) Waterproofing
(8) Scaffolding
(9) Pumping
(10) Hoisting
(11) Bricklaying (including structural tile, cement block, glass block)
(12) Tuck pointing
(13) Stone setting (including artificial stone)
(14) Marble setting (including structural glass)
(15) Terrazzo
(16) Asbestos work (including pipe covering)
(17) Tile setting (ceramic and encaustic tile, paving tile)
(18) Slate and tile roofing
(19) Built-up roofing
(20) Lathing
(21) Plastering
(22) Structural steel fabrication
(23) Structural steel erection
(24) Ornamental metal work (including miscellaneous iron, metal sash, metal doors)
(25) Steel stairs
(26) Sheet metal work
(27) Rough carpentry (including rough hardware)
(28) Finished carpentry
(29) Finished wood floors
(30) Stair building
(31) Cabinetwork
(32) Kitchen cabinets
(33) Finished hardware
(34) Weather stripping
(35) Insulating
(36) Overhead doors
(37) Plumbing (including gas fitting)
(38) Sprinkler installation
(39) Heating and steam fitting (including boilerwork)
(40) Burner or stoker installation
(41) Ventilating and air conditioning
(42) Electrical wiring
(43) Electrical fixtures
(44) Elevator installation
(45) Elevator doors and closers
(46) Elevator cabs
(47) Ranges
(48) Refrigerators
(49) Glazing
(50) Painting and decorating
(51) Paper hanging
(52) Linoleum
(53) Composition tile

b. TYPICAL SUBCONTRACTS ON A SMALL DETACHED HOUSE

(1) Excavating and grading
(2) Landscaping
(3) Masonry (including concreting, chimney and fireplace construction, waterproofing)
(4) General carpentry (including finished floors, insulation, rough and finished hardware, form work, miscellaneous iron and steel, overhead garage doors)
(5) Cabinetwork
(6) Weather stripping
(7) Lathing and plastering
(8) Tile setting
(9) Linoleum (including composition tile)
(10) Roofing (slating, shingling, or rolled roofing)
(11) Sheet metal
(12) Painting (including paper hanging)
(13) Plumbing (including gas fitting)
(14) Heating (including burner installation, and air conditioning)
(15) Electric wiring (including fixtures)
(16) Glazing
(17) Range
(18) Refrigerator

Source: Based on the opinions of persons familiar with residential construction. Subcontracts are listed in approximate accordance with the sequence of work at the job site.

8. Profits in the Construction Industry

As indicated in the text, it is impossible to determine profits realized in housebuilding as distinct from those derived in other types of construction. Even for the construction industry as a whole, only an approximation is possible because of the large number of small builders whose profits are negligible and difficult to trace, and many of whom can scarcely be classified as builders because they move in and out of the business so frequently.

Table 21 below presents data supplied by the Bureau of Foreign and Domestic Commerce which for the first time give an indication of the volume of profits in the contract construction industry as a whole, including both general and subcontracting. Since it is desired to show only the profits accruing to builders, no consideration is here given to general income-producing factors in the industry, such as wages and salaries and interest payments. An important exception, as indicated in Table 21, is the inclusion of returns for personal services of proprietors of unincorporated businesses. In these businesses, the major return is, of course, that received by the proprietor for his own services.

The inclusion of such compensation results in an inflated figure for the "rate of return," i.e., the ratio of net income to gross value, as shown in the last column. It actually makes it impossible to compare the rate of return in construction with that of other industries where the proportionate share of total income accruing to unincorporated businesses is much lower. Thus, in 1940, BFDC data indicate that for all business activity combined about 72 per cent of total "net" income (as defined above) was derived from unincorporated businesses. If agriculture is excluded, only about 61 per cent total net income is so derived.[36] In the contract construction industry, because of the prevalence of small-scale operators, some 86 per cent of total net income accrues to unincorporated businesses, as is shown in Table 21.

36. Gilbert and Yntema, *op. cit.,* Table 8, p. 17.

It may be that a more realistic conception of the true "rate of return" can be obtained from an analysis of data for corporations alone. In these data, "net" income is calculated after payment of wages and salaries and hence they more accurately represent the profitableness of the building industry. The available statistics, which are based on income tax returns, are presented in Table 22 of this appendix and discussed in the text (Chapter 3). These figures provide another advantage over those in Table 21 in that they are apparently for *building* construction rather than for all construction combined. Because of changes in classifications, the information in Table 22 cannot be extended beyond 1937.

However, the reclassification beginning in 1938 did provide an interesting break between general contractors and subcontractors. The data are shown in Table 23 below. Also given in this table are data for total manufacturing to provide a basis for comparison. As already suggested, such comparison must be made with care, since the degree to which incorporated firms are representative of a given industry as a whole varies greatly from one industry to another. Also, the proportion of incorporated firms that are represented in income tax returns varies as between different industries and different years. As a further point, the 1938 reclassification involved certain important inclusions, as indicated in note "b" to Table 23.

TABLE 21

ESTIMATED TOTAL CONSTRUCTION AND NET INCOME, CONTRACT CONSTRUCTION INDUSTRY, SELECTED YEARS, 1929–1940

Year	Estimated Gross Value of All Construction	Net Income: Total	Net Income: Incorporated Business	Net Income: Unincorporated Business[a]	Ratio of Total Net Income to Gross Value
			(In Millions)		*(Per Cent)*
1929	$7,938	$537	$92	$445	6.8
1933	1,553	22	—57[b]	79	1.4
1937	4,095	314	20	294	7.7
1938	4,021	297	20	277	7.4
1940	5,269	396	55	341	7.5

Source: Bureau of Foreign and Domestic Commerce.
a. Includes returns for personal services of owners.
b. Net loss.

9. SEASONAL FLUCTUATION IN CONSTRUCTION CONTRACTS AWARDED IN 37 EASTERN STATES

Data given in Table 24 below represent computed seasonal factors for construction contract awards in 37 eastern states, as reported by the F. W. Dodge Corporation. The basic method of computation involves the calculation of ratios of individual monthly items to a free-hand curve, and averaging the ratios. The period covered by the data varies somewhat, but in all cases at least eight years are available, thus providing a period sufficient for the calculation of seasonals. The seasonal factors shown are those for 1940 except where otherwise specified. A more detailed discussion of the methods used appears in the *Federal Reserve Bulletin* for October 1938, p. 836.

Contract awards do not provide a very satisfactory measure of seasonality in building construction. First, they are deficient in coverage, having reference only to the 37 eastern states; a considerable volume of railroad and public utility construction is not included, and low-cost housing is covered only in part. Coverage for the latter item has improved in recent years since the minimum contract included has been reduced from $5,000 to $2,000.

Second, the construction time on different types of operations varies considerably.

TABLE 22

BUILDING CONSTRUCTION CORPORATIONS FILING INCOME TAX RETURNS, 1929, 1933, AND 1937

	1929	1933	1937
		(Value Figures in Thousands)	
All active firms			
Number of returns	12,868	11,599	10,744
Gross receipts	$1,641,377	$531,430	$1,004,374
Net income or deficit (—) after taxes	$33,349	$—39,718	$5,412
Per cent net income to gross receipts	2.0		0.5
Returns with net income			
Number of returns	7,097	1,404	3,629
Per cent of total active firms	55.0	12.0	34.0
Gross receipts	$1,158,728	$131,353	$627,381
Net income after taxes	$68,762	$5,303	$19,919
Per cent net income to gross receipts	5.9	4.0	3.2
Returns with no net income			
Number of returns	5,771	10,195	7,115
Per cent of total active firms	45.0	88.0	66.0
Gross receipts	$482,649	$400,077	$376,993
Net deficit	$35,413	$45,021	$14,507
Per cent net deficit to gross receipts	7.3	11.3	3.8

Source: Bureau of Internal Revenue, *Statistics of Income* for years indicated.

In a study of 1931 construction in 14 cities, the Bureau of Labor Statistics found that the average construction period for 4,862 one-family frame dwellings was 92 days. One-family brick dwellings numbering 2,580 averaged 141 days. Other types of structures showed extreme variations, depending, among other things, on the size of structure.

These data were presented in "Elapsed Time in Building Construction," *Monthly Labor Review,* January 1933, pp. 158-167.

There is also a time lapse between awarding the contract and beginning work. The study mentioned above indicates that the lag between issuance of the building permit and the initiation of construction averaged only six days for 7,442 one-family dwellings (more than one half of these were started within three days) and only eight days for commercial buildings. While data on the lag between contract award and initiation of construction are lacking, it obviously could not be greater than the lapse between issuance of permit and start of work. In fact, contracts are sometimes awarded after the beginning of operations.

The second consideration mentioned above is particularly important in comparing

TABLE 23

CONSTRUCTION INDUSTRY CORPORATIONS FILING INCOME TAX RETURNS COMPARED WITH TOTAL MANUFACTURING, 1938

Income Tax Return Items	Construction Industry: Total Construction [a]	Construction Industry: General Contractors [b]	Construction Industry: Special Trade Contractors	Total Manufacturing
	(Value Figures in Thousands)			
All active firms				
Number of returns	16,341	7,861	8,369	82,155
Gross receipts	$1,964,134	$1,374,229	$577,472	$48,614,851
Net income or deficit (—) after taxes	$15,441	$18,196	$—3,375	$1,243,204
Per cent, net income of gross receipts	0.8	1.3	—0.6	2.6
Returns with net income				
Number of returns	5,057	2,698	2,330	33,044
Per cent of total active firms	31.0	35.0	28.0	40.0
Gross receipts	$1,255,862	$935,299	$310,965	$32,519,433
Net income after taxes	$52,975	$42,142	$10,039	$2,034,932
Per cent, net income of gross receipts	4.2	4.5	3.2	6.3
Returns with no net income				
Number of returns	11,284	5,163	6,039	49,111
Per cent of total active firms	69.0	65.0	72.0	60.0
Gross receipts	$708,272	$438,930	$266,487	$16,095,418
Net deficit	$37,534	$23,946	$13,414	$791,728
Per cent, net deficit of gross receipts	5.3	5.5	5.0	4.9

Source: Bureau of Internal Revenue, *Statistics of Income,* 1938.

a. Includes unallocable contractors.

b. Includes building, highway, bridge, and heavy construction, marine construction (not including shipbuilding), water-well drilling, and airport construction contractors.

the magnitude of seasonal fluctuations for the different types of construction. Also important, but not subject to measurement, is the difference in construction patterns on the several classes of construction. The distribution of work over the building period may vary considerably from one type of project to another, but information on the subject is restricted to public construction, with a complete lack of data on private residential work.

TABLE 24

SEASONAL FLUCTUATION IN CONSTRUCTION CONTRACTS AWARDED IN 37 EASTERN STATES, 1929, 1932, 1940

(*Monthly Average = 100*)

Month	Private Residential: Total Private Residential			Private Residential: One- and Two-Family Dwellings: For Sale or Rent	Private Residential: One- and Two-Family Dwellings: Owner-Occupied	Private Residential: Apartments, Hotels, Dormitories, and "Other" Shelter	Privately Financed Construction Other Than Residential	Streets and Highways
	1929	1932	1940	1940	1940	1940	1940	1940
January	75	71	67	75	53	84	76	65
February	82	72	71	80	61	70	74	53
March	114	108	110	119	98	114	108	80
April	124	121	120	121	119	122	115	100
May	128	123	121	120	127	110	114	130
June	108	119	117	110	127	104	118	129
July	95	112	111	102	124	102	123	130
August	94	107	106	100	115	96	108	120
September	93	102	100	96	110	86	98	125
October	112	110	109	106	112	112	100	105
November	96	90	91	94	87	96	84	80
December	90	70	77	77	67	104	82	83

Source: Board of Governors of the Federal Reserve System.

TABLE 25

SEASONAL FLUCTUATION IN RESIDENTIAL CONSTRUCTION AND APPROXIMATE AVERAGE TEMPERATURES, BY MONTHS, IN SELECTED AREAS, 1930–1938

Region	Jan.	Feb.	March	April	May	June	July	Aug.	Sept.	Oct.	Nov.	Dec.
				Permits Issued for New Residential Construction (Average for Each Region = 100)								
New England	54	29	66	115	131	131	132	127	110	125	103	78
New Jersey	50	53	114	114	111	111	120	100	112	118	113	85
Ohio	57	55	104	116	126	125	129	123	120	107	81	58
Minnesota	41	37	80	129	137	132	111	136	114	121	103	59
Colorado	52	73	121	141	121	121	118	111	116	95	85	47
Washington	68	75	130	128	130	105	96	109	117	102	84	56
California	79	83	116	118	117	105	99	106	108	105	87	78
Florida	95	94	108	108	104	108	122	108	91	105	85	72
N. Carolina	77	72	118	139	115	109	105	111	106	110	84	54
Tennessee	59	80	102	120	113	102	138	140	110	121	78	37
Missouri	50	72	125	125	130	115	107	120	125	103	78	48
Louisiana	79	106	126	121	113	100	100	99	112	92	94	59
Texas	99	99	113	109	105	100	106	109	96	111	81	74
				(Approximate Daily Average Temperature, in Degrees)								
New England	28°	29°	36°	46°	57°	66°	72°	70°	63°	54°	42°	32°
New Jersey	32	33	40	51	62	70	75	74	68	57	45	36
Ohio	28	30	38	50	61	69	74	73	66	56	42	32
Minnesota	13	16	29	46	58	67	72	69	61	49	33	18
Colorado	30	33	39	47	56	66	72	71	63	51	40	32
Washington	35	36	43	49	55	61	66	66	59	51	42	36
California	53	54	56	57	60	62	64	65	65	63	58	54
Florida	61	63	67	71	76	80	82	81	79	74	67	62
N. Carolina	35	38	45	54	63	69	72	70	65	56	45	38
Tennessee	41	44	52	62	71	78	81	79	74	64	53	44
Missouri	30	33	44	56	66	75	79	78	70	59	45	34
Louisiana	54	57	63	69	75	81	82	82	79	71	62	56
Texas	50	53	60	68	74	81	84	84	79	70	59	52

Source: Federal Home Loan Bank Board. Temperature data represent averages of city reports made by the Weather Bureau. Construction data refer to residential permits issued in all cities of 10,000 or more, as reported by the Bureau of Labor Statistics. The seasonals for permits are computed by the link relative method, from data covering the period 1930-1938. In the computation, cyclical trend was eliminated by fitting a log curve to the averages of the month-to-month link relatives.

APPENDIX D

1. Tenure of Employment in the Construction Industry

Data used in Figure 20, p. 107 to show the tenure of employment in construction as compared with other industries, are compiled by the Social Security Board from the quarterly reports of taxable wages paid to individual workers under the Old-Age and Survivors' Insurance provisions of the Social Security Act. The following table shows, for selected industries, what proportion of all workers were employed at some time during each of the four quarters of 1938: [1]

Industry	Percentage of Full-Time Workers to All Workers
General contracting, building	54
General contracting, other	42
Special trade contracting	64
Motor vehicles and equipment	69
Basic lumber industries	68
Finished lumber products	77
Stone, clay and glass products	80
Iron and steel and their products	84

Only workers who had taxable wages in the fourth quarter of 1938 are included in this table. For all industries combined, such workers totaled about 77 per cent of all 1938 workers. The remaining 23 per cent had some employment during any one, or more, of the first three quarters of 1938, but as they did not also receive taxable wages in the fourth quarter they are not included. Out of the total of workers receiving taxable wages in the fourth quarter, those who received wages in each of the four quarters, regardless of the length of time employed in any one quarter, are assumed to be "full-time" workers for purposes of this table. The "total" includes, in addition to workers engaged in all four quarters, those who worked for any period *less* than four quarters but including the fourth quarter.

The data give some indication of the unfavorable position of the construction worker, and the true situation is probably even worse than it here appears. Thus in this presentation, a worker engaged in each of the four quarters might nevertheless work only a few weeks at a time. This is much more likely to be true in the building industry than in most other lines of trade.

This conclusion is reinforced by the following statistics of labor turnover: [2]

1. Social Security Board, *Old-Age and Survivors' Insurance Statistics: Employment and Wages of Covered Workers, 1938*. Table 205, *et seq.*, of this publication contain data for a number of additional industries.

2. Social Security Board, Bureau of Old-Age and Survivors' Insurance.

Industry	Average Number of Jobs Per Worker — Quarters: First	Second	Third	Fourth
In all industries	1.115	1.139	1.143	1.128
General contracting				
Building construction	1.417	1.529	1.533	1.469
Other than building	1.302	1.398	1.416	1.358
Special trade contracting	1.343	1.438	1.445	1.337

These statistics were derived from a sample of some 6.5 million workers, classified according to their employment in the third quarter of 1939. The sample is adequate (about 20 per cent of the workers in all industries covered by the Social Security Act) but, because of mechanical problems in tabulation, the data are subject to some limitations: (a) The classification of workers according to their employment in the third quarter does not provide any information regarding shifts by individual workers from one industry to another during the year, a procedure believed to be common in the building industry. (b) The quarterly ratios cannot be added to give turnover ratios for the year as a whole. This is because an employer is required to submit separate reports of the taxable wages paid to each individual worker for each quarter in which he was employed. A worker employed in each of the four quarters of 1939, therefore, would be counted four times if the quantity ratios were added, while a worker employed in one quarter would be counted only once. (c) The classifications for construction are rather broad, and there may be considerable variation within the individual classes of employment. The turnover of workers in residential construction, for example, may be somewhat greater than in other building construction, due to the smaller average size of job.

2. Concentration of Ownership and the Rigidity of Prices in the Building Materials Industry

As made clear in the text (pp. 111-112), there is ample evidence that prices of building materials are, in the aggregate, more rigid than those of other commodities (see also Table 27 below). Concentration of control over the supply of goods is frequently advanced as the explanation for price rigidities in general and for building materials in particular. A comprehensive report of the Temporary National Economic Committee tends to disprove this, first by presenting evidence that concentration of ownership is less, rather than greater, among manufacturers of building materials than among producers of other commodities; and second, by demonstrating that in *all* commodities there is no predictable relationship between the degree of concentration of ownership and the extent to which prices are rigid.[3]

In comparing concentration of ownership among building materials manufacturers and other manufacturers, the measure of concentration is the proportion of the total value in 1937 of each product accounted for *by the four largest producers,* according to Census of Manufactures data. The data have reference only to the concentration of

3. Walter F. Crowder, "The Concentration of Production in Manufacturing," Pt. V, *The Structure of Industry,* TNEC Monograph No. 27.

ownership and do not take into consideration the effective concentration of control that may result from various kinds of understandings among producers. The figures are compiled on a company basis; a company represents a combination of all establishments under common ownership. Thus, all establishments operated from a central administrative office were considered as a single producing unit or company. It should

TABLE 26

NUMBER OF WORKERS BY TRADES AND BY NUMBER OF WEEKS WORKED ON A UNITED STATES HOUSING PROJECT OF 83 UNITS

Number of Weeks Worked	Number of Workers						
	Carpenters	Brick Masons	Plumbers	Concrete Finishers	Painters	Hod Carriers	Laborers
More than 0	23	21	13	24	17	14	47
" " 1	22	20	12	23	17	14	46
" " 2	22	19	11	21	13	14	43
" " 6	16	16	9	18	10	13	35
" " 10	15	13	8	16	9	10	26
" " 14	13	8	6	12	8	8	25
" " 18	12	8	3	7	6	7	23
" " 22	8	5	2	5	5	5	23
" " 26	7	1	2	3	4	2	22
" " 30	5	—	2	2	2	—	21
" " 34	2	—	2	1	—	—	20
" " 38	1	—	2	1	—	—	18
" " 42	1	—	—	—	—	—	14
" " 46	1	—	—	—	—	—	5
" " 50	—	—	—	—	—	—	—

Source: Bureau of Labor Statistics.

Note: Data are derived from a frequency distribution, by trades, of the number of men at work during each week of construction operations. The trades given accounted for 82 per cent of the total "man-weeks" required for the job. The project examined consisted of 41 buildings containing 83 dwelling units and 368½ rooms. Contracts let were valued at $243,393. Derivation of the data is as follows: The frequency distribution for carpenters, for example, indicated that in the maximum week of operations, 23 workers were engaged. In the next most active week, 22 carpenters were at work. It is assumed, therefore, that 23 carpenters had one week's work, and that 22 carpenters had more than one week's work. By a process of successive elimination, tenure for the balance of the workers was obtained.

It should be noted that the tabulation gives no consideration to hours worked or labor turnover. Thus, the carpenter who received only one week's work may in fact have worked less than a week. Also, the 22 carpenters working more than one week may have been a partially different group than was engaged in the most active week. The table thus provides only a mechanical means of determining the best possible record as to continuity of employment. This "best" obviously leaves much to be desired, and in actuality, the situation is even less favorable.

also be clear that the data cover manufacturing operations only. Concentration through ownership or otherwise, as applied at the successive stages of distribution, is not here taken into consideration.

The sample used in the TNEC report consists of 1,807 individual products, of which 283 are building materials. It is not possible to determine the representativeness of the building materials sample since the product data give no clue as to usage. For example, some 27 per cent of all manufactured forest products are included, but no information is available to indicate the representativeness of these data in the consumption of manufactured finished products as a whole. Separate data for residential construction are, of course, likewise unavailable. The 283 building materials are for the most part

TABLE 27

PATTERN OF CHANGE IN AVERAGE REALIZED PRICES OF BUILDING MATERIALS COMPARED WITH OTHER PRODUCTS, 1929-1933 AND 1933-1937

(*Based on 70 Building Materials and 337 Other Products*)

Per Cent of Base Year (1929 or 1933)	1933 Compared with 1929 Building Materials		1933 Compared with 1929 Other Products		1937 Compared with 1933 Building Materials		1937 Compared with 1933 Other Products	
	(*Number*)	(*Per Cent*)	(*Number*)	(*Per Cent*)	(*Number*)	(*Per Cent*)	(*Number*)	(*Per Cent*)
More than 255	—	—	—	—	—	—	—	—
" " 240	—	—	—	—	—	—	4	1.2
" " 225	—	—	—	—	—	—	7	2.1
" " 210	—	—	—	—	—	—	14	4.2
" " 195	—	—	—	—	2	2.9	19	5.7
" " 180	—	—	—	—	2	2.9	28	8.4
" " 165	—	—	—	—	4	5.8	41	12.3
" " 150	—	—	—	—	6	8.7	55	16.5
" " 135	4	5.7	3	0.9	11	15.8	99	29.6
" " 120	7	10.0	5	1.5	32	45.8	172	51.1
" " 105	11	15.7	16	4.8	45	64.4	244	72.4
" " 90	21	30.0	41	12.2	56	80.1	304	90.2
" " 75	49	70.0	134	39.8	64	91.5	331	98.2
" " 60	62	88.6	250	74.2	68	97.2	335	99.4
" " 45	64	91.4	315	93.5	69	98.6	336	99.7
" " 30	70	100.0	334	99.1	70	100.0	337	100.0
" " 15	70	100.0	337	100.0	70	100.0	337	100.0

Source: Walter F. Crowder, "The Concentration of Production in Manufacturing," Pt. V, *The Structure of Industry,* TNEC Monograph No. 27, Appendix E, Table 1E, pp. 562-571.

Note: The table is interpreted as follows: In 1933, the average realized prices of 10 per cent of all building materials remained 20 per cent or more above 1929, while only 1.5 per cent of all other products remained 20 per cent or more above 1933; the average realized prices of 70 *per cent* of all building materials either increased, or showed declines of less than 25 per cent, while only 39.8 per cent of all other products showed a similar degree of rigidity over this period. Prices of building materials also showed resistance to price change from 1933 to 1937—prices of 64.4 per cent of the building materials showed gains of more than 5 per cent, while prices of 72.4 per cent of all other products showed similar increases.

scattered among seven of the fourteen census industry groups, with the greatest concentration in the stone, clay, and glass products group. Each of the seven groups includes, to a varying degree, products other than building materials.

Table 28 below indicates the relative concentration of ownership in building materials as compared with other manufactured products. Thus, the four leading producers of 68 per cent of the 283 building materials account for more than 50 per cent of the total output of each; but 78 per cent of the 1,524 other manufactured products are produced under similar conditions of concentration.

It is interesting to note also that concentration in the hands of the largest *single* producer is not particularly high among the building materials. While data for individual building materials are not readily available, the TNEC data show that in only 10 per cent of the products included in the stone, clay and glass group does the largest producer account for more than 50 per cent of the total output. The same percentage

TABLE 28

CONCENTRATION OF PRODUCTION OF BUILDING MATERIALS COMPARED WITH ALL OTHER PRODUCTS, 1937

(Based on 283 Building Materials and 1,524 Other Products)
(Cumulative Percentages)

Per Cent of Production Accounted for by the 4 Largest Producers	Number of Products		Value of Products	
	Building Materials	Other	Building Materials	Other
More than 0.1	100.0	100.0	100.0	100.0
" " 10.0	98.9	99.7	97.4	97.6
" " 20.0	96.4	97.7	94.7	93.2
" " 30.0	88.6	93.2	67.6	85.2
" " 40.0	77.6	87.2	52.4	70.6
" " 50.0	67.7	78.1	41.5	58.6
" " 60.0	58.2	67.9	33.0	49.6
" " 70.0	42.4	55.7	18.7	40.7
" " 80.0	29.0	41.2	12.3	26.9
" " 90.0	16.6	29.2	7.3	19.6
a	9.2	19.8	3.6	8.5
b	2.1	11.1	0.2	2.1

Source: Walter F. Crowder, "The Concentration of Production in Manufacturing," Pt. V, *The Structure of Industry,* TNEC Monograph No. 27. Data for building materials are derived from Table 9D, p. 561; those for "other products" are obtained by subtracting building materials from "all products" as shown in Table 3D, p. 555.

a. Withheld to avoid disclosure of operations of any one of the four leading companies.

b. Withheld to avoid disclosing the operations of companies other than the four leaders.

Note: This table is interpreted as follows: For building materials the four leading producers of 67.7 per cent of the 283 products accounted for more than 50 per cent of the total output of each, according to the 1937 Census of Manufactures. At the same time the four leading producers of only 41.5 per cent of the total value of these 283 products accounted for more than 50 per cent of the total value of each.

is shown for rubber products, leather and its manufactures, iron and steel, and nonferrous metals. Chemicals, forest products, and machinery show percentages as high as 17 per cent, while paper products, petroleum and coal, foods, and textiles range from 6 to 8 per cent.[4]

Moreover, it has been shown that among all products the relative importance of the leader tends to increase directly with the degree of control exercised by the four leading

4. Crowder, *op. cit.,* Table 4, pp. 294–295.

producers. "The dominant and general feature throughout the industry groups is the tendency for the leader to be more important in the total value of products with high concentration and less important in the case of products with low concentration ratios." [5] Since the concentration ratios have been shown to be relatively low among building materials, it probably follows that the degree of control exercised by a single producer of a particular building material is also low, relative to other industries.

But, regardless of the relative *degree* of concentration in building materials manufacture as compared with other products, there is no evidence that rigid prices are associated with high concentration or that flexible prices are uniformly found to accompany dispersed ownership.

When concentration ratios and price changes of 1929-1933 for individual products are compared, there is no apparent tendency for products with high concentration ratios to be associated with small price declines or for products with low concentration ratios to be associated with large price declines. Also, there is no indication that large declines in output are associated with high concentration ratios, or vice versa. Apparently neither prices nor production are directly influenced by the concentration of ownership. Products with high concentration ratios and with low concentration ratios experience similar changes in price and output.[6]

3. Distribution Costs of Building Materials

"Distributive operations are a part of every step in the entire process beginning with the production of raw materials and ending with the final sale of the finished article." [7] For building materials, here considered as final products, this process encompasses a tremendously intricate and variable pattern which cannot be traced on a comprehensive basis. Thus at the raw materials stage we do not even have information as to the quantities of such materials that eventuate in manufactured building materials,[8] much less information on the distribution expenses that were incurred in producing and moving them to consuming factories.

At the manufacturing level, the data are somewhat better, but still not satisfactory for the problem at hand. Thus, the Census of Distribution for 1929, 1933, and 1935 gives operating expenses by type of manufacturer, and individual industry sales distributed by type of outlet. The data, however, are of very limited usefulness in the determination of distribution costs. Comparable information on profits is not available and, moreover, the figures for the distribution of sales are according to types of intermediary buyers, and have no reference to final consumers. For example, the distribution of sales of planing-mill products shows the proportion of sales to wholesalers, retailers, industrial users, etc., but does not show the proportion going to the residential construction industry, or even to the construction industry as a whole (Table 29). It is

5. *Ibid.*, p. 289.

6. This is the general conclusion of the TNEC report as regards commodities in general. It applies with equal force to building materials, according to scatter diagrams plotted from the Crowder data, *op. cit.*, Appendix E, Table 1E, pp. 562–571.

7. *Does Distribution Cost Too Much?*, The Twentieth Century Fund, New York, 1939, p. 7.

8. An exception to this may be noted in the case of certain aggregates such as sand and gravel, which, in the 1929 Census of Mines and Quarries, are segregated by type of consumer. Even here, however, no distinction is or can be made between aggregates used in residential and in nonresidential work, and in any event, distribution costs are not segregated.

TABLE 29

Distribution of Manufacturers' Sales in Selected Industries, 1935

Industry	Amount of Sales	Percentage Distribution of Sales: Total Sales	To Own Wholesale Branches	To Wholesalers and Jobbers	To Retailers [a]	To Industrial and Other Large Users	To Household Consumers
	(In Millions)						
Cement	$115	100.0	23.9	24.9	25.7	25.5	—
Clay products (other than pottery)	102	100.0	9.4	22.6	11.0	54.0	3.0
Doors, shutters, window sash, etc.	25	100.0	[b]	10.6	2.7	86.7	[c]
Hardware	107	100.0	3.7	30.3	15.5	50.3	0.2
Lumber and timber products	485	100.0	8.5	41.7	13.2	33.6	3.0
Paints, pigments and varnishes	393	100.0	35.0	12.7	18.2	32.9	1.2
Planing-mill products	205	100.0	3.9	23.4	21.6	37.5	13.6
Plumbers' supplies	66	100.0	14.0	63.6	8.5	13.7	0.2
Roofing	77	100.0	50.2	33.4	7.5	8.2	0.7
Sheet metal work	114	100.0	11.5	19.5	17.2	45.7	6.1
Steam and hot water heating apparatus	111	100.0	34.6	35.7	5.1	23.7	0.9
Structural metal work	173	100.0	12.1	3.2	1.9	81.9	0.9
Wallboard and plaster	23	100.0	15.2	38.5	20.6	24.2	1.5
Wallpaper	18	100.0	—	66.4	33.6	[d]	—
Window shades and fixtures	21	100.0	5.3	19.4	43.2	17.9	14.2

Source: Census of Business: 1935, *Distribution of Manufacturers' Sales.*

a. Includes sales to chain stores, and to manufacturers' own retail stores.

b. Combined with sales to wholesalers and jobbers to avoid disclosure.

c. Combined with sales to industrial users to avoid disclosure.

d. Less than 1/10 of one per cent.

apparent that an error would be involved in applying over-all distribution cost ratios to that proportion of planing-mill products which eventually go into housing.

Practically the same limitations apply at the wholesale and retail level. Data on profits are not collected by the census, and the compiled distribution of sales is too broad to bring out the flow of residential-construction materials from the wholesaler to subsequent points in the distribution system. Also, the industrial classifications are on an establishment basis, and since a considerable volume of building material is handled by distributors whose principal business is in other lines, it is not possible to get a complete picture of total wholesale and retail costs of operations. Thus the census classification of Builders Supplies covers only part of the building material sold at wholesale. Another large segment of total sales is included in the classification of Plumbing and Heating Equipment, and the balance is scattered among other types of outlets such as hardware stores, electrical-goods stores, general-merchandise stores, and a number of others. As a final limitation, throughout the whole process of distribution, nothing is known of the extent to which the usual distribution charges are by-passed by contractors purchasing directly from manufacturers or wholesalers rather than through retailers. In some lines of trade, too, the retailing function is so enmeshed with the building subcontractor's function that separation of operating expenses is not possible. For example, tile setters purchase directly from the manufacturers; they, in effect, perform all of the functions of the wholesaler, retailer and subcontractor. Division of an individual subcontractor's operating cost according to these three activities is obviously impractical.

In view of all these limitations, it is possible to present only very rough indications of the over-all picture. According to the 1935 Census of Distribution, the operating costs of manufacturers producing building materials were about 11.6 per cent of sales value.[9] These expenses include salaries and wages paid to plant employees devoting all or a major portion of their time to distribution activities, traveling expenses of salesmen, advertising, credit and collection expense, bad debts, and an allocation for rent, interest, and general administration. For transportation cost the only information is a special survey of 312 manufacturers made in 1931. This study included a group of manufacturers of building materials who reported transportation and warehousing costs as 2.4 per cent of net sales.[10] Such costs may have been about the same, on a ratio basis, in 1935. According to data from the Bureau of Internal Revenue, industries classified in the Stone, Clay and Glass group showed only a small profit in 1935, and this was more than offset by a considerable loss in the Forest Products industries. These two industrial classifications are much broader than that given above for industries reporting operating expenses, but it can be safely assumed that in 1935 producers of building materials on the whole operated without a profit. The distribution expenses of manufacturers of building materials were thus about 14 per cent of net sales (operating costs 11.6 per cent, transportation and warehousing costs 2.4 per cent), which represents a markup of a little more than 16 per cent over cost of goods sold. The reader is again cautioned that this does not necessarily indicate the manufacturers' distribution cost

9. In view of the earlier discussion, it will be clear that in many of these industries only a small part of their output, broadly classified here as Building Materials, actually goes into residential construction. See Census of Business: 1935, *Distribution of Manufacturers' Sales*.

10. *An Analysis of the Distribution Costs of 312 Manufacturers,* Association of National Advertisers and the National Association of Cost Accountants, New York, 1933, pp. 64, 106 (reprinted in *Does Distribution Cost Too Much?,* The Twentieth Century Fund, New York, 1939, Table U, p. 394).

of materials actually going into residential structures. Also, it does not include any of the costs of distribution incurred prior to the manufacturing stage.

Operating expenses of wholesale establishments which the census classifies as lumber and construction materials amounted to 16.7 per cent of net sales in 1935 and for plumbing and heating equipment and supplies establishments 19.8 per cent—or 17.7 per cent of the net sales of these two types of establishments combined.[11] Such expenses comprise administrative, selling, warehouse, and occupancy expenses, interest on bank loans, and losses from bad debts. Also included are delivery expenses. Data on profits of wholesalers in 1935 are available for a small sample; for lumber, net profits were 1.7 per cent of sales, for plumbing and heating equipment, 0.6 per cent, for hardware 1.4 per cent, and for electrical parts and supplies, 1.1 per cent.[12] Conservatively, it is assumed that profits in all lines averaged one per cent of net sales. The markup, which

TABLE 30

CITIES OVER 25,000 POPULATION HAVING COMPREHENSIVE ZONING ORDINANCES, CONTROL OF PLATS AND MASTER PLANS, FEBRUARY 1942

City Size	Total	Comprehensive Zoning Ordinance	Control of Plats	Master Plan [a]
Total over 25,000	412	294 [b]	266	221
Over 1,000,000	5	5	4	5
500,000—1,000,000	9	9	8	7
250,000—500,000	23	21	19	18
100,000—250,000	55	46	45	41
50,000—100,000	107	81	70	57
25,000—50,000	213	132	120	93

Source: The Municipal Year Book, 1942, The International City Managers' Association, Chicago, pp. 364-379.

a. Includes master plans in all stages of completion.

b. An additional 48 cities had partially complete zoning ordinances, i.e., regulation pertaining to only one or two of the three subjects (use, height, and area) covered by zoning.

at the wholesale level can be charged entirely to cost of distribution, is thus about 23 per cent.

For combined retail establishments classified by the census as lumber and building material dealers, heating and plumbing equipment dealers, and paint, glass and wallpaper stores, operating expenses (comprising the same items of expense listed for wholesalers) amounted to about 24.8 per cent of net sales.[13] For a small sample of lumber and building material dealers, Dun & Bradstreet, Inc., found that net profits in 1936 amounted to 3.7 per cent of net sales.[14] Assuming this figure to be representative of heating and plumbing equipment dealers and paint, glass and wallpaper stores,[15]

11. Census of Business: 1935, *Wholesale Distribution,* Vol. VI, Table 1.

12. Roy A. Foulke, *The Balance Sheet of the Future,* Dun & Bradstreet, Inc., New York, 1941, pp. 92, 94.

13. Census of Business: 1935, *Retail Operating Expense,* p. 8.

14. *Retail Credit Survey, 1936,* Dun & Bradstreet, Inc., New York.

15. This probably does not follow, since operating expenses show considerable variation as between the three types of outlets. Census of Business: 1935, *Retail Operating Expense.*

TABLE 31

States Having Licensing Laws Applicable to Building Trades and Occupations

States	Trade or Occupation				
	Architects	Contractors	Electricians	Plumbers	Others
New England					
Maine				x	
New Hampshire				x	
Vermont					
Massachusetts			x	x	
Rhode Island	x				
Connecticut	x		x	x	
Middle Atlantic					
New York	x		x	x	
New Jersey	x			x	
Pennsylvania	x			x	
North East Central					
Ohio	x		x[a]	x	
Indiana	x		x[a]	x[a]	
Illinois	x		x[a]	x	
Michigan	x	x[b]	x	x	
Wisconsin	x		x[a]	x	painters
West North Central					
Minnesota	x		x	x	painters and steam fitters
Iowa	x			x	
Missouri				x	
North Dakota	x	x[c]	x	x	
South Dakota	x		x	x	
Nebraska	x			x	
Kansas		x		x	
South Atlantic					
Delaware	x	x[c]		x	
Maryland	x	x[d]		x	
District of Columbia	x			x	
Virginia	x	x		x	steam fitters[d]
West Virginia	x				
North Carolina	x	x	x	x	tile[a] heating[a]
South Carolina	x	x		x	
Georgia	x		x[a]	x[a]	tinning[a] steam fitting[a]
Florida	x			x	
East South Central					
Kentucky	x	x		x	
Tennessee	x	x	x	x	
Alabama	x	x		x	
Mississippi	x	x[d]	x[d]	x	sheet metal[d]
West South Central					
Arkansas	x	x		x	
Louisiana	x	x		x	
Oklahoma	x			x	
Texas	x			x	

TABLE 31 (*continued*)

States	Trade or Occupation				
	Architects	Contractors	Electricians	Plumbers	Others
Mountain					
Montana	x	x[c]		x	
Idaho	x	x[c]			
Wyoming					
Colorado	x			x	
New Mexico	x	x			
Arizona	x	x			
Utah	x	x		x	
Nevada					
Pacific					
Washington	x	x[d]	x		
Oregon	x		x	x	
California	x	x	x	x	

Source: Library of Congress, Legislative Reference Section; and National Bureau of Standards, Building and Codes Section.

a. Contractors only.
b. Residential building only.
c. Public contracts only.
d. License tax only.

total expenses for these types of stores can be placed at 28.5 per cent of net sales. As at the wholesale level, such expenses can be charged in their entirety to distribution costs. They indicate a markup over wholesale cost amounting to nearly 40 per cent.

With all of the qualifications discussed, distribution costs of building materials are indicated by the manufacturers' markup (over production cost) of 16 per cent, the wholesalers' markup of 23 per cent, and the retailers' markup of 40 per cent. This represents a total markup over production cost of about 100 per cent. That is, the retail cost to the contractor is about double the cost of production.

No attempt has been made to compare this estimate with distribution expenses in other industries. In view of the complications outlined it is clear that the figures given are subject to considerable qualification and the same difficulties would likely be encountered in other industries. Of even greater importance is the difficulty of interpreting such data for different industries, since relative costs of distribution can be judged only after proper consideration of services rendered. In the construction industry as it is now constituted, the services rendered by the various types of distributors are obviously indispensable in large degree. In other industries they may be either more or less essential, and the extent of the services rendered likewise differs from that provided by distributors of building materials.

Further difficulties arise because of the geographical variations in building materials prices. Manufacturers quote different prices in different localities, which cannot be accounted for by freight charges; they are rather determined by the local competitive situation. Retail markups also vary from locality to locality and for the same reasons.[16]

16. For examples see *Geographical Differentials in Prices of Building Materials,* TNEC Monograph No. 33, Table 29, p. 77 and Table 51, p. 111.

Even if reliable over-all figures for distribution costs were available, they would in fact be typical of nothing at all, so far as individual products are concerned. Nevertheless, while the pattern for individual products would be concealed, it remains true that reliable over-all figures, if they were statistically possible, would make it feasible to appraise the total bill for the distribution costs of materials used in residential construction. Even then, however, the cost of distribution from the standpoint of the ultimate consumer, i.e., the homeowner, would be understated. Operating expenses and profits of the building contractor and the real-estate broker should be included to obtain a complete picture.

APPENDIX E

TABLE 32

TRADES AND CITIES IN WHICH UNION AGREEMENTS PROVIDE SEPARATE WAGE SCALES FOR RESIDENTIAL CONSTRUCTION, JUNE 1, 1940

Asbestos Workers
- Kansas City (Mo.)
- Newark (N. J.)
- Philadelphia

Bricklayers and Hod Carriers
- Philadelphia
- St. Louis

Building Laborers
- Philadelphia
- St. Louis

Carpenters
- Buffalo
- Houston
- Jacksonville
- Milwaukee
- Philadelphia
- Rochester
- St. Louis

Cement Finishers
- Oklahoma City
- Philadelphia

Composition Roofers
- Reading

Electricians
- Atlanta
- Grand Rapids
- Houston
- Indianapolis
- Jackson (Miss.)
- Little Rock
- Louisville
- Milwaukee
- Nashville
- New Orleans
- Philadelphia
- Phoenix
- Reading

Lathers
- Detroit
- Jackson (Miss.)
- New York
- Philadelphia
- Rochester
- St. Louis
- Seattle

Painters
- Columbus (Ohio)
- Grand Rapids
- New Haven
- New Orleans

Paper Hangers
- Grand Rapids

Plasterers and Plasterers' Laborers
- Detroit
- New York
- Philadelphia
- St. Louis

Plumbers and Plumbers' Laborers
- New Orleans
- New York
- Philadelphia
- St. Louis

TABLE 32 (*continued*)

Sheet Metal Workers	Steam Fitters and Helpers
Philadelphia	New Orleans
	New York
Slate and Tile Roofers	Philadelphia
New York	
Philadelphia	Tile Layers and Helpers
Toledo	Philadelphia

Source: Special tabulation by the Bureau of Labor Statistics, Industrial Relations Division. Data are derived from records for 70 selected cities, and hence may not include a few places in which special agreements are in effect.

APPENDIX F

TABLE 33

PROPORTION OF FAMILIES IN 33 CITIES IN LOWER-, MIDDLE-, AND UPPER-INCOME GROUPS, 1929 COMPARED WITH 1933

Annual Income Group	1929			1933		
	(*Number*)	(*Per Cent*)		(*Number*)	(*Per Cent*)	
Total	213,522	100.0		241,207	100.0	
Less than $150	10,271	4.8		23,925	9.9	
$150—$349	8,130	3.8		25,820	10.7	
$350—$549	11,068	5.2	25.1	25,665	10.7	49.6
$550—$749	11,218	5.2		22,575	9.3	
$750—$949	13,031	6.1		21,638	9.0	
$950—$1,149	15,750	7.4		20,847	8.6	
$1,150—$1,349	19,099	8.9		19,396	8.0	
$1,350—$1,549	17,477	8.2	37.8	15,932	6.6	32.7
$1,550—$1,749	11,297	5.2		10,582	4.4	
$1,750—$1,949	17,184	8.1		12,375	5.1	
$1,950—$2,149	15,443	7.3		9,530	3.9	
$2,150—$2,349	6,856	3.2		4,755	2.0	
$2,350—$2,549	13,198	6.2		6,692	2.8	
$2,550—$2,749	4,936	2.3		2,899	1.2	
$2,750—$3,149	11,584	5.4		5,875	2.5	
$3,150—$3,549	5,295	2.5	37.1	2,966	1.2	17.7
$3,550—$3,949	4,650	2.2		2,000	0.8	
$3,950—$4,949	6,572	3.1		3,157	1.4	
$4,950—$5,949	3,611	1.7		1,723	0.7	
$5,950—$6,949	2,181	1.0		944	0.4	
$6,950—$7,949	1,227	0.6		511	0.2	
$7,950 and over	3,444	1.6		1,400	0.6	

Source: David L. Wickens, *Residential Real Estate,* National Bureau of Economic Research, New York, 1941, Table Cl, p. 146. Data are derived from the *Financial Survey of Urban Housing.*

Note: The table shows that in 1933 each income group up to $1,149 comprised a larger proportion of the total number of families than in 1929, while in each income group above $1,149 the proportion declined. However, the 33 cities included in this table are heavily weighted with large ones; and no allowance has been made for differences in the size of the samples. Consequently the percentage figures do not constitute an accurate picture of the level of family income in urban areas. The data should only be interpreted as showing changes in the distribution of families among broad income groups in prosperity and depression. If complete data or a more representative sample were available, the break between proportionate increase and proportionate decrease in families from 1929 to 1933 might have come elsewhere than at the $1,149 income level.

TABLE 34

Dwelling Units for Which Building Permits Were Issued in Six Selected Cities, 1870-1940

Year	Boston	Brooklyn	Manhattan	Detroit	San Antonio	Los Angeles
1870	—	—	7,049	—	—	—
1871	—	—	9,973	—	—	—
1872	2,371	—	6,920	—	—	—
1873	1,662	106	6,539	—	—	—
1874	2,284	1,177	6,205	—	—	—
1875	1,144	[a]	6,307	—	—	—
1876	813	3,065	5,360	—	—	—
1877	676	2,484	4,447	—	—	—
1878	419	2,435	4,488	—	—	—
1879	641	1,944	5,719	454	—	—
1880	632	2,119	9,288	545	—	—
1881	914	2,870	10,364	1,048	—	—
1882	1,015	3,809	9,464	1,401	—	—
1883	1,300	4,971	13,964	1,279	—	—
1884	1,861	6,618	15,828	1,437	—	—
1885	2,449	8,488	16,745	1,402	192	—
1886	2,432	9,212	20,874	1,437	[a]	—
1887	2,860	9,292	22,729	1,704	287	—
1888	3,087	10,320	14,293	1,779	287	—
1889	3,782	11,867	17,182	1,745	503	—
1890	3,624	12,587	15,292	2,021	990	—
1891	3,632	10,208	11,219	1,997	733	—
1892	4,268	11,999	10,856	2,358	689	—
1893	3,605	7,936	7,667	1,873	474	—
1894	3,766	7,911	8,609	1,137	339	—
1895	5,015	6,831	19,376	1,191	288	—
1896	5,145	5,622	9,184	1,054	217	—
1897	5,559	8,220	15,769	1,290	212	—
1898	3,725	7,213	17,110	1,272	175	—
1899	3,700	9,966	29,447	1,278	222	—
1900	2,378	5,939	8,996	1,323	323	—
1901	2,569	7,012	19,745	1,620	629	—
1902	2,165	4,392	5,766	2,200	566	3,821
1903	1,279	7,323	11,356	2,499	578	5,194
1904	1,513	16,456	20,135	2,707	711	5,740
1905	2,304	28,199	34,847	3,321	783	7,007
1906	2,475	27,429	26,058	4,136	904	6,590
1907	2,202	26,395	9,008	4,272	1,268	4,713
1908	2,984	14,134	6,771	3,688	1,718	4,583
1909	4,087	19,778	15,907	4,257	1,580	5,457
1910	3,412	10,074	7,598	5,379	1,163	6,397
1911	5,385	10,531	6,898	6,947	1,219	8,605
1912	5,226	13,395	6,472	8,134	1,440	12,163
1913	3,315	9,820	5,389	10,242	1,263	10,254
1914	3,483	15,224	4,733	8,430	1,033	6,578
1915	4,116	16,676	6,251	10,021	963	4,334
1916	4,013	12,943	6,973	18,284	745	3,900
1917	1,146	4,964	794	8,638	900	3,122
1918	27	2,064	197	1,373	1,068	2,221
1919	509	11,004	2,149	13,002	1,397	5,422

TABLE 34 (*continued*)

Year	Boston	Brooklyn	Manhattan	Detroit	San Antonio	Los Angeles
1920	320	3,917	22	6,266	1,054	10,986
1921	878	16,636	4,837	6,266	1,718	19,572
1922	3,434	32,234	8,389	16,813	1,654	28,033
1923	3,577	43,289	11,808	22,764	1,587	43,842
1924	4,682	33,609	11,384	25,752	1,913	29,894
1925	5,940	40,727	12,009	26,173	1,873	22,072
1926	3,882	45,663	11,910	26,421	1,964	20,017
1927	5,316	33,172	9,502	15,614	2,171	11,801
1928	6,805	28,938	15,983	15,929	2,784	21,081
1929	2,583	7,758	8,684	12,198	2,233	15,185
1930	1,353	8,346	7,846	3,989	950	11,469
1931	1,338	8,541	1,835	2,131	667	6,645
1932	311	1,198	471	308	334	2,810
1933	306	984	1,598	263	228	2,392
1934	156	2,127	395	407	160	1,726
1935	147	5,491	917	1,663	367	4,019
1936	213	4,991	2,574	4,452	620	8,852
1937	486	5,828	3,886	4,264	549	9,736
1938	356	6,583	2,918	6,763	619	12,437
1939	304	7,598	3,698	8,992	962	15,570
1940	4,971	9,306	4,172	24,815	7,441	40,108

Source: Bureau of Labor Statistics, Building Permit Survey. Special tabulation made for The Twentieth Century Fund.

a. Data not available.

1. THE RELATION OF NEW BUILDING AND DEPRECIATION TO THE TOTAL SUPPLY

Data showing the approximate annual building rate in the nonfarm areas on several bases are presented in Table 35 below. Table 36 shows for the 1930-1940 decade the building rate by price classes, the value changes which occurred in the housing supply and the relation between old and new houses in the 1940 supply by price classes; it also attempts to indicate what would have occurred had more houses been built during the decade and had they been distributed differently.

In determining the annual building rate over an extended period of time, it is necessary to know the volume of building over the period, and the number of units standing at either the beginning or end of that period. Thus, from 1900 to 1939, a total of 18,645,000 new and converted dwelling units were provided in the nonfarm area, an average of about 465,000 units per year. Related to the number of units standing at the beginning of the period this indicates a building rate of about 4.4 per cent. In terms of the number standing at the end of the period, however, the indicated rate is only 1.6 per cent. The spread between these two rates, either of which appears applicable, is such that a more refined method of measurement is needed. Ideally, this would be in the form of an average annual building rate in which the number of units built in each year would be related to the number standing at the beginning of that year, and then averaged. Lacking such information, it is still possible to secure a better over-all rate by computing an average of decade rates. This involves determining the number of units built and converted during each decade, and the number standing at the end of each decade. Data for the number of new units built and converted in each decade are those discussed in Appendix C, 1. The number standing at the beginning and end of each decade was derived by projecting backwards the number of nonfarm dwelling units reported by the 1940 Census of Housing. Thus, 29,706,000 units were standing in 1940. A total of 3,459,000 new and converted units were built from 1930 to 1939,

TABLE 35

ANNUAL BUILDING RATES IN NONFARM AREAS, 1900-1939

Item	1900-1909	1910-1919	1920-1929	1930-1939	Averages 1900-1939
			(Thousands of Units)		
Number of units standing, beginning of decade[a]	11,797	15,533	19,112	25,692	
New units built during decade	3,952	3,890	7,035	2,734[b]	
Converted units built during decade	81 } 4,033	103 } 3,993	125 } 7,160	725[b]	} 4,411
Makeshift units provided during decade	—	—	—	952[b, c]	
Units demolished during decade	297	414	580	397[b]	
Number of units standing, end of decade[a]	15,533	19,112	25,692	29,706[d]	
			(Average Annual Percentages[e])		
Units added per year, as percentage of number at beginning of decade	3.4	2.6	3.7	1.4	2.6
Units added per year, as percentage of number at end of decade	2.6	2.1	2.8	1.2	2.1
Units added per year, as percentage of average standing during decade	3.0	2.3	3.2	1.3	2.3

Source: Based on Census of Housing: 1940; "Housing and the Increase in Population," *Monthly Labor Review,* April 1942; and David L. Wickens, *Residential Real Estate,* National Bureau of Economic Research, New York, 1941.

a. Derived by projecting backwards the number of nonfarm dwelling units reported by the 1940 Census of Housing. Thus, 29,706,000 units were standing in 1940. According to the BLS, a total of 3,459,000 new and converted units were built from 1930 to 1939 (see Appendix F, 1), and according to the same report, 952,000 makeshift units were added, and 397,000 units were demolished. The total standing in 1930 was thus 25,692,000. For earlier decades the same procedure was followed, using data for new and converted units and demolitions as reported in *Residential Real Estate,* Table EM5, p. 54.

b. Estimated by BLS.

c. Included with "New units built" in earlier decades; *excluded* from annual percentages here shown. If included, annual percentages are increased as follows: units added to number in 1930, 1.7 per cent; units added to number in 1939, 1.5 per cent; units added to average of number in 1930 and in 1939, 1.6 per cent.

d. 1940 Census of Housing, preliminary estimate.

e. The indicated computations are here given on an annual basis. Thus, new and converted units added during 1900-1909 totaled 4,033,000, or 403,300 per year. This amounted to 3.4 per cent of the units standing at the beginning of the period.

and in addition, 952,000 families found accommodations in makeshift quarters. Also, 397,000 units were demolished. Combining these figures and deducting them from the 1940 total gives a total of 25,692,000 units standing in 1930. The same procedure was followed for earlier decades.

In the last three lines of Table 35, the final computations are shown. For each decade, new and converted units were reduced to an annual basis and stated as a percentage of (a) the number standing at the beginning of the decade, (b) the number standing at the end of the decade, and (c) the average number standing during the decade, i.e., the average of those at the beginning and at the end of the decade. Averages of the rates for the four decades are also given.

Table 36, Section A, below, estimates the relation between new and existing urban dwellings during the 1930-1940 decade by price classes. It also estimates the amount of filtering down which occurred during the decade. William K. Wittausch of the Federal Housing Administration has made similar computations for nonfarm dwellings during the 1900-1940 period.[1] Because his computations were made before 1940 Census data became available, and because of the paucity of information for the first three decades of this century, they are valuable chiefly because of "the methods and relationships applied" rather than because of "the absolute figures derived therefrom." [2]

The computations set forth in Table 36 have utilized the method developed by Wittausch. Greater accuracy has been achieved by using the newly available 1940 Census data and by confining the calculations to urban dwellings and to the last decade. Two major steps are involved: (1) the distribution by rent-value classes of all urban dwelling units in 1930 and 1940 (columns 1 and 8), and (2) a corresponding distribution of the number of new and converted units built in the period 1930-1939 (columns 2 and 3).[3] The balance of the calculations are derived from these steps. Thus in the

1. See "Used Homes in the Low Cost Housing Market," *The Journal of Land & Public Utility Economics,* August 1942.

2. *Ibid.*

3. The distribution by rent-value classes of all dwelling units in 1930 is on the basis of 1930 Census data for families. The distribution of families is taken to represent the distribution of occupied dwelling units, and vacant units are distributed in proportion. Monthly rentals on tenant-occupied units are assumed to equal one per cent of the value of owner-occupied houses.

The distribution of 1940 dwelling units is 1940 Census data of contract rents for all tenant-occupied units, estimated rents for vacant units and rental equivalents of the value of owner-occupied units.

The number of new units, net conversions and makeshift dwellings added as well as the number of units demolished during the decade are derived from "Housing and the Increase in Population," *Monthly Labor Review,* Vol. 54, No. 4, April 1942, p. 880, Table 2.

The distribution of new units built is on the basis of a special Bureau of Labor Statistics building permit survey covering operations in a large number of cities in 1938. This distribution is slightly different from that shown in Table 17 of Appendix C, 5. As explained in that appendix, building permit values in 72 cities were connected to selling prices in each of three regions (North, South, and West) and cities in two size groups (over 100,000 population and under 100,000 population). For each of these six groups of cities, frequency distributions of selling prices were determined. These in turn were combined to obtain a total distribution for the 72 cities. Here, however, the frequency distributions for each of the six groups of cities were weighted, according to the 1938 volume of building in all urban places, in order to obtain a frequency distribution of selling prices for all urban areas rather than for just 72 cities.

Lacking data, net conversions are distributed in the same way as new construction, while demolitions are all taken out of the lowest price class and makeshift dwellings placed there. The error involved, however, in placing too many conversions at the top of the price scale is partly offset by placing all demolitions at the bottom.

TABLE 36

Effect of New Building and Depreciation on the Urban Housing Supply and Under Assumed Conditions as to the Quality and Quantity of New Houses Built, 1930-1940

(Thousands of Dwelling Units)

A. Changes in the Urban Housing Supply in the Decade 1930-1940

	1	2	3	4	5	6	7	8
					Depreciation of Existing Houses			
Rent-Value Group [a]	Dwelling Units Standing 1930 [b]	New Units Added 1930-1939 [c]	Net Conversions 1930-1939 [d]	Makeshift Dwellings Added 1930-1939	Added	Deducted [e]	Change in Number of Dwelling Units 1930-1939	Dwelling Units Standing 1940
Total	18,984	1,735	650	595	—	—	+2,632	21,616
$50 and over	7,081	1,046	392	—	—	5,517	—4,079	3,002
$30-$50	5,316	408	153	—	5,517	4,786	+1,292	6,608
$20-$30	3,227	116	43	—	4,786	2,706	+2,239	5,466
Under $20	3,360	165	62	595	2,706	348 [g]	+3,180	6,540

B. Greater Production, Same Distribution of New Supply

	1	2	3	4	5	6	7	8
Total	18,984	5,613	650	595 [f]	—	—	+2,632	21,616
$50 and over	7,081	3,385	392	—	—	7,856	—4,079	3,002
$30-$50	5,316	1,319	153	—	7,856	8,036	+1,292	6,608
$20-$30	3,227	376	43	—	8,036	6,216	+2,239	5,466
Under $20	3,360	533	62	595 [f]	6,216	4,226 [g]	+3,180	6,540

C. Greater Production, Redistribution of New Supply

Total	18,984	5,613	650	595[f]	—	—	+2,632	21,616
$50 and over	7,081	376	44	—	—	4,499	−4,079	3,002
$30–$50	5,316	779	90	—	4,499	4,076	+1,292	6,608
$20-$30	3,227	1,260	146	—	4,076	3,243	+2,239	5,466
Under $20	3,360	3,198	370	595[f]	3,243	4,226[g]	+3,180	6,540

a. Owner-occupied units converted to rent equivalent on assumption of 100 to 1 relationship between value and monthly rent.

b. Total dwelling units standing plus net reclassifications and annexations into the urban area between 1930 and 1939, distributed according to the census distribution of occupied units.

c. Distributed in accordance with a special Bureau of Labor Statistics study of selling prices of one-family houses in 72 cities in 1938.

d. Distributed in the same manner as new units.

e. The difference between column 8 and the sum of columns 1 to 5 inclusive.

f. Since under this assumption there would probably be no makeshift dwellings, the 595,000 such units should be added to the number of new units in the lowest rent-value group.

g. Demolitions.

$50-and-over class, 1,438,000 new and converted units were added to the 7,081,000 existing in 1930, making a total of 8,519,000; but since only 3,002,000 units remained in that price class in 1940, the balance or 5,517,000 units must have declined in value. It is assumed that these moved down to the next lowest price group. They are then added to the 5,316,000 houses existing in the $30-$50 group in 1930 and the 561,000 new and converted units added, and the whole is then subtracted from the 6,608,000 dwellings standing in that price class in 1940. The derivative, 4,786,000 units, is then added to the next lowest price class. And so on, until the derivative in the lowest price class is assumed to be demolished.

Sections B and C of Table 36 are derived from assuming certain conditions as to the number of new units built and the rent-value classes in which they are built. Section B purports to show what would have happened in the 1930-1940 decade to the depreciation pattern and to the distribution between old and new dwellings by price classes had as many houses been produced as in the twenties. Section C indicates what would have happened had production been both increased and redistributed so as to place the bulk of new construction in the lowest price class.

TABLE 37

INDEXES OF PERMITS ISSUED FOR RESIDENTIAL AND NONRESIDENTIAL CONSTRUCTION, 1856-1936

Year	Number of Cities	Index of Residential Units	Index of Nonresidential Buildings [a]
		(1920–1930 = 100)	
1856	1	23	16
1857	1	19	16
1858	1	19	12
1859	1	25	16
1860	1	30	12
1861	1	22	4
1862	1	32	12
1863	2	31	23
1864	2	16	16
1865	2	22	23
1866	2	31	28
1867	2	44	26
1868	2	56	26
1869	2	66	26
1870	2	64	26
1871	2	78	26
1872	2	58	37
1873	3	58	26
1874	4	41	13
1875	5	41	12
1876	5	34	12
1877	5	37	9
1878	6	26	10
1879	7	23	12

TABLE 37 (*continued*)

Year	Number of Cities	Index of Residential Units	Index of Nonresidential Buildings [a]
1880	8	19	8
1881	9	27	9
1882	9	30	9
1883	10	37	10
1884	10	42	11
1885	10	53	12
1886	10	60	12
1887	12	64	15
1888	12	61	14
1889	12	74	16
1890	12	70	15
1891	13	56	13
1892	13	65	16
1893	13	50	12
1894	13	46	13
1895	13	56	13
1896	17	49	13
1897	17	55	11
1898	20	36	10
1899	21	38	11
1900	21	28	9
1901	22	36	13
1902	22	33	14
1903	22	36	16
1904	22	48	17
1905	22	66	20
1906	23	72	21
1907	24	65	21
1908	26	60	19
1909	26	79	20
1910	27	72	28
1911	28	71	29
1912	29	66	29
1913	29	60	28
1914	29	61	29
1915	29	69	34
1916	29	69	41
1917	29	34	36
1918	29	14	32
1919	29	65	70
1920	29	37	75
1921	29	75	83
1922	29	123	103
1923	29	143	121
1924	29	149	129
1925	29	164	128
1926	29	133	122
1927	29	101	106

TABLE 37 (*continued*)

Year	Number of Cities	Index of Residential Units	Index of Nonresidential Buildings [a]
1928	29	87	93
1929	29	54	80
1930	29	32	60
1931	29	31	52
1932	29	10	29
1933	29	7	22
1934	29	7	23
1935	29	18	28
1936	29	32	35

Source: Clarence D. Long, Jr., *Building Cycles and the Theory of Investment,* Princeton University Press, Princeton, 1940, Appendix B, Section 3, pp. 228-229.

a. Philadelphia data, 1887-1912, excluded because of excessive number of miscellaneous structures.

1. Philadelphia.
2. Includes Philadelphia, Manhattan and Bronx.
3. Boston added.
4. Brooklyn added.
5. Washington added (wards 23 and 24 of Bronx added).
6. Newark added.
7. Salem added.
8. Detroit added.
9. New Haven added.
10. Providence added.
12. Minneapolis and Cambridge added.
13. Indianapolis added.
17. Bridgeport, Atlanta, Louisville and Waltham added (remainder of Bronx annexed in 1895).
20. Watertown, Queens and Richmond Boroughs added.
21. New Bedford added.
22. Baltimore added.
23. Rochester added.
24. Portland added.
26. Cleveland and Richmond, Va., added.
27. St. Louis added.
28. Springfield added.
29. Kansas City added.

Note: The indexes are derived from link relatives in order to compensate for the increase in the number of cities over the index period. For identical cities, year-to-year relatives are first computed, i.e., the percentage change from a given year to the next year. These percentage changes are then linked together by successive multiplication to obtain the indexes.

2. Multiple Determinants of the Volume of Residential Building Activity

The measurement of the combined influence of several factors on the volume of residential building has been attempted by several authorities. It is here intended to review briefly some of their work and compare the results, in so far as this is possible.

The general method used is that of multiple correlation wherein the several determinants or independent variables, such as rents, family incomes, family formation, etc., are combined mathematically in such a manner as to produce a theoretical curve for residential building. This theoretical curve is then compared with the actual volume of residential building year by year in order to discover the extent to which the selected independent variables operate as determinants in the volume of residential building.

Maximum or perfect correlation would require that the theoretical and actual building curves be identical. In that event, the *coefficient of multiple correlation* would, in statistical terminology, be 1.0. Deviations between the two curves would be measured on the scale of 0 to 1.0. The theoretical curve, as here conceived, is comprised of several independent variables, such as rents, costs, incomes, etc. Each of these may be compared with the curve of actual building, and, as in the determination of multiple relationships, the individual coefficients of correlation can be calculated. By means of a mathe-

TABLE 38

SALES OF ONE-FAMILY DETACHED HOUSES IN LUCAS COUNTY (TOLEDO), OHIO, CLASSIFIED BY AGE OF HOUSE AT TIME OF SALE, 1917–1938

(*Annual Average of Number of Sales in Periods Specified*)

Age at Time of Sale	War	Post-War	Depres-sion	Boom	Decline	Depres-sion	Recovery
Years	1917-1918	1919-1920	1921	1922-1928	1929-1930	1931-1935	1936-1938
			(*Number of Sales*)				
Total	2,956	5,475	3,487	5,137	3,942	1,765	3,255
New [a]	675	630	622	1,614	912	195	401
1–4	594	1,276	656	857	875	160	95
5–9	430	871	543	695	545	423	419
10–19	532	1,244	706	769	650	449	1,070
20–29	423	824	535	604	384	208	482
30–39	179	407	267	373	283	175	365
40 and over	123	223	158	225	293	155	423
			(*Percentage Distribution*)				
Total	100.0	100.0	100.0	100.0	100.0	100.0	100.0
New [a]	22.8	11.5	17.8	31.4	23.1	11.0	12.3
1–4	20.1	23.3	18.8	16.6	22.2	9.1	2.9
5–9	14.5	15.9	15.6	13.5	13.8	24.0	12.9
10–19	18.0	22.7	20.3	15.0	16.5	25.4	32.9
20–29	14.3	15.1	15.3	11.8	9.7	11.8	14.8
30–39	6.1	7.4	7.7	7.3	7.2	9.9	11.2
40 and over	4.2	4.1	4.5	4.4	7.5	8.8	13.0

Source: William Hoad, *Real Estate Prices* (unpublished doctoral dissertation submitted to the University of Michigan, 1942). Data are based on all transfer records available, covering bona fide transfers in the period 1917–1938, of 50 per cent of the one-family detached houses standing in Lucas County, Ohio, in 1938.

a. Includes houses purchased new and houses built on contract.

Note: Annual average sales are derived by weighting annual sales by the number of houses standing at the end of each year in the period.

TABLE 39

Annual Sales of New and Old One-Family Detached Houses in Lucas County (Toledo), Ohio, Classified by Age of House at Time of Sale, 1917–1938

(Number of Units)

Year	Total Stock	Total Sales	New Houses a	Old Houses, Age in Years at Time of Sale: Total	1-4	5-9	10-19	20-29	30-39	40 and Over
1917	32,416	2,883	770	2,113	479	387	551	401	180	115
1918	32,745	2,848	400	2,448	708	474	513	445	177	131
1919	33,349	5,260	675	4,585	1,178	830	1,187	828	373	189
1920	33,845	5,690	586	5,104	1,374	913	1,300	820	440	257
1921	34,377	3,487	622	2,865	656	543	706	535	267	158
1922	35,314	4,439	1,027	3,412	548	759	818	737	358	192
1923	36,647	5,461	1,423	4,038	838	821	973	741	424	241
1924	38,140	5,507	1,583	3,924	903	822	848	738	395	218
1925	39,833	5,000	1,783	3,217	806	653	705	577	311	165
1926	41,587	5,058	1,844	3,214	1,007	543	680	501	345	138
1927	43,515	5,324	2,018	3,306	837	597	689	458	396	329
1928	45,050	5,169	1,625	3,544	1,060	672	669	473	380	290
1929	46,190	4,487	1,234	3,253	940	541	740	415	334	283
1930	46,619	3,398	591	2,807	809	549	561	353	232	303
1931	46,816	2,078	393	1,686	350	420	442	214	129	131
1932	46,793	1,355	179	1,176	208	324	264	120	151	109
1933	46,685	1,484	98	1,386	128	396	385	173	167	137
1934	46,569	1,807	120	1,687	69	509	541	213	204	151
1935	46,618	2,098	185	1,913	45	464	612	321	223	248
1936	46,817	3,137	314	2,823	55	732	979	442	352	263
1937	47,215	4,024	526	3,498	111	402	1,344	607	433	601
1938	47,494	2,603	363	2,240	118	123	888	396	311	404

Source: William Hoad, *op. cit.* Data are based on all transfer records available, covering bona fide transfers in the period 1917-1938, of 50 per cent of the one-family detached houses standing in Lucas County, Ohio, in 1938.

a. Includes houses purchased new and houses built on contract.

TABLE 40

Annual Number of Families Added in Nonfarm Areas, 1900–1939

(In Thousands)

Year	Families Added	Year	Families Added	Year	Families Added
1900	272	1914	475	1928	419
1901	289	1915	451	1929	474
1902	373	1916	496	1930	306
1903	394	1917	532	1931	234
1904	334	1918	294	1932	112
1905	407	1919	498	1933	380
1906	488	1920	612	1934	553
1907	530	1921	561	1935	551
1908	329	1922	582	1936	572
1909	477	1923	630	1937	585
1910	406	1924	515	1938	456
1911	388	1925	529	1939	520
1912	436	1926	542		
1913	500	1927	465		

Source: Housing—The Continuing Problem, National Resources Planning Board, December 1940, Table I, p. 22. Since publication therein, considerable revision has been made by the compilers. These changes are here incorporated.

matical process, these individual coefficients in effect become the weights applied to the individual independent variables in the computation of the coefficient of multiple correlation. Thus, if rents and building have a higher degree of correlation than do costs and building, then rent will receive a greater weight in the calculation of the coefficient of multiple correlation.

According to Chawner's development [4] the economic conditions (independent variables) which, during the period 1914-1937, appeared to have influenced the volume of building are indicated by:

(1) A series measuring conditions in the market for existing units. This is derived by taking the product of the occupancy ratio (ratio of total nonfarm families to total available nonfarm dwelling units) and an index of rent changes for the annual period immediately preceding by three months that shown for the number of units built.

(2) A measure of the number of families added during the year immediately preceding that shown for the number of units built.

(3) A measure of the ratio of income per family to cost of ownership (interest rate plus taxes, weighted and multiplied by building costs) for the annual period immediately preceding by three months that shown for the number of units built.

The theoretical building curve derived from these three independent variables follows very closely the actual residential building curve. The coefficient of multiple correlation between the two curves is 0.96, indicating in statistical terminology that the three independent variables taken in combination account for 93 per cent of the variation (coefficient of multiple correlation squared) in the number of units started annually over the period 1914-1937, which is the time interval covered by the data.

As explained above, the relative importance of the several independent variables is indicated by the closeness with which they are individually correlated with the volume of building. Their relative importance in turn determines the weight which each receives in the determination of the coefficient of multiple correlation. In the Chawner calculations, the series representing the ratio of income per family to costs of ownership is found to be more closely correlated with actual building than are either of the other two series; hence, it is of greater importance in the determination of the volume of building than either market conditions (item 1 above) or family formation (item 2 above). Stated as simply as possible, this means that, of the *factors considered,* it was found that the relation of income to cost of ownership is the most important determinant in the volume of building—or, that nothing is quite so favorable to building as an increase in this ratio (incomes increasing more rapidly than costs, or costs declining more rapidly than incomes). But, the calculations also indicate that conditions in the market are almost as important. In other words, rents and vacancies exert nearly as much influence as the income-cost relationship.[5]

Family formation appears to be considerably less important than either of the other two determinants. It may be pointed out that not only is it less important, but it may also to some extent be an intermediate reflection of the trend in income. Thus, it can be said that changes in the number of new families added each year have a certain effect on the volume of building, as pointed out in the text, but it must be recognized that the formation of families is to a great extent dependent upon the level of income. As sug-

4. Lowell J. Chawner, "The Residential Building Process," *Housing—The Continuing Problem,* National Resources Planning Board, December 1940, pp. 30-31.

5. *Ibid.,* p. 31.

gested later, a similar interrelationship probably also exists between income on the one hand and rents and vacancies on the other. The full importance of income consequently is only partly reflected, some of its influence being measured by changes in the rate of net family formation and changes in rents.

Derksen in his analysis finds residential building most closely correlated with rents, which have about twice the influence of costs.[6] This is not necessarily contrary to Chawner's conclusion, although variations in basic data used and in the manner in which they were combined make it impossible to say to what extent the two writers are in agreement. Derksen places rents as the most important determinant, by a wide margin—Chawner, as it will be recalled, places rents multiplied by the occupancy ratio in second position, but by a narrow margin only. Derksen omits both interest rates and the occupancy ratio from his calculations and this may partly account for the difference in results. Also, he evaluates family incomes and construction costs separately; in a ratio, they might assume an importance more nearly comparable to that suggested by the Chawner calculations.

In the Derksen computations, as well as in those of Chawner, the importance of family income is only in part shown directly. Independently it is only about one third as important as rents. But the level of rent is to a considerable extent a function of family income, i.e., Derksen shows that the most important determinant in the level of rent is the ratio of the number of families to the number of dwelling units.[7] As already suggested, the level of income has a considerable influence on family formation. Furthermore, Derksen's second most important independent variable is family income. With these considerations, the level of family income, as in the analysis of the Chawner calculations, assumes much greater importance in the determination of the volume of building than its direct measurement indicates.

The multiple correlation technique as used here has certain limitations forced on it by the multiplicity of the factors involved and by the limitations to the data themselves both with respect to their accuracy and to the extent to which they represent a random sample. There is always the possibility that new factors may be inroduced. Such new factors, of course, in no way invalidate conclusions reached as regards past experience; rather, they represent one of the imponderables which must be contended with in attempting to forecast the volume of building. Also, the independent variables must be selected on a purely a priori basis. Actually it is only *assumed* that the independent variables are determinants in the volume of building. The assumptions being made, the correlation technique can only show the net result of the combined fluctuations of these variables, and the relative importance of these variables to each other.

It is not intended to detail here the limitations inherent in the data themselves. Most of the independent variables which investigators must use are crude, and even the data on the number of dwelling units built are subject to a considerable margin of error. For all of the series such errors become progressively larger the further back the data are extended. Finally, the successful use of the correlation technique presupposes the use of a random sample. In many fields of investigation the analyst can *select* a sample. If, for example, he wishes to determine the effect of temperature, moisture and

6. J. B. D. Derksen, "Long Cycles in Residential Building," *Econometria,* Vol. 8, No. 2, University of Chicago Press, April 1940, pp. 97-116. Data used cover the period 1914-1938.

7. Earlier calculations by Chawner, *op. cit.,* pp. 25-26, and by J. Tinbergen, *Statistical Testing of Business-Cycle Theories,* Vol. II, League of Nations, Geneva, 1939, p. 56, show the same results.

the quantity of fertilizer used on the yield of corn, he can take a random sample of yields, and for each item in the sample he can obtain information as to each of the three independent variables. Moreover, he may be able to vary the size of the sample. In a time-series analysis, such as residential building, the "sample" comprises the experience in each of the years for which data are available. It can never be known whether all of these years taken together represent a random sample of years. The best that can be said is that in both of the cases examined here they cover slightly more than a complete building cycle, i.e., 1914-1937.

TABLE 41

COST OF LIVING COMPARED WITH AVERAGE RENTS, 1914-1941

(Monthly Average 1923 = 100)

Year	Combined Index of Cost of Living	Rent	Year	Combined Index of Cost of Living	Rent
1914	61.3 [a]	57.7 [a]	1928	100.6	93.7
1915	61.0 [a]	57.7 [a]	1929	100.1	92.0
1916	65.4 [a]	58.6 [a]	1930	96.7	89.5
1917	77.6 [a]	60.6 [a]	1931	87.2	82.4
1918	94.2 [b]	67.9 [b]	1932	77.9	72.4
1919	102.3 [c]	74.7 [c]	1933	74.9	63.8
1920	118.2	89.2	1934	79.4	64.8
1921	102.3	97.7	1935	82.2	70.3
1922	97.4	95.9	1936	84.1	77.9
1923	100.0	100.0	1937	87.8	86.5
1924	101.3	106.3	1938	85.7	87.0
1925	103.7	104.1	1939	84.5	86.3
1926	104.3	101.3	1940	87.0	86.9
1927	102.0	97.8	1941	89.0	88.5

Source: Compiled by National Industrial Conference Board and republished in *Survey of Current Business,* 1940 Supplement, p. 11, issue of January 1941, p. 18, and subsequent monthly issues. Annual indexes shown are averages of monthly figures, except as indicated in footnotes below.

a. Indexes are for month of July only.

b. Indexes are averages of the two months, June and November.

c. Indexes are averages of the three months, March, July and November.

APPENDIX G

TABLE 42

AVERAGE SETTLEMENT CHARGES COMPARED WITH PROPERTY VALUATION, NEW SINGLE-FAMILY HOUSES INSURED BY FEDERAL HOUSING ADMINISTRATION SEPTEMBER-DECEMBER, 1939

Property Value Classes	Settlement Charges	Charges as Per Cent of Value
All Classes	$124.57	2.31
Under $3,000	82.23	3.12
$3,000–$3,999	99.52	2.83
$4,000–$4,999	110.37	2.49
$5,000–$5,999	118.96	2.21
$6,000–$6,999	133.91	2.13
$7,000–$7,999	157.65	2.15
$8,000–$9,999	184.66	2.13
$10,000–$14,999	248.29	2.17
$15,000 and over	359.78	1.95

Source: Division of Research and Statistics, Federal Housing Administration.

Note: Data are based on a sample of single-family houses securing 6,000 mortgages insured by FHA. Depending on the situation in each case, closing charges as given here may include any or all of the following items: FHA appraisal fee, mortgagee's appraisal fee, cost of title search, title insurance, cost of abstracting, survey charges, attorney's charges, recording and filing fees, revenue stamps, initial service charge, photograph and credit report and notary fees.

APPENDIX H

TABLE 43

TREND OF HOME OWNERSHIP IN SELECTED TYPES OF CITIES, 1900-1940
(*In Per Cent of Dwellings Owned*)

	Six Large Cities			
Year	Total	Three "Old"[a]	Three "New"[b]	Six Small Cities[c]
1900	18.8	15.2	28.0	45.4
1910	20.1	15.5	30.7	45.1
1920	23.1	19.0	30.7	45.5
1930	30.3	27.0	35.3	51.7
1940	24.3	20.4	30.2	44.7

Source: 1940 Census of Housing, preliminary data, and Decennial Census of Population for years indicated.

a. New York City, Philadelphia, and Boston.

b. Chicago, Detroit and Los Angeles.

c. Lafayette, Indiana; Cumberland, Maryland; Attleboro, Massachusetts; Adrian, Michigan; Laconia, New Hampshire; and Alameda, California.

TABLE 44

RATIO OF 1940 TAXES TO AVERAGE ORIGINAL LOANS MADE BY HOME OWNERS' LOAN CORPORATION ON 400,000 PROPERTIES

Less than 1 Per Cent	1–2 Per Cent	2–3 Per Cent	3–4 Per Cent	4–5 Per Cent	5–6 Per Cent
Louisiana	Alabama	Illinois	Arizona	Colorado	New Jersey
	Arkansas	Iowa	California	Maine	
	Delaware	Kansas	Connecticut	Massachusetts	
	District of Columbia	Michigan	Idaho	Montana	
	Florida	Nebraska	Maryland	New Hampshire	
	Georgia	New Mexico	Minnesota	New York	
	Indiana	North Carolina	Nevada	Vermont	
	Kentucky	Ohio	North Dakota		
	Mississippi	Oregon	Pennsylvania		
	Missouri	South Carolina	Rhode Island		
	Oklahoma	Texas	South Dakota		
	Tennessee	Utah	Wisconsin		
	Virginia	Wyoming			
	Washington				
	West Virginia				

Source: Federal Home Loan Bank Review, July 1941, Table 2, p. 336.

TABLE 45

RELATION BETWEEN ANNUAL INCOME AND PROPERTY TAXES FOR A GROUP OF FEDERAL HOUSING ADMINISTRATION RENTAL PROJECTS, 1939-1940

Location	Annual Income		Property Taxes		
	Potential[a]	Actual	Total Amount	Per Cent of Potential Income	Per Cent of Actual Income
District of Columbia					
Washington	$231,488	$255,569	$22,790	10	9
Washington	118,652	141,544	13,096	11	9
Florida					
Miami Beach	66,096	39,829	8,957	14	22
Georgia					
Atlanta	90,223	86,014	11,000	12	13
Illinois					
Chicago	131,047	142,842	16,101	12	11
Indiana					
Indianapolis	39,075	43,572	4,273	11	10
Indianapolis	25,101	27,014	2,165	9	8
Indianapolis	46,030	41,579	2,927	6	7
Maryland					
Annapolis	41,520	22,171	5,484	13	25
Baltimore	223,930	249,887	31,986	14	13
Dundalk	121,617	143,520	10,931	9	8
Silver Springs	170,340	221,228	15,819	9	7
Silver Springs	135,226	153,117	9,977	7	6
Minnesota					
Minneapolis	29,883	29,700	6,535	22	22
New Jersey					
Tenafly	32,702	26,840	3,989	12	15
New York					
Bronx (borough)	33,048	32,294	3,426	10	11
Brooklyn (borough)	—	51,879	18,996	—	37
Greensburgh	55,550	53,147	6,356	12	12
Jackson Heights	136,325	131,653	22,413	16	17
Yonkers	151,550	116,187	20,156	13	17
North Carolina					
Charlotte	44,086	41,408	4,012	9	10
Durham	75,330	64,307	7,936	11	12
Greensboro	51,192	55,021	4,996	10	9
Raleigh	84,488	89,390	8,860	11	10
Raleigh	85,230	89,403	9,923	13	11
Winston-Salem	64,966	59,725	5,310	8	9
Pennsylvania					
Mount Penn	30,000	28,522	2,046	7	7
York	26,085	23,419	3,114	12	13
Texas					
Dallas	48,556	38,357	6,703	14	17
Houston	78,570	71,652	9,257	12	13
Virginia					
Arlington	306,020[b]	321,674	21,525	7	7
Arlington	53,940[b]	56,119	3,595	7	6
Arlington	109,536[b]	184,016	10,831	10	6
Arlington	120,700[b]	122,504	6,839	6	6
Arlington	173,232[b]	174,310	8,887	5	5
Newport News	54,924	55,562	2,708	5	5

TABLE 45 (*continued*)

Location	Annual Income		Property Taxes		
	Potential [a]	Actual	Total Amount	Per Cent of Potential Income	Per Cent of Actual Income
Norfolk	$97,825	$105,419	$11,926	12	11
Richmond	93,504	81,462	11,021	12	14
Washington					
Seattle	167,157	157,159	19,540	12	12

Source: Federal Housing Administration, Rental Housing Division.

a. Based on 90 per cent occupancy.

b. Based on 100 per cent occupancy.

TABLE 46

AVERAGE TIME REQUIRED TO COMPLETE FORECLOSURE COMPARED WITH AVERAGE FORECLOSURE COSTS, HOME OWNERS' LOAN CORPORATION EXPERIENCE [a]

State	Average Time Months	Average Time Days	Average Cost	State	Average Time Months	Average Time Days	Average Cost
Alabama	25	3	$47.95	Montana	15	2	$161.74
Arizona	8	27	202.38	Nebraska	5	26	112.19
Arkansas	5	4	123.18	Nevada	15	12	223.01
California	14	26	161.34	New Hampshire	1	27	70.82
Colorado	7	18	102.65	New Jersey	4	21	222.29
Connecticut	4	4	111.00	New Mexico	13	0	175.38
Delaware	3	12	120.93	New York	3	17	312.54
District of Columbia	1	3	68.75	North Carolina	1	16	64.07
				North Dakota	16	4	114.94
Florida	3	22	158.16	Ohio	3	24	125.46
Georgia	0	27	56.70	Oklahoma	9	20	139.93
Idaho	15	1	170.98	Oregon	15	10	130.37
Illinois	19	16	354.30	Pennsylvania	1	19	158.27
Indiana	14	0	185.61	Rhode Island	2	10	44.72
Iowa	15	14	129.35	South Carolina	2	28	123.25
Kansas	11	14	90.88	South Dakota	13	25	70.84
Kentucky	6	3	149.23	Tennessee	1	11	77.51
Louisiana	4	11	125.23	Texas	0	22	5.18
Maine	12	25	21.32	Utah	14	23	158.33
Maryland	1	11	157.56	Vermont	8	27	97.14
Massachusetts	2	6	29.08	Virginia	0	8	94.48
Michigan	15	1	90.52	Washington	16	6	134.40
Minnesota	13	25	96.11	West Virginia	1	6	56.93
Mississippi	1	24	58.81	Wisconsin	16	0	169.94
Missouri	1	16	44.83	Wyoming	15	1	174.11

Source: Federal Home Loan Bank Review, November 1937, Table 1, p. 42 and Table 2, p. 45.

a. Data are based on as near 100 foreclosures as possible for each state, which were taken as representative of experience in 1937.

TABLE 47

MORTGAGES OUTSTANDING ON NONFARM 1-4-FAMILY DWELLINGS, CLASSIFIED BY TYPE OF LENDER, 1925-1940

(In Millions)

Year	Total	Savings and Loan Associations	Insurance Companies	Mutual Savings Banks	Commercial Banks and Trust Companies	Individuals and Others	Home Owners' Loan Corporation
1925	$13,216	$4,204	$837	$2,375	$800	$5,000	—
1926	15,272	4,810	1,062	2,650	1,250	5,500	—
1927	17,492	5,488	1,254	2,900	1,850	6,000	—
1928	19,605	6,060	1,445	3,125	2,375	6,600	—
1929	21,058	6,507	1,626	3,225	2,500	7,200	—
1930	21,259	6,402	1,732	3,300	2,425	7,400	—
1931	20,685	5,890	1,775	3,375	2,145	7,500	—
1932	19,242	5,148	1,724	3,375	1,995	7,000	—
1933	17,878	4,437	1,599	3,200	1,810	6,700	$132
1934	17,857	3,710	1,379	3,000	1,189	6,200	2,379
1935	17,510	3,293	1,281	2,850	1,189	6,000	2,897
1936	17,225	3,237	1,245	2,750	1,230	6,000	2,763
1937	17,344	3,420	1,246	2,700	1,400	6,180	2,398
1938	17,646	3,555	1,320	2,670	1,600	6,332	2,169
1939	18,216	3,758	1,490	2,680	1,810	6,440	2,038
1940	19,123	4,104	1,758	2,700	2,095	6,510	1,956

Source: Federal Home Loan Bank Review, September 1941, Table 2, p. 412.

Note: These data, as well as those in Table 48 below, are based on a regular monthly survey by the Federal Home Loan Bank Board of all nonfarm mortgages ($20,000 and under) made in 600 counties and localities, together with information collected by the Federal Deposit Insurance Corporation, Comptroller of the Currency, and the Board of Governors of the Federal Reserve System, and data prepared by insurance companies for the hearings of the Temporary National Economic Committee. The figures are not an entirely accurate representation of home financing, since in some instances the funds obtained by mortgagors are used for other purposes. This explains in part the relatively high level of commercial bank activity in the late twenties. It should also be noted that the data include construction loans. To some extent, this may result in duplications in the data for mortgages made, i.e., the construction loan and the permanent loan will both be included. This also may result in some distortion of the totals for certain types of lenders. Thus, a construction loan made by a savings and loan association is more likely to be extended to permanent financing than a similar loan made by a commercial bank.

TABLE 48

MORTGAGES MADE ON NONFARM 1-4-FAMILY DWELLINGS, CLASSIFIED BY TYPE OF LENDER, 1925-1940

(In Millions)

Year	Total	Savings and Loan Associations	Insurance Companies	Mutual Savings Banks	Commercial Banks and Trust Companies	Individuals and Others	Home Owners' Loan Corporation
1925	$4,763	$1,620	$400	$863	$760	$1,120	—
1926	5,321	1,824	465	809	943	1,280	—
1927	5,733	1,895	500	834	1,144	1,360	—
1928	5,778	1,932	525	915	1,156	1,250	—
1929	5,088	1,791	525	612	1,040	1,120	—
1930	3,536	1,262	400	484	670	720	—
1931	2,175	892	169	350	364	400	—
1932	1,092	543	54	150	170	175	—
1933	865	414	10	99	110	100	$132
1934	3,070	451	16	80	110	150	2,263
1935	2,011	564	77	80	264	443	583
1936	2,158	755	140	100	430	605	128
1937	2,499	897	232	120	500	723	27
1938	2,455	798	242	105	560	669	81
1939	2,873	986	274	112	610	740	151
1940	3,322	1,200	324	133	689	865	111

Source: Federal Home Loan Bank Board, Division of Research and Statistics.
Note: See note to Table 47 above.

APPENDIX I

SUMMARIES OF FINANCIAL OPERATIONS OF FEDERAL HOUSING AGENCIES, 1932–1940

TABLE 49

Financial Interest of the Federal Government in Housing to June 30, 1940

Agency	Outlays: Investments	Outlays: Loans	Outlays: Expenditures	Receipts: Return of Outlay	Receipts: Interest, Dividends and Fees	Liabilities, Contingent and Contracted for
Total	$410,041,000	$150,912,669	$362,206,124	$59,024,247	$26,381,189	$6,224,625,835
Home Owners' Loan Corporation	200,000,000[a]	30,000,000[b]	—	30,000,000[b]	86,749[b]	2,634,808,900[c]
The RFC Mortgage Company	25,000,000[d]	34,049,821[e]	—	—	6,596,541[f]	—
Federal Home Loan Bank System	124,741,000[g]	—	—	—	11,183,336[h]	—
Federal Savings and Loan Associations	49,300,000[i]	—	815,944[j]	15,162,900[k]	8,448,174[l]	—
Federal Savings and Loan Insurance Corporation	m	—	—	—	—	—
Federal Housing Administration	—	—	80,389,608[n]	9,861,347[o]	—	2,128,473,643[p]
Federal National Mortgage Association	10,000,000[q]	62,862,848[r]	1,000,000[q]	—	s	—
Public Works Administration	—	—	149,470,636[t]	—	—	—
United States Housing Authority	1,000,000[u]	24,000,000[v]	6,398,562[w]	4,000,000[v]	66,389[x]	1,461,343,292[y]
Farm Security Administration	—	—	124,131,374[z]	s	s	—

Source: Financial Statements of Certain Government Agencies: in response to Senate Res. 292, 76th Cong., 3d sess., 1940 (mimeographed). Annual reports and officials of the agencies concerned.

a. By Reconstruction Finance Corporation. From Table 50, "Capital stock sold."
b. From Table 50, "Expenses," footnote a.
c. Outstanding bonded indebtedness, guaranteed by U. S. Government. From Table 50, "Borrowings."
d. By Reconstruction Finance Corporation. From Table 51, "Capital stock sold."
e. By Reconstruction Finance Corporation. From Table 51, "Borrowings."
f. By Reconstruction Finance Corporation. From Table 51, "Expenses."
g. From Table 52, "Capital stock sold."
h. From Table 52, "Costs," footnote b.
i. In addition, the HOLC purchased capital stock in the net amount of $168,130,800. From Table 53, "Capital stock sold."
j. From Table 53, "Treasury appropriation."
k. From Table 53, "Capital stock repurchased."
l. From Table 53, footnote a.
m. Capital stock in the amount of $100,000,000 purchased by HOLC and paid for in HOLC bonds.
n. Mostly Reconstruction Finance Corporation funds, including some loans. From Table 55, "Federal funds received."
o. Includes some interest. From Table 55, "Returned to treasury."
p. Total insurance in force and debentures outstanding. From Table 55, "Insurance written, Contingent liabilities and Debentures."
q. By Reconstruction Finance Corporation. From Table 56, "Capital stock sold" and footnote a.
r. By Reconstruction Finance Corporation. From Table 56, "Borrowings."
s. No data.
t. Does not include administrative expenses, but includes $9,469,023 expended by the Puerto Rico Reconstruction Administration, of which $744,407 was from PWA funds. From Table 57, "Federal funds expended, PWA operations," and footnote a.
u. From Table 58, "Capital stock."
v. From Table 58, "Borrowings," footnote c.
w. Unexpended funds transferred from PWA. Not included in outlays to PWA. From Table 58, "Unexpended PWA balance," and "PWA unexpended administrative fund."
x. From Table 58, "Expenses," footnote b.
y. Estimated maximum subsidy on projects contracted for as of June 30, 1940, calculated at $25,195,574 per year for 58 years.
z. Period ending December 31, 1940. From Table 59, "Public funds contributed."

TABLE 50

Summary of Financial Operations of the Home Owners' Loan Corporation to June 30, 1940

Capital Stock		
Capital stock sold to Reconstruction Finance Corporation		$200,000,000.00
Expenses and Reserves, and Earnings		
Expenses		
Interest, etc., on bonded debt[a]	$446,017,618.74	
Administrative and general	208,835,873.04	
Property expense	62,619,049.05	
Losses on sale of furniture, etc.	43,895.38	
Total		717,516,436.21
Provision for losses		
On mortgage loans	186,137,153.25	
For fidelity and casualties	1,077,146.24	
For fire and other hazards	32,663.00	
Total		187,246,962.49[b]
Total expenses and reserves		904,763,398.70
Earnings		
Interest on loans	727,206,149.60	
Interest on investments	26,490,508.65	
Property income	72,939,967.66	
Other income	1,674,160.28	
Total		828,310,786.19
Net loss from operations		76,452,612.51
Loss on Property Accounts		
Expenditures on acquired property		
Unpaid principal balance on acquired property (including sold property reacquired)		
Property subsequently sold	393,865,831.17	
Property still owned	343,023,865.70	
Total		736,889,696.87
Net expenditures on acquired property (including unpaid interest capitalized)		
Property subsequently sold	108,449,767.49	
Property still owned	81,161,345.76	
Total		189,611,113.25
Total expenditures		926,500,810.12
Receipts from property sales		
Principal payments	87,010,903.01	
Less balance of advances and partial sales	617,438.52	
Total receipts		86,393,464.49
Net expenditures on property		840,107,345.63
Assets remaining from property accounts		
Capitalized value of property owned and in process of acquiring title	424,185,211.46	
Unpaid principal of property sold	277,239,129.17	
Total		701,424,340.63
Loss on property accounts		138,683,005.00

TABLE 50 (*continued*)

Borrowing and Lending Operations		
Borrowings [c]		
Bonds issued		$3,469,453,550.00 [d]
Bonds retired		834,644,650.00 [e]
Outstanding bonded debt		2,634,808,900.00
Loans		
Original loans made		3,246,633,609.89
Principal repayments	$776,798,955.74	
Balances transferred to property and other accounts [f]	734,951,572.10	
		1,511,750,527.84
Original loans outstanding		1,734,883,082.05
Vendee accounts [g]		277,239,129.17
Unposted advances		638,222.99
Total loans outstanding		2,012,760,434.21
Investments		
Capital stock of Federal Savings and Loan Associations		
Purchased	176,289,800.00	
Sold	13,159,000.00	
Balance held		163,130,800.00
Capital stock of state chartered savings and loan associations		
Purchased	44,398,410.00	
Sold	4,505,000.00	
Balance held		39,893,410.00
Capital stock of Federal Savings and Loan Insurance Corporation		100,000,000.00
Total investments		303,024,210.00

a. Includes interest of $86,748.85 paid on $30,000,000 worth of HOLC bonds held by Treasury but disposed of prior to June 30, 1940.

b. Losses have been written off to the amount of $138,683,005.00, as detailed under "Loss on Property Accounts"; balance in reserve thus amounts to $48,563,957.49.

c. Exclusive of refundings.

d. Includes Treasury purchase of $30,000,000.00 worth of HOLC bonds.

e. Includes matured bonds to the total of $31,449,200.00, on which interest has ceased.

f. Represents chiefly balances due on foreclosed properties.

g. Mortgages held on resold foreclosed properties.

TABLE 51

Summary of Financial Operations of The RFC Mortgage Company to June 30, 1940

Capital Stock		
Capital stock sold to Reconstruction Finance Corporation		$25,000,000.00
Earnings and Expenses		
Earnings		
Interest and discounts	$9,736,995.71	
Premiums, service fees, and commitment charges	1,274,372.97	
Total		11,011,368.68
Expenses		
Administrative [a]	4,095,808.48	
Interest and commitment fee expenses [b]	6,596,541.09	
Losses on assets	6,174.16	
Reserves	100,139.17	
Total		10,798,662.90
Net earnings		212,705.78
Borrowing and Lending Operations		
Borrowings		
RFC loan on 4 per cent notes		34,049,821.18
Loans		
Mortgage loans	67,910,501.37	
Other loans	94,572.36	
Insured mortgages purchased	89,272,771.24	
Other mortgages purchased	1,711,000.00	
Total		158,988,844.97
Repayments		
Mortgage loans	24,997,631.37	
Other loans	27,402.94	
Insured mortgages	73,962,233.40	
Other mortgages	402,000.00	
Total	99,389,267.71	
Loans in default	4,948,271.71	
Total repayments and defaults		104,337,539.42
Total outstanding loans		54,651,305.55

a. Includes service charges.

b. Paid to RFC.

TABLE 52

Summary of Financial Operations of Federal Home Loan Bank System to June 30, 1940

Capital Stock		
Capital stock sold to Treasury		$124,741,000.00[a]
Earnings and Expenses		
Earnings		
Interest, etc.		37,550,530.90
Costs		
Operating, general, interest, etc.		13,013,731.19
Net earnings		24,536,799.71[b]
Borrowing and Lending Operations		
Borrowings		
Consolidated Federal Home Loan Bank Debentures issued	$142,700,000.00	
Debentures retired at maturity	94,200,000.00	
Debentures outstanding		48,500,000.00
Loans		
Advances to members	631,033,291.77	
Principal repayments	473,636,244.61	
Advances outstanding		157,397,047.16

a. Additional stock has been purchased by members to the amount of $42,632,475.00.

b. Of this amount, $5,810,375.14 represents reserves, and $4,453,661.25 undivided profits. The balance, $14,272,763.32, has been paid out in dividends, including $11,183,336.00 paid to the Treasury.

TABLE 53

Summary of Federal Government Investment in Federal Savings and Loan Associations to June 30, 1940

Capital Stock		
Capital stock sold to Treasury		$49,300,000.00[a]
Capital stock repurchased		15,162,900.00
Balance held by Treasury		34,137,100.00[b]
Treasury appropriation to promote and organize Federal Savings and Loan Associations	$850,000.00	
Unexpended balance	34,056.09	
Net expenditures for promotion		815,943.91

a. Dividends have been paid to the Treasury in the amount of $8,448,174.00.

b. The major sources of funds were as follows: Home Owners' Loan Corporation purchases of capital stock, $163,130,800.00 (net) and $1,268,048,000.00 private repurchasable capital.

TABLE 54

Summary of Financial Operations of Federal Savings and Loan Insurance Corporation to June 30, 1940

Earnings and Expenses		
Earnings		
Insurance premiums	$9,117,982.69	
Admission fees	234,120.89	
Interest on invested reserves	1,113,686.13	
Interest on Home Owners' Loan Corporation bonds	18,034,755.26	
Profit on sale of securities	111,200.72	
Miscellaneous	291.02	
Total		$28,612,036.71
Expenses		
Operating and general expenses	1,038,700.87	
Losses	917,198.94	
Dividends on capital stock	3,035,326.09	
Total		4,991,225.90
Net income		23,620,810.81[a]

a. This amount, together with original capital in the amount of $100,000,000.00, obtained through the sale of capital stock to the HOLC (paid for in HOLC bonds) constitutes an insurance reserve for the protection of depositors in insured institutions. The potential liability of the corporation on insured share accounts up to $5,000 and creditor obligations in 2,235 insured institutions is $2,056,000,000.00. This is not guaranteed by the United States government. In addition, the HOLC is entitled to cumulative dividends on the FSLIC's capital stock held by it. Of the net income of $23,620,810.81 the FSLIC has set aside $15,000,000 for this purpose.

TABLE 55

Summary of Financial Operations of Federal Housing Administration to June 30, 1940

Net Public Funds Contributed		
Federal funds received		
Contribution from Reconstruction Finance Corporation to establish the Mutual Mortgage Insurance Fund	$10,000,000.00	
Administrative expenses from RFC and National Recovery Administration funds	42,780,726.47	
Title I claims and loans from RFC funds	27,608,881.50	
Total		$80,389,607.97
Returned to Treasury		
Cash	5,710,629.64	
Property valued at	3,862,782.95	
Loans	141,000.00	
Surplus property valued at	18,355.67	
Interest and miscellaneous receipts	128,579.13	
Total		9,861,347.39
Net public funds contributed		70,528,260.58
Expenses and Earnings		
Expenses		
Administrative expenses	64,682,549.06	
Title I claims and loans	27,608,881.50	
Reserve for losses on small homes and mortgage insurance	1,205,160.70 [a]	
Reserve for losses on rental projects mortgage insurance	555,655.24 [b]	
Total		94,052,246.50
Earnings		
Premiums, fees, etc., from insurance on small homes	41,768,585.06	
Premiums, fees, etc., from insurance on rental projects	1,600,968.19	
Recoveries and revenues from Title I, and miscellaneous	13,025,459.35	
Total		56,395,012.60
Net loss from operations		37,657,233.90 [c]
Insurance Written, Contingent Liabilities, and Debentures		
Valuation of insured property		
Title I		1,073,132,387.00
Small homes		2,288,347,588.00
Rental projects		121,081,775.00
Total		3,482,561,750.00
Contingent liabilities		
Title I		48,077,858.00
Small homes		1,965,811,111.00
Rental projects		107,083,719.00
Total		2,120,972,688.00
Debentures issued for foreclosed properties		
Small homes		7,373,129.17
Rental projects		2,023,910.62
Total		9,397,039.79

TABLE 55 (*continued*)

Debentures outstanding		
Small homes		$5,477,105.28
Rental projects		2,023,850.00
Total		7,500,955.28
Reserve Accounts		
Mutual Mortgage Insurance Fund [d]		
Receipts		
RFC allocation	$10,000,000.00	
Premiums, fees, etc.	41,768,585.06	
Total	51,768,585.06	
Expenses		
Administrative expenses	21,051,571.84	
Transferred to Housing Insurance Fund	1,000,000.00	
Reserve for losses	1,205,160.70 [e]	
Total	23,256,732.54	
Balance in Fund		28,511,852.52
Housing Insurance Fund [f]		
Receipts		
Transferred from Mutual Mortgage Insurance Fund	1,000,000.00	
Premiums, fees, etc.	1,600,968.19	
Total	2,600,968.19	
Expenses		
Reserve for losses	555,655.24 [g]	
Balance in Fund		2,045,312.95
Title I account		
Receipts		
Premiums and fees	3,164,111.96	
Appraised value of notes held	2,258,577.41	
Total	5,422,689.37	
Expenses		
Administrative	850,250.77	
Balance		4,572,438.60
Assets in furniture, stores, etc.		1,099,920.14
Net worth		36,229,524.21

a. The actual losses on small homes mortgage insurance as of June 30, 1940 amounted to $914,-800.23. The difference, $290,360.47, represents reserve for losses on properties still on hand.

b. As of June 30, 1940 there were no losses sustained on rental housing projects. This amount represents the reserve for losses on property still on hand.

c. Offsetting items against the net loss are (a) Title I notes on hand appraised (June 30, 1940) at $2,258,577.41, and (b) furniture, stores, etc., valued at $1,099,920.14.

d. Small homes under Title II only.

e. See note a.

f. Rental projects only.

g. See note b.

TABLE 56

Summary of Financial Operations of Federal National Mortgage Association to June 30, 1940

Net Public Funds Contributed		
Capital stock sold to Reconstruction Finance Corporation [a]		$11,000,000.00
Earnings and Expenses		
Earnings		
Interest	$11,481,412.49	
Commitment fees	41,757.00	
Service fees	43,641.52	
Miscellaneous	3,409.18	
Total		11,570,220.19
Expenses		
General and administrative	1,794,347.87	
Interest	3,795,422.53	
Service charge expense	1,495,388.92	
Losses	6,673.37	
Reserves for appraisal of Federal Housing Administration claim certificates	17,016.97	
Total		7,108,849.66
Net earnings		4,461,370.53
Borrowing and Lending Operations		
Borrowings		
RFC loan on 2 per cent notes		62,862,847.67
Public sale of 1 5/8 and 2 per cent notes		85,240,000.00
Total		148,102,847.67
Lending		
Direct insured mortgage loans	2,621,500.00	
Principal repayments	35,625.17	
Balance outstanding		2,585,874.83
Insured mortgages purchased	176,630,541.79	
Repayments	15,325,239.80	
Total		161,305,301.99
		163,891,176.82
Less: Credits from foreclosed and acquired property		1,099,402.38
Balance outstanding		162,791,774.44

a. Includes $1,000,000.00 paid-in surplus.

TABLE 57

Summary of Financial Operations of Public Works Administration Housing Division to June 30, 1940

Net Public Funds Contributed		
Federal funds received		
Allocated to PWA	$146,139,533.49	
Allocated to Puerto Rico projects	744,406.96 [a]	
Total		$146,883,940.45
Federal funds expended		
PWA operations		
Development cost of public projects	127,525,461.24	
Loss on sale of unused land	1,997,781.38	
Loans to limited-dividend corporations	10,478,369.95 [b]	
	140,001,612.57	
Allocations for Puerto Rico projects	744,406.96 [a]	
Net public funds expended		140,746,019.53 [a]
Unexpended balance transferred to United States Housing Authority, November 1, 1937		6,137,920.92
Revenues and Expenses		
Revenues		
Income from federally operated projects	5,456,167.55	
Rents from leased projects	2,654,973.86	
Principal on limited-dividend projects	1,043,455.98 [c]	
Interest on limited-dividend projects	1,025,139.97 [d]	
Miscellaneous	14,224.04	
Total		10,193,961.40
Expenditures		
Operation of projects	4,480,077.01	
Central office expenses, November 1, 1937-June 30, 1940	1,627,360.37 [e]	
Furniture, etc., bought after November 1, 1937	11,025.30	
Total		6,118,462.68
Net return from operations		4,075,498.72

a. Federal funds allocated to Puerto Rico projects totaled $9,469,023.11. Of this amount, $744,-406.96 was spent by PWA and the balance by the Puerto Rico Reconstruction Administration.

b. Principal repayments on these loans did not revert to the Treasury but were transferred to PWA and USHA.

c. Does not include $336,187.58 principal repaid prior to November 1, 1937, which was apparently absorbed in central office expense of PWA.

d. Does not include interest paid prior to November 1, 1937, which was apparently absorbed in central office expense of PWA.

e. Prior to November 1, 1937 these expenses were for the most part paid from Treasury appropriations.

TABLE 58

Summary of Financial Operations of United States Housing Authority to June 30, 1940

Public Funds Contributed		
Capital stock purchased by Treasury	$1,000,000.00	
Unexpended Public Works Administration balance	6,137,920.92	
Net public funds contributed		$7,137,920.92
Other funds made available		
Net receipts transferred from PWA program	1,420,524.86 [a]	
PWA unexpended administrative fund	260,640.89	
Total		1,681,165.75
Total funds available for USHA operations		8,819,086.67
Expenses and Revenues		
Expenses		
Administrative expenses	8,640,811.48	
Furniture and equipment	336,715.47	
Interest on borrowings [b]	2,290,054.99	
Total		11,267,581.94
Revenues		
Interest on loans		3,598,758.84
Net loss from operations		7,668,823.10
Borrowing and Lending Operations		
Borrowings		
Five-year 1 3/8 per cent notes [c]		114,157,000.00
Loans		
To local authorities (2¾-3¼ per cent)		78,204,518.22

a. Represents net receipts from PWA projects, amounting to $4,075,498.72, less rents of $2,654,-973.86 from leased projects. See Table 57 above.

b. Includes $66,388.73 interest paid to Treasury.

c. Of this amount, $24,000,000.00 was bought by the Treasury, of which $4,000,000.00 was retired.

TABLE 59

Summary of Federal Government Investment in the Farm Security Administration Housing Program[a] to December 31, 1940

Public Funds Contributed		
Direct expenditures		
For farm and suburban housing	$81,711,261.34	
For migratory camps	10,769,286.74	
Total		$92,480,548.08[b]
Loans		
To individuals	25,602,986.73	
To associations	6,047,839.46	
Total		31,650,826.19[c]
Public funds contributed		124,131,374.27

a. Data include rural and suburban housing activities of the Agricultural Adjustment Administration, the Federal Emergency Relief Administration, the Subsistence Homesteads Division of the Department of the Interior, and the Resettlement Administration, all of which are now co-ordinated in the FSA. Data do not include central office expenses.

b. Data relating to funds returned to the Treasury are not available, since FSA does not maintain separate records for its housing operations.

c. No data available on either principal or interest repayments.

TABLE 60

Average Cost Per Dwelling Unit of United States Housing Authority-Aided Projects Compared with Public Works Administration Projects

Cost Items	USHA (To February 28, 1942)	PWA
Land	$270	$429
Land acquisition	17	14
Net construction	2,711	3,740
Dwelling equipment	111	140
Site improvement	395	518
Nondwelling facilities	101	313
Preoccupancy	43	17
Architectural and engineering	201	175
Administrative, carrying and contingencies	385	72[a]
Average over-all cost of new dwellings[b]	4,234	5,418
Land for future development	8	0
Other than land acquisition	21	16
Slum buildings	293	482
Demolition	10	5
Relocation of tenants	16	0
Administrative and carrying	22	6
Average cost of slum clearance and land for future development[b]	370	509
Average total development cost	4,604	5,927

Source: United States Housing Authority, Division of Research and Statistics.

a. Administrative costs only.

b. As defined by USHA.

TABLE 61

Status of the Federal War Housing Program as of December 15, 1942

Type of Accommodation and Source of Funds	Programmed		Under Construction	Completed
		(*Number of Dwelling Units*)		
Total	$1,717,567,000 [a]	552,118	216,976	187,210
Units for families of three or more	1,501,361,000	376,816	141,902	139,855
Public, No. 671 [b]	142,710,000	29,909	11,133	17,913
Public, No. 781 [c]	57,667,000	16,040	1,129	14,911
Public, No. 849 [d]	839,891,000	223,556	62,495	90,336
Public, No. 9 [e]	253,674,000	65,765	47,653	4,312
Public, No. 522 [f]	43,931,000	9,742	328	414
Public, No. 649 [g]	385,000	200	200	0
USHA converted	115,232,000	23,006	13,510	8,825
Defense Homes Corp.	47,871,000	8,598	5,454	3,144
Dormitory apartments for two-person families	96,120,000	39,126	12,596	5,439
Public, No. 849 [d]	85,567,000	35,534	9,654	5,064
Public, No. 9 [e]	10,553,000	3,592	2,942	375
Dormitory units for single persons	82,545,000	112,317	55,538	30,613
Public, No. 781 [c]	219,000	296	0	296
Public, No. 849 [d]	34,183,000	51,679	25,463	7,739
Public, No. 9 [e]	28,321,000	36,726	16,999	17,231
Public, No. 522 [f]	7,038,000	8,712	7,935	0
Public, No. 649 [g]	7,946,000	11,716	3,040	4,260
Defense Homes Corp.	4,838,000	3,188	2,101	1,087
Trailers				
Public, No. 9 [e]	37,541,000	23,859	6,940	11,303

Source: Federal Public Housing Authority, Statistics Division.

a. This constitutes 85 per cent of the amount available.
b. 76th Cong., June 28, 1940.
c. 76th Cong., September 9, 1940.
d. 76th Cong., October 14, 1940, and amendments.
e. 77th Cong., March 1, 1941, and amendments.
f. 77th Cong., April 10, 1942.
g. 77th Cong., July 2, 1942.

BIBLIOGRAPHY

Books and Monographs

Abrams, Charles, *Revolution in Land.* New York and London: Harper & Bros., 1939.
Achinstein, Ascher, "Recent Efforts of the Federal Government in the Field of Low-Rental Housing," in *Economic Essays in Honor of Wesley Clair Mitchell.* New York: Columbia University Press, 1935.
Armstrong, Robert H. and Hoyt, Homer, *Decentralization in New York City: A Preliminary Report to The Urban Land Institute.* Chicago: 1941.
Arnold, Thurman W. *The Bottlenecks of Business.* New York: Reynal & Hitchcock, 1940.
Bassett, Edward M. *The Master Plan.* New York: The Russell Sage Foundation, 1938.
———. *Zoning.* New York: The Russell Sage Foundation, 1940.
Bauer, Catherine, *Modern Housing.* New York: Houghton Mifflin Co., 1934.
———, *A Citizen's Guide to Public Housing.* Poughkeepsie: Vassar College, 1940.
Bemis, Albert Farwell, *The Evolving House.* Cambridge: Massachusetts Institute of Technology, Technology Press, 3 vols.
Vol. I. *A History of the Home.* 1933.
Vol. II. *The Economics of Shelter.* 1934.
Vol. III. *Rational Design.* 1936.
Burchard, John, with the help of Haible, Wm. E., Hopkins, Margaret, Mayer, Davis and Weese, Harry, *A Method for Analyzing the Economic Distribution of Shelter.* Cambridge: Albert Farwell Bemis Foundation, Massachusetts Institute of Technology, June 1940.
Burns, A. F. *Production Trends in the United States Since 1870.* Washington: National Bureau of Economic Research, 1934.
Citizens' Housing Council of New York, *Ailing City Areas.* New York: May 1941.
———, *Local Taxation and Housing.* New York: July 1939.
Clark, Appleton P., Jr. "Origin of the Building Regulations," in Columbia Historical Society, *Records* . . . Vol. 4. Washington: 1901.
Cornell Agricultural Experiment Station, *An Economic Study of Farm Buildings in New York.* Bulletin 478. Ithaca: May 1920.
Drellich, Edith Berger and Emery, Andrée, *Rent Control in War and Peace.* New York: National Municipal League, 1939.
Ebenstein, William, *The Law of Public Housing.* Madison: University of Wisconsin Press, 1940.
Eyre, Virginia L. *A Study of Tax Delinquency in the Second Ward of Detroit with Special Reference to Apartment House Properties.* Detroit: Social Science Research Council of Wayne University, Report No. 3, 1934.
Federated American Engineering Societies, Committee on Waste in Industry, *Waste in Industry.* New York: McGraw-Hill Book Co., 1921.
Fisher, Ernest M. *Advanced Principles of Real Estate Practice.* New York: The Macmillan Co., 1930.

———. *Real Estate Subdividing Activity and Population Growth in Nine Urban Areas.* Michigan Business Studies, Vol. I, No. 9. Ann Arbor: University of Michigan, 1928.

Fisher, Ernest M. and Smith, Raymond F. *Land Subdividing and the Rate of Utilization.* Michigan Business Studies, Vol. IV, No. 5. Ann Arbor: University of Michigan, 1932.

Ford, James, in collaboration with Morrow, Katherine and Thompson, George N. *Slums and Housing, with Special Reference to New York City.* Cambridge: Harvard University Press, 1936.

Fortune, Editors of, *Housing America.* New York: Harcourt Brace & Co., 1932.

Haber, William, "Building Construction," in *How Collective Bargaining Works.* New York: The Twentieth Century Fund, 1942.

———, *Industrial Relations in the Building Industry.* Cambridge: Harvard University Press, 1930.

Harvard City Planning Studies. Cambridge: Harvard University Press.

Vol. III. Whitten, Robert and Adams, Thomas, *Neighborhoods of Small Houses.* 1931.

Vol. IV. Bartholomew, Harland, *Urban Land Uses.* 1932.

Vol. V. Comey, Arthur C. *Transition Zoning.* 1933.

Vol. VI. Adams, Thomas, *The Design of Residential Areas.* 1934.

Vol. VII. Bassett, Edward M., Williams, Frank B., Bettman, Alfred and Whitten, Robert, *Model Laws for Planning Cities, Counties, and States.* 1935.

Vol. VIII. Black, Russell VanNest, *Building Lines and Reservations for Future Streets.* 1935.

Vol. X. McNamara, Katherine, *Bibliography of Planning, 1928-1935.* 1936.

Vol. XII. Walker, Mabel L. *Urban Blight and Slums.* 1938.

Hegemann, Werner, *City Planning and Housing.* 2 vols. New York: Architectural Book Publishing Co., 1936 and 1937.

Hill, Octavia, *House Property and Its Management.* New York: The Macmillan Co., 1921.

Hoad, William M. "Real Estate Prices: A Study of Residential Real Estate Transfers in Lucas County, Ohio" (unpublished doctoral dissertation, University of Michigan, 1942).

Hoagland, Henry E. *Real Estate Principles.* New York: McGraw-Hill Book Co., 1940.

Holden, Arthur C. *Money in Motion.* New York and London: Harper & Bros., 1940.

Hoyt, Homer, *One Hundred Years of Land Values in Chicago.* Chicago: University of Chicago Press, 1933.

Kuznets, Simon, *National Income and Capital Formation, 1919-1935.* New York: National Bureau of Economic Research, 1937.

———, *Seasonal Variations in Industry and Trade.* New York: National Bureau of Economic Research, 1933.

Lautner, Harold W. *Subdivision Regulations.* Chicago: Public Administration Service, 1941.

Long, Clarence D., Jr., *Building Cycles and the Theory of Investment.* Princeton: Princeton University Press, 1940.

MacChesney, Nathan William, *The Principles of Real Estate Law.* New York: The Macmillan Co., 1927.

McKenzie, R. D. *The Metropolitan Community.* New York and London: McGraw-Hill Book Co., 1933.

Mohaupt, Rosina K. and Lenz, Alger W. *A Description of the English System for the Taxation of Real Property on an Income Basis.* Detroit: Detroit Bureau of Governmental Research, *circa* 1934.

Monchow, Helen Corbin, *Seventy Years of Real Estate Subdividing in the Region of Chicago.* Evanston and Chicago: Northwestern University, 1939.

———, *The Use of Deed Restrictions in Subdivision Development.* Chicago: The Institute for Research in Land Economics and Public Utilities, 1928.

Montgomery, R. E. *Industrial Relations in the Chicago Building Trades.* Chicago: University of Chicago Press, 1927.

National Housing Committee, *The Housing Market.* Washington: December 3, 1937.

Newman, William H. *The Building Industry and Business Cycles.* Chicago: University of Chicago Press, 1935.

Perry, Clarence Arthur, *Housing for the Machine Age.* New York: The Russell Sage Foundation, 1939.

The President's Conference on Home Building and Home Ownership. Gries, John M. and Ford, James (editors), Washington.

Vol. I. *Planning for Residential Districts.* 1932.

Vol. II. *Home Finance and Taxation.* 1932.

Vol. III. *Slums, Large-Scale Housing and Decentralization.* 1932.

Vol. IV. *Home Ownership, Income and Types of Dwellings.* 1932.

Vol. V. *House Design, Construction and Equipment.* 1932.

Vol. VI. *Negro Housing.* 1932.

Vol. VII. *Farm and Village Housing.* 1932.

Vol. VIII. *Housing and the Community—Home Repair and Remodeling.* 1932.

Vol. XI. *Housing Objectives and Programs.* 1932.

General Index, Final Reports. 1933.

The President's Conference on Unemployment, *Seasonal Operation in the Construction Industries.* New York: McGraw-Hill Book Co., 1924.

Robinson, Herbert W. *The Economics of Housing.* London: P. W. King & Son, 1939.

Rosahn, Beatrice G. *Housing Management, Its History and Relation to Present Day Housing Problems.* New York: National Municipal League, 1935.

Rosahn, Beatrice G. and Goldfeld, Abraham, *Housing Management: Principles and Practices.* New York: Covici-Friede, 1937.

Ryan, Frederick L. *Industrial Relations in the San Francisco Building Trades.* Norman: University of Oklahoma Press, 1936.

Semenow, Robert W. *Survey of Real Estate Brokers' License Laws.* Chicago: National Association of Real Estate Boards, 1936.

Shire, A. C. "Rationalization of the Home Building Industry," in *Urban Blight and Slums.* Vol. XII, Harvard City Planning Studies. Cambridge: Harvard University Press, 1938.

Simpson, Herbert D. and Burton, John E. *The Valuation of Vacant Land in Suburban Areas.* Studies in Public Finance, Research Monograph No. 2. Chicago: Institute for Economic Research, Northwestern University, 1931.

Slichter, Sumner H. *Union Policies and Industrial Management.* Washington: The Brookings Institution, 1941.

Strauss, Michael W. and Wegg, Talbot, *Housing Comes of Age*. New York: Oxford University Press, 1938.

Tax Policy League, *Property Taxes* (symposium conducted December 27-29, 1939, in Philadelphia). New York: 1940.

Thorp, Willard Long, *Business Annals*. New York: National Bureau of Economic Research, 1926.

Trull, Edna, *The Administration of Regulatory Inspection Services in American Cities*. New York: Municipal Administration Service, Publication No. 27, *circa* 1932.

The Twentieth Century Fund, *Does Distribution Cost Too Much?* New York: 1939.

———, *Facing the Tax Problem*. New York: 1937.

———, *Housing for Defense*. New York: 1940.

Unwin, Sir Raymond, *Town Planning in Practice*. New York: The Century Co., 1932.

Wickens, David L. *Residential Real Estate*. New York: National Bureau of Economic Research, 1941.

Wickens, David L. and Foster, Ray R. *Non-Farm Residential Construction, 1920-1936*. New York: National Bureau of Economic Research, Bulletin 65, 1937.

Wilson, F. Vaux, Jr. *Tomorrow's Homes*. Trenton, New Jersey: The Homasote Corporation, 1939.

Wood, Edith Elmer, *Recent Trends in American Housing*. New York: The Macmillan Co., 1931.

Wright, Henry, *Rehousing Urban America*. New York: Columbia University Press, 1935.

FEDERAL GOVERNMENT

Agriculture, Department of. *The Farm-Housing Survey (1934)*. Miscellaneous Publication No. 323, 1939.

———. Purves, C. M. and Gibbons, C. A. "Expenditures for and Depreciation of Permanent Improvements on Farms, 1910-1940," in *Income Parity for Agriculture*, Pt. II, *Expenses of Agricultural Production*. 1941 (preliminary).

———. Farm Security Administration. *Report of the Administration of the Farm Security Administration, 1940*.

———. *Small Houses*. 1939.

———. Forest Service. Hallauer, Frank J. *Lumber Requirements for Nonfarm Residential Construction*. Miscellaneous Publication No. 347, May 1939.

———. Luxford, R. F. *Progress Report on Prefabricated House System Under Development by the Forest Products Laboratory*. December 1937.

———. Trayer, George W. *Forest Products Laboratory Prefabrication System, A New Departure in All-Wood Housing*. May 1935.

Commerce, Department of. Advisory Committee on City Planning and Zoning. *Standard State Zoning Enabling Act*. 1926.

———. *Planning Enabling Act*. 1928.

———. *Preparation of Zoning Ordinances*. 1931.

Commerce, Department of. Bureau of the Census. *Biennial Census of Manufactures, 1937*. 2 vols.

———. *Census of Manufactures: 1939* (preliminary releases).

———. *Census of American Business: 1933:*

Retail Distribution. Vols. I-VIII.
Wholesale Distribution. Vols. I-VII.
———. *Census of Business: 1935:*
Construction Industry, Vol. I, *Work Performed, Personnel, Pay Roll and Cost of Material.*
Distribution of Manufacturers' Sales.
Real Estate Agencies.
Retail Distribution. Vols. I-VI.
Retail Operating Expense.
Wholesale Distribution, Vol. VI, *Business-Size Groups and Analysis of Operating Expenses.*
———. *Census of Business*: *1940, Construction: A Summary of the United States* (preliminary release).
———. *Thirteenth Census of the United States: 1910, Population*. Vols. I-III.
———. *Fourteenth Census of the United States: 1920, Population*. Vols. I-IV.
———. *Fifteenth Census of the United States: 1930:*
Census of Distribution.
Construction Industry.
Manufactures: 1929, Vol. I, *General Report: Statistics by Subject.*
Metropolitan Districts: Population and Area.
Mines and Quarries: 1929.
Population. Vols. I-VI.
———. *Sixteenth Census of the United States: 1940:*
Housing (preliminary releases).
Population (preliminary releases).
———. *Financial Statistics of Cities, 1937.*
———. *Realty Tax Delinquency*, Vol. 2, *Urban Tax Delinquency*. 1934.
———. *A Social-Economic Grouping of the Gainful Workers of the United States, 1930*. 1938.
Commerce, Department of. Bureau of Foreign and Domestic Commerce, Chawner, Lowell J. *Construction Activity in the United States, 1915-37.*
———. "Construction and Real Estate—Construction Contracts Awarded in 37 States—(F. W. Dodge Corporation)," *Survey of Current Business*, 1940 Supplement.
———. Ehlers, J. H. *The Conservation of Critical Materials in Construction*. December 1, 1941 (mimeographed).
———. *Financial Survey of Urban Housing*. 1937.
———. Gilbert, Milton and Yntema, Dwight B. "National Income Exceeds 76 Billion Dollars in 1940," *Survey of Current Business*, June 1941.
———. Horton, Donald C. *Long-Term Debts in the United States*. Series No. 96, 1937.
Commerce, Department of. National Bureau of Standards. *Minimum Live Loads Allowable for Use in the Design of Buildings*. 1925.
———. *Recommended Building Code Requirements for Working Stresses in Building Materials.*
———. *Recommended Minimum Requirements for Fire Resistance in Building.*
———. *Recommended Minimum Requirements for Masonry Wall Construction*. 1925.
———. *Recommended Minimum Requirements for Plumbing for Dwellings and Similar Buildings*. 1923 (revised later to cover all classes of buildings and published

as *Recommended Minimum Requirements for Plumbing,* with Supplement containing Progress Revisions to May 1931).

———. *Recommended Minimum Requirements for Small Dwelling Construction.* Building and Housing Publication No. 18, 1932.

———. *Recommended Practice for Arrangement of Building Codes.*

———. Report of the Subcommittee on Plumbing, Central Housing Committee on Research, Design, and Construction. *Plumbing Manual.* Building Materials and Structures Report BMS66, 1940.

———. *Simplified Practice—Its Purpose and Application.* Letter Circular LC 690, April 15, 1940 (mimeographed).

———. Thompson, George N. *Preparation and Revision of Building Codes.* Building Materials and Structures Report BMS19, May 1939.

———. *Variety Reduction Effected by the Application of Simplified Practice.* Letter Circular LC 504, September 3, 1937 (mimeographed).

Congress. United States House of Representatives. Select Committee to Investigate Real Estate Bondholders' Reorganization. (74th Cong. 1st-2d sess. H. Rept. 35) Preliminary Report and Supplemental Report.

———. United States Senate. Senate Select Committee on Reconstruction and Production. Report issued 1921 (66th Cong., 3d sess. Senate Report 829).

———. *Financial Statements of Certain Government Agencies:* information collected pursuant to Senate Resolution No. 292, 76th Cong., 3d sess., 1940. 2 vols.

Federal Emergency Administration of Public Works. *Urban Housing; The Story of the PWA Housing Division, 1933-1936.* 1936.

———. Wood, Edith Elmer, *Slums and Blighted Areas in the United States.* Bulletin No. 1, 1935.

Federal Home Loan Bank Board. *Annual Reports.* 1933-1940.

———. *Federal Home Loan Bank Review.* "Interest Rates," November 1937.

———. "Nominal and Effective Interest Rates," December 1937.

———. "Home Financing in Relation to Business Fluctuations," April 1938.

———. "Seasonal Variations in the Residential Construction Index," October 1938.

———. "A Trend in Dividend Rates," November 1939.

———. "Dividend Rates of Savings and Loan Associations," May 1940.

———. "Real Estate Taxes in the Home Owners' Budget," July 1941.

———. "Three States Tackle the Urban Rehabilitation Problem," September 1941.

———. *Waverly— A Study in Neighborhood Conservation.* 1940.

Federal Housing Administration. *Annual Reports.* 1934-1940.

———. Fisher, Ernest M. and Ratcliff, Richard U. *European Housing Policy and Practice.* 1936.

———. *Four Decades of Housing With a Limited Dividend Corporation.* 1939.

———. *Low Rental Housing for Private Investment.* 1940.

———. *Minimum Construction Requirements* (individually for each Insuring Office).

———. *Modern Design.* Technical Bulletin No. 2 (revised March 1, 1941).

———. *Preliminary Report on a Study of House Standardization.* Technical Bulletin (Form No. 2373).

———. *Principles of Planning Small Houses.* Technical Bulletin No. 4 (revised July 1, 1940).

———. *Property Standards Circular No. 2* (individually for each Insuring Office).

———. *Recent Developments in Dwelling Construction.* Technical Bulletin No. 1 (revised July 1, 1940).

———. *Rental Housing Manual.* 1940.

———. *Report of the Committee on Current Real Estate Data.* May 25, 1935 (mimeographed).

———. *Structure and Growth of Residential Neighborhoods in American Cities.* 1939.

———. *A Survey of Apartment Dwelling Operating Experience in Large American Cities.* 1940.

———. Taylor, James S. "City Growth and Real Estate Cycles," *Insured Mortgage Portfolio,* July 1937.

———. *Underwriting Manual.* 1938.

Federal Security Agency. Social Security Board. *Old-Age and Survivors' Insurance Statistics: Employment and Wages of Covered Workers, 1938.*

Federal Trade Commission. *Report of the Federal Trade Commission on Lumber Manufacturers' Trade Association.* 1922.

———. *Report of the Federal Trade Commission on Northern Hemlock and Hardwood Manufacturers Association.* May 7, 1923.

———. *Report of the Federal Trade Commission on Western Red Cedar Association, Lifetime Post Association, Western Red Cedarmen's Information Bureau.* January 24, 1923.

———. *Trade Practice Conferences.* 1929.

Federal Works Agency. *Annual Reports.* 1940, 1941.

———. *Suggested General Principles Governing Execution and Operation of Mutual Home Ownership Projects.* Form 7530 (revised October 17, 1941).

Labor, Department of. Bureau of Industrial Housing. *Report of the United States Housing Corporation.* 2 vols. 1919.

———. Bureau of Labor Statistics. *Building Construction, 1921 to 1938.* Bulletin No. 668, 1940.

———. *Union Wages, Hours, and Working Conditions in the Building Trades.* Bulletin 674, June 1, 1939.

———. *Monthly Labor Review.* "Relative Cost of Material and Labor in Building Construction, 1931-32," October 1932.

———. "Elapsed Time in Building Construction," January 1933.

———. "Labor and Material Costs in Small-House Construction," May 1939.

———. "Labor and Unit Costs in PWA Low-Rent Housing," September 1939.

———. "Builders of 1-Family Houses in 72 Cities," September 1940.

———. "Union Wages and Hours in the Building Trades," November 1940.

———. "New Dwelling Units in Nonfarm Areas During 1940," April 1941.

———. "Operations of Urban Home Builders," May 1941.

———. "Housing and the Increase in Population," April 1942.

National Recovery Administration. *Code of Fair Competition for the Builders' Supplies Trade Industry.* 1934.

———. *Code of Fair Competition for the Construction Industry.* 1934.

———. *Code of Fair Competition for the Electrical Division.* 1934.

———. *Code of Fair Competition for the Painting, Paperhanging and Decorating Division.* 1934.

———. *Code of Fair Competition for the Retail Lumber, Lumber Products, Building Materials, and Building Specialties Trade*. 1934.
———. *Code of Fair Competition for the Roofing and Sheet Metal Division*. 1934.
———. *Code of Fair Competition for the Tile Division*. 1934.
National Resources Planning Board [National Resources Committee prior to 1940]. *Consumer Expenditures in the United States*. 1938.
———. *Consumer Incomes in the United States*. 1938.
———. *Our Cities; Their Role in the National Economy*. 1937.
———. *The Problems of a Changing Population*. 1938.
———. *State Legislation on Planning and Zoning*. Circular No. XII, June 1, 1938.
———. *Urban Planning and Land Policies*. Vol. II of the Supplementary Report of the Urbanism Committee. 1939.
———. *Housing—The Continuing Problem*. 1940.
Office of Emergency Management. Division of Defense Housing Coordination. *Emergency Plumbing Standards for Defense Housing*. January 1942.
The President's Conference on Unemployment. *Seasonal Operations in the Construction Industry*. 1924.
Resettlement Administration. *Annual Report*. 1936.
———. *Greenbelt Towns*. 1936.
Securities and Exchange Commission. *Report on the Study and Investigation of the Work, Activities, Personnel and Functions of Protective and Reorganization Committees. Pursuant to Section 211 of the Securities Exchange Act of 1934. Part III, Committees for the Holders of Real-Estate Bonds*. 1936.
Temporary National Economic Committee:
———. Hearings. Part 1. *Economic Prologue*. 1939.
———. Part 11. *Construction Industry*. 1939.
———. Part 31-A. *Supplemental Data Submitted to the Temporary National Economic Committee*. 1941.
———. Monographs. No. 8. Stone, Peter A. and Denton, R. Harold, *Toward More Housing*. 1940.
———. No. 27. Crowder, Walter F. *The Structure of Industry*. 1941.
———. No. 33. Keim, Walter G. *Geographical Differentials in Prices of Building Materials*. 1940.
Treasury, Department of the. Bureau of Internal Revenue. *Annual Report of the Secretary of the Treasury on the State of the Finances for the Fiscal Year Ended June 30, 1940*.
———. *Statistics of Income, 1929, 1933, 1937,* and *1938*.
United States Housing Authority. *Annual Reports,* 1938, 1939.
———. *Planning the Site*. Policy and Procedure Bulletin No. 11. 1939.
———. *Dwelling Unit Planning*. Policy and Procedure Bulletin No. 12. 1939.
———. *Income Limits and Rents for USHA-Aided Projects*. Policy and Procedure Bulletin No. 24 (revised December 14, 1940).
———. *Public Housing*. 1938-1941.
———. *What Does the Housing Program Cost?* March 1940.
Works Progress Administration. Stapp, Peyton, *Urban Housing: A Summary of Real Property Inventories Conducted as Work Projects, 1934-1936*. 1938.

LOCAL AND STATE GOVERNMENT

Birmingham, Alabama. Jefferson County Board of Health, *Report of Blighted Areas, Showing Some Comparative Figures for the Years 1933 and 1935*. December 1, 1936.

Boston, Massachusetts. The Finance Commission of the City of Boston, *A Report on the Building Department of the City of Boston*. 1912.

California. California State Planning Board, *Tax Delinquent Land in California*. Sacramento: 1938.

Cleveland, Ohio. Cleveland Metropolitan Housing Authority, *An Analysis of a Slum Area in Cleveland*. 1934.

Detroit, Michigan. Michigan Planning Commission, *A Study of Subdivision Development in the Detroit Metropolitan Area*. Lansing: June 1939.

District of Columbia. Alley Dwelling Authority. *Annual Reports*. 1935-1941.

Illinois. *Report of Illinois Building Investigation Commission*. 1923.

Los Angeles, California. Regional Planning Commission, *Land Use Survey, County of Los Angeles*. May 1938.

New Jersey. New Jersey Agricultural Experiment Station. Lee, Alvin T. M. *Land Utilization in New Jersey*. Bulletin 665, July 1939.

———. New Jersey State Planning Board, *Land Subdivision in New Jersey, Its Extent, Quality, and Regulation*. Trenton: 1938.

———, *Premature Land Subdivision a Luxury*. Trenton: 1941.

New York City. *The Report of the Tax Department and the Tax Commission of the City of New York*. July 1, 1939.

New York State. Cornick, Philip H. *Problems Created by Premature Subdivision of Urban Lands in Selected Metropolitan Districts*. A Report to the State Planning Council of New York. Albany: February 1938.

———. *Final Report of the Joint Legislative Committee on Housing*. Legislative Document (1923) No. 48.

———. *Intermediate Report of the Joint Legislative Committee on Housing*. Legislative Document (1922) No. 60.

———. New York State Tax Commission, *The Assessment of Real Property in the United States*. Special Report No. 10, 1936.

———. *Report of the Joint Legislative Committee to Investigate the Guaranteed Mortgage Situation*. Legislative Document (1938) No. 87.

———. State Commissioner of Housing [State Board of Housing prior to 1939], *Annual Reports*. 1927-1941.

Rochester, New York. Rochester Bureau of Municipal Research, *Report on the Administration of the Bureau of Buildings in the Department of Public Safety in the City of Rochester, N. Y.* 1921.

St. Louis, Missouri. City Planning Commission. Harland Bartholomew, Engineer, *Urban Land Policy, St. Louis, Missouri*. September 1936.

Westchester County, New York, *Land Use and Local Finance*. Prepared for the Westchester County Commission on Government by the Institute of Public Administration. December 1935 (mimeographed).

PERIODICALS AND YEAR BOOKS

Achinstein, Ascher, "Operating Cost Variables in a Low Rental Housing Program," *Journal of the American Statistical Association,* Vol. XXIX, No. 185A, March 1934 Supplement.

Alexander, W. W. "Housing Activities of the Resettlement Act," *Housing Yearbook, 1937.*

American Builder, "It's Not the First Cost But the Upkeep—'Bargain Homes' Are Costly to Own," April 1941.

The American City, "Full Value vs. Market Value in Real Estate Assessments," March 1940.

The Annals of The American Academy of Political and Social Science, "Zoning in the United States," Vol. 155, Pt. II, May 1931.

———, "Current Developments in Housing," Vol. 190, March 1937.

Architectural Forum, "Economics of Site Planning," August 1932.

———, "The Integrated House," April 1937.

———, "Home," October 1940.

———, "Survey of Builder Importance," December 1940.

———, "Plumbing Progress," February 1941.

———, "Plywood," March 1941.

———, "Building for Defense . . . Prefabricators Put on a Show," September 1941.

———, "House of 194X," September 1942.

Architectural Record, "Contributions of Science and Technology to Building," February 1941.

Arnaud, Leopold, "Buildings the Future Will Demand," *Pencil Points,* January 1943.

Augur, Tracy B. and Blucher, Walter H. "The Significance of the Greenbelt Towns," *Housing Yearbook, 1938.*

Bacon, Edmund N. "A Diagnosis and Suggested Treatment of an Urban Community's Land Problems," *The Journal of Land & Public Utility Economics,* Vol. XVII, No. 1, February 1940.

Bodfish, Morton, "A Sound System of Mortgage Credits in Relation to Banking Policy," *The Journal of Land & Public Utility Economics,* Vol. XI, No. 3, August 1935.

Bridewell, David A. "The Effects of Defective Mortgage Laws on Home Financing," *Law & Contemporary Problems,* Vol. V, No. 4, Autumn 1938.

Building Standards Monthly, "History of Building Regulations," October 1937.

———, "Building Department Salaries and Operating Costs," March-May 1938.

———, "Building Permit Survey Completed," January 1939.

Buttenheim, Harold S. "Possible Modification of Urban Land Policies in America," *The Journal of Land & Public Utility Economics,* Vol. XI, No. 1, May 1935.

———, "Unwise Taxation as a Burden on Housing," *Yale Law Journal,* Vol. 47, No. 2, December 1938.

Buttenheim, Harold S. and Cornick, Philip H. "Land Reserves for American Cities," *The Journal of Land & Public Utility Economics,* Vol. XIV, No. 3, August 1938.

Chase, Stuart, "The Case Against Home Ownership," *Survey Graphic,* May 1938.

Chawner, Lowell J. "Construction Cost Indexes as Influenced by Technological Change and Other Factors," *Journal of the American Statistical Association,* Vol. XXX, No. 191, September 1935.

Davison, Robert L. "New Construction Methods," *Architectural Record,* October 1929.

Derksen, J. B. D. "Long Cycles in Residential Building," *Econometria,* Vol. 8, No. 2, April 1940.

Dickey, Raymond R. "The New World of Plastics," *Pencil Points,* January 1943.

Dunn, Samuel O. "Building Activity, Employment and Taxable Wealth," *American Builder,* July 1941.

Fahey, John H. "Functions and Objectives of the Federal Home Loan Bank Board," *Housing Officials' Yearbook, 1935.*

Fisher, Ernest M. "Speculation in Urban Lands," *American Economic Review,* Vol. 23, No. 1, March 1933 Supplement.

Flynn, John T. "Gangsters Don't Build Houses," *Collier's,* September 23, 1939.

Foley, E. H., Jr., "Low Rent Housing and State Financing," *University of Pennsylvania Law Review,* Vol. 85, No. 3, January 1937.

Fortune, "The House Not-So-Beautiful," May 1938.

———, "The Trouble With Building Is—," June 1938.

———, "Plywood: $80 Million Industry That Wants to Revolutionize the Construction of Everything," January 1940.

———, "American Radiator & Standard Sanitary Corp.," March 1940.

———, "New Age of Wood," October 1942.

———, "Magnesium Production by Dow," December 1942.

———, "Technology and Postwar Life," December 1942.

French, David M. "The Contest for a National System of Home Mortgage Finance," *The American Political Science Review,* Vol. 35, No. 1, February 1941.

Garfield, Frank R. and Hoad, William M. "Construction Costs and Real Property Values," *Journal of the American Statistical Association,* Vol. 32, No. 200, December 1937.

Gill, Corrington, "Construction Statistics," *Journal of the American Statistical Association,* Vol. XXVIII, No. 181, March 1933.

Glick, Philip M. "The Federal Subsistence Homestead Program," *Yale Law Journal,* Vol. 44, No. 8, June 1935.

Goble, Emerson, "Better Houses Can Cost Clients Less," *Architectural Record,* July 1941.

Gray, Howard A. "Public Housing and Taxes," *American City,* April 1937.

Grebler, Leo, "The Home Mortgage Structure in Transition," *Harvard Business Review,* Vol. XXVIII, No. 3, Spring 1940.

———, "Housing Policy and the Building Cycle," *The Review of Economic Statistics,* Vol. XXIV, No. 4, May 1942.

Hallauer, F. J. "Population and Building Construction," *The Journal of Land & Public Utility Economics,* Vol. X, No. 1, February 1934.

Harper's Magazine, "Facing the Facts on Housing," March 1937.

Hoagland, H. E. "Government and the Changing Mortgage Structure," *American Economic Review,* Vol. XXVI, No. 2, June 1936.

Holden, Arthur C. "A Basis for Procedure in Slum Clearance," *Architectural Record,* March 1933.

———. "Removing the Obstacles to Group Rehabilitation of Real Properties," *The Journal of Land & Public Utility Economics,"* Vol. XII, No. 2, May 1936.

———. "Housing Can Be Financed," *The Atlantic Monthly,* June 1938.

Holden, Thomas S. "No Santa Claus in Housing," *The Atlantic Monthly,* March 1938.

———. "America Can Build," *The Atlantic Monthly,* March 1940.

The International City Managers' Association, *Municipal Year Book, 1941,* Chicago.

Kahn, Ernest, "Economics of Housing in the United States," *Architectural Forum,* August and September, 1935.

Keyes, Scott, "Converted Residences and the Supply of Housing," *The Journal of Land & Public Utility Economics,"* Vol. XVI, No. 1, February 1940.

Knight, C. L. "Blighted Areas and Their Effects Upon Urban Land Utilization," *The Annals of The American Academy of Political and Social Science,* Vol. 148, Pt. I, March 1930.

Law & Contemporary Problems, Duke University School of Law, "Low-Cost Housing and Slum Clearance," Vol. I, No. 2, March 1934.

———, "The Collection of Real Property Taxes," Vol. III, No. 3, June 1936.

———, "Home Financing," Vol. V, No. 4, Autumn 1938.

Long, Clarence D., Jr. "Long Cycles in the Building Industry," *Quarterly Journal of Economics*, Vol. 53, May 1939.

McCornack, Walter R. "Effect of Obsolete Municipal Codes on Building Costs," *Building Standards Monthly,* January 1938.

McDougal, Myres S. and Brabner-Smith, John W. "Land Title Transfer: A Regression," *Yale Law Journal,* Vol. 48, No. 7, May 1939.

Maverick, Lewis A. "Cycles in Real Estate Activity," *The Journal of Land & Public Utility Economics,* Vol. XXVII, No. 2, May 1932, and Vol. XXVIII, No. 1, February 1933.

Mayer, Albert, "A Technique for Planning Complete Communities," *Architectural Forum,* January and February, 1937.

Mendershausen, Horst, "The Elimination of Seasonal Fluctuations in the Building Industry," *International Labour Review,* Vol. XXXVI, No. 8, August 1937.

Merrill, David H. "The Effect of Building Code Adoption on Fire Insurance Rates," *Building Standards Monthly,* February 1938.

Mumford, Lewis, "Mass-Production and the Modern House," *Architectural Record,* January and February, 1930.

National Association of Housing Officials, *Housing Officials' Yearbook,* 1935-1941, Chicago.

Olzendam, Roderic, "After the War . . . Wood," *Pencil Points,* January 1943.

Pink, Louis H. "Life Insurance Company Investment in Housing," *Real Estate Record,* August 10, 1935.

Poteat, J. Douglass, "State Legislative Relief for the Mortgage Debtor During the Depression," *Law & Contemporary Problems,* Vol. V, No. 4, Autumn 1938.

Riggleman, John R. "Building Cycles in the United States, 1875-1932," *Journal of the American Statistical Association,* Vol. XXVIII, No. 182, June 1933.

Shire, A. C. "Industrial Organization of Housing: Its Costs and Methods," *The Annals of the American Academy of Political and Social Sciences,* March 1937.

Stevenson, Charles, "Housing, A National Disgrace," *The Atlantic Monthly,* December 1938, January 1939.

Stine, Charles M. A. "Tomorrow We Will Produce to Build," *Pencil Points,* January 1943.

———. "Molders of a Better Destiny," *Chemical and Engineering News,* 1942 (reprint by the American Chemical Society).

Stolper, Wolfgang F. "British Monetary Policy and the Housing Boom," *Quarterly Journal of Economics,* Vol. LVI, No. 1, Pt. II, November 1941.

Straus, Nathan, "Housing, A National Achievement," *The Atlantic Monthly,* February 1939.

Taylor, James S. "Construction Cost Statistics," *Journal of the American Statistical Association,* Vol. XXIX, No. 185A, March 1934 Supplement.

Terborgh, George, "The Present Situation of Inadequate Housing," *The American Economic Review,* Vol. 27, No. 1, March 1937 Supplement.

Thomas, Raymond D. "Exemption of Homesteads from Taxation: A Case Study in Oklahoma," *The Journal of Land & Public Utility Economics,* Vol. XI, No. 3, August 1935.

Thompson, George N. "The History of Building Regulations," *Building Standards Monthly,* October 1937.

Tugwell, Rexford G. "Housing Activities of the Resettlement Act," *Housing Yearbook, 1936.*

———. "The Meaning of Greenbelt Towns," *New Republic,* February 17, 1937.

Unwin, Sir Raymond, "Land Values in Relation to Planning and Housing in the United States," *The Journal of Land & Public Utility Economics,* Vol. XII, No. 1, February 1941.

Van Antwerpen, F. J. "Chemistry," *Pencil Points,* January 1943.

Vermilya, Howard P. "Building Codes:—Administration and Techniques," *The Journal of Land & Public Utility Economics,* Vol. XVII, No. 1, March 1941.

Wells, F. C. "Chemistry—Farming—Building," *Pencil Points,* December 1942.

Wenzlick, Roy, "The Problem of Analyzing Local Real Estate Cycles," *Journal of the American Statistical Association,* Vol. XXVIII, No. 181A, March 1933 Supplement.

Wilson, M. L. "The Place of Subsistence Homesteads in Our National Economy," *Journal of Farm Economics,* Vol. XVI, No. 1, January 1934.

Wood, Edith Elmer, "A Century of the Housing Problem," *Law & Contemporary Problems,* Vol. I, No. 2, March 1934.

Woodbury, Coleman, "Some Suggested Changes in the Control of Urban Land Development," *The Journal of Land & Public Utility Economics,* Vol. V, No. 3, August 1929.

Wright, Henry, "What Does the Architect Know About Small House Costs?" *Architectural Record,* December 1931, February 1932.

Yale Law Journal, "A Comparison of Land and Motor Vehicle Registration," Vol. 48, No. 7, May 1939.

Zeigler, Carl F. "Concrete," *Pencil Points,* January 1943.

RELEASES, PAMPHLETS, CONFERENCES, ADDRESSES, ETC.

Allen, W. D. M. *Jerry-Built Mortgages,* Proceedings of Building Officials' Conference, 1938.

Arnold, Thurman W. *Restraints of Trade in the Building Industry,* Address before the New York Building Congress, June 21, 1939.

Babcock, George N. *Engineering Management of Project Planning and Construction,* Address before Engineers' Club of Hampton Roads, Virginia, September 27, 1940 (mimeographed).

Bruce, Alfred and Sandbank, Harold, *A History of Prefabrication,* New York: John B. Pierce Foundation, Housing Research 3, July 1943 (reprinted from *Architectural Forum,* December 1942, *et seq.*).

Burton, F. *History of Building Codes,* Proceedings of Building Officials' Conference, 1929.

Chicago Homes Economic Council, *The Economic Fallacy of the Peak Leasing Seasons, circa* 1928 (circular).

Colean, Miles L. *Can America Build Houses?* New York: Public Affairs Pamphlet No. 19, 1938.

———, *The Role of the Housebuilding Industry,* National Resources Planning Board, July 1942.

Committee for Economic and Social Progress, *Government Opportunities and Responsibilities in a National Home-Building Program,* 1937.

Congress of Industrial Organizations, *Memorandum to the National Defense Advisory Committee,* October 14, 1940 (mimeographed).

———, *Memorandum to the Office of Emergency Management,* April 14, 1941 (mimeographed).

———, *Memorandum to the Office of Production Management,* January 23, 1941 (mimeographed).

Construction League of the United States, *Construction Industry Code Manual,* Vol. 1, No. IV. Washington: April 1935.

Dun & Bradstreet, *Business Failures, 1939-1940,* New York.

———, *Retail Credit Survey, 1936,* New York.

———, *1940 Retailers' Operating Cost Survey,* New York.

Edwards, Corwin D. *The Antitrust Laws as an Aid to the Building Industry,* Address before the New York Association of Master Plumbers, May 9, 1940 (mimeographed).

———. *Restraints in Building Codes,* Address before the Central Housing Committee, November 28, 1940, with introductory statements by Thompson, George N. Central Housing Discussion Papers: G: 1940 Series, Washington (mimeographed).

Fisher, Ernest M. *The Problem of Stabilization of the Residential Construction Industry,* Report of the Sixth Annual Research Conference on Economics and Statistics, Cowles Commission, 1940.

Greer, Guy and Hansen, Alvin H. *Urban Redevelopment and Housing,* National Planning Association, Planning Pamphlet No. 10, 1941.

Holden, Thomas S. (President, F. W. Dodge Corporation), *Integration of the Housing Function,* Paper read before the annual meeting of the American Statistical Association in Philadelphia, December 28, 1939.

Husband, William H. *Taxation and Security,* Address before the National Conference of Real Estate Taxpayers, Washington, April 26, 1941.

Johns-Manville Sales Corporation, Housing Guild Division, Hood, Arthur A. *Management Handbook and Sales Manager's Guide for Retail Building Material Executives.* New York: 1940.

Lavanburg, Fred L. *Practices and Experiences of the Lavanburg Homes,* April 1934.

Mackie, J. E. *Uniform Building Code of the Pacific Coast,* Proceedings of Building Officials' Conference, 1927.

Metzenbaum, James, *Zoning—Its Evolution and Development,* Proceedings of Building Officials' Conference, 1930.

National Association of Real Estate Boards, Proposed *Code of Fair Competition for the Land Development and Home Building Industry* (revised draft, June 19, 1934, mimeographed), and accompanying statement to National Recovery Administration.

National Electrical Manufacturers Association, *Summary of Existing State Electrical Laws and Statistical Report on Municipal Electrical Ordinances,* December 31, 1939.

National Elevator Manufacturing Industry, *List of Codes in Effect in Various Cities and States,* May 28, 1940.

New York Building Congress, Land Utilization Committee, Holden, Arthur C. and Fisher, Oscar (editors), "Group Action for Property Control IV-V," in *Land Usage, Housing and City Planning, 1936,* New York: 1937.

———, *Problems Affecting Housing,* New York: March 1938.

Purdue University, Better Homes in America, *Home Information,* Bulletins 1-32, 1936-1937.

Stegner, C. M. *Standardization of Building Codes,* Proceedings of Building Officials' Conference, 1930.

Terborgh, George, *Fluctuations in Housing Construction,* Address delivered September 29 [1935?] at meeting of the Cyclical Variations Section of the Central Housing Committee (mimeographed).

Thompson, George N. *Status of Building Codes,* Proceedings of Building Officials' Conference, 1930.

United States Chamber of Commerce, Construction Industry Conference, *Building Code Revision to Lower Costs,* December 5, 1940 (mimeographed).

Unwin, Sir Raymond, *Nothing Gained by Overcrowding,* London: The Garden City & Town Planning Association, Pamphlet No. 13, 1932.

Washington Committee on Housing, *Proceedings of the Conference on Methods of Reducing the Cost of Residential Construction,* October 24, 1936.

INDEX

ABERTHAW COMPANY, construction cost indexes, 359
Adams, Thomas, land planning, 19
Alabama, licensing laws, 402; mortgage foreclosures, 244, 245, 425; taxes, 423
Alexander, W. W., "greenbelt" towns, 284
Alterations, *see* Repairs and alterations
Amalgamated Clothing Workers, co-operatives, 234
American Appraisal Company, construction cost indexes, 359
American Federation of Labor, Building Trades Department, 72, 152, 372-73; prefabrication, 152-54; trade restraints, 162; wages, 152, 374, 375
American Institute of Architects, standard fees, 97
American Society of Planning Officials, building codes, 161
American Standards Association, Building Code Correlating Committee, 160; building codes, 127; dimensional standards, 133-34
Amortization, *see* Mortgages
Apartments, construction, contracts awarded, 391, New York City, 46, subcontracts required, 386-87; co-operative, 233 ff.; economies, 56-57; garden, 45, New York City, 30-31; height, 56-58; standardization, 135-36
Architects, 97-98, 314; contributions, 98; fees, 97; licensing, 129, 402-03; number, 97
Armstrong, Robert H., decentralization, 18, 23, 239
Army, *see* War Department
Arnold, Thurman W., trade restraints, 104
Associated General Contractors of America, construction cost indexes, 359
Atlanta, decentralization, 35; land improvements, 350; wage agreements, 405
Augur, Tracy B., "greenbelt" towns, 284
Augusta (Ga.), decentralization, 347, 348
Automobile industry, employment compared with building industry, 107; prices and sales, 61, 362

BACON, EDMUND N., land planning, 16
Baltimore, decentralization, 347, 348; ground rent, 215, 222; land values, 23; Roland Park, 31; Waverly, 36, 158
Banks, commercial, 119, 252, 253, 426-27; for co-operatives, 282; savings, 119, mutual, 252, 253, 426-27
Bartholomew, Harland, city planning, 21
Bassett, Edward M., zoning, 123-24
Bathrooms, flush toilet, 45, 46; lack of, 6
Bemis, A. F., design, 132, 133; mortgages, 248; *see also* Modular Service Association
Bemis Foundation, research, 164
Bettman, Alfred, city planning, 124
Bid peddling, *see* Trade restraints
Birmingham, Jemison development, 31
Blighted areas, *see* Decentralization; Land; Slums
Blucher, Walter H., "greenbelt" towns, 284
Bodfish, Morton, mortgages, 254; TNEC testimony, interest rates, 249, 250
Boeckh, E. H., and Associates, construction cost indexes, 49, 357 ff.
Boston, building cycles, 408-09; decentralization, 347, 348; homeownership, 229, 423
Bridewell, David A., mortgage foreclosures, 244
Brokers, real-estate, fees, 220; function, 209 ff., 217-20; licensing, 218; number, 219
Brookings Institution, 7, 62, 92, 110
Bruère, Henry, TNEC testimony, interest rates, 249, 250
Buhl Foundation, rental housing, 232
Builders, combinations with jobbers, 104; effect of war on, 91; financial resources, 80 ff.; of multifamily houses, 76-78, 379 ff.; number, 75 ff., 377 ff.; profits, 83-84, 93, 387-88; relations with labor, 103, 106 ff.; of single-family houses, 75-78, 377 ff.; size, 75 ff., 377 ff.; types, 95 ff., 314-15; *see also* Contractors; Subcontractors
Builders' Association of Chicago, wages, 374, 375
Building codes, 22, 125 ff., 159-60, 161, 318, 323; electrical, 125-26, 129; Ohio, 125, 126; plumbing, 125, 127; Wisconsin, 125-126; *see also* Licensing laws
Building Construction Corporations, income, 389
Building cycles, 180-81, 185-206, 408-09, 414 ff.; and business cycles, 194-97; and prices, 200-02; Toledo, 187-89; underlying factors, 189-94, 416 ff.
Building industry, *see* Housebuilding
Building materials, distribution costs, 68-70, 398 ff.; distributors, 64, 115-17, 315, as dealer-builders, 145, 295, markup, 117; new developments, 156-57; prefabricated, 140-42; prices, 111-14, 394 ff.; producers, 64, 111-15, 315, 398 ff., concentration of production, 112, 394 ff., markup, 117, 401, 403; standardization,

Building Materials, *continued*
132-34, 323, 324; variety, 42-43, 354-56; weight, 39-40, 352, 353
Building methods, *see* Housebuilding, methods
Building permits issued, selected areas, 392, (1870-1940), 181, 408-09, (1856-1936), 185-87, 414-16
Building Permit Survey (Bureau of Labor Statistics), 409, 411, rental housing, 231-32
Building Trades Department (AF of L), 72, 152, 372-73
Bureau of Agricultural Engineering, 123, 306
Bureau of Foreign and Domestic Commerce, construction cost indexes, 359; Financial Survey of Urban Housing, 123; national income, 370-72, 376, 387-88; Real Property Inventory, 123
Bureau of Home Economics, farm housing, 123, 306
Bureau of Internal Revenue, tax returns, 389-90
Bureau of Labor Statistics, 123; building trades, 372; construction volume, 361 ff., 392, 409, 410 ff.; employment, 395; number of builders, 382 ff.; rental housing, 231-32; size of builders, 378 ff.; wages, 152, 374 ff., 406
Burns, Arthur F., building trends, 187
Burton, F., building codes, history, 120
Burton, John E., land planning, 14, 15
Business cycles, 194-97

CALIFORNIA, equity investment, 300; licensing laws, 403; mortgages, financing, 273, foreclosures, 245, 425; seasonal fluctuation in building, 87, 392; taxes, 423
Cambridge (Mass.), tax delinquency, 21
Carpenters, employment, 395; equipment, 83, 385; location of work, 81, 384
Chawner, Lowell J., building cycles, 192, 193, 363, 367, 418-20
Chicago, decentralization, 18, 35; homeownership, 229, 423; Lake Forest development, 31; land use, 30; land values, 23; mortgage interest rates, 248; rental housing, 231-32; Riverside development, 31; surplus land, 14-15; taxes, 238; Urban Land Institute, The, 18
Cincinnati, "greenbelt" towns, 283; tax delinquency, 21
Cincinnati Model Homes Corporation, 232
City planning, *see* Land, planning
Clark, J. M., building cycles, 195
Cleveland, decentralization, 16-18; land improvements, 351; land values, 23; size of builders, 379; tax delinquency, 21
Climate, average temperatures by areas, 87, 392; and construction methods, 44; and construction volume, 85-87, 392
Code of fair competition for the construction industry (NRA), 62, 63
Combinations, *see* Trade restraints
Commercial banks, 119, 252, 253, 426-27
Committee on Elimination of Waste in Industry (1921), 92
Committee of the President's Conference on Unemployment (1924), off-season construction, 88
Communities, depreciation of, *see* Depreciation, of neighborhoods
Congress of Industrial Organizations, prefabrication, 152-54
Connecticut, licensing laws, 402; mortgage foreclosures, 245, 425; taxes, 423
Construction industry, definition, 62; employment, 79, 393-94; income, 389, 390; profits, 84, 387-88; seasonal fluctuation, 85; *see also* Housebuilding
Contractors, employment by, 107; financial resources, 80 ff.; functions, 60, 98-99, 314; income, 390; licensing, 129, 402-03; localism, 80, 81, 384; profits, 84, 387-88; seasonal fluctuation in contracts, 88; size, 79-80, 382 ff., 393-94; value of equipment, 82-83, 385; *see also* Builders; Subcontractors
Co-operative ownership, 233-35
Cornick, Philip H., land planning, 15
Cost of living (1914-1941), 199, 421
Costs, 46-52; construction, indexes, 49, 357 ff.; decline in, 50-52; distribution, 221; land, 23-30, improvements, 26-28, 29, 350-51; maintenance and operation, 47-48, *Committee recommendations,* 339-41; production, 47 ff., 352 ff., 357-60, labor, 68, 70-72, materials, 68-70, 398 ff.
Cover, John H., business cycles, 194
Craft restrictions, 72, 92, 109 ff.; *see also* Labor; Trade restraints
Credit, *see* Finance; Mortgages
Credit unions, federal, 282
Crowder, Walter F., TNEC testimony, building materials prices, 111, 112, 394 ff.

DAVIS-BACON ACT, 374, 375
Davison, Robert L., construction methods, 54
Decentralization, 16-18, 35-37, 316, 347, 348
Defense Homes Corporation, 286-87, 288, 289, 440
Defense Housing Coordination, Division of, 288, 289; plumbing codes, 161
Demand, *see* Housing market
Demountable houses, 53
Density of urban dwellings, 30-31
Denton, R. Harold, 41, 42, 149, 377
Denver, land values, 23
Department of Agriculture, Extension Service, 306; Forest Products Laboratory, 122, 123, 164
Department of Commerce, Division of Building and Housing, research, 121, 122; Building Code

Committee, 160; *see also* Bureau of Foreign and Domestic Commerce; National Bureau of Standards
Department of the Interior, Division of Subsistence Homesteads, 283
Department of Justice, bid depositories, 102, 105; combinations and trade restraints, 101, 103, 104, 122, 162-63
Depreciation, of houses, 5-7, 183-85, 203-05, 240-41, 409-14; of neighborhoods, 32-33
Derksen, J. B. D., building cycles, 191, 420
Des Moines, decentralization, 347, 348
Deterioration, *see* Depreciation
Detroit, building cycles, 181, 408-09; decentralization, 35, 347, 348; homeownership, 229, 423; land use, 30; land values, 23; surplus land, 15-16; tax delinquency, 21; wage agreements, 405
Distribution, building materials, 115-17, costs, 117; houses, costs, 221, *see also* Housing market
Distributors, types, 217 ff.; *see also* Brokers; Operative builders; Prefabrication, dealers; Real estate, brokers, operators
District of Columbia, *see* Washington, D. C.
District of Columbia Alley Dwelling Act, 274-75
Dodge, F. W., Corporation, contract values, 49; seasonal fluctuation in construction contracts, 388-89, 391; size of building operations, 379-80
Douglas, Paul H., unemployment, 377
Drellich, Edith B., rent control, 273
Duluth, decentralization, 347, 348
Dunn, Samuel O., labor, 91

ECKSTEIN, HENRY J., TNEC testimony, investment, 301
Edwards, Corwin D., building codes, 127, 128, 129; TNEC testimony, trade restraints, 162
Ehlers, J. H., building materials, 127
Electrical facilities, costs, 358; lack of, 6; percentage use, 46; weight, 353
Electrical trades, building codes, 125-26, 129; contractors, 81, 83, 384, 385; licensing, 129, 402-03; profits, 401
Electric Home and Farm Authority, *Committee recommendations,* 339
Electric washers, prices and sales, 61, 362
Emergency Crop and Feed Loan Offices, 282
Emergency Relief and Construction Act (1932), 276
Emery, Andrée, rent control, 273
Employees, *see* Labor
Employers, *see* Builders; Contractors; Operative builders; Special trade contractors; Subcontractors
Employment, regularity, 107-08; *see also* Labor
Epstein, Henry, trade restraints, 163
Equitable Life Assurance Society, 274
Equity investment, availability, 225-35, 300 ff., for owner-occupancy, 225-30, for rental, 231-33; deterrents, 235-42, depreciation, 240-41, nonliquidity, 235-36, taxes, 236-40; *see also* Mortgages
Evans, Mercer G., wages, 377
Eyre, Virginia L., tax delinquency, 21

FACTORY PREFABRICATORS, *see* Prefabrication
Fahey, John H., TNEC testimony, HOLC experience, 260, 261, interest rates, 249, 250
Family formation, 192-93, 198, 418-20
Family income levels, 130, 178, 179, 407
Farm Credit Administration, 282-83; *Committee recommendations,* 338-39
Farm dwellings, *Committee recommendations,* 336-39; condition, 6; construction and repairs, 67, 366-68; demand, 169-71, postwar, 6-8; federal aid, 258, 282-85, 305-06, 322, agencies, 282-85, unification, 305-06; number, 6; ownership, 228
Farm Security Administration, *Committee recommendations,* 338-39; financial operations, 428, 439; functions, 283-84, 285, 289; prefabrication, 122; rural housing program, 170, 289
Farm Tenant Purchase Act (1937), 284
Federal Deposit Insurance Corporation, 264
Federal Farm Mortgage Corporation, functions, 259, 282-83; *see also* Federal Land Banks; Land Bank Commissioner
Federal government, financial aid, 121-22, 257 ff., 262 ff., 276 ff., 303 ff., 428-40, emergency measures, 258-62, 319 ff., farm housing, 258, 282-85, 305-06, 322, urban housing, 257 ff., 276-82, 305; housing agencies, 121 ff., 258 ff., 319 ff., 428-40; local-federal co-operation, 279-80, 306-07; regulation, 123 ff., 159 ff.; research, 121-23, 160-61, 164-66; 323; *see also* Government; National Bureau of Standards; and various agencies
Federal Home Loan Bank Act, amended, 271
Federal Home Loan Bank Administration, 98, 123, 262, 264, 270, 272-73, 289, 320; *Committee recommendations,* 333
Federal Home Loan Bank Board, 258, 288, 289; climate and construction, 392; *Committee recommendations,* 339; construction cost indexes, St. Louis, 49, 357 ff.; functions and affiliates, 262-64; Home Owners' Loan Corporation, 259-60, 261, 262; mortgage interest rates, 249; nonfarm mortgages, 426, 427; Registered Home Service, 97-98; Waverly development, 36, 158; *see also* Federal Home Loan Bank System; Federal Savings and Loan Associations; Federal Savings and Loan Insurance Corporation; Home Owners' Loan Corporation

Federal Home Loan Bank System, 121, 258; *Committee recommendations,* 333; conflict with Federal Housing Administration, 269-73; financial operations, 428, 432; functions, 262-64, 320-21
Federal Housing Administration, bidders' building estimates, 42; *Committee recommendations,* 333-34, 339; conflict with Federal Home Loan Bank System, 269-73; Division of Economics and Statistics, 74, 165; financial operations, 428, 434-35; functions, 265 ff., 319-20; Land Planning Division, 351; land subdivision, 30-31; loans, conditional commitment, 119, in new areas, 35, for rural housing, 284, 306; location criteria, 18-19; mortgages, insurance, 251, interest rates, 121, 192, 248, loan ratio, 226; nonfarm dwelling computations, 411; and operative builders, 142-43; and prefabrication, 122, 147; projects, density, 31, rental, 237-38, 424-25; property valuation, 50-52, 349; Rental Housing Division, 47, 425; settlement charges, 216-17, 422; standards, 58, 122, 128-29; Technical Division, 40, 352, 353, 358; wartime powers, 287-89
Federal housing agencies, conflicts, 269-73; co-ordination, 304 ff.; financial operations, 428-40, summary, 428; functions, 121 ff., 257-90, 319 ff.; local-federal co-operation, 279-80, 306-07; *see also* under various agencies
Federal Intermediate Credit Banks, 282
Federal Land Banks, 258, 259, 282-83; *see also* Federal Farm Mortgage Corporation
Federal Loan Agency, 288
Federal National Mortgage Association, 250, 271, 272, 428, 436; *Committee recommendations,* 333
Federal Public Housing Authority, 278, 289, 306, 321, 440; *Committee recommendations,* 336; *see also* United States Housing Authority
Federal Reserve System, construction contracts, 391
Federal Savings and Loan Associations, 262; financial operations, 428, 432; functions, 263-64
Federal Savings and Loan Insurance Corporation, 262; financial operations, 428, 433; functions, 264
Federal Trade Commission, unfair practices, 122
Federal Works Agency, 278, 289; and prefabrication, 147; seasonal fluctuation in building, 85-86; wartime housing, 286
Filtering-down, *see* Depreciation
Finance, equity investment, 225-42, for co-operative ownership, 233-35, deterrents, 235-42, in rental housing, 231-33, 300 ff.; government operations, 257-90, 428-40, insurance of sales contracts, 303-04; housebuilding, 117-20; long-term credit, 242-56, 316-18; marketing, 225 ff., *Committee recommendations,* 331 ff., new types of sales contracts proposed, 303-04; *see also* Banks; Insurance companies; Mortgages; Savings and loan associations; and various agencies
Financial Survey of Urban Housing, 123
Fisher, E. M., brokers' licenses, 218; land planning, 15, 187
Flint (Mich.), decentralization, 347, 348
Florida, licensing laws, 402; mortgage foreclosures, 245, 425; seasonal fluctuation in building, 87, 392; taxes, 423, 424
Ford Foundation development, 33
Foreclosures, costs, 244, 245, 425; time required, 244, 245; 425; *see also* Mortgages
Forest Products Laboratory (Department of Agriculture), research, 122, 123, 164
Foster, Ray R., production volume, 361 ff.
Foulke, Roy A., profits on materials and equipment, 401
Foundation, cost, 358; weight, 353
Frame, balloon, 43, 44; braced, 43; platform, 43; weight, 353
Frankfurter, Felix, trade restraints, 163
F. W. Dodge Corporation, contract values, 49; seasonal fluctuation in construction contracts, 388-89, 391; size of building operations, 379-80

GARDEN-CITY COMMUNITIES, 283-84
Georgia, licensing laws, 402; mortgage foreclosures, 244, 245, 425; taxes, 423, 424
Gibbons, C. A., farm dwellings, 366, 368
Gilbert, Milton, national income, 370-72, 376, 377, 387
Goble, Emerson, costs, 47
Goerl, Martin, building codes, 127
Government, *Committee recommendations on public aid and activity,* 334-36; in housebuilding, 120 ff., 157 ff., 315, 318 ff.; in marketing, 257 ff., 318 ff., competition with private enterprise, 281-82, 305, financial operations, 257 ff., 276 ff., 303 ff., 428-40, local-federal co-operation, 279 ff., 306-07; *see also* Federal government; Municipal government; State government; and various agencies
Gray, Richard J., AF of L and prefabrication, 153
Green, Howard W., decentralization, 17
"Greenbelt" towns, 283-84
Gridiron pattern, 19
Ground rent, 215, 222

HABER, WILLIAM, handicraft methods, 137-38; union organization, 73, 110
Hallauer, Frank J., lumber, 70
Handicraft methods, 54, 92, 137-38
Harper, R. F., building codes, history, 120
Harvard City Planning Studies, land planning, 19; urban blight, 18; zoning, 124

Heating, contractors, 81, 83, 384, 385; equipment, 43, 57, 353, 358, 401; lack of, 6
Hoad, William M., real estate cycles, 187, 190, 417-18
Holden, Thomas S., F. W. Dodge Corporation, 380
Homeownership, demand, 88, 176, 227 ff., 423 ff.; in large cities, 227, 229, 423; *vs.* renting, 205-06, 228, 230; in small cities, 227, 229, 423; *see also* Owners
Home Owners' Loan Act, 320
Home Owners' Loan Corporation, 262; financial operations, 428, 429-30; functions, 259 ff., 319; mortgages, foreclosures, 244, 245, 425, interest rates, 191-92, 248, loan ratio, 226, volume, 252, 253, 426-27; seasonal buying demand, 90; tax studies, 236-37, 238, 239, 423; Waverly development, 36
Housebuilding, capacity, 90-92; *Committee recommendations,* 329-30; construction cost indexes, 49, 357 ff.; description, 59 ff.; economic importance, 64 ff., in terms of expenditures, 68, gross national product, 69, 368-70, national income, 7, production, 45, 64 ff., 181, 198, 361 ff., profits, 83-84, 93, 387-88, wages, 71, 370-72; management, 95 ff., and finance, 117-20, and government, 120 ff., 157 ff., labor, 106-11, materials manufacture and distribution, 111-17, subcontracting, 99-101, trade restraints, 101-06; market demand, 166-71, 183-85, 203-05, 291 ff., 409-14; methods, 43-44, 138-42, drywall, 137, effect of climate and seasons, 44, 84-90, 388-92, handicraft *vs.* mechanization, 54, 92, 137-38, local practices, 44, precutting, 138, 139, stressed panel, 140-41, *see also* Prefabrication, Standardization; problems, 149 ff., backwardness, 45-46, 154-55, 313-15, lack of integration, 60, of leadership, 149-51, 315, of mechanization, 54, 137-38, of specialization, 62 ff., localism, 80, 81, waste, 92; trends, 131 ff., 149 ff., 323-25; *see also* Builders; Building cycles; Building materials; Costs; Houses; Housing market; Labor
Houses, 38-58; bulk and weight, 39-40, 53, 352, 353; complex arrangement, 40-41, 54-55; durability, 45-46; equipment and parts, 41-42, 43; fixed location, 38-39; maintenance and operation, 47-48, 56-57; materials and structure, 42-44, 53-54, 354-56; mutability, 52 ff.; types, 44-45, 54-56; *see also* Apartments; Building materials; Costs; Farm dwellings; Housebuilding; Housing market; Low-priced houses; New houses; Nonfarm dwellings; Prices; Row houses; Single-family houses; Urban dwellings; Used houses
Housing Committee Program, conclusions, 311-25; recommendations, 325-43, financing of urban housing, 331-34, industrial reorganization, 329-30, integration of production, distribution and maintenance, 330-31, maintenance and operating costs, 339-41, public aid and activity, 334 ff., regulation of land use, 326-29, rural and farm housing, 336-39, timing of program, 341-43
Housing market, *Committee recommendations,* 330-31; demand, 7, 176 ff., custom, 167-68, mass, 168-69, new, 294-96, rental, 169, rural, 169-71; description, 166-71, 175 ff.; distribution, costs, 221, methods, 207 ff., 294 ff.; finance, 225 ff.; fluctuations, 66-68, 176-78, 180-81, 185-97, 207 ff., 414 ff., relation to prices, 200-02; and government, 257 ff.; and housebuilding, 166 ff., 291 ff.; supply, 178-85, 208-09, redistribution, 183-85, 203-05, 409-14, surplus, 202-03; *see also* Finance; Houses; Real estate
Housing problem, 3-5, 291 ff.; *Committee recommendations, program,* 325-43, *timing,* 341-43
Houston, prices, 32-33; River Oaks development, 31, 32-33
Hoyt, Homer, decentralization, 18, 23-24, 239; interest rates, 191; land planning, 14, 187
Hubbard, J. B., building cycles, 195
Husband, William H., tax rates, 238

ILLINOIS, licensing laws, 402; mortgage foreclosures, 244, 245, 425; redevelopment legislation, 275; taxes, 423, 424
Indianapolis, land improvement, 351; wage agreements, 405
Institute for Research in Land and Public Utility Economics, mortgage interest rates, 248
Insurance companies, housing investment, 119, 252, 253, 426-27, 300-02; insurance company law, 273-74, 300
Interest rates, *see* Mortgages

JIG TABLE, 141-42
John B. Pierce Foundation, framed panel system, 141, 157; research, 164
Joint Stock Land Banks, 282

KANSAS, licensing laws, 402; mortgage foreclosures, 244, 245, 425; taxes, 423
Kansas City (Mo.), Country Club development, 31; taxes, 238; wage agreements, 405
Knickerbocker Village, 276
Kuznets, Simon, national income, 70, 368, 369

LABOR, 70-74; employment, average, 77-79, 383, 393-94, regularity, 107, 395; and management, 103, 105, 106-11; in nonfarm residential building, 70, 72; policies, 151-54, 162-63, 314; skilled, 72; unions, effectiveness, 108-11, number, 72-74, 372-73, working rules, 109-10; wages, earnings, 374-77, scales, 74, 373 ff.,

Labor, *continued*
405-06, total paid, 70-71; and the war, 91; *see also* American Federation of Labor; Trade restraints
Land, 13-37; costs, 23-33, 297-99, improved, 25-30, 349-51, raw, 28, 30; planning, 19-20, 22, 157-59, *Committee recommendations,* 326-29, government regulation, 33-35, 123-25, 318-19, 401, reassembly, 36, 159, 275, 298 ff.; vacant, 13 ff., 316, and decentralization of cities, 16-18, 35-37, 316, for low-priced houses, 157-58, 296-97, 315, and subdivision, 14-16, 19-20, 30-33, 315-16, and tax delinquency, 20-22, 159; *see also* Real estate
Land Bank Commissioner, loans, 259, 283; *see also* Federal Farm Mortgage Corporation; Federal Land Banks
Lanham Act, war housing, 285-86
Lautner, Harold W., subdivision regulations, 34, 124
Leases, 215
Licensing laws, builders, 129-30, 402-03; brokers, 218
Limited-dividend housing legislation, 274, 275, 276, 277
Location of housing developments, criteria, 18-19
Long, Clarence D., Jr., building cycles, 191, 195, 363, 416; interest rates, 247
Los Angeles, building cycles, 181, 408-09; home-ownership, 229, 423; land values, 23; rental housing, 231-32
Los Angeles County, surplus land, 15-16, 18
Lots, *see* Land; Subdividers
Louisiana, licensing laws, 402; mortgage foreclosures, 245, 425; taxes, 423
Louisville, decentralization, 347, 348; wage agreements, 405
Low-priced houses, 177, 183-85, 203-06, 311 ff.; *see also* Land
Luxford, R. F., prefabrication, 140
Lyon, Leverett S., building codes, 62, 63

MacChesney, Nathan W., co-operatives, 234
MacChesney Act, brokers' licenses, 218
McFadden Act (1927), mortgage credit, 252, 254
McKenzie, R. D., decentralization, 18
Maintenance and operation, *Committee recommendations,* 339-41; costs, 47-48, 56-57; repairs and alterations, 5-6, 8, 67, 167-68, 265-66, 319-20
Management, *see* Architects; Builders; Contractors; Labor; Operative builders; Owners; Subcontractors; Subdividers
Manchester (N. H.), decentralization, 347, 348
Manufacturers, building materials, *see* Building materials, producers
Maryland, licensing laws, 402; mortgage foreclosures, 245, 425; taxes, 423, 424
Massachusetts, equity investment, 300; financial aid to housing, 273; licensing laws, 402; mortgage foreclosures, 245, 425; taxes, 423
Massachusetts Homestead Commission, suburban homes for workers, 273
Massachusetts Trust, trustee ownership, 234-35
Materials, *see* Building materials
Maverick, Lewis A., real-estate cycles, 187
Mechanics' lien, 119
Mechanization, 54, 137-38, 323-24
Metropolitan districts, decentralization, 16, 17, 347-49
Metropolitan Life Insurance Company, Parkchester development, 57, 96, 112, 114, 144
Miami, land values, 23
Michigan, licensing laws, 402; mortgage foreclosures, 245, 425; redevelopment legislation, 275; taxes, 423
Miller, Rudolph P., building codes, 127, 128
Miller, William S., real-estate taxes, 24
Milwaukee, co-operative housing, 273; "greenbelt" towns, 283; tax delinquency, 21; wage agreements, 405
Minnesota, licensing laws, 402; mortgage foreclosures, 245, 425; seasonal fluctuation in building, 87, 392; taxes, 423, 424
Modular Service Association, dimensional standards, 133-34
Monchow, Helen C., real-estate cycles, 187
Montgomery, R. E., trade restraints, 104
Mortgages, 118-19, 225 ff., 242 ff., 302 ff., 316-18, 426-27; amortization, 246 ff., 302-03, 319; British system, 255; FHA *versus* FHLBS systems, 269-73; foreclosure, 244, 245, 425; insurance, 251, 266 ff.; interest rates, 191-92, 247-51; legal aspects, 243-44; lending agencies, 251 ff., 258 ff., 428 ff.; outstanding, 253, 426; volume, 252, 253; *see also* Equity investment; Finance; and various agencies
Multifamily houses, number, 66, 76-78, 366, 379 ff.; types, 45; *see also* Apartments
Municipal government, bulding codes, 125 ff., 159-60, 318; land regulation, 123 ff.
Mutual Mortgage Insurance Fund, 267
Mutual Ownership Defense Housing Division, 289

National Association of Real Estate Boards, brokers' licenses, 218, 220; Co-operative Division, 233; housebuilding industry, 63; mortgage interest rates, 248
National Bureau of Economic Research, construction, costs, 49, volume, 361 ff., 410; family income levels, 407; national income, 70, 368, 369
National Bureau of Standards (Department of Commerce), building codes, 126, 127, 160-61, 323, 403; frames, 43; research, 122-23; Simplified Practice Recommendations, 132-33, 164

National Capital Housing Authority, 274-75; land policy, 299-300
National Farm Loan Associations, 282
National Housing Act (1934), 265 ff.; Title I, 265-66; Title II, 266 ff.; Title III, 271
National Housing Agency, 269, 278, 305, 321, 323; *Committee recommendations,* 330, 332, 333-34, 335, 338, 340-41; subsidiaries, 288-89
National Industrial Conference Board, cost of living compared with rents, 421
National Lumber Manufacturers' Association, lumber prices, 112
National Recovery Act, Subsistence Homesteads Division, 283
National Recovery Administration, building codes, 62, 63, 104-05
National Resources Committee, land planning, 16, 21, 123-24
National Resources Planning Board, building cycles, 192, 363, 418-20; mortgages, 244; research, 122; wages, 377
Navy Department, housing activities, 285, 286, 289
New England, licensing laws, 402; seasonal fluctuation in building, 87, 392
New England Building Officials' Conference, building codes, 161
New Hampshire, licensing laws, 402; mortgage foreclosures, 245, 425; taxes, 423
New Haven, decentralization, 347, 348; wage agreements, 405
New houses, market, 294-96; sales in Toledo, 187 ff., 417-18; supply, 182-85
New Jersey, decentralization, 347, 348; licensing laws, 402; mortgage foreclosures, 245, 425; seasonal fluctuation in building, 87, 392; surplus land, 15-16; taxes, 238, 423, 424
Newman, William H., building cycles, 191, 192, 195
New Orleans, land improvements, 350; wage agreements, 405-06
New York City, apartments, construction, 46, height, 30-31, 57-58; building cycles, 181, 408-09; Citizens' Housing Council, 21; City and Suburban Homes Corporation, 232; decentralization, 18, 347, 348; dividend rates, 249; homeownership, 229, 423; Knickerbocker Village, 276; land, subdivision, 30-31, surplus, 15, values, 23-24, 239; mortgage interest rates, 248; Parkchester development, 57, 112, 114, 144; public housing projects, 275; rental housing, 231-32, 273-74; size of building operations, 378-81; taxes, 239, 424, delinquency, 21; wage agreements, 405-06
New York City Housing Authority, height of buildings, 58; public housing, 363, 365
New York Federal Reserve Bank, construction cost indexes, 359
New York State, aid to housing, 273-74, 276, 301; insurance company law, 273-74, 300; licensing laws, 402; limited-dividend legislation, 274, 275; mortgage foreclosures, 244, 245, 425; public housing projects, 275, 280; Redevelopment Companies Act, 275, 294; taxes, 238, 423, 424; Urban Redevelopment Corporations Act, 275, 328-29
New York State Planning Council, 15
Nonfarm dwellings, condition of, 5-7; demand, 168-69, postwar, 6-8; expenditures, 8; federal aid, 276 ff.; mortgages, 252, 253, 426-27; number, 6; ownership, 228; vacancies, 6; volume, 65, 66, 67, 182 ff., 197 ff., 361 ff., 409 ff., 418 ff.; *see also* various agencies
North Carolina, licensing laws, 402; mortgage foreclosures, 245, 425; taxes, 423, 424

OBSOLESCENCE, *see* Depreciation
Ohio, building codes, 125, 126; licensing laws, 402; mortgage foreclosures, 245, 425; seasonal fluctuation in building, 392; taxes, 423
Old houses, *see* Used houses
Operation, *see* Maintenance and operation
Operative builders, functions, 142-44, 222-23; value of equipment, 83, 385
Overman Act, 288
Owner-occupied housing, *see* Homeownership
Owners, 95-96; conservatism, 154-55; co-operative, 233-35; inexperience, 209 ff.; limitations of ownership, 211 ff.; *see also* Homeownership

PACIFIC COAST BUILDING OFFICIALS' CONFERENCE, building codes, 161
Parkchester development (New York City), 57, 96, 112, 114, 144
Parons, Raymond V., building materials, 352
Pennsylvania, licensing laws, 402; mortgage foreclosures, 245, 425; taxes, 423, 424
Perry, Clarence A., land planning, 32
Philadelphia, decentralization, 347, 348; homeownership, 229, 423; land improvements, 350; land values, 23; rental housing, 231-32; wage agreements, 405-06
Pierce, John B., Foundation, framed panel system, 141, 157; research, 164
Pittsburgh, decentralization, 18; land improvements, 350
Planning laws, *see* Land, planning; Zoning laws
Platting, *see* Land; Subdividers
Plumbing, building codes, 125, 127, 161; contractors, 81, 83, 384, 385; costs, 358; employment, 395; licensing, 129, 402-03; supplies, 399, 400, 401; weight of fixtures, 353
Plywood, in prefabrication, 140-41
Portland (Me.), decentralization, 347, 348

Postwar, demand, 5-8, 166, 195, 312-13, 325, for rural housing, 170-71; readjustments in housebuilding, 91-92
Poteat, J. Douglass, mortgage foreclosures, 244, 258
Prefabrication, 151, 324; dealers, 223-24; distributing methods, 295-96; factory *vs.* site, 146-48; and FHA, 122, 147; labor's attitude towards, 152-54; materials, 140-41; methods, 138-42; size of business, 147-48
President's Conference on Home Building and Home Ownership, mortgage interest rates, 248, 258
Prices, of building materials, 111-14, 394 ff.; of houses, 177-78, 183-85, 197-206, 381, 412-13, stickiness, 197-203; of land, 23 ff., 31-33, 298-99, 349
Production, *see* Housebuilding; Building materials
Production Credit Association, 282
Production Credit Corporations, 282
Public Buildings Administration, 289
Public housing, 276 ff.; *Committee recommendations,* 334-36; competition with private enterprise, 281-82, 305; employment, 395; unit costs, PWA, USHA, 51, 280-81, 439; volume, 67, 321, 367; *see also* Public Works Administration; United States Housing Authority
Public Works Administration, Housing Division, 276-78, 321; average dwelling unit costs, 51, 277, 281, 439; financial operations, 428, 437; wages, 375
Purdue University, research, 164
Purves, C. M., farm dwellings, 366, 368

Real estate, brokers, 209 ff., 217-20; cycles, 187; leases, 215; limitations of ownership, 211 ff., operators, 221-22, taxes, 236-40; titles, 212-15; transaction costs, 215-17, settlement charges, 216-17, 422; *see also* Land
Real Property Inventory, 123, homeownership, 227; rental housing, 208, 210
Reassembly of land, *see* Land, planning
Reclamation, Bureau of, 285
Reconstruction Finance Corporation, 276; rental housing, 287; repairs and replacements, 285
Redevelopment of land, *see* Land, planning
Refrigerators, lack of, 6; prices and sales, 61
Rental housing, 176; demand, 88, 169, 205-06; FHA projects, 237-38, 424-25; investment, 231-33, 300-02, yield insurance, 301-02; leases, 215; mortgage insurance, 268-69; *vs* owner-occupied, 228, 230-31; problems, 232-33; rent fluctuations, 198-99, 421; supply, 208, 210
Reorganization Act (1939), 269
Repairs and alterations, dollar volume, 8, 67, 367, 368; federal aid, 265-66, 285, 319-20; need, 5-6, 167-68
Research, Bemis Foundation, 164; government, 122-23, 160-61, 164-66, 323; John B. Pierce Foundation, 164; Purdue University, 164
Resettlement Administration, 283-84
Residential construction, *see* Housebuilding
Restriction of output, 9
RFC Mortgage Company, financial operations, 271, 428, 431; functions, 260; rental housing, 287
Riggleman, J. R., building cycles, 195
Rogers, R. R., TNEC testimony, interest rates, 249, 250
Roos, Charles F., business cycles, 193
Rosenwald, Julius, rental housing, 232
Row houses, 44-45; construction, 46; economies, 27, 29, 55-56
Rural dwellings, *see* Farm dwellings; Nonfarm dwellings
Rural Electrification Administration, 285, 306; *Committee recommendations,* 338, 339
Russell, Horace, mortgages, 244
Russell Sage Foundation, land planning, 32; zoning, 123-24
Ryan, Frederick L., trade restraints, 104

Sacramento, decentralization, 347, 348
St. Louis, construction costs, 48-49, 357 ff.; decentralization, 35, 347, 348; surplus land, 15-16; tax delinquency, 21; wage agreements, 405
San Antonio, building cycles, 408-09
Savings banks, 119; mutual, 252, 253, 426-27
Savings and loan associations, 119; mortgage volume, 252, 253, 426-27
Seasonal fluctuation in housebuilding, 84-90, 388-92; average temperatures by areas, 87, 392
Seattle, decentralization, 347, 348; taxes, 425; wage agreements, 405
Securities and Exchange Commission, 120
Segregation of social groups, 4
Semenow, Robert W., broker's licenses, 218
Servicing, *see* Maintenance and operation
Settlement charges, 216-17, 422
Simplified Practice Recommendations (National Bureau of Standards), 132-33, 164
Simpson, Herbert D., land planning, 14, 15
Single-family houses, detached, 44, 46, 55; FHA insured, 51; number, 66, 75-77, 88, 366, 379 ff., 391; semiattached, 44-45; standardization, 136-37; valuation, 349; *see also* Row houses
Site, *see* Location of housing developments
Slichter, Sumner H., labor, 110
Slums, causes, 4; clearance, 298-99, tax delinquency, 21-22
Smith, Bernard, new types of sales contracts, 304
Smith, Raymond F., land planning, 15
Social Security Board, building contractors, 382 ff., 393-94

South Bend, decentralization, 347, 348
Special trade contractors, 81, 314, 384, 390; *see also* Subcontractors
Spokane, decentralization, 347, 348
Standardization, 131 ff., 167; dimensions, 133-34; dwelling units, 134-37; materials and parts, 132-34, 323, 324; Simplified Practice Recommendations, 132-33, 164, 323
State government, building codes, 125-29, 318; licensing laws, 129-30; mortgage moratorium laws, 258; planning and zoning laws, 123-25, 159; relations with federal government, 279-80, 306-07; urban housing aid, 273 ff.
Stolper, Wolfgang F., mortgage rates, 191, 255
Stone, Peter A., 41, 42, 89, 149, 377
Subcontracting system, 99 ff., apartment building, 386-87; effects, 100-01; *see also* Subcontractors
Subcontractors, financial resources, 82 ff.; functions, 60, 99-100; localism, 80, 81, 384; profits, 84, 387-88; size, 78-80, 382 ff., 393-94; value of equipment, 82-83, 385; *see also* Special trade contractors
Subdividers, 96-97, 315; *see also* Land
Subdivision Regulation Law, 124
Subsistence Homesteads Division (Department of the Interior), 283
Superior (Wis.), decentralization, 347, 348
Supply, *see* Housing market

DE TARNOVSKY, IVAN, new types of sales contracts, 304
Taxation, 236 ff., 423-25; British system, 239-40; delinquency, 20-22; inequalities, 237-38; and land planning, 159; method, 238-39
Taylor, James S., real-estate cycles, 187
Technological development, new materials, 156-57; problems, 155-57
Temperature, *see* Climate; Housebuilding; Seasonal fluctuation
Temporary National Economic Committee, hearings, assets of construction corporations, 82; building materials, distribution, 115, prices, 111-12; 394 ff., 403; contract insurance, 304; Home Owners' Loan Corporation, 259-61; house parts, 41; interest rates, 249, 250; investment, 301; trade restrictions, 149, 162; union labor, 73-74, 108; wages, 377
Tenement House Law (1901), 18
Tennessee, licensing laws, 402; mortgage foreclosures, 245, 425; seasonal fluctuation in building, 87, 392; taxes, 423
Tennessee Valley Authority, housing activities, 285
Texas, licensing laws, 402; mortgage foreclosures, 244, 245, 425; seasonal fluctuation in building, 87, 392; taxes, 423, 424
Thompson, George N., building codes, 126, 127
Thorp, Willard L., TNEC testimony, assets of construction corporations, 82; building materials, distribution, 115, prices, 111
Tinbergen, Jan, business cycles, 193, 420
Titles, real-estate, 212-15; leases, 215
Toilet, flush, 45, 46
Toledo, building cycles, 187-89, 417-18; wage agreements, 406
Torrens system of land-title registration, 213-14, 333
Tracy, D. W., TNEC testimony, union labor, 73-74, 108
Trade restraints, 101-06; bid depositories, 102-03; bid peddling, 102; building codes, 126-27; effects, 105-06; elimination, 162-63; licensing laws, 129-30; practices under NRA, 104-05; purpose, 101-02; *see also* Craft restrictions; Labor
Trayer, George W., prefabrication, 140
Trull, Edna, building codes, 128
Trustee ownership, 234-35
Tugwell, R. G., Resettlement Administration, 284
Turner Construction Company, construction cost indexes, 359
Twentieth Century Fund, distribution costs, 115, 398, 400; labor, 73; taxation, 237; wartime housing, 286, 364, 365
"Typical" house, costs, 48-49

UNITED STATES HOUSING ACT, *Committee recommendations,* 336
United States Housing Authority, 277-82, 289, 321; average dwelling unit costs, 51, 280-81, 439; competition with private enterprise, 281-82; co-operation with local authorities, 279-80; financial operations, 428, 438; loans and subsidies, 278-81; projects, average density, 31; rural housing program, 284-85, 306; union labor, 74; volume, 280-81; wartime housing, 286
United States Housing Corporation, World War I, 289, 364, 365
Unwin, Sir Raymond, land planning, 15
Urban dwellings, *Committee recommendations,* 331-34; condition of stock, 6; demand, 168, 183-85, 203-05, 409-14; density, 30-31; federal aid, 257 ff., 276-82, unification, 305; number, 6; ownership, 227, 229; state aid, 273-75; volume, 65, 361 ff.
Used houses, market, 292-94; sales, 208, in Toledo, 187 ff., 417-18; supply, 182-85
Utilities, connections, 27, 29, costs, 26-30, 350-51; regulation, 34, 35

VIRGINIA, equity investment, 300; licensing laws, 402; mortgage foreclosures, 244, 245, 425; taxes, 423, 424-25

WAGES, *see* Labor
Walker, Mabel L., urban blight, 18, 21
Wall, wood-frame, 54
War Department, housing activities, 285, 286, 289
Wartime housing, 9-10, 40, 91-92, 257; codes, 161; co-ordination under National Housing Agency, 288-89; Defense Homes Corporation, 286-87; demountable, 53; Federal Housing Administration, 287-88; Lanham Act, 285-86, prefabrication, 152, 153; program, 289-90, 322-23, 440; shortages, 180, 312
Washington, D. C., Alley Dwelling Act, 274-75; decentralization, 35; "greenbelt" towns, 283; land boom, 24; licensing laws, 402; mortgage foreclosures, 245, 425; rental housing, 231-32; subdivision practices, 34; taxes, 423, 424
Washington Sanitary Housing Company, rental housing, 232
Washington Sanitary Improvement Company, rental housing, 232
Washington (State), land policies, 299; licensing laws, 403; mortgage foreclosures, 245, 425; seasonal fluctuation in building, 87, 392; taxes, 423, 425
Waverly, 36, 158
Weather, *see* Climate; Housebuilding; Seasonal fluctuation
Wenzlick, Roy, real-estate cycles, 187
Westbrook, Laurence, TNEC testimony, contract insurance, 304
Westchester County, land improvements, 350; tax delinquency, 20-21
Whitten, Robert, city planning, 19, 124
Wichita, decentralization, 347, 348
Wickens, David L., construction, costs, 49, volume, 361 ff., 410; equity, 226; income levels, 407; mortgages, 247
Williams, Frank B., city planning, 124
Wilmington, decentralization, 347, 348; land improvements, 350
Wisconsin, building codes, 125, 126; licensing laws, 402; mortgage foreclosures, 245, 425; taxes, 423
Wittausch, William K., nonfarm dwellings (1900-1940), 411
Wood, Edith E., mortgage financing, 273
Work Projects Administration (Works Progress Administration), building materials prices, 89; electrical facilities, 46; labor, 121, wages, 374

YIELD INSURANCE, 301-02
Yntema, Dwight B., national income, 370-72, 376, 377, 387

ZONING LAWS, 22, 123-25, 318-19, 401, *Committee recommendations,* 326-29; *see also* Land, planning